Contending
Theories
of International
Relations

THE LIPPINCOTT SERIES
IN INTERNATIONAL POLITICS
under the editorship of
STEVEN MULLER
The Johns Hopkins University

Contending Theories

of International Relations

James E. Dougherty/ Robert L. Pfaltzgraff, Jr.

St. Joseph's College
Philadelphia

Fletcher School of Law and
Diplomacy, Tufts University

J. B. Lippincott Company

Philadelphia   New York   Toronto

9   8   7   6   5

Copyright © 1971 by J. B. LIPPINCOTT COMPANY. All rights reserved.

With the exception of brief excerpts for review, no part of this book may be reproduced in any form or by any means without written permission from the publisher.

Library of Congress Catalog Card Number: 70–134865

Paperbound: ISBN–0–397–47237–4

Clothbound: ISBN–0–397–47236–6

Printed in the United States of America

Cover and interior design by Peter Bertolami

The authors acknowledge research assistance from the Foreign Policy Research Institute.

To Robert

Preface

The present volume is an outgrowth of the authors' teaching experience for nearly a decade in graduate and undergraduate honors seminars in international relations. Rather than choosing any *one* major theoretical approach for study, in our teaching we have striven to acquaint students with *all* the major efforts, both traditional and contemporary, normative and behavioral, qualitative and quantitative, to theorize about international relations. Believing that many of the theorizing efforts of international relations are, or can be, mutually reinforcing, we have sought not only to avoid ideological and methodological extremism, but to strike a judicious balance among contending theoretical approaches.

Convinced of the need for an interdisciplinary approach to international relations, we cite, throughout the book, the contributions of many disciplines—political science, history, economics, psychology, biology, and sociology—to the development of international relations theory. By its arrangement of topics, the book is designed to provide a detailed examination of the development of international relations as a field of study and to suggest avenues of future scholarly investigation. Throughout the volume, emphasis is placed upon the examination of similarities and differences among authors within each of the major approaches, as well as intellectual continuities and discontinuities among the major theories. Each chapter contains the authors' critical evaluation of the contribution, and the limitations, of major theories to the study of international relations, together with copious references directing the reader to other relevant literature.

As an inventory, summary, and analysis of international relations theory, this book is designed to offer to scholars, teachers, and policymakers alike a guide to the principal theories which have shaped international relations and the work of persons, both in the academic and policy communities, who have influenced international relations as a field for investigation by scholars and a field for action by policymakers. Thus, the book is intended for the general community of persons interested in international relations, including policymakers, as well as the academic community of scholars, teachers, and students at the graduate and undergraduate levels. It is our intention to provide the student of international relations with access to virtually all the important ideas and leading writers in the field. We have endeavored to make it possible for the reader not only to survey the vast literature of international relations, but also to choose for further study among the many contending theories of international relations.

During the last fifteen years, the authors' understanding of international relations has been immeasurably enhanced as a result of discussions with the following associates, past and present, of the Foreign Policy Research Institute: Dr. William Y. Elliott, Dr. Feliks Gross, Dr. Morton A. Kaplan, Dr. William R. Kintner, Dr. Hans Kohn, Dr. Lawrence Krause, Dr. Philip E. Mosely, Dr. Norman D. Palmer, Dr. Stefan T. Possony, Dr. Froelich Rainey, Dr. Frank Trager, Dr. Arthur P. Whitaker, and Dr. J. K. Zawodny, as well as Mr. Robert C. Herber, managing editor of *Orbis*. The authors have also benefited considerably from discussions following upwards of a score of lectures between 1967 and 1970 to seminars of mid-career officers at the Foreign Service Institute, Department of State, Washington, D.C., where for several years, under the able direction of Dr. John W. Bowling and Dr. Paul Kattenberg, theorists and practitioners of international affairs have been brought into vigorous and mutually profitable interaction.

Over the years, Dr. Dougherty has benefited greatly from conversations with colleagues in various organizational contexts: the International Studies Association; the International Arms Control Symposia held in Ann Arbor and Philadelphia; the Strategy for Peace Conferences at Arden House and Airlie House; the Catholic Association for International Peace; the United States Arms Control and Disarmament Agency; the Washington consultations of the Council on Religion and International Affairs; the National War College and the Inter-American Defense College; the International Affairs Committee of the United States Catholic Conference; the National Strategy Information Center; and the World Affairs Council of Philadelphia. Specifically, among those who have influenced his views of the world, he would like to thank Dr. Donald G. Brennan, Professor Hedley Bull, Professor Joseph I. Coffey, Professor Frank X. Gerrity, Mr. Amrom Katz, Mr. A. William Loos, Professor William V. O'Brien, Professor Paul Ramsey, Professor Thomas C. Schelling, Professor Louis B. Sohn, Mr. C. Maxwell Stanley, Terrence Toland, S.J., president of St. Joseph's College, Professor Thomas C. Wiegele, the participants in the Hogan Hall course on conflict and two men named Murray, both among the faithful departed.

Dr. Pfaltzgraff has received beneficial insights into problems of International Relations theory from many colleagues in discussions under the auspices of the International Studies Association, the Fourth International Arms Control Symposium; the Inter-American Defense College; the International Studies Institute (Westminster College) and the Foreign Service Institute, Department of State. For their valuable comments on draft chapters, he is indebted to Professor Harold Guetzkow, Northwestern University, and Professors Neal Cutler and Willard Keim, both of the University of Pennsylvania. In addition, Dr. Pfaltzgraff wishes to thank Professors Philip E. Jacob and Alvin Z. Rubinstein of the University of Pennsylvania for insights over the years as to the prospects and limitations of theory-building at the international level.

The authors have benefited from discussions with members, past and present, of the Foreign Policy Research Institute: Dr. Alvin Cottrell; Dr. Morton Gorden; Mr. Walter T. Hahn; Dr. David C. Schwartz and Mr. Harvey Sicherman.

We appreciate the research assistance rendered by Miss Annette Binnendijk and Mrs. Janet Howell during the process of readying this work for publication. In the typing of the manuscript, the authors received extraordinary service from Miss Barbara Maser and Mrs. Teresa Torelli.

We acknowledge enthusiastically the intellectual stimulation provided by many excellent students, graduate and undergraduate whom it has been our privilege to teach, and to learn from, during the past decade.

Last, but not least, we owe a considerable debt to Dr. Robert Strausz-Hupé, formerly director of the Foreign Policy Research Institute, and later United States Ambassador to Ceylon, both for his guidance as an exponent of interdisciplinary theorizing and for his exacting taskmastership as a theorist and analyst of international politics.

In the preparation of this book, Dr. Dougherty drafted the introductory chapter as well as the chapters on theories of conflict, decision-making theories, and game theory, bargaining and simulation. Dr. Pfaltzgraff drafted the chapters on man-milieu relationships, political realism, systemic theories, theories of integration, regionalism and alliance cohesion, and the concluding chapter. Both thoroughly reviewed the entire manuscript together and contributed substantively to each other's work. Both accept full responsibility for every sentence in the text.

James E. Dougherty
Robert L. Pfaltzgraff, Jr.

Philadelphia, Pa.
December 29, 1970

Table of Contents

Table of Contents

CHAPTER 1
Theoretical Approaches to International Relations

Most political scientists and other students of international relations realize that their subject areas are appallingly vast and complex. They are aware also that despite the many nostrums advertised for the world's ills, it is no less difficult to find a permanent solution for conflict and war than a cure for cancer. Understanding either the biological processes of the human organism or the political processes of the international system—in such a way as to control them for moral and rational ends—profoundly challenges man's intellect. Yet only through profound understanding can a theory for purposeful action arise. Throughout centuries, and with greater urgency certainly in modern times, men have tried to make sense of the shifting-sand relationships of larger social groupings on the world scene. By surveying the theories which have been advanced, any reader—whether student, policymaker, journalist, or casual observer—may improve his understanding of international relations. This book, therefore, is designed to trace for the reader the development of international relations as a field of systematic study as well as to guide him through the best in theory.

Early Approaches to International Relations Theory

Efforts at theorizing about the nature of interstate relations are quite old; some in fact go back to ancient times in India, China and Greece. Although Plato's and Aristotle's reflections on the subject are quite sketchy, the ancient Greek historian Thucydides' *History of the Peloponnesian War* is a classic treatise any student of international relations can still read profitably.[1] Machiavelli's *The Prince,* a harbinger of modern analysis of power and the state system, emphasized a "value-free" science of foreign policymaking and statecraft.[2] Dante's *De Monarchia* became one of the first and most powerful appeals in Western political literature for an international organization capable of enforcing the peace.[3] Other early proponents of a confederation or league of nation-states were Pierre Dubois (French lawyer and political pamphleteer of the late fourteenth and early fifteenth centuries), Émeric Crucé (French monk of the late sixteenth and early seventeenth centuries), the Duc de Sully (minister of France's Henry IV), William Penn, Abbé de Saint Pierre (French publicist and theoretical reformer of the late seventeenth and early eighteenth centuries), Jean-Jacques Rousseau, Jeremy Bentham, and Immanuel Kant.[4]

Yet despite these classical writings no systematic development, comparable to that in internal political theories of the state, occurred in international theory before World War I. Martin Wight has noted that if by "international theory" we mean a "tradition of speculation about relations between states, a tradition imagined as the twin of speculation about the State to which the name 'political theory' is appropriated," it does not exist.[5] Wight suggests that a reason for this situation is that since Grotius (1583–1645), the Dutch jurist and statesman, and Pufendorf (1632–1694), the German jurist and historian, nearly all speculation about the international community fell under the heading of international law. He notes that most writing on interstate relations before this

1. Thucydides, *The Peloponnesian War,* trans. Rex Warner (Harmondsworth: Penguin Books, 1954). See also William T. Bluhm, *Theories of the Political System: Classics of Political Thought and Modern Political Analysis* (Englewood Cliffs, N.J.: Prentice-Hall, 1965), Chapter II; John H. Finley, Jr., *Thucydides* (Cambridge: Harvard University Press, 1942); Charles Norris Cochrane, *Thucydides and the Science of History* (London: Oxford University Press, 1929); Peter J. Fliess, *Thucydides and the Politics of Bipolarity* (Baton Rouge: Louisiana State University Press, 1966).

2. Niccòlo Machiavelli, *The Prince and The Discourses* (New York: Random House [Modern Library], 1940); James Burnham, *The Machiavellians* (New York: John Day Company, 1943); Herbert Butterfield, *The Statecraft of Machiavelli* (New York: Macmillan Company, 1956); Friedrich Meinecke, *Machiavellism: The Doctrine of Raison d'État and Its Place in Modern History,* trans. Douglas Scott (New Haven: Yale University Press, 1957).

3. Dante Alighieri, *On World Government,* trans. Herbert W. Schneider, 2nd rev. ed. (New York: Liberal Arts Press, 1957); Étienne Gilson, *Dante and Philosophy,* trans. David Moore (New York: Harper and Row [Torchbooks], 1963), Part III.

4. See Daniel S. Cheever and H. Field Haviland, *Organizing for Peace* (Boston: Houghton Mifflin Company, 1954), Chapter 2. For additional reading on the history of international political theory, see F. H. Hinsley, *Power and the Pursuit of Peace: Theory and Practice in the History of Relations between States* (Cambridge: Cambridge University Press, 1967), pp. 13–149; Frank M. Russell, *Theories of International Relations* (New York: D. Appleton-Century Company, 1936), pp. 99–113 and Chapter IX; Kenneth N. Waltz, "Political Philosophy and the Study of International Relations," William T. R. Fox, ed., *Theoretical Aspects of International Relations* (Notre Dame: University of Notre Dame Press, 1959).

5. Martin Wight, "Why Is There No International Theory?" *International Relations,* II (April, 1960), 35–48, 62.

century was contained in the political literature of the peace writers cited above, buried in the works of historians, cloistered in the peripheral reflections of philosophers, or harbored in speeches, despatches and memoirs of statesmen and diplomats. Wight concludes that in the classical political tradition "international theory, or what there is of it, is scattered, unsystematic, and mostly inaccessible to the layman," as well as being "largely repellent and intractable in form." [6]

The period of European history from 1648 to 1914 was the golden age of diplomacy, the balance of power and international law. Nearly all political thought focused upon the sovereign nation-state—the origins, functions and limitations of governmental powers, the rights of individuals within the state, the requirements of order, the imperatives of national self-determination and independence. Various branches of socialist thought, however, formed the major exception. Socialists, despite their professed internationalism, did not really produce a coherent international theory. They advanced a theory of imperialism borrowed largely from John A. Hobson (1858–1940), the British economist, and thus derivative from an economic theory indigenous to the capitalist states. [7] Until 1914, international theorists almost uniformly assumed that the structure of international society was unalterable, and that the division of the world into sovereign states was necessary and natural. [8] The study of international relations consisted almost entirely of diplomatic history, international law and political theory, rather than of investigation into the processes of survival.

Modern Approaches to International Relations Theory

Some impetus to the serious study of international relations in this country came when the United States emerged as a world power. But ambiguities in American foreign policy and the trend toward isolationism during the 1920s and 1930s hindered the development of international relations as an intellectual discipline. A dichotomy developed between intellectual idealists, who shared Woodrow Wilson's vision of the League of Nations, and politicians who, feeling pressures for a "return to normalcy," blocked United States entry into the world organization. Americans demanded a moral and peaceful world order, but they were unwilling to pay the price. This dichotomy between noble impulses and tendencies toward isolationism was clearly reflected in the Kellogg-Briand Treaty of 1928, which "outlawed" war by moralistic declaration but provided no adequate means of enforcement. Countless educators

6. *Ibid.,* pp. 37–38.

7. See in Chapter 6 below the section on the Marxist-Leninist theories of imperialism.

8. Wight, *op. cit.,* p. 40.

considered it their mission to keep the younger generation from repeating the older one's mistakes.[9]

For a decade or more after Versailles, the two most popular approaches to teaching world affairs in American universities included courses in current events and courses in international law and organization. Current events courses were designed more to promote international understanding than to apply social science methodologies to good advantage. Courses in international law emphasized discrepancies between the formal obligations of states (especially League members) and their actual conduct in an era of struggle between powers anxious to preserve the international status-quo and those determined to overturn it.[10]

An awareness that the study of international relations must go beyond the study of international law and organization was evident in the writings of scholars in England and the United States during the 1930s. While Brierly, Eagleton, Fenwick, Hill, Lauterpacht, Moore, Oppenheim and Potter [11] persisted in a theory of international relations based on law and organization and drew upon legal case materials and international administrative experience, many other writers looked beyond the field of law for more dynamic, comprehensive explanations of forces and events in interstate relations.

After World War I, leading diplomatic historians on both sides of the Atlantic searched for the "causes" or "origins" of the great conflict.[12] Hayes,

9. Grayson Kirk, *The Study of International Relations in American Colleges and Universities* (New York: Council on Foreign Relations, 1947), p. 4; Foster Rhea Dulles, *America's Rise to World Power, 1898–1954* (New York: Harper and Row, 1963), pp. 158–161. For an excellent treatment of the dichotomy, see Robert E. Osgood, *Ideals and Self-Interest in America's Foreign Relations* (Chicago: University of Chicago Press, 1953).

10. Kenneth W. Thompson, "The Study of International Politics: A Survey of Trends and Developments," *Review of Politics*, XIV (October, 1952), 433–443.

11. James L. Brierly, *The Law of Nations*, 2nd ed. (New York: Oxford University Press, 1936); Clyde Eagleton, *International Government* (New York: Ronald Press, 1932); Charles G. Fenwick, *International Law*, 2nd ed. (New York: D. Appleton-Century Company, 1934); Norman L. Hill, *International Administration* (New York: McGraw-Hill Book Company, 1931); Hersch Lauterpacht, *The Function of Law in the International Community* (New York: Oxford University Press, 1933); J. B.

Moore, *A Digest of International Law* (Washington: Government Printing Office, 1906); Lassa F. L. Oppenheim, *International Law: A Treatise*, 4th ed. (London: Longmans, Green, and Company, 1928); Pitman B. Potter, *An Introduction to the Study of International Organization*, 3rd ed. (New York: D. Appleton-Century Company, 1928).

12. Sidney B. Fay, *The Origins of the World War*, 2nd ed. (New York: Macmillan Company, 1930); G. P. Gooch, *History of Modern Europe, 1878–1919* (New York: Henry Holt, 1923); R. B. Mowat, *European Diplomacy, 1815–1914* (New York: Longmans, 1922); Bernadotte E. Schmitt, *The Coming of the War, 1914* (New York: Charles Scribner's Sons, 1930); Raymond J. Sontag, *European Diplomatic History, 1871–1932* (New York: Century, 1933); G. P. Gooch and Harold W. Temperley, *British Documents on the Origins of the War, 1898–1914* (London: His Majesty's Stationery Office, 1928). For an historiographical appraisal of the work of American historians, see Warren I. Cohen, *The American Revisionists: The Lessons of Intervention in World War I* (Chicago: University of Chicago Press, 1967).

Contending Theories of International Relations

Kohn, and other historians explored the emotional-ideological content of nationalism, regarded by many as the most potent political force in the modern world despite the advent of universalist ideologies.[13] Specialized writings appeared in a number of areas: on the problems of security, war and disarmament—Baker, Shotwell and Wheeler-Bennett;[14] on imperialism—Moon and Priestley;[15] on diplomacy and negotiation—Nicolson;[16] on the balance of power—Friedrich and Vagts;[17] on the geographical aspects of world power (building on the work of Alfred Thayer Mahan and Sir Halford Mackinder)— Fairgrieve and Spykman;[18] on the history of international relations theories— Russell;[19] on economic factors in warfare, the strategic significance of raw materials, and the role of economics in international relations—Angell, Simonds, Emeny, Robbins, Einzig and Staley.[20] During the interwar period,

13. Carlton J. H. Hayes, *Essays on Nationalism* (New York: Macmillan Company, 1926); Hans Kohn, *A History of Nationalism in the East* (London: George Routledge and Sons, 1929), *Nationalism and Imperialism in the Hither East* (London: George Routledge and Sons, 1932), *Nationalism in the Soviet Union* (London: George Routledge and Sons, 1933), and *The Idea of Nationalism* (New York: Macmillan Company, 1944).

14. Philip J. Noel Baker, *Disarmament* (New York: Harcourt, Brace, and Company, 1926); James T. Shotwell, *War as an Instrument of National Policy* (New York: Harcourt, Brace, and Company, 1929); J. W. Wheeler-Bennett, *Disarmament and Security Since Locarno, 1925–1931* (New York: Macmillan Company, 1932).

15. Parker T. Moon, *Imperialism and World Politics* (New York: Macmillan Company, 1926); Herbert I. Priestley, *France Overseas: A Study of Modern Imperialism* (New York: Appleton-Century Company, 1938).

16. Harold Nicolson, *Peacemaking, 1919* (Boston: Houghton Mifflin Company, 1933) and *Diplomacy* (London: Oxford University Press, 1939).

17. Carl J. Friedrich, *Foreign Policy in the Making: The Search for a New Balance of Power* (New York: W. W. Norton Company, 1938); Alfred Vagts, "The United States and the Balance of Power," *Journal of Politics,* III (November, 1941), 401–449.

18. James Fairgrieve, *Geography and World Power* (New York: E. P. Dutton and Company, 1921); Nicholas J. Spyk-

man, "Geography and Foreign Policy I," *American Political Science Review,* XXXII (February, 1938), 213–236, and the following two books: *America's Strategy in World Politics* (New York: Harcourt, Brace, and Company, 1942) and *The Geography of the Peace* (New York: Harcourt, Brace, and Company, 1944). Spykman also wrote two articles with Abbie A. Rollins, "Geographic Objectives in Foreign Policy I," *American Political Science Review,* XXXIII (June, 1939), 391–410, and "Geographic Objectives in Foreign Policy II," *ibid.* (August, 1939), 591–614. The theories of Mahan and Mackinder are treated in Chapter 2. For a discussion of Spykman's theories, see Chapter 3, pp. 72–74.

19. Frank M. Russell, *Theories of International Relations* (New York: Appleton-Century-Crofts, 1936).

20. Norman Angell, *The Great Illusion* (New York: G. P. Putnam's Sons, 1933) and *Raw Materials, Population Pressure and War* (New York: National Peace Conference, 1936); Frank H. Simonds, *The ABC of War Debts* (New York: Harper and Brothers, 1933); Brooks Emeny, *The Strategy of War Materials* (New York: Macmillan Company, 1936); Lionel Robbins, *Economic Planning and International Order* (New York: Macmillan Company, 1937); Paul Einzig, *Finance and Politics* (London: Macmillan Company, 1932) and *The Economics of Rearmament* (London: Routledge and Kegan Paul, 1934); and Eugene Staley, *World Economy in Transition* (New York: Council on Foreign Relations, 1939). Angell's well-known hypothesis concerning the possibility of eliminating

several textbooks on international relations, in describing the "states system" (as it was then called), tried to bring a knowledge of political, historical, economic, demographic, geographic and strategic factors to bear upon the effort to understand the actual evolution of foreign policies among the Great Powers.[21] Other important sources of this era include *Foreign Affairs* (the distinguished quarterly journal of the Council on Foreign Relations), *International Conciliation* (published monthly by the Carnegie Endowment for International Peace), the fortnightly *Foreign Policy Reports* (published by the Foreign Policy Association) and the *American Journal of International Law.*

E. H. CARR AND THE CRISIS OF WORLD POLITICS

By the 1930s there was a growing recognition among international relations teachers of the gap between the "utopians" and the "realists." The academic climate after World War I made it conducive for "utopians" and "realists" to concern themselves with the means of preventing another international war. Consequently, this task spurred the serious study of international relations. Both schools of thought then clashed over the best means of guaranteeing the peace. No scholar in that period more trenchantly analyzed the philosophical differences between "utopians" and "realists" than Edward Hallett Carr in his celebrated work,[22] which, although published in 1939, did not make its deserved impact in America until after World War II. Most of the following comparative analysis draws heavily from that work.

Carr saw the "utopians," for the most part, as intellectual descendants of eighteenth-century Enlightenment optimism, nineteenth-century liberalism, and twentieth-century Wilsonian idealism. Utopianism is closely associated with a distinctly Anglo-American tendency to assume that statesmen enjoy

war by educating men to its economic futility is discussed in Chapter 5, pp. 158–159.

21. Raymond L. Buell, *International Relations* (New York: Henry Holt and Company, 1929); Charles Hodges, *The Background of International Relations* (New York: John Wiley and Sons, 1932); R. B. Mowat, *The European States System: A Study of International Relations* (London: Oxford University Press, 1929); Frederick L. Schuman, *International Politics: An Introduction to the Western States System* (New York: McGraw-Hill Book Company, 1933); Frank H. Simonds and Brooks Emeny, *The Great Powers in World Politics* (New York: American Book Company, 1935); Frederick S. Dunn, *Peaceful Change: A Study of International Procedures* (New York: Council on Foreign

Relations, 1937); Francis J. Brown, Charles Hodges and Joseph S. Roucek, *Contemporary World Politics* (New York: John Wiley and Sons, 1940); Edward Hallett Carr, *International Relations Since the Peace Treaties* (London: Macmillan Company, 1937); Georg Schwarzenberger, *Power Politics: An Introduction to the Study of International Relations and Post-War Planning* (London: Jonathan Cape, Ltd., 1941), *Power Politics: A Study of International Society,* 2nd ed. (New York: Frederick A. Praeger, 1951), and *Power Politics: A Study of World Society,* 3rd ed. (New York: Frederick A. Praeger, 1964).

22. *The Twenty-Years' Crisis, 1919–1939: An Introduction to the Study of International Relations* (London: Macmillan Company, 1939; New York: Harper and Row [Torchbooks], 1964).

broad freedom of choice in the making of foreign policy.[23] Marred by a certain self-righteousness, the utopians clung to the belief that the United States had entered World War I as a disinterested, even reluctant, champion of international morality. Emphasizing how men ought to behave in their international relationships rather than how they actually behave, the American utopians disdained balance of power politics (historically identified with Europe), national armaments, the use of force in international affairs and the secret treaties of alliance and spoils-division attendant on World War I. Instead, they stressed international legal rights and obligations, the natural harmony of national interests—reminiscent of Adam Smith's "invisible hand" [24]—as a regulator for the preservation of international peace, a heavy reliance upon reason in human affairs, and confidence in the peace-building function of the "world court of public opinion."

"Realists," on the other hand, stressed power and interest, rather than ideals in international relations. Realism is basically conservative, empirical, prudent, suspicious of idealistic principles, and respectful of the lessons of history. It is more likely to produce a pessimistic rather than an optimistic view of international politics. Realists regarded power as the fundamental concept in the social sciences (such as energy in physics); although they admitted that power relationships are often cloaked in moral and legal terms. The realist viewed theories as rationalizing, rather than shaping, events. He criticized the utopian for allowing his visionary goals to distort his scientific techniques of analysis.

To the realist of the 1930s, appeals to reason and to public opinion proved woefully weak supports for keeping the peace: for example, they did not save Manchuria and Ethiopia from aggression. Thus, while the idealist hoped for change that might permit disarmament, the realist continued to worry about national security and the need for military force to support diplomacy.

The argument pitting utopianism and realism is classic. Carr's analysis of this dialectic is still timely: "The inner meaning of the modern international crisis," he contended, "is the collapse of the whole structure of utopianism based on the concept of the harmony of interests." [25] In his view, the international morality of the interwar years merely justified the interests of the dominant English-speaking status-quo powers, of the satisfied versus the unsatisfied, of the "haves" versus the "have-nots." Carr, a pragmatist, took utopians *and* realists to task. He saw that whereas the utopians ignore the lessons

23. Arnold Wolfers, "Statesmanship and Moral Choice," *World Politics,* I (January, 1949), 175–195, and "Political Theory and International Relations," Arnold Wolfers and Lawrence Martin, eds., *The Anglo-American Tradition in Foreign Affairs* (New Haven: Yale University Press, 1956); Kenneth W. Thompson, "The Limits of Principle in International Politics: Necessity and the New Balance of Power," *Journal of Politics,* XX (August, 1958), 437–467.

24. Adam Smith and other eighteenth-century economists, following in the individualistic steps of John Locke, taught that men in a competitive system, when they seek their own private gain, are led by an "invisible hand" to promote the interest of the whole society.

25. Carr, *op. cit.,* p. 62. See especially Chapters 1–6. For a fuller exposition of the realist theories, see Chapter 3 below.

of history, the realists often read history too pessimistically. Whereas the idealist exaggerates freedom of choice, the realist exaggerates fixed causality and slips into determinism. While the idealist may confuse national self-interest with universal moral principles, the realist runs the risk of cynicism and "fails to provide any ground for purposive and meaningful action" [26]—i.e., he denies that human thought modifies human action. Purpose precedes observation; the vision of a Plato comes before the analysis of an Aristotle. The vision may even seem totally unrealistic. Carr cites the alchemists who tried to turn lead into gold, noting that when their visionary project failed they began examining "facts" more carefully, thus giving birth to modern science.[27] He concludes that sound political theories contain elements of utopianism and realism, of power and moral values.[28]

INTERSTATE RELATIONS AND THE POLITICAL ORDER

During the 1930s, academicians on both sides of the Atlantic tried to come to grips with the nature and scope of international relations as a field of study within the university. In 1935, Sir Alfred Zimmern, professor of international relations at Oxford University, suggested that "the study of international relations extends from the natural sciences at one end to moral philosophy . . . at the other." He defined the field not as a single subject or discipline but as a "bundle of subjects . . . viewed from a common angle." [29]

Debate on scope, emphasis, and methodology in the discipline of international relations reached a point of intensity before World War II and continues today. Nicholas J. Spykman, among the first to propose a rigorous definition, used the term "interstate relations," which, however, he did not expect to gain wide acceptance: "International relations are relations between individuals belonging to different states, . . . international behavior is the social behavior of individuals or groups aimed, . . . or influenced by the existence or behavior of individuals or groups belonging to a different state." [30] Loosely defined, the

26. *Ibid.*, p. 92.

27. *Ibid.*, pp. 5–6.

28. *Ibid.*, pp. 10, 20–21, 93–94.

29. Alfred Zimmern, "Introductory Report to the Discussions in 1935," Alfred Zimmern, ed., *University Teaching of International Relations,* Report of the Eleventh Session of the International Studies Conference (Paris: International Institute of Intellectual Cooperation, League of Nations, 1939), pp. 7–9. Later, C. A. W. Manning prepared a pamphlet for UNESCO on the university teaching of international relations in which he took a similar position. There

is an international relations complex which has to be viewed from a "universalistic angle" and none of the established disciplines as traditionally taught can be relied upon to supply this necessary perspective. See P. D. Marchant, "Theory and Practice in the Study of International Relations," *International Relations,* I (April, 1955), 95–102.

30. Nicholas J. Spykman, "Methods of Approach to the Study of International Relations," *Proceedings of the Fifth Conference of Teachers of International Law and Related Subjects* (Washington: Carnegie Endowment for International Peace, 1933), p. 60.

term "international relations" could encompass many different activities— international communications, business transactions, athletic contests, tourism, scientific conferences, educational exchange programs, and religious missionary activities. The political scientist is interested in such phenomena as world's fairs, Telstar, the Olympic Games, multinational corporations, fluctuations in the pattern of Japan's foreign trade, or the Vatican's relations with Israel and the Arab states—insofar as these have implications for international political relations. The political scientist, as such, cannot learn much from the facts surrounding a single transnational telegram, a periodical subscription, a wedding or real estate purchase. Yet significant increases or decreases of these items in the aggregate might have potential political meaning, just as the conclusion of agreements for an international motion picture distribution, a television rerun, a professor and student exchange program, and oceanic ecology might have. Because governments and international organizations are important in international relations and "interdisciplinary" in outlook and interests, political scientists, adhering to the Aristotelian tradition, insist that their field is the queen of the international relations sciences. In fact, the study of international relations in an American university has usually been organized within the department of political science.[31] Thus, a definition of "international relations" depends on a definition of politics.

Political action, a distinctive dimension of human social life, cannot be reduced to any other sphere, such as the economic or the psychological. The most frequently cited of the modern definitions, that of David Easton—that politics is the process whereby societal values are authoritatively allocated [32]— is too limited for our usage. It presupposes the organization of a society under an effective government. It cannot encompass international politics because there is no effective authority at this level. True, conceiving of politics as an activity within and among groups covers both intranational and international politics. The political process involves organizing and directing social power in many forms, in order to accomplish objectives desired by the group. Political activity aims at policymaking on group goals, procedures and leadership. The values and interests of the groups shape both the ends and means of politics. As Morton A. Kaplan has suggested, "politics is the regulation of the system. It involves action manifesting capabilities or 'power'; it may involve restructuring the relationship of the roles in the system or creating or eliminating roles; and it also allocates goods or values." [33] Power is merely a capability

31. Quincy Wright, *The Study of International Relations* (New York: Appleton-Century-Crofts, 1955), p. 28.

32. David Easton, *The Political System* (New York: Alfred A. Knopf, 1959), pp. 129–131. See also Bruno Leoni, "The Meaning of 'Political' in Political Decisions," *Political Studies,* V (October, 1957), 225–239.

33. Morton A. Kaplan, *Macropolitics: Selected Essays on the Philosophy and Science of Politics* (Chicago: Aldine Publishing Company, 1969), p. 68. Kaplan holds that politics occurs within a political system which, "like many other social systems, has recognizable interests which are not identical—though not necessarily opposed and perhaps complementary—with those of the members of the

of attaining ends, although power may at times become an end in itself. This holds internally, within nations, and externally, in the world at large. But we must not lose sight of the crucial structural difference between national societies, where the normal tendency is toward the centralization of power and values, and international society, where power and values are decentralized.[34]

POST-WORLD WAR II REALISM

Not surprisingly World War II and its immediate aftermath shifted Western thinking on international relations from idealism to realism, from law and organization to the elements of power. There seems to be at least a partial vindication of the Hegelian dialectic (in which history is seen to develop through the clash of opposites) in the fact that war increases man's desire for peace. But when millions engage in military conflict on the scale of World War II, when entire politico-socioeconomic systems of modern nation-states are geared for total war, and when war aims impel scientists and engineers to create new weapons by researching the fundamental mysteries of matter, inevitably the postwar generation regards international politics as a power struggle. Even idealistically inclined analysts become skeptical of pure utopian programs and instead call for a merger of international law and organization with effective power to insure international peace, the security of nations, and the equitable settlement of disputes.

Throughout the post-World War II period, the United States' global responsibilities generated within American universities a heightened interest in the study of international relations. War veterans in college showed a keen concern over "foreign affairs." Under the impact of critical international developments, often associated with the East-West "cold war," the United States government greatly expanded its operations in the areas of national military security, alliances and other international organizations, and economic development assistance to foreign countries—all these operations, of course, increased the need for trained personnel. National political leaders and career public servants emphasized the importance of Americans assuming a world outlook to prevent

system and within which there are regularized agencies and methods for making decisions concerning those interests. The rules for decision-making, including the specification of the decision-making roles and the general constitutional rules governing the society, are enacted within the political system." Morton A. Kaplan, *System and Process in International Politics* (New York: John Wiley and Sons, 1957), pp. 13–14.

34. See Vernon Van Dyke, *Political Science, A Philosophical Analysis* (Stanford:

Stanford University Press, 1960), pp. 133–135. On the difference between domestic and international politics, with emphasis on the lack of a common power and the legality of force in the interstate arena, see Raymond Aron, "What Is a Theory of International Relations?" *Journal of International Affairs,* XXI (No. 2, 1967), 190; Stanley Hoffmann, *The State of War* (New York: Frederick A. Praeger, 1965), Chapter 2; and Roger D. Masters, "World Politics as a Primitive Political System," *World Politics,* XVI (July, 1964), 595–619.

a return to the isolationism of the interwar period. For the first time, many American businessmen became aware of international trade and investment possibilities. Scientists, alarmed at the implications of the new nuclear technology which they had just produced, entered politics as crusading novices, warning of the dangers confronting mankind. Civic-minded persons zealously organized councils and associations across the land to educate and exhort—all by way of making citizens more aware of the international dimension.

Several works published in the late 1940s emphasized the power approach to the study of international relations. Martin Wight noted that

> *what distinguishes modern history from medieval history is the predominance of the idea of power over the idea of right; the very term 'Power' to describe a state in its international aspect is significant; and the view of the man in the street, who is perhaps inclined to take it for granted that foreign politics are inevitably 'power politics,' is not without a shrewd insight.*[35]

Another English scholar, Georg Schwarzenberger, analyzed power as a prime factor in international politics. In the absence of genuine international community, he asserted, groups within the international system can be expected to do what they are physically able to do rather than what they are morally exhorted to do. Power, in Schwarzenberger's view, is by no means a wanton, destructive thing. It is a combination of persuasive influence and coercive force, but those who wield power, while maintaining and exhibiting an ability to impose their wills on the noncompliant, normally prefer to achieve their ends merely by posing the threat of effective sanctions, without actually resorting to physical force.[36]

To say that international politics is predicated on the concept of power does not necessarily imply the simplistic cynicism that individuals and groups are constantly seeking to maximize their power; that all states are potentially aggressive and expansionist; that the nature of international politics is always "red in tooth and claw." Building up power does not necessarily imply even intending to apply pressure against other states. The pursuit of political power is balanced against other drives of an economic, psychological, social and cultural nature. Men's efforts to attain these nonpolitical wants often impose limits on their ability to pursue political power beyond their national boundaries.[37] Several states use the greater part of their power for self-development and improvement in the quality of their social and cultural life. Some of the lesser states located near larger powers focus on power in an inverted manner,

35. Martin Wight, *Power Politics,* "Looking Forward" Pamphlet No. 8 (London: Royal Institute of International Affairs, 1946), p. 11.

36. Georg Schwarzenberger, *Power Politics: A Study of World Society* (New York: Frederick A. Praeger, 1951), pp. 13–14. (The third edition of this work appeared in 1964.)

37. Vernon Van Dyke, *International Politics* (New York: Appleton-Century-Crofts, 1957), p. 10.

Theoretical Approaches to International Relations   11

seeking security through noninvolvement, isolation, neutrality, appeasement, or the acceptance of a dependent buffer or satellite status.

Even the "Great Powers," who historically have set the competitive tone of international politics, are not perpetually at each other's throats. The history of interstate relations is one of conflict *and* cooperation. The peace among larger rivals may be tense and precarious at times, but rivals do experience fairly long periods of relative peace during which their tacit cooperation, though less visible, may be more significant than their public contentiousness. Nevertheless, Great Powers in modern history have either resorted to force or at least threatened the use of force to defend or advance what they considered their basic interests against other states. Perhaps the most fundamental fact of the international system is that both power and values are still decentralized. Certainly an international system—i.e., a complex set of variables in inter-action—does exist. But at most it is only a society of national political communities which are aware of each other and which produce effects upon each other. There is, as yet, no international community in which political values are shared sufficiently on a global scale to facilitate the emergence of an orderly set of behavioral expectations in respect to regulation, cooperative relations, adjudicating conflict relations, and controlling or eliminating violence.

The textbooks published during the two decades after World War II reflected an increasing recognition in the United States that "power" in myriad forms holds a central place in the analysis of international relations. The text which had the greatest impact upon the university teaching of international relations—that of Hans J. Morgenthau—defined national interest in terms of power.[38] The other important textbooks of that period all devoted substantial attention to the nature of power and power politics.[39] Nearly all

38. Hans J. Morgenthau, *Politics Among Nations* (New York: Alfred A. Knopf, 1948, 1954, 1960, 1967).

39. Frederick L. Schuman, *op. cit.*, 4th and 5th eds. (New York: McGraw-Hill Book Company, 1948, 1953); Robert Strausz-Hupé and Stefan T. Possony, *International Relations* (New York: McGraw-Hill Book Company, 1950, 1954); Norman D. Palmer and Howard C. Perkins, *International Relations* (Boston: Houghton Mifflin Company, 1953, 1957, 1969); Norman J. Padelford and George A. Lincoln, *The Dynamics of International Politics* (New York: Macmillan Company, 1962); Ernst B. Haas and Allen S. Whiting, *Dynamics of International Relations* (New York: McGraw-Hill Book Company, 1956); Harold and Margaret Sprout, *Foundations of National Power* (Princeton: D. Van Nostrand Company, 1945, 1951) and *Foundations of International Politics* (Princeton: D. Van Nostrand Company, 1962); Quincy Wright, *op. cit.*; Vernon Van Dyke, *International Politics, op. cit.*; Charles P. Schleicher, *Introduction to International Relations* (Englewood Cliffs, N.J.: Prentice-Hall, 1954) and *International Relations: Cooperation and Conflict* (Englewood Cliffs, N.J.: Prentice-Hall, 1962); Frederick H. Hartmann, *The Relations of Nations* (New York: Macmillan Company, 1957, 1962); A. F. K. Organski, *World Politics* (New York: Alfred A. Knopf, 1958); Lennox A. Mills and Charles H. McLaughlin, *World Politics in Transition* (New York: Henry Holt and Company, 1956); Fred Greene, *Dynamics of International Relations* (New York: Holt, Rinehart and Winston, 1964); W. W. Kulski, *International Politics in a Revolutionary Age* (Philadelphia: J. B. Lippincott Company, 1964, 1967).

devoted at least a chapter or more to a discussion of the nature of power. In addition they devoted on the average another two chapters to analyzing the various elements or factors of national power such as geography, population, and raw materials.

Most texts persisted in providing chapters on those subjects which had been the primary concerns up to World War II—international law and morality, international organization and peaceful settlement of disputes, diplomacy and the conduct of foreign relations. A plethora of new categories and concepts appeared: nationalism, imperialism, colonialism and the emergence of the Third World, and ideology and propaganda. Some texts contained chapters on alliances, regional or functional integration, disarmament and arms control, and specific techniques of foreign policy such as nonalignment and isolation. Several texts included an account of the historic or modern foreign policies of selected leading powers.[40]

The expanding interest in theoretical analysis was even more evident in works other than these descriptive textbooks. Quincy Wright's *The Study of International Relations,* although often used as a text, belongs more properly to this theoretical category. Morton A. Kaplan and Charles A. McClelland theorized on the international system. Kenneth W. Thompson grappled with the issues of political realism. Richard C. Snyder and his colleagues concentrated on foreign policy decision-making. John H. Herz approached the issue of international politics in the nuclear age. Ernst B. Haas dealt with functional integration. Richard N. Rosecrance analyzed international politics in terms of action and reaction processes in various diplomatic periods, while Karl W. Deutsch approached it as a development in social communication. Thomas C. Schelling handled the subject in terms of conflict strategy and George Liska in terms of equilibrium theory—to mention only a few.[41] Moreover, in the early 1960s several anthologies in international theory facilitated the burgeoning interest in this field.[42]

40. The reader's attention is called to the following excellent reviews of the leading international relations texts: Richard C. Snyder, "Toward Greater Order in the Study of International Politics," *World Politics,* VII (April, 1955), 461–478; Fred A. Sondermann, "The Study of International Relations: 1956 Version," *ibid.,* IX (October, 1957), 102–111; Robert W. Tucker, "The Study of International Politics," *ibid.,* X (July, 1958), 639–647.

41. The bibliographical data for these and several other related works will be found in succeeding chapters where the various theoretical approaches are treated in depth.

42. William T. R. Fox, ed., *Theoretical Aspects of International Relations* (Notre Dame: University of Notre Dame Press, 1959); Charles A. McClelland, William C. Olson, and Fred A. Sondermann, eds., *The Theory and Practice of International Relations* (Englewood Cliffs, N.J.: Prentice-Hall, 1960); Stanley Hoffmann, ed., *Contemporary Theory in International Relations* (Englewood Cliffs, N.J.: Prentice-Hall 1960); Ivo D. Duchacek, ed., with the collaboration of Kenneth W. Thompson, *Conflict and Cooperation Among Nations* (New York: Holt, Rinehart and Winston, 1960); Klaus Knorr and Sidney Verba, eds., *The International System: Theoretical* (World Politics, XIV [October, 1961]) (Princeton: Princeton University Press, 1961); James N. Rosenau, ed., *International Politics and Foreign Policy: A Reader in Research and Theory* (New York: Free Press, 1961);

As William T. R. and Annette Baker Fox have shown, in recent decades remarkable efforts have been directed toward methodologies and techniques for research and analysis in international relations.[43] Government-supported "think tanks" such as the RAND Corporation, a dozen or so university-centered research institutes, and a few private organizations and conferences have had a significant effect on trends of thought in the field. Such periodicals as *World Politics, Review of Politics, Orbis,* the *Journal of Conflict Resolution,* the *Journal of Peace Research,* and *International Studies Quarterly* have supplemented the older, more general publications. Advanced weapons technology has necessitated specifically dealing with deterrence, arms control, and disarmament. Scholars have concentrated on the following specifically defined problems—the nature of bipolarity, the diplomacy of alliances, experiments in regional integration (notably in Western Europe), the politics of development and of developing countries, decolonization and the rise of the Afro-Asian states, and international economic policies in an age of ideological conflict. Investigations have concentrated on psychological strategy, conflict resolution, the role of foreign policy elites, and the nature of the decision-making process. Methodology has been the issue in the "Great Debates" between realists and idealists, between traditionalists and behaviorists (to be dealt with in Chapters 3 and 13).

By the mid-1960s courses and seminars in international theory had become rather common in university programs, particularly at the graduate level. Some concentrated on a single favorite theoretical approach or on only a few

Horace V. Harrison, ed., *The Role of Theory in International Relations* (Princeton: D. Van Nostrand Company, 1964).

43. William T. R. Fox and Annette Baker Fox, "The Teaching of International Relations in the United States," *World Politics,* XIII (July, 1961), 339–359: See also Quincy Wright, *op. cit.,* Chapters 3, 4; Grayson Kirk, *op. cit.;* Waldemar Gurian, "On the Study of International Relations," *Review of Politics,* VIII (July, 1946), 275-282; Frederick L. Schuman, "The Study of International Relations in the United States," *Contemporary Political Science: A Survey of Methods, Research and Training* (Paris: United Nations Educational, Scientific, and Cultural Organization, 1950); Frederick S. Dunn, "The Present Course of International Relations Research,"

World Politics, II (October, 1949), 142–146; Kenneth W. Thompson, *op. cit.;* L. Gray Cowen, "Theory and Practice in the Teaching of International Relations in the United States," in Geoffrey L. Goodwin, ed., *The University Teaching of International Relations* (Oxford: Basil Blackwell, Ltd. 1951); John Gange, *University Research on International Relations* (Washington: American Council on Education, 1958); Richard N. Swift, *World Affairs and the College Curriculum* (Washington: American Council on Education, 1959); Edward W. Weidner, *The World Role of Universities,* The Carnegie Series in American Education (New York: McGraw-Hill Book Company, 1962), especially the chapters dealing with student-abroad programs, exchange programs, and international programs of university assistance.

theories; others became more comprehensive. However aesthetically satisfying a neat, logically unified theoretical system might be, no theory adequate to the complexity of international reality presently exists. The theoretical analyst who makes a significant contribution to the field works within a unified intellectual schema. But the beginning student must master a body of existing knowledge before striking out on his own. Therefore he would be wise to survey the field of international relations theory rather than prematurely select a single theory.

THE SCOPE, NATURE AND FUNCTION OF INTERNATIONAL THEORY

Most general texts published after 1945 presented international relations theory or theories only peripherally and in a piecemeal, if not haphazard, fashion. Textbook writers seldom concerned themselves with the development of a systematic, single, coherent theory. The notable exception was Hans J. Morgenthau, who came closest to setting forth a closely reasoned and internally consistent explanation of nation-state behavior based upon a classical, near Thucydidean-Augustinian form of "realism." This orientation to classical realism was ardent in its theory of human nature and its theory that national interest (defined in terms of power) is the normal objective pursued by governments. Naturally, all textbook writers were obliged to discuss specific theories or summarize previous theoretical speculations and controversies about such subjects as power, the state system, the balance of power, imperialism, the impact of modern military technology on international relations, and so forth. But seldom was there an effort to draw precise linkages between the theories discussed in one chapter with the theories discussed in another, or to find out whether any of them could be fitted together in a larger whole.[44] This is not to suggest that the textbook authors themselves lacked an underlying, informing theory of international relations. A student with a critical philosophical bent, by carefully analyzing any textbook's concepts and assumptions, might be able to reconstruct the writer's theory fairly accurately. Usually, however, an overarching theory was not made explicit in the texts. Perhaps this was inevitable, given the scope and complexity of the field to which the texts were designed to introduce the student.

A very important contribution of the textbooks to the development of international relations theory is often overlooked. Taken in the aggregate, they provide a crude, discursive definition of the scope of the field. Before we can develop theory, we must have at least a vague consensus within the commun-

44. Horace V. Harrison, writing in 1964, criticized not only the textbooks but nearly all writing in international theory as being partial, implicit rather than explicit, too narrowly focused, designed to serve particular professional interests, and incapable of providing a guide either to research or to action. He added, however, that some progress toward more general theories had begun since the latter 1950s. See his Introduction to the book he edited, *op. cit.*, pp. 8–9.

ity of scholars as to what the field of international relations entails. Textbooks and other significant works published over a few decades furnish us with a comprehensive view and thus prevent us from accepting too hastily a neatly phrased, yet intellectually-confining definition. Frederick S. Dunn once warned that the word *scope* is dangerously ambiguous because it implies clearly discernible boundaries as readily identifiable as a surveyor's mark.

> *A field of knowledge does not possess a fixed extension in space but is a constantly changing focus of data and methods that happen at the moment to be useful in answering an identifiable set of questions. It presents at any given time different aspects to different observers, depending on their point of view and purpose. The boundaries that supposedly divide one field of knowledge from another are not fixed walls between separate cells of truth but are convenient devices for arranging known facts and methods in manageable segments for instruction and practice. But the foci of interest are constantly shifting and these divisions tend to change with them. . .*[45]

We are, at this point, on the threshold of defining the field in order to develop a systematic theory. Every good scholar has views on what the field encompasses, and the authors do not wish to impose any dogmatic conceptions. Their definitive presentations are designed to encourage the reader to broaden his own animated debate with teachers and students by including the theories of recognized authorities in the field. The end of this debate will hopefully be not to memorize the *views* of these authorities but to clarify the discipline in which we wish to theorize.

What are we studying? Although international relations scholars cannot at present agree on what is included in and excluded from the field, the student must be satisfied in his own mind regarding the phenomena he is investigating. Dunn says that international relations "may be looked upon as the actual relations that take place across national boundaries, or as the body of knowledge which we have of those relations at any given time." [46] This is a fairly standard approach, but is it adequate? It is comprehensive. It does not limit the subject to official relations between states and governments. But returning to a previously raised question, is this delineation too broad, and would it be better to qualify the transnational relations on the basis of their political significance, e.g., by focusing upon the power relations among the world's basic political units? When doing this, of course, we accept the political order as the central organizing framework for our study. It is possible also

45. Frederick S. Dunn, "The Scope of International Relations," *World Politics,* I (October, 1948), 142.

46. *Ibid.,* p. 143. Stanley Hoffmann warns against excessive preoccupation with the problem of defining scope. A definition, he says, is useful if it merely suggests the proper area of inquiry. It need not pretend to penetrate to the essence of the subject, especially in the social sciences. *Contemporary Theory in International Relations, op. cit.,* pp. 4–6.

that this definition may be too restrictive. "Relations across national boundaries" may not cover all phenomena that would come within the bounds of international relations, e.g., linkages between domestic and foreign politics.

What are the units of study and our level of analysis? At first glance, this seems easy to answer, but it becomes more difficult as we proceed. Even after answering the earlier question concerning the scope of the field in a manner calculated to gather the economic, cultural and other extra-political relations of states, governments and peoples, one often has a tendency when thinking about "units" and "levels of analysis" to go back to states and governments alone. Thus, international relations become interstate relations—at least at times—in our thinking, as Nicholas Spykman once hoped they would. But even at a purely political level, we encounter problems. The units themselves undergo constant historic changes. Even over the short course of a half century from the eve of World War I to the early 1960s, the political map of the world underwent drastic changes as empires gave way to successor states. Should we restrict the scope of the field to relations between sovereign states? What about colonies, protectorates, trusteeships, partitioned states and other territories with an extraordinary status? What about intergovernmental organizations (such as the United Nations, the North Atlantic Treaty Organization, the European Economic Community, and the Arab League)—entities with which governments themselves may have substantial diplomatic dealings? Quincy Wright reached this conclusion: "Clearly international relations includes relations between many entities of uncertain sovereignty. As a subject of study it is not limited by the legal formalism which alone could at any moment precisely define what entities are sovereign and what are not." [47]

Several other additions or alternatives to organized political communities have been suggested as proper units of study or "actors" in this field. Within nations, one might examine the role of such organizations, institutions and groups as political parties, churches, ethnic minorities, the press, and economic interest groups (labor, farmers, and industries anxious to export or to achieve protection against foreign imports). Arnold Wolfers pointed out that recent decades have witnessed a reaction against the traditional "states-as-sole-actors approach" in which all significant events and changes in the international scene were attributed to the policies of national governments.

> *This reaction has taken two distinct forms: one new theory has placed individual human beings in the center of the scene that had previously been reserved to the nation-states; the other emphasized the existence, side by side with the state, of other corporate actors, especially international organizations. . . .*
> *The "individuals-as-actors" approach first appeared in the form of*

47. *The Study of International Relations,* p. 5. The authors of this text would note that in an ideologically divided world, there may not be any precise way of formally defining sovereignty. For example, does "international society" recognize North Korea, North Vietnam and East Germany as sovereign states?

Theoretical Approaches to International Relations

what has been called the "minds-of-men theory of international politics." It was soon to be followed by the "decision-making" approach. . . . It was the aim of the new theories to replace the abstract notion of the state with the living realities of human minds, wills, and hearts. But the result, on the whole, was to substitute one set of abstractions for another, because, in politics, it is also an abstraction to examine the individual apart from the corporate bodies by means of which he acts politically.[48]

According to Wolfers, it is wrong to assume that because private individuals in Country A pursue the same goals of personal welfare, happiness and social advancement as private individuals in Country B, it should be a simple matter to eliminate political hostility and promote harmonious relations between the two countries by setting the good, peaceful interests of individuals against the evil power designs of governments. He found the exclusive minds-of-men approach highly misleading because, even though it is true in a sense that international relations takes place "in here" (in the minds of citizens) and not just "out there" (in the world), nevertheless "psychological events are not the whole stuff out of which international politics is formed," and thus the psychologist alone, without the political scientist, cannot adequately explain an international reality which proceeds not merely from individuals but also from organized groups of many magnitudes.[49]

This brings us to one of the most crucial and enduring dilemmas in all the social sciences: the relationship between the "macrocosmic" and the "microcosmic," between collective power structures and individual personalities.[50] Stewart E. Perry has attempted to bridge the gap between the two polar levels of international analysis—to integrate psychological data with political concepts—by highlighting the role of the national, "the role played by a person when interacting with others who are not citizens of his own nation."[51] But the nation, too, has been put in some doubt as a result of modern technological developments. In 1957, John H. Herz argued that the territorial nation-state could be the basic unit of the international political system only so long as its "hard shell" defense enabled it to claim impenetrability and thus to

48. Arnold Wolfers, "The Actors in International Politics," in William T. R. Fox, ed., *op. cit.*, p. 84. A full discussion of decision-making theories will be found in Chapter 11 and of regional or functional integration with accompanying corporate actors in Chapter 10.

49. *Ibid.*, p. 89.

50. See J. David Singer, "Man and World Politics: The Psychological Interface," *Journal of Social Issues*, XXIV (July, 1968), 127–156; and Heinz Eulau, *Micro-Macro Political Analysis*, (Chicago: Aldine Publishing Company, 1970). See

also below the discussion on this point in chapters 5–9, especially pp. 142–143 and 197–199, with particular reference to the writings of Herbert C. Kelman and Werner Levi. See also Singer's earlier essay, "The Level of Analysis Problem in International Relations," in Knorr and Verba, eds., *op. cit.*

51. Stewart E. Perry, "Notes on the Role of the National: A Social-Psychological Concept for the Study of International Relations," *Journal of Conflict Resolution*, I (December, 1957), 346–363.

afford security and protection to its population. With the advent of nuclear weapons, he said, the territorial state has begun to experience a new permeability "which tends to obliterate the very meaning of unit and unity, power and power relations, sovereignty and independence."[52] Arnold Toynbee, as a result of his monumental *A Study of History,* suggests (more implicitly than explicitly) that the nation-state does not constitute a viable unit either of historical or political study, and should be replaced by the civilizational area.[53] Morton A. Kaplan offers for our contemplation the whole international system as the most appropriate object of analytical investigation.[54] George Modelski advances the hypothesis that there are two basic models of social and economic organization—Agraria and Industria—each having distinctive implications for the foreign policy of nations and for international politics as a whole.[55] William H. Riker points to the importance of political coalitions for theory-building purposes.[56]

In any event we face a choice between the micro-level and the macro-level of analysis; this choice can be not only extremely difficult but also highly controversial within the discipline. J. David Singer directs attention to the problem in the following trenchant passage:

> *In the vernacular of general systems theory, the observer is always confronted with a system, its sub-systems, and their respective environments, and while he may choose as his system any cluster of phenomena from the most minute organism to the universe itself, such choice cannot be merely a function of whim or caprice, habit or familiarity. . . . We have, in our texts and elsewhere, roamed up and down the ladder of organizational complexity with remarkable abandon. . . . And though most of us have tended to settle upon the nation*

52. John H. Herz, "The Rise and Demise of the Territorial State," *World Politics,* IX (April, 1957), 474. Herz later admitted that his earlier deprecation of the role of the state was probably premature, and that the same nuclear developments which had rendered the territory of states theoretically vulnerable had also, paradoxically, made all force, even conventional force, "unavailable" in the relations between major powers and their alliance blocs, thus producing trends toward a "new territoriality." See his "The Territorial State Revisited: Reflections on the Future of the Nation-State," James N. Rosenau, ed., *op. cit.,* rev. ed., 1969, pp. 76–89.

53. Toynbee in an earlier period between the wars emphasized the nation-state. This was also his more "idealistic" phase in his theory of international relations. Later he shifted his attention to

civilizations and the world religions, as he became more "realistic" in his advocacy of the balance of power. See his "Encounters Between Civilizations," *Harper's,* CXCIV (April, 1947), 289–294; and "The International Outlook," *International Affairs,* XXIII (October, 1947), 463–476. See also Kenneth W. Thompson, "Toynbee and the Theory of International Politics," *Political Science Quarterly,* LXXXI (September, 1956), 365–386.

54. Morton A. Kaplan, *op. cit.* See also the references to Kaplan's work in Chapter 4 below.

55. George Modelski, "Agraria and Industria: Two Models of the International System," Knorr and Verba, eds., *op. cit.*

56. William H. Riker, *The Theory of Political Coalitions* (New Haven: Yale University Press, 1962).

Theoretical Approaches to International Relations

as our most comfortable resting place, we have retained our propensity for vertical drift, failing to appreciate the value of a stable point of focus. Whether this lack of concern is a function of the relative infancy of the discipline or the nature of the intellectual traditions from which it springs, it nevertheless remains a significant variable in the general sluggishness which characterizes the development of theory in the study of relations among nations.[57]

Should study and theory focus on contemporary international reality? There is an inescapable attractiveness about the present international system for purposes of research. Materials and funding support usually come easier when the subject under study is of relatively contemporary concern—i.e., a phenomenon that falls within the time span since World War II. Yet despite the lure of the present, most experienced scholars in international relations realize that if the development of theory is ever to lead to a predictive capability, a knowledge of international relations in the past is essential, since it broadens and strengthens the data base from which projections are to be made.

The argument concerning the value of historical knowledge can only be partially correlated with the argument between "traditionalists" and "behaviorists." Hedley Bull has censured the practitioners of the scientific approach charging that "their thinking is certainly characterized by a lack of any sense of inquiry into international politics as a continuing tradition to which they are the latest recruits."[58] But this is not entirely so. Although most behaviorists, given their preferred methodologies, rarely engage in research requiring a mastery of historiographical techniques, it is not accurate to suggest that all scientific theorists are experimental behaviorists who are impervious to history. Morton Kaplan, for example, opens his principal work with a tribute to history: "There is one respect in which a science of international politics must always be indebted to history. History is the great laboratory within which international action occurs."[59] Kaplan also calls for investigations into the ancient Greek city-state system, the Italian state system of the Renaissance, and the balance-of-power system that dominated Europe during the eighteenth and nineteenth centuries in order to compare typical system behaviors in different eras.[60] (Kaplan's models of the international system have been used in

57. J. David Singer, "The Level-of-Analysis Problem in International Relations," Knorr and Verba, eds., *op. cit.*, pp. 77–78.

58. Hedley Bull, "International Theory: The Case for a Classical Approach," *World Politics*, XVIII (April, 1966), 375–376.

59. Kaplan, *System and Process in International Politics*, p. 3. In an article written as a rejoinder to Bull's criticism of the scientific writers, Kaplan accused the traditionalists of using history in-

eptly, of falling into the trap of "overparticularization and unrelated generalization," and of being unaware that many writers in the modern scientific school regard history as a laboratory for the acquisition of empirical data. See his "The New Great Debate: Traditionalism vs. Science in International Relations," *World Politics*, XIX (October, 1966), 15–16.

60. Morton A. Kaplan, "Problems of Theory Building and Theory Confirmation in International Politics," Knorr and

such studies which are discussed in Chapter 4). The international theorist should be interested in all international systems, past, present, future and hypothetical.[61] Thus he should not confine his attention exclusively to the existing nation-state system. Indeed, he cannot fully understand what exists unless he has some knowledge of what existed formerly, out of which present reality evolved, and what might exist, toward which the present seems to be moving and by which the present can be evaluated. A history of international relations is not an international theory; it *is* the essential raw material with which the theoretician works.[62]

What is the relationship between theory and practice? Aristotle distinguished between knowing and doing, between the speculative intellect which seeks to understand and the practical intellect which chooses a specific course of action under a concrete set of circumstances.[63] David Hume, too, went further, drawing a sharp contrast among three classes of knowledge—(a) deductive reasoning which relates to the logical and necessary truths of mathematics and metaphysics; (b) empirical knowledge which pertains to apparently causal relationships that are not really rationally necessary; and (c) value judgments which derive from an accumulation of historical facts as they have affected human emotions and intuitions. For Hume, politics and morals must always be inextricably bound with value judgments and hence can be neither deductive nor empirical.[64] To state the problem of theory and practice in

---

Verba, eds., *op. cit.,* p. 23; Morton A. Kaplan, *New Approaches to International Relations* (New York: St. Martin's Press, 1968), pp. 399–404. See also George Modelski, "Comparative International Systems," *World Politics,* XIV (July, 1962), 662–674, in which he reviews Adda B. Bozeman, *Politics and Culture in International History* (Princeton: Princeton University Press, 1960). See also Hoffmann, *op. cit.,* pp. 174–180.

61. Kaplan, *System and Process,* Chapter 2. See also the reference below, p. 30 to Quincy Wright's fourfold approach to all social studies.

62. "The substance of theory is history, composed of unique events and occurrences. An episode in history and politics is in one sense never repeated. It happens as it does only once. . . . In this sense, history is beyond the reach of theory. Underlying all theory, however, is the assumption that these same unique events are also more concrete instances of more general propositions. The wholly unique, having nothing in common with anything else, is indescribable. . . ." Kenneth W. Thompson, "Toward a Theory

of International Politics," *American Political Science Review,* XLIX (September, 1955), 734.

63. "Nor again does Practical Wisdom consist in a knowledge of general principles only, but it is necessary that one should also know the particular details, because it is apt to act, and action is concerned with details; for which reason sometimes men who have not much knowledge are more practical than those who have. . . . Since then Practical Wisdom is apt to act, one ought to have both kinds of knowledge, or, if only one, the knowledge of details rather than of Principle." *The Ethics of Aristotle,* trans. D. P. Chase (New York: E. P. Dutton and Company, 1950), Book VI, p. 147.

64. David Hume, A Treatise of Human Nature, Part III, "Of Probability and Knowledge," in *The Essential David Hume,* intro. by Robert P. Wolff (New York: New American Library, 1969), pp. 53–99. See Sheldon S. Wolin, "Hume and Conservatism," *American Political Science Review,* XLVIII (December, 1954), 999–1016. Michael Polanyi, too, has

Humean terms, we might say that whereas the pure theorist is usually concerned principally with deductive thought processes and with empirical knowledge that will lead by inductive processes to generalized formulations, the policymaker is usually concerned with the empirical, inductive knowledge derived from his own personal experience rather than from any systematic research effort. He concerns himself also with the subtle details of the political values, forces and preferences operating in a particular situation, so that he can make a decision addressed to this particular situation in all its existential reality rather than to a universal abstraction or probability. Whereas the social theorist wishes to concentrate primarily upon elements common to many situations, the decision-maker invariably wants greater information about those elements that are unique to the case at hand. But lest anyone receives the wrong impression, it should be stressed that the differing emphases of theorist and practitioner do not alter the desirability that each should try to appreciate the modes of knowledge peculiar to the other. Neither can afford to dismiss generalized or particularized knowledge.

The interface between theory and practice leads logically to several corollary questions. Did statesmen of relatively long experience—Talleyrand, Metternich, Canning, Disraeli, Bismarck, Theodore Roosevelt, Wilson, Churchill, Lenin, Stalin, Franklin Roosevelt and de Gaulle—have an international theory worthy of study? When Metternich engineered the post-Napoleonic restoration of a Europe legitimate and in balance; when Disraeli ordered the purchase of the Khedive's Suez Canal Company shares; when Bismarck concluded the Reinsurance Treaty with Russia; when Wilson presided over the dissolution of the Austro-Hungarian Empire and worked to have the League of Nations made an integral part of the Versailles peace settlement; when de Gaulle arrested the progress of the "federalizers" in the European Economic Community—were these men acting on the basis of a coherent theory, of which they were intellectually aware? Or were they acting merely on the basis of pragmatic evaluations in reaction to political pressures of the moment? This is difficult to answer. Some leaders tend more toward theoretical reflections than others. Metternich and Churchill entertained a balance of power theory, Wilson emphasized the principle of national self-determination, and Lenin and Stalin theorized on the relations of capitalistic imperialism with the colonial areas of the world. But to what extent their decisions responded to situations and to what extent their decisions flowed from theories remain subjects of debate. Some conclusions seem tenable. Most statesmen probably reach the majority of their foreign policy decisions through some theoretical reflection, perhaps weighing, even mixing, different theories in their effort to understand, choose and predict. The theories on which they act may not always be the theories that they articulate publicly. In some cases, they may be able to predict trends and outcomes without the aid of very sophisticated theories. They

treated the difference between the theory of affairs and the practice of affairs. *Personal Knowledge* (Chicago: University of Chicago Press, 1958), pp. 49 ff.

are likely to think that their own theories, arising out of reflection on their own personal experience, or out of the accumulated experience of institutions of which they have long been a part (such as the British Foreign Office or the U. S. Department of State) [65] are more reliable guidelines for policy choices than the more abstract theoretical constructs that have been developed in academic circles and couched, as they often are, in a terminology unfamiliar to policymakers. This discussion leads to the question of whether we are studying and theorizing about foreign policy or international relations, and the implications of this question for the "policy sciences" and for "pure theory."

Is the study of international relations the same as the study of foreign policy? The theory-practice dichotomy correlates partially, though not perfectly, with the distinction between foreign policy and international relations. First we must explain the latter distinction and then use this explanation to clarify the theory-practice dichotomy.

Undoubtedly some writers, past and present, have assumed that the study of foreign policy and the study of international relations are synonymous. Even when they did not equate their own country's foreign policy with international relations, they identified the latter field with the sum total of the foreign policies of all states (theoretically) or of the states in which they were for all practical purposes interested. It is true that the relations of any two states can provide part of the data input into our empirical study of international relations,[66] although we would not wish to develop a generalized theory from such a narrow base. But the moot question is whether, if we consider only two states, we can conclude that their "international relations" can be fully understood merely by examining their foreign policies regarding each other, and somehow by adding them. We think not.

Even granting that foreign policy decision-makers are compelled to take action-reaction processes into account, to receive "feedback" from abroad in the wake of their decisions, and to modify their policies accordingly,[67] nevertheless we do not think that "international relations" is merely the sum of the nations' foreign policies. The concept of "foreign policy" refers to the formulation, implementation and evaluation of external choices *within* one country, viewed from the perspective of that country. If we consider the whole inter-

65. For an example of "institutionalized" theory out of the British Foreign Office, the student should read the famous Eyre Crowe memorandum on Anglo-German relations dated January 1, 1907. See G. P. Gooch and Harold V. Temperley, eds., *British Documents on the Origins of the War, 1898–1914* (London: His Majesty's Stationery Office, 1928), III, 402–420.

66. The concept of international relations need not be restricted to those aspects of reality which affect all the elements of the system simultaneously. Thus we do consider it possible to study the interna-tional relations of a region, such as Latin America or the Middle East, so long as the region is recognized as a subsystem of the whole international system. See Leonard Binder, "The Middle East as a Subordinate International System," *World Politics,* X (April, 1958), 408–429; and Michael Brecher, "The Subordinate State System of Southern Asia," *World Politics,* XV (January, 1963), 213–235.

67. This idea is further elaborated below in our discussion of decision-making theories in Chapter 11.

national system, there must always be something inward about foreign policy, no matter how "internationalist" a country's policies might be. Foreign policy is made inside; international relations take place outside, somewhere between two or more countries. (This is not to deny the significant linkage between international and domestic politics.) Moreover, whereas foreign policy is something of which policymakers are aware, international relations involve a confluence of forces and the net results of interactive processes to which foreign policymakers may not even be sensitive. In other words, "international relations" embraces more than the aggregate of national foreign policies; it focuses primarily on the larger interactive process rather than on the way national participants view that process. Still, we quickly add that much of our substantive knowledge about international relations has always come and will continue to come from studies of national foreign policies.[68]

How does international relations differ from policy science? First, what are the policy sciences? A policy science is a form of theory. But it is not "pure theory," which aims solely at understanding. A policy science aims at action. The policy scientist wishes to understand in order to improve his ability to choose wisely. The problem which the policy scientist wishes to solve is often one his society wants solved. The policy scientist's theoretical efforts usually take the form of an "if-then" proposition: If we assume that this particular community wishes to achieve this particular objective, then the following describes the most effective and available means of doing so under existing circumstances. The policy scientist does not really define the goal, even though he may favor it; he assumes some goals as givens and merely provides a technical prescription for the aptest means thereto. (If he allows himself to become too emotionally attached to the attainment of the goal, this might conceivably have an adverse effect upon his expert judgment concerning the policy means to be adopted.) [69]

A policy scientist may address himself to problems either in foreign policy or international relations. Typical foreign policy problems for an American policy scientist would be: finding means of controlling the proliferation of nuclear weapons to nations not already possessing them; promoting tourism to the United States from countries with which we are having balance-of-payments difficulties; improving U.S. relations with NATO allies; enhancing the effectiveness of U.S. aid or information programs abroad in terms of U.S. national interests and objectives; increasing the invulnerability, reliability,

68. The foregoing section owes a great deal to the essay by Fred A. Sondermann, "The Linkage between Foreign Policy and International Politics," James N. Rosenau, ed., *op. cit.*, pp. 8–17.

69. Daniel Lerner and Harold D. Lasswell, eds., *The Policy Sciences: Recent Development in Scope and Method* (Stanford: Stanford University Press, 1951).

According to W. T. R. Fox and Annette Baker Fox, the study of policy problems "is not a threat to objectivity so long as the preferences of the disciplined scholar are permitted to operate only in the selection of the problem and not in the mode of observation and analysis." *Op. cit.*, p. 343. To what extent this can be achieved in practice is another matter.

credibility or some other quality of the U.S. strategic deterrent; and improving the image of the United States in the United Nations. Typical problems likely to interest an international relations policy scientist would be: the achievement of world peace through world law, the elimination of international war, general and complete disarmament, the maintenance of stable equilibrium through mutual deterrence, the construction of international peace-keeping machinery, the expansion of communications and the promotion of regional integration in several regions of the world. A man who is interested in both foreign policy and international relations policy problems may be more interested in one set than the other. Both types of policy scientists are interested in international theory. But instead of playing a creative role in the origination of international theory, both are likely to borrow existing pure theory and adapt it (or bend it, as the case may be) to their policy purposes. Both have legitimate perspectives, which are value-laden rather than value-free: each is committed not only to understanding reality but also to acting upon it for the purpose of achieving certain preselected goals. "To think policy-wise," wrote Lasswell, "is to invent or assess alternative courses of action (or inaction)." [70]

What is, and what should we expect of, a theory of international relations? At the simplest level a theory—any theory—is a general explanation of certain selected phenomena set forth in a manner satisfactory to someone acquainted with the characteristics of the reality being studied. Even this elementary definition, of course, is fraught with difficulties arising out of the problem of objective and subjective knowledge: a theory might satisfy its expounder and horrify his listener, and yet both may claim to be experts concerning the "characteristics of reality." The authors of this text will refrain from attempting to settle the profound questions of epistemology which have remained unsettled for centuries. For us, theory is a way of organizing our knowledge so that we can ask questions worth answering, and guide our research toward valid answers. We can now proceed to speak about "theory" as this term is usually employed in the "exact" sciences and in the "social" (sometimes called the "nonexact") sciences. [71]

70. Harold D. Lasswell, "The Scientific Study of International Relations," *The Yearbook of World Affairs 1958,* London Institute of World Affairs (New York: Frederick A. Praeger, 1958), p. 3. See also Philip E. Mosely, "Research on Foreign Policy," in *Research for Public Policy,* Brookings Dedication Lectures (Washington: Brookings Institution, 1961).

71. Anatol Rapoport, "Various Meanings of 'Theory,'" *American Political Science Review,* LII (December, 1958), 972. Rapoport illustrates the meaning of the-

ory in an exact science by citing the example of the pendulum. The problem is to explain its motion, and this introduces the notions of "why" and "because." The questions asked flow from what is singled out for observation. The question "why does the pendulum move around?" is too vague. "The first task of an exact science, therefore, is to make the questions precise. The question, 'Why does the pendulum move *as it does?*' is more to the point. But the phrase 'as it does' now lays the questioner open to a counterquestion: 'What do you mean, "as it does?"' This is a challenge to describe

In literature on the philosophy of science the term *theory* has assumed a specific meaning. A theory is defined as a symbolic construction, a series of interrelated constructs or concepts, together with definitions, laws, theorems and axioms. A theory sets forth a systematic view of phenomena by presenting a series of propositions or hypotheses which specify relations among variables in order to present explanations and make predictions about the phenomena. In the natural sciences a theory may be viewed as a system consisting of the following elements: (a) a set of axioms whose truth is assumed and can be tested only by testing their logical consequences—an axiom cannot be deduced from other statements contained in the system; (b) statements, or theorems, that are deduced from the axioms, or from other theorems and definitions; (c) definitions of descriptive terms contained in the axioms.[72] A theory is a group of laws which are deductively connected. Some of the laws are premises from which other laws are deduced. Those laws serving as premises are termed the axioms of the theory. Those laws deduced from the axioms are the theorems of the theory. Whether or not a law is an axiom or a theorem depends on its position in a theory.

A theory does not depend necessarily upon empirical referents for validity. It need only state logically deduced relationships among the phenomena with which the theory is concerned.[73] According to Abraham Kaplan, the ability to apply the theory successfully is not a necessary condition for its success, since the failure of application may be traceable to many factors external to the theory itself.[74] But the development of empirical referents makes possible the verification of a theory.

A scientific theory might therefore be likened to a complex spatial network: Its terms are represented by the knots, while the threads connecting the latter correspond, in part, to the definitions and, in part, to the fundamental and derivative hypotheses contained in the theory. The whole system floats, as it were, above the plane of observation and is anchored to it by rules of interpretation. These might be viewed as strings which are not part of the network but link certain parts of the latter with specific places in the plane of observation. By virtue of those interpretive connectors, the network can function as a scientific theory. From certain observational data, we may ascend, via an interpretive string, to some point in the theoretical network, thence

how in fact the pendulum does move, and this temporarily turns the attention away from (explanation) toward description." Before we can explain, we must first carefully circumscribe, and thus we face the requirement of exact mathematical measurement of that which we wish to explain. *Ibid.,* p. 974.

72. See Fred N. Kerlinger, *Foundations of Behavioral Research* (New York:

Holt, Rinehart and Winston, 1966), p. 11, and Robert Brown, *Explanation in Social Science* (Chicago: Aldine Publishing Company, 1963), p. 174.

73. Gustav Bergmann, *The Philosophy of Science* (Madison: University of Wisconsin Press, 1958), pp. 31–32.

74. Abraham Kaplan, *The Conduct of Inquiry* (San Francisco: Chandler Publishing Company, 1964), p. 319.

proceed, via definitions and hypotheses, to other points from which another interpretive string permits a descent to the place of observation.[75]

Although students in the social sciences have tried in recent years to develop theories as formally stated as those of the natural sciences, the term *theory* has had several meanings in the social sciences in general and international relations in particular:

a. A deductive system in which propositions are set forth, which purportedly contain internal logical consistency. Although such theoretical systems may be free of direct linkages with the real world, they may be compared with the real world. The systems of Morton H. Kaplan and George F. Modelski are illustrative of such a conception of theory. (See Chapter 4.)

b. A taxonomy, classificatory scheme, or conceptual framework which provides for the orderly arrangement and examination of data. Data gathered from the real world may be placed in the categories, or slots, provided in the framework. Parsons's social system, Almond and Easton's political systems, and Snyder's decision-making framework are illustrative of such taxonomies. (See Chapters 4 and 11 respectively.)

c. Series of propositions about political behavior inductively derived either from empirical studies or the comparative examination of case materials from the past. The historical comparison made by Deutsch and his associates of the integration of national units in the North Atlantic area represents an effort to develop a series of propositions concerning conditions essential for types of integration. (See Chapter 10.)

d. The development of a series of statements about rational behavior based upon a dominant motive such as power. Such a theory provides a description of the political behavior of rational actors. Such behavioral patterns can then be compared with the real world in one or more historical periods. Morgenthau, for example, holds to such a theory of politics which, "by the very fact of painting a rational picture of the political scene, points to the contrast between what the political scene actually is and what it tends to be, but can never completely become." [76] (See Chapter 3.)

e. A set of norms or values indicating how political actors ought to behave, the study of international relations from the perspective of "ethical desiderata." [77] Traditionally, much of political philosophy consists of such theory. Normative theory establishes sets of standards against

75. Carl G. Hempel, *Fundamentals of Concept Formation in Empirical Science* (Chicago: University of Chicago Press, 1952), p. 36.

76. Hans J. Morgenthau, "The Nature and Limits of a Theory of International Relations," William T. R. Fox, ed., *op. cit.*, p. 17.

77. Kenneth W. Thompson, "Toward a Theory of International Politics," *American Political Science Review*, XLIX (September, 1955), 740.

which existing conduct can be measured and toward which political behavior ought to aspire. Generally speaking, the phenomena of international war in the nuclear age, revolutionary guerrilla conflict and counterinsurgency, and the economic development gap between the richer and poorer nations have led to an increased emphasis in the United States on ethical factors in the analysis of international relations during the last two decades.

    f. A set of proposals of action for the statesman. Such prescriptions are usually: (a) assumptions about the international system such as the existence of a balance of power (variously defined) in which political actors supposedly take one or another course of action to achieve a particular kind of goal; or (b) policy recommendations based upon the results of the study of one or several instances of a particular kind of political behavior.

Traditionalists and behaviorists often disagree on their approaches to theory. J. David Singer has given succinct expression to one salient difference between traditionalists and behaviorists by referring to the "N/V ratio," in which N stands for the number of cases studied and V the number of variables examined. The typical traditional scholar minimizes the N and maximizes the V, while the typical behavioral scientist does just the reverse. Singer also notes that each approach has its disadvantages. If the scholar investigates for only one or a few variables in the whole universe or system of nation-states, he runs the risk of over-homogenizing the various units and of bypassing significant differences among them. He may uncover interesting correlations, but he dare not adduce causality. On the other hand, the scholar who dwells upon only one or a few nation-states often lapses into the opposite distortion of over-emphasizing the uniqueness of each nation-state, of exaggerating differences rather than similarities, and of concluding not only that the search for general laws of universal political behavior is futile but that the correlations which the behaviorist calls "statistically significant" are not really all that significant to the political analyst. Singer himself regards the tendency to overhomogenize less dangerous in terms of scientific method than the tendency to over-differentiate.[78]

Students in the social sciences have theorized at different levels of observation and analysis. The development of "grand theories" is illustrative of theorizing in which interrelationships among a few or many variables purportedly explain a wide range of phenomena. The attempts of such writers as Parsons and Easton to develop frameworks for the organization of data concerning social and political systems illustrate grand theory in the sense that their

---

78. J. David Singer, "The Behavioral Science Approach to International Relations: Payoff and Prospects," *SAIS Review* (School of Advanced International Studies of the Johns Hopkins University), X (Summer, 1966), 12–20, especially p. 14; and "The Level-of-Analysis Problem in International Relations," in Klaus Knorr and Sidney Verba, eds., *op. cit.,* pp. 81–83.

taxonomies encompass most, if not all, of political behavior. In international relations the work of realist writers such as Aron and Morgenthau rank as efforts toward grand theory.

Other writers have focused upon the development of "middle-range" theories, theories designed to explain or study a limited range of political phenomena with a few variables. Writers focusing specifically on the study of conditions of political integration, conflict, or the behavior of nations in alliance, engage in middle-range theorizing. Their preoccupation is the development of islands of theory which at some future time may be linked into a grand theory of international relations.

The student of international relations usually has little difficulty in grasping the meaning of middle-range theories. Most of the theoretical problems in the field of international relations are in the mid-range. Why does functional integration in specific economic sectors lead to (or not lead to) political integration among nation-states? How are informal, tacit, unilateral arms control measures related to the process of negotiating formal arms control agreements? What are the dynamics of Great Power involvement (economic, political and military) in Third World revolutionary insurgencies? When one member of a coalition withdraws, what effect does this have upon the other members? The student can readily supply for himself several testable hypotheses which would be illustrative of mid-range theoretical problems. The meaning of a "general theory" or "grand theory" of international relations is often much more difficult even for the experts to understand.

According to Quincy Wright, "a general theory of international relations means a comprehensive, comprehensible, coherent, and self-correcting body of knowledge contributing to the understanding, the prediction, the evaluation, and the control of relations among states and of the conditions of the world." [79] Wright elaborates on his definition by arguing that the theory must cover all aspects of the field. It should be expressed in generalized propositions as clear, as accurate, and as few as possible. In other words, the theory should be parsimonious, and not so diffuse and complicated as to be confusing. (Scientists have always been predisposed to equate scientific truth with aesthetic beauty, and the latter with intellectual simplicity.) Every part of the general theory should be logically consistent with every other part. The theory should be formulated in a style conducive to continual improvement and updating. Instead of being purely speculative, its theses should be capable of constant verification on the basis of available evidence. It should contribute to an objective understanding of international reality, rather than one distorted by national perspective. It should enable us to predict at least some things, and it should also help us to arrive at value judgments—even if the process of moral valuation may not be entirely consistent with the value-free tradition of the scien-

79. Quincy Wright, "Development of a General Theory of International Relations," in Horace V. Harrison, ed., *op. cit.*, p. 20.

tific method. Thus does Wright comment upon the attributes which he predicated of the general theory.[80] He himself concedes—and we agree with him—that a theory fulfilling all these ideal requirements will be extremely difficult to achieve.

Quincy Wright has advanced some ideas which cast light upon the study and theory of international relations. In his major work, *A Study of International Relations,* after admitting that the field of international relations is still "an emerging discipline manifesting little unity from the point of view of method and logic," [81] he suggests that the field might best be understood if approached through four basic intellectual perspectives: history, art, science, and philosophy. In his opinion, all social reality can be conveniently divided into four categories: a) the *actual* (what was or what is, known through the method of description); b) the *possible* (what can be, known through the method of theoretical speculation); c) the *probable* (what will be, known through the method of prediction); and d) the *desirable* (what ought to be, known through the method of ethical or valuational or normative reflection). These four categories, says Wright, correspond to history, art, science and philosophy.[82] The authors find this a categorization worth pondering.

Traditional Theory: Balance of Power

As an example of a traditional theory, let us consider one of the oldest, most persistent and most controversial of all theories of international politics—the "balance of power." It was recognized at least implicitly in ancient India and in ancient Greece, although it was never formally articulated. David Hume noted that although the term "balance of power" may be modern, "the maxim of preserving the balance of power is founded so much on common sense and obvious reasoning, that it is impossible it could altogether have escaped antiquity," concluding that it had been practiced from ancient times to the eighteenth century.[83]

Insofar as it could be called a formal theory of international politics, the

80. *Ibid.,* pp. 21–23.

81. Wright, *A Study of International Relations,* p. 26.

82. *Ibid.,* p. 11 and Chapters 8, 9, 10 and 11. In addition to these four basic intellectual perspectives, Wright dwells at length on the root disciplines of international relations in Chapter 5—international law, diplomatic history, military science, international politics, international organization, international trade, colonial government and the conduct of foreign relations—and in Chapter 6 on "disciplines with a world point of view" —such as world history, world geography, the sociology and social psychology of international relations, and studies of population, technology, etc.

83. David Hume, *Essays and Treatises on Several Subjects* (Edinburgh: Bell and Bradfute, and W. Blackwood, 1825), I, 331–39. Reprinted in Arend Lijphart, ed., *World Politics* (Boston: Allyn and Bacon, 1966), pp. 228–234.

modern concept of balance of power was associated with the Newtonian conception of a universe in equilibrium. (Frequently a social science theory has been adapted from a physical science theory or at least influenced by developments of one.) Actually, the notion of equilibrium is basic to many sciences. Chemists speak of a solution in stable equilibrium. Economists perceive a balance of countervailing forces, such as supply and demand. Biologists warn against human activities which disturb the "balance of nature" between organisms and environment. Political writers often analyze the interaction of interest groups or of governmental branches within national society in terms of "checks and balances." [84] Naturally theorists of international social reality employ "balance" as a central organizing concept for the power relations of nation-states and then to assume that the latter are driven, almost by a law of their own nature, to seek their security by some form of power-balancing.

Balance of Power: Problems of Definition

The term "balance of power" has been roundly criticized for causing considerable semantical confusion. Richard Cobden said of it:

> It is not a fallacy, a mistake, an imposture—it is an undescribed, indescribable, incomprehensible nothing; mere words, conveying to the mind not ideas, but sounds like those equally barren syllables which our ancestors put together for the purpose of puzzling themselves about words . . . .[85]

Ernst B. Haas found at least eight distinct meanings for the term: a) any distribution of power; b) an equilibrium or balancing process; c) hegemony or the search for hegemony; d) stability and peace in a concert of power; e) instability and war; f) power politics in general; g) a universal law of history; and h) a system and guide to policymakers.[86] "The trouble with the balance of power," says Inis L. Claude, Jr., "is not that it has no meaning, but that it has too many meanings." [87]

It is true that the concept of "balance of power" is riddled with ambiguities. Many statesmen have sought a unilateral superiority rather than an objective bilateral balance with their principal rival. Nevertheless, it is theoretically possible to conceive of the balance of power as a situation or condition, as

84. All these examples are cited in Hans J. Morgenthau, *Politics Among Nations*, pp. 161–166.

85. Richard Cobden, *Political Writings*, 2nd ed. (London: William Ridgeway, 1868), I, 259.

86. Ernst B. Haas, "The Balance of Power: Prescription, Concept or Propaganda?" *World Politics*, V (July, 1953), 442–477.

87. Inis L. Claude, Jr., *Power and International Relations* (New York: Random House, 1962), p. 13.

a universal tendency or law of state behavior, as a guide for statesmanship, and as a mode of system-maintenance characteristic of certain types of international systems. As long as we think in terms of equilibrium rather than superiority, these four usages need not be inconsistent with one another.

Conceived as a situation or a condition, balance of power implies an objective arrangement in which there is relatively widespread satisfaction with the distribution of power. The universal tendency or law describes a probability—and enables one to predict—that members of a system threatened by the emergence of a "disturber of the balance," i.e., a power seemingly bent upon the establishment of an international hegemony, will form a countervailing coalition. Balance of power as a policy guide prescribes to statesmen who would act "rationally" that they should maintain eternal vigilance and be prepared to organize a countervailing coalition against the disrupter of equilibrium. Balance of power as a system refers to a multi-national society in which all essential actors preserve their identity, integrity and independence through the balancing process.[88]

Balance of Power: Purposes and Functions

Various purposes and functions were attributed to the balance of power in classical theory as expounded by Bolingbroke, Gentz, Metternich and Castlereagh. It was supposed to: a) prevent the establishment of a universal hegemony; b) preserve the constituent elements of the system and the system itself; c) insure stability and mutual security in the international system; and d) strengthen and prolong the peace by deterring war—i.e., by confronting an aggressor with the likelihood that a policy of expansion would meet with the formation of a counter-coalition. The traditional methods and techniques of maintaining or restoring the balance were: a) the policy of divide and rule (working to diminish the weight of the heavier side); b) territorial compensations after a war; c) creation of buffer states; d) the formation of alliances; e) spheres of influence; f) intervention; g) diplomatic bargaining; h) legal and peaceful settlement of disputes; i) reduction of armaments; j) armaments competition or races; and k) war itself.

88. This paragraph and the one following constitute a synthesis from several different sources. For fuller treatments of the balance of power, see Inis L. Claude, Jr., op. cit.; Edward V. Gulick, Europe's Classical Balance of Power (Ithaca: Cornell University Press, 1955); Sidney B. Fay, "Balance of Power," Encyclopedia of the Social Sciences (New York: Macmillan Company, 1930), II; Alfred Vagts, "The Balance of Power: Growth of an Idea," World Politics, I (October, 1948), 82–101; Paul Seabury, ed., Balance of Power (San Francisco: Chandler Publishing Company, 1965). See also the chapters on the balance of power in the following textbooks, all cited previously: Schleicher, Morgenthau, Palmer and Perkins, Hartmann, Organski.

Contending Theories of International Relations

A review of the list of objectives and methods will show that there were internal inconsistencies in the theory and in the practice, but that they were probably unavoidable, given the historic oscillation between stable and unstable equilibria within the nation-state system. If the balance of power had worked perfectly as all statesmen expected, and if the existing distribution of power had posed no threat to their national security, then the balance of power as situation, law, policy and system would almost certainly have contributed to the prolongation of peace. But the dynamics of the international political system were conducive neither to serene stability nor to prudent rational decision-making at all times. Moreover, statesmen pursuing only what they considered their own legitimate national interest—a term closely associated with the balance of power system—may have appeared in the eyes of other statesmen as conspiring to overturn the international system and gain predominance. Or conversely, a government embarked upon a hegemonial course might not provoke the formation of a counter coalition until too late to prevent a large-scale war declared to restore the balance. In theory the balance helped preserve the peace and identity of member-states; but in practice balance of power policy sometimes led to war and to the partitioning of "less essential" actors (such as Poland in the 1790s). But keeping the peace and preserving all the lesser members intact were subordinate to the more fundamental aims of preserving the multi-state system by observing the maxim expressed by Friedrich Gentz:

> That if the states system of Europe is to exist and be maintained by common exertions, no one of its members must ever become so powerful as to be able to coerce all the rest put together.[89]

Another key concept in the classical theory must be mentioned. Under normal circumstances, with several nations seeking to maximize their power position through the various methods and techniques of balance of power politics, no one nation gains hegemony, and a precarious equilibrium is maintained. But for various reasons the balance might conceivably break down. Perhaps some states will react lethargically to any power trying to upset the balance. At this point, the system is fortunate if it has an impartial and vigilant "holder of the balance" strong enough to restore the balance swiftly once it is disturbed. Historically, England played this role in the European state system. In a famous memorandum published on January 1, 1907, Sir Eyre Crowe said that it had "become almost an historical truism to identify England's secular policy with the maintenance of this balance by throwing her weight now in this scale and now in that, but ever on the side opposed to the political dictatorship of the strongest single state or group at a given time." [90] Winston Churchill reiterated this as a fundamental tenet of British

9. Quoted in Edward V. Gulick, *op. cit.,* p. 34.

). "Memorandum on the Present State of British Relations with France and Germany," in G. P. Gooch and Harold V. Temperly, eds., *op. cit.,* III, 402.

foreign policy in 1936.[91] Perhaps the theory of the balance of power—as policy guide to statesmen—is a distinctively British theory.

Critiques of Balance of Power

In recent decades, the balance of power theory has encountered much crit cism even from traditional analysts, and for reasons other than the semant cal vagueness mentioned earlier. Nicholas J. Spykman held that the theor inadequately explained the practice:

> *The truth of the matter is that states are interested only in a balance (imbalance) which is in their favor. Not an equilibrium, but a generous margin is their objective. There is no real security in being just as strong as a potential enemy; there is security only in being a little stronger. There is no possibility of action if one's strength is fully checked; there is a chance for a positive foreign policy only if there is a margin of force which can be freely used.*[92]

Hans J. Morgenthau finds the balance of power deficient on several ground It has failed on a number of occasions since the end of the eighteenth centur to preserve the independent existence of states. The multistate system preclud ing a single state from achieving universal dominion has been preserved onl at the price of frequent and costly wars. He finds the balance of power 1) *ur certain* because no completely reliable means of measuring, evaluating an comparing power exist; 2) *unreal* because statesmen try to compensate for i uncertainty by aiming for superiority; 3) *inadequate* for explaining nation: restraint during most of the years from 1648 to 1914 because it does n give credit to the restraining influence of the basic intellectual unity an moral consensus then prevailing in Europe.[93]

Charles P. Schleicher has suggested that "peace is most in jeopardy whe power is rather evenly balanced and war less likely when there is a preponder ant power." [94] A. F. K. Organski denies that a "holder of the balance" wa ever primarily motivated by a desire to maintain the balance rather than b self-interest, and warns against "elevating the public relations statements c sixteenth-century monarchs and nineteenth-century diplomats to the statu of scientific theory." [95] Ernst B. Haas has observed that using the balance c power as a policy guide assumes a high degree of flexibility in national decisior making. The vigilant statesman must engage in a constant power calculu:

91. Winston S. Churchill, *The Gathering Storm* (Boston: Houghton Mifflin Company, 1948), pp. 207–210.

92. Nicholas J. Spykman, *American Strategy and World Politics* (New York:

Harcourt, Brace, and Company, 1942 pp. 21–22.

93. Morgenthau, *op. cit.*, Chapter 14.

94. Schleicher, *op. cit.*, p. 368.

95. Organski, *op. cit.*, pp. 299 and 28.

Contending Theories of International Relation

e must be ready to intervene or enter into coalition almost immediately to reserve the balance—and do this regardless of ideological affinities, economic interests and domestic political attitudes. Haas has questioned the degree to which policymakers, especially in democratic countries, can enjoy the kind of flexibility which the balance of power theory would seem to demand.[96] Several writers, including the classical theorists, have insisted that the cultural homogeneity of the European state system from the seventeenth through the nineteenth century was an important precondition for the successful operation of the balance of power.[97] All international analysts have recognized that in this century the state system encompasses states with very different cultural backgrounds. Moreover, universalist ideologies now challenge what for a long time has been the most powerful political force on the world scene—nationalism. William G. Carleton observed in 1947 that in modern times nation-centered loyalties have generally proved stronger than internationalist ideologies. But he noted that the rise of ideological conflicts within and between national societies undoubtedly helped complicate the operation of the balance of power. He cautioned that international politics in the latter part of this century may be conducted less along national and more along ideological lines.[98]

Balance of Power: Contemporary Models

Nevertheless, it would be erroneous to suggest that, because the balance of power theory has been buried by an avalanche of criticism, it is dead. Several "modern," "nontraditional" and "scientific" theoreticians have found it attention-worthy. Morton A. Kaplan makes it one of his six heuristic models of international systems. He devotes more space to the balance of power system with its essential rules than to any of the other systems.[99] (For a discussion of Kaplan's systems models, see Chapter 4.) Arthur Lee Burns, after studying the problem of the system in stable balance, concludes that "the most stable arrangement would seem to be a world of five or some greater odd number of Powers, independent and of approximately equal strength," since these would not be readily divisible into two equal sides.[100] For simplicity in

96. Ernst B. Haas, "The Balance of Power as a Guide to Policy-Making," *Journal of Politics*, XV (August, 1953), 370–398.

97. Gulick, *op. cit.*, pp. 10–15.

98. William G. Carleton, "Ideology or Balance of Power?" *Yale Review*, XXXVI (June, 1947), 590–602.

99. Kaplan, *System and Process*, pp. 22–

36. Particularly important to his theory is the list of six essential rules of the balance of power system on p. 23.

100. Arthur Lee Burns, "From Balance to Deterrence: A Theoretical Analysis," *World Politics*, IX (July, 1957), 505. Whereas Burns prefers five as the optimal number for security, Kaplan says that five is the minimal number required for security, but that security increases

calculating relationships, and for the certainty and stability which such sim plicity would yield, Burns holds that, optimally, the most stable system woul be a world of "five roughly equal blocs, each including a family of exchange able client nations." [101] Some analysts in the field of nuclear deterrence an arms control theory have updated the categories of balance of power think ing.[102] And although many intellectuals and academicians regard the balanc of power theory as a crude, unsophisticated, naïvely simplistic or obsolet theory of international politics, large numbers of statesmen, politicians, diplo mats, pundits, journalists and men-in-the-street still regard it as an adequat explanation of what actually happens in the international system and of th basis on which foreign policy ought to be formulated and conducted.

Can There Be a "Scientific" International Theory?

Posing such a question just after discussing the balance of power theory doe not imply that the latter was "unscientific." The meaning of "scientific" : relative. The term "science" connotes nothing more than a body of know edge and a way of discovering new knowledge. Whatever satisfies intelliger men in any age as the optimum means of enlarging their intellectual frontier will pass muster as "scientific."

Genuine scientific progress is usually made when one starts out by accept ing that knowledge of the field which is already in general circulation amon scholars. Each individual may wish to reorganize the existing body of know edge somewhat to enhance his own working comprehension of it. But he mu take something as given—something already based upon empirical observa tion, experience and human reflection. If learning is social, the individua cannot begin every day to create his own universe de novo.

Once the investigator has mastered the existing knowledge, and organize it for his purposes, he pleads a "meaningful ignorance": "Here is what know; what do I not know that is worth knowing?" This is a very importan question. If it were asked more often there would be much less social scienc research of low-level value. Once an area has been selected for investigatior the question should be posed as clearly as possible, and it is here that quant fication can prove useful,[103] provided that mathematical methods are com

---

with the number of states up to some as-yet-undetermined upper limit. "Tradi tionalism vs. Science in International Re lations," op. cit., p. 10.

101. Arthur Lee Burns, op. cit., p. 508.

102. See Glenn H. Snyder, "Balance of Power in the Missile Age," Journal of International Affairs, XIV (No. 1, 1960);

John H. Herz, "Balance Systems an Balance Policies in a Nuclear and B polar Age," ibid.; and the books an articles cited below in the extended di cussion on deterrence and arms contr in Chapter 9.

103. For examples of quantitative studie in international relations, see Morton A

ined with carefully constructed taxonomic schemes. Achieving a satisfactory merger of appropriate tools of statistical analysis with solid typologies is one of the most difficult aspects of formulating a worthwhile and testable hypothesis in the realm of political reality, where the names we call things and the words we use are of crucial importance. Surveying the field of international relations, or any sector of it, we see many disparate elements and keep sifting them through various permutations in our minds, wondering whether there may be any significant relationships between A and B, or between B and C. By a process which we are compelled to call "intuition" until we learn much more about it than we now know, we perceive a possible correlation, hitherto unsuspected or not firmly known, between two or more elements. At this point, we have the ingredients of a hypothesis which can be expressed in measurable referents and which, if validated, would be both explanatory and predictive. (In the strictest scientific sense, what we cannot predict we cannot fully explain.) [104]

From here on, the scientific method is quite simple. The hypothesis must be validated through testing. This demands the construction of a verifying experiment or the gathering of empirical data in other ways. In either case every effort must be made to eliminate the influence of the unknown, and to make certain that the evidence sought pertains to the hypothesis and to nothing else. The results of the data-gathering effort are carefully observed, recorded and analyzed, after which the hypothesis is discarded, modified, reformulated or confirmed. Findings are published, and others are invited to duplicate this knowledge-discovering adventure, and to confirm or deny. This, very roughly, is what we usually mean by "the scientific method." At every step of the way there is emphasis upon precision of thought and language and upon a distinction between that which is assumed and that which is empirically verifiable.

Application of this scientific method during the last 250 years has produced some very impressive results in the "hard sciences"—particularly in the form of universal uniformities or generalized laws. In physics, astrophysics, chemistry, biology and certain areas of psychology a high degree of predictability

---

Kaplan, ed., *New Approaches to International Relations* (New York: St. Martin's Press, Inc., 1968); Richard L. Merritt and Stein Rokkar, eds., *Comparing Nations: The Use of Quantitative Data in Cross-National Research* (New Haven: Yale University Press, 1966); John E. Mueller, ed., *Approaches to Measurement in International Relations: A Non-Evangelical Survey* (New York: Appleton-Century-Crofts, 1969); James N. Rosenau, ed., *International Politics and Foreign Policy* (New York: Free Press, 1969); Rudolph J. Rummel, *et al., Di-*

mensions of Nations (Evanston: Northwestern University Press, 1967); Bruce Russett, *International Regions in the International System* (Chicago: Rand McNally and Company, 1967); J. David Singer, *Quantitative International Politics: Insights and Evidence* (New York: Free Press, 1968).

104. Carl G. Hempel and Paul Oppenheim, "Studies in the Logic of Explanation," *Philosophy of Science,* XV (1948), 135–175.

has been achieved. But even the "exact" sciences, with all their powerful methodologies, reach limits to what can be known at any given moment. According to Werner Heisenberg's principle of indeterminacy, for example, it is not possible to determine simultaneously both the position and the movement of a particle of matter.[105]

Theory and Predictability

The crucial question is whether there can be a theory of action (behavior) in the social sciences comparable to the theory of action in the exact sciences. Is it possible to formulate generalized laws of human behavior, either for individuals or for social aggregates, which will provide a predictive capability —at least one which can be expressed in terms of probabilities, "other things being equal?" The authors cannot answer this question with any certitude. To date our capability for predicting social and political developments has hardly been impressive: neither "traditionalists" nor "nontraditionalists" have worthy reputations for foresight. It would be interesting to hold an international conference of international relations specialists to ascertain whether a consensus could be reached as to what social scientists are capable of predicting over periods of, say, ten, twenty, or thirty years. What will most likely increase or decrease? (One sometimes gets the erroneous impression that in the social sciences all curves are constantly rising!) Let us suppose that the conferees were trying to look ahead to the first decade of the twenty-first century. They might ask themselves what aspects of reality in the 1970s could reasonably have been foreseen in the late 1940s, and what aspects of current reality have evolved from the advent of forces which very probably could not have been forecast thirty years ago.

As we pointed out earlier, scientists are dubious of a capability to explain unaccompanied by a corresponding capability to predict. Most social scientists readily concur with the historians' judgment that unique human events and choices lie beyond predictability. We cannot assign a precise probability to a "discrete event"—for example, whether nuclear war will or will not occur or whether a military coup will occur in a specific country within a specified time period. But when we turn from the unique to aggregates, man's predictive ability improves considerably. Across the whole universe of political communities, we are better able to establish correlations between conditions (necessary and sufficient) and events, to define trends, and to say that some

105. Werner Heisenberg, *Physics and Philosophy* (New York: Harper, 1958), pp. 179, 183, 186. It should be pointed out that the principle of indeterminacy is often referred to less accurately by social scientists as "the uncertainty principle."

Contending Theories of International Relations

pes of policy problems will probably increase while others decrease. Even here the calculus of probabilities gives us trouble, we may be able to fore-ll accurately the range of possibilities. Thus while we cannot predict indi-idual decisions, we might have a fairly accurate prevision of the environment which decisions will be made (but even here perfect prevision is not possi-le). Some things are less difficult to predict than others. Often it is easier to redict negatively—i.e., to narrow the range of possibilities by ruling some ut. At times, certain economic, biological, technological and cultural trends ay be identified and accepted as to their validity (or even "inevitability") or a country, a region, or the world as a whole. Examples include projec-ons of population growth, the expansion of specific sectors of international ade, the worldwide diffusion of technical communications media, and an crease in the number of countries capable of producing nuclear weapons. ut in the realm of international politics we must remember that the total stem-with-environment is both complex and subtle, modifiable not only by uman decisions but also by a variety of factors whose significance may arcely be perceived at the time of prediction.[106]

he Search for Recurring Patterns

nyone claiming to be a "scientific" theorist—whether "traditional" or future-iented "behaviorist"—is bound to search for regularities. But we should member that there are peculiar difficulties confronting all social scientists, d if we keep these in mind we are more likely to make intellectual progress an if we ignore or forget them.

The scientist studying human affairs encounters problems concerning the lation of the observer to the observed to a greater degree than the scientist dying atoms, molecules or stars. The physical scientist requires certain struments and techniques which are fairly standardized and which work the me way for all. The physical scientist, no matter how excited he might be out his work, usually avoids that kind of emotional involvement with the served phenomenon which might influence his perception and his judgment.

the investigation of human society, objective observation is much more ely to be infused with subjective purpose. A physicist or a chemist who

6. For an analysis of the types of prob-ms involved in the effort to look ahead, Herman Kahn, "The Alternative orld Futures Approach," in Morton A. plan, ed., *New Approaches to Inter-tional Relations* (New York: St. Mar-'s Press, 1968); Bruce M. Russett, he Ecology of Future International litics," *International Studies Quarterly,* (March, 1967), 12–31; Daniel Bell,

"Twelve Modes of Prediction: A Prelim-inary Sorting of Approaches in the Social Sciences," *Daedalus,* XCIII (Summer, 1964), 845–880; Bertrand de Jouvenel, "Political Science and Prevision," *American Political Science Review,* LIX (March, 1965), 29–38; "Toward the Year 2000" Issue of *Daedalus,* XCVI (Summer, 1967).

happens to be an ardent pacifist in his personal outlook is not prone to b swayed by this conviction in his analytic approach to the more fissionab atoms as compared with other atoms. But social scientists who have stron preconceptions about such subjects as war, guerrilla terror, national value world population and hunger, disarmament and international organizatio or the conflict between democracies and dictatorships are much more like to run into difficulty in their efforts to achieve that complete detachment whic the scientific method presupposes. (There is, in the view of the authors, r need for social scientists to apologize for this "human involvement.") Whi the method is supposed to be "value-free," the phenomenon being examine is often overladen with value implications which influence the intellectual ar psychological set of the observer-analyst. Social scientists hardly agree c which of these two attitudes produces the greater perceptual distortion in tl study, let us say, of the problems of war and peace: a purely neutral or no ethical desire to "understand" human aggressiveness for the purpose of e plaining it and predicting its manifestations, or a moral commitment to stud war with a view toward abolishing it in order to make the world a bett place. Undoubtedly the effort to build a scientific international theory w continue to be characterized by the interpenetration of these two distin purposes, both within individual minds and within the field as a whole.[1]

The peculiarities of the observer-observed relationship in the social scienc give rise to additional difficulties. Some of these are well known and frequent cited—such as the inability to conduct controlled experiments to isolate t factors for studying. Even the most ruthless totalitarian regime, whatever t efficiency of the technical means of social control at its disposal, would l extremely hard-pressed to conduct a strictly controlled scientific experime with a single nation, not to mention two or more. The point is that in attemp ing to study any large social aggregates scientifically, the conditions of contr for the sake of exactitude must be established primarily through the clarific tion of one's own thought processes, rather than in the confusion and unco trollability of the international *complexe*.

Other problems are less readily recognized. Given the comprehensibility the field, the sheer mass of pertinent data seems to exceed the bounds human mastery. Many data are inaccessible and remain so either for a ve long time (in governmental archives) or forever (in the minds of men who fc get or die before they transmit to scholars all they know about what rea happened). The scholar and theorist, therefore, often arrive at generaliz

107. See Quincy Wright, *A Study of International Relations,* Chapter 7, "Educational and Research Objectives"; Ladis K. D. Kristof, "Political Laws in International Relations," *Western Political Quarterly,* XI (September, 1958), 598–606. Another penetrating discourse on the role of normative theory in contrast to purely value-free approach to intern tional relations is to be found in Char A. McClelland, "The Function of Theo in International Relations," *Journal Conflict Resolution,* IV (Septemb 1960), 311–314.

onclusions from sketchy evidence that might be unreliable on grounds quite apart from its incompleteness.

Especially in the 1960s, scholars turned to the computer, with its capacity or the statistical manipulation of vast amounts of data, for the building of theories of international relations. Although other such theory-building efforts are described elsewhere in this book, we turn now to an example of the uses to which the computer can be put in this field—a study of the relationship between intranational and international conflict.

Case Study in Quantitative Methodology

In a project designed to find recurrent political patterns within and between nations, Rudolph J. Rummel collected data for 236 variables about 82 nations for one year, 1955. These data were analyzed through a technique known as factor analysis.[108] In the first phase of the Dimensionality of Nations (DON) project, three separate analyses were applied to the data: (1) the foreign conflict behavior variables were intercorrelated and factor analyzed separately; (2) the foreign conflict behavior variables were regressed upon dimensions of national characteristics and domestic conflict dimensions (to "regress" means to determine how well data on one variable can be predicted from data in a set of variables); and (3) the foreign conflict and domestic conflict variables were factor analyzed together.

Of the 236 variables, 94 were measures of such aspects of international relations as trade, membership in international organizations, treaties signed, aid given and received, and votes with the United States in the United Nations.

It was found that conflict behavior did not correlate with the degree of a nation's involvement in foreign affairs. Stated differently, nations may be heavily engaged in foreign affairs without necessarily resorting to conflict. In factor analysis of all variables, domestic conflict variables appeared in patterns distinct from foreign conflict variables.

However, these conclusions were based upon a method which does not

108. Developed in mathematics, used first in psychology, later in economics, and more recently in political science, factor analysis is a statistical technique by which a large number of variables can be clustered on the basis of their intercorrelation. Factor analysis enables the researcher to identify patterns among variables. The results of factor analysis, the factors defining the different patterns, are often termed "Dimensions." Hence the use of the word "Dimensionality" in the DON Project. For a detailed discussion of factor analysis, see Harry H. Harmon, *Modern Factor Analysis* (Chicago: University of Chicago Press, 1967); R. J. Rummel, *Applied Factor Analysis* (Evanston: Northwestern University Press, 1970); L. L. Thurstone, *Multiple Factor Analysis* (Chicago: University of Chicago Press, 1965).

differentiate among the nations under consideration. Jonathan Wilkenfel reevaluated Rummel's data using a different method which involved "the re arrangement of the nations under consideration into groups, according to typ of nation, in an effort to determine whether type of nation has any bearing o the relationship between internal and external behavior." [109] A group o seventy-four nations was divided into three groups, based on differences i leadership—personalist (or dictatorial), centrist (centralized government and polyarchic (representative government, including two or more parties All possible pairs of domestic conflict behavior dimensions and foreign con flict behavior dimensions were correlated for these groups. Moreover, th possibility of time lags was considered. The results indicated that there is relationship between internal and external conflict behavior. The nature the relationship depends upon the type of nation and the dimension of con flict: "As we shift our attention from the personalist, to the centrist, an finally to the polyarchic group, the particular dimensions of conflict behavic which are related change. Indeed, there is no one particular relationship be tween any pair of internal and external conflict dimensions which holds fo all groups equally well. . . . . Nations in the international system do no behave solely on the basis of the givens of the international situation. De pending upon the type of nation, we must look beyond the internation; sphere to the internal situation in the participating nation, to determine tha nation's reactions." [110]

(The reader is referred to the discussion of the findings of R. J. Rumm and Raymond Tanter concerning the correlation of internal and external con flict in Chapter 8, pp. 235–236).

Quincy Wright, to whom Rummel owes a considerable intellectual deb develops a so-called field theory consisting of geographic and analytic fields.[11] Defined by time-space coordinates, Wright's geographic field describes th real world, with its distribution of population, resources, agricultural an industrial production, and political and economic power and their change in time. Wright's so-called analytic field consists of two fields—values an capability. Wright bases his value field and the capability field on the assump tion that decision-makers formulate and follow policies which relate value

109. Jonathan Wilkenfeld, "Domestic and Foreign Conflict Behavior of Nations," *Journal of Peace Research,* I (1968), 57.

110. *Ibid.,* p. 66.

111. In his field theory, Quincy Wright was influenced by Kurt Lewin, a psychologist whose contributions in determining the methodological and conceptual prerequisites for a science of human behavior are said to be relevant to all the social sciences. Lewin characterized field theory as "a method of analyzing causal rela-

tions and of building scientific constructs Lewin argued that the realm of determ nants of human behavior should t treated in a single, interdependent fie and not separated into traditional "disc plines." He insisted that the determinar of human behavior could be represente in rigorous mathematical terms. Accor ing to Lewin, all behavior can be co ceived as a change of some state of field in a given unit of time. Kurt Lewi *Field Theory in Social Science* (Ne York: Harper and Brothers, 1951), p. 4

capabilities. Wright attempts to "locate each state or other system of action at a point in these multidimensional fields which reflects its position in respect to each of the selected co-ordinates." [112] In the value field, for example, Wright suggests the rise of co-ordinates setting forth a range of behavior from narrow identification to a broad conception of national interests from politics of passivity to strategies of intervention in world affairs.[113]

The principal assumption of field theory is that a so-called field can be described at any moment in history, but that systems of action within each field may move over time to new positions in the field and thus form new relationships with each other. Again, to quote Wright:

> The field may be tending to become a consistent legal system, a stable equilibrium, an efficient organization, or even a harmonious community. But the theory does not commit itself to any of these outcomes. It is not a developmental model for building a philosophy or practicing the art of international relations, but a formulating model for building a science or explaining the history of international relations.

Thus field theory is a form of spatial analysis, in which an effort is made to study problems related to distance, relative position, accessibility, connectivity and the place characteristics of two or more variables.

In Rummel's study, the foreign conflict variables were regressed upon other dimensions of national characteristics. The findings were that the magnitude of a nation's characteristics or attributes has little relationship to its foreign conflict behavior. In other words, such factors as the level of economic or technological development, the level of international communications, totalitarianism, power, instability, military capabilities, ideology, or values of any individual nation were not found to correlate importantly with its foreign conflict behavior.

The Atoms and Language of International Politics

The units we study, whatever small groups, socioeconomic classes, institutions, governments, nations, states, intergovernmental entities or cultures, undergo constant change. This fact makes the social sciences much less stable enterprises than the physical sciences and compounds the difficulty of conducting research such as that described above. Even though the theories in the "exact sciences" are always being developed and refined as more knowledge is discovered, the phenomena investigated are stable, enduring, and

112. Quincy Wright, "Development of a General Theory of International Relations." In Horace V. Harrison, ed., The Role of Theory in International Relations (Princeton: D. Van Nostrand Company, 1964), p. 38.

113. For a more complete examination of co-ordinates in field theory see Quincy Wright, The Study of International Relations (New York: Appleton-Century-Crofts, 1955), pp. 540–567.

duplicable. A hydrogen atom is the same in the Soviet Union as in the Unite States and scientists in both countries have an abundant supply to stud Theorizing about interstate relations might be compared with theorizing abou a small container in which several atoms are in motion. No two atoms ar alike. Each is unique, having a distinctive atomic weight at any given momen yet constantly changing positions. Some atoms are quite heavy; some are i the middle range; most are light. The total number of atoms in the containe is not fixed. Occasionally a small number of atoms of approximate sizes mov together as if to form a molecule. A light atom spins off from a heavier on At times a heavier atom may break into a half dozen or so atoms, manifestin a long period of weakness and instability after separation. Sometimes sever atoms polarize around the two heaviest. The heavier atoms appear to avoi each other but they become agitated in their motion when lighter atoms i relatively distant parts of the container collide with each other. Atoms of a weights often engage in intraatomic and interatomic behavior which puzzl scientific observers. Every analogy limps, but this one might furnish a point (departure for initial reflection and discussion concerning the behavior of th "international system."

Finally, we come to the problem of language in which all theory must b couched. Even the exact sciences have not been immune from difficulties i relating language to observation, or verbal symbols to experience. It is ina curate to say that the exact sciences require quantitative symbols while th social sciences rely on qualitative symbols. Every physical science and ever social science requires some empirical foundation, and the method is n empirical unless it entails the essential functions of naming and countin In all the sciences, counting is a very simple thing. An important separat between the physical sciences and the social sciences is the realm of qualit tive language or the naming process. No one debates the meaning of suc terms as "liquid," "vapor," "magnetic," "electrically charged," "sodiu chloride," or "nuclear fission." But in analyzing the social universe, we co stantly face terms such as "democratic," "aggressive," "revolutionary "illegal," "discriminatory," and "violent." Not one of these terms is investe with scientific objectivity. Thus while all social scientists can count, and great many understand the process of statistically correlating dependent ar independent variables, or of performing factor analysis, there is reason believe that the basis of agreement on what is being counted or measured the field of international relations is very narrow and precarious indeed.

Conclusion

To sum up then, the essential function of international theory is to enable to improve our knowledge concerning international reality, whether for th

ke of "pure understanding" or for the more active purpose of changing
at reality. Theory helps us to order our existing knowledge and to discover
w knowledge most efficiently. It provides a framework of thought in which
e define research priorities and select the most appropriate available tools
r the gathering and analysis of data. Theory directs our attention to signifi-
nt similarities and differences, and suggests relationships not previously
rceived. Done well, theory serves as a proof that man has applied his powers
' mind to a problem at hand with precision, imagination and profundity, and
is proof inspires others to further efforts either in agreement or disagreement.

There is no one model for theory. Social theorizing occurs at many levels
d through many discipline-perspectives, with several experiments at inter-
sciplinary approaches under way. International theory, which goes beyond
oreign policy" theory, contains components which are descriptive, specula-
ve, predictive and normative. A single scholar may stress any one of these,
t the more highly developed the field of international theory as a whole
comes, the more likely will it involve a synthesis of "what is," "what might
," "what probably will be" and "what ought to be." Good theory may be
ductive or deductive; micro or macro; highly specific, mid-range or "grand"
the sense of being as comprehensive as the state of our knowledge at any
ven time permits. All of these approaches are valid and useful when handled
th intelligence and methodological care. But we should remember that
eory properly conceived always aims at generalization. It looks, therefore,
the universal and the uniform rather than to the unique, the particular, the
screte. The latter is by no means held in disdain by the sound theorist. He
spects the singular and he studies its subtle complexities, always aware that
ese may reveal something of value which might deepen his grasp of the
rger pattern.[114]

4. See Charles A. McClelland, "The
nction of Theory in International Re-
ions," *Journal of Conflict Resolution,*
' (September, 1960), 303–336; and
Theory and the International System
(New York: Macmillan Company, 1966),
pp. 1–32.

CHAPTER 2
Man-Milieu Relationships

The Role of Environment in International Relations

The growing interest among social scientists with environmental problem reflects an age-old concern, that of man-milieu relationships. As a definitio of milieu, Harold and Margaret Sprout suggest the "whole spectrum of er vironing factors, human as well as non-human, intangible as well as tangible." Aristotle believed man and his environment are inseparable, and that man affected by both geographical circumstances and political institutions. Loc tion near the sea stimulated commercial activity which expanded into th city-state; temperate climate favorably affected the development of nation character, human energy and intellect.[2] Jean Bodin, too, maintained tha climatic circumstances influence national characteristics, even determinin their foreign policies. The extremes of northern and tropical climates off conditions most favorable to building a political system based on law an justice. Northern and mountainous regions encourage greater political disc pline than southern climes which fail to spark initiative.[3] Montesquieu, to pointed to various climatic factors which he felt influenced man's politic behavior and vitality. The small scale of the political divisions of Wester Europe, in contrast to the great plains of Asia and Eastern Europe, contri

1. Harold and Margaret Sprout, *The Ecological Perspective on Human Affairs with Special Reference to International Politics* (Princeton: Princeton University Press, 1965), p. 27. The Sprouts set forth the following definitions: Environment may be defined as a generic concept under which are subsumed all external forces and factors to which an organism or aggregate of organisms is actually or potentially responsive. Or environment may be limited to the material and spa-

tial aspects of the surrounding world the exclusion of the melee of huma social relations.

2. Aristotle, *The Politics of Aristot* trans. Ernest Barker (Oxford: Clarend Press, 1961), pp. 289–311.

3. Jean Bodin, *Six Books of the Co monwealth,* trans. E. J. Tooley (Ne York: Macmillan Company, 1955), p 145–157.

tes to a spirit of political independence. Islands can preserve their freedom
ore than continental countries because they are protected from foreign influ-
ces.[4] Ecological perspectives have made inroads into modern political
eory as well. Both Mahan and Mackinder found a close relationship between
ographical factors and national political capabilities. The German geo-
olitical school correlated *Lebensraum* and national power.

Both "utopians" and "realists" in international relations (examined in
hapters 1 and 3 respectively), discussed man in relation to his environment.
ut they broadened the notion of "environment" to include the products of
uman culture as well as the physical features of the earth. Drawing upon the
ritings of theorists of the Enlightenment, utopians claimed that international
ehavior could be altered by transforming the institutional setting. Schemes
r international organization and world government, as well as for estab-
shing norms for international conduct, were designed to alter human be-
avior by changing the international environment. In contrast, as the analysis
ndertaken in Chapter 3 reveals, "realists" in international relations often
eld that the geographical location of states conditions, if not determines,
olitical behavior. If the political behavior of national units is in large part
e product of the environmental circumstances, including geography, in
hich nations find themselves, the statesman's perennial task is to work within
e parameters established by the environment.

Excluding ecological perspectives would certainly be incongruous with his-
orical precedent. Man's relationship to his environment remains a focal point
f analysis. Writers who have studied politics as a general systems theory have
mphasized environment. Systems models, discussed in Chapter 4, may be
rouped as both "open" or "closed." The "open" systems—both biological
nd social—by definition are susceptible to, and dependent for their survival
n, inputs from their environment. Those writers who have developed so-called
closed" or self-contained systems have eliminated inputs from an external
nvironment but they have often incorporated environmental factors of great
mportance right into their models of the system.

UCKLE AND HUNTINGTON: CLIMATIC FACTORS

lany nineteenth- and twentieth-century scholars were as convinced as the
assical writers of the importance of climate as a conditioner of political
ehavior. Henry Thomas Buckle (1821–1862), a British historian, realized
at climate, food, and soil closely depend on each other. Climate influences
e kinds of crops grown; the quality of the food depended on the soil. Buckle
xplained the vigor of the northern laborer as a result of the food supply
vailable in a cold climate. In nations in cold climates, "there is for the most

Baron de Montesquieu, *The Spirit of*   I, 154–159, 259–274.
aws (Worcester: Isaiah Thomas, 1802),

part displayed, even in the infancy of society, a bolder or more adventurou character, than we find among those other nations whose ordinary nutrimen . . . is easily obtained, and indeed is supplied to them, by the bounty of natur gratuitously and without a struggle." Buckle added that the sparseness of po ulation and thus inflation of wages and living standard fluctuates with foc supply,

> advancing when the supply is plentiful, halting or receding when the supply is scanty. The food essential to life is scarcer in cold countries than in hot ones; and not only is it scarcer, but more of it is required; so that on both grounds smaller encouragement is given to the growth of that population from whose ranks the labour-market is stocked. To express, therefore, the conclusion in its simplest form, we may say, that there is a strong and constant tendency in hot countries for wages to be low, in cold countries for them to be high.

Civilizations with hot climates, and therefore low wage levels, produce lar and depressed working classes, with attendant social and economic cons quences. Great inequality in the distribution of wealth, political power a social influence, according to Buckle, led many ancient civilizations to rea a "certain stage of development and then to decline."[5]

Ellsworth Huntington (1876–1947), the American geographer and e plorer, found climate a determinant not only of man's health, activity, le of food production and other resource availabilities, but of the migration peoples and their racial mixtures as well. Only the most physically fit, intel gent, and adventurous survive migration. And only those subject to econom distress due to poor harvest and food shortages attempt migration. To supp this view, Huntington cited as an example, the desiccation of central Asia different periods of history which led to the invasion of Europe by the ba barians, the Dorian and Ionian invasions of ancient Greece, and the Mong incursion into southeast Asia. The Arab migration led by Mohammed, a strengthened by religious motivation, represented a movement from parch deserts to more fertile lands. Improved economic conditions, stimulated climatic factors, liberated large parts of a population from the tasks of gathe ing and producing food, and permitted them to develop new and advanc ideas in the fields of art, literature, science and political life. Huntington su ported the supposition of man's disinclination to strenuous labor in hot c mates with the statistic that most of the world's major civilizations develop where the annual average temperature neared the optimum necessary maximum human productivity (65–70° Fahrenheit).[6] Great civilizations witl

5. Henry Thomas Buckle, *History of Civilization in England* (London: Longmans, Green and Company, 1903), I, 39–151.

6. Ellsworth Huntington, *Mainsprings of*

Civilization (New York: John Wiley Sons, 1945), especially pp. 250–275; *Civilization and Climate* (New Hav Yale University Press, 1924), especia pp. 1–29; 387–411.

Contending Theories of International Relati

he tropic zones have risen only on temperate plateaus or along cool seacoasts where the temperature in no season far exceeded the optimum temperature, .g., the Mayas in Mexico and in Guatemala, the Khomens in Indochina, and he ancient Javanese and Singhalese.

TOYNBEE: ENVIRONMENTAL CHALLENGE AND RESPONSE

Arnold Toynbee held that civilizations are born in environments that are unusually difficult, in response to challenges posed by environments.[7] He examined five types of challenging stimuli. Two of these were physical—hard country, i.e., country possessing a harsh climate, terrain, and soil; and new ground, that is, the exploration, opening up, and development of a wilderness into productive land. The three nonphysical stimuli include: (1) external blows from another state; (2) continuous external pressure against a state; and (3) a stimulus of penalizations, that is, if a state loses the use of a particular component it is likely to respond by increasing correspondingly the efficiency of another component. Toynbee adds that overly severe physical challenge can arrest the development of civilization. The Polynesian, Eskimo, Nomad, Spartan and Osmanli civilizations were retarded as a result of physical challenges which they could not meet.

Civilizations grow when a society undergoes a catapulting series of challenges. The challenged civilization develops an *élan vital,* which carries it through equilibrium toward another challenge thereby inspiring another response. The challenge-response cycle is potentially infinite. A criticism of the challenge-response hypothesis is that it is retrospective, not allowing us to predict the potential response to a challenge.

The breakdown of civilizations results from the degeneration of the creative minority into a "dominant minority which attempts to retain by force position that it has ceased to merit." This, in turn, provokes a "secession of proletariat which no longer admires and imitates its rulers and revolts against its servitude." [8] Thus the society loses its social cohesiveness.

Vertical schisms between geographically segregated communities and horizontal schisms between classes or groups geographically contiguous but socially segregated—these characterize the disintegration of a civilization. The horizontal schism may occur when a dominant minority retains its ruling

. For an examination of Toynbee's challenge-response hypothesis, see *A Study of History,* abridgement of Volumes I–IV, by D. C. Somervell (London: Oxford University Press, 1956), pp. 60–39. Andrew M. Scott has proposed the challenge-response concept as a central approach to the study of international affairs, closely related to the balance-of-power idea. "Challenge and Response: A Tool for the Analysis of International Affairs," *Review of Politics,* XVIII (1956), 207–226.

8. *Ibid.,* p. 246. Toynbee defines breakdown as the termination of growth.

position by force but loses its right to that role as a result of its loss of cre
ativity. Toynbee's schema is related to modern, more complex theories o
social revolution. (The correlations and distinctions are made in Chapter 8.

Geographic Factors of National Power

For the most part, those writers concerned with the interaction between man
and his environment have tended to stress the importance of environmenta
factors as determinants, or at least conditioners, of political behavior. Environ
ment not only limits human conduct, it provides opportunities. Of particula
importance are climatic and geographical factors. These theorists assume tha
uneven distribution of resources and differences in geographical and climati
endowments affect the potential power of a nation. The size of the countr
influences the availability of natural resources; and the climate affects th
mobilization of human resources necessary for exploiting these natural re
sources. Variations in these factors may crucially affect the structure c
political systems, even influencing their ability to survive under stress.

If political behavior is affected by environment, man has the capacity t
alter political behavior by manipulating the environment. Of particular im
portance to writers such as Alfred Thayer Mahan (1840–1914), an America
naval officer and historian, and Sir Halford Mackinder (1861–1947), a Britis
geographer, as well as the Sprouts, is the impact of technological change upo
man's environment. Technology, it is suggested, does not render environ
mental factors unimportant, or obsolete. Rather, it alters the importance c
environmental factors once considered crucial, replacing them with still an
other set. Mahan saw naval power as the key to man's control of space
Mackinder saw the technology of land transport as crucial; and the technolog
of airpower and outer space exploration are two other environmental factor
in space control. Even in this age of intercontinental ballistic missiles (ICBMs
analysts engaging in the constant calculus of deterrence consider a country'
size and population distribution, and weapon deployments which confor
to the configuration of land and sea.

Though possessing a limited capacity to change his environment, man'
behavior remains circumscribed by environmental factors. A French schoc
of geographic "possibilist" thought, represented by Lucien Febvre and Vid
de la Blache, rejected the determinism of Anglo-American and Germa
environmental theories. Drawing upon the intellectual heritage of the Enligh
enment, French students of geography suggested that man can modify hi
natural environment. In fact, human free will ultimately determines the op
tions open to man. Environment, geography in particular, is but one of man

Contending Theories of International Relation

rces governing the development of man's activity.[9] Twentieth-century geo-
olitical writers fall somewhere between a strictly determinist and possibilist
nterpretation. If environment does not determine the boundaries of human
onduct, it provides nevertheless an important, if not crucial, conditioning
nfluence. As Ladis K. D. Kristof has suggested, "the modern geopolitician
oes not look at the world map in order to find out what nature *compels* us
o do but what nature advises us to do, given our preferences." [10]

We turn now to the writings of geopolitical theorists from the United States
nd Europe. Among the Americans we focus on Mahan and the Sprouts.
Mahan concentrated on the impact of naval power upon national political
otential. The Sprouts probed the implications of a broad range of environing
actors for political behavior. In addition to Mahan and the Sprouts, a list of
ne most eminent American students of geopolitical relationships includes
uch diverse writers as Frederick Jackson Turner, Homer Lea, Nicholas J.
pykman, Ellen Churchill Semple, General William Mitchell, George F. Ken-
an, Karl A. Wittfogel, Owen Lattimore, Alexander P. de Seversky, Stephen
. Jones, and Robert Strausz-Hupé. Moreover, as we shall note in Chapter 3,
ealist writers have directed attention to geopolitical relationships.

MAHAN, THE SEAS AND NATIONAL POWER

Mahan wrote during the period of the last great wave of European expansion
nd the rise of the United States to the status of a world power. He was a
lose friend and advisor of Theodore Roosevelt on military and naval affairs.
s assistant secretary of the navy and, later, as president, Theodore Roosevelt
ade a major contribution to the development of the United States as a
ading naval power. Mahan's analysis of maritime history, particularly the
rowth of British global influence, led him to conclude that control of the
eas, and especially of strategically important narrow waterways, was crucial
o great power status.[11] Mahan based his theory on the observation that the

See Sprout and Sprout, *The Ecological
erspective on Human Affairs,* pp. 83–
8; Lucien Febvre, *A Geographical In-
oduction to History* (New York: Alfred
. Knopf, 1925), pp. 358–368; P. W. J.
idal de la Blache, *Principles of Human
eography.* Edited by Emmanuel de Mar-
nne (New York: Henry Holt and Com-
any, 1926). O. H. K. Spate, "How De-
rmined Is Possibilism?" *Geographical
udies,* IV (1957), 3, 8; George Tatham,
Environmentalism and Possibilism." In
riffith Taylor, ed., *Geography in the
wentieth Century* (New York: Philo-
ophical Library, 1951), pp. 128ff, 151ff.
0. Ladis K. D. Kristof, "The Origins

and Evolution of Geopolitics," *Journal of
Conflict Resolution,* IV (March, 1960),
19.

11. Alfred Thayer Mahan, *The Influence
of Seapower Upon History, 1660–1783*
(Boston: Little, Brown and Company,
1897), especially pp. 281–329. See also
Margaret Tuttle Sprout, "Mahan: Evan-
gelist of Sea Power," Edward Mead
Earle, ed., *Makers of Modern Strategy:
Military Thought from Machiavelli to
Hitler* (Princeton: Princeton University
Press, 1943), pp. 415–445; Harold and
Margaret Sprout, *The Rise of American
Naval Power* (Princeton: Princeton Uni-
versity Press, 1942).

rise of the British Empire and the rise of the British navy had occurred simul taneously. The world's principal sea routes had become the Empire's internal communication links. Except for the Panama Canal, Britain controlled all the world's major waterways: Dover, Gibraltar, Alexandria, the Cape of Good Hope, and the Straits of Malacca at Singapore. The ocean commerce of Northern Europe passed either through the narrow Strait of Dover under British guns or round the northern tip of Scotland, where the British navy maintained constant vigil. Britain and the United States enjoyed greater access to the oceans than Germany and Russia. The facility for sea transport was easier than movement over land, and the land masses were surrounded by oceans. States with ready access to the oceans had greater potential for great power status than states which were landlocked. Islands had an advantage over land-bordered states. Maritime states formed alliances more for purpose of commerce than aggression.

Mahan advocated a large United States navy to deal with the inevitable international conflicts resulting from commercial rivalries. He recognized the influence of additional factors of geographic position, land configuration, population and government on a country's capacity to achieve great power status. A nation such as Britain or Japan, isolated by water, had the strategic advantage of concentrating its defenses in one roving navy. Whereas nations such as France or Italy, with two coastlines and a land border, found their energies dissipated by the dispersal of their forces. Thus, land was a geophysi cal factor in Mahan's philosophy. Harbors and rivers played a role in provid ing ports necessary to international trade. In Mahan's analysis the length of the coastline and quality of harbors were more crucial factors than square mileage. Similarly, he concerned himself not with raw population statistics but with analyses of the labor force available for shipbuilding and occupations related to naval power. Mahan held that an aptitude for commercial pursuits, particu larly those of international trade, indicated a capacity in a nation to become a major power. To summarize, Mahan correlated national power and geo graphical mobility. Because the "frictionless" seas afforded greater mobility than land at the time he wrote, naturally Mahan attached great importance to seapower.

MACKINDER AND THE HEARTLAND

Like Mahan, Mackinder saw an intimate relationship between geography and technology. If the technology of the nineteenth century had enhanced the mobility of seapower over land power, the technology of the twentieth century restored landpower to the dominant position. The railroad effectuated rapid transportation across the vast expanses of Eurasia. Until then the inner regions

Contending Theories of International Relations

f the Eurasian land mass were landlocked. Eurasia's river system drains into one of the major seas of the world. The Arctic freezes much of the northern Eurasian coast. With the coming of the railroad, the Middle East was now as accessible to Germany by land as it had been to Britain by sea. India and the Far East were accessible to Russia as well as Britain. While Britain, as a small island, was the legatee of a depreciating estate, the major Eurasian powers sat astride the greatest human and natural resources available to man. Mackinder saw the struggle between the landpower and the seapower as a unifying theme of history. The first cycle in the evolution of seapower was completed in the closing of the Mediterranean Sea by the Macedonians. Mackinder traced the next cycle in the evolution of seapower in noting that Rome, a land power, defeated maritime Carthage and once again the Mediterranean became a closed sea." [12] In both these cycles in the ancient era—the Macedonian-Greek and the Roman-Carthaginian—a land power had successfully challenged a seapower. In modern times Britain, initially a seapower, dominated the sea. In the twentieth century, however, Britain found it difficult, if not impossible, to withstand pressures from land powers. In the contemporary world, seapower was dominant for only a passing era. Land power was becoming more significant. Technology, once favorable to seapower, was now tipping the advantage to land power.

Mackinder suggested twice that the "pivot area" of international politics would be the East European and Siberian plains. He suggested it first in a famous paper read before the Royal Geographic Society of London in 1904, and later, at the end of World War I, in his book *Democratic Ideals and Reality*.

> *As we consider this rapid review of the broader currents of history, does not a certain persistence of geographical relationship become evident? Is not the pivot region of the world's politics that vast area of Euro-Asia which is inaccessible to ships, but in antiquity lay open to the horse-riding nomads, and is today about to be covered with a network of railways?* [13]

This area, which coincided with the tsarist Russian Empire "occupies the central strategical position" and possesses "incalculably great" resources. This "pivot area" Mackinder called the Heartland.) This region, he suggested, was surrounded by the "inner crescent," which includes such countries on the periphery of Eurasia as Germany, Turkey, India, and China. This region, in turn, is surrounded by the Outer Crescent, which includes such countries as Britain, South Africa, and Japan.

Mackinder formulated the famous dictum:

12. Halford Mackinder, *Democratic Ideals and Reality* (New York: W. W. Norton and Company, 1962), pp. 35–39.

13. Mackinder, "The Geographical Pivot of History," *Geographical Journal,* XXIII (April, 1904), 434.

Who rules East Europe commands the Heartland
Who rules the Heartland commands the World Island (Eurasia)
Who rules the World Island commands the world.[14]

Mackinder feared the rising power of Germany and later the Soviet Union
for both countries might be able not only to rule the Heartland, but to becom
great naval powers and thus to threaten Britain. While emphasizing the grow
ing importance of land power, Mackinder did not deprecate the role of sea
power. Seapower was as vital to world power as it had ever been. In th
twentieth century, however, broader land bases were necessary for seapowe
than had been needed in the nineteenth century. The World Island had th
potential to become the greatest seapower, though its "heartland" woul
remain invulnerable to attack by seapower. In the twentieth century the powe
controlling the "heartland" and hence the World Island would control sea
power in the same way as Macedonia and Rome, though primarily lan
powers, had gained control of the seas.

In fact, he foresaw international politics of the twentieth century as
struggle between Germany and Russia for control of the Heartland and adja
cent areas on the Eurasian land mass.

Mackinder's geopolitical framework is similar to that of certain reali
writers examined in Chapter 3. The realists, like Mackinder, considering th
Eurasian land mass the key to world power, dealt with this so-called Worl
Island as a major factor in the balance of power. Without referring to Mac
kinder or stating their assumptions as explicitly, American policymakers hav
aimed, through the twentieth century, to prevent the domination of the Eu
rasian land mass by a hostile power.

During World War II Mackinder reassessed and revised his geopolitica
theory. In 1943, he saw in an Atlantic community a counterpoise to the aggre
gation of power in the Eurasian land mass. Although the Soviet Union woul
emerge from World War II as the "greatest land power on the globe" an
"in the strategically strongest defensive position," the nations of the Nort
Atlantic basin would form a counterpoise.[15] Together, Britain, France, an
the United States could provide power adequate both to prevent a resurgenc
of Germany and to balance the Soviet Union. Other writers, such as Nichola
J. Spykman and Stephen B. Jones, suggested that the "rimland" of Eurasi
might prove strategically more important than the Heartland if new center
of industrial power and communications were created along the circumferenc
of the Eurasian land mass. The "rimland" hypothesis lays the theoretica
foundations of George F. Kennan's famous postwar proposal for a "policy c
containment." [16]

14. Mackinder, *op. cit.,* p. 150. See also
Hans W. Weigert, "Mackinder's Heartland," *The American Scholar,* XV (Winter, 1945), 43–54.

15. Halford J. Mackinder, "The Round

World and the Winning of the Peace
Foreign Affairs, XXI (July, 1943), 60

16. See Stephen B. Jones, "Global Strat
gic Views," *Geographical Review,* XL
(October, 1955), 492–508; Nicholas

Contending Theories of International Relation

Geopolitics: The Political Significance of Space

Friedrich Ratzel (1844–1904), a German geographer, coined the term *Anthropogeographie,* which meant a synthesis of geography, anthropology and politics. Thus the new discipline of political geography was born in Germany in the nineteenth century. The new discipline was directed to the study of man, the state and the world as organic units. The state was seen as a living organism which occupies space and which grows, contracts and eventually dies. Ratzel stopped short of imputing to the state an objective reality, asserting instead that states "are not organisms properly speaking but only aggregate-organisms," the unity of which is forged by "moral and spiritual forces." [17]

Political geographers addressed themselves to the question of man's relationship to nature. They concerned themselves with the implications of climate, topography, and natural resources for civilization. In fact, Ratzel attributed the development of superior civilizations, European civilization in particular, to favorable climatic conditions. He contended that mankind was engaged in an unending struggle for living space. A nation's land area indicates its power position. Nations strive to extend their territorial frontiers. The urge to territorial expansion is greatest among strong nations. Boundaries, therefore, are constantly shifting. They form the zones of conflict between nations. Geopoliticians referred to this concept as "dynamic frontiers." In twentieth-century German geopolitical writings and in Spykman's work,[18] boundaries are viewed as demarcations of zones where expansion has temporarily ceased.

Rudolf Kjellén (1864–1922), a Swedish geographer, first used the term "geopolitics" when describing the geopolitical bases of national power. Adhering to an organic theory of the state, he held that states, like animals in Darwinian theory, engage in a relentless struggle for survival. States have boundaries, a capital, and lines of communication, as well as a consciousness and a culture. Though Kjellén writes metaphysically and imputes to the state the quality of a living organism, he nevertheless concludes that "the life of the state is, ultimately, in the hands of the individuals." [19] He considered the

---

Spykman, *The Geography of the Peace* New York: Harcourt, Brace and Company, 1944), p. 43; and George F. Kennan, "The Sources of Soviet Conduct," *Foreign Affairs,* XXV (July, 1947), 566–82. Spykman, in discussing the value of the "heartland's interior lines" with respect to the periphery or "rimland," suggested that the relations between center and circumference are of one sort if the maritime powers are trying to apply their leverage around the rimland from afar; but these relations are changed if local centers of power and communications are developed around the rimland. *Op cit.,* p. 40.

17. Friedrich Ratzel, *Anthropogeographie,* 2nd ed. (Stuttgart: J. Engelhorn, 1899), Part I, p. 2. See Kristof, *op. cit.,* p. 22.

18. See, in particular, Nicholas J. Spykman and Abbie A. Rollins, "Geographic Objectives in Foreign Policy, I," *American Political Science Review,* XXXIII (June, 1939), 391–393.

19. Rudolf Kjellén, *Der Staat als Lebensform,* trans. M. Langfelt (Leipzig: S. Hirzel Verlag, 1917), pp. 218–220. See Kristof, *op. cit.,* p. 22.

emergence of a few great powers a result of efforts of strong states to expand.

In the interwar period, the followers of Kjellén and Ratzel used geopolitic to develop a framework for German national expansion. Karl Haushofer (1869–1946), a retired army officer, founded the German Academy at the University of Munich in 1925, together with the journal *Zeitschrift für Geo politik.* Both received active support from the Third Reich.[20] Haushofer' influence was considerable in military circles and he was credited with being one of Hitler's key political advisors.

Haushofer considered that geopolitics involved the correlation of politica phenomena with geographical data. He believed that geopolitics would enable German leaders to establish national objectives and policies.

German geopolitical thinking expressed the need for great nations to enlarge their frontiers, to obtain *lebensraum,* self-sufficiency in raw materials, industry and markets and population growth. Extensive geographic space and nationa power were synonymous. Haushofer drew upon Ratzel's writings on the rela tionship between space and power. Moreover, Haushofer based his recom mendations for achieving *lebensraum* on Japan's successful expansion in th 1930s. He was indebted to Mackinder's conception that the Heartland wa the key to global mastery. Warning of the danger posed by an expansionis Nazi Germany, Robert Strausz-Hupé suggested that geopolitics "represent a revolutionary attempt to measure and to harness the forces which make for expansionism." [21] German geopolitical theorists considered conflict among leading states inevitable. This conflict would pit a continental European group ing dominated by Germany in alliance with a Pacific grouping led by Japan against an Atlantic grouping under the leadership of Britain and the United States. The continental and Pacific groupings would fight for a more favorable distribution of living space.

Haushofer's organic theory of boundaries contains a second major com ponent of German geopolitical thinking. He proposes in this theory that a state strives to achieve a frontier which contains a zone of sparse settlement— a zone outside the living space, separating the state from neighboring states

20. For a discussion of the development of the German Academy, see Donald H. Norton, "Karl Haushofer and the German Academy, 1925–1945," *Central European History,* I (March, 1968), 82. According to its rules and regulations, the objectives of the Academy were "to nourish all spiritual expressions of Germandom and to bring together and strengthen the unofficial cultural relations of Germany with areas abroad and of the Germans abroad with the homeland, in the service of the all-German folk-consciousness." Quoted in *ibid.*

21. Robert Strausz-Hupé, *Geopolitics: The Struggle for Space and Power* (New York: G. P. Putnam's Sons, 1942), p vii. Ladis K. D. Kristof suggests th following definition: "Geopolitics is th study of political phenomena (1) in thei spatial relationship and (2) in their rela tionship with, dependence upon, and in fluence on, earth as well as on all thos cultural factors which constitute the sub ject matter of human geography (anthro pogeography) broadly defined. In othe words, geopolitics is what the word itsel suggests etymologically: geographical pol itics, that is, politics and *not* geography— politics geographically interpreted or an alyzed for its geographical content. Kristof, *op. cit.,* p. 34.

Contending Theories of International Relation

Haushofer and his followers considered the world to consist of renovating and decadent nations. British "decadence" was exemplified by Britain's inability to halt tendencies in her empire toward self-government. In another war, Haushofer believed, Britain could not be assured of the loyalty and support of the self-governing parts of the British Empire. Finally, the German geopolitical theorists developed geostrategy, a military science. All relevant information about an opponent was gathered so that a *blitzkrieg,* a quick and decisive attack, could be mounted.

German geopolitical writings contained five concepts: (1) Autarchy, national economic self-sufficiency, precluding the need for foreign products; (2) *Lebensraum,* sufficient land area and natural resources to support the population of a nation; (3) Pan-regions, or geographic areas, to replace the traditional concept of national frontiers; (4) the assumption that the land mass of Eurasia-Africa, being the most populous and the largest combination of land power and seapower, has therefore the potential for world domination; and (5) that the state has the right to "natural frontiers, or boundaries set forth by nature." [22]

The Sprouts and Man-Milieu Relationships

Of all who have written about man's relationship to his human and nonhuman environment, Harold Sprout, professor of geography and international relations at Princeton, and his wife, Margaret, have contributed most toward clarifying concepts, developing hypotheses, and presenting frameworks for examining man-milieu relationships. Although the Sprouts have long believed in the importance of geography in explaining political behavior,[23] they contend that most, if not all, human activity is affected by the uneven distribution of human and nonhuman resources.[24]

Human and nonhuman environmental factors affect human activities in only two respects. First, they can influence human decisions only if human beings perceive them. Second, environmental factors can limit the human individual's performance.[25] The Sprouts regard geographic science as "concerned with the arrangement of things on the face of the earth, and with the association of things that give character to particular places." And they believe that geography affects all human and nonhuman, tangible and intangible phe-

22. Derwent Whittlesey, "Haushofer: The Geopolitician," Edward Mead Earle, ed., *Makers of Modern Strategy: Military Thought from Machiavelli to Hitler* (Princeton: Princeton University Press, 1943), pp. 398–406.

23. Harold and Margaret Sprout, *The Ecological Perspective on Human Affairs with Special Reference to International Politics* (Princeton: Princeton University Press, 1965), p. 9.

24. Harold and Margaret Sprout, *An Ecological Paradigm for the Study of International Politics* (Princeton: Center for International Studies, 1968), Monograph No. 30, p. 21.

25. *Ibid.,* p. 11.

nomena that "exhibit areal dimensions and variations upon or in relations to the earth's surface." [26]

Every political community has a geographic base. Each political community is set on a territory which is a unique combination of location, size, shape, climate and natural resources. Thus, most transactions among nations entail significant, even crucial, geographic considerations. The Sprouts noted that international statecraft exhibits in all periods "more or less discernible patterns of coercion and submission, influence and deference; patterns reflected in political terms with strong geographic connotations." [27]

COGNITIVE BEHAVIORALISM AND THE OPERATIONAL MILIEU

Important to the Sprouts is the concept of cognitive behavioralism. This concept assumes that a person consciously responds to his milieu through perception "and in no other way." [28] Erroneous ideas of the milieu may be just as influential as accurate ideas in forming moods, preferences, decisions and actions. The Sprouts proceed to distinguish, somewhat imprecisely, between the environment as the observer perceives it and the environment as it actually exists. The ecologists compare the so-called psycho-milieu to Plato's shadows in the cave, "images or ideas which the individual derives from interaction between what he selectively receives from his milieu, by means of his sensory apparatus, and his scheme of values, conscious memories, and subconsciously stored experience." [29] Failure to perceive the limiting condition may result in severe consequences. Inflated illusions about and misinterpretations of geographic circumstances may have similar unfortunate effects.[30] Popular attitudes, as well as the decisions of statesmen, are based upon geographic conceptions which "depend in no small degree upon the kinds of maps to which they are accustomed." Therefore, an analysis of political behavior models must account for assumptions that political leaders make about their milieu. However, such models are limited by the assumptions from which they are derived.

The Sprouts object to the concept of the "state's motivation" and "the state's needs." They do not apply psychoecological concepts to social organization for much the same reason that they reject giving human attributes to the national or international system. They attribute these concepts only to human beings. They believe that political discussion on such an abstract level muddies rather than clarifies one's understanding of the workings of international politics.[31]

26. *Ibid.*, p. 13. The definition is quoted by the Sprouts from Preston E. James, *et al*, *American Geography: Inventory and Prospect* (Syracuse: Syracuse University Press, 1954), p. 4.

27. Sprout and Sprout, *The Ecological Perspective on Human Affairs*, p. 15.

28. *Ibid.*, p. 140.

29. *Ibid.*, p. 28.

30. See Sprout and Sprout, *An Ecological Paradigm for the Study of International Politics*, pp. 39–41. For the implications of perception in foreign policy decision-making, see Chapter 11.

31. *Ibid.*, p. 42.

Contending Theories of International Relations

Though political decisions are based on statesmen's perceptions of their milieu, results of these decisions are limited by the objective nature of the operational milieu as well. The operational milieu is "the situation as it actually exists and affects the achievements and capabilities of the entity in question (whether a single individual, group, or community as a whole)." [32] It is a real form, though perhaps unknown to the political actor. But it is important to remember that so far as decisionmaking is concerned, the Sprouts do not see the geographical factor as "conditioning," "drawing" or "compelling" the policymaker and "dictating" his choices. The rational decisionmaker is merely presumed to take into account the opportunities and limitations inherent in the perceived involvement.

The entity, acting within the operational milieu and having a psychomilieu,[33] is an environed organism (an individual or a population), not an abstraction (the state), which is the principal concern to the social scientist and the particular concern of the student of international relations.

The ecological perspective provides a framework for the consideration of three types of phenomena: ecological concepts of the psychological behavior of persons, their undertakings, and the outcomes of their efforts.[34] The three fundamental concepts of ecology include environment, environed entities and entity-environment relationships. Ecology includes the study of human as well as nonhuman organisms.[35]

While the student may disagree about the importance of geography, he must, nevertheless, recognize the important part that it plays in the Sprouts's paradigm. The Sprouts's schema assumes political accomplishment is limited by geographic configuration and the "distribution and arrangement of phenomena over the earth's surface." [36]

LIMITATIONS OF GEOPOLITICAL THEORIZING

The Sprouts emphasize that technology and social change play a large role in man-milieu relationships. Although technology has obviously not altered the physical layout of lands and seas, it has added elements to the international environment. Although geopolitical speculation has enriched our understanding of the international system, the most serious defect has been the "almost universal failure of the geopolitical theorists to anticipate and allow for the rate of technological and other changes." An accurate assessment of the tools, skills and technological innovations available to the interacting communities is crucial to all geopolitical theorizing. The Sprouts adduce the ecological principle that substantial change in one sector of the milieu can be expected

32. Sprout and Sprout, *An Ecological Paradigm for the Study of International Politics*, p. 34.

33. *Ibid.*, p. 11.

34. Sprout and Sprout, *The Ecological Perspective on Human Affairs*, p. 8.

35. Sprout and Sprout, *An Ecological Paradigm for the Study of International Politics*, p. 62.

36. *Ibid.*, p. 14.

to produce "significant, often unsettling, sometimes utterly disruptive consequences in other sectors." [37]

Technological advance has to make limitations imposed by the social order relatively more significant politically than the natural obstacle. To be sure, the time lag between environmental change and general awareness of such change is not new. The rate of technological change today, however, widens the gap between image and reality, with portents more dangerous than in any period since the formation of the modern international system.

Geography, environed organisms, the psychomilieu, technology, the operational milieu, and beliefs all affect each other. "Substantial changes either in the environment or in the genetic makeups of the organisms involved are likely to start chain reactions that ramify throughout the entire 'web-of-life' within the 'biotic community' ".[38] The interrelatedness of the ecological paradigm has grown increasingly with the mounting complexity of modern society resulting from expanding populations and advanced technology. It is increasingly difficult to "isolate and classify human political events as merely domestic matters or foreign affairs, or as political, sociological, or economic." In fact, the complexity of interrelatedness "within and between national communities, and the increasing irrelevance of the time honored distinction between domestic and international questions, constitute major datum points in the ecological perspective on international politics." [39] The focal point for empirical analysis in the past decade has increasingly been the "linkage" between domestic politics and foreign policy. In their study of man-milieu relationships, the Sprouts have drawn four major conclusions. First, the ecological perspective and frame of reference provide a fruitful approach to the analysis of foreign policy and the estimation of a state's capabilities. Second, it is helpful to distinguish analytically between the relation of environmental factors to policy decisions and to the operational results of decisions. In the Sprouts' judgment, much of the confusion clouding the discussion of environmental factors in international politics stems from the failure to make this distinction explicit. Third, the ecological approach is a useful complement to the study of both the foreign policy and the international capabilities of states. The Sprouts' paradigm entails the examination of such limiting conditions as the level of available technology, cognition of essential factors, and the ratio of available resources to commitments.[40] Finally, they see the ecological approach as broadening the study of international politics by integrating into it relevant theories and data from geography, psychology, sociology, and other systems of learning.

Current Empirical Research and Environmental Factors

Although the present generation of international relations scholars has not given great weight to geographical factors, some writers have focused on the

37. *Ibid.*, p. 55.
38. *Ibid.*, p. 20.

39. *Ibid.*, p. 56.
40. *Ibid.*, p. 64.

relationship between environment and political behavior. In an effort to determine the impact of insular status on nations, two authors have compared the policies of Britain, Ceylon, and Japan.[41] Their analysis revealed that insular polities have a "more active involvement" with other countries than noninsular polities. Insular polities are more limited than noninsular polities in the range of foreign policies available to them. The authors found similarities in the foreign policies of Britain and Japan. Both countries attempted to occupy sections of the mainland, especially those areas from which invasions might be mounted. Both tried to maintain a balance of power among mainland nations by supporting the weaker coalition. Both sought alliances with powers outside the region to strengthen their position *vis-à-vis* continental national units.

In assessing the effect of noncontiguity on the integration of political units, Richard Merritt's study of territorially discontinuous polities indicated centrifugal forces increasing with the distance.[42] Peoples tend to communicate more with neighboring than with physically distant peoples. The noncontiguous polity depends on the external environment to preserve communication links among its physically separated parts. Daily dependence upon communications makes noncontiguous polities sensitive to shifts in international environment which affect communications. Such polities have been concerned with the application of international law to internal waters, territorial and high seas, air rights, and land access, to cite only the modern history of problems experienced by Malaysia, Pakistan, the United Arab Republic (Egypt-Syria) and the West Indies Federation. Some of these polities did not endure.

Critiques of Environmental Theories

Even critics of "environmental theories" acknowledge a minimal influence of environment on political behavior. In fact, the Sprouts chide writers who engage in "environmentalistic rhetoric" and assume uncritically that attitudes or decisions are "determined" or "influenced" or in some other way causally affected by environmental factors.[43] Although the Sprouts reject environment as a determinant of politics, they conceive as crucial (a) the actor's percep-

41. Robert T. Holt and John E. Turner, "Insular Polities," James N. Rosenau, ed., *Linkage Politics* (New York: Free Press, 1969), pp. 199–236.

42. Richard L. Merritt, "Noncontiguity and Political Integration," in *Ibid.,* pp. 237–272.

43. Harold and Margaret Sprout, *Foundations of International Politics* (Princeton: D. Van Nostrand Company, 1962),

p. 54. Examples of such rhetoric include: "The mountains of Japan have pushed the Japanese out upon the seas *making* them the greatest seafaring people of Asia." "England, *driven* to the sea by her sparse resources to seek a livelihood and to find homes for her burgeoning population, and sitting athwart the main sea routes of Western Europe, seemed *destined by geography* to command the seas." Italics are those of the Sprouts.

tion of environmental factors; and (b) limitations to human activity posed by the environment.[44]

According to Strausz-Hupé, geographic conditions have been modified by man throughout history: "Geographic conditions determine largely *where* history is made, but it is always man who makes it." [45] Though deriving his own work from the geopolitical concepts in Mackinder's writings, Spykman criticized Mackinder for overestimating the potentialities of the Heartland and underestimating those of the Inner Crescent. According to Spykman, "if there is to be a slogan for the power politics of the Old World, it must be: 'Who controls the Rimland rules Eurasia; who rules Eurasia controls the destinies of the world.' " [46] Spykman also noted that a combination of sea-powers had never been aligned against a grouping of land powers. "The historical alignment has always been in terms of some members of the Rimland with Great Britain against some members of the Rimland with Russia, or Great Britain and Russia together against a dominating Rimland power." [47] Strausz-Hupé in his analysis of the German geopolitical school says that "there is, in short, no historical evidence in support of the causal nexus alleged by the advocates of *lebensraum* . . . to exist between population pressure and national growth in space." [48] Historically, national expansion has resulted from conditions other than population pressure. For example, Japanese expansionism in Asia antedated the upsurge in Japan's population. Nor does large space necessarily equal national power, although "whenever large space was thoroughly organized by a state, small nations . . . were not able to withstand its expansive force." [49]

Finally, it is often asserted that technological change has rendered both Mackinder's "Heartland" concept and Haushofer's geopolitical theory obsolete. In the discussion following Mackinder's presentation of his paper, "The Geographical Pivot of History" to the Royal Geographic Society, Leopold Amery said: "Both the sea and the railway are going in the future . . . to be supplemented by the air as a means of locomotion, (and) when we come to that, a great deal of this geographical distribution must lose its importance, and the successful powers will be those who have the greatest industrial basis." [50] According to Strausz-Hupé: "If it [the Heartland] ever was a valid concept [for which there is no convincing evidence], there is no guarantee that modern technology will not invalidate it. It may, indeed, have done so already." [51]

44. Sprout and Sprout, *The Ecological Perspective on Human Affairs*, p. 11.

45. Strausz-Hupé, *Geopolitics*, p. 173.

46. Spykman, *The Geography of the Peace*, p. 43.

47. *Ibid.*, p. 181.

48. Strausz-Hupé, *op. cit.*, pp. 164–165.

49. *Ibid.*, p. 181.

50. *Geographical Journal*, XXIII (April, 1904), 441.

51. Strausz-Hupé, *op. cit.*, pp. 189–190. A half century after Leopold Amery made his comment about the airplane, long-range bombers carrying nuclear bombs had become prime symbols of international power, and analysts were still arguing, not quite conclusively, as to whether the advent of air power and

The Sprouts criticize the theories of both Mahan and Mackinder as being outmoded as a result of innovations in military technology and "paramilitary and non-military forms of political interaction." [52] Kristof criticizes geopolitical writers for having "marshalled facts and laws of the physical world to justify political demands and support political opinions. One of the best examples of the hopelessly contradictory arguments to which this may lead is a concept akin in spirit to that of the 'natural boundary,' namely, the concept of the 'harmonic state.' " [53] A "natural boundary/harmonic state" is a relative concept.

Technology, Population Growth and Environmental Issues

Although they had to alter their views to account for the impact of technology on environment, the environmentalists contributed greatly to thought about international politics. Technological changes may have altered the significance of the theorizing of certain of the writers examined in this chapter. Still, advanced technology has rendered relationships between man and his environment ever more important. As many writers have suggested, modern science and technology have transformed the environment in ways intended, but also in ways unintended, by man.[54] Science and technology have brought "uninvited guests" in such forms as air pollution and traffic congestion. In the twentieth century, the pace of scientific-technological innovation has quickened beyond any historical precedent and peoples in all parts of the globe have been drawn into the orbit of modern technology. Whether changes wrought by technology are affecting the environment in ways beyond the means of coping with them remains debatable.

The 1970s opened on a note of growing concern over the pollution of the human environment. This concern was demonstrated especially, but not exclusively, by youth. It is difficult to say whether this preoccupation was only a fad or whether it would become, at least in some of the more technically advanced nations, an enduring concern. Increasing numbers of people are

---

nuclear energy had rendered the Heartland concept obsolete. See W. Gordon East, "How Strong is the Heartland?" *Foreign Affairs,* XXIX (October, 1950), 78–93; and Charles Kruszewski, "The Pivot of History," *Foreign Affairs,* XXXII (April, 1954), 388–401.

52. Sprout and Sprout, *Foundations of International Politics,* pp. 338–339.

53. Kristof, *op. cit.,* p. 29.

54. See, for example, Robert Strausz-Hupé, "Social Values and Politics: The

Uninvited Guests," *Review of Politics,* XXX (January, 1968), 60–61. Another writer, George F. Kennan, who, like Strausz-Hupé, is examined in the following chapter, has suggested the need for an international organization for the collection, storage, and retrieval and dissemination of information and the coordination of research and operational activities on environmental problems at the international level. See George F. Kennan, "To Prevent a World Wasteland," *Foreign Affairs,* XLVIII (April, 1970), 404.

aware that population growth, modes in urbanization and the chemical waste of products of industrial civilization are causing profound changes in the ecology of human civilization. Scientists worry about the contamination of the land, of lakes, rivers and oceans, of the air we breathe, even of outer space. Unreplenishable mineral resources are constantly being converted into energy, and waste products are spoiling our finite atmosphere. In countless ways, human interventions are upsetting the "balance of nature." This has always been true. The novelty lies in the greater awareness of the ecological consequences of human behavior and scientific technology and in the acceleration of impact.[55]

It seems likely that the problems of polluted environment will bring new issues into national and international politics. Controversy will obviously arise between those desiring to control pollution and those whose activities will be restrained by such controls. Whether or not to curb an activity will require a weighing of consequences—human needs served versus human interests harmed. Allocations of gains and costs must be made, as they are central to politics.[56] The future will probably witness a tendency of political leaders to devote greater attention to such problems as reducing pollution of oceans and beaches, providing effective safeguards against the disposal of radioactive wastes, regulating population growth, renewing the urban atmosphere, and otherwise bringing under control those forms of environmental pollution which threaten health and the quality of human life. Such issues have important implications for national security policy and international scientific cooperation in an age when national governments still jealously guard their prerogatives.[57]

55. The literature on ecology and environmental pollution is voluminous, and there is no need in a book of this sort to cite a large number of books on the subject. Some of the more important writers include Rene Dubos, Garrett Hardin, Rachel Carson, Robert and Leona Ellul, Lynn White, Jr., and Garrett De Bell. The student is referred to the bibliography in Garrett De Bell, ed., *The Environmental Handbook* (New York: Ballantine Books, 1970).

56. As early as 1963, the conclusion of the Partial Nuclear Test Ban Treaty (covering the atmosphere, the oceans and outer space) reflected in part an effort to control the dangers of radioactive fallout.

57. See, for example, Lord Ritchie-Calder, "Mortgaging the Old Homestead," *Foreign Affairs,* XLVIII (January, 1970), 207–230; "The Chemistry and Cost of Contamination," Symposium by R. Stephen Berry and Norman F. Ramsey, *Bulletin of the Atomic Scientists,* XXVI (April, 1970), 2–5, 34–41; Daniel S. Cheever, "Marine Science and Ocean Politics," *ibid.* (February, 1970), 22, 29–34; Frank M. Potter, Jr., "Everyone Wants to Save the Environment But No One Knows Quite What to Do," *The Center Magazine,* III (March-April, 1970), 37–40.

Contending Theories of International Relations

CHAPTER 3
Political Realism
at the International Level

Realism vs. Utopianism

Realism, as a reaction to utopianism, dominated the study of international relations in America from 1940 to 1960. International relations teachers in American universities used textbooks by realist scholars and their other writings, often policy-oriented, which had wide currency in official and academic circles. Indeed, much of international relations theory is the product of the political realists or of their critics.

Realism, like utopianism, is normative and policy-oriented; to a greater degree than utopianism, its generalizations about international behavior come from the study of history. But much of realist theory is a critique of utopianism. Realism, unlike utopianism, holds that public opinion is easily changed and is thus an unreliable policymaking guide. In contrast to utopianism, with its emphasis upon the development of norms of international behavior based on law and organization, realism stresses the nation-state as the principal unit of analysis. Unlike the utopians, realists assume there is no essential harmony of interests among nations. Instead, they posit that nation-states often have conflicting national objectives, some of which lead to war. The capabilities of nations are crucial for the outcome of international conflict and a nation's ability to influence another's behavior. But seldom, if ever, is the notion of capabilities, or power, synonymous in realist theory with strictly military capabilities. Power has both military and nonmilitary components, and realist theorists have schemes for classifying the elements of national power. In their analyses, realists try to assess national capabilities which include not only military forces, but levels of technology, population, natural resources, geographical factors, form of government, political leadership, and ideology.

Theoretical Assumptions of Realism

Realist theorists assume that certain largely immutable factors shape inter national conduct. In contrast to utopianism, realism holds that human nature is essentially constant, or at least not easily altered. Man is not innately good or perfectible. There are severe limitations in the extent to which political reform or education can alter human nature. Man is evil, sinful, power-seeking

Realist writers generally agree that a nation's location affects its national capabilities and its foreign policy orientation. Because of geography, certain nations are more vulnerable than others to foreign conquest. Some nations occupy more strategically important geographical positions than others. Ac cess to important waterways and the exposure or protection of frontier influence a nation's foreign policy. Location affects the climate and length of the growing season for crops, as well as a nation's ability to mobilize against other nations.

Because of the difficulty of achieving peace through international law and organization, or even world government, it is necessary to devise other ar rangements for the management of power. Most realists agree that the balance of power furnishes an important regulatory device. When power is balanced among several nations, no one nation can achieve international hegemony

Realists assume that moral principles cannot be applied to political actions To what extent, it must be asked, has the statesman succeeded in achieving his major foreign policy objectives without endangering the state he represents Because the statesman acts in an international environment—distinguishable from a national environment by the absence of authoritative political institu tions, legal systems, and commonly accepted standards of conduct—his moral standards differ from those governing behavior within a national unit. Al though all realists do not consider the statesman *qua* statesman as amoral they nevertheless place less emphasis than the utopian upon morality in inter national conduct. According to the realists, politics is not a function of ethics Political theory is derived from political practice and from historical ex perience.

Power as a Determinant of International Behavior

Power is one of the words most frequently used in the study of political sci ence, especially in international relations. In international relations, the absence of institutions and procedures for resolving conflict comparable to those in most domestic political systems makes the so-called power element more obvious than at the domestic level. In a textbook first published in 1933 Frederick L. Schuman held that in an international system lacking a common government, each unit "necessarily seeks safety by relying on its own power and viewing with alarm the power of its neighbors." [1] According to Nicholas J. Spykman, "all civilized life rests in the last instance on power. Power is the ability to move men in some desired fashion, through "persuasion, purchase, barter, and coercion." [2] Hans J. Morgenthau even defines international politics, and indeed all politics, as a "struggle for power." Thus, power becomes a means and an end. In Morgenthau's theory, power is "man's control over the minds and actions of other men." [3] Robert Strausz-Hupé maintains that international politics is "dominated by the quest for power," and that "at any given period of known history, there were several states locked in deadly conflict, all desiring the augmentation or preservation of their power." [4] Arnold Wolfers argued that power is "the ability to move others or to get them to do what one wants them to do and not to do what one does not want them to do." Moreover, he deemed it important "to distinguish between power and influence, the first to mean the ability to move others by the threat or infliction of deprivations, the latter to mean the ability to do so through promises or grants of benefits." [5]

Antecedents of Realism

Like utopianism in international relations theory, realism has its intellectual roots in the older political philosophy of the West and in the writings of non-Western ancient authors such as Mencius and the Legalists in China and Kautilya in India. In his analysis of interstate relations in the Italian system of the sixteenth century, Machiavelli derived a theory of politics from the observation of the political practice of his time. Machiavelli's emphasis on the need for the ruler to adopt moral standards different from those of the individual in order to insure the state's survival, his concern with power, his assumption that politics is characterized by a clash of interests, his pessimistic view of human nature—all these clearly place him within the realist framework. [6]

1. See Frederick L. Schuman, *International Politics,* 4th ed. (New York: McGraw-Hill Book Company, 1969), p. 71; Klaus Knorr, *The War Potential of Nations* (Princeton: Princeton University Press, 1956). For an analysis of the various components of national power, see Klaus Knorr, *Military Power and Potential* (Lexington, Mass.: D. C. Heath and Company, 1970).

2. Nicholas J. Spykman, *America's Strategy in World Politics* (New York: Harcourt, Brace and Company, 1942), p. 11.

3. Hans J. Morgenthau, *Politics among Nations,* 4th ed. (New York: Alfred A. Knopf, 1967), pp. 25–26.

4. Robert Strausz-Hupé and Stefan T. Possony, *International Relations* (New York: McGraw-Hill Book Company, 1954), pp. 5–6.

5. Arnold Wolfers, *Discord and Collaboration* (Baltimore: Johns Hopkins Press, 1962), p. 103.

6. Niccòlo Machiavelli, *The Prince and the Discourses* (New York: Random House [Modern Library], 1950), pp. 52–53.

Thomas Hobbes, like Machiavelli, viewed power as crucial in human behavior. Man has a "perpetual and restless desire of power after power, that ceaseth only in death." [7] Hobbes believed that "covenants, without the sword, are but words and of no strength to secure a man at all." [8] Without a strong sovereign, chaos and violence follow: "if there be no power erected, or not great enough for our own security; every man will and may lawfully rely on his own strength and art for caution against all other men." [9]

Like the modern realists, Hobbes concerned himself with the underlying forces of politics and with the nature of power in political relationships. Although Hobbes believed that a strong sovereign was mandatory for maintaining order within the political system, he saw little prospect for fundamentally changing man's behavior or his environment. He differs from modern realism in his emphasis on political institutions in managing power and preventing conflict. In this regard, Hobbes, paradoxically enough, is closer to proponents of world government than to realists who stress a balance of power among major political groups.

Hegel, more than any other political philosopher, elevated the position of the state. Although realist writers reflect little Hegelianism, Hegel's belief that the state's highest duty is its own preservation is a fundamental of realist theory. Hegel reasoned that "since states are related to one another as autonomous entities and so as particular wills on which the validity of treaties depends, and since the particular will of the whole is in content a will for its own welfare it follows that welfare is the highest aim governing the relation of one state to another." [10] Moreover, Hegel held that the state has an "individual totality" which develops according to its own laws. The state has objective reality; that is, it exists apart from its citizens. Moreover, the state has moral standards different from, and superior to, those of the individual. The idea that the state creates its own morality and acts to assure its survival permeates modern realist writings in international relations.

Realism in Twentieth-Century International Relations Theory

REINHOLD NIEBUHR

Although many scholars, past and present, have shaped the development of realist international relations theory, the writings of the Protestant theologian Reinhold Niebuhr (1892–1971) have had a major impact on realist writing

7. Thomas Hobbes, *Leviathan,* ed. and intro. Michael Oakeshott (Oxford: Basil Blackwell Ltd., 1946), p. 64.

8. *Ibid.,* p. 109.

9. *Ibid.*

10. G. W. F. Hegel, *Philosophy of Right* (Oxford: Clarendon Press, 1942), p. 264; Friedrich Meinecke, *Machiavellism: The Doctrine of Raison d'État and its Place in Modern History* (New York: Frederick A. Praeger, 1965), p. 360.

n America.[11] Crucial to Niebuhr's theory is his biblical concept of man who s tainted by original sin and therefore capable of evil. Man's sinfulness stems rom his anxiety. "Anxiety is the inevitable concomitant of the paradox of reedom and finiteness in which man is involved." [12] Man is sinful because he lenies his finiteness, pretending to be more than he really is.[13]

Man's effort to usurp God's position "inevitably subordinates other life to ts will and thus does injustice to other life." Moreover, man has a "will-to-ive" which leads to a "will-to-power." Since man's "will-to-live" transcends a mere will to assure physical survival, he invariably seeks security against the perils of nature and history by enhancing his individual and collective power.

> The conflicts between men are thus simple conflicts between compet- ing survival impulses. They are conflicts in which each man or group seeks to guard its power and prestige against the peril of competing expressions of power and pride. Since the very possession of power and prestige always involves some encroachment upon the prestige and power of others, this conflict is by its very nature a more stub- born and difficult one than the mere competition between various sur- vival impulses in nature.[14]

Like relations among small groups, international politics is a struggle for power. Discussing the nature of power in groups and nations, Niebuhr asserts that national power is the projection of the individual's "will-to-power." When there are fewer moral restraints upon the individual as a member of a group, or a nation, than upon him as an individual, greater violence results at the group, or national, level. An individual acting as a member of a group loses his identity, becoming instead a member of an anonymous mass.[15] Thus his tendencies toward power become magnified at the group, or national, level. The hypothesis that individual aggressiveness is eventually displaced to the national level is treated in Chapter 6.)

11. In discussing the realist intellectual debt to Niebuhr, Kennan allegedly called him "the father of us all." See Kenneth W. Thompson, *Political Realism and the Crisis of World Politics: An American Approach to Foreign Policy* (Princeton: Princeton University Press, 1960), pp. 3–25.

12. Harry K. Davis and Robert C. Good, eds., *Reinhold Niebuhr on Politics: His Political Philosophy and its Application to Our Age as Expressed in his Writings* (New York: Charles Scribner's Sons, 1960), p. 75.

13. "In the Christian view, then, for man to understand himself truly means to be- gin with a faith that he is understood from beyond himself, that he is known and loved of God and must find himself

in terms of obedience to the divine will. This relation of the divine to the human will make it possible for man to relate himself to God without pretending to be God and to accept his distance from God as a created thing, without believing that the evil of his nature is caused by this finiteness." Davis and Good, eds., *op. cit.*, p. 74. See also Reinhold Niebuhr, *Christianity and Power Politics* (New York: Charles Scribner's Sons, 1940), p. 64; and his *Christian Realism and Politi- cal Problems* (New York: Charles Scrib- ner's Sons, 1953).

14. David and Good, eds., *op. cit.*, p. 77.

15. Reinhold Niebuhr, *Moral Man and Immoral Society* (New York: Charles Scribner's Sons, 1947), pp. xi–xii.

Like George F. Kennan and Charles Burton Marshall, Niebuhr criticize what he considers historic American attitudes toward foreign policy. In particular, Americans have been unaware of the power motive in international politics because their nation enjoyed a long period of isolation from the power confrontations of other nations. The "irony" of American history is that the Founding Fathers' dreams of the United States developing into a uniquely virtuous nation have been shattered. Instead, the United States entered into a struggle for world power. "Our age is involved in irony because so many dreams of our nation have been so cruelly refuted by history." [16] The "irony" is heightened by the "frantic efforts of some of our idealists to escape this hard reality by dreaming up schemes of an ideal world order which have no relevance to either our present dangers or our urgent duties." [17]

In criticizing proponents of world government, Niebuhr implies that political theory derives from political practice.

> *Governments cannot create communities for the simple reason that the authority of government is not primarily the authority of law nor the authority of force, but the authority of the community itself. Laws are obeyed because the community accepts them as corresponding, on the whole, to its conception of justice.*[18]

Because the forces of cohesiveness are minimal, the prospects for world government are not promising.

There are elements of free will and determinism in Niebuhr's view of man. If man is tainted with original sin and is power-seeking, he has capacities for both good and evil. Although his "will-to-live" may lead him to dominate other men, it may also be transformed into a "will-to-self-realization." Paradoxically, the highest form of self-realization is self-giving. Man's will-to-live may lead him to choose one form of behavior or another.

Although believing that conflict is inherent in intergroup and international relations, Niebuhr does not agree that the statesman *qua* statesman is amoral. He suggests, instead, that realism must be tempered with morality, that "nations must use their power with the purpose of making it an instrument of justice and a servant of interests broader than their own." [19] Moreover, he criticizes those realists who overemphasize the "national interest," because a

---

16. Reinhold Niebuhr, *The Irony of American History* (New York: Charles Scribner's Sons, 1952), p. 2. See also Gabriel Fackre, *The Promise of Reinhold Niebuhr* (Philadelphia: J. B. Lippincott Company, 1970), pp. 60–64; Charles Burton Marshall, *The Limits of Foreign Policy* (New York: Henry Holt and Company, 1954).

17. *Ibid.*, p. 40.

18. Reinhold Niebuhr, "The Illusion of World Government," *Bulletin of the*

Atomic Scientists, V (October, 1949), 290. See also Charles Burton Marshall, *op. cit.*, p. 122, where he says: "Legitimate government, let us remember, must rest on a tradition of kingship or aristocracy, or on a popular consensus. . . Those proposing to solve all the problems by the magic of world government are invariably hazy on the most serious underlying question of government—how to make it legitimate."

19. Niebuhr, *op. cit.*, p. 40.

he national as well as the individual level, "egotism is not the proper cure for n abstract and pretentious idealism." [20] Since each nation interprets justice rom its own perspective rather than a competing state's, it becomes difficult o give operational meaning to the rule that statesmen must always frame poli- ies based upon the "national interest." For Niebuhr, the balance of power is he organizational device for achieving a semblance of justice. "Some balance of power is the basis of whatever justice is achieved in human relations. Where he disproportion of power is too great and where an equilibrium of social orces is lacking no mere rational or moral demands can achieve justice." [21]

Perhaps we can better understand Niebuhr if we review the evolution of his utlook during the period between the two world wars. In a sense, Niebuhr eflected the dilemma of American pacifism when faced by Nazism. Although isillusioned by the consequences of World War I, he had never been an bsolute religious pacifist. He once distinguished between "absolute pacifism" espoused by religious perfectionists) and "pragmatic pacifism" (based more pon political preferences than upon the Gospel ethic), and eventually identi- ed himself with the latter.[22] Even so, he admitted that some coercion might e necessary in the domestic social struggle against the status quo (thereby evealing his somewhat Marxist leanings). But for a time he refused to justify ny type of international armed conflict. In the early 1930s, while chairman of he Fellowship of Reconciliation, he declared that members of that pacifist rganization would not fight in an international war.[23]

Following Italy's invasion of Ethiopia in 1935, however, Niebuhr disassoci- ted himself from international pacifism and condemned the policy of appease- ient which bought today's peace at the price of tomorrow's war.[24]

By 1938, at the time of the Munich settlement, he broke completely with lealist pacifism. Without chiding religious perfectionists who bear witness to he Gospel spirit, he criticized Western idealist pacifists as follows:

> We may say that the pacifists are right in their conviction that our civilization stands under the judgment of God; no one can have an easy conscience about the social and political anarchy out of which the horrible tyrannies of our age have arisen. But they are wrong in assuming that we have no right or duty to defend a civilization, de- spite its imperfections, against worse alternatives. . . .
>
> The pacifists rightly recognize that it may be very noble for an individual to sacrifice his life or interests rather than participate in the claims and counterclaims of the struggle for justice. . . . They are

). *Ibid.*, p. 148.

1. Davis and Good, eds., *op. cit.*, p. 65.

2. John C. Bennett, "Reinhold Nie- ihr's Social Ethics," Charles W. Kegley id Robert W. Bretall, eds., *Reinhold iebuhr* (New York: Macmillan Com- iny, 1956), p. 64; and Reinhold Nie- ihr, "A Critique of Pacifism," *Atlantic*

Monthly, CXXXIX (May, 1927), 637– 641.

23. Reinhold Niebuhr, "Why I Leave the F. O. R.," *The Christian Century*, LI (January 3, 1934), 17–19.

24. Reinhold Niebuhr, "Which Way Great Britain?" *Current History*, XLV (November, 1936), 35–39.

wrong in making no distinction between an individual act of self-abnegation and a political policy of submission to injustice, whereby lives and interests other than our own are defrauded or destroyed.[25]

After World War II, Niebuhr continued noting that political leaders constantly faced moral ambiguities. He insisted that the United States must contain the expansion of communism and at the same time prevent nuclear war. For all its shortcomings, constitutional democracy (of which the "free enterprise" system, he maintains, is not an intrinsic part) is a clearly superior form of political organization to communist oligarchy which, by unscrupulously centralizing absolute power, promotes far greater injustices than those the communists attribute to the free society.[26] But Niebuhr frequently warns Americans against thinking that they are innocent of the power drives which have motivated other peoples of the world. The United States, he says, has engaged in its own imperialist ventures, but a democratic nation with a strong sense of international mission is always reluctant to admit to itself that its actions spring from any but the noblest of motives. Niebuhr contends that although the mission of preserving and extending democratic self-government has greater validity than some other forms of national messianism, Americans must abandon their illusion of a special national innocence and righteousness and must resist the temptation to "claim more virtue for the exercise of our power than the facts warrant." [27]

NICHOLAS J. SPYKMAN

Several realist writers support the idea that conflict rather than cooperation is more typical of international relations than of intrastate relations. Nicholas J. Spykman (1893–1943), professor of international relations at Yale, assumed that conditions which characterized relations among groups within a state only during crises and breakdowns of central authority are normal for relations among states in the international system. States exist because they are strong or have other states protecting them. In the international system, as in other social groupings, Spykman saw basic processes operating: cooperation, accommodation, and opposition. To assure their survival, states "must make the preservation or improvement of their power position a principal objective of

25. Reinhold Niebuhr, "The Christian Faith and the World Crisis," *Christianity and Crisis*, I (February 10, 1941), 4.

26. Reinhold Niebuhr, *Christian Realism and Political Problems* (New York: Charles Scribner's Sons, 1953), p. 36; and Reinhold Niebuhr, "Coexistence or Total War," *The Christian Century*, LXXI (August 18, 1954), 972–974.

27. Niebuhr, *The Irony of American History*, p. 35; Reinhold Niebuhr and Alan Heimert, *A Nation So Conceived* (New York: Charles Scribner's Sons, 1963), pp. 129–139, and 144 (where the above quotation appears); and Reinhold Niebuhr, "American Hegemony and the Prospects for Peace," *Annals of the American Academy of Political and Social Science*, CCCXLII (July, 1962), 15

heir foreign policy." [28] Because power is ultimately the ability to wage war, tates have always emphasized the building of military establishments.

Spykman's geopolitical and balance of power concepts are crucial to his ealism. According to Spykman, expansion follows the line of least resistance. "New territories are conquered, held, assimilated, and serve as a starting point or new advance. There is a correlation between the amount of expansion and ase of movement." The limits to expansion are set by natural barriers such as oceans, rivers, and mountains, as well as a tendency to expand up and down river valleys, to seek access to the sea, and to dominate strategic points near communications routes. At any time in history, the frontiers of states indicate their relative power relationship. The potential for conflict increased, Spykman held, as the world became more densely populated and nations encroached upon each other. A country's geographic location determines its problems. Therefore, geography is a conditioner of a country's foreign policy.

Drawing upon Mackinder's geopolitical theory, Spykman advanced his conception of the goals which should guide American foreign policy during and after World War II. Because the Western Hemisphere did not contain economic, military, and technological resources capable of withstanding the combined resources of the Eurasian land mass, it was crucial for the United States to preserve a balance of power in Europe and Asia.[29] Writing before United States entry into World War II, Spykman concluded that just as the German-Japanese alliance represented a threat to America's security, other powers, namely Russia and China, would pose security problems for the United States in the postwar period. "A Russian state from the Urals to the North Sea can be no great improvement over a German state from the North Sea to the Urals." [30] In Asia, Spykman suggested, the United States may face a "modern, vitalized and militarized China" which would not only threaten the position of Japan but also that of the Western powers in Asia. Just as the United States twice came to the aid of Britain so "that the small offshore island might not have to face a single gigantic military state in control of the opposite coast of the mainland," the United States would "have to adopt a similar protective policy toward Japan" to preserve a balance of power in Asia. Moreover, Spykman acknowledged that an "equilibrium of forces inherently unstable,

8. Nicholas J. Spykman, *America's Strategy in World Politics: The United States and the Balance of Power* (New York: Harcourt, Brace and Company, 1942), p. 7; Nicholas J. Spykman and Abbie A. Rollins, "Geography and Foreign Policy," *American Political Science Review*, XXXIII (June, 1939), 392.

9. "The Old World is two and one half times as large as the New World and contains seven times the population. It is true that, at present, industrial productivity is almost equally divided, but in terms of self-sufficiency, the Eurasian Continent with the related continents of Africa and Australia is in a much stronger position. If the thin land masses of the Old World can be brought under the control of a few states and so organized that large unbalanced forces are available for pressure across the ocean fronts, the Americas will be politically and strategically encircled." Spykman, *op. cit.*, pp. 447–448.

30. *Ibid.*, p. 460.

always shifting, always changing," is an "indispensable element of an interna
tional order based on independent states." [31]

Implicit in Spykman's thought is the pursuit of limited national objectives
He urged the United States to seek only the removal of the then-existing
regimes of Germany and Japan, not to have as an objective their destruction
as states, since they must play a major role in restraining other powers which
one day will vie for hegemony in the Eurasian land mass. Thus he relates the
pursuit of limited national interest to balance of power and geopolitical
concepts.

FREDERICK L. SCHUMAN

Another writer of the 1930s, Frederick L. Schuman (1904–   ), professor
of government at Williams College, suggested, like Spykman, that the Western
state system is composed of sovereignties—autonomous political entities whose
followers acknowledge no higher authority, and pursue their own interests by
fighting and bargaining. Supporting this view with historical examples, he
claims that self-preservation is each state's ultimate objective. If several states
each sovereign and desiring survival, compose the system, Schuman believes
that their behavior will be predictable. He terms this behavioral system a
"design for anarchy." [32]

Distrust is the inevitable basis of interstate behavior. "Since each has no
control over the acts of the others, enjoys no participation in any effective
merging of local purposes into a larger polity, and accordingly has no assur
ance of what others may do, all must suspect the worst of each." [33] Thus, each
state, to preserve its autonomy, must compete with the others and extinguish
all possible threats from its neighbors and rivals. If it has sufficient power, it
will, with almost mathematical certainty, defeat the states that cannot resist
it.[34]

In the final analysis, Schuman views power as military strength or fighting
capacity. The only rational, justifiable policy in such a system is national
power "to be preserved against threats, to be maintained against contingen
cies, and to be enlarged and extended when opportunities present themselves
for so doing without unreasonable risk." [35] Peace itself, therefore, is never the
policy objective, but it may be a necessary condition for enhancing relative
power. When considering courses of action, policymakers "will weigh the con

31. *Ibid.,* p. 472. The view that the bal
ance of power in Asia, as well as in
Europe, is an essential ingredient of the
national interest of the United States
was subsequently advanced by Walt W.
Rostow in *The United States in the
World Arena* (New York: Harper, 1960),
Appendix A, pp. 543–550.

32. Frederick L. Schuman, *International
Politics,* 4th ed. (New York: McGraw
Hill Book Company, 1969), p. 63. First
edition published in 1933.

33. *Ibid.,* p. 271.

34. *Ibid.,* pp. 272–273.

35. *Ibid.,* p. 554.

Contending Theories of International Relations

sequences of acts less in terms of the 'merits' of any given controversy than
in terms of the probable effects of alternative solutions on the total balance of
power." [36] Moral principles are of value only for propaganda purposes or
when they coincide with national power.[37]

In this type of international system, as described by Schuman, the balance
of power is an important regulatory mechanism. To maintain their self-defense,
the members will unite against any potential menace to all, and invariably a
coalition of the prospective victims represses the aspirant to world power.
Thus, each power retains its independence, the state system is preserved, and
an equilibrium, or balance of power, results.[38]

Small states can preserve their independence by carefully aligning themselves in the balance system. Whether they can achieve interests in addition to
survival depends upon their skill and how indispensable their power is in
maintaining the balance. For example, sometimes small states can remain
neutral or isolated when the great powers are so evenly balanced that they
are deadlocked. Geographical position often influences the actions of small
states in the balance system. Although this system lends stability to the state
system, conflict is inevitable because the balancing process is imprecise and
constantly fluctuates. (The reader is referred back to the discussion of the
balance of power in Chapter 1.)

Hans J. Morgenthau

More explicitly than other realists, Hans J. Morgenthau (1904–   ), professor of political science at the University of Chicago, advances several principles of realism. First, he suggests that political relationships are governed by
objective rules deeply rooted in human nature. Since these rules are "impervious to our preferences, men will challenge them only at the risk of failure." [39]
If these rules themselves cannot be changed, Morgenthau's determinism holds
that society can be improved by first understanding the laws which govern
society, and then by basing public policy on that knowledge.

In theorizing about international politics it is necessary to employ historical
data for examining political acts and their consequences. In systematizing these
vast historical data, the student of politics must place himself "in the position
of a statesman who must meet a certain problem of foreign policy under certain circumstances," and ask himself "what the rational alternatives are from
which a statesman may choose who must meet this problem under these circumstances (presuming always that he acts in a rational manner), and which
of these rational alternatives this particular statesman, acting under these
circumstances, is likely to choose. It is the testing of this rational hypothesis

36. *Ibid.,* p. 277.
37. *Ibid.*
38. *Ibid.,* p. 273.

39. Hans J. Morgenthau, *Politics Among
Nations,* 4th ed. (New York: Alfred A.
Knopf, 1967), p. 4.

against the actual facts and their consequences that gives meaning to the facts of international politics and makes a theory of politics possible." [40]

Second, Morgenthau contends that statesmen "think and act in terms of interest defined as power" and that historical evidence proves this assumption.[41] This concept, central to Morgenthau's realism, gives continuity and unity to the seemingly diverse foreign policies of the widely separated nation-states. Moreover, the concept "interest defined as power" makes evaluating the actions of political leaders at different points in history possible. To describe Morgenthau's framework in more contemporary language, it is a model of interaction within an international system. Using historical data, Morgenthau compares the real world with the interaction patterns within his model.

In his view, international politics is a process in which national interests are adjusted.

> *The concept of the national interest presupposes neither a naturally harmonious, peaceful world nor the inevitability of war as a consequence of the pursuit by all nations of their national interest. Quite to the contrary, it assumes continuous conflict and threat of war, to be minimized through the continuous adjustment of conflicting interest by diplomatic action.*[42]

Third, Morgenthau acknowledges that the meaning of "interest defined as power" is an unstable one. However, in a world in which sovereign nations vie for power, the foreign policies of all nations must consider survival as their minimum requirement. All nations are compelled to "protect their physical, political and cultural identity against encroachments by other nations." Thus national interest is identified with national survival. "Taken in isolation, the determination of its content in a concrete situation is relatively simple; for it encompasses the integrity of the nation's territory, of its political institutions, and of its culture." [43] As long as the world is divided into nations, Morgenthau asserts, the "national interest is indeed the last word in world politics." Interest, then, is the essence of politics.

Once its survival is assured, the nation-state may pursue lesser interests. Morgenthau assumes that nations ignore the national interest only at the risk of destruction. Yet in twentieth-century foreign policy formulation, lesser interests have sometimes preceded the national interest.[44] Had Great Britain in 1939 based her policy toward Finland upon legalistic-moralistic considerations, backed with large-scale military aid against Soviet aggression, then

40. *Ibid.*, p. 5.

41. *Ibid.*

42. Hans J. Morgenthau, "Another 'Great Debate': The National Interest of the United States," *American Political Science Review,* LXVI (December, 1952), 961–998.

43. *Ibid.* See also Hans J. Morgenthau,

In Defense of the National Interest (New York: Alfred A. Knopf, 1951); Charles A. Beard, *The Idea of the National Interest* (New York: Macmillan Company, 1934). The idea of the national interest as a basis for decision-making is examined in Chapter 11).

44. *Politics among Nations*, pp. 11–14.

Britain's position might have been so weakened as to assure her destruction by Nazi Germany. Britain would have neither restored Finland's independence nor safeguarded her most vital national interest, physical survival. All foreign policies, Morgenthau insists, must "be subjected to rational scrutiny which will determine, however tentatively, their approximate place in the scale of national value." [45] Only when the national interest most closely related to national survival has been safeguarded can nations pursue lesser interests.

Fourth, Morgenthau states that "universal moral principles cannot be applied to the actions of states in their abstract, universal formulation, but that they must be filtered through the concrete circumstances of time and place." [46] In pursuit of the national interest, nation-states are governed by a morality which differs from the morality of the individual in his personal relationships. In the actions of statesmen *qua* statesmen, the political consequences of a particular policy become the criteria for judging it. To confuse an individual's morality with a state's morality is to court national disaster. Because the statesman's primary official responsibility is the survival of the nation-state, his obligations to his citizenry require a different morality from that of the individual.

Fifth, Morgenthau asserts that political realism does not identify the "moral aspirations of a particular nation with the moral laws that govern the universe." [47] In fact, if international politics is placed within a framework of defining interests in terms of power, "we are able to judge other nations as we judge our own." [48] The influence of Augustinian theology through Niebuhr is evident in this aspect of Morgenthau's realism.

Sixth, and finally, Morgenthau stresses the autonomy of the political sphere. Political actions must be judged by political criteria. "The economist asks: 'How does this policy affect the welfare of society, or a segment of it?' " The lawyer asks: "Is this policy in accord with rules of law?" The moralist asks: "Is this policy in accord with moral principles?" And the political realist asks: "How does this policy affect the power of the nation?" [49]

In power struggles, nations follow policies designed to preserve the status-quo, to achieve imperialistic expansion, or to gain prestige. In Morgenthau's view, domestic and international politics can be reduced to one of three basic types: "A political policy seeks either to keep power, to increase power, or to demonstrate power." [50]

Although the purpose of a status-quo policy is to preserve the existing distribution of power, the nation adopting such a policy does not necessarily act to prevent all international change. Instead, status-quo nations try to thwart change which may cause fundamental shifts in the international distribution of power. Morgenthau cites the Monroe Doctrine as an example of

45. *Ibid.*
46. *Ibid.*, p. 10.
47. *Ibid.*

48. *Ibid.*, p. 11.
49. *Ibid.*
50. *Ibid.*, p. 36.

a status-quo policy that fulfills his two criteria. First, it was designed to preserve the prevailing power balance in the Western Hemisphere. Second, it expressed the United States's unwillingness to prevent all change. Instead, the United States would act only against change which threatened the existing distribution of power. Likewise, treaties concluded at the end of wars would be invariably designed to preserve the prevailing status-quo.

Imperialism is the second major alternative available to nations. This is a policy designed to overthrow the status-quo and achieve a "reversal of the power relations between two or more nations." [51] The goals of imperialist powers include local preponderance, continental empire, or world domain. Nations may adopt imperialistic policies as a result of victory, defeat, or the weakness of other nations. A nation whose leaders expect victory may alter its objectives from the restoration of the status-quo to a permanent change in the distribution of power. Moreover, a defeated nation may adopt an imperialistic policy to "turn the scales on the victor, to overthrow the status-quo created by his victory, and to change places with him in the hierarchy of power." [52] Finally, the existence of weak states may prove irresistible to a strong state.

To attain imperialistic objectives, nations may resort to military force or to cultural and economic means. Military conquest is the oldest and most obvious form of imperialism. Economic imperialism is not as effective a technique as military conquest. If a nation cannot assume military control over another people, it may attempt economic control instead. Cultural imperialism is an attempt to conquer and control men's minds "as an instrument for changing the power relations between two nations." [53]

A policy of prestige is the third alternative. In contrast to the other two policies, this policy is "one of the instrumentalities through which the policies of status-quo and of imperialism try to achieve their ends." [54] Its objective is to "impress other nations with the power one's own nation actually possesses or with the power it believes, or wants the other nations to believe, it possesses." [55] Morgenthau suggests two specific techniques of this policy: diplomatic ceremonial and the display of force. A policy of prestige succeeds when a nation gains such a reputation for power that the actual use of power becomes unnecessary.

Morgenthau is concerned not only about the quest for power but the conditions for international peace. His concept of international order is closely related to his concept of national interest. Pursuing national interests that are nonessential to national survival contributes to international conflict. In the twentieth century, especially, nations have substituted global objectives for more limited goals that are vital to national interests. The development of

51. *Ibid.,* p. 42.

52. *Ibid.,* p. 51.

53. *Ibid.,* p. 57. For a survey of other meanings of "imperialism" and theoreti-

cal controversies concerning its nature see Chapter 6.

54. *Ibid.,* p. 69.

55. *Ibid.,* p. 70.

Contending Theories of International Relations

modern nationalism, combined with messianic ideologies, has obscured the national interest. In the guise of extending communism or "making the world safe for democracy" nations intervene in the affairs of regions not vital to their security. Like Kennan, Morgenthau opposed American military intervention in South Vietnam because Southeast Asia lay beyond the vital interests of the United States, and because the United States would find it impossible, except perhaps with a vast expenditure of resources, to maintain a balance of power in Southeast Asia. Thus Morgenthau contends that the return of nations to the pursuit of limited national interest is a crucial factor in attaining a more peaceful world.

Even in an international system without ideologically motivated foreign policies, competition between opposing nation-states is possible. As many other realists, Morgenthau views the balance of power as the most effective technique for managing power. He defines balance of power as follows: (1) a policy aimed at a certain state of affairs; (2) an actual state of affairs; (3) an approximately equal distribution of power; and (4) any distribution of power. However, it is not the balance of power itself, but the international consensus upon which it is built, which preserves international peace. "Before the balance of power could impose its restraints upon the power aspirations of nations through the mechanical interplay of opposing forces, the competing nations had first to restrain themselves by accepting the system of the balance of power as the common framework of their endeavors." Such a consensus "kept in check the limitless desire for power, potentially inherent, as we know, in all imperialisms, and prevented it from becoming a political actuality." [56]

The international consensus which sustained the balance of power before the twentieth century no longer exists. Moreover, structural changes in the international system have limited the effectiveness of the balance of power. In Morgenthau's view, the balance of world power through the early 1960s rested with two nations, the United States and the Soviet Union, rather than with several great powers. In such a bipolarization allies of one superpower may shift their support to the other side, but they can no longer significantly alter the distribution of power. Nor is there any third power capable of intervening on either side and greatly changing the power distribution.

Like the balance of power, diplomacy plays a crucial role in the preservation of peace. In fact, a precondition for the creation of a peaceful world is the development of a new international consensus, in the formation of which diplomacy can contribute to "peace through accommodation." [57] Morgenthau decries the "deprecation of diplomacy" in the twentieth century. The diplomat's role has been diminished by the development of advanced communications, by public disparagement of diplomacy and diplomats, and by the tendency of heads of government to conduct their own negotiations. The rise to importance of international assemblies, the substitution of open diplomacy for secrecy, and the inexperience on the part of the superpowers have con-

56. *Ibid.,* p. 214.   57. *Ibid.,* p. 519.

tributed to the decline of diplomacy. Thus, Morgenthau clearly prefers a diplomacy similar to that of the international system before the twentieth century. His views on traditional diplomacy as a means for adjusting national interests resemble those of Sir Harold Nicolson, a leading twentieth-century British diplomatist and theoretician of diplomatic practice.[58]

Diplomacy, to be revived as an effective technique for managing power must meet four conditions: (1) Diplomacy must be divested of its crusading spirit. (2) Foreign policy objectives must be defined in terms of national interest and must be supported with adequate power. (3) Nations must view foreign policy from the point of view of other nations. (4) Nations must be willing to compromise on issues that are not vital to them. If diplomacy can be restored to a position of importance, Morgenthau believes, it may not only contribute to "peace through accommodation," but to building an international consensus upon which more adequate world political institutions can be built.[59]

GEORGE F. KENNAN

To the extent that he bases his theory of international relations upon historical materials, in this case from the eighteenth and nineteenth centuries, George F. Kennan (1904–   ), former United States ambassador to Russia and Yugoslavia and now a Princeton professor, shows considerable similarity to Morgenthau. If Morgenthau's model is derived largely from a European context, Kennan's is based on American diplomacy from 1776 to 1812. Kennan divides United States foreign policy into two periods: the first he dates from the American Revolution to the mid-nineteenth century; the second he extends from that time to the present.

In the first period, for which Kennan clearly shows preference, the United States evolved basic goals that found expression in such documents as the Declaration of Independence and the Constitution. American statesmen developed a foreign policy designed to achieve their objectives. In defining and shaping the limits of foreign policy, American leaders concluded that:

> *The first and obvious answer was: that we ought to protect the physical intactness of our national life from any external or political intrusions—in other words, that we ought to look to the national security. . . . Secondly, one could see to it that insofar as the activities of our citizens in pursuit of their private interests spilled over beyond our borders and into the outside world, the best possible arrangements were made to promote and protect them.*[59]

58. See, for example, Harold Nicolson, *Evolution of Diplomatic Method* (New York: Macmillan Company, 1962); *The Congress of Vienna* (London: Constable Ltd., 1946); Morgenthau, *Politics among Nations*, pp. 540–548.

59. George F. Kennan, *Realities of American Foreign Policy* (New York: W. W. Norton and Company, 1966), p. 11.

Contending Theories of International Relations

According to Kennan, American goals were fixed, limited, and devoid of pretentions of international benevolence or assumptions of moral superiority or inferiority on the part of one nation or another. Like Morgenthau, he derives his model from historical data in a period when limited, rather than universalist, concepts of the national interest prevailed.

Erroneously, in Kennan's estimation, Americans projected to the international arena assumptions based upon their own national experience. Because they believed that the United States political and legal framework had contributed decisively to domestic tranquility, American statesmen focused on the creation of an international legal framework designed to minimize the likelihood of conflict.

> *I see the most serious fault of our past policy formulation to lie in something that I might call the legalistic-moralistic approach to international problems. This approach runs like a red skein through our foreign policy of the past fifty years. It has in it something of the old emphasis on arbitration treaties, something of the Hague Conferences, and schemes for universal disarmament, something of the more ambitious American concepts of international law, something of the Kellogg Pact, something of the idea of a universal "Article 51," something of the belief in World Law and World Government. . . . It is the belief that it should be possible to suppress the chaotic and dangerous aspirations of governments by the acceptance of some system of legal rules and restraints.[60]*

Moreover, Kennan asserts that American statesmen in this first period frankly and confidently dealt with power realities.[61] Recognizing the importance of power factors in international politics, United States leaders strove to restrain the European powers in their territorial ambitions in the Western Hemisphere. They encouraged movements toward political independence and gave U.S. guarantees to new countries which had severed their links with European powers. "All of this involved power considerations. Yet none of it was considered evil or Machiavellian, or cynical. It was simply regarded as a response to the obvious and logical requirements of our situation." [62]

Against this first period, Kennan assesses United States policy in a later period, when Americans allegedly lost sight of the power factor and substituted legalistic-moralistic assumptions and objectives for earlier foreign policy goals. If Americans forgot the power factor in the nineteenth century, this was only "natural and inevitable." Geographically separated from Europe, shielded by the British navy from Continental European powers, and preoccupied with

---

60. George F. Kennan, *American Diplomacy, 1900–1950* (New York: Mentor Books, 1957), pp. 93–94. See also Charles Burton Marshall, *op. cit.,* p. 56: ". . . [o]ur national experience has been such as to root in our minds an excess of confidence in the political efficacy of documents—in the capability of statesmen to resolve the future by agreement on the written word."

61. George F. Kennan, *op. cit.,* p. 13.

62. *Ibid.,* p. 14.

domestic development, Americans especially in the second half of the nine
teenth century cultivated a spirit of romanticism:

> *We were satisfied, by this time, with our own borders; and we found
> it pleasant to picture the outside world as one in which other peoples
> were similarly satisfied with theirs, or ought to be. With everyone thus
> satisfied, the main problem of world peace, as it appeared to us, was
> plainly the arrangement of a suitable framework of contractual en-
> gagements in which this happy status-quo, the final fruit of human
> progress, could be sealed and perpetuated. If such a framework could
> be provided, then, it seemed, the ugly conflicts of international poli-
> tics would cease to threaten world peace.*[63]

In addition to criticizing the American assumption of an international har
mony of interests, Kennan asserts that Americans lost sight that the rule
governing personal morality are not necessarily adequate criteria for foreign
policy decisions. Governmental behavior cannot be subjected to the same
moral judgments that are applied to human behavior.

> *Moral principles have their place in the heart of the individual in
> the shaping of his own conduct, whether as a citizen or as a govern-
> ment official . . . But when the individual's behavior passes through
> the machinery of political organization and merges with that of mil-
> lions of other individuals to find its expression in the actions of govern-
> ment, then it undergoes a general transformation, and the same moral
> concepts are no longer relevant to it. A government is an agent, not a
> principal; and no more than any other agent may it attempt to be the
> conscience of its principal.*[64]

Nevertheless, even though the use of force in international affairs canno
be completley ruled out, this "does not constitute a reason for being indiffer
ent to the ways in which force is applied—to the moral implications of weap
ons and their use." [65] Finally, Kennan objects to a concept of international
affairs that leads one nation to consider its own purposes moral and those of
its opponent immoral. "A war fought in the name of high moral principle finds
no end short of some form of total domination." [66] Thus the introduction of
moralistic principles leads nations to pursue unlimited national objectives, to
choose total war, and to impose laws of unconditional surrender upon defeated
opponents. In sum, the pursuit of moralistic principles is incompatible with
the pursuit of essentially limited foreign policy objectives.

As most other writers examined in this chapter, Kennan believes that
human nature is "irrational, selfish, obstinate and tends to violence." [67] It is
difficult, if not impossible, to effect basic changes in man, and few people wil

63. *Ibid.*, p. 16.

64. *Ibid.*, p. 48.

65. George F. Kennan, "World Problems in Christian Perspective," *Theology
Today,* XVI (July, 1959), 155–172.

66. Kennan, *American Diplomacy,* p. 87

67. Kennan, *Realities of American For
eign Policy,* p. 48.

ver "have an abstract devotion to the principles of international legality capa-
le of competing with the impulses from which wars are apt to arise." [68]
Moreover, it is by no means certain that governments in their foreign policies
xpress the aspirations of their peoples. "Every government represents only
ne momentary product of the never-ending competition for political power
within the respective national framework. In the most direct sense, therefore,
 speaks only for a portion of the nation: for one political faction or coali-
on of factions." [69] In foreign policy, public opinion cannot play a role similar
o its role in national politics, since "international affairs are, after all, a mat-
er of relations between governments and not peoples." [70]

The many and varied causes of international conflict are not easily elimi-
ated by human action. Lack of uniformity in the cultural, political, economic,
nd social development of nations contributes to conflict. Moreover, Kennan
elieves that "just as there is no uncomplicated personal relationship between
ndividuals, so . . . there is no international relationship between sovereign
tates which is without its elements of antagonism, its competitive aspects." [71]

Like Morgenthau, Kennan assigns to diplomacy a major role in the mitiga-
on of international conflict. Through diplomacy, nations have been able to
djust differences. Thus diplomacy contributes to peaceful change in the inter-
ational system. In fact, Kennan is critical of schemes for world government
nd international law, because

> *the function of a system of international relationships is not to in-*
> *hibit this process of change by imposing a legal straight jacket upon it*
> *but rather to facilitate it; to ease its transition, to temper the asperities*
> *to which it often leads, to isolate and moderate the conflict to which it*
> *gives rise, and to see that these conflicts do not assume forms too un-*
> *settling for international life in general.[72]*

Moreover, to expect the United Nations to play a major role in the resolution
f East-West problems is to impose on it burdens it cannot bear.[73]

Like most realist theorists, Kennan bases his realism upon geopolitical
oncepts. He assumes that military strength on a scale capable of reaching
ne United States can be mobilized only in several parts of the world, namely
n "those regions where a major industrial power, enjoying adequate access to
aw materials, is combined with large reserves of educated and technically
killed manpower." These geographically important regions include the North
tlantic Community, Japan, Germany, and the immediately contiguous indus-

8. *Ibid.*, p. 36.

9. George F. Kennan, "History and
iplomacy as Viewed by a Diplomatist,"
eview of Politics, XVIII (April, 1956),
73.

9. George F. Kennan, "World Prob-
ms in Christian Perspective," p. 156.

1. George F. Kennan, *Russia and the*

West under Lenin and Stalin (New York:
New American Library, 1960), p. 367.

72. Kennan, *American Diplomacy, 1900–
1950*, p. 96.

73. George F. Kennan, *Russia, the Atom
and the West* (New York: Harper and
Brothers, 1958), p. 27.

trial regions, and the Soviet Union.[74] For Kennan, the relationship between Germany and Russia is crucial to United States security.

Kennan, both as a diplomat and scholar, has been preoccupied largely with East-West problems. As chairman of the State Department's Policy Planning Staff in the early postwar period, he played a major role in the development of United States policy toward the Soviet Union. It was his assumption that the Soviet leaders were influenced in large part by communist ideology. Because of their ideology, the Soviets were in no hurry to administer a *coup de grace* to the West, since capitalism supposedly contained the seeds of its own destruction. In fact, Lenin's teachings advise caution and flexibility in pursuing foreign policy objectives. The Soviet Union, Kennan reasoned, would press its advantage wherever the West appeared vulnerable, and would seek to fill any power vacuum which appeared. Given their belief in the inevitability of the Communist triumph, together with Lenin's strategic principles, the Soviets have "no compunction about retreating in the face of superior force." [75]

The problem confronting the United States was, in the short run, to prevent the extension of Soviet power into regions of the world which were threatened in the early postwar period. In the longer run, the United States faced the difficult problem of effecting change within the Soviet Union. If the Soviet leadership could be induced to abandon its ideology, the Soviet Union might substitute limited foreign policy objectives for universalist goals. By a policy of containment, Kennan concluded, the United States could respond effectively to the short- and long-term problems of Soviet-American relations. By denying the Soviet Union foreign policy gains the United States would eventually lead Soviet leaders not only to question and reject their ideology, but to adopt limited foreign policy objectives.

A decade after his formulation of the rationale for containment, Kennan discerned changes both within the Soviet Union and the communist states of East Central Europe. In calling for the disengagement of U.S. forces in Germany, Kennan reasoned that pressures upon the Soviet Union would lead to a similar withdrawal of Soviet forces from East Central European countries. The removal of Soviet troops would contribute to internal liberalization of communist regimes, as well as greater independence from the Soviet Union in foreign policy. Thus Soviet influence in a region of the world vital to the United States would be reduced.[76]

Given the importance of the German-Soviet relationship and his belief in

---

74. Kennan, *Realities of Foreign Policy*, pp. 63–64.

75. (Kennan), "X," "The Sources of Soviet Conduct," *Foreign Affairs*, XXV (July, 1947), p. 514. Charles Burton Marshall was in substantial agreement when he wrote: "The best hopes lie in creating the circumstances for a heightening of the dilemma within the Soviet framework, eventually to move it along the course of accommodation and thereby toward its own transformation." *Op. cit.* p. 97.

76. Kennan, *Russia, the Atom, and the West*, pp. 41–45.

he pursuit of limited foreign policy objectives, Kennan saw no great urgency about the problems of less developed areas.[77] As in the case of economic assistance, the United States had no overriding interest in responding around the world to communist wars of national liberation. In fact, Kennan views disdainfully subsequent efforts to extend the containment doctrine to new geographic regions. He objects to the universalization of containment to situations and times different from those during which he formulated it, just as he opposed in his writings other offers to develop and apply abstract principles to all foreign policy problems.[78]

ARNOLD WOLFERS

There are, of course, important differences among the realist theorists. Although the late Arnold Wolfers, formerly professor at Yale and Johns Hopkins Center for Foreign Policy, may, for example, be included in a survey of realist thought, his focus differs from that of other proponents of realism. While acknowledging that a key point for the study of international relations is the "behavior of states as organized bodies of men," he calls for "concentration on human beings upon whose psychological reactions the behavior credited to states ultimately rests." [79] The international behavior of states is the amalgam of conflicting pressures. Moreover, subnational, transnational and supranational actors intrude into international politics, and must be the object of scholarly analysis.

In their relationships nation-states exhibit various kinds of behavior from amity to enmity, depending upon their international goals. Nations set for themselves differing sets of goals: (1) "possession" goals, such as national independence, physical survival, and territorial integrity, or (2) "milieu" goals, designed to affect the environment beyond a nation's boundaries. Moreover, Wolfers delineates three basic clusters of foreign policy objectives, namely objectives related to (1) national self-extension, (2) national self-preservation, and (3) national self-abnegation, such as international solidarity, lawfulness, or peace. Goals of national self-abnegation transcend, although they do not necessarily conflict with, goals of national self interest. For example, the United States in 1918 was powerful enough to permit President Wilson to indulge in self-abnegation goals without harm to its vital national interests. A nation's foreign policy thus includes overlapping goals. The pursuit of goals related to national self-preservation often makes necessary the pursuit of goals of national self-extension. In fact, increasing international interdependence contributes to the pursuit among nations of goals of national self-

---

77. *Ibid.,* pp. 66–71.

78. George F. Kennan, *Memoirs, 1935–1950* (Boston: Atlantic–Little, Brown and Company, 1967), p. 367.

79. Arnold Wolfers, *Discord and Collaboration* (Baltimore: Johns Hopkins Press, 1962), p. 9.

Political Realism at the International Level

extension in order to achieve goals of national self-preservation, thus rendering difficult the return to foreign policies based upon limited objectives, as Kennan, Kissinger and Morgenthau have urged.

According to Wolfers, a nation's foreign policy is the amalgam of many factors. Although a policymaker is guided by his conception of the national interest, this concept holds differing meanings for different peoples. At the minimum, national interest encompasses a nation's territorial integrity, independence, and national survival. Yet the goal of "national survival itself is given a wide variety of interpretations by different countries or countries facing different conditions." [80] Security is a value some countries prize to a greater extent than others. The level of security sought by states is not always identical. In fact, political leaders are often confronted with a dilemma as to whether a given increment in defense conflicts with other values.[81] As an official decision-maker the political leader is constantly confronted with difficult choices in which he is unable to separate interest from morality. In fact, his calculus of interest is based upon a hierarchy of values, since "the 'necessities' in international politics, and for that matter in all spheres of life, do not push decisions and actions beyond the realm of moral judgment; they rest on moral choices themselves. If a statesman decides that the dangers to the security of his country are so great as to make necessary a course of action that may lead to war, he has placed an exceedingly high value on an increment of national security." [82]

Wolfers viewed the balance of power as a useful concept in describing the contemporary international system. Although the term balance of power has been given various meanings, Wolfers used the term to mean "an equilibrium or a roughly equal distribution of power between two opponents, the opposite, then, of hegemony or domination." [83] The contemporary balance of power consists of two "hub" states—the United States and the Soviet Union, each of which is at the center of a global alliance. Outside the respective alliances of the two superpowers, neutralist states are able to extract concessions from the United States and the Soviet Union, each of which competes for their favor. For the United States the problem arises of reconciling policies toward allies and neutralists, since policies toward allies affect policies toward neutralists. Wolfers preferred foreign policy priorities which favor allies.

Wolfers concluded that "ideological conflict, concentration of power in the hands of two antagonistic superpowers, and the introduction of nuclear weapons have deepened the gulf between nations and made world unity more remote." [84] Whatever its deficiencies, therefore, the balance of power commends itself as a technique for the management of power. Nation-states have shown little inclination to make use of collective security schemes in the resolution of international conflict. Examination of British and French

80. *Ibid.*, p. 73.
81. *Ibid.*, p. 60.
82. *Ibid.*

83. *Ibid.*, p. 118.
84. *Ibid.*, p. 131.

Contending Theories of International Relations

olicy between the two world wars shows that France conceived of the League
of Nations collective security framework as supplementary to the French alliance system against Germany. If alliances failed to deter Germany, France
could rely upon collective security under League auspices against Germany.
In contrast, Wolfers maintained, Britain viewed her commitment to collective
security as a commitment against any power which breached the peace.[85]

In Wolfers' estimation, a commitment to collective security requires a
degree of national self-abnegation which few, if any, powers are prepared to
make. In collective security, nations commit themselves to divert scarce resources to action against a breach of the peace in parts of the world where
it may have few, if any, interests. Nations find themselves pledged to participate in collective action against a country with which they have important
trading links, and to support a mechanism in which the collective power of
nations could be brought to bear against its own self-justified use of force.
The history of collective security does not provide evidence of the willingness of nations to respond to an outbreak of aggression wherever it occurs.
The action of the United States, together with other nations, in Korea cannot
be interpreted as an example of collective security. Instead, Wolfers views
the Korean conflict as an instance in which the United States used the United
Nations to achieve a major foreign policy objective in Asia, namely, the prevention of communist expansion.

It was the United Nations that identified itself with the United States's action
in Korea. The United States's resort to force against North Korea strengthened the United States's power position *vis-à-vis* her major opponent, the
Soviet Union, and thus did not depart from older patterns of international
politics. In sum, Wolfers rejected collective security and viewed balance of
power as the technique for the management of power most in keeping with
the contemporary international system. In contending that nation-states engage in a spectrum of behavior from enmity to amity, he rejected the proposition that all states are motivated to increase their power. In claiming the
existence of several kinds of behavior, Wolfers provided insights and hypotheses for further testing in efforts to develop theory from the comparative study
of foreign policy decision-making.

HENRY A. KISSINGER

Another scholar who has drawn from history, in this case European diplomatic history, is Henry A. Kissinger (1923–   ), former Harvard professor
and later special assistant for national security affairs to President Richard
Nixon. Kissinger develops two models for the study of international relations:
the first is that of a stable system; the second is that of a revolutionary system.

85. Arnold Wolfers, *Britain and France between the Two Wars* (Hamden, Conn.: Archon Books, 1963), pp. 11–19, 201–222.

He contends that stability has resulted not "from a quest for peace, but from a generally accepted legitimacy." [86] By Kissinger's definition, legitimacy means "no more than an international agreement about the nature of workable arrangements and about the permissible aims and methods of foreign policy." [87] Legitimacy implies an acceptance of the framework of the international order by all major powers. Agreement among major powers upon the framework of international order has not eliminated international conflicts, but it has limited their scope. Conflict within the framework has been more limited than conflict *about* the framework. Diplomacy, which Kissinger defines as "the adjustment of differences through negotiation," becomes possible only in international systems where "legitimacy obtains." [88] In Kissinger's model the primary objective of national actors is not to preserve peace. In fact, "wherever peace—conceived as the avoidance of war—has been the primary objective of a power or a group of powers, the international system has been at the mercy of the most ruthless member of the international community." [89] In contrast, "whenever the international order has acknowledged that certain principles could not be compromised even for the sake of peace, stability based on an equilibrium of forces was at least conceivable." [90]

An understanding of the characteristics of a revolutionary world order can be derived from Kissinger's model of stability. Any order in which a major power is so dissatisfied that it seeks to transform it is revolutionary. In the generation before 1815, revolutionary France presented a major challenge to the existing order.

> *Disputes no longer concerned the adjustment of differences within an accepted framework, but the validity of the framework itself; the political contest had become doctrinal: the balance of power which had operated so intricately throughout the eighteenth century suddenly lost its flexibility and the European equilibrium came to seem an insufficient protection to powers faced by a France which proclaimed the incompatibility of its political maxims with those of the other states.[91]*

Tracing the diplomacy of European powers between 1812 and 1822, Kissinger concludes that the restoration of a stable order depends on several factors: (1) The willingness of supporters of legitimacy to negotiate with a revolutionary power while at the same time being prepared to use military power; (2) the ability of supporters of legitimacy to avoid the outbreak of "total" war, since such conflict would threaten the international framework which status-quo powers wish to preserve; (3) the capacity of national units to use limited means to achieve limited objectives. No power is compelled

---

86. Henry A. Kissinger, *A World Restored—Europe After Napoleon: The Politics of Conservatism in a Revolutionary Age* (New York: Grosset and Dunlap [Universal Library], 1964), p. 1.
87. *Ibid.*

88. *Ibid.*, p. 2.
89. *Ibid.*, p. 1.
90. *Ibid.*
91. *Ibid.*, p. 4.

o surrender unconditionally. Powers defeated in limited war are not elimi-nated from the international system. No power, whether victorious or van-quished, is completely satisfied or completely dissatisfied. Limitations placed upon means and goals make possible the restoration of a balance of power between the victorious and the vanquished.

In other writings Kissinger has applied concepts derived from his study of early nineteenth-century European diplomatic history to the contemporary international system. The problems posed by the great destructive potential of nuclear weapons have been of great concern to him. As in the past, it is necessary for nations to develop limited means to achieve limited objectives. "An all or nothing military policy will . . . play into the hands of the Soviet strategy of ambiguity which seeks to upset the strategic balance by small degrees and which combines political, psychological, and military pressures to induce the greatest degree of uncertainty and hesitation in the mind of the opponent." [92] If U.S. policymakers are to have a choice other than "the dread alternatives of surrender or suicide," [93] they must adopt concepts of lim-ited war derived from the experience of nineteenth-century warfare. At that time the objective of warfare "was to create a calculus of risks according to which continued resistance would appear more costly than the peace terms sought to be imposed." [94] A strategy of limited warfare would provide the United States with the means "to establish a reasonable relationship between power and the willingness to use it, between the physical and psychological components of national policy." [95]

If the United States is to avoid the stark alternatives of suicide or surrender, it must have both large-scale conventional forces and tactical nuclear weap-ons. Kissinger establishes three requirements for limited war capabilities.

1. The limited war forces must be able to prevent the potential aggressor from creating a *fait accompli;*
2. They must be of a nature to convince the aggressor that their use, while invoking an increasing risk of all-out war, is not an inevitable prelude to it;
3. They must' be coupled with a diplomacy which succeeds in conveying that all-out war is not the sole response to aggression and that there exists a willingness to negotiate a settlement short of unconditional sur-render.[96]

If nations are to evolve a limited war strategy, they must develop an under-standing of those interests which do not threaten national survival. Decision-makers must possess the ability to restrain public opinion if disagreement

92. Henry A. Kissinger, *Nuclear Weap-ons and Foreign Policy* (New York: Har-per and Brothers for the Council on Foreign Relations, 1957), p. 16.

93. Henry A. Kissinger, *The Necessity for Choice* (New York: Harper and Brothers, 1961), p. 63.

94. Kissinger, *Nuclear Weapons and For-eign Policy,* p. 89.

95. *Ibid.,* p. 84.

96. Kissinger, *The Necessity for Choice,* p. 65.

arises as to whether national survival is at stake. Given a tacit understanding among nations about the nature of limited objectives, it is possible to fight both conventional conflicts and limited nuclear wars without their escalation to total war.

In the adjustment of differences among nations, Kissinger, like most other realists, assigns an important role to diplomacy. Historically, negotiation was aided by the military capabilities a nation could bring to bear if diplomacy failed. The vast increase in destructive capabilities has contributed to the perpetuation of disputes. "Our age faces the paradoxical problem that because the violence of war has grown out of all proportion to the objectives to be achieved, no issue has been resolved." [97]

Moreover, the reduction in the number of powers of approximately equal strength has increased the difficulty of conducting diplomacy.

> *As long as no nation was strong enough to eliminate all the others, shifting coalitions could be used for exerting pressure or marshaling support. They served in a sense as substitutes for physical conflict. In the classical periods of cabinet diplomacy in the eighteenth and nineteenth centuries, a country's diplomatic flexibility and bargaining position depended on its availability as a partner to as many other countries as possible. As a result, no relationship was considered permanent and no conflict was pushed to its ultimate conclusion.*[98]

Although wars occurred, nations did not risk national survival and were able instead to use limited means to achieve limited objectives.

Like Morgenthau, Kissinger views with disfavor the injection of ideology into the international system. Ideology not only contributes to the development of unlimited national objectives, but it eventually creates states whose objective is to the overthrow of the existing international system. In the absence of agreement among powers about the framework for the system—or its legitimacy—the conduct of diplomacy becomes difficult, even impossible.

Finally, in Kissinger's view the Atlantic Alliance is crucial to United States security. Neither the United States nor the nation-states of Western Europe alone can resolve the problems confronting the West. Without the cohesion of the Atlantic Alliance, the "future of freedom is dim." Kissinger proposed the following changes in the Atlantic Alliance: (1) development of a "political mechanism" for the planning of long-range policies, crisis management and the control of nuclear weapons. Such a mechanism might be formed by the creation of an Executive Committee of the NATO Council consisting of the United States, Britain, France, the German Federal Republic, and Italy, together with a rotating representative from smaller NATO countries; (2) formation of a group of senior officers from the United States, Britain, France

97. *Ibid.*, p. 170.   98. *Ibid.*, p. 171.

nd the German Federal Republic to provide military advice to the long-
ange planning committee; (3) the creation of an Allied Nuclear Force from
he nuclear capabilities of the United States, Britain and France.[99]

ROBERT STRAUSZ-HUPÉ

Although prescriptions for action by the statesman can be found in most
ealist writings, the works of Robert Strausz-Hupé, in particular, have empha-
ized the relationship between power and values, between power and the
ransformation of the international system. Strausz-Hupé (1903–   ), former
irector of the Foreign Policy Research Institute at the University of Penn-
ylvania and later United States Ambassador to Ceylon, has had as a major
oncern the nature of power as well as its exercise and control. In his study
f international relations, he contends: "Power is the staff of orderly govern-
ent. Without the exercise of power, political order could neither be estab-
shed nor maintained. Power guards society against anarchy. Yet power
pawns tyranny and violence, corrupts the mighty and crushes freedom." [100]

Although international conflict is attributable to several causes, it stems
argely from the human "power urge," which is "derived from the more basic
rge of self-aggrandizement or self-assertion." [101] The power urge may take
ny one of several forms: "personal ambition, a quest for prestige and
ratification, or simply a desire to profit from other people's work." [102] In the
odern world, power is more important than before. Population growth, the
mergence of organizational structures with intermediate layers of power
olders, and the growth of the physical force of power—all of these enhance
e importance of power. Moreover, the religious and metaphysical limitations
hich once restrained powerholders have broken down. Deification of the
ate and development of Darwinian theories have strengthened the power
rge. Rapid social change, together with the alienation of men from older
ollectivities, has produced states of anxiety and anomie, which stimulates in
dividuals and groups of men suicidal tendencies and increases the incidence
f war and aggressiveness.[103]

The individual's quest for power has the effect of making the entire society
ore aggressive. Domestic power struggles spill over into the international
ystem. In international politics, the power urge reveals itself in several kinds
f conflict. The attempt of one state to impose its political ideology on an-

. Henry A. Kissinger, *The Troubled
artnership: A Re-Appraisal of the At-
ntic Alliance* (New York: McGraw-
ill Book Company, 1965), pp. 170–171.

0. Robert Strausz-Hupé, *Power and
ommunity* (New York: Frederick A.
raeger, 1956), p. 3.

101. Robert Strausz-Hupé and Stefan T.
Possony, *International Relations* (New
York: Mc-Graw-Hill Book Company,
1954), p. 11.

102. *Ibid.*

103. *Ibid.*, p. 18.

other state; psychological differences, especially fear, hatred or divergent man
ners or customs; differences in social structure and culture; population pres
sures; conflicts over economic issues; territorial claims; conflicting securit
interests; and differences between political systems account for internationa
conflict. As a result, a state may seek one of several kinds of objectives: th
redrawing of its own borders; the modification of another state's politica
social and cultural system; an increase in its security by removing possibl
threats and establishing its own power superiority.

In achieving foreign policy objectives, decision-makers must choose amon
alternative means. Their choice depends upon their degree of motivation t
achieve a particular goal, the time available for its attainment, the cost, th
risk, and the extent to which one goal conflicts with other goals. Conflic
management has many aspects. Four basic techniques are available for shap
ing an opponent's behavior: evolution (the gradual transformation of an op
ponent's intention or his ruling class) revolution from above, revolution fron
below, and war.

Like several other theorists examined in this chapter, Strausz-Hupé i
concerned with geographical location, manpower, and natural resources, a
well as scientific and technological proficiency, national psychology, an
political institutions as elements of national power. Size and structure of pop
ulation are vital measurements of national power. A decline in populatio
usually precedes a decline in a nation's international position. Those coun
tries which are most powerful "possess an adequate supply of all 'essential
'strategic,' and 'critical' materials or . . . are able, by virtue of their master
over transportation routes, to import, in time of war, materials inadequatel
supplied at home." [104] Political, economic and military organization "trans
forms these elements of power into world-political realities." [105]

Despite changes in technology, geography remains an important factor i
the power equation. As a student of geopolitical relationships, Strausz-Hup
attached particular significance to Sir Halford Mackinder's concept of th
Heartland. "If domination of the land-locked plains-lands of European Russi
is joined to the domination of East Central Europe between the Baltic, Adr
atic, and Aegean, then the condition obtains which Sir Halford conceived a
the final step to the mastery of Europe." [106] Because the "political unificatio
of the European continent under a single power would profoundly alter th
distribution of technological and economic potentials," [107] the defense of Wes
ern Europe is vital to the security of the United States.

Conflict can be traced to the conditions which attend the breakdown c
political systems. It is possible to trace a series of "systemic" revolution
which have transformed political institutions and practices. According t
Strausz-Hupé, the first systemic revolution "started with the Peloponnesia

104. Robert Strausz-Hupé, *The Balance
of Tomorrow* (New York: G. P. Putnam's Sons, 1945), p. 119.

105. *Ibid.,* p. 173.
106. *Ibid.,* p. 262.
107. *Ibid.,* p. 234.

Contending Theories of International Relation

War and reached its climax in the Roman Civil Wars which pitted first Pompey against Caesar and then Caesar's heirs against one another. The revolution . . .,was not confined to any one city or country. It rolled over the entire Mediterranean region—the universe of the ancients. When it had run its course of four centuries, the state system had changed from one of many city-states into one of a single universal empire." [108] With the dawn of the modern period with the Renaissance and the Reformation, the feudal system gave way to the nation-state system. This system, in turn, is in decline. In the twentieth century, the world once again is passing through a systemic revolution. The nation-state is no longer adequate to the demands imposed upon it. Ultimately, the systemic revolution ushers in the development of larger political units, and even the unification of the globe. The struggle between the United States and the Soviet Union is but the contemporary expression of pervasive conflict that encompasses all lands, all peoples, and all levels of society. The systemic revolution obeys a law of the dialectic. Within each period there are forces which contend with and eventually lead to the destruction of the existing system. One system gives way to another system which in turn contains forces which lead eventually to its transformation. Upon the outcome of the systemic revolution depends the future of political organization in the world.

Although Strausz-Hupé attaches great importance to the power urge as well as to certain environmental factors as conditioners of behavior, he believes that man can shape his political institutions and relationships. In the outcome of the systemic revolution the peoples of the West, and the United States in particular, can play a role of decisive importance. The Atlantic Alliance is the core of the West's federative power and its mightiest bulwark against the Soviet Union, the primary contender of the United States for shaping the future world order.

Because of the importance which he attaches to the outcome of the systemic revolution, Strausz-Hupé has addressed himself to the nature of communist strategy, as well as the strategic concepts adequate to the challenges facing the West. One of his principal preoccupations has been the study of communist strategic concepts, which call for the use of a variety of techniques, most of them nonmilitary, to achieve foreign policy objectives. Strausz-Hupé has been attracted to the study of the limited means employed by communist states to attain their goals without resorting to all-out conflict. In the systemic revolution, the Soviet Union is engaged in a "protracted conflict."

> *The salient characteristics of the doctrine of protracted conflict are: the total objective, the carefully controlled methods and the constant shifting of the battleground, weapons systems and operational tactics for the purpose of confusing the opponent, keeping him off balance*

108. Robert Strausz-Hupé, William R. Kintner, James E. Dougherty, and Alan J. Cottrell, *Protracted Conflict* (New York: Harper and Brothers, 1959), pp. 8–9.

and wearing down his resistance. The doctrine of protracted conflict prescribes a strategy for annihilating the opponent over a period of time by limited operations, by feints and maneuvers, psychological manipulations and diverse forms of violence. . . . . In Communist theory, various techniques of political warfare and graduated violence are so co-ordinated as to form a spectrum that reaches all the way from the clandestine distribution of subversive literature to the annihilating blow delivered with every weapon available.[109]

As a student of communist strategy and proponent of a Western strategy adequate to the difficult task of mastering the forces sweeping the international system, Strausz-Hupé is concerned with the means by which man shapes his destiny in a revolutionary age. As a scholar and policy scientist, he has urged the development of United States strategic superiority and military flexibility the strengthening of alliance systems, the integration of Western Europe within an Atlantic federation, and the exploitation of communist vulnerabilities. In an age when biological survival has been a dominant concern of many men, he has given primacy to the development of a world order emphasizing the values of Western civilization, and in doing so has attempted to restore a balance of thought between the defense of values and the defense of life. As a realist, his effort has been to understand those forces which inhere in the contemporary world and the distant past as well as the strategies by which man may mold the future.

RAYMOND ARON

Because of his attempt in the monumental work, *Peace and War,* to synthesize much of the past and contemporary writings in international relations, Raymond Aron, (1904–   ) noted French philosopher, does not fall easily into a realist category of international theorists. Aron engages in what he terms a four-fold analysis of international relations: theory, sociology, history, and praxiology. What he calls theory corresponds to "ordering of data, selection of problems, and variables." [110] His conceptualization includes the development of propositions about diplomacy and strategy, the nature of power, notions of equilibrium, and models of multipolar and bipolar international systems, and homogeneous and heterogeneous systems.

109. *Protracted Conflict,* p. 2.

110. Raymond Aron, *Peace and War* (New York: Doubleday, 1966), p. 2. For contrasting analyses of Aron's writings on international relations, see Stanley Hoffmann, *The State of War: Essays in the Theory and Practice of International Relations,* New York: Frederick A. Praeger, 1965, pp. 22–53; Oran R.

Young, "Aron and the Whale: A Jonah in Theory," Klaus Knorr and James N. Rosenau, eds., *Contending Approaches to International Politics* (Princeton: Princeton University Press, 1969), pp. 129–143. For a recent examination of Aron as an intellectual, see Milton Viorst, "Talk with 'a Reasonable Man,' " *New York Times Magazine,* April 5, 1970, p. 341.

Contending Theories of International Relations

In Aron's view, theory provides an enumeration of "effect-phenomena, the determined factors, for which the sociologist is tempted to seek cause-phenomena, the determinants." [111] In the section of his work termed sociology, he is concerned with causality and the determinants of international behavior. In particular, Aron addresses himself to the problems of spatial relationships, population, resources, and the origins of war, as well as what he terms the nation, the civilization and humanity as collectivities which affect conduct at the international level. Aron's examination of history, his third level of conceptualization, consists of an effort to relate his theory and sociology to the international system since 1945. Finally, praxiology (or normative theory) represents Aron's attempt to derive a series of prescriptions for international conduct from his analytic framework as applied to contemporary history.

According to Aron, international relations consists of relations among the political units into which the world is divided at any given time, from the Greek city states to the modern nation-states. Although a science or philosophy of politics would include the study of international relations, the case for the uniqueness of international relations stems from the fact that it deals with "relations between political units, each of which claims the right to take justice into its own hands and to be the sole arbiter of the decision to fight or not to fight." [112]

Because of the existence of several or many autonomous political units, the principal objective of each unit is to insure its safety, and ultimately its survival. Given this preoccupation, the political leaders can never fully develop a rational diplomatic-strategic behavior. Nevertheless, Aron seeks to develop a "rational type of theory, proceeding from fundamental concepts (strategy and diplomacy, means and ends, power and force, power, glory, and idea) to systems and types of systems."

In international relations the diplomat-strategist faces the risk of war since he confronts opponents in a situation of "incessant rivalry in which each side reserves the right to resort to the *ultima ratio,* that is, to violence." [113] In Aron's conceptualization relations among nations are often marked by conflict. Essentially, relations among political units consist of the alternatives of war and peace, since every collectivity exists among friends, enemies, neutrals, or indifferent parties. The status of political units is determined by the material or human resources that they can allocate to diplomatic-strategic action. The extent to which political units mobilize such resources depends upon many factors, including, of course, accessibility to them, but also the objectives which political leaders choose to pursue. Aron asserts that political units do not desire power for its own sake, but rather as a means toward achieving some goal, such as peace or glory, or in order to influence the future of the international system. Many kinds of circumstances, such as changes in military or economic technique, the transformation of institutions or ideologies,

111. *Ibid.,* p. 178. 113. *Ibid.,* p. 16.
112. *Ibid.,* p. 8.

affect the goals of political leaders. Technological innovations modify previously held spatial concepts, including the strategic value of geographical positions and the economic importance of certain natural and human resources. But Aron acknowledges that political units which have the greatest influence on others are not always those which most consciously attempt to impose themselves on others. Although it is possible, as Aron attempts, to examine, even quantify, elements of national power, it is more difficult to assess their effectiveness in attaining the goals set by political leaders.

Moreover, the conduct of nations toward each other is the product not only of the relation of forces but also of the ideas and emotions that influence the actions of decision-makers. It is necessary, as Aron himself does in his theory, to provide for geographical relationships, alliances, and military structures. But it is essential as well to assess the relationship between the capabilities of political units and the objectives sought by political leaders.

Here Aron introduces two models of the international system, the so-called homogeneous system and the heterogeneous system. In the homogeneous system "states belong to the same type, obey the same conception of policy." In the heterogeneous system, the "states are organized according to different principles and appeal to contradictory values." [114] In homogeneous systems political leaders are in agreement about the kinds of objectives to be pursued. Conflict occurs within the system, but the continued existence of the system itself is not at stake. Thus, Aron suggests that from the end of the Thirty Years War in 1648 until the French Revolution, the international system was homogeneous. Since 1945, however, the international system has been heterogeneous, since much of the conflict has been concerned with the system itself, not just the attainment of goals within the system.

Although Aron gives great prominence in his theory to power as a means toward the attainment of national objectives, he sets forth explicitly a system framework for the analysis of international politics. An international system, he suggests, is "the ensemble constituted by political units that maintain regular relations with each other and that are capable of being implicated in a generalized war." [115] In addition to homogeneous and heterogeneous systems, it is possible to distinguish bipolar and multipolar systems, depending on whether the majority of political units are grouped around two states of·far greater strength, or the system includes several political units relatively similar in strength.

Both the bipolar and multipolar systems contain equilibrating mechanisms. At its highest level of abstraction, equilibrium consists of the tendency, found also in other theories, of a state or combination of states to attempt to prevent any state or coalition that seems capable of achieving preponderance. Although this rule, according to Aron, is applicable to all international systems, it is necessary to construct models according to a configuration of forces in

114. *Ibid.,* p. 100.   115. *Ibid.,* p. 94.

order to elaborate rules for the operation of equilibrium. In the multipolar system the essential rule of equilibrium is that "the state whose forces are increasing must anticipate the dissidence of certain of its allies, who will rejoin the other camp in order to maintain the balance." [116] In the bipolar system, the most general law of equilibrium is that "the goal of chief actors is to avoid finding themselves at the mercy of a rival." [117] The principal goal of each of the chief actors is that of preventing the other from acquiring capabilities superior to its own. The chief actor, the leader of a coalition, seeks simultaneously to prevent the growth of the opposing coalition and to maintain the cohesiveness of its own coalition.

In Aron's theory, there are three types of peace—equilibrium, hegemony or empire. In any historical period, the forces of the political units are in one of three conditions: (1) they are in balance; (2) they are dominated by those of one of the units; or (3) they are outclassed by the forces of one of the political units. Between peace by equilibrium and peace by empire, Aron places what he terms peace by hegemony. The incontestable superiority of one political unit is acknowledged by other members of the international system. Although the smaller states are unable to change the status quo, the hegemonic state does not attempt to absorb them. Germany, for example, in the period after the Franco-Prussian War of 1870–71, possessed a kind of hegemony in the continent which Bismarck sought to make acceptable to other European states.

If peace is the "more or less lasting suspension of violent modes of rivalry between political units," conflict, in Aron's theory, consists of the dialectics of antagonism—deterrence, persuasion, and subversion.

Deterrence is related both to the material means which a state possesses to prevent action by another political unit, and the resolution which one state is able to convey to another which threatens it. "Today as yesterday, the essential problem of deterrence is both psychological and technological. How can the state diplomatically on the defensive convince a state diplomatically on the offensive that it will carry out its threat?" [118] If the credibility of a threat depends upon the perceived intention of the state making a threat to carry it out, the threat becomes less convincing as its execution appears to be contrary to the interests of those who make it. The advent of weapons of mass destruction increases the risk of executing a threat and thus reduces the interests for which the use of force can be credibly threatened. Aron outlines a system, similar to Morton Kaplan's unit veto system, in which each state will be in a position to exterminate all others. Thus, in this model, technology affects the credibility of threats made by political actors.

What Aron terms persuasion, in his dialectics of antagonism, consists of methods designed to modify behavior in some desired fashion and, indeed,

116. *Ibid.,* p. 128.
117. *Ibid.,* p. 36.
118. *Ibid.,* p. 405.

includes the strategy of subversion. What Aron describes as subversion is the use of violence to attain an objective. "Abstractly," he suggests, "the goal of subversion is to withdraw a population from the administrative and moral authority of an established power and to integrate it within other political and military frameworks, sometimes in and by conflict." [119]

According to Aron, conflict, in the most general sense, results whenever two individuals, social groups, or political units covet the same property or seek incompatible goals. Aron holds that the human animal is aggressive, but that man does not fight by instinct. War is an expression, but not a necessary expression, of human aggressiveness. Although, given the nature of man, it is impossible to eliminate all conflict, it is not "proved that these conflicts must be manifested in the phenomenon of war, as we have known it for thousands of years, with organized combatants, utilizing increasingly destructive weapons." [120]

Although Aron's theoretical framework is similar in many respects to those of American realists, he contrasts American realism with the work of earlier European scholars such as the German historian Heinrich von Treitschke (1834–1896). In contrast to Treitschke, "the American authors who are commonly regarded as belonging to the realist school declare that states, animated by a will to power, are in permanent rivalry, but that they are not self-congratulatory about the situation and do not regard it as a part of the divine plan. The refusal of states to submit to a common law or arbitration seems to them incontestable, intelligible, but not sublime, for they hold neither war nor the right to draw the sword as sublime." [121] But American realists, according to Aron, are "located on the margin of the idealist situation" since, although they criticize the utopian or idealist conception, the realists unconsciously "follow the example of those whom they oppose." Realists, too, develop a normative theory of international relations.

In the portion of his work entitled praxiology, Aron himself engages in normative theorizing. He believes that the political leader ought to remember that international order is the result of a balancing of forces which support the preservation of the system with those which seek its transformation. If the statesman is unable to calculate correctly such forces, he fails to perform his primary responsibility: the security of the persons and values entrusted to his care. For the statesman immorality, in Aron's conception, is a condition in which the political leader "obeys his heart without concerning himself with the consequences of his acts." Thus Aron suggests, as American realists have held, that the morality of the political leader as a political leader differs from that of the citizen within a political unit.

Aron prefers an international community based on world law and order. Such a community is not possible without what he terms a homogeneity of

119. *Ibid.*, pp. 166–167. 121. *Ibid.*, p. 592.
120. *Ibid.*, p. 366.

states and a similarity of constitutional practices. States must reduce their levels of armaments, cease to suspect each other of the worst intentions, abandon the resort to force to resolve disputes, and give respect to the same legal and moral ideas.

Realism: Its Limitations and Contributions

No theoretical approach to the study of international relations is without its critics. Realism evoked criticism because of the boldness with which its proponents stated assumptions about political behavior, as well as policy proposals, at variance with those of utopianism. Indeed, realists have criticized each other, largely because of disagreement on policy proposals. Although each theorist examined in this chapter has his supporters and critics, the following critique relates principally to concepts shared by more than one realist, but not necessarily by all realists.

For several reasons, the "national interest" concept has been the object of considerable criticism. According to one critique: "That national interest is a necessary criterion of policy is obvious and unilluminating. No statesman, no publicist, no scholar would seriously argue that foreign policy ought to be conducted in opposition to, or in disregard of, the national interest." [122] Moreover, it is difficult to give operational meaning to the concept national interest. Different political leaders interpret national interest differently. Diverse national experiences promote differing conceptions of the national interest. The statesman is constrained, or given freedom, by many forces, in interpreting the national interest. He is often the captive of his predecessors' policies. He interprets national interest as a result of his cultural training, values and the data made available to him as a decision-maker. According to Professor Stanley Hoffmann of Harvard:

> [T]he conception of an objective and easily recognizable national interest, the reliable guide and criterion of national policy, is one which makes sense only in a stable period in which the participants play for limited ends, with limited means, and without domestic kibbitzers to disrupt the players' moves. In a period when the survival of states is at stake to a far greater extent than in former times, the most divergent courses of action can be recommended as valid choices for survival. Ordinarily less compelling objectives, such as prestige, or an increment of power in a limited area, or the protection of private citizens abroad, all become tied up with the issue of survival, and the most frequent

122. Thomas I. Cook and Malcolm Moos, "The American Idea of International Interest," *American Political Science Review,* XLVII (March, 1953), 28.

argument against even attempting to redefine a hierarchy of national objectives so as to separate at least some of them from survival is the familiar fear of a 'chain of events' or a 'row of dominoes.' [123]

Therefore, in the absence of empirically based studies, it is difficult to determine what the "national interest" means at any specific time.

Realist writers have been criticized for their efforts to draw from the past a series of political concepts for the analysis of the contemporary international system. Pursuit of limited national objectives, the separation of foreign policy from domestic politics, the conduct of secret diplomacy, the use of balance of power as a technique for the management of power, and the pleas for nations to place reduced emphasis on ideology as a conditioner of international conduct, have little relevance to the international system today. By urging that nations return to the practices of an earlier period, some realist writers overestimate the extent to which such change in the present international system is possible. If nations obey laws of nature, which the realist purports to have discovered, why is it necessary to urge them, as realists do, to return to practices supposedly based upon such laws? [124] Although history provides many examples of international behavior which substantiate realist theory, historical data offer deviant cases. In calling upon the statesman to alter his behavior, the realist becomes normative in theoretical orientation and fails to provide an adequate explanation as to why political leaders sometimes do not adhere to realist tenets in foreign policy.

In emphasizing power as the principal motivation for political behavior, realists have made themselves the object of criticism. Critics have suggested that realist writers, for the most part, have not clearly conceptualized power. There are formidable problems of measuring power. There is no common unit into which power is converted for measurement in realist writings. Moreover, power must be related to the objective for which it is to be used. The amount and type of power varies with national goals. In addition, realists have been criticized for allegedly having placed too much emphasis on power, to the relative exclusion of other important variables. In Hoffmann's view, "it is impossible to subsume under one word variables as different as: power as a condition of policy and power as a criterion of policy; power as a potential and power in use; power as a sum of resources and power as a set of processes." [125]

The use of the term balance of power in realist writings has evoked criticism. According to Inis Claude and Ernst Haas, the balance of power, as used in contemporary writings, has various meanings: (1) a policy directed toward the attainment of certain goals in foreign relations; (2) a description of an actual state of affairs; (3) an equal distribution of power, or equilibrium, in the

123. Stanley Hoffmann, *Contemporary Theory in International Relations* (Englewood Cliffs, N.J.: Prentice-Hall, 1960), p. 33.

124. Cecil V. Crabb, *American Foreign Policy in the Nuclear Age* (New York: Harper and Row, 1965), pp. 458–459.

125. Hoffmann, *op. cit.*, p. 32.

international system; (4) a description of any distribution of power; (5) a search for hegemony; or (6) a description of a universal law of history.[126] Because of its many meanings, the utility of the term balance of power is limited, unless writers using it set forth clearly their definition. Unfortunately, Claude suggests: "The frustrations of the student who seeks to understand and evaluate the concept of balance of power are almost intolerably heightened by the tendency of many writers to slide blissfully from one usage of the term to another and back again, frequently without posting any warning that plural meanings exist." [127]

Despite its critics, realism ranks as the most important attempt thus far to isolate and focus on a key variable in political behavior, namely power, and to develop a theory of international relations. To a far greater extent than their predecessors, realist students of international relations attempted to construct theory from historical data. In addition to their efforts to determine how nations in fact behaved, realists developed a body of normative theory addressed particularly to policymakers. Having isolated what they considered to be the important determinants of political behavior in the past, they compared contemporary international politics with a model based on their study of history. The problems to which realist thought has addressed itself—of the interaction and behavior of human beings as decision-makers, the nature of power, the foreign policy goals, the techniques for managing power, the impact of environment upon political behavior, and the purposes and practices which ought to guide political leaders—are central to the study of international politics. Other approaches are addressed to similar problems. Social-psychological theories of international behavior have focused on the study of power. In systems frameworks the study of demand-response relationships is essentially the study of the efforts of one national unit to bring influence to bear upon another national unit in either a conflictual or collaborative situation. The study of decision-making is essentially an examination of the interpretation in a given instance of the national interest. The decision-making system, like all social systems, is "open," that is, it is subject to a variety of inputs from its environment. Hence environment, or political ecology, becomes important not only to the realist, but to the student of systems theory, as a potential conditioner of political behavior. In sum, in addition to its contribution to international relations theory, realism provides a series of propositions about political behavior which can be subjected to further examination with the use of other frameworks and methodologies.

126. Inis L. Claude, Jr., *Power and International Relations* (New York: Random House, 1962), p. 25; Ernst B. Haas, "The Balance of Power: Prescription, Concept, or Propaganda," *World Politics,* V (July 1953), 422–477.

127. Claude, *op. cit.,* p. 22.

CHAPTER 4
Systemic Theories of Politics and International Relations

Definition, Nature and Approaches to Systems Theory

System is probably the most widely used term in political science and international relations literature today. *System* describes (a) a theoretical framework for the coding of data about political phenomena; (b) an integrated set of relationships based on a hypothetical set of political variables, e.g., an international system involving world government; (c) a set of relationships among political variables in an international system, alleged in academic discussions and writings to have existed, e.g., the bipolar system of the 1950s; and (d) any set of variables in interaction.

This chapter will focus on systems theory, rather than systems analysis. It would be desirable, but perhaps not possible, to distinguish the two terms. The latter properly applies to the procedures that the RAND Corporation and the Department of Defense developed for efficient allocation of resources among alternative weapons systems. Systems analysis describes a variety of techniques, such as cost-effectiveness studies, which are designed to allow rational choice in decisions regarding the allocation of resources. But in the literature of political science, "systems analysis" has often been used interchangeably with "systems theory" insofar as it is employed to describe conceptual frameworks and methodologies for understanding the operation of political systems. It aids in determining a political system's capacity for maintaining its equilibrium in the face of stress and for adapting to changes that are forced internally and externally. We prefer to call this systems theory, which we define as a series of statements about relationships among independent and dependent variables which are assumed to interact with each other; that is, changes in one or more variables are accompanied, or followed, by changes in other variables or combinations of variables. As Anatol Rapoport has suggested, "a whole which functions as whole by virtue of the interdependence of its parts is called a *system,* and the method which aims at discovering how this is brought about in the widest variety of systems has been called general systems theory." [1] The human nervous system, a car motor, the Hilton Hotel chain, an Apollo spacecraft, the Federal Reserve System, a fishtank in a marine ecology experimental project, and the "balance of power" system— all of these are *systems*.

A system can be described in its successive states. It may be loosely or tightly organized. It may be stable or unstable. Smaller systems (or subsystems) may exist within larger systems. Every system has boundaries which distinguish it from its operating environment. Every system is, in some sense, a communications net which permits the flow of information leading to a self-adjusting process. Every system has inputs and outputs; the output of one system may become the input of another with which it is coupled. When systems are coupled in two directions, we speak of the occurrence of "feedback." We usually distinguish the "state of a system" from the "characteristic behavior" of a system. Some inputs may affect the state of the system and create disturbances in its equilibrium, after which the system returns to its former normal state. Other inputs may have such an impact as to transform the characteristic behavior of the system; instead of returning to its former state of equilibrium, it might achieve equilibrium at a different level and under different characteristic operating conditions. These and other basic notions associated with systems will be elaborated as we proceed.

Although in the past decade systems theory has reached a pinnacle of importance in the study of politics, the idea of systems was not unknown to earlier political writers. For example, Thomas Hobbes, in Chapter 22 of his *Leviathan* writes of systems.[2] Modern students of politics have adapted the concept of systems from the physical sciences and the social sciences on which systems theory has had a major impact. The social sciences imported the modern concept of system from homeostatic physics and biology.

One of the most important exponents of systems theory is Ludwig von Bertalanffy, professor of theoretical biology at the University of Alberta, Canada, whose work in this field dates from the 1920s. He suggests that the ever-increasing specialization within modern science begets fragmentation in the discipline as a whole: "The physicist, the biologist, the psychological and the social scientist are, so to speak, encapsulated in a private universe, and it is difficult to get a word from one cocoon to the other." [3] The growth of dis-

1. Anatol Rapoport, "Foreword," Walter Buckley, ed., *Modern Systems Research for the Behavioral Scientists* (Chicago: Aldine Publishing Company, 1968), p. xvii. Italics are the author's.

2. Hobbes defines system as follows: "By systems I understand any numbers of men joined in one interest or one business of which some are regular and some irregular." Thomas Hobbes, *Leviathan,*

introduction by Michael Oakeshott (Oxford: Basil Blackwell, 1946), p. 146.

3. Ludwig von Bertalanffy, "General Systems Theory," General Systems, I (1956), 1–10, reprinted in J. David Singer, ed., *Human Behavior and International Politics: Contributions from the Social-Psychological Sciences* (Chicago: Rand McNally and Company, 1965), p. 21. See also Roy R. Grinker, ed., *Toward*

ciplines and greater academic specialization threaten to fragment the scientific community into isolated enclaves unable to communicate. Systems theory represents a response to this threat. Rapoport suggests that the systems approach has the potential of reestablishing approaches which emphasize the functional relationship between parts and whole without sacrificing scientific rigor. The analogies established or conjectured in systems theory are not mere metaphors. According to Rapoport, they are rooted in actual correspondences between systems or theories of systems.[4] Bertalanffy discerns similar viewpoints and conceptions in various fields.

Disciplines such as physics and chemistry study phenomena in dynamic interaction. In biology, there are problems of an organismic nature. In such seemingly diverse disciplines, it is essential, according to Bertalanffy, to "study not only isolated parts and processes, but the essential problems are the organizing relations that result from dynamic interaction and make the behavior of parts different when studied in isolation or within the whole." [5]

In short, Bertalanffy, like Rapoport, sees structural similarities or isomorphism [6] in the principles which govern the behavior of intrinsically dissimilar entities. This is because they are in certain respects "systems," i.e., "complexes of elements standing in interaction." Because of such similarities, general systems theory offers a "useful tool *providing, on the one hand, models that can be used in, and transferred to, different fields, and safeguarding, on the other hand, from vague analogies* which have often marred the progress in these fields." [7]

KENNETH BOULDING

From his work in economics and general systems theory, Kenneth Boulding has attempted to classify systems according to levels of increasing complexity: mechanical, homeostatic, biological, equivalent to higher animals, and human.[8] The gathering, selecting, and using of information essential to preservation is far more complex in the human system than in a simple system. A thermostat,

---

a Unified Theory of Human Behavior (New York: Basic Books, 1956).

4. Rapoport, *op. cit.*, p. xxi.

5. Singer, *op. cit.*, p. 21. Bertalanffy has suggested that a "system" implies any arrangement or combination of parts or elements in a whole which may apply to a cell, a human being, or a society. "General Systems Theory: A New Approach to Unity of Science," *Human Biology,* XXIII (1951), 302–304.

6. Isomorphism may be defined as "a one-to-one correspondence between ob-

jects in different systems which preserves the relationship between the objects." A. Hall and R. Fagen, "Definition of a System," *General Systems,* I (1956), 18.

7. *Ibid.*, p. 22. Italics in original.

8. Kenneth E. Boulding, *The Image: Knowledge in Life and Society* (Ann Arbor: University of Michigan Press, 1956), p. 8. "Political Implications of General Systems Research," *General Systems Yearbook,* VI, (1961), 1–7. For a treatment of image theory and international conflict, see Chapter 7, pp. 224–226.

or example, reacts only to changes in temperature, and ignores other data. The simpler the system, the fewer data essential for survival. In contrast to simple systems, humans have a capacity of self-knowledge, which makes possible the selection of information on the basis of a particular cognitive structure, or "image." The "image" can cause the restructuring of the information, or stimulus, into something fundamentally different from the information itself. The resulting human behavior is a response not to a specific stimulus, but to a knowledge structure effecting a comprehensive view of the environment. Difficulties in the prediction of system behavior arise to account for the intervention of the "image" between stimulus and response. To a far greater extent than simple systems, complex systems have a potential to collapse because the "image" has screened out information essential for survival.

Social and political systems are structured from the "images" of participant human actors. Boulding gives the term "folk knowledge" to the collective "images" of the members of political systems. The decisions of political leaders conform to the dictates of "folk knowledge," screening out conflicting information. The information-gathering apparatus of both national and international systems usually serves to confirm both the "images" of the leading decision-makers and also the "folk knowledge" of the system. Boulding is convinced that the elimination of the influence of "folk knowledge" in decision-making would have as great an effect on international behavior as removing medieval notions about cosmology had on developing modern science. Clearly, Boulding considers the idea of "image" a crucial concept in understanding systems, and in studying such political phenomena as conflict and decision-making.

Boulding contends that general systems theory aids interdisciplinary studies at a level "between the highly generalized constructions of pure mathematics and the specific theories of the specialized disciplines." [9] He proposes two approaches in using general systems theory to organize knowledge across disciplines.

The first approach starts with the empirical universe of disciplines, locates the general phenomena common to different disciplines, and constructs theoretical models relevant to at least two different fields of study. For example, as Boulding suggests, nearly all disciplines have examples of populations consisting of aggregates of individuals that interact among themselves. In addition, births and deaths add and subtract from populations. Models of population change and interaction can be used in many different fields. Patterns of interaction among the population, even including patterns of competition and cooperation, can be examined by analyzing populations comprised of animals, social classes, molecules, or commodities.

A second approach to general systems theory consists of the development of a spectrum of theoretical constructs arranged in a nine-level hierarchy of

9. Kenneth E. Boulding, *Beyond Economics* (Ann Arbor: University of Michigan Press, 1968), p. 83.

complexity. This hierarchy includes (1) the level of static structures, which sets out the elementary framework of perceived reality by describing the mapping of the geography and anatomy of the universe. (This framework includes the patterns of electrons around a nucleus, the solar system, and also descriptive social science. "Without accuracy in this description of static relationships no accurate functional or dynamic theory is possible"); [10] (2) the "level of clockworks," which refers to the simple dynamic system whose motions are predetermined. This level includes both simple equilibrium systems and stochastic dynamic systems leading to equilibria; (3) the "level of the thermostat," which is distinguishable from the clockwork system by the fact that its operation depends on the transmission and interpretation of information. (This entails a control mechanism. It is a cybernetic system.); (4) the "open system," which is self-maintaining or self-reproducing. (This includes cellular and atomic structures); (5) the genetic-societal level, distinguished by a division of labor among differentiated, yet mutually dependent, cells in a cell-society. This level includes plant life; (6) the "animal" level, characterized by self-awareness, with receptors such as eyes and ears and having a capacity to absorb and structure information; (7) the "human" level, differing from the "animal" level because of man's possession of self-consciousness and capacity for language and symbolism; (8) the level of social organizations, differing from the previous level in that the unit is the role rather than the person. Social systems are conceived as "a set of roles tied together with channels of communication."); [11] (9) transcendental systems, including what Boulding terms "the ultimates and absolutes and the unescapable unknowables," [12] which have "systematic structure and relationship." [13]

Thus, according to Boulding, systems theory provides a framework for placing seemingly diverse disciplines into a more coherent structure. Within the hierarchy of systems it is possible to inventory the current theoretical and empirical knowledge which ranges many disciplines.

TALCOTT PARSONS

In sociology, Talcott Parsons has been the foremost student of systems theory, and his work has influenced thought on systems in political science. He has developed an "action system" to be used as an analytical tool. Parsons postulates an actor oriented toward attaining anticipated goals by means of a normatively regulated expenditure of energy. [14] Since the relationships between the actor and his situation have a recurrent character or system, therefore, all action occurs in systems. Although Parsons recognizes that action can occur

10. Boulding, *op. cit.*, p. 89.
11. Boulding, *op. cit.*, p. 93.
12. *Ibid.*, p. 93.
13. *Ibid.*, p. 94.

14. Talcott Parsons and Edward A. Shils, eds., *Toward a General Theory of Action* (New York: Harper and Row [Torchbooks], 1962), p. 53.

Contending Theories of International Relations

between an individual and an object, he is more concerned with action in a societal context. Therefore, Parsons' action system places persons both in the role of subjects and in the role of objects. Subject (*alter*) and object (*ego*) interact in a system. If actors gain satisfaction, they develop a vested interest in the preservation and functioning of the system. Mutual acceptance of the system by the actors creates an equilibrating mechanism in the system.

At any given time, a person is a member of several action systems such as his family, his employer and his nation-state. Three subsystems comprise the Parsonian system: (1) the personality system, (2) the social system, and (3) the cultural system. These subsystems are interconnected within the "action system" so that each mutually affects the other. In sum, Parsons conceives of society as an interlocking network of acting systems. A change in one subsystem affects the other subsystems and the whole action system.

It is possible, Parsons suggests, to distinguish and study the actions which persons, or actors, perform as members of a specific system of action. Action is based on the choices among alternative courses which the actor believes to be open to him. In Parsons' view, action is "a set of oriented processes," in which there are two major "vectors," the motivational orientations and the value-orientations. Supposedly, the course of action which the actor adopts is based on a previous learning experience as well as on his expectations about the behavior of the person with whom he is interacting. According to Parsons, interaction makes the development of culture possible at the human level, and provides culture with a significant determinant of patterns of action in a social system. Interaction among acting subjects is crucial to Parsons' framework. In a perfectly integrated social system the actors gratify each other's specific needs.[15]

Parsons proposed a set of five dichotomous pattern variables as constituting the basic dilemmas that actors face in all social action. These variables describe the alternatives available to actors confronted with problematic situations. The pattern variables are grouped as follows: (1) universalism-particularism; (2) ascription-achievement; (3) self-orientation-collectivity-orientation; (4) affectivity-affective neutrality; (5) specificity-diffuseness. The universalism-particularism dichotomy distinguishes between judging objects in terms of a general frame of reference, and judging them in terms of a particular scheme.

---

15. Parsons defines a social system as a "system of interaction of a plurality of actors, in which the action is oriented by rules which are complexes of complementary expectations concerning roles and sanctions. *As a system,* it has determinate internal organization and determinate patterns of structural change. It has, furthermore, as a system, a variety of mechanisms of adaptation to changes in the external environment. These mechanisms function to create one of the important properties of a system, namely, a tendency to maintain boundaries. A total social system which, for practical purposes, may be treated as self-sufficient— which, in other words, contains within approximately the boundaries defined by membership all the functional mechanisms required for its maintenance as a system—is here called a *society*." Italics in original. Parsons and Shils, *op. ct.,* pp. 195–196.

Whereas the impartial dispensation of justice under law is universalistic; kinship behavior is particularistic. The ascription-achievement dichotomy refers to values governing human advancement in social and political systems —whether, for example, birth and wealth count far more than intellectual ability and education. The self-orientation-collectivity-orientation dichotomy categorizes action as taken in behalf of the unit initiating action or as initiated on behalf of other units. Businesses, for example, tend to be self-oriented, while governments are collectively-oriented. The affectivity-affective neutrality variable indicates an individual's sensitivity or insensitivity to emotional stimuli. The specificity-diffuseness variable distinguishes between those relationships which are diffuse and all-encompassing, such as a marriage, and those which are, on the other hand, specific and highly structured, such as interaction between a sales clerk and customer. While diffuseness characterizes traditional societies, specificity of function is a mark of modernized societies.

Parsons' pattern variables provide a framework for describing recurring and contrasting patterns in the norms of social systems. Many authors deem the Parsonian pattern variables as useful in examining social and political systems. For example, Parsons suggests that a bureaucracy is built on universalistic and achievement norms, and that the contractual relationships among business corporations are based on norms of specificity. Such variables may be used either in a discussion of international relations or political parties at the national or local level in the United States.[16]

In his theory, Parsons attaches great importance to equilibrium as a means of measuring fluctuations in the ability of a social system to cope with problems that affect its structure.[17]

Systems theory assumes the interdependence of parts in determinate relationships, which impose order upon the components of the system. Although equating order with equilibrium, Parsons asserts that equilibrium is not necessarily equated with "static self-maintenance or a stable equilibrium. It may be an ordered process of change—a process following a determinate pattern rather than random variability relative to the starting point. This is called a moving equilibrium and is well exemplified by growth." [18] Social systems are characterized by a multiple equilibrium process, since social systems have many subsystems, each of which must remain in equilibrium if the larger system is to maintain equilibrium.

Parsons is concerned with how social systems endure stress, how they

16. F. X. Sutton, "Analyzing Social Systems," in *A Systems Approach to Political Development*, p. 22.

17. Talcott Parsons, "An Outline of the Social System," Talcott Parsons, Edward A. Shils, Kaspar Naegele, and Jesse R. Pitts, eds., *Theories of Society* (New York: Free Press of Glencoe, 1961), p. 37.

18. Parsons and Shils, *Toward a General Theory of Action*, p. 107. Parsons defines "process" as "any mode in which a given state of a system or a part of a system changes into another state." *The Social System*, p. 201.

enhance their position, how they disintegrate. If societal equilibrium and ultimately the social system itself, are to be maintained, four functional prerequisites must be performed: (1) *Pattern maintenance*—the ability of a system to insure the reproduction of its own basic patterns, its values and norms. (2) *Adaptation* to the environment and to changes in the environment. (3) *Goal Attainment*—the capacity of the system to achieve whatever goals the system has accepted or set for itself. (4) *Integration* of the different functions and subsystems into a cohesive, coordinated whole. In Parsons' social system, families and households are the subsystems which serve the function of pattern maintenance. Adaptation occurs in the economy and in areas of scientific and technological change. The polity—the government in particular—performs the function of goal attainment. The cultural subsystems, which include mass communications, religion, and education, fulfill the integrative function. Parsons' functional prerequisites have been adapted, in varying forms, to the study of politics, which is itself one of his subsystems; and they have influenced those international systems writers who are considered in this chapter.[19] Although Parsons briefly addresses himself to the concept of international systems, he sees in the international system patterns of interaction similar to those within the action system at the domestic level. The major problem for the international system, as well as for the domestic system, is that of maintaining the equilibrium or order, which is important if a system is to manage its inner tensions.[20]

The existence of a bipolar international system increases the difficulty of maintaining equilibrium. According to Parsons, the formulation of common values which cut across national boundaries is essential to international order. Although the international system is deficient in such values, the importance attached to economic development and national independence in many parts of the world over the past generation represents their emergence at least in rudimentary form as consensus-building forces at the global level. Parsons sees the need for the development of procedural consensus—agreement among participants in international politics about the institutions and procedures for the settlement of problems and differences. He also calls for the differentiation

19. According to Parsons, the traditional focus of political science has been on such concrete phenomena as government and constitutions rather than on conceptual schemes such as system. Classical political theory has consisted primarily of the normative and philosophical problems of government instead of empirical analysis of its processes and determinants. Parsons acknowledges that government, which is "one of the most strategically important processes and foci of differentiated structures within social systems," forms therefore one of the most crucial disciplines of the social sciences. But Parsons calls for a shift in focus of the study of political science from the concrete phenomena of government to a more sharply theoretical and empirical emphasis. *Ibid.,* p. 29.

20. Talcott Parsons, "Order and Community in the International Social System," in James N. Rosenau, ed., *International Politics and Foreign Policy* (New York: Free Press of Glencoe, 1961), pp. 120–121. For the implications of Parsons' work for sociological theories of conflict, see Chapter 5, Footnote 10, pp. 143–144.

of interests among peoples in a pluralistic fashion so that they will cut across the historic lines of partisan differentiation. In domestic political and social systems, peoples achieve greater unity as a result of the fact that they have crosscutting cleavages, i.e., some Catholics are Republicans, while others are Democrats, and some Protestants are Democrats and others Republicans. Such pluralistic differentiation at the international level would enhance the prospects for international stability. In holding to such views, Parsons addresses himself in some detail to a problem of central concern in his writings, namely, how to build a social and political community.[21] Ideas such as those discussed in Parsons' work are found in the writings of those authors who have addressed themselves specifically to the question of how peoples attain cohesiveness in political communities. (For this discussion, see Chapter 10.)

DAVID EASTON AND OTHERS

Several political scientists have developed, adapted and employed system theory. These scholars have preoccupied themselves with the "political system," which has been defined by Gabriel Almond as "that system of interactions to be found in all independent societies which performs the functions of integration and adaptation (both internally and *vis-à-vis* other societies) by means of the employment, or the threat of employment, of more or less legitimate physical compulsion."[22] Karl Deutsch, who also adheres to the functional prerequisites of Parsons, holds that a system is characterized by transactions and communications. He is concerned with the extent to which political systems are equipped with adequate facilities for collecting external and internal information as well as for transmitting this information to the points of decision-making. Those political systems which survive stress can receive, screen, transmit, and evaluate information.[23] According to David Easton, professor of political science at the University of Chicago, systems theory is based on the idea of political life as a boundary maintaining set of interactions imbedded in and surrounded by other social systems which constantly influence it.[24] According to Easton, political interactions can be distinguished from other kinds of interactions by the fact that they are oriented principally toward the "authoritative allocation of values for a society."[25]

Herbert Spiro, professor of political science at the University of Pennsyl-

21. Talcott Parsons, *Sociological Theory and Modern Society* (New York: Free Press, 1967), pp. 467–488.

22. Gabriel Almond, "Introduction," Gabriel Almond and James S. Coleman, eds., *The Politics of the Developing Areas* (Princeton: Princeton University Press, 1960), p. 7. See also Gabriel A. Almond and G. Bingham Powell, Jr., *Comparative Poiltics: A Developmental Approach* (Boston: Little, Brown and Company, 1966), especially Chapter 2.

23. Karl W. Deutsch, *The Nerves of Government* (New York: Free Press, 1964), pp. 250–254.

24. David Easton, *A Framework for Political Analysis* (Englewood Cliffs, N.J.: Prentice-Hall, 1965), p. 25.

25. *Ibid.*, p. 50.

vania and subsequently a member of the Policy Planning Council, Department of State, holds that a political system can exist wherever people either cooperate or engage in conflict to solve common problems. A political system is a community that is processing its issues. A problem has entered the political system when members of the community have recognized it and begun to disagree about it. A problem leaves the political system after a solution has been recognized.[26]

Almond, Deutsch, Easton, and Spiro share an interest in functions performed by the political system—an interest in the means by which the system converts inputs into outputs. Easton, in particular, has been identified with what is termed input-output analysis. In his scheme, the principal inputs into the political system are demands and supports, while the principal outputs are the decisions allocating system benefits. Almond addresses himself to the question of how political systems engage in political socialization, interest articulation and aggregation, and political communication. Such factors represent means for making demands on the political system; therefore, they are input functions. Almond is particularly concerned with political output functions involving rule making, rule application and rule adjudication. His output functions, in the case of the United States' political system, correspond to the executive, legislative and judicial branches.

Deutsch suggests that political systems might be categorized according to their ability to respond effectively to demands upon them.[27] All political systems might be divided into four categories: (a) self-destroying systems, which are likely to break down even in relatively favorable environments; (b) nonviable systems, which are not likely to survive under the range of difficulties found in most environments; (c) viable systems, which are likely to survive over a limited range of environmental conditions; and (d) self-enhancing systems, which are able to increase their probability of survival over a growing variety of environments.

Easton is concerned, as well, with the capacity of political systems to respond to their environments. Demands arise either in the environment outside the system, or within the system itself. Supports include those resources which enhance the political system's ability to respond to the demands upon it. In Easton's model, output consists of decisions or policies.

The system represents an effort to cut across the boundaries separating seemingly discrete disciplines. Political scientists who have embraced systems theory try to transcend the divisions within their field. Easton, for example, maintains that at the international level, no less than at the national level, it is possible to find sets of relationships through which values are authoritatively allocated. Unlike certain other systems, the international system lacks universal, or even strongly held, feelings of legitimacy; nevertheless, its mem-

26. Herbert J. Spiro, *World Politics: The Global System* (Homewood, Ill.: Dorsey Press, 1966), p. 51.

27. Deutsch, *op. cit.,* pp. 248–249.

bers make demands with the anticipation that these demands will be con verted into outputs. According to Easton, authorities in this case are much "less centralized than in most modern systems, less continuous in their oper ation and more contingent on events, as in the case of primitive systems But nonetheless, historically the great powers and, more recently, various kinds of international organizations, such as the League of Nations and the United Nations, have been successful, intermittently, in resolving differences that were not privately negotiated and in having them accepted as authori tative." [28] Employing his system model, Easton suggests the possibility o studying and categorizing political systems, at both the national and interna tional levels, according to their capacity for authoritatively allocating values In Spiro's framework, the political process consists essentially of four phases 1) the formulation of issues arising from problems; 2) the deliberation o issues; 3) the resolution of issues; 4) the solution of the problem that pro voked the issue.[29]

Although all political systems perform these functions, they vary widely depending on the political style of the actors. In turn, political style is derived from four basic goals toward which political systems are more or less deliber ately directed—stability, flexibility, efficiency, effectiveness.[30] The successful political system achieves an equilibrium among these goals. Spiro views prob lems as constituting the input of political systems, and solutions as the output of political systems.

Moreover, a successful political system depends on the style of its actors Spiro suggests a fourfold categorization of style—legalism, pragmatism, ideol ogism, violence. A system whose style was legalistic might devote itself to the promulgation of laws and institutions and to the abstract deliberation of issues Those systems whose styles are violent resort frequently to armed conflict to resolve issues. For the most part, however, political systems contain a variety of styles: for example, both pragmatism and legalism in the United States and both pragmatism and violence in Stalinist Russia. Like Easton's model, Spiro's framework applies to many levels of political analysis.

Systems theory, the work of Gabriel Almond in particular, and comparative studies of political systems all share a basic concern with structural-functiona analysis which attempts to examine the performance of certain kinds of func tions within a biological organism or a political system. Contemporary scholars who employ structural-functional analysis are indebted to the early twentieth century work of anthropologists Bronislaw Malinowski (1884–1942) and A. R Radcliffe-Brown (1881–1955). Subsequently, Robert K. Merton of the Co lumbia University Bureau of Applied Social Research developed a framework

28. David Easton, *A Systems Analysis of Political Life* (New York: John Wiley and Sons, 1965), pp. 284–285, 484–488. See also N. B. Nicholson and P. A. Reynolds, "General Systems, the International System and the Eastonian Analysis" *Political Studies*, XV (No. 1, 1967), 12–31.

29. Spiro, *op. cit.*, p. 51.

30. *Ibid.*

or structural-functional analysis in the field of sociology.[31] Proponents of structural-functional analysis assume that it is possible, first, to specify a pattern of behavior which satisfies a functional requirement of the system and, second, to identify "functional equivalents" in several different structural units. Structural-functional analysis contains as concepts structural and functional requisites. A functional requisite is a generalized condition essential for maintaining the type of unit under consideration, given the level of generalization of the definition and the unit's general setting.[32] A structural requisite is a pattern or observable uniformity of action necessary for the continued existence of the system.[33] Moreover, an effort is made to distinguish between functions (or what Levy calls eufunctions) and dysfunctions. According to Merton, "eufunctions are those observed consequences which make for the adaptation or adjustment of a given system; and dysfunctions, those observed consequences which lessen the adaptation or adjustment of the system.[34] Thus, structural-functional analysis may enable the researcher to avoid the pitfall of associating particular functions with particular structures and, for this reason, may prove useful in comparative research and analysis.

Both the Parsonian functional prerequisites and the functions set forth by Almond and Easton can be located and described within a given political system. Such functions relate to the system's goals, to the system's maintaining an equilibrium, and to the system's ability to interact with and adapt to changes within the environment. Structural-functional analysis provides, at the minimum, a classificatory scheme for examining political phenomena. Structural-functional analysis and, indeed, general systems theory would be acclaimed an empirically-based theory were it possible to operationalize the variables vital to maintaining the system and to understanding relationships among such variables.[35]

Systems frameworks have been applied to studies in international integration, foreign policy decision-making, and conflict. Systems frameworks have been used at several analytical levels of immediate interest to the student of international politics: (1) the development of models of international systems

31. See Robert K. Merton, *Social Theory and Social Structure* (Glencoe, Ill.: Free Press, 1957).

32. Marion J. Levy, Jr., "Functional Analysis," *International Encyclopedia of Social Sciences* (New York: Macmillan Company and The Free Press, 1968), VI, 23.

33. *Ibid.*

34. Merton, *op. cit.,* p. 51. In addition, Merton distinguishes between manifest and latent functions. Manifest are those whose patterns produce consequences which are both intended and recognized by the participants. Latent functions consist of patterns whose results are unintended and unrecognized by participants.

35. See A. James Gregor, "Political Science and the Uses of Functional Analysis," *American Political Science Review,* LXII (June, 1968), 434–435. Even though the point is not central to international theory, the student should be aware of the important distinction drawn in recent years by scholars of comparative politics between static or equilibrium models of the system with dynamic or developmental models. See Gabriel A. Almond, "A Developmental Approach to Political Systems," *World Politics,* XVII (January, 1965), 183–214.

in which patterns of interaction are specified; (2) the study of the processes by which decision-makers in one national unit, interacting with each other and responding to inputs from the domestic and international environment formulate foreign policy; (3) in the study of interaction between a national political system and its domestic subsystems, such as public opinion, interest groups, and culture, in order to analyze patterns of interaction; (4) the study of external "linkage groups," i. e., other political systems, actors or structures in the international system with which the national system under examination has direct relations; (5) the examination of the interaction between external "linkage groups" [36] and those internal groups most responsive to external events, such as foreign affairs elites, the military and businessmen engaged in world trade.

These analytic foci are by no means mutually exclusive: an understanding of decision-making processes and systems at the national level is essential to an understanding of interaction between the national units of the international system. Focusing on national decision-making emphasizes the study of a sub system of the international system; focusing on the international system involves studying the interaction between foreign policies of a series of national units, or subsystems. In this chapter we are concerned in particular with those theorists who concentrate on the international system. In subsequent chapters on decision-making and integration theory, we shall examine the application of systems theory at yet another level of analysis.

The Nature of Systems at the International Level

In the study of international relations, Morton A. Kaplan suggests the existence of a system of action which he defines as "a set of variables so related in contradistinction to its environment, that describable behavioral regularities characterize the internal relationships of the set of individual variables to combinations of external variables." [37] According to another student of international relations, Charles A. McClelland, systems theory is a technique for developing an understanding of relationships among nation-states:

> *The strategy, first of all, of conceiving of many kinds of phenomena in terms of working relations among their parts, and then labeling them* systems *according to a definition of what part of the problem*

36. Rosenau has defined "linkage" as "any recurrent sequence of behavior that originates in one system and is reacted to in another." James N. Rosenau, "Toward the Study of National-International Linkages," James N. Rosenau,

ed., *Linkage Politics* (New York: Free Press, 1969), p. 45.

37. Morton A. Kaplan, *System and Process in International Politics* (New York: John Wiley and Sons, 1962), p. 4

Contending Theories of International Relations

is most relevant, is the key to the approach. Then, the procedures of by-passing many complexities in order to investigate relationships between input and output, of systematically moving to different levels of analysis by recognizing the link of sub-systems to systems, of being alert to "boundary phenomena" and the ranges of normal operations of sub-systems and systems, and of taking into account both "parameters" and "perturbations" in the environments of systems are other major parts of the general systems apparatus.[38]

ı McClelland's work, systems theory is simply a technique for identifying, measuring, and examining interaction within a system and its subsystems. ystems theory provides for the examination of linkages, or recurrent sequences of behavior that originate in one system and are reacted to in another. f such sequences can be isolated and examined, it may be possible to gain heoretical insights into the nature of the interdependence of national and ıternational systems.

George Modelski, professor of political science at the University of Washingon, defines an international system as a social system having structural and ınctional requirements. International systems consist of a set of objects, ogether with the relationships between these objects and between their ttributes. International systems contain patterns of action and interaction etween collectivities and between individuals acting on their behalf.[39] Richard Rosecrance, professor of political science at Cornell University, concludes that , system is comprised of disturbance inputs, a regulator which undergoes hanges as a result of the disturbing influence, environmental constraints vhich translate the state of the disturbance and the state of the regulator into table or unstable outcomes.[40]

The systems approach has many adherents because supposedly it furnishes ı framework for organizing data, integrating variables, and introducing materials from other disciplines. Kaplan maintains that systems theory permits the ntegration of variables from different disciplines.[41] Rosecrance believes that ystems theory helps link "general organizing concepts" with "detailed empirical investigation." In his work the concept of system provides a framevork for the study of the history of a particular period and enhances the prospects for the development of a "theoretical approach which aims at a legree of comprehensiveness."[42] Dissatisfied with past approaches to the

8. Charles A. McClelland, "System Theory and Human Conflict," Elton B. McNeil, ed., *The Nature of Human Conflict* (Englewood Cliffs, N.J.: Prentice-Hall, 1965), p. 258.

39. George Modelski, "Agraria and Industria: Two Models of the International Systems," in Klaus Knorr and Sidney Verba, eds., *The International System,*

Theoretical Essays (Princeton: Princeton University Press, 1961), pp. 121–122.

40. Richard N. Rosecrance, *Action and Reaction in World Politics* (Boston: Little, Brown and Company, 1963), pp. 220–221.

41. Kaplan, *op. cit.,* p. xii.

42. Rosecrance, *op. cit.,* p. 267.

study of international relations, McClelland favors a systems framework be cause there is a need "to gather the specialized parts of knowledge into coherent whole." [43]

Modelski emphasizes the study of systems because he believes that th study of past and present international systems, as well as those of the hypo thetical future, have heuristic value. Since international society and ever international system change, systems and change within systems must be th object of study of international relations.[44]

Writers on international systems develop what are termed concrete or phys ical systems and analytic systems. A concrete system describes a pattern c interaction among human actors which supposedly exists, or existed, in th *real* world. In contrast, an analytic system is a heuristic device for the analysi of possible future systems, for comparison between some existing systems an a kind of ideal or analytical system.[45] Kaplan's systems are models in the sam sense in which a theory of molecular structure could be translated into a mode which, if a correct model, would relate to the observable real world. They ar theoretical models which can be applied to real systems, but which in principl can also be expressed in purely logical form. Modelski's models, Agraria an Industria, are analytic systems. Rosecrance's, derived from the analysis o historical data, are concrete systems. Both Kaplan's and Modelski's model are macro-models of international politics.

Just as there are similarities in their definitions of systems, those writer discussed in this chapter whose work has dealt primarily with the internationa level have common elements in their respective international systems frame works. Each has a concern with those factors that contribute to stability o instability in the international system. Second, there is a common concer with what are the adaptive controls, by which the system remains in equi librium or "steady state." Such preoccupation in the study of political an social systems is analogous to the interest of biologists in homeostasis in livin organisms. Third, there is a shared interest in assessing the impact upon th system of the existence of units with a greater or lesser ability to mobiliz resources and to utilize advanced technology. Fourth, there is a consensu among writers that domestic forces within the national political units exer a major effect on the international system. Fifth, they are concerned, as par of their preoccupation with stability, with the capacity of the internationa

43. Charles A. McClelland, "Systems History in International Relations: Some Perspectives for Empirical Research and Theory," *General Systems, Yearbook of the Society for General Systems Research,* III (1958), 221–247.

44. Knorr and Verba, *op. cit.,* p. 121.

45. According to Oran Young, "member-ship (i.e., concrete) systems are those whose basic components are human beings and that can therefore be though of as collections of individuals. Analyti systems, on the other hand, are abstrac tions that focus on selected elements o human behavior. In this context we ma distinguish a wide range of types of ana !ytic system such as political, economic or religious systems." *Systems of Politica Science* (Englewood Cliffs, N.J.: Pren tice-Hall, 1968), pp. 37–38.

ystem to contain and deal effectively with disturbances within it. This leads
hem to share an interest in the role of national and supranational actors
s regulators of the system. They are in accord that the international system
s characterized by change, rather than by static qualities.

All are concerned with the role of elites, resources, regulators and environ-
ient as factors that enhance or detract from stability in the system. Moreover,
he flow of information is crucial in the systems framework of each writer.
n fact, systems theory owes much to principles of cybernetics developed by
Jorbert Wiener and applied by scholars such as Karl W. Deutsch to the study
f politics. (See Chapter 10.) Interaction among the units of a system occurs
s a result of a communications process. Communications are crucial to the
reservation of the system. Modelski refers to information as the international
ulture and communication which comprise all contacts among states from
liplomacy to the everyday routine communication among states. According
o Rosecrance, communication among the elites of the national units takes
lace within the regulator mechanism. Moreover, Kaplan, Rosecrance, and
Modelski all attach importance to the role of elites. According to Rose-
rance, feelings of insecurity among the elites contribute to instability in the
nternational system. In his work, Modelski gives emphasis to the composition
f the elite, i. e., a singular authority in Agraria or a pluralistic authority in
ndustria, with the latter forming a stabilizing factor in the system. In Kaplan's
nodel, the elites determine whether or not the government of the actor state
vill be directive (authoritarian) or nondirective (democratic). In Kaplan's
nodels, the nature of the governments of national units is of considerable
mportance to the stability of the international system. In contrast, McClelland
loes not address himself specifically to the question of an elite, although he
loes discuss domestic forces which affect the international system.

The ability of actors to mobilize resources and the degree of specializa-
ion and advanced technology are important in the work of each theorist.
[n Rosecrance's model, the availability of disposable resources to the elite is
 dynamic determinant in the international system; that is, it will affect the
tability of the system, since insecure elites will not be able to resist using
esources that can be easily mobilized. In Modelski's models of Agraria and
[ndustria, which respectively are international systems based on agricultural
and industrialized national units, the ability to mobilize resources by the elites
affects the nature of the system. Because of the vast amount of resources
available to the elites of Industria, it is essential to the stability of the system
that the ruling elites be pluralistic in nature and hence subject to democratic
control and that they use available resources for purposes other than the
destruction of neighboring states. In Kaplan's models of the international system, resources and the states' ability to use resources to attain goals are considered as capability variables. According to McClelland, the specialization of
functions leads to an increase in the volume of communications, and makes
necessary a highly-trained elite.

McClelland and, to a lesser extent, Kaplan deal with the impact of domestic groups on the international system. However, Rosecrance and Modelski are concerned with the impact of such domestic forces as nationalism upon the international system. In fact, Rosecrance contends that elites who feel their domestic positions are threatened contribute to a system's instability. Such elites are prone to take aggressive action against other states in order to strengthen their domestic position. According to Modelski, the elite's ability to mobilize domestic forces as well as the homogeneous population of Industria makes possible the articulation of the interests of domestic groups. Kaplan addresses himself to domestic subsystems especially in his hierarchical international and universal international systems.

The capacity of the system to contain and cope with disturbance is of concern to each writer. One of Rosecrance's principal preoccupations is the capacity of the system to contain disturbance, in part through the regulator mechanism. Explicit in Modelski's Industria is the assumption that this model would be better able to cope with disturbance than would be possible under an Agrarian system. Kaplan's concern with this problem is illustrated by his interest in transformation rules, i.e., rules which specify the conditions under which an international system having certain characteristics (e.g., tight bipolar) changes to an international system having other characteristics (e.g. loose bipolar). McClelland writes of the international system as being subject to manipulation and exposed to disturbances. His emphasis on an "open and adaptive" system, as well as the communication of information, suggests a concern with the system's ability to change in order to cope with disturbance.

In short, writers who use systems theory are concerned in varying degree with several categories of questions, concepts, and data: (1) the internal organization and interaction patterns of complexes of elements hypothesized or observed to exist as a system; (2) the relationship and boundaries between a system and its environment and, in particular, the nature and impact of input from and outputs to the environment; (3) the functions performed by systems, the structures for the performance of such functions, and their effect upon the stability of the system; (4) the homeostatic mechanisms available to the system for the maintenance of steady-state or equilibrium; (5) the classification of systems as open or closed, or as organismic or nonorganismic systems; and (6) the structuring of hierarchical levels of systems, the location of subsystems within systems, the patterns of interaction among subsystems themselves, and between subsystems and the system itself.

This latter category may be restated as the problem of level of analysis, including international subsystems, or "subordinate state systems" to which students of international relations have addressed themselves at considerable length over the past generation.[46] (Reference has previously been made to

46. See J. David Singer, "The Level-of-Analysis Problem in International Relations," Klaus Knorr and Sidney Verba, eds. *The International System: Theoretical Essays* (Princeton: Princeton University Press, 1961), pp. 77–92. See

Contending Theories of International Relations

he level-of-analysis problem in Chapter 1.) Several scholars have attempted
o specify patterns of interaction models and political units in the North Atlan-
ic area, and specifically Western Europe, the Middle East, and southern Asia.
Regions have been treated as subsystems of the international system, and
fforts have been made to link integration theory to general systems theory.
Research on international subsystems has had several focal points: (1) an
ttempt to specify as precisely as possible patterns of interaction among units
n one international subsystem; (2) an effort to compare two or more inter-
ational subsystems; and (3) studies of relationships between a subsystem
nd the international system.[47]

CHARLES A. McCLELLAND

One writer in particular, Charles A. McClelland, has attempted linking sys-
ems theory explicitly to the problem of delineating levels of analysis for the
tudy of international relations. McClelland's model of the international sys-
em is an expanded version of two interacting states. He believes that exchanges, transactions, contacts, flows of information, and actions occurring at
he present influence future interactions. The international system is multidimensional in character. In order to understand McClelland's systems framework, it is necessary to imagine nations of the world having a wide range of
official and unofficial contacts with each other. For the most part such contacts
are demand-response relationships, in which an action by one nation elicits
a response from another, in turn calling forth a response from the nation
which initiated the action. Thus interaction between nations forms one level
of analysis for students of international politics. According to McClelland,
conditions and events in the international system result from sources generated within nations, from subsystems within the national unit such as public
opinion, interest groups, and political parties. Therefore, McClelland's model
includes not only interaction at the international level, but interaction between
the national unit and its subsystems. He suggests that a nation's "international
behavior, in the system perspective, is a two-way activity of taking from and
giving to the international environment. All the giving and taking, when con-

International Studies Quarterly, (special
issue on international subsystems) XIII
(December, 1969).

47. For studies on international subsystems, see Michael Brecher, The States of
Asia: A Political Analysis (New York:
Oxford University Press, 1963), pp. 88–
111; Leon N. Lindberg, "The European
Community as a Political System," Journal of Common Market Studies, V (June,
1967), 348–387; Karl Kaiser, "The U.S.
and EEC in the Atlantic System: The

Problem of Theory" in ibid, pp. 388–
425; Stanley Hoffmann, "Discord in
Community: The North Atlantic Area
as a Partial International System," Francis O. Wilcox and H. Field Haviland, Jr.,
The Atlantic Community: Progress and
Prospects (New York: Frederick A.
Praeger, 1963), pp. 3–31; International
Studies Quarterly (special issue on international subsystems) XIII (December,
1969).

sidered together and for all the national actors, is called the international system." [48] A systems framework, McClelland contends, provides an orderly procedure for shifting perspective from one level to another in the study of international politics.

Although the international system is multidimensional, the most promising prospect for theory building lies in the focus of attention upon one level of analysis at a time. McClelland concentrates on interaction between the national units, rather than interaction between the national unit and its domestic sub systems or foreign policy decision-making. He is concerned only with inter action observable outside the "black-boxes" which constitute the national units, with their complex and obscure decision-making processes. In McClelland's scheme, transactions between the national units are recorded and analyzed. Both routine and nonroutine activity between nations may be studied, since the "performance of the participants—the interaction sequences—are reliable indicators of active traits of participating actors . . . . Our basic assumption is that the kind of social organization developed in a nation-state fundamentally conditions its crisis behavior." [49]

In McClelland's own work the "acute international crisis" as a subsystem of the international system, is the object of examination by interaction analysis. He asks the following research questions: Is it possible to detect a "change of state" in the activities of a system in the transition from a noncrisis to a crisis period? Is a designated subsystem that is part of a more general system of action responsive to major disturbances in the general system? McClelland offers three propositions for examination: (1) that acute international crises are "short burst" affairs and are marked by an unusual volume and intensity of events; (2) that the general trend in acute international crises will be toward "routinizing" crisis behavior, that is, dealing with problems by means of increasingly "standard" techniques; and (3) that participants will be reluctant to allow the level of violence to increase beyond that present at the onset of the crisis.

In McClelland's scheme the significant variation in the flow of action within the system is of central interest. McClelland suggests that "information concerning conditions created at a certain moment by the effects of interaction and by factors of the environment is returned to the participating actors. The latter are presumed to receive and process such 'output' information and to feed the processed results (as inputs) into the next phase of participation in the particular and relevant 'system of action,' " [50] In acute international crisis,

48. Charles A. McClelland, *Theory and the International System* (New York: Macmillan Company, 1966), p. 90.

49. Charles A. McClelland, "The Acute International Crisis," Knorr and Verba, *op. cit.*, p. 194.

50. Charles A. McClelland, "The Acute International Crisis," In *ibid.*, p. 194. McClelland's analysis suggests the possibility that in an acute international crisis the intensification of communication which accompanies such a phenomenon might give rise to a condition of "system overload."

sequences of action can be traced since the time span and the focus of inquiry are narrowed. Because there is little delay between demand and response, sequences of action can be examined and patterns ascertained. The objective of the study of acute international crises is to identify patterns of interaction for purposes of comparison in several crises. Thus, McClelland has coded events and traced the sequences of action in crises, focusing in the Berlin crisis on interferences, harassments, and delays on access routes, as well as the responses to these actions: arrests and detainment of personnel, disputes between governing authorities, and decrees, decisions and regulations affecting Western freedom of movement within the city.[51]

RICHARD N. ROSECRANCE

Although students of international relations have traditionally turned to historical materials for the construction and validation of theories, their work has been faulted often for its noncomparability or for failure to develop adequate criteria for the selection of data. Proponents of systemic theories of politics, such as Rosecrance and Kaplan, have made use of historical materials in an effort to construct and validate models of international behavior. Rosecrance bases his systems analysis on the study of nine historical systems.[52] He divides West European history from 1740–1960 into nine periods or systems, each of which is demarcated by significant changes in diplomatic techniques and objectives. In work reminiscent of Arnold Toynbee, because of its emphasis upon the uniformities of history, Rosecrance discerns the existence of recurring phenomena in the nine international systems periods between 1740 and 1960, from which he develops two models. Concerned with the conditions for international stability, he selects as his basic elements: disturbance input, the regulator mechanism which reacts to the disturbance, the environmental restraints which influence the range of possible outcomes, and finally the outcomes themselves. Disturbance input includes such forces as ideologies, domestic insecurity, disparities between nations in resources, and conflicting national interests. The regulator mechanism consists of capabilities such as the Concert of Europe, the United Nations, or an informal consensus which, it is often pointed out by historians, the major European nations shared in the eighteenth century. The third element, the presence of environmental restraints, limits the range of possible outcomes. He judges systems to be equilibrial or

51. Charles A. McClelland, "Access to Berlin: The Quantity and Variety of Events, 1948–1963," J. David Singer, ed., *Quantitative International Politics: Insights and Evidence* (New York: Free Press, 1968), pp. 160–161.

52. Rosecrance lists past international systems as follows: (1) 18th Century, 1740–1789, (2) Revolutionary Imperium, 1789–1814, (3) Concert of Europe, 1814–1822, (4) Truncated Concert, 1822–1848, (5) Shattered Concert, 1848–1871, (6) Bismarckian Concert, 1871–1890, (7) Imperialist Nationalism, 1890–1918, (8) Totalitarian Militarism, 1918–1945, (9) Post-War, 1945–1960.

Systemic Theories of Politics and International Relations

disequilibrial, depending upon whether the regulator or the disturbance was stronger. From these elements, Rosecrance develops and examines four basic determinants for each of his nine systems: elite direction (attitudes), degree of elite control, resources available to the controlling elites, and the capacity of the system to contain disturbances. Given his choice of determinants, it is evident that Rosecrance attaches considerable importance to the domestic sources of international behavior.

Among his domestic determinants Rosecrance emphasizes the elites of national units. Was the elite satisfied with its position domestically or did it feel threatened by events in the international system? Second, the control or security of the elite within the society which it commanded was a determinant in each of Rosecrance's international systems. Did the elites perceive a weakening in their internal position? Third, emphasis is placed upon the availability of disposable resources to the elite and its ability to mobilize them. Finally, Rosecrance views the system's capacity to mitigate and contain disturbances as a determinant.[53]

From Rosecrance's work, it is possible to construct essentially two models of the international system: the first, a model with characteristics of stability. A stable system is based on a comparison of systems I, Eighteenth Century, 1740–1789; III, Concert of Europe, 1814–1822; IV, Truncated Concert, 1822–1848; VI, Bismarckian Concert, 1871–1890; and IX, Post-War, 1945–1960. In these systems the amount of disturbance was at a minimum and the regulator, be it Concert, League or informal consensus, was able to cope with actor disturbance. The elites were satisfied with the status-quo, both within their own respective national units and in the international system in general. In their political views they were not strongly influenced by ideology except, perhaps, in System IX (1945–1960). Even in this system, however, the elites were willing for the most part to resolve problems by means short of war. Because of feelings of relative security, the elites were not tempted to mobilize resources or to use whatever means at their disposal to effect changes in the system. Although a state may have been willing to mobilize resources to improve its position *vis-à-vis* another state, it was not prepared to disrupt the entire system. In a stable system the environmental restraints were usually sufficient to ease whatever disturbance occurred. Territorial ambitions, if they existed, were either transferred to colonial areas, or could be satisfied without affecting the vital interests of other states. Since a bipolar system characterized three of the four unstable periods, it may be inferred that a multipolar system, or perhaps a tripolar system, is characteristic of a stable system. A stable system is one in which there is an emphasis upon diplomacy and other conventional methods of negotiation and the goals of national units are limited. Although a state would not undertake to improve its own position at a cost of disrupting the entire system, it might attempt to do so at the expense

53. Rosecrance, *op. cit.*, pp. 280–296, *passim*.

Contending Theories of International Relations

of only one or two states, but even then not if it was necessary to inflict major losses upon other states.

The characteristics of an unstable system may be derived from a comparison of systems II, Revolutionary Imperium (1789–1814), V, Shattered Concert (1848–1871), VII, Imperialist Nationalism (1890–1918), and VIII, Totalitarian Militarism (1918–1945). In these systems, actor disturbance was high relative to the ability of the regulator to cope with it and the variety of means at the disposal of the regulator was minimal. The elites were dissatisfied with the status quo and harbored feelings of insecurity. They sought to improve their own internal and external positions *vis-à-vis* the international system and other actors. Elites were able to mobilize resources through appeals to nationalism and ideology. Because of their feelings of insecurity, governing elites could often not resist the urge to resort to such appeals. Environmental restraints failed to play a role in restraining disturbances.

Although Rosecrance concludes that it is impossible to predict future events on the basis of a limited number of variables and that those variables with which he was concerned in this study may not be crucial in future international systems, his major conclusion is that there is a correlation between international instability and the domestic insecurity of elites.[54] His work is notable for his effort both to develop and apply a systems framework to the analysis of materials which for the most part have been the preserve of the historian.

GEORGE MODELSKI

Other writers have set forth international system models whose parameters and patterns of interaction are carefully specified. George Modelski presents two models designed to make possible a comparative analysis of international systems. The models represent respectively international systems at each end of a spectrum extending from agrarian to industrial societies. These models draw upon and combine elements of international systems from the past and present, and provide a framework in which processes of change or intermediate systems may be studied in relation to the extremes of the spectrum. In Modelski's view, Agraria corresponds to the twenty-one civilizations studied by Arnold Toynbee, while Industria has no comparable historical counterpart. Modelski's two models are "conceptual devices or constructs which draw upon and combine properties of international systems but do not in themselves necessarily represent any concrete international system." [55] Therefore, an interna-

54. *Ibid.,* p. 304.

55. "Agraria and Industria: Two Models of the International System," in Knorr and Verba, eds., *op. cit.,* p. 124. For an effort to develop a similar typology in the field of public administration, see Fred

W. Riggs, "Agraria and Industria: Toward a Typology of Comparative Administration," William J. Siffin, ed., *Toward the Comparative Study of Public Administration* (Bloomington: Indiana University Press, 1957), pp. 23–116.

tional system in the real world is likely to embody some of the characteristics of both models.

Industria, as an international system, has a large population. Its resources are more easily mobilized than those of Agraria. Society is largely homogeneous with politically conscious citizens and elites who are specialists. Because a person's position depends upon skill and achievement rather than ascriptive values, Industria is a meritocracy. In Industria, world organizations and improved communications networks provide information and contribute to the development of a world culture.[56] In Industria, power is based upon industrial organization. In contrast to Agraria, in Industria the political community is coexistent with the population. There is a level of integration of the masses of people into a common political form which is lacking in Agraria. An industrial society cannot tolerate recourse to war, as Agraria did, as a means of settling grievances because the destructive capabilities of Industria are such that war might result in the total destruction of the society. Because of the vast amount of destructive power at its disposal, bargaining, subtle coercion, and maneuvers, rather than recourse to war, must be used to obtain goals.

Drawing upon Parsons's framework, Modelski suggests that each of his international systems is distinguished by the way in which it performs four basic functions:

> 1. Allocation of Resources. *In Agraria there are minimal allocation structures and fused role functions. Industria has many specialized facilities, including the governments of national units and international organizations, for the allocation of role functions.*
> 2. Authority. *Whereas in Agraria the exercise of authority is the prerogative of sovereigns and princes, and the elite structure is simple, in Industria, there are many elites, whose authority role is based upon achievement.*
> 3. Solidarity. *While a ruling elite of Agraria maintains solidarity by an extended kinship system perpetuated by the inter-marriage of royalty, Industria's leadership achieves cohesiveness through loyalty to a nationalist, universalist order. Rank is determined largely by achievement, and achievement is based upon excellence in science and technology.*
> 4. Culture. *In Agraria culture is communicated and diffused by the courts of the nobles. Industria has superior facilities, including a world press, a diplomatic circuit, and international institutions, for the development of a universal culture.*

Thus Modelski, employing a structural-functional approach akin to that of Parsons, posits that international systems are social systems consisting of sets of objects with relationships among themselves; that all international systems have structures, or relatively stable system responses to the need to satisfy functional requirements; and that the same functional requirements are satis-

56. Modelski, *op. cit.*, pp. 138–139.

Contending Theories of International Relations

fied in all international systems, namely, resource allocation, authority, solidarity, and culture.

MORTON A. KAPLAN

Of all writers Morton A. Kaplan has made the greatest effort to specify rules and patterns of interaction within his models of the international system. According to Kaplan, the classic statement of systems theory is to be found in the work of W. Ross Ashby on the human brain.[57] Although Ashby is concerned with the human brain and Kaplan with international politics, both are preoccupied in their respective fields with a system as a set of interrelated variables, distinguishable from its environment, and with the manner in which the set of variables maintains itself under the impact of disturbances from the environment.

Accordingly, Kaplan has constructed six models of hypothetical international systems which provide a theoretical framework within which hypotheses can be generated and tested.[58] Within each model he has developed five sets of variables: the essential rules, the transformation rules, the actor classificatory variables, the capability variables, and the information variables. The so-called "essential" rules are essential because they describe the behavior necessary to maintain equilibrium in the system.[59] The transformation rules

57. W. Ross Ashby, *Design for a Brain* (New York: John Wiley, 1952). Kaplan makes this assertion in "Systems Theory," James C. Charlesworth, ed., *Contemporary Political Analysis* (New York: Free Press, 1967), p. 150.

58. According to Kaplan: "The conception that underlies *System and Process* is fairly simple. If the number, type and behavior of nations differ over time, and if their military capabilities, their economic assets, and their information also vary over time, then there is some likely interconnection between these elements such that different structural and behaviorial systems can be discerned to operate at different periods of history. This conception may turn out to be incorrect, but it does not seem an unreasonable basis for an investigation of the subject matter. To conduct such an investigation requires systematic hypotheses concerning the nature of the connections of the variables. Only after these are made can past history be examined in a way that illuminates the hypotheses. Otherwise the investigator has no criteria on the basis of which he can pick and choose from among the infinite reservoir of facts available to him. These initial hypotheses indicate the areas of facts which have the greatest importance for this type of investigation; presumably if the hypotheses are wrong, this will become reasonably evident in the course of attempting to use them." Morton A. Kaplan, "The New Great Debate: Traditionalism vs. Science in International Relations," *World Politics,* XX (October, 1967), 8.

59. According to Kaplan: "The models are not equilibrium models in the Parsonian sense. Thus they are not static but respond to change, when it is within specified limits, by maintaining or restoring system equilibrium. Equilibrium does not have an explanatory function within such systems. Rather it is the equilibrium that is to be explained; and the model itself constitutes the explanation by indicating the mechanisms that restore or maintain equilibrium." Morton A. Kaplan, "The Systems Approach to International Politics," Morton A. Kaplan, ed., *New Approaches to International Relations* (New York: St. Martin's Press, 1968), p. 388.

Systemic Theories of Politics and International Relations

specify the changes that take place as inputs other than those necessary for equilibrium enter the system. The actor classificatory variables set forth the structural characteristics of actors. Capability variables indicate armament levels, technologies and other elements of power available to actors. Information variables refer to the levels of communication within the system. The rules, to be specified in greater detail in a later examination of each of his models, refer to the kinds of actors, their capabilities, motivations and goal orientations, their style of political behavior, and the structural characteristics of each of Kaplan's six systems—the balance of power, loose bipolar, tight bipolar, universal, hierarchical, and unit veto—which can be ranged along a scale of integrative activity. The unit veto system is least integrated and the hierarchical system most integrated.

In Kaplan's models, changes in the system are the result of changes in the value of the parameters or constants. He acknowledges that few, if any, existing international systems conform fully with any of his models of hypothetical systems. Nevertheless, he is prepared, so long as the theory set forth in the model explains behavior when "suitable adjustments are made for the parameters of the system," to continue to employ that model. The system has changed when a different theory, or systems model, is needed to account for its behavior. Thus the utility of Kaplan's models lies in the extent to which they permit the student to compare behavior within any given existing international system with one or another of the six models. Moreover, by specifying rules for system change, a step level function (i.e., a system response to a disturbance input of such a nature as to transform the system itself), Kaplan claims to have built into his models a means of understanding how international systems are transformed.

Kaplan's balance of power system resembles the international system that realist writers such as Morgenthau describe.[60] It is distinguished by an international social system, but lacks a political subsystem, since it does not have regularized agencies and methods for making decisions concerning interests beyond these of the component national units. The balance of power system, like the European state system of the nineteenth century, has five major powers, or "essential actors," whose presence is crucial to the operation of the system.

> *The balance of power system in its ideal form is a system in which any combination of actors within alliances is possible so long as no alliance gains a marked preponderance in capabilities. The system tends to be maintained by the fact that even should any nation desire to become predominant itself, it must, to protect its own interests, act to prevent any other nation from accomplishing such an objective. Like Adam Smith's "unseen hand" of competition, the international system*

60. Hans J. Morgenthau, *Politics among Nations,* 4th ed. (New York: Alfred A. Knopf, 1967), pp. 161–211.

is policed informally by self-interest, without the necessity of a political subsystem.[61]

The modal behavior of units is found in Kaplan's rules for the balance of power system: (1) Actors increase their capabilities, but negotiate with each other rather than fight; (2) Actors fight rather than pass up an opportunity to increase their capabilities; (3) Actors stop fighting rather than eliminate another essential actor; (4) Actors oppose any coalition or single actor who threatens to assume a position of predominance within the system; (5) Actors seek to constrain those actors who subscribe to supranational organizational principles; and (6) Actors permit defeated or constrained essential actors to reenter the system as acceptable role partners, or bring a previously inessential actor within the essential actor category.[62]

The second of Kaplan's models, the loose bipolar, resembles in many respects the international system of the post-World War II period. This model includes major bloc actors (such as NATO and the Warsaw Pact), a leading national actor within each bloc (such as the United States and the Soviet Union), nonbloc national actors (such as India); and universal actors (such as the United Nations).

In its operation, the loose bipolar system reflects the internal organization of bloc actors. If both blocs are hierarchical, their membership becomes rigid, and only uncommitted states, by aligning themselves with one bloc or the other, change the existing alignments. If the blocs are not hierarchically organized, the loose bipolar system resembles the balance of power system, although there are fewer shifts in alignment.

Kaplan posits several rules for the loose bipolar system, including: (1) Blocs subscribing to directive hierarchical or mixed hierarchical integrating principles eliminate the rival bloc, negotiate rather than fight, fight minor wars rather than major wars, and fight major wars rather than fail to eliminate the rival bloc; (2) Bloc actors increase their capabilities in relation to those of the opposing bloc; (3) Bloc actors subscribing to nonhierarchical or nondirective hierarchical organizational principles negotiate rather than fight to increase capabilities, but refrain from initiating major wars for this purpose; (4) Bloc actors engage in a major war rather than permit the rival bloc to gain preponderant strength; (5) Bloc members subordinate the objectives of universal actors to the objectives of their bloc; (6) Universal actors reduce the incompatibility between blocs and mobilize nonbloc member national actors against cases of major deviation, such as resorting to force, by a bloc actor.

The tight bipolar system, although Kaplan's third model, is similar, in many

61. Morton A. Kaplan, "Some Problems of International Systems Research," *International Political Communities: An Anthology* (New York: Doubleday and Company, Inc., 1966), p. 478.

62. Kaplan, *System and Process in International Politics*, pp. 22–23.

respects, to the loose bipolar system, but it has important differences. The tight bipolar system has fewer types of actors. The structure of the blocs affects the stability of the system. If both bloc actors are nonhierarchically organized, the system will tend to be transformed to a loose bipolar system. The system is stable if both bloc actors are hierarchically organized. Within the system integrating mechanisms are weak or nonexistent. In this model the rules are the same as the bloc-directed rules of the loose bipolar system.

The universal-international system, the fourth of Kaplan's models, could conceivably develop as a result of the extension of the functions of the universal actor found in the loose bipolar system. The universal-international system differs from other models thus far discussed in that it has as a subsystem a political system which can allocate prestige and rewards both to national actors and individuals according to their "specific achievements rather than because of special qualities they possess, such as race." The universal-international system possesses integrating mechanisms which perform judicial, political, economic and administrative functions. It has the following rules: (1) All national actors attempt to increase their rewards and access to facilities; (2) all national actors attempt to increase the resources and productive base of the international system; (3) when rules (1) and (2) conflict, rule (1) is to be subordinated to (2), and if rule (1) threatens minimal standards of any national actor, it is subordinated to considerations involving the ascriptive base of the total society; (4) all actors use peaceful methods to obtain their objectives; (5) individuals who have functions in organs of the international system make decisions in accordance with requirements of the international system.

In the universal-international system, value structures of the national actors are such that the international system is able to coordinate and integrate them. The international system possesses facilities and resources superior to those of any national actor system and is able to give hope of improvement to underdeveloped national actors. However, this system may be subject to a long period of instability, since it is unlikely initially to have succeeded in integrating the domestic values of the various national actors within a common system. There is the prospect that national actors may wish to change the system to hierarchical, bipolar, or balance of power system because they may not wish to make the necessary changes in their political and social structures or prove unable to make the sacrifices necessary for this type of system to function effectively.[63]

Kaplan's fifth model, the hierarchical international system, may be either nondirective or directive.[64] It will operate directly upon individuals, since national actors will be territorial subdivisions of the international system

---

63. *Ibid.,* pp. 45–58.

64. According to Kaplan: "The nondirective international system functions according to political rules generally op-

erative in democracies. The directive hierarchial system is authoritarian in character." *Ibid.,* p. 48.

rather than independent political systems. Interest groups, rather than national units, are the primary actors. The system will be solidary, linking rewards and access to facilities to the system's criteria. If the hierarchical system is imposed by force upon a bipolar or universal system, it is likely to be a directive rather than a nondirective system. If the hierarchical system is formed as a result of world conquest by a national actor, rewards will be allocated according to ascriptive criteria such as the qualities of the actors, including race and color. If the system is formed under other conditions, rewards may be based upon achievement criteria, as in the case of the universal system. The hierarchical international system is characterized by great stability. Channels of communication facilitate central control, and render almost impossible any attempts by local regions to revolt or secede. Whatever minor changes are made in the distribution of rewards will be functional, rather than territorial. Since there will be no outside political system capable of aiding a localized revolt, once a hierarchical system is established it will become almost impossible to displace it.[65]

In Kaplan's sixth system, the unit veto, there are no universal actors. It is, Kaplan suggests, a Hobbesian system, in which "the interests of all were opposed—were, in fact, at war—but in which each actor responded to the negative golden rule of natural law by not doing to others what he would not have them do to him." [66] The only condition under which the unit veto system is possible is if all actors have weapons capable of destroying any other actor. Even if one actor attacks and destroys another actor, in so doing he may assure his own destruction. So long as national units are prepared to retaliate in case of attack, and their ability to do so forms a credible deterrent to attack by another national unit, the system is stabilized. There is a "stand off" in which the existing state of affairs is preserved. However, the system will be changed if any actor is successfully blackmailed. In this case the number of national units will be reduced. If one member successfully blackmails all other national units, the unit veto system will become a hierarchical system.

Kaplan readily admits that his six systems by no means exhaust the possibilities for useful model building for analytical purposes in international politics. Instead, they represent positions along a spectrum of schemes of international political organization. Moreover, in his scheme national actors are classified according to structural categories: directive or nondirective systems, which in turn may be system dominant or subsystem dominant.

In each of his models Kaplan is concerned with (1) the organizational focus of decisions, including the nature of actors' objectives and the instruments available to attain them; (2) the allocation of rewards, including the extent to which they are allocated by the system or the subsystem; (3) the alignment preferences of actors; (4) the scope and direction of political activity; (5) the flexibility or adaptability of units in their behavior.

65. *Ibid.*, pp. 49–50.   66. *Ibid.*, p. 50.

Kaplan and his associates have only begun the formidable task of "investigating reality" with models set forth in *Systems and Process*. Their objective is to use historical materials for purposes of comparison with systems models. In this research endeavor, the models are tested for formal logical consistency with the uses of mathematical tools and the computer.[67] The model is then compared with historical materials, such as the Chinese warlord system of the early twentieth century and the Italian city-state system of the fourteenth and fifteenth centuries. The author of a study of the Chinese warlord system found that this was "basically a 'balance of power' system operating under many unfavorable parameters." Moreover, this was a "balance of power system in which the actors either deliberately or unwittingly violated many of the essential behavioral rules that are necessary for the stability of such a system." [68] Among the conclusions of a study of the Italian city-state system were that, by and large, essential rules contained in the "balance of power" model were not violated; essential and even nonessential actors were preserved; the territorial capabilities of actors did not change greatly; equilibrium became both less static and less stabile, and inevitably the system disintegrated.[69]

Thus Kaplan's models, although less complex than the international system of the real world, are designed to facilitate comparison with the real world to contribute to a meaningful ordering of data, and to build theory at the macro-level. Only two of them—the balance of power and the loose bipolar—can be clearly discovered in history, but the case can be made that a third model (the unit veto system) is partially validated in the contemporary role of the nuclear powers while a fourth model (the universal-international system) enjoys a kind of quasi-existence in the rhetoric of statesmen and the thinking of intellectuals who assume either that it already exists or that it can and will eventually come into existence.

Theories of Bipolarity, Multipolarity and International Stability

The relationship between the distribution of power and the incidence of war in the international system has been the object of theorizing both in traditional and contemporary writings. Although Kaplan, in his models, has focused on "essential rules" for the operation of several international systems, other scholars, including Karl W. Deutsch, J. David Singer, Kenneth N. Waltz, and Richard N. Rosecrance, have theorized about the implications of multipolarity

67. See Donald L. Reinken, "Computer Explorations of the 'Balance of Power': A Progress Report," Morton A. Kaplan, ed., *New Approaches to International Relations*, pp. 459–481.

68. Hsi-Sheng Chi, "The Chinese Warlord System as an International System." *Ibid.*, p. 424.

69. Winfried Franke, "The Italian City-State System as an International System." *Ibid.*, p. 449.

and bipolarity for the frequency and intensity of war. Deutsch and Singer contend that "as the system moves away from bipolarity toward multipolarity, the frequency of war should be expected to diminish." [70] They assume that coalitions or blocs of nations reduce the freedom of alliance members to interact with outside countries. The greater the number of actors who are not alliance members, the greater the number of possible partners for interaction in the international system. Although alliance membership minimizes both the range and intensity of conflict among those countries which are alliance members, the range and intensity of conflicts with actors outside the alliance is increased.

Although interaction among nations is as likely to be competitive as it is to be cooperative, the more limited the possibility for interaction, the greater the potential for instability. Deutsch and Singer assume that the international system is but a special case of the pluralism model, namely, that "one of the greatest threats to the stability of any impersonal social system is the shortage of alternative partners." Interaction with a great number of nations produces crosscutting loyalties which induce hostility between any single dyad of nations.

Another hypothesis in support of a correlation between the number of actors and war is based on the "degree of attention that any nation in the system may allocate to all of the other nations or to possible coalitions of nations.[71] The greater the number of dyadic relationships, the less the amount of attention which an actor can give to any one dyadic relationship. If some minimal percentage of a nation's external attention is needed for "behavior tending toward armed conflict, and the increase in the number of independent actors diminishes the share that any nation can allocate to any other single actor, such an increase is likely to have a stabilizing effect upon the system." [72] Multipolarity is said to reduce the prospects for an arms race, since a country is likely to respond only to that part of the increase in armaments spending of a rival power which appears to be directed toward it.

70. Karl W. Deutsch and J. David Singer, "Multipolar Power Systems and International Stability," *World Politics,* XVI (April, 1964), 390. For an earlier theoretical analysis of multipolarity and international stability, see Arthur Lee Burns, "From Balance to Deterrence: A Theoretical Analysis," *World Politics,* IX (July, 1957), 494–529. Burns examines several propositions, including the following: The closer the Alliance between any two or more Powers, the greater the increase of opposition or "pressure" (other things being equal) between any one of the two and any third Power or group of Powers; Other things being equal, considerations of long-run security determine an optimum degree of short-run security; any system embodying the balance of power has some intrinsic tendency to diminish the number of its constituent Powers or blocs, and no intrinsic tendency to increase that number; a deterrent state or system will emerge from a power-balancing system whenever the development of military technology makes (1) the physical destruction of all of an opponent's forces impossible, and (2) the physical destruction of his economy very easy.

71. Deutsch and Singer, *op. cit.,* p. 392.

72. *Ibid.,* p. 400.

Empirical studies by Singer and Melvin Small yielded conclusions not fully in support of the hypothesis about bipolarity-multipolarity and the outbreak of war. Analyzing historical data for the period 1815–1945 for possible correlations between alliance aggregation and the onset of war, Singer and Small tested the following hypotheses: (1) the greater the number of alliance commitments in the system, the more war the system will experience; and (2) the closer the system is to bipolarity, the more war it will experience.[73]

For the entire period under examination, the hypothesis about alliance aggregation and the outbreak of war was not confirmed. In the nineteenth century, alliance aggregation and amount of war correlated inversely, while in the twentieth century the variables covaried. In addition, the authors discovered that regardless of "whether we measure amount of war by number of wars, the nation-months involved, or battle deaths incurred, alliance aggregation and bipolarity predict strongly away from war in the nineteenth century and even more strongly toward it in the twentieth." [74] In short, for the period 1815–1899, the evidence presented by Singer and Small failed to support the theory about bipolarity and conflict presented earlier by Deutsch and Singer.

Although such a study using aggregate data can show the existence of correlations, it cannot, as Singer and Small acknowledge, establish a causal relationship. Conceivably, a third variable, such as the perception of national decision-makers, is the causal factor which affects the other two variables. For example, leaders may "step up their alliance building activities as they perceive the probability of war to be rising." [75]

There is little agreement among scholars about the relationship between multipolarity-bipolarity and international stability. In marked contrast to

73. International wars (in which at least one participant on each side is an independent and sovereign member of the international system) with total battle-connected deaths of more than 1,000 were included in the data. To "operationalize" the dependent variable, the duration, magnitude, and intensity of wars were gradated. The magnitude of each war was measured by "the nation-months-of-war measure; the sum of the months which all nations individually experienced as participants in the war." Furthermore, distinction was made between major and minor powers, and their wars and nation-months calculated separately.

To operationalize and quantify this independent variable, namely, "the extent to which alliance commitments reduced the interaction opportunities" two dimensions were considered: (1) the nature of the obligation (whether it was a defense

pact, neutrality pact, or entente); and (2) the nature of the signatories' power status (whether it was between 2 major, 2 minor, or 1 major and 1 minor power).

After the alliances were discovered and classified, the data on each type of alliance for each year were converted into a percentage figure as follows:
  1) % of All in Any Alliance
  2) % of All in Defense Pact
  3) % of Majors in Any Alliance
  4) % of Majors in Defense Pact
  5) % of Majors in Any Alliance with Minor.
J. David Singer and Melvin Small, "Alliance Aggregation and the Onset of War," J. David Singer, ed., *Quantitative International Politics* (New York: The Free Press, 1968), pp. 247–286.

74. *Ibid.,* p. 283.

75. *Ibid.,* p. 284.

Contending Theories of International Relations

Deutsch and Singer, Kenneth Waltz argues that a bipolar international system, with its inherent disparity between the superpowers and the lesser states, is more stabilizing than a multipolar system. Having the capacity to inflict and control violence, the superpowers are "able both to moderate others' use of violence and to absorb possibly destabilizing changes that emanate from uses of violence that they do not or cannot control." [76] Both superpowers, following their instinct for self-preservation, continually seek to maintain a balance of power based upon a wide range of capabilities, including military and technological strength. Military power is most effective when it deters an attack. Hence Waltz sees utility in the maintenance of strength by each of two competing superpowers in a bipolar system, since states "supreme in their power have to use force less often." [77] According to Waltz: "bipolarity is expressed as the reciprocal control of the two strongest states by each other out of their mutual antagonism . . . each is very sensitive to the gains of the other." [78]

Offering an alternative system, Richard N. Rosecrance is critical of both the Deutsch-Singer and Waltz models, respectively, of multipolarity and bipolarity, and argues instead for bi-multipolarity. Criticizing Waltz's formulation of bipolarity, Rosecrance contends that a bipolar world in which the two superpowers are intensely and vitally interested in the outcome of all major international issues is essentially a zero sum game. Hence the motivation for expansion and the potential for conflict between the bloc leaders is greater in a bipolar system than it is in a multipolar world. According to Rosecrance, two contradictory notions of bipolarity are employed in its favor. A strict, zero-sum notion of bipolarity is incompatible with the looser, détente idea of bipolarity. The choice is between a system in which change can take place without drastic action by the two major groups of nations, even though, as a result, disequilibrium can occur; or a system in which a taut balance is maintained by constant counter pressure with great antagonism between the camps." [79]

Although the intensity of conflict may be lower in a multipolar world than in a bipolar system, the frequency of conflict will be greater because of a greater diversity of interests and demands. "If a multipolar order limits the consequences of conflict, it can scarcely diminish their number. If a bipolar system involves a serious conflict between the two poles, it at least reduces or eliminates conflict elsewhere in the system." [80] Another criticism is that, while reducing the significance of any change in the power balance, multipolarity increases the uncertainty as to what the consequences will be. Thus it makes policymaking complex and the achievement of stable results difficult.

76. Kenneth N. Waltz, "International Structure, National Force, and the Balance of World Power," *Journal of International Affairs*, XXI (No. 2, 1967), 229.

77. *Ibid.*, p. 223.

78. *Ibid.*, p. 230.

79. Richard N. Rosecrance, "Bipolarity, Multipolarity, and the Future," *Journal of Conflict Resolution*, X (September, 1966), 318.

80. *Ibid.*, p. 319.

The alternative system proposed by Rosecrance combines the positive features of bipolarity and multipolarity without their attendant liabilities. In bi-multipolarity, "the two major states would act as regulators for conflict in the external areas; but multipolar states would act as mediators and buffers for conflict between the bipolar powers. In neither case would conflict be eliminated, but it might be held in check." [81] The bipolar nations, and in particular the superpowers, would seek to restrain each other from attaining predominance, while acting together from a mutual interest in restraining conflict or challenge in the multipolar region of the globe. The multipolar states, although having rivalries stemming from a diversity of national perspectives and interests, would have a common interest in resisting the ambitions of the bipolar powers. Therefore, the probability of war would be lower in a bimultipolar system than in either a strictly bipolar or multipolar system. Nevertheless he concludes that the increase of multipolarity would enhance the prospects for détente between the superpowers, and thus for collaboration between them on the resolution of problems of a multipolar nature.

As an alternative to each of the foregoing models, Oran R. Young, associate professor of politics at Princeton University, suggests the need for a model which emphasizes "the growing interpenetration of the global or system-wide axes of international politics on the one hand and several newly emerging but widely divergent regional areas or subsystems on the other hand." [82] Critical of the bipolar and multipolar models for their focus on essentially structural problems to the neglect of the dynamics of international systems, Young develops a "discontinuities model" which encompasses the concurrent influence of global and regional power processes in patterns that are strongly marked by elements of both congruence and discontinuity.[83] Young uses the concepts of congruence and discontinuity to refer to the degree to which "patterns of political interests and relationships of power are similar or dissimilar as between the global area and various regional areas and as between the different regional areas themselves." [84] Some actors, including the superpowers, and certain issues, such as communism, nationalism, and economic development, are relevant throughout the international system. Yet the regional subsystems of the international system have unique features and patterns of interaction. Young proposes a model in which the existence of discontinuities is emphasized. The discontinuities model is designed to generate useful insights about the variety and complexity of interpenetration among subsystems, the trade-offs and the possibilities for manipulation across subsystems, the problems of incompatibility of the actors with systemwide interests, and the relationships between various subsystems and the global patterns of international politics.

81. *Ibid.,* p. 322.

82. Oran R. Young, "Political Discontinuities in the International System." *World Politics,* XX (April, 1968), 369.

83. *Ibid.,* p. 370.

84. *Ibid.*

Although general systems theory has had such an impact as to make it the dominant contemporary approach to the study of politics, it is not without its critics. According to Harold and Margaret Sprout, some systems theorists (of whom they cite McClelland as an example) "explicitly introduce the 'organismic' concept (reminiscent of Hegelian doctrine) into their discussions of the state and the international system." Although they acknowledge that "most systems theorists would stop far short of claiming that social and biological structures and functions are isomorphic in any but a purely metaphysical sense," the Sprouts question "whether one derives clearer and richer insights into the operations of political organizations by endowing them even metaphorically with pseudobiological structures and pseudopsychological functions." [85] The Sprouts caution against the reification of abstractions.

Another critic, Stanley Hoffmann, contends that systems theory does not provide a framework for achieving predictability. By combining the ideal of a deductive science with the desire to achieve predictability, Hoffmann claims that systems theorists become tautological.

If one builds a model of the behavior of certain groups (for instance nations) based on a set of hypotheses about the variables which are supposed to determine the behavior of the groups, if, further, some of these hypotheses are highly questionable, and if, finally, the model rests on the assumption that these groups are interchangeable, then the "predictions" about the groups' behavior will be a mere restatement in the future tense of the original hypotheses, and thus comprise a totally arbitrary set of propositions about the groups concerned. Such is the danger of "formal models of imaginary worlds, not generalizations about the real world." It is the triumph of form over substance.[86]

In Hoffmann's critique is the contention that systems theorists use inappropriate techniques borrowed from other disciplines such as sociology, economics, cybernetics, biology and astronomy. At the same time, Hoffmann faults models which posit specific patterns of interaction, such as those of Kaplan and Modelski, for being deficient in empirical referents.

85. Harold and Margaret Sprout, *The Ecological Perspective on Human Affairs with Special Reference to International Politics* (Princeton: Princeton University Press, 1965), p. 208; Harold and Margaret Sprout, *An Ecological Paradigm for the Study of International Politics,* Research Monograph No. 30, Center of International Studies, Princeton University (1968), pp. 2–10.

86. Stanley Hoffmann, "Theory as a Set of Questions," Stanley Hoffmann, ed., *Contemporary Theory in International Relations.* The quotation in this excerpt is from Ralph Dahrendorf, "Out of Utopia: Toward a Reorientation of Sociological Analysis," *American Journal of Sociology,* LXIX (September, 1958), 120.

The construction of purely abstract hypotheses based on a small number of axioms, from which a number of propositions are deduced, either is a strange form of parlor game, too remote from reality to be "testable," or else rests on postulates about the behavior of the included variables, which are either too arbitrary or too general: the choice is between perversion and platitude.[87]

Hoffmann contends that systems models, because they aim at a high level of generalization and use tools from other disciplines, do not "capture the stuff of politics." The emphasis of many systems models on communications theory reduces men and societies to communications systems to the relative neglect of the substance of the messages which these networks carry. Moreover, the tendency to reduce a theory to as few hypotheses as possible "and to prefer a single hypothesis to a complex one, because such simplicity makes a theory easier to use even though it might imply sheer formalism and the tendency to reduce politics to what it is not, entail a loss of such vital elements as institutions, culture, and the action of individuals as autonomous variables rather than social atoms." [88] In response to Hoffmann's critique, it may be suggested that proponents of systems theory, because they are preoccupied with the development of macro-theory, do not concern themselves with many substantive problems, the study of institutions, or the "stuff of politics." But this is not to suggest that systems theorists necessarily hold that such studies have no place in the field of international relations. For the quantitative study of politics, systems theory presents problems of operationalization. It is often difficult to develop operational indicators for the verification of concepts contained in systems theory. Moreover, there is disagreement about the extent to which, in the relative absence of empirical studies using hypotheses from systems theory, it is possible to develop criteria of significance in order to judge isomorphic relationships. In addition to this criticism of fundamental proportions because of the importance of isomorphisms in systems theory, there is an apparent lack of hypotheses and propositions except at an abstract level.[89]

Because of its emphasis upon notions of stability, equilibrium, steady-state, and pattern maintenance, systems theory has been criticized for its alleged ideological bias in favor of the status quo, although equilibrium theory does not connote a bias against change. This criticism has been leveled against structural-functionalism in particular, although in response Merton has argued that its proponents could be accused of having a bias in favor of change because of the essentially mechanistic nature of structural-functional analysis and its susceptibility, therefore, to social engineering.[90]

So-called systemic studies have been faulted for having failed allegedly either

87. Stanley Hoffmann, "International Relations: The Long Road to Theory," James N. Rosenau, ed., *International Politics and Foreign Policy* (New York: Free Press of Glencoe, 1961), p. 426.

88. *Ibid.*, p. 48.

89. See Young, *Systems of Political Science*, pp. 24–26.

90. See Merton, *Social Theory and Social Structure*, pp. 37–42.

to specify or to clarify adequately their epistemological bases. Without such preliminary investigation, writers on systems theory have turned at an early stage of their work to substantive statements about power and stability and without having set forth definitions or clearly specified variables. According to Oran Young, such a tendency to dispense with preliminaries "leads to obscurity with regard to conceptual choices" and to ambiguities and confusion within the works of a single writer.[91] For example, there is confusion among writers about the distinction between concrete and analytical constructs, the relevance of concepts such as environment, and the use of organismic analogies. There is disagreement among students of systems theory about deductive and inductive studies, quantitative techniques for the manipulation of data, and the relative merits of comparative analyses and historical studies.[92] Thus the problems of definition, scope and method which divide proponents of systems theory resemble those which beset the study of international relations and political science. Because of such discord among students of systems theory, its contribution to the methodological and conceptual advance of international relations is uncertain. But undoubtedly the comprehensiveness of systems theory will continue to attract the attentive effort of scholars who are seeking powerful international theories at the macro-level.

91. Oran R. Young, *A Systemic Approach to International Politics,* Research Monograph No. 33, Center of International Studies (Princeton University, 1968), p. 1.

92. *Ibid.,* pp. 2–3.

CHAPTER 5
The Older Theories of Conflict

Prerequisites of a General Theory of Conflict

At this time no single general theory of conflict exists which is acceptable to social scientists in the several disciplines, much less to authorities in other scientific fields from which analogous concepts might be borrowed. The student of human conflict can gain insights into the phenomenon from a wide variety of intellectual disciplines. If a comprehensive general theory should ever be developed, it would require inputs from biology, psychology, social psychology, sociology, anthropology, history, political science, geography, economics, communications and organization theory, games and simulation theory, strategic and decision-making theory, integration theory and systems theory—even ethical philosophy and religious-theological reflection.

Until recently, authorities in each of these fields have tended to approach the phenomenon of conflict within the confines of their own discipline. Each field has adhered to its own ways of perceiving, defining, classifying, correlating, measuring and evaluating social phenomena. Within the last decade, the pattern has changed remarkably. Interdisciplinary approaches are under way. Social scientists now borrow insights, methodologies and analogies (hopefully isomorphic) from related fields—and sometimes undiscriminatingly from fields still difficult to relate. Nevertheless, most students still agree that synthesizing is a long and difficult process. There is considerably less agreement that within the foreseeable future—say, within the intellectual lifespan of the current generation of students—the social sciences will achieve an aesthetically and scientifically unified general theory capable of *explaining* "why men fight." We cannot, within the realm of science, explain unless we can predict and control. If there are any satisfying explanations which go beyond human capabilities of prediction and control, we cannot call them "scientific."

The Nature of Conflict

The term *conflict* usually refers to a condition in which one identifiable group of human beings (whether tribal, ethnic, linguistic, cultural, religious, socio-economic, political or other) is engaged in conscious opposition to one or more other identifiable human groups because these groups are pursuing what are or appear to be incompatible goals. Lewis A. Coser (1913–   ), professor of sociology at Brandeis University, defines conflict as a "struggle over values and claims to scarce status, power and resources in which the aims of the opponents are to neutralize, injure or eliminate their rivals." [1] Conflict is an interaction involving humans; it does not include the struggle of man against his physical environment. Conflict implies more than mere competition. Men may compete with each other for something that is in shortage without being fully aware of their competitors' existence, or without seeking to prevent the competitors from achieving their objectives. Competition shades off into conflict when the parties try to enhance their own position by reducing that of others, try to thwart others from gaining their own ends, and try to put their competitors "out of business" or even to destroy them. Conflict may be violent or nonviolent (i.e., in terms of physical force), dominant or recessive, controllable or uncontrollable, resolvable or insoluble under various sets of circumstances. Conflict is distinct from "tensions" insofar as the latter term usually implies latent hostility, fear, suspicion, the perceived divergence of interests, and perhaps the desire to dominate or gain revenge, but it does not necessarily extend beyond attitudes and perceptions to encompass actual overt opposition and mutual efforts to thwart one another. Tensions often precede and always accompany the outbreak of conflict, but they are not the same as conflict, and are not always incompatible with cooperation. The "causes" of tension, however, are probably closely related to the "causes" of conflict. Moreover, if tensions become powerful enough they themselves may become a contributory or preliminary "cause" of the occurrence of conflict insofar as they affect the decision-making process.

What Coser provides above is a sociological definition. He is interested in conflict between groups. Other analysts insist that the term must embrace not only intergroup but interpersonal and intrapersonal phenomena. Society would not have to be concerned about conflict within the individual if it were not for the plausible assumption that there is a significant relation between conflicts within the psychic structure of the individual and conflict in the external social order. No theory of conflict can ignore this relationship. This is not to suggest that all internal conflicts can be explained only in terms of external forces, or that all external conflicts can be explained only in terms of inner psychic

1. Lewis A. Coser, *The Functions of Social Conflict* (New York: Free Press, 1956), p. 3.

forces. The internal and the external can never be completely separated. Neither can the one ever be reduced completely to the other and derived solely from it. Psychological states alone cannot explain social behavior, and social conditions alone cannot explain individual behavior.

Micro- and Macro-Theories of Conflict

Most social sciences can be roughly divided into two groups, depending upon whether they adopt the "macro" or the "micro" approach to the study of the human universe. Do we seek the origins of conflict in the nature of man or in his institutions? Generally speaking, psychologists, social psychologists, biologists, games theorists and decision-making theorists take as their point of departure the behavior of individuals, and from this they draw inferences to the behavior of the species. Moreover, sociologists, anthropologists, geographers, organization and communication theorists, political scientists and international relations analysts and systems theorists typically examine conflict at the level of groups, collectivities, social institutions, social classes, large political movements, religious or ethnic entities, nation-states, coalitions and cultural systems. Some scholars—economists, for example—might divide their efforts between the macro and the micro dimensions. One historian might prefer to study the clash of nation-states, while another might prefer to concentrate on the unique factors in the personality, background and crisis behavior of an individual statesman that prompted him to opt for war or peace in a specific set of circumstances.

Historically, the intellectual chasm between the macro and the micro perspectives of human conflict was nowhere better illustrated than in the earlier polarity of psychology and sociology. The former analyzed conflict from a knowledge of individual, the latter from a knowledge of collective behavior. The psychologist tended to approach human problems as arising from the inner psychic structure of the individual, from where he thought that complexes, tensions and other disorders were projected into the external social situation. The sociologist, conversely, was disposed to begin his analysis of all human problems at the level of social structures and institutions, and to trace the effects of disorders at that level back to the psychic life of individuals. The sharpness of the cleavage as it was perceived around the turn of the century is reflected in Émile Durkheim's statement that "every time that a social phenomenon is directly explained as a psychic phenomenon, one may be sure that the explanation is false." [2] The longstanding antipathy of Freudian anal-

2. Quoted in Abram Kardiner and Edward Preble, *They Studied Man* (New York: New American Library [Mentor Books], 1963), p. 102. Elsewhere Durkheim wrote: "Social facts do not differ from psychological facts in quality

ysis toward the Marxian dialectic (so severe that for several decades Freudian psychology was completely taboo in the Soviet Union) provides a well-known if somewhat extreme example of the divergent perspective of the two fields.[3]

In the twentieth century, especially in the last two decades, the fields have narrowed the distance between them. Psychologists have recognized the importance of institutions, groups and the total cultural environment in the shaping of the individual's psychic life. For their part, sociologists have paid increasing attention to the role of psychic factors in social processes. Social psychologists, in particular, have sought to bridge the gap between the two parent disciplines. But it would be going too far to conclude that the gap has yet been fully bridged, for social psychologists still contend that they are more interested in individual than in collective behavior.[4] Nevertheless, increasing numbers of social scientists are becoming convinced that it is impossible to construct an adequate theory of conflict without fusing the macro and the micro dimensions into a coherent whole.[5]

Interpersonal Conflict and International Conflict

In any event, social psychologists are more hesitant today than were their predecessors two or three decades ago to extrapolate the explanations of complex social behavior—particularly at the level of international relations—from their knowledge of individual psychic behavior. In the past, some psychologists who were concerned with the problem of conflict assumed too readily that the explanation of group aggression is a mere corollary of the explanation of individual aggression. They took the Platonic notion that the state is the individual "writ large" and converted this into a pseudoscientific analogy under which society came to be uncritically regarded as the psychological organism "writ large." Social psychologists are now much less confident in this respect. J. K. Zawodny, professor of political science at the

---

only: *They have a different substratum; they evolve in a different milieu; they depend on different conditions. . . . The mentality of groups is not the same as that of individuals; it has its own laws.*" Author's preface to the second edition, *The Rules of Sociological Method*, S. A. Solvay and J. K. Mueller, trans., G. E. G. Catlin, ed. (Glencoe, Ill.: Free Press, 1938), p. xlix.

3. See Reuben Osborn, *Freud and Marx* (London: Victor Gollancz, Ltd., 1937), and *Marxism and Psycho-Analysis* (London: Barrie and Rockliff, Ltd., 1965).

4. See the editor's introduction in Harold Proshansky and Bernard Seidenberg, eds., *Basic Studies in Social Psychology* (New York: Holt, Rinehart and Winston, 1965), pp. 4–5.

5. See, e.g., the collection of essays from various social science disciplines in Elton B. McNeil, ed., *The Nature of Human Conflict* (Englewood Cliffs, N.J.: Prentice-Hall, 1965); also J. David Singer, "Man and World Politics: The Psycho-Cultural Interface," *Journal of Social Issues*, XXIV (July, 1968), 127–156.

University of Pennsylvania, has noted that "while there is a remarkable massing of data, particularly for individual behavior, scientists are justifiably cautious against inferring applicable parallels between patterns of behavior in an individual, a group, and a nation." [6] Stephen Withey, professor of psychology and program director of the Institute of Social Research at the University of Michigan, and Daniel Katz, professor of psychology at the University of Michigan, have warned against the attempt to "explain the functioning of social systems by a simple reduction of a macroscopic process to a similar microscopic process." [7] Herbert C. Kelman, professor of social ethics at Harvard University, has also pointed out that much earlier writing on war and peace by psychologists and psychiatrists was not germane to the interactions of nation-states. Kelman holds that the earlier writers tended to overemphasize individual aggressive impulses. They took it for granted that the behavior of states is merely the aggregate of individual behaviors, ignoring the fact that individuals differ widely in their roles, interests and ability to influence final decisions. The behavior of such a large collectivity as a nation, according to Kelman, cannot be considered a direct reflection of the motives of either its citizens or its leaders.

Kelman suggests that there can be no such thing as an autonomous psychological theory of war and international relations, but only a general theory of these phenomena in which the findings of psychology play their part. Although in war many individuals engage in aggressive behavior, they do not necessarily act from aggressive motives. For strategic reasons leaders may behave aggressively, and the population of a state may manifest such behavior in order to conform socially. Kelman acknowledges that from the findings of psychology valuable insights about international relations can be gained. However, only by analyzing international relations, not by automatically applying psychological findings about the individual, can we identify those points at which such application is relevant. Kelman defines war as a societal and intersocietal action conducted within a national and international political context. Of crucial importance in the study of international relations is the process by which nations develop their national policies and decide upon war. In part, such an explanation includes the motivations and perceptions of individuals as policymakers and relevant publics playing various roles as part of a larger society. But Kelman cautions that psychological analysis is useful to the study of aggressive behavior in an international context only if we know where and how such individuals fit into the larger political and social framework of the nation and the international system as well as the constraints under which they operate. [8]

6. J. K. Zawodny, *Man and International Relations* (San Francisco: Chandler Publishing Company, 1967), I, 2.

7. Stephen Withey and Daniel Katz, "The Social Psychology of Human Conflict," Elton B. McNeil, ed., *The Nature of Human Conflict* (Englewood Cliffs, N.J.: Prentice-Hall, 1965), p. 65.

8. Herbert C. Kelman, "Social-Psychological Approaches to the Study of Inter-

Contending Theories of International Relations

Most specialists in the fields of political science and international relations would heartily endorse Kelman's conclusion, which is pertinent not only to the problem of international war but to all forms of large-scale social conflict that have engrossed many American scholars in recent years—such as revolutions, coups, insurgencies and civil disorders. Psychological factors alone might go a long way toward explaining instances of anomic violence (i.e., apparently spontaneous and irrational outbursts by either a crowd or an individual) but even in these cases social scientists are now more wary of the "fallacy of the single factor." At more complex levels of politicized conflict, where violence reflects to a much greater degree planning, organization, management and perhaps even institutionalization, the need for circumspection in the explanation of phenomena by reference to purely psychological factors becomes commensurately greater.

Conflict and Social Integration

Social scientists are divided on the question whether social conflict should be regarded as something rational, constructive and socially functional or something irrational, pathological and socially dysfunctional. Most Western psychologists and social psychologists in modern times, for example, seem inclined to regard all violent forms of politicized aggression as irrational and undesirable. Virtually all law-oriented thinkers and most ethical philosophers would agree with them on this.[9] By way of contrast, most modern sociologists and anthropologists both in Europe and America (with the notable exception of the Parsonian school) have been willing to attribute a constructive purpose to conflict, insofar as it helps to establish group boundaries, strengthens group consciousness and sense of self-identity, and contributes toward social integration, community-building and economic development.[10] Many economists

national Relations," Herbert C. Kelman, ed., *International Behavior: A Social-Psychological Analysis* (New York: Holt, Rinehart and Winston, 1965), pp. 5–6. See also the references to the work of Werner Levi in the following chapter.

9. By way of exception, however, it should be noted that Western moralists are under increasing pressure to distinguish between justifiable and unjustifiable violence, including revolutionary terror. Whereas the traditional Christian doctrine was that only the public authority of government could legitimately invoke the use of force against human life, today in some quarters the assumption is growing that the use of force by governmental authority is usually presumptively unjust whereas revolutionary violence against an unjust established system is not only permitted but necessary. Since 1966, *Worldview,* a publication of the Council on Religion and International Affairs, has devoted several articles to the moral doctrine of revolutionary violence. See especially the October, 1968 issue devoted to "Revolution and Violence."

10. See M. Jane Stroup, "Problems of Research on Social Conflict in the Area of International Relations," *Journal of Conflict Resolution,* IX (September,

and political scientists would undoubtedly regard violent conflict as irrational, while others would judge it "good" or "bad" depending upon the context in which it arises, the economic issues or political values at stake, the costs incurred, and the net economic or political outcome for the contesting groups, the nation and the international system. Games theorists, strategists and decision-making analysts might emphasize the rational elements involved in wishing and planning for a "win" or the accomplishment of an objective through the waging of conflict, but they would readily concede that irrational forces and erroneous perceptions can significantly influence the calculations of "players" who opt for war or revolution.

Varieties of Conflict

Several other salient questions occur at the outset of our inquiry. Should we study the phenomenon of conflict in terms of conscious motivations? Do men

1965), 413–417. See also Coser, *op. cit.,* pp. 15–38; Jessie Bernard, "Parties and Issues in Conflict," *Journal of Conflict Resolution,* I (June, 1957), 111–121; and Raymond W. Mack and Richard C. Snyder, "The Analysis of Social Conflict—Toward an Overview and Synthesis," *ibid.,* I (June, 1957), 212–248. For the argument that Talcott Parsons's "structural-functional" approach, relegating conflict to the realm of the abnormal, deviant and pathological, renders itself incapable of explaining social change and conflict, see Ralf Dahrendorf, "Toward a Theory of Social Conflict," *Journal of Conflict Resolution,* II (June, 1958), 170–183. According to Dahrendorf, Parsons was more interested in the maintenance of social structures and order than in change. The Parsonians focused attention upon problems of adjustment rather than of change. For them, social conflict was essentially disruptive and dysfunctional. Dahrendorf in his sociology stresses change rather than persisting configurations; conflict rather than integration; constraint rather than consensus. He presents his postulates not to overturn the Parsonian view but rather to complement it with an organic model of different emphases. He believes that neither model alone, but only the two taken synthetically, can exhaust social reality and supply us with a complete theory of society in its changing as well as in its enduring aspects. For the earlier views of the German sociologist Georg Simmel, see

Nicholas J. Spykman, *The Social Theory of Georg Simmel* (New York: Atherton Press, 1966), especially pp. 3–127; Lewis A. Coser, ed., *Georg Simmel* (Englewood Cliffs, N.J.: Prentice-Hall, 1965), especially pp. 1–77. See also *Conflict,* trans. by Kurt H. Wolff, in *Conflict* and *The Web of Group Affiliations* (Glencoe, Ill.: Free Press, 1955), p. 13. Simmel wrote: "Just as the universe needs 'love and hate,' that is, attractive and repulsive forces, in order to have any form at all, so society, too, in order to attain a determinate shape, needs some quantitative ratio of harmony and disharmony, of association and competition, of favorable and unfavorable tendencies." (*Ibid.,* p. 15) "A certain amount of discord, inner divergence and outer controversy is organically tied up with the very elements that ultimately hold the group together . . ." (pp. 17–18). Even in relatively hopeless situations, the opportunity to offer opposition can help to render the unbearable bearable: "opposition gives us inner satisfaction, distraction and relief, just as do humility and patience under different psychological conditions." (p. 19) See also R. C. North and others, "The Integrative Functions of Conflict," *Journal of Conflict Resolution,* IV (September, 1960), 355–374, and Lewis A. Coser, "Some Social Functions of Violence," *Annals of the American Academy of Political and Social Science,* CCCLXIV (March, 1966), 8–18.

eally fight about what they say they are fighting about? Or must we go beyond tated reasons, regard them with the greatest suspicion as mere self-rationali- ations, and try to penetrate to the "real"—i.e., unconscious, murky and ordid impulses which drive men to aggressive behavior? Is this a false dichot- omy? Probably. If we look carefully, we shall see that micro scientists are more inclined to probe beneath the surface into the unconscious, the innate, he "instinctive" (to use an obsolete term), whereas macro scientists are some- what more willing to lend credence to conscious motivations, for these latter pertain to thought, language and communications patterns which, in contrast to internal psychic forces, are products of society. Given man's nature as a symbolic animal, words are crucial links between the unconscious and the conscious, between macro and micro.

International war is one form of social conflict—undoubtedly the most important single form in terms of its potential consequences for man in the nuclear age. But there are many other forms of social conflict—civil war, revo- lution, coup, guerrilla insurgency, political assassination, sabotage, terror, riots, demonstrations, strikes and strike-breaking, threats, displays of force, formal protests, economic sanctions and reprisals, psychological warfare, propaganda, legislative lobbying for contrary purposes, vendettas, tavern brawls, labor-management disputes, flareups at collegiate sports events, di- vorce contests and legal wrangling over the custody of children, student sei- zure of university buildings, intrafamily fights, and felonious assault or homicide.

A crucial question, which arises frequently in the social sciences regardless of the phenomenon under investigation, is this: Are we dealing with the *one* or the *many*? Can we understand war as a separate conflict phenomenon in isolation, or must we study it as one highly organized manifestation, at a specific social-structural level, of a general phenomenon? Social scientists are far from agreement as to whether human conflict can be satisfactorily ex- plained as a continuum in which violent outbursts differ only by such acci- dents as the nature of the parties, the size, the duration, the intensity, the nature of the issues and the objectives sought, the processual modes of con- flict, the weapons employed, and so forth, but not in their underlying "causes," or whether human conflict is an indefinite series of discrete phenomena each of which, despite a superficial external resemblance to the others, requires its own unique theoretical explanation.

Should we try to explain religious strife in Northern Ireland according to the same general theory of conflict that we would use to explain the Mideast June 1967 war, food riots in India, a guerrilla insurgency in Angola, a taxicab rate war in Chicago, or a general strike of workers and students in France? Does conflict differ by type? If so, how many types are there?

The answer is that we do not know partly because it was only during the decade of the 1960s that American social scientists in any substantial numbers became seriously interested in applying quantitative methodologies to the study of such phenomena as "internal war," "low-level" violence and "civil strife." [11] Social scientists have not yet come forth with a generally accepted taxonomy for distinguishing, classifying and arranging coherently various types of conflict. Many proposals have been offered. But at the present time, we still lack universal crosscultural classifications. What we cannot classify, we cannot measure, and what we cannot measure we cannot correlate. In fact we can hardly gather data pertaining to human conflict. The problems of data-gathering are very serious, much more serious than social scientists who study the phenomenon of conflict on an international scale usually care to admit.[12]

As to the question whether each form of conflict is unique and whether all forms of conflict can be incorporated into a unified explanatory scheme, the authors still maintain an open mind. They would admit that in some respects there does seem to be a universal phenomenon of conflict. Certainly the history of mankind up to the present time would indicate that conflict in one form or another is a permanent and ubiquitous phenomenon in the social universe—an apparently inescapable aspect of the human condition. Religious prophets may envisage an era in which men are no longer given to war; utopians may describe a halcyon age in which reason has eliminated violence; and the revolutionary children of the Enlightenment may speak confidently of the "final conflict" which will usher in the era of peace, justice, plenty, knowledge and human perfection. Even the most objective social scientists usually have their own mystical or philosophical or political preconceptions of what the ideal world ought to be. But insofar as they weigh empirical evidence, they are likely to predict the indefinite continuation of conflict in myriad modes. The authors agree with Kenneth Boulding's contention that it is important to examine both the similarities and the differences in the various types of conflict, and that it is possible for social scientists eventually to derive a general theory of conflict from diverse sources and disciplines.[13]

The Older Theories of War, its Causes and its Laws

Some of man's earlier "prescientific" efforts to arrive at theoretical explanations of war and conflict now strike social scientists as unsophisticated. But

11. See the editor's introduction in Harry Eckstein, ed., *Internal War: Problems and Approaches,* New York: Free Press of Glencoe, 1964, p. 1; and Ted Robert Gurr, "Psychological Factors in Civil Violence," *World Politics,* XX (January, 1968), 245–246. See also the references to the studies of conflict behavior within and between nations by Rudolph Rummel, Raymond Tanter and Ted Robert Gurr in Chapter 8 below, p. 235.

12. See Jessie Bernard, "Parties and Issues in Conflict," *Journal of Conflict Resolution,* I (June, 1957), 111–121; Raymond W. Mack and Richard C. Snyder, "The Analysis of Social Conflict—Toward an Overview and Synthesis," *ibid.,* 212–248; and Clinton F. Fink, "Some Conceptual Difficulties in the Theory of Social Conflict," *ibid.,* XII (December, 1968), 412–460. The latter is the most comprehensive summary of the problem yet published.

13. Kenneth E. Boulding, *Conflict and Defense: A General Theory* (New York: Harper and Brothers, 1962), p. 2.

some of the older theories are still perceptive and useful, insofar as they reflect conscious motivations for and rationalizations of war, and thus serve to remind contemporary man of certain aspects of the phenomenon which, in his preoccupation with underlying forces and more rigorous methodologies, the intellectual is often prone to ignore. Whereas modern social scientists often approach the study of conflict through mathematical models which are abstracted (and thus removed) from experience, earlier thinkers often examined conflict at a more "natural" and less artificial level of immediate human observation.

War between societies is one of mankind's oldest scourges. It is the form of conflict to which philosophers in previous ages have most often addressed themselves. If today we are not impressed with the "scientific" profundity achieved by the great minds of Western culture prior to the nineteenth century in their reflections on the problem of war, we should remember two facts: 1) they possessed a relatively small data base and crude methodology for performing scientific analysis; 2) they were much more interested in religious and philosophical evaluations (or what we would now call "normative analysis") than in "scientific" explanations of human social behavior inferred from empirical evidence. For millenia before the rise of Darwinism, men had been convinced of the reality of good and evil, of the "why and wherefore" which move men to act in a moral universe of rational causality which is but a reflection of the Divine.[14] Men enjoyed freedom of choice, and they were responsible for their decisions. The causes of war lay deep in the wills of individuals, whose motives were good or bad. War, then, resulted from a moral deficiency in man. Plato held that men go to war simply because they are unwilling to live within the limits of necessity; since men refuse to live like pigs and demand a luxurious existence, even an ideal republic must contain military guardians to defend the polity against external aggressors.[15]

WAR IN THE ANCIENT RELIGIOUS CIVILIZATIONS

In nearly all the prescientific religious civilizations, the problem of war was recognized, at least by some thinkers, as one of spiritual and moral dimensions. Poets were prompted by the specter of social conflict to ponder what man has made of man. Religious teachers cautioned rulers to be slow in resorting to force, lest they become indistinguishable from savage beasts. Philosophers and legalists condemned certain modes of warfare as immoral, illegal, or uncivilized. Prophets held forth visions of a day when swords would be beaten into ploughshares and men would no longer be given to war. Thus, we

14. See Daniel Lerner, "On Cause and Effect," the introduction to the work which he edited, *Cause and Effect* (New York: Free Press, 1965), especially pp. 1–5.

15. Plato, *The Republic,* Charles M. Bakewell, ed. (New York: Charles Scribner's Sons, 1956), Book II, pp. 69–71.

might say that the efforts to understand and control conflict are very old, but throughout history the path of intellectual comprehension lay through the conscience of the individual decision-maker, who in all ages has heard ethical teachers counsel against excessive reliance on arms or preach a doctrine of benevolence toward other living beings.

In ancient China, Confucius and Mencius warned rulers not to engage in aggressive wars. Mo-Ti preached a doctrine of universal love with which the waging of war between states was deemed incompatible. According to Lao Tsu, anyone who lived in accordance with the Tao, or the "way of original simplicity," must abstain from every form of self-assertiveness, including war. Far from taking delight in conquest or enjoyment in the slaughter of men, he viewed military victory as a cause for sorrow rather than exultation.[16] It sometimes comes as a surprise to learn that ancient Indian culture was more militarist and less pacifist than Chinese in the expression of its ideals. There were, of course, some Hindu and Buddhist teachers who protested against war on pragmatic grounds, but even Buddhist rulers took war for granted as a natural political phenomenon. *Ahimsa* (or harmlessness toward all living things) is an ancient Indian doctrine, now famous as the source from which Gandhi in modern times has derived the creed of nonviolence, but in the ancient period it was never taken to forbid the waging of war.[17] Neither in China nor in India (with the notable exception of Asoka) did rulers generally shun war for ethical reasons. More often than not they followed the advice of Kuan Chung or Kautilya—"The Machiavellis of the East" who stressed the strategic elements of power, foreign policy and war.[18]

16. See Mousheng Lin, *Men and Ideas: An Informal History of Chinese Political Thought* (New York: John Day Company, 1942); Arthur Waley, *Three Ways of Thought in Ancient India* (London: Allen and Unwin, 1939 [Anchor Edition, 1956]); H. G. Creel, *Chinese Thought from Confucius to Mao Tse-tung* (New York: New American Library, 1960), especially pp. 51–53, 113–121 and 129–130; and Ch'u Chai and Winberg Chai, eds., *The Humanist Way in Ancient China: Essential Works of Confucianism* (New York: Bantam Books, 1965).

17. In other words, *ahimsa* promoted vegetarianism long before it promoted pacifism in India. But undoubtedly in this century the Gandhian concept of *ahimsa* has had a considerable impact upon the development of pacifist thought throughout the world, and rather notably in Western Christian intellectual circles. For further discussion of historic Indian attitudes toward war, see D. Mackenzie Brown, *The White Umbrella: Indian Political Thought from Manu to Gandhi* (Berkeley: University of California Press, 1953), especially Part One; U. N. Goshal, *A History of Hindu Political Theories* (London: Oxford University Press, 1923); A. L. Basham, "Some Fundamentals of Hindu Statecraft," Joel Laurus, ed., *Comparative World Politics: Readings in Western and Pre-Modern Non-Western International Relations* (Belmont, Calif.: Wadsworth Publishing Company, 1964), especially pp. 47–52.

18. A good example of Machiavellian analysis can be found in *The Book of Lord Shang*, written by a Legalist. The author recognized that the common people dislike war; his solution was to make the peasant's ordinary life so hard with work that he would welcome release from it for military service. See H. G. Creel, *op. cit.*, pp. 129–130; also the two excellent chapters on "Ancient China" and "Ancient India" in Frank M. Russell, *Theories of International Relations* (New York: Appleton-Century-Crofts, 1936),

Contending Theories of International Relations

By way of contrast to the more mystic, detached and quietistic religions of the Orient, Islam furnishes an illustration of a religious civilization which in its historical roots experienced no contradiction between ethical theory and political practice. The prophet Mohammed preached the holy war (*jihad*) as a sacred duty and a guarantee of salvation, and for several centuries Moslem theorists, accepting the reality that Arab rulers were for the most part a war-minded group, assumed that the world is divided into the *dar al-Islam* (the peaceful abode of the true believers and those who submitted to their tolerant rule) and the *dar al-harb* (the territory of war). Inasmuch as Islam was a universalist system of belief, the two territories were always theoretically at war with each other, for war was the ultimate device for incorporating recalcitrant peoples into the peaceful territory of Islam. The *jihad,* therefore, was a form of *bellum justum* ("just war") not entirely unlike that of medieval Christian writers. The concept of the *jihad* as a permanent state of war against the non-Moslem world has become obsolete in modern times. This became evident with the utter failure of the Caliph's call for a holy war against the Allied powers in World War I, but the concept has regained some relevance in the period of the Arab-Israeli conflict. Today writers stress that the term refers not only to international war but also to the spiritual struggle for perfection within the heart of man.[19] Mahatma Gandhi declared that he was able to perceive the origins of the doctrine of nonviolence and love for all living things not only in the sacred Hindu writings and the Bible, but also in the Koran.[20]

The predominant historical attitudes toward war which are found in Western culture are a product of several different sources, including the Judaeo-Christian religious tradition, Greek philosophy, Roman legalism, European feudalism, Enlightenment pacifism, and modern scientism, humanitarianism and other ideologies. The ancient Jewish scriptures reflect the paradox of human yearning for a peaceful existence amidst the constant recurrence of war. Surrounded by hostile peoples, the Israelites relied heavily upon a combination of religious prophetism and military organization for nation-building, defense and territorial expansion. Such warrior leaders of the Old Testament as Joshua, Gideon, Saul and David demonstrated that they were instruments

pp. 16–50; Norman D. Palmer, "Indian and Western Political Thought: Coalescence or Clash?" *American Political Science Review,* LXIX (September, 1955), 747–761; George Modelski, "Kautilya: Foreign Policy and International System in the Ancient Hindu World," *ibid.,* LVIII (September, 1964), 549–560. Modelski, like many writers, calls attention to the similarities between Kautilya's *Arthasastra* and Machiavelli's *The Prince,* inasmuch as both are concerned with how a ruler gains, consolidates and expands his power. *Ibid.,* p. 550.

19. Hamilton A. R. Gibb, *Mohammedanism: An Historical Survey* (New York: The New American Library, 1955), pp. 57–58. Majid Khadduri has written two very fine expositions of the subject—*War and Peace in the Law of Islam* (Baltimore: Johns Hopkins Press, 1955) and "The Islamic Theory of International Relations and Its Contemporary Relevance," in J. Harris Proctor, ed., *Islam and International Relations* (New York: Frederick A. Praeger, 1965), pp. 24–39.

20. Brown, *op. cit.,* p. 143.

of Yahweh largely by their prowess in defeating the enemies of God's Chosen People.[21]

WAR AND CHRISTIANITY

The early Christians, whose founder had distinguished between religion and politics more sharply than had been common in the Jewish theocratic culture, were divided in their attitude toward the use of military force by the State, partly, no doubt, because on the one hand the new Christian religion was an alien substance in the Roman Empire and did not depend upon the latter for the dissemination of the Gospel, while on the other hand the early Christians preferred, within the framework of their own religious consciences, to be regarded as good citizens rather than as enemies of the State. Thus it is not surprising that the early Christian thinkers split over the issue. A radical minority, stronger at times and weaker at others, but always tending toward an apocalyptic vision, insisted that the Christian in all his actions both as a private person and as a member of society must emulate the submissiveness of the Prince of Peace and respond to injury by turning the other cheek, regardless of the consequences for the State.[22]

Pacifism, however, did not become the orthodox Christian doctrine. The more influential patristic writers, recognizing that Christ had been for the most part silent on the subject of warfare and that the Gospel does not explicitly censure the military profession, refused to hold that the law of force had been abrogated by the law of love. Christ had certainly disdained the use of force in his own mission, which involved a kingdom not of this world, but they were far from certain that the Master's example of self-abnegation on Calvary was intended as an appropriate model for political communities or a guide for the action of citizens in states. The dominant view among the fathers of the church in both East and West was that the political authority of the state was established by God for the benefit of man. War was one of the four institutions of the *ius gentium*—along with coercive government, private property and slavery—which flowed not from rational human nature in the abstract but from the sinfulness of human nature in the concrete and from a voluntary

21. See Joshua, ch. 1:5–9; 23: 2–6; Judges, Ch. 6: 6–18; Samuel, Chs. 13–18.

22. Marcion, when confronted with the military realities of Jewish history, denied the relevance of that experience for Christianity, and contrasted the stern God of Justice revealed in some books of the Old Testament with the merciful God of Love revealed in the New. Johannes Quasten, *Patrology* (Westminster, Md.: Newman Press, 1950), I, 270. Tertullian asserted that there can be no agreement between God's sacrament and man's, between Christ's standard and the Devil's, between God and Caesar—and he concluded that no believer could take to military service, nor could a soldier be admitted to the Church. Ernest Barker, ed. and trans., *From Alexander to Constantine* (Oxford: Clarendon, Ltd., 1956), pp. 456–457. Origen, too, was a pacifist, but less of an absolutist than Tertullian. See Franziskus Stratmann, *War and Christianity Today* (Westminster, Md.: Newman Press, 1956), p. 105.

introduction by man. Coercive power was a divinely appointed remedy for sin, designed to be used as an instrument of justice to put men into the right path. Hence when force was used justly, it was a good, not an evil.

The typical view of the fathers of the church was that the individual Christian who seeks perfection should turn the other cheek when his own private rights are violated; charity prompts him to abjure reliance on force where his own rights are concerned. But the organized political community, charged with safeguarding a human common good which has its primary meaning within the temporal sphere, cannot seek its perfection in the same way as the person seeks salvation beyond history. Having no destiny hereafter, the state protects itself when it is threatened, and Christians cannot categorically deny the necessity of the state to resort to force at times. Thus, although many Chrisians did refuse to perform military service for the empire, the early church did not impose a burden upon the soldier's conscience by requiring him to abandon the military profession upon conversion to Christianity.[23]

The medieval Christian period was dominated by the doctrine of the "just war" which had been elaborated during the fourth and fifth centuries by Saint Ambrose and Saint Augustine. Ambrose taught that not only does the state have a right to make war (*ius belli*) but under certain circumstances there might be a positive moral obligation to undertake it.[24] Augustine, although he fully appreciated the tragic aspects of human war and roundly condemned its gladiatorial features, nevertheless conceded that there are times when men

23. See Cecil John Cadoux, *The Early Church and the World* (Edinburgh: T. & T. Clark, 1925), especially pp. 51–57; Franziskus Stratmann, *The Church and War* (New York: Sheed and Ward, 1928); Joan D. Tooke, "The Development of the Christian Attitude to War before Aquinas," Chapter I in *The Just War in Aquinas and Grotius* (London: Society for the Propagation of Christian Knowledge, 1965), pp. 1–20; and James E. Dougherty, "The Catholic Church, War and Nuclear Weapons," *Orbis*, IX (Winter, 1966), especially pp. 845–850. Saint Augustine denied that Christian practice condemned war in general. Letter No. 138 to Marcellinus, *Saint Augustine: Letters*, Sister Wilfred Parsons, trans., Roy J. Deferrari, ed. (New York: Fathers of the Church, 1953), III, 47. If Christians did not enter the Roman army in significant numbers, the reason must be sought not only in the pacifist tendencies of the Christian conscience but in other causes unrelated to the Christian attitude toward war. Christians were not deemed particularly suitable for conscription; they refused to take an oath that could be construed as an act of religious homage to the Emperor; and they did not wish to serve in an organization which was often employed to persecute, torture and kill Christians. Two historians of the early Church call it a "great exaggeration to say that the ordinary practice of Christians was to refuse military service." Such refusal, they add, "was, for a century, a theory of moralists, not the teaching of the ecclesiastical magisterium, and not the ordinary reaction of the faithful to the question when it arose." Jules Lebreton and Jacques Zeiller, *The History of the Primitive Church* (New York: Macmillan Company, 1949), II, 1159.

24. "Man has a moral duty to employ force to resist active wickedness, for to refrain from hindering evil when possible is tantamount to promoting it." But St. Ambrose insisted that war may be waged only for a just cause and by fair methods, and that any punishment meted out to an adversary should be proportionate to the degree of injustice perpetrated by him. See F. Homes Dudden, *The Life and Times of Saint Ambrose* (Oxford: Clarendon Press, 1945), II, 538–539.

have no choice but to resort to war. "War and conquest . . . are a sad necessity in the eyes of men of principle . . . [yet] it would be still more unfortunate if wrongdoers should dominate just men." [25] He assigned to war a deep spiritual meaning, not that he deemed it the exhilarating experience which certain nineteenth-century writers took it to be, but because he saw that war reflects both a profound restlessness in man and a fundamental craving for peace. If men are willing to fight with arms, he wrote, this does not necessarily mean that they love peace less, but rather that they love their own kind of peace more.[26] We might say, therefore, that Augustine was one of the earliest Western writers to perceive that the confrontation of widely differing cultural value systems can produce a sense of threat which may in itself constitute a "cause" of violent social conflict.

SCHOLASTIC REFINEMENTS: THE "JUST WAR" DOCTRINE

Scholastic philosophers in the Middle Ages considerably refined the "just war" doctrine. The decision to initiate violent hostilities could not be taken by a private individual, but only by public authority, which was invested with a divinely instituted character. Thus an individual Christian who, acting in a private capacity, could never morally intend to kill a human being, may do so when he is acting as an agent of the state. But rulers were enjoined against resorting to war unless they were morally certain that their cause was just— i.e., that their juridical rights had been violated by a neighboring ruler. Even then, they were exhorted to exhaust all peaceful means of settling the dispute before initiating the use of force, and this usually meant arbitration. Furthermore, there had to be a reasonable prospect that the resort to force would be more productive of good than of evil and would restore the order of justice. The war had to be waged throughout with a right moral intention, and had to be conducted by means that were not intrinsically immoral, for what begins as a just war could become unjust in its prosecution. These were the common teachings of such medieval writers as Antoninus of Florence and St. Thomas Aquinas.[27]

25. Augustine, *The City of God,* Book IV, Chapter 15, Demetrius B. Zema, S. J. and Gerald G. Walsh, S. J., trans. (New York: Fathers of the Church, 1950), p. 193.

26. *Ibid.,* Book XIX, Chapter 12.

27. See Frank M. Russell, *Theories of International Relations* (New York: Appleton-Century Company, 1936), pp. 91–97; Quincy Wright, *A Study of War* (Chicago: University of Chicago Press, 1942), I, 198; Coleman Phillipson, *The International Law and Custom of Ancient Greece and Rome* (New York: Macmillan Company, 1911), II, 5–8; Bede Jarrett, *Social Theories of the Middle Ages 1200–1500* (Westminster, Md.: Newman Press, 1942), pp. 201–202. The most thorough exposition of the medieval doctrine of the "just war" is to be found in Joan D. Tooke, *op. cit.* Most of the interpretations of the doctrine in this century have been presented by Catholic writers. See, e.g., "The Ethics of War," reprinted from *The Code of International Ethics* of the Catholic Social Guild, in John A. Ryan and Francis J. Boland, *Catholic*

Throughout the Middle Ages, the church attempted to impose ethical controls upon the conduct of war by specifying times when fighting could not be carried on, sites where battle was prohibited, types of weapons that could not legitimately be employed, and classes of persons that were either exempted from the obligation of military service or immune as targets of military action. This effort to "soften" the cruelty of warfare was by no means new in Western culture. The ancient Greeks and Romans had been familiar with such agreed rules of war as those forbidding wanton destruction of populations, the burning of cities, and the severance of water supplies. Many circumstances of medieval European culture, including the nature of feudalism, prevailing economic conditions, and the crude state of the military sciences actually reinforced the moral efforts of the Church to mitigate the harshness of warfare during the medieval period.[28] When the chivalric code was observed, warfare often took on the aspect of a tournament. This was not surprising in an environment in which legal and political institutions, as well as cultural and religious values, were relatively homogeneous. The sort of ideological differences which often make for absolute struggles to the death were lacking *within* Europe before the fourteenth century. The outcome of a feudal war often determined *who* should wield authority over a particular piece of territory, but it did not affect the *how* of life. People rarely if ever became emotionally involved in the issues over which wars were fought.

In the period of transition from medieval to modern Europe, three outstanding exceptions to the dominant theory and practice of morally limited warfare can be perceived. These were invariably expressions of ideological

---

Principles of Politics (New York: Macmillan Company, 1940), pp. 251–271; Cyprian Emmanuel, O. F. M., *The Ethics of War* (Washington: Catholic Association for International Peace, 1932); Luigi Sturzo, *International Community and the Right of War* (London: George Allen and Unwin, 1929); Heinrich A. Rommen, *The State in Catholic Thought* (St. Louis: B. Herder Book Company, 1947), pp. 641–671. For a discussion of the "just war" doctrine in the nuclear age, see below, pp. 167–171.

28. Since medieval society exalted cavalry over infantry, only a limited number of full-fledged warriors was available. Given the low level of the armor-making arts, the fully equipped mounted knight represented a considerable investment. Monarchs lacked the financial and organizational resources to raise and maintain large professional armies. Europe, with population sparse and agricultural methods poor, was usually preoccupied

with basic problems of survival. Furthermore, the intricate feudal network of land-loyalty relationships gave rise to many conflicts of fealty among vassals and lords. In a society of delicately balanced bargaining relationships, wars were frequent but they were waged on a small scale for strictly limited objectives. See Henri Pirenne, *Economic and Social History of Medieval Europe* (New York: Harcourt, Brace and Company, 1937); Joseph R. Strayer and Rushton Coulborn, *Feudalism in History* (Princeton: Princeton University Press, 1956); F. L. Ganshof, *Feudalism* (London: Longmans Green, Ltd., 1952); and Carl Stephenson, *Medieval Institutions: Selected Essays* (Ithaca: Cornell University Press, 1955). For an account of the rules of warfare laid down by the Church during the twelfth century under the "Truce of God" and the "Peace of God," see Arthur Nussbaum, *A Concise History of the Law of Nations* (New York: Macmillan Company, 1954), p. 18.

conflict which ran counter to the distinctive tendencies of medieval culture: 1) the Crusades of the twelfth and thirteenth centuries, fought against an alien and infidel civilization; 2) the wars of the fourteenth and fifteenth centuries, especially between the French and English, in which the forces of national feeling made themselves felt for the first time on a large scale; and 3) the religious wars which followed the Reformation. In all of these cases, war ceased to be a rational instrument of monarchical policy for the defense of juridical rights. The concept of war as a small-scale affair of skirmish and maneuver lost its primacy when large numbers of nonprofessional (i.e., nonchivalric) warriors, both volunteers and mercenaries, became enmeshed with cultural, national or religious antipathies. When a cherished set of values or a way of life was thought to hinge upon the outcome of an encounter, war became an all-consuming psychological and moral experience. Hence the battles of Antioch, Crecy, Poitiers, Agincourt and Magdeburg were bitter and bloody in the extreme.

THE PHILOSOPHICAL THEORIES OF THE NATION-STATE PERIOD

During the classical period of the balance of power which was ushered in by the Peace of Westphalia in 1648, the concept of limited war regained currency in Europe. At the beginning of the modern nation-state period in the sixteenth and seventeenth centuries, the traditional Western doctrine of the "just war" was reaffirmed by Scholastic theologians and philosophers, such as Victoria and Suarez, as well as by the earliest systematic expounders of international law—Grotius, Ayala, Gentilis and others. For these writers, the just war emerged as a substitute juridical proceeding—a sort of lawsuit in defense of the legal rights of the state, prosecuted by force in the absence of an effective international judicial superior capable of vindicating the order of justice. Virtually all the classical European writers on international war insisted upon the necessity of sparing the lives of the innocent in war. The slaying of the guiltless could never be directly intended; at best, it was permitted as incidental to the legitimate operations of a just war.[29]

In the latter half of the seventeenth century, after the violence of the religious wars had subsided, the pendulum swung back again toward more moderate forms of warfare. From then on through most of the eighteenth century, wars were less ideological and more instrumental in the traditional sense.

29. See Francisco de Victoria, *De Indis et De Iure Belli Relectiones*, John P. Bate, trans. (Washington: Carnegie Endowment for International Peace, 1917); Francisco Suarez, *De Triplici Virtute Theologica*, Disp. VIII, "De Bello," in *Selections from Three Works* (Oxford: Clarendon Press, 1925); Balthazar Ayala, *Three Books on the Law of War, the Duties Connected with War and Military Discipline* (Washington: The Carnegie Institution, 1912); and Albericus Gentilis, *De Iure Belli,* John C. Rolfe, trans. (Oxford: Clarendon Press, 1933). All of these works are in the Classics of International Law Series, edited by James Brown Scott.

Contending Theories of International Relations

Professor John U. Nef, founder and former chairman of the Committee on Social Thought at the University of Chicago, suggests a number of factors which influenced this development: a growing distaste for violence; a raising of the comfort level among the European bourgeoisie; the improvement of manners, customs and laws by an aristocracy which now admired gentility, agility and subtlety more than prowess in battle; the pursuit of commerce; and the growth of the fine arts, combined with zealous efforts to apply reason to social affairs. All these factors, Nef concludes, helped to weaken the will for organized fighting.[30]

Down to the time of the French Revolution, the nations of Europe were not willing to pursue objectives which required inflicting a great deal of destruction upon the enemy. This period witnessed the emergence of economic motivations for conflict but, while it is true that colonial and commercial rivalries were added to dynastic feuds as causes of international disputes, the rise of the bourgeoisie helped buttress pacifist rather than militarist sentiments, for the bourgeoisie desired more than anything else an orderly international community in which conditions of trade would be predictable. The very fact that the leading commercial nations of Western Europe were also developing naval power helped to soften the effects of warfare in the eighteenth century insofar as naval forces could carry on hostile engagements without directly involving land populations. Such land warfare as did take place was usually characterized by adroit maneuver, surprise, march and countermarch, and rapier thrusts at the enemy's supply lines, as exemplified in the campaigns of Turenne, Frederick the Great and Marlborough. War, in the century of "drawing room culture," was not entirely unrelated to the game of chess or the minuet. The prevailing sense of restraint led to a slowdown in the innovation rate of military technology. Encounters between armies in the field were often looked upon as mere adjuncts to the diplomatic process, designed to strengthen or weaken the bargaining positions of envoys during prolonged negotiations.

The Origins of Modern Pacifism

Meanwhile, the post-Renaissance and Enlightenment periods had witnessed the rise in Europe of a school of pacifist thought which rejected the medieval moral-legal doctrine of war. The pacifist writers—Erasmus, More, Comenius, Crucé, Fenelon, Penn, Voltaire, Rousseau and Bentham—took their stand either on stoic and early Christian radical positions or on the newer European ideals of cosmopolitanism, humanitarianism and bourgeois internationalism. Practically all of them exhibited a pronounced skepticism in their attitudes

30. John U. Nef, *War and Human Progress* (Cambridge: Harvard University Press, 1950), pp. 250–259.

toward war and the military profession. It was particularly fashionable to compare unfavorably the destructive life of the soldier with the useful life of the merchant. The abolition of force from international politics came to be looked upon as the noblest objective of statesmen. The quest for human happiness unmarred by any trace of the tragic became for European intellectuals the great goal of life.[31]

The *philosophes* were not agreed among themselves as to whether happiness was to be achieved through the application of scientific and technical reason or through man's return to nature and rediscovery of his original simplicity. But rationalists and romantics alike were convinced that society was about to break the shackles of traditional authority and superstition, dispel the historic curses of ignorance, disease and war, and embark—in the vision of Condorcet—upon the absolutely indefinite perfectibility of man, which knows no other limit than the duration of the globe upon which nature has placed us.[32] "The people, being more enlightened," wrote Condorcet, "will learn by degrees to regard war as the most dreadful of all calamities, the most terrible of all crimes." [33] The era was marked by a bitter cynicism concerning the concept of the "just war," which was regarded as mere propaganda calculated to cloak the aggressive urges of ambitious kings. No one at the time denounced the stupidity and incongruities of war with more scathing sarcasm than Voltaire, who poked fun at the two kings each of whom had *Te Deums* sung in his own camp after the battle.[34] There was an anticipation, reflected in the writings of Montesquieu and others, that the transition from monarchical to republican institutions would be accompanied by a shift from the spirit of war and aggrandizement to that of peace and moderation. The period abounded in projects for abolishing war and establishing perpetual peace.[35]

The hopes of the Enlightenment writers proved ill-founded in the latter part of the eighteenth century. The emergence of liberal nationalist ideologies, sparked by the French Revolution and the Napoleonic aftermath, led once again to an intensification of warfare. Citizen armies, backed by a steadily growing industrial base, fought ferociously for nationalist ideals. Napoleon

31. Paul Hazard, *European Thought in the Eighteenth Century*, J. Lewis May, trans. (New York: World Publishing Company, 1963), p. 18.

32. Kingsley Martin, *French Liberal Thought in the Eighteenth Century*, 2nd ed. (New York: New York University Press, 1954), Chapter XI.

33. *Outlines of an Historical View of the Progress of the Human Mind, 1794.* Excerpts from an English translation of 1802 in Hans Kohn, *Making of the Modern French Mind* (Princeton: D. Van Nostrand Company [Anvil Books], 1955), pp. 97–98.

34. *Candide,* Chapter 3, in Edmund Fuller, ed., *Voltaire: A Laurel Reader* (New York: Dell Publishing Company, 1959), pp. 13–14.

35. William Penn wrote an *Essay toward the Present and Future Peace of Europe;* Abbé de St. Pierre, *A Project for Making Peace Perpetual in Europe;* Jean Jacques Rousseau, *A Lasting Peace through the Federation of Europe;* Immanuel Kant, *Perpetual Peace;* and Jeremy Bentham, *Plan for a Universal and Perpetual Peace.*

upset the European balance of power. The conservative reaction of 1815, based on the principle of a return to monarchical legitimacy, restored the classical idea of the balance of power—a Newtonian notion of an international universe in equilibrium—to a central place in the thinking of European statesmen.[36] This restoration helped to minimize the harsh effects of a developing war technology for another hundred years. The era of the Concert of Powers, of which the *Pax Britannica* was an important feature, was marked by astute diplomacy and chessboard military moves rather than by violent conflict. Throughout the nineteenth century, Europe experienced no conflict so bloody as the American Civil War, which was in many respects an ideological war fought for absolute objectives.

The latter part of the nineteenth century witnessed the spread of universal conscription in Europe, the mass production of new automatic weapons, armaments races, the creation of alliances, increasing colonial and commercial rivalries among the Powers, and the growth of a popular press which could be converted into a powerful instrument for stirring belligerent sentiments. The rise of modern war industry had an ambiguous significance. It served on the one hand to make war more frightful and more unprofitable, and hence less readily undertaken. On the other hand, it served to make it much more likely that war, when it did come, would be total in nature, absorbing all available energies. The closely packed battle, in which mass is multiplied by velocity, became the central feature of modern European military thought.[37] For the first time in history, men were coming into possession of constantly expanding means of waging absolute war for unlimited objectives.

Throughout the nineteenth century, the pacifist movement slowly extended its influence in England and the United States. Jonathan Dymond, an English Quaker, argued that war, like the slave trade, would begin to disappear when men would refuse to acquiesce in it any longer and begin to question its necessity. Dymond denied that the patriotic warrior celebrated in song and story for having laid down his life for his country deserves such praise. The officer, he said, enters the army in order to obtain an income, the private because he prefers a life of idleness to industry. Both fight because it is their business, or because their reputation is at stake, or because they are compelled to do so. Dymond anticipated the contentions of the socialists and the later exponents of the "devil theory of war" by insinuating that the industrialists who profit from war combine forces with the professional military for the purpose of promoting war. He declared that the Christian Scriptures require man to refrain from violence under all circumstances. All distinctions between just

36. An analysis of the balance of power as a theory was presented in Chapter 1. On this see Henry A. Kissinger, *A World Restored—Europe After Napoleon: The Politics of Conservatism in a Revolutionary Age* (New York: Grosset and Dunlap [Universal Library], 1964).

37. R. A. Preston, *et al., Men in Arms: A History of Warfare and Its Interrelationships with Western Society* (New York: Frederick A. Praeger, 1956), Chapter 12.

The Older Theories of Conflict

and unjust war, between defensive and aggressive war, he dismissed as being in vain. War must be either absolutely forbidden or else permitted to run its unlimited course.[38] Dymond is one of the early voices of that modern movement of uncompromising pacifism which seeks not only to give religious advice to the conscience of the individual but also to exert an influence upon the policy of states—or at least those states in which the climate of opinion is sufficiently liberal to permit the propagation of the pacifist doctrine.

The aversion of moden intellectual pacifists to war cannot be explained purely in terms of religious and humanitarian factors. Since the nineteenth century, economic considerations, either liberal or socialist in their foundation, have entered into the thinking of most pacifists on the subject of war and peace. From Richard Cobden down to very recent times, many liberal pacifists have been convinced that there exists an intrinsic and mutually causal relationship between free trade and peace, and that the abolition of trade barriers is the only means of effecting permanent peace.[39]

SIR NORMAN ANGELL AND WAR AS AN ANACHRONISM

The Liberal view that war represents the greatest threat to the economic health of modern industrial civilization reached its culmination in the writings of Norman Angell, an English publicist who achieved prominence in the 1920s and 1930s. Shortly before World War I, Angell argued that warfare in the industrial age had become an anachronism. The economic futility of military power, he declared, had been amply demonstrated by recent history, which showed that even when victory in war seems at first glance to bring with it substantial economic gains, such appearances are deceptive. Nearly everyone thought that the Germans had reaped an advantage from the huge indemnity which France was forced to pay after being defeated in the Franco-Prussian War of 1870–71, but, Angell argued, the indemnity actually induced an inflation which hurt the German economy. No nation, he went on to say, can genuinely improve its economic position either through war or through those imperialistic operations which involve costly preparations for military defense. Angell was convinced that "the factors which really do constitute prosperity have not the remotest connection with military or naval power, all our political jargon notwithstanding." [40]

38. Jonathan Dymond, *An Inquiry into the Accordancy of War with the Principles of Christianity and an Examination of the Philosophical Reasoning by Which it is Defended,* 3rd ed. (Philadelphia: Brown, 1834).

39. Helen Bosanquet, *Free Trade and Peace in the Nineteenth Century* (New York: G. P. Putnam's Sons, 1924).

40. Norman Angell, *The Great Illusion: A Study of the Relation of Military Power to National Advantage* (New York: G. P. Putnam's Sons, 1910), p. 71. One of the arguments employed by Angell to prove that economic prosperity can be separated from military capability was that the national bonds of small non-military states were sought after by investors as more secure than bonds of the

Contending Theories of International Relations

In the final analysis, Angell was a rationalist who believed that war could be eliminated through the growth and progressive application of human reason to international affairs. The modern technical state could no longer expect to profit from waging war, but could only anticipate the disintegration of its own society and the virtue of its individual members. Once men become convinced that war has lost its meaning except as a form of mutual suicide, thought Angell, disarmament and peace would be possible. He was confident that peace was primarily a matter of educating the publics of democratic societies, and he chose to couch his homilies in terms of the economic self-interest of an interdependent European community rather than in terms of traditional religious morality. But he had no doubt that once men fully realized the irrelevance of military force for the attainment, promotion and preservation of prosperity, or socioeconomic well-being, then political wars would cease as religious wars did in the West a long time ago.[41]

Perhaps Angell (who won the Nobel Peace Prize in 1933) failed to realize that, just as the wars of the late Middle Ages may have been fought for reasons more complicated than purely religious ones, so the wars of the modern nation-state system, up to and including World War I, may not have been completely comprehensible under the rubric of economic causality. Economics, though a "dismal science," is nonetheless highly rational for all that. But the danger of rational analysis is always overrationalization, not to mention oversimplification. This caveat leads to other major strands of modern philosophical-economic thought, besides Liberalism, which have exerted an intellectual influence upon Western pacifism—i.e., anarchism and the Marxist-socialist theories of imperialism and conflict. But before we turn to these latter theories, a word is in order about the antithesis of pacifism in the modern era prior to World War I.

Bellicist Theories

Modern Western theories of conflict and war, including those of utopian pacifism, cannot be understood without some reference to the appearance, following the French Revolution, of a militarist school of thought within the West. Bellicism, as this school might be called, developed at least partly in conscious reaction to idealistic pacifism. Perhaps it would be more accurate to say that the two tendencies in Western thought fed upon each other as

larger military powers. In rebuttal to Angell, Professor J. H. Jones of the University of Glasgow pointed out that it was the military expenditures of the larger powers which created the conditions of international stability and secur-

ity on which smaller nations depended. *The Economics of War and Conquest* (London: King and Son, Ltd., 1915), p. 25.

41. Angell, *op. cit.*, p. 335.

polar opposites. Western culture has never lacked thinkers who stressed conflict and tension over cooperation and harmony in social reality. In ancient Greece, Empedocles and Heraclitus had postulated endless strife as the underlying process of reality.[42] Toward the close of the Middle Ages, Niccòlo Machiavelli had shocked his contemporaries by exhorting the ruler never to let his thoughts stray too far from the subject of war, and by setting forth what he considered a scientific view of statecraft that was really tantamount to a process of power accumulation through the rather cynical manipulation— by political, psychological, economic and military means—of human foibles.[43]

Most Western theorists of military strategy from the period of the French Revolution until the latter 1950s (when the emphasis shifted from conventional and nuclear strategies to the study of guerrilla warfare and counterinsurgency) showed a distinct preference for direct over indirect strategies, for the bludgeoning attack of the massed army over the graceful rapier thrust, for the frontal assault and the quick decision over the more patient strategy of maneuver, encirclement, attrition and negotiation. Karl von Clausewitz expressed, more vividly than any other writer up to his time, the concept of absolute war pushed to its utmost bounds. The chief object of military strategy, he wrote, is to break the enemy's will to resist. He denied that there is any chance of disarming and defeating the enemy without a good deal of bloodshed. "If bloody slaughter is a horrible spectacle, then it should only be a reason for treating war with more respect, but not for making the sword we bear blunter and blunter by degrees from feelings of humanity, until once again someone steps in with a sword that is sharp, and hews away the arms from our body." [44]

More important than Clausewitz were the nineteenth-century philosophers

42. Empedocles did not go quite as far as Heraclitus. The former held that the separating force of Strife and the attracting force of Love are in constant interaction. These two forces alternate in the ascendancy. At any given time the ascendant force is expanding and driving out the other, but the one driven out eventually returns to gain its own ascendancy, and the cycle recurs endlessly. John Burnet, *Greek Philosophy: Thales to Plato* (New York: Macmillan Company, 1961) (reprinted from the 1914 edition), pp. 72–74. According to Heraclitus, if war should perish the universe would be destroyed, for strife is justice, through which all things come into being and pass away. See Bertrand Russell, *A History of Western Philosophy* (New York: Simon and Schuster, 1945), p. 42.

43. Machiavelli was a man of intellectual virtues and vices. He attempted to give political analysis more of an empirical foundation than it had hitherto possessed, and he was for many centuries the most incisive of all Western writers on international politics and on the relationship between politics and military-strategic factors. But he was dogmatic in the exposition of the maxims and principles of statecraft. More than that, his brilliance was vitiated by a moral and metaphysical vacuity, a failure to understand the relationship between means and ends, as well as between power and value. See *The Prince,* especially Chapters 14 and 18; also Herbert Butterfield, *The Statecraft of Machiavelli* (New York: Macmillan Company, 1956).

44. Karl von Clausewitz, *On War,* trans. O. J. Mathhijs Jolles (New York: Random House [Modern Library], 1943), p. 210.

Hegel, Nietzsche, Treitschke and Bernhardi. These writers, carrying to extremes ideas which had been adumbrated by Machiavelli, Hobbes and Bacon, seemed at times to exalt power and war as ends in themselves. Hegel, for whom reality was the dialectical clash of ideas, regarded the nation-state as the concretization of the absolute in history, "the march of God in the world." On the subject of war, he has perhaps been misunderstood. He did not glorify war and its brutality, but since he valued the nation so highly he accepted war as a phenomenon which could contribute to national unity. Hegel left himself open either to misunderstanding or to justifiable criticism when he said that through war "the ethical health of nations is maintained . . . just as the motion of the winds keeps the sea from the foulness which a constant calm would produce." [45]

The harshest nineteenth-century critic of the values which underlay not only the Western Christian civilization of his day but even of pure original Christianity was Friedrich Nietzsche. Emphasizing as he did the "will-to-power" as the basic determinant of human behavior, Nietzsche looked upon the Christian ethos, marked by self-denial, resignation, humility, respect for weakness and the renunciation of power, as the foe of the truly creative impulses in man—a religion of failure which inhibits the full development of "Superman." [46] Even more than Hegel, war for Nietzsche plays an indispensable role in the renewal of civilizations. In the following passage, published in 1878, the German philosopher—undoubtedly one of the most important of all nineteenth-century thinkers—seemed to adumbrate in a very stark way the theory of the "moral equivalent of war" which William James would express more optimistically in 1912:

For the present, we know of no other means whereby the rough energy of the camp, the deep impersonal hatred, the cold-bloodedness of murder with a good conscience, the general ardor of the system in the destruction of the enemy, the proud indifference to great losses, to one's own existence and that of one's friends, the hollow earthlike convulsion of the soul, can be as forcibly and certainly communicated to enervated nations as is done by every great war . . . . Culture can by no means dispense with passions, vices and malignities. When the

45. G. W. F. Hegel, *Philosophy of Right and Law*, par. 324, in Carl J. Friedrich, ed., *The Philosophy of Hegel* (New York: Random House [The Modern Library], 1953), p. 322.

46. "What is good? All that enhances the feeling of power, the Will to Power, and power itself in man. What is bad? All that proceeds from weakness. What is happiness? The feeling that power is increasing—that resistance has been over-come. Not contentment, but more power; not peace at any price, but war; not virtue, but efficiency . . . . The weak and the botched shall perish: first principle of our humanity. And they ought even to be helped to perish. What is more harmful than any vice? Practical sympathy with all the botched and the weak—Christianity." From *The Twilight of the Idols* (1888) in Geoffrey Clive, ed., *The Philosophy of Nietzsche* (New York: New American Library, 1965), p. 427.

The Older Theories of Conflict

Romans, after having become Imperial, had grown rather tired of war, they attempted to gain new strength by beast-baitings, gladiatorial combats, and Christian persecutions. The English of today, who appear on the whole to have also renounced war, adopt other means in order to generate anew those vanishing forces; namely, the dangerous exploring expeditions, sea voyages, and mountaineerings, nominally undertaken for scientific purposes, but in reality to bring home surplus strength from adventures and dangers of all kinds. Many other such substitutes for war will be discovered, but perhaps precisely thereby it will become more and more obvious that such a highly cultivated and therefore necessarily enfeebled humanity as that of modern Europe not only needs wars, but the greatest and most terrible wars—consequently occasional relapses into barbarism—lest, by the means of culture, it should lose its culture and its very existence.[47]

Lesser minds than Nietzsche's followed in his tracks. The German historian Treitschke, who spoke for the Prussian military caste, drew his inspiration from such figures as Machiavelli and Bismarck. Convinced that the independent sovereign nation-state is the highest political achievement of which man is capable, he rejected as intolerable the concept of a genuine universal political community. War is frequently the only means available to the state to protect its independence, and thus the ability and readiness to wage war must be preserved in a carefully honed condition. The state ought to be oversensitive in matters of national honor, so that the instinct of political

47. *Human, All Too Human*, Vol. I (1878). *Ibid.*, pp. 372–373. According to William James, peaceful activities involving a challenge to strenuous exertion and sacrifice could serve as a substitute for war in providing the "social vitamins" generated by war. The philosopher-psychologist recognized that war and the military life met certain deep-rooted needs of societies and summoned forth human efforts of heroic proportions. He did not think it possible to attenuate the proclivity to war until these same energies could be redirected—e.g., by training young men to fight not other human beings but such natural forces as diseases, floods, poverty and ignorance. If the nation is not to evolve into a society of mollycoddles, youth must be conscripted to hardship tasks to "get the childishness knocked out of them." See William James, "The Moral Equivalent of War," in his *Memories and Studies* (New York: Longmans, 1912); and *A Moral Equivalent for War* (New York: Carnegie Endowment for International Peace, 1926).

Later, Aldous Huxley was to popularize the hypothesis that many people find an exhilaration in war because their peacetime pursuits are humiliating, boring and frustrating. War brings with it a state of chronic enthusiasm, and "life during wartime takes on significance and purposefulness, so that even the most intrinsically boring job is ennobled as 'war work.'" Prosperity is artificially induced; newspapers are filled with interesting news; and the rules of sexual morality are relaxed in wartime. But Huxley, writing just before World War II, conceded that the conditions of modern war have become so appalling that not only the civilians on the home front but "even the most naturally adventurous and combative human beings will soon come to hate and fear the process of fighting." *Ends and Means* (New York: Harper and Brothers, 1937). Excerpted in Robert A. Goldwin *et al.*, eds., *Readings in World Politics* (New York: Oxford University Press, 1959), pp. 13–14.

Contending Theories of International Relations

self-preservation can be developed to the highest possible degree. Whenever the flag is insulted, there must be an immediate demand for full satisfaction, and if this is not forthcoming, "war must follow, however small the occasion may seem." [48] There is nothing reprehensible in this, for in Treitschke's eyes war itself was majestic and sublime.[49] Above all, a state should not neglect its military strength in order to promote the idealistic aspirations of mankind, for if it does this "it repudiates its own nature and perishes." [50]

The ideas voiced by Clausewitz, Hegel, Nietzsche and Treitschke were echoed by several philosophers of military history in Europe and in the United States. General Friedrich von Bernhardi, strongly influenced by the Darwinian concept of "survival of the fittest" (which he understood only superficially), correlated war with human progress, holding that "those intellectual and moral factors which insure superiority in war are also those which render possible a general progressive development" among nations.[51] The geopolitical writings of Kjellén and Ratzel, as well as the twentieth-century German students of geopolitics represented by Haushofer, were indebted intellectually to Darwinian concepts. (See Chapter 2 where the geopolitical theories are discussed.) Alfred Thayer Mahan also saw history as a Darwinian struggle in which fitness is measured in terms of military strength. The habits of military discipline, he thought, are necessary underpinnings of an orderly civilian structure. He viewed the nations of the world as economic corporations locked in a fierce survival competition for resources and markets. Unlike the Marxists, however, he attributed this not merely to the impulses of competition but rather to the nature of man and the fact that the supply of economic goods is finite. Contradictions of national self-interest, along with wide and irreducible discrepancies of power, opportunity and determination, produce the conditions of permanent conflict and render it unrealistic to expect violence to be eliminated from international affairs. Mahan deemed futile all efforts to substitute law for force, since all law depends for its efficacy upon force. Finally Mahan defended the institution of war against the accusation that it was immoral and un-Christian. He argued that war is the means whereby nation-states carry out the mandates of their citizens' consciences. A state should go to war only when it is convinced of rightfulness, but once it has committed its conscience, there is no choice but war (not even arbitration),

48. Heinrich von Treitschke, *Politics* (New York: Macmillan Company, 1916), II, 595.

49. "We have learned to perceive the moral majesty of war through the very processes which to the superficial observer seem brutal and inhuman. The greatness of war is just what at first sight seems to be its horror—that for the sake of their country men will overcome the natural feelings of humanity, that they will slaughter their fellow men who have done them no injury, nay whom they perhaps respect as chivalrous foes. Man will not only sacrifice his life, but the natural and justified instincts of his soul; . . . here we have the sublimity of war." *Ibid.*, pp. 395–396.

50. *Ibid.*, I, p. 24.

51. Quoted in Russell, *op. cit.*, p. 245.

The Older Theories of Conflict

for "the material evils of war are less than the moral evil of compliance with wrong." [52]

Bellicist and Pacifist Polarize

As the nineteenth century gave way to the twentieth, the intellectual polarization of Western pacifists and bellicists became complete, and the philosophical debate between them, notwithstanding occasionally brilliant flashes of insight on both sides, often generated more heat than light. Neither side seemed to enjoy a monopoly of wisdom. The bellicists had history as well as the more important names in the total Western philosophical tradition on their side. The pacifists, who preferred to discount the lessons of the past and to look optimistically toward the future, took their stand more on the basis of religious idealism, an optimistic philosophical-ethical view concerning the improvability of man and his social institutions, and an abstract logic, somewhat Voltairean, which is used most effectively to focus attention on the anomalies inherent in the existing order.

The bellicist doctrines may be summarized as follows: 1) Realistic positivism, represented by such turn-of-the-century Italian writers as Vilfredo Pareto (1848–1923) and Gaetano Mosca (1858–1941). Pareto, an economist and sociologist, and Mosca, a political scientist, both expounded the concepts of rule by the elite, the importance of coercive instruments in the maintenance of social unity and order, and the inevitable recurrence of revolution. Mosca was not as antihumanitarian and antidemocratic as Pareto but he shared Pareto's prejudice against pacifism, fearing that if war should be eliminated nations would grow soft and disintegrate.[53] 2) Social Darwinists and nationalists with proclivities toward Social Darwinism, such as the sociologists William Graham Sumner and Ernst Haeckel and the jurist Oliver Wendell Holmes.[54] 3) Certain pessimistic philosophers of history, including Oswald Spengler (1880–1936) and Bendetto Croce (1866–1952). Spengler, a German his-

52. Alfred Thayer Mahan, *Armaments and Arbitration* (1912), p. 31. Quoted in Charles D. Tarlton, "The Styles of American International Thought: Mahan, Bryan and Lippmann," *World Politics,* XVII (July, 1965), 590. The foregoing summary of Mahan is based largely upon Tarlton's analysis. For an analysis of Mahan's work on the relationship between seapower and national power, see Chapter 2.

53. Vilfredo Pareto, *The Mind and Society,* A. Bongiorno and A. Livingston, trans. (New York: Harcourt, Brace Company, 1935), IV, pp. 2170–75 and 2179–2220; Gaetano Mosca, *The Ruling*

Class, H. D. Kahn, trans. (New York: McGraw-Hill Book Company, 1939). For interesting and valuable assessments of both Pareto and Mosca, see Parts III and VI of James Burnham, *The Machiavellians: Defenders of Freedom* (New York: John Day Company, 1943).

54. Holmes glorified war as a romantic adventure and as a necessary corrective for the irresponsible and sybaritic tendencies of modern youth. See Edward McNall Burns, *Ideas in Conflict: The Political Theories of the Contemporary World* (New York: W. W. Norton and Company, 1960), p. 54.

torian, was particularly fascinated by the will to power, the virility of barbarians, the subjugation of weaker peoples, and the law of the jungle, while he suffered from a special dread of a worldwide revolution of the colored people against the whites.[55] Croce, an Italian philosopher and statesman, although a critic of the excesses of militarism, regarded war as a necessary tragedy of the human condition, indispensable to human progress, and the dream of perpetual peace as fatuous.[56] 4) The forerunners and crypto-representatives of racist theory and fascism, as well as the actual archetypes of those ideologies. Writers in these categories included Houston Stewart Chamberlain, Arthur de Gobineau, Giovanni Gentile, Alfredo Rocco, Gabriel d'Annunzio and Benito Mussolini. It would be unfair to insinuate that all the foregoing schools of thought should be linked with the fascists, but all exalted, in varying degrees, the role of force in social processes. The individuals mentioned above are more appropriately treated in works on political theory or intellectual (and anti-intellectual) history, but the serious student of international relations cannot afford to ignore the impact which they had on the thinking of their time, nor should he overlook the "causative" role of conscious ideas and persisting attitudes in decision-making and social conflict.

Anarchism and the Marxist Socialists

Finally, there were the anarchists and the Marxist socialists. These two movements of an extremist nature, antithetical in many respects, produced contrary offshoots, some theoretical and some practical. Both movements helped dialectically to strengthen the theory of pacifism and the practice of politicized violence as an instrument either of abolishing the state or of promoting class revolution as prelude to the establishment of a cooperative or a socialist order. The Marxist-socialist theory of imperialism and war will be examined in the next chapter. Here a brief word about anarchism is in order, because it is often misunderstood by the public at large and because it constitutes a more significant component of the contemporary mind, especially the youthful mind in the West, than is generally recognized.

Anarchism is the doctrine which opposes political authority in all its forms. The anarchist views life as a moral drama in which the individual is arrayed against the state and all the oppressive instruments of coercion which he associates with government—bureaucracies, courts, police, and the military, as well as the institutions of private property and religion. He seeks liberation

55. Oswald Spengler, *The Decline of the West*, trans. Charles F. Atkinson (New York: Alfred A. Knopf, c. 1926–1928), 2 vols., and *The Hour of Decision*, trans. Charles F. Atkinson (New York: Alfred A. Knopf, 1934).

56. See Burns, *op. cit.*, pp. 265–266.

from these and all forms of external constraint upon human freedom. Firmly convinced of man's innate goodness and reasonableness, a benign anarchist who follows Kropotkin believes that the basic law of society is not conflict but mutual aid and cooperation. According to Irving Louis Horowitz, the anarchist, in addition to being antipolitical, is also antitechnological and anti-economic.[57] Thus he is essentially a foe of capitalist and socialist alike: if the former keeps government merely to protect his bourgeois interests and manage his affairs, the latter would replace capitalist tyranny with socialist tyranny —the "dictatorship of the proletariat."

Some branches of anarchism—notably collectivist, communist, syndicalist and conspiratorial—openly espoused the use of violence both in theory and as a tactical necessity. Sergei Nechaev (1847–1882), a disciple of Mikhail Bakunin (1814–1876), a Russian revolutionary agitator, adopted a creed of "propaganda by deed" and "universal pan-destruction." He advocated the nihilistic tactic of assassination for its effects of psychological terror and the demolition of existing institutions.[58] Errico Malatesta (1850–1932), an Italian journalist, regarded well-planned violence as an apt means of educating the working classes as to the meaning of the revolutionary struggle.[59] Similarly, the French journalist Georges Sorel (1847–1922) perceived value in proletarian acts of violence which serve to delineate the separation of classes. Such violence, he said, helps to develop the consciousness of the working class and keeps the middle class in a chronic state of fear, always ready to capitulate to the demands made upon it rather than run the risk of defending its position by resort to force.[60]

Not all anarchists have been advocates of violence. Individualist anarchists in America, such as Henry David Thoreau (1817–1862) and Benjamin R. Tucker (1854–1939), eschewed violence as unrespectable. They preferred to emphasize nonviolent civil disobedience. The two most influential pacifist anarchists of modern times—Mahatma Gandhi (1869–1948) and Leo Tolstoi (1828–1910)—radically opposed a pure religious ethic to man's willingness to submit to the State, which they excoriated for brutalizing the masses and converting military heroism into a virtue. Deeming it imperative that the law of force be superseded by the law of love, yet finding this impossible within the framework of the existing nation-state system, they insisted that the latter must give way to a universal society.[61]

Anarchism has sometimes been quite trenchant in its moral criticism of

57. Irving Louis Horowitz, ed., *The Anarchists* (New York: Dell Publishing Company, 1964), from the editor's introduction, p. 22.

58. See the excerpt from Thomas G. Masaryk in *ibid.*, pp. 469–473.

59. Horowitz, *op. cit.*, pp. 44–55.

60. Georges Sorel, *Reflections on Violence* (New York: Collier-Macmillan,

1961), pp. 77–79, and 115. See his Chapter 2, "Violence and the Decadence of the Middle Classes." See also Part IV, "Sorel: A Note on Myth and Violence," in Burnham, *op. cit.*, and William Y. Elliott, *The Pragmatic Revolt in Politics: Syndicalism, Fascism and The Constitutional State* (New York: Howard Fertig, 1968), pp. 111–141.

61. Horowitz, *op. cit.*, pp. 53–54.

Contending Theories of International Relations

existing institutions, but it has not made a significant contribution toward a scientific understanding of the sources of human conflict. Where one finds in anarchist writings a keen insight into group sociology (e.g., in Sorel's awareness of the group-integrating function of externally-directed violence), this usually reflects a borrowing from more dispassionate social scientists (e.g., Sorel was strongly influenced by Durkheim). In our day, the chief appeal of anarchist theories in the United States, whether pacifist or proviolence, has been to intellectuals, students and black militants. Much of the current suspicion of "The Establishment," of the police, of "the military-industrial complex," of national security and defense policies, and of middle and working class demands for "law and order" which marks a portion of our university population cannot be fully understood without some reference to the long tradition of intellectual anarchism in America.[62]

Older Theories of Conflict in Retrospect

In sum, in international relations, and in the social sciences in general, we have many theories of conflict. As this chapter has shown, certain writers have focused on the development of macro-level theories of conflict, while others have centered their attention on micro-theories. In addition, some writers have attempted to draw inferences about international conflict from the study of interpersonal conflict, while others have cautioned against the use of small-group models to explain conflict at the level of the collectivity. Because of the crucial importance of conflict, and its management, for political relationships, writers have engaged in normative analysis of conflict, seeking for example to develop concepts of "just war." Finally, certain older theories of conflict have had as a focal point the development of tactics and strategies for the use of conflict for the transformation of political, social, and economic systems. All of these older theories of conflict examined in this chapter provide intellectual antecedents to conflict as studied, and practiced, in the twentieth century.

The "Just War" Theory in the Nuclear Age

Since considerable attention was devoted earlier in this chapter to the "just war" doctrine as a set of normative constraints limiting the way a state may act in pursuit of its "necessities" (survival, independence, the preservation

62. See, e.g., Irving Louis Horowitz, "The Struggle Is the Message," *The Center Magazine,* II (May, 1969), 37–42.

of its common good and the defense of its rights), reference should be made here to the revival of the debate over the ethics of warfare in the twentieth century.

Several writers have argued that in view of the destructive power of modern military technology, especially nuclear weapons, the conditions of the "just war"—specifically the requirement that the amount of force employed must be proportionate to the political objectives sought—can no longer be validated. According to the "nuclear pacifist" school, even though it may have been theoretically possible to justify the use of force by states in earlier historical periods, nuclear war is potentially fraught with such monstrous consequences that it cannot be deemed politically or morally justifiable under any circumstances. Moreover, the fact that political leaders in all states and at all times have invoked the justice of their cause when they went to war, combined with the fact that history furnishes scanty evidence of religious leaders in any nation questioning or denying the justice of their government's policies during wartime, has contributed to a growing skepticism toward the "just war" theory even in respect to nonnuclear war. Finally, the inhumanity of modern warfare has prompted increasing numbers of theologians and ethicians to ask whether the waging of war can ever be made compatible with the imperatives of the Christian conscience.[63]

The typical contemporary pacifist is appalled by what he regards as the stupidity, futility or immorality of nuclear war. Such conflict threatens not only mutual extinction for the nations engaging in a large-scale nuclear exchange but also grave dangers of widespread radioactive fallout and genetic mutations for the rest of mankind. The pacifist is usually skeptical of all theories of nuclear deterrence and of the decision-makers' presumed rationality on which deterrence is supposed to be based. He abhors the international competition in armaments (or "arms race") which in his view, even if it does not lead inevitably to war, piles up an "overkill" capability, produces an international climate of neurotic fear, wastes vast amounts of economic and scientific-technological resources which could otherwise be channeled into development assistance for the poorer nations, and generally dehumanizes man, stifling his impulse to love his fellow man. Some writers, after contemplating the tragic situation into which the nations have drifted, advocate unilateral disarmament and nonviolent resistance as the only ways of breaking

63. For a repesentative sample of the voluminous literature reflecting these attitudes, see Roland H. Bainton, *Christian Attitudes toward War and Peace* (Nashville: Abingdon Press, 1960); Franziskus Stratmann, *op. cit.*; John C. Bennett, ed., *Nuclear Weapons and the Conflict of Conscience*, (New York: Charles Scribner's Sons, 1962); Gordon Zahn, *An Alternative to War* (New York: Council on Religion and International Affairs, 1963); Walter Stein, ed., *Nuclear Weapons and Christian Conscience* (London: Merlin, 1961); James Finn, ed., *Peace, the Churches and the Bomb* (New York: Council on Religion and International Affairs, 1965); and Donald A. Wells, *The War Myth* (New York: Pegasus, 1967).

through the vicious circle. Erich Fromm, Mulford Q. Sibley and Gordon Zahn see nonviolent resistance less as a form of helpless passivity than as a psychic or spiritual "soul" force capable of effecting a significant attitude change or "conversion" on the part of the aggressor.[64]

Even in the nuclear age with all its potential horrors, the mode of rational analysis embodied in the "just war" tradition has not lacked spokesmen. Without denying that the theory has often been abused in history, its modern proponents generally take the position that past distortions, while they should make us wary of the self-rationalizing tendency of nations, do not warrant our discarding an intellectual type of ethical analysis which seeks to chart a middle course between the extremes of pacifism and bellicism. Theorists in this group include John Courtney Murray, Paul Ramsey, Robert E. Osgood, Richard A. Falk, Robert W. Tucker, William V. O'Brien and others.[65]

The "just war" writers are convinced that, no matter how far efforts in this area may fall short of an ideal model of moral action, it is still better for men to engage in this kind of evaluation than to try to achieve a sense of inner purification by washing their hands of advanced weapons technology, thereby allowing it to develop according to its own dialectic. That nuclear power exists is a fundamental fact of contemporary political reality which cannot be conjured away by pious rhetoric or wishful thinking. This massive power, wrote the Jesuit theologian John Courtney Murray in 1959, demands a master strategic concept based upon a high sense of moral and political direction.

64. See Erich Fromm, "The Case for Unilateral Disarmament," in Donald G. Brennan, ed., *Arms Control, Disarmament and National Security* (New York: George Braziller, 1961), pp. 187–197; Mulford Q. Sibley, "Unilateral Disarmament," in Robert A. Goldwin, ed., *America Armed* (Chicago: Rand McNally and Company, 1961), pp. 112–140; Gordon Zahn, *op. cit.*

65. See John Courtney Murray, *Morality and Modern War* (New York: Church Peace Union, 1959) and republished as "Theology and Modern War" in *Theological Studies*, XX (March, 1959), 40–61; Paul Ramsey, *War and the Christian Conscience* (Durham, N.C.: Duke University Press, 1961) and *The Limits of Nuclear War* (New York: Council on Religion and International Affairs, 1963); Robert E. Osgood, "The Uses of Military Power in the Cold War," in Robert A. Goldwin, ed., *America Armed, op. cit.*, pp. 1–21; Richard A. Falk, *Law, Morality and War in the Contemporary World*, Princeton Studies in World Politics No. 5 (New York: Frederick A. Praeger, 1963); Robert W. Tucker, *The Just War* (Baltimore: Johns Hopkins Press, 1960) and *Just War and Vatican II: A Critique* (New York: Council on Religion and International Affairs, 1966); William V. O'Brien, *Nuclear War, Deterrence and Morality* (Westminster, Md.: Newman Press, 1967). See also Joseph C. McKenna, "Ethics and War: A Catholic View," *American Political Science Review*, LIV (September, 1960), 647–658; Thomas E. Murray, *Nuclear Policy for War and Peace* (Cleveland: World Publishing Company, 1960), Chapters 2 and 3; William J. Nagle, ed., *Morality and Modern Warfare* (Baltimore: Helicon Press, 1960); and James E. Dougherty, "The Catholic Church, War and Nuclear Weapons," *op. cit.*; "The Morality and Strategy of Deterrence, *Catholic World*, CXCIV (March, 1962), 337–344; "The Christian and Nuclear Pacifism," *Catholic World*, CXCVIII (March, 1964), 336–346.

This sense of direction cannot be found in technology; of itself, technology tends toward the exploitation of scientific possibilities simply because they are possibilities. . . . It is the function of morality to command the use of power, to forbid it, to limit it; or, more in general, to define the ends for which power may or must be used and to judge the circumstances of its use.[66]

The general consensus of the "just war" writers can be summed up in the following propositions: 1) In the absence of effective international peace-keeping institutions, the moral right of states to resort to war under certain circumstances cannot be denied. 2) Although aggressive war (which was permitted under the traditional doctrine to punish offenses and to restore justice) is no longer considered a lawful means available to states for the vindication of violated rights, there still exists the right to wage defensive war against aggression and to give aid to another party who is a victim of aggression.[67] 3) Modern military technology cannot be allowed to render entirely meaningless the traditional distinction between "combatant forces" and "innocents" even in strategic war. (This issue arose during the 1960s in the somewhat inconclusive strategic debate over "counterforce" versus "countercity" or "countervalue" strategies.) 4) The "just war" theorist denies that in war the end justifies the means and that once a war starts a government may employ any and every instrument at its disposal in an unlimited quest for victory. Even when the state has the moral right to wage war (*ius ad bellum*), there is an obligation to adhere to the law governing the means used in war (*ius in bello*).[68] 5) While there is reason to hope that deterrence will succeed and nuclear war will not occur, the "just war" writers insist that a posture of massive deterrence through the threat of massive retaliation is not sufficient. There is a heavy moral obligation upon political leaders to assure an operational readiness, in case deterrence fails, to wage war (including nuclear war) in a limited and discriminating rather than an all-out manner. Ramsey argues that "traditional and acceptable moral teachings concerning legitimate military targets require the avoidance of civilian damage as much as possible even while accepting this as in some measure an unavoidable indirect effect." [69] 5) Thus nuclear weapons cannot be held intrinsically evil (*malum in se*). Their strictly controlled use against primarily military targets, under conditions calculated to avoid escalation to uncontrollable levels, is morally conceivable, especially where this seems necessary to contain aggression quickly and bring about early negotiations. But their indiscriminate use against whole cities cannot be morally justified—not even in retaliation.[70]

The "just war" theorists recognize that they face several dilemmas. In the

66. Murray, *op. cit.*, p. 61.

67. O'Brien, *op. cit.*, pp. 34–41.

68. *Ibid.*, pp. 23–26 and Chapter 5, "Morality and Nuclear Weapons Systems."

69. Ramsey, *The Limits of Nuclear War, op. cit.*, p. 10.

70. This point was made by Pope Pius XII in 1954. See O'Brien, *op. cit.*, pp. 34 and 45.

past, some of them have denied the right of the Christian to be a conscientious objector and to refuse to bear arms to defend the common good in a just war. But the Second Vatican Council recommended that humane legal provision be made for conscientious objectors, provided that they agree to serve the human community in some other way.[71] More recently, just war theorists have engaged in a debate as to whether the Christian, instead of presuming the justice of a war declared by lawful political authority, should be allowed to be a "selective conscientious objector" against a particular war which he deems unjust. With a rise in the worldwide incidence of revolutionary guerrilla insurgency and counterinsurgency interventions by governments, the moral analysis of the kinds of force which are morally justifiable either to overthrow an unjust regime or to suppress guerrilla terrorism has undoubtedly gained a new lease on life. In short, despite frequent assertions that the "just war" doctrine had become obsolete in a nuclear era of unlimited destructive capability, there have been numerous instances of limited conventional and unconventional warfare to which the traditional analysis of the conditions needed for the moral justification of force is quite relevant and—what is more—frequently applied in the public political debate.

71. *Pastoral Constitution on the Church in the Modern World,* Chapter V, Sec. 1, in Walter M. Abbott, S. J., ed., *The Documents of Vatican II* (New York: America Press, 1966), p. 292. This constitution, building on Pope John XXIII's Encyclical, *Pacem in Terris,* and other sources, deals with such subjects as the legitimate right to self-defense, guerrilla warfare, the dangers of the arms race, the relation between peace and nuclear deterrence, and the need for negotiated disarmament with adequate safeguards.

Most "just war" theorists today have no difficulty in respecting the right of the Christian to be a conscientious objector, but they would argue that at the level of interstate relations the causes of neither peace nor justice can be made dependent upon the religious or ethical dispositions of individual consciences, and that governments charged with responsibilities for the defense of societies cannot be expected to adopt "pacifist" policies and renounce the right to resort to force at times.

CHAPTER 6
Economic Theories of Imperialism and War

In studies of the essential conditions for world peace and the causes of international conflict, economic factors have held a position of considerable importance. Implicit, if not explicit, in many theories of international relations is the assumption that rising living standards and national economic growth contribute to peace among nations. In modern liberal thought, writers such as Adam Smith, John Stuart Mill, and Richard Cobden, considered free trade to be a guarantor of peace. Free trade would create a division of labor based on international specialization in an international economy in which nations were so interdependent as to make virtually impossible the resort to war. The growth of individual and national prosperity would divert public attention from military ventures because of their potentially disruptive effects on economic growth and prosperity. In marked contrast to the proponents of free trade based upon economic competition, other writers have argued that economics is a principal determinant of international conflict.

Marx and Engels

Over large portions of the globe today the most popular theory among intellectuals for the explanation of imperialism, social revolutionary conflict and international war derives from the philosophical system of Karl Marx and from the pronouncements, both consistent and contradictory, of his numerous socialist and communist descendants, notably Lenin, Stalin, Khrushchev and Mao. The main elements of this theory are more than a century old; its origins date back to 1848. Yet the theory has shown a remarkable ability to survive into the third quarter of a century which is often harshly critical of abstractions inherited from the past. Perhaps it survives more as faith than

172

science, but survive it does. Consciously or unconsciously, a good many Western intellectuals and students of international relations have for several decades accepted the Marxist analysis of the causes of war and revolution. A surprising number of otherwise very bourgeois American college and university students, when asked to comment upon the reasons for the entry of the United States into World War I or for the contemporary appearance of revolutionary stirrings in Latin America, will readily give a rather orthodox rendition of the Marxist-Leninist hypothesis. Since World War II, there has been a widespread tendency among the elites of Asia, Africa and Latin America to assume the validity of the Marxist interpretation of imperialism. As one might expect, since Marxism itself is a product of Western culture, and since communism has singled out capitalism as its principal foe, not only the most sophisticated formulations but also the most incisive criticisms of the Marxist analysis have come from the West.

Marxism-Leninism is an admixture of metaphysics (dialectical materialism), theory of history (economic determinism), economic and sociological science, political ideology, theory and strategy of revolution, social ethics and an eschatalogical moral theology which looks toward a secular salvation: the advent of a classless social order of perfect justice in which conflict ceases and the psychology of a "new man" is generated. If Newton contributed toward an explanation of international conflict in terms of mechanistic equilibrium in the "Golden Age" of the balance of power, if Hegel to the personification of nations and the philosophy of national sentiment and clashes, if Darwin to a conception of international politics based on the notion of biological struggle from which the fittest survive, and if Freud to the concept of social conflict as a result of the projection outward of dark psychological forces from the inner depths of man, then Marx more than any other individual strengthened the idea that conflict arises inevitably out of the life-and-death struggle of socioeconomic classes. In the cosmic drama of redemption, capitalism is the sin from which man strives to be liberated; the grace which enables man to overcome sin is the knowledge of the inexorable dialectical laws of historical-social development; communism is the hoped-for Beatific Vision of complete happiness; and Marx is the way, the truth and the light which will lead the children of men to the promised land once they put aside the self-defeating delusion that they are the children of God.[1]

MARX AND DIALECTICAL MATERIALISM

Karl Marx spent much of his adult life in England, where he observed at firsthand the acceleration of the Industrial Revolution during the nineteenth

1. See especially Jules Monnerot, *Sociology and Psychology of Communism,* trans. Jane Degras and Richard Rees (Boston: Beacon Press, 1953), Chapters 1 and 2.

century. He perceived the emergence of an urban working class and a widening gap between the rich and the poor. Marx evolved a theory of history based on dialectical materialism, in which the system of economic production determines the institutional and ideological structure of society.[2] He who controls the economic system controls the political system. Marx and Engels's study of history and of nineteenth-century Britain led them to conclude that each period of history contains clashing forces, or a dialectic, from which a new order emerges. "In ancient Rome, we have patricians, knights, plebeians, slaves; in the Middle Ages, feudal lords, vassals, guild-masters, journeymen, apprentices, serfs; in almost all of these classes, again, subordinate gradations." [3]

All history is the history of class struggle between a ruling group and an opposing group, from which comes a new economic, political and social system. Marx's "model" for the study of society and its transformation contains a thesis (ruling group) and an antithesis (opposing group) which clash and produce a synthesis (new economic, political and social system).

Before the emergence of capitalism, ownership of land had been the basis of political power. The feudal system was challenged by a growing commercial class, a bourgeoisie, whose economic strength derived from trade and manufacturing and who lived in towns and cities, rather than on landed estates. From this clash of opposing forces emerged a new synthesis, capitalism. The bourgeoisie has concentrated population in large cities, centralized the means of production, and gathered wealth in a few hands. Formerly independent or loosely connected provinces which once had their separate legal systems, economic interests, and governments, have been organized into one nation with a central government and customs tariff.

Like the system which preceded it, capitalism contained the seeds of its own destruction. Marx foresaw the growing impoverishment of the working class, or proletariat, which would lead to a revolution to overthrow the ruling capitalist class. The lower strata of the middle class are absorbed into the proletariat, since they do not have the capital to compete on the scale of their larger counterparts and their specialized skills become worthless as a result of new methods of production. As the ranks of the proletariat are increased, the struggle with the bourgeoisie grows in intensity. Initially the struggle is conducted by individual workers, then by the laborers in one factory, against individual members of the exploiting capitalist class. Marx foresaw a series of clashes of increasing intensity between the proletariat and bourgeoisie until

---

2. For a detailed examination of this concept, see Gustav A. Wetter, *Dialectical Materialism: A Historical and Systematic Survey of Philosophy in the Soviet Union* (New York: Frederick A. Praeger, 1963).

3. Karl Marx and Friedrich Engels, *Manifesto of the Communist Party* (New York: International Publishers Company, 1932), p. 9.

the eruption of a revolution which results in the overthrow of the bourgeoisie.

Marx developed in elaborate detail his doctrine of surplus value. Stated briefly, the socially useful labor which produces it is considered to be the only measure of the worth of a commodity. Capitalists themselves produce nothing. Instead, they live like parasites from the labor of the producing class. The capitalist pays the laborer a subsistence wage and keeps the rest. According to Marx, the vast mass of the population become wage slaves in a capitalist society. The proletariat produces goods and services for which it receives no return. In a capitalist system, the bourgeoisie, which controls the means of production, exploits the worker and widens the gap, or surplus value, between the price paid the worker for his labor and the price obtained by the bourgeoisie in the market place for the goods or services produced by the proletariat.[4]

The coming clash between the capitalist, bourgeoisie class (thesis) and the proletariat (antithesis) would lead to a socialist order. There would be a period of extensive government controls over production and distribution until the last vestiges of capitalism were removed. Finally, Marx foresaw the withering away of the state with the development of a communist economic, political and socialist order.

Thus the Marxist views all political phenomena, including imperialism and war, as projections of underlying economic forces. Here all forms of consciousness are subordinated to the economic. Religious, humanitarian, political, cultural and military-strategic motives for any kind of power relationship between a stronger and a weaker community are explained by the Marxist as rationalizations designed to disguise the economic substructure. This has been essentially true throughout human history, Marx held, but it becomes most luminous in the case of capitalism. In a passage noted more for its ideological passion than its social science objectivity, Marx and Engels declared:

> The bourgeoisie . . . has left no other bond between man and man than naked self-interest, than callous "cash payment." It has drowned the most heavenly ecstacies of religious fervor, of chivalrous enthusiasm, of philistine sentimentalism, in the icy water of egotistical calculation. . . . The bourgeoisie has stripped of its halo every occupation hitherto honored and looked up to with reverent awe. It has converted the physician, the lawyer, the priest, the poet, the man of science, into its paid wage-laborers.[5]

4. See Karl Marx, *Capital: A Critique of Political Economy* (New York: Random House [Modern Library], n.d.), especially Chapters 1, 7, 9, 11, 12, 16, 18, and 24 for Marx's most extensive treatment of the concept of surplus value.

5. Karl Marx and Friedrich Engels, *Manifesto of the Communist Party*, p. 11.

Although Marx fully appreciated the worldwide scope of capitalist opera-tions for acquiring raw materials and marketing manufactures, he himself did not elaborate a theory of imperialism. This task was left for his twentieth-century intellectual heirs—Rudolph Hilferding (1877–1941), a German Social Democrat; Rosa Luxembourg (1870–1919), a German Socialist agi-tator; and Lenin, whose views will be examined presently.

Hobson on Imperialism

Curiously enough, most of the clues to the communist theory of imperialism in this century were provided by the English economist, J. A. Hobson. Hob-son, who was in several respects a forerunner of Lord Keynes, argued that imperialism results from maladjustments within the capitalist system, in which a wealthy minority oversaves while an impoverished or "bare subsistence" majority lacks the purchasing power to consume all the fruits of modern indus-try. Capitalist societies are thus faced with the critical dilemma of overpro-duction and underconsumption. If capitalists were willing to redistribute their surplus wealth in the form of domestic welfare measures, there would be no serious structural problem. But the capitalists seek instead to reinvest their surplus capital in profit-making ventures abroad. The result is imperialism, "the endeavor of the great controllers of industry to broaden the channel for the flow of their surplus wealth by seeking foreign markets and foreign invest-ments to take off the goods and capital they cannot sell or use at home." [6]

Hobson was aware that there were noneconomic forces at work in late nineteenth-century European expansion abroad—forces of a political, military, psychological and religious-philanthropic character. He insisted, however, that the essential ingredient in imperialism is finance capitalism, which galvanizes and organizes the other forces into a coherent whole.

> *Finance manipulates the patriotic forces which politicians, soldiers, philanthropists and traders generate; the enthusiasm for expansion which issues from these sources, though strong and genuine, is irregu-lar and blind; the financial interest has those qualities of concentration and clear-sighted calculation which are needed to set imperialism at work.* [7]

In Hobson's view, imperialism in the case of Britain had not been necessary to relieve population pressure, for Britain was not overpopulated and its growth rate at the turn of the century was declining toward a stationary level.

6. J. A. Hobson, *Imperialism: A Study* (London: George Allen and Unwin, 1902), p. 85.

7. *Ibid.*, p. 59.

Furthermore, he noted, Englishmen did not seem at all anxious to resettle in most areas of the Empire acquired after 1870.[8]

Hobson condemned late nineteenth-century imperialism as irrational and as bad business policy for the nation as a whole, even though it was rational and profitable for certain groups—bourses, speculative miners, engineers, the shipbuilding and armaments industries, the export industries, contractors to the military services, and the aristocratic classes that sent their sons to be officers in the army, navy, and colonial service.[9] Although the economic activities of these classes comprised but a small fraction of Britain's total enterprise, the groups benefiting from imperialism were well organized to advance their interests through political channels. Imperialism, said Hobson, involves enormous risks and costs to the nation compared to the relatively meager results it brings in the form of increased trade, and hence the rationale for it must be sought in the advantages it brings to special groups within the society. "To a larger extent every year Great Britain is becoming a nation living upon tribute from abroad, and the classes who enjoy this tribute have an ever-increasing incentive to employ the public policy, the public purse and the public force to extend the field of their private investments. . . ."[10] E. M. Winslow (1896–1966), professor and chairman of the department of economics at the Tufts University, evaluating the significance of Hobson's study, concluded: "No other book has been so influential in spreading the doctrine of economic imperialism."[11]

Hobson anticipated the later Leninist attack upon capitalist profiteering as a major factor in the causation of international war. Policies of aggressive imperialism and war lead to vast arms budgets, public debts and the fluctuation of the values of securities from which the skilled financier benefits most. "There is not a war, a revolution, an anarchist assassination, or any other public shock, which is not gainful to these men; they are harpies who suck their gains from every new forced expenditure, and every sudden disturbance of public credit."[12] To be sure, Hobson here is not saying that the capitalists are responsible for the wars from which they profit. Almost certainly he would not contend that capitalists lurked behind every anarchist assassin. But the unmistakable thrust of his reasoning—which would be made more explicit by Lenin—was that if the behavior of capitalists is primarily motivated by

8. *Ibid.,* p. 41–45. Later, Italy and Germany employed the argument concerning population pressure to justify their quest for colonies in Africa prior to World War I, and the Japanese did likewise in their Manchurian venture in the early 1930s. But in all the cases where the *Lebensraum* argument was employed, subsequent movement of population to the conquered areas proved negligible. See N. Peffer, "The Fallacy of Conquest," *International Conciliation* (New York: Carnegie Endowment for International Peace, No. 318, 1938).

9. Hobson, *op. cit.,* p. 46–51.

10. *Ibid.,* pp. 53–54.

11. E. M. Winslow, *The Pattern of Imperialism* (New York: Columbia University Press, 1948), p. 106.

12. Hobson, *op. cit.,* p. 58.

Economic Theories of Imperialism and War

the desire to gain profits, and if certain segments of capitalist society can profit from imperialistic wars, then these elements can be expected to bend every effort to bring about war when the circumstances call for it. In the passage quoted last, the tone of Hobson's moral indignation becomes less scholarly and more ideological, not unlike that which runs through the writings of Marx and his followers.

LENIN: IMPERIALISM AND INTERNATIONAL CONFLICT

Rosa Luxembourg (1870–1919), a German Socialist agitator, closely followed Hobson's analysis, while Hilferding sought to refine it by attributing the export of capital to the operation of cartel and monopoly systems which limit domestic investment possibilities. The best known theorist of imperialism in modern times, of course, was Lenin. The architect of the Bolshevik Revolution was neither the scholar nor the original thinker that Hobson was. In addition to borrowing ideas from Hobson, Lenin relied upon Hilferding's analysis of the role of monopoly capitalism.

> *Imperialism is capitalism in that stage of development in which the dominance of monopolies and finance capital has established itself; in which the export of capital has acquired pronounced importance; in which the division of the world among the international trusts has begun; in which the division of all territories of the globe among the great capitalist powers has been completed.*[13]

Monopoly capitalism, which he equated with imperialism, Lenin derived from four factors: the concentration of production in combines, cartels, syndicates and trusts; the competitive quest for sources of raw materials; the development of banking oligarchies; and the transformation of the "old" colonial policy into a struggle for spheres of economic interest in which the richer and more powerful nations exploit the weaker ones. Thus Lenin took strong exception to Karl Kautsky's thesis that imperialism was merely the "preferred policy" of capitalist states; for Lenin it was inevitable. Moreover, in the Leninist interpretation the receipt of monopoly profits by the capitalists of certain industries enables them to corrupt the workers in those industries, who for the sake of a higher standard of living ally themselves with the bourgeoisie against their fellow workers of the exploited, imperialized countries.

Since finance capitalism is the source of imperialism, it also becomes for the Marxists the principal source of international wars in the capitalist era, or at least the only source in which the Marxists are interested. If there are other sources of conflict, Marxists prefer not to call much attention to them. Hobson, who was a liberal rather than a Marxist, had conceded that there

13. V. I. Lenin, *Imperialism: The Highest Stage of Capitalism* (New York: International Publishers Company, 1939), p. 89.

Contending Theories of International Relations

are "primitive instincts" in the human race which played a part in nineteenth century imperialism—the instinct for the control of land, the "nomadic habit" which survives as love of travel, the "spirit of adventure," the sporting and hunting instincts, and the "lust of struggle," which in the age of spectator sports is transformed into gambling on the outcome of athletic games and into jingoism in war.[14] But Hobson circumvented the theoretical difficulty implicit in a plurality of factors merely by accusing the dominant classes in capitalistic societies of advancing their own interests by playing upon the primitive instincts of the race and channeling them into imperialistic ventures. Lenin, too, recognized that there had been imperialism in the world before the highest stage of capitalism had been reached, but he was not interested in the analysis of imperialism as a general phenomenon of all ages apart from reference to socio-economic systems and especially capitalism.

Lenin's contribution to communism was twofold: First, he imparted an organizational theory in which the Communist party became the "vanguard of the proletariat" to hasten the coming of the revolution which Marx had foreseen as inevitable. Second, drawing heavily upon the work of Hobson described above, Lenin developed a theory of imperialism, which ranks as the principal communist theory of international relations in an international system consisting of capitalist states.[15]

Looking back upon the history of Europe in the decades after Marx published his *Communist Manifesto,* Lenin concluded that the proletariat would not revolt spontaneously, as Marx had believed, against the ruling bourgeoisie. In his famous tract entitled *What Is to be Done?,* Lenin held that a strong, tightly-knit, highly-motivated party of professional revolutionaries was essen-

14. "Jingoism is merely the lust of the spectator, unpurged by any personal effort, risk, or sacrifice, gloating in the perils, pains, and slaughter of fellow-men whom he does not know, but whose destruction he desires in a blind and artificially stimulated passion of hatred and revenge. . . . The arduous and weary monotony of the march, the long periods of waiting, the hard privations, the terrible tedium of a prolonged campaign play no part in his imagination; the redeeming factors of war, the fine sense of comradeship which common personal peril educates, the fruits of discipline and self-restraint, the respect for the personality of enemies whose courage he must admit and whom he comes to realize as fellow-beings—all these moderating elements in actual war are eliminated from the passion of the Jingo. It is precisely for these reasons that some friends of peace maintain that the two most potent checks of militarism and of war are the obligation of the entire body of citizens to undergo military service and the experience of an invasion." Hobson, *op. cit.,* p. 215.

15. For the complete works of Lenin, see V. I. Lenin, *Collected Works* (Moscow: Foreign Language Publishing House, 1963), 44 vols. For biographical accounts of Lenin's life, see Louis Fischer, *The Life of Lenin* (New York: Harper and Row [Colophon Books], 1965); Robert Payne, *The Life and Death of Lenin* (New York: Simon and Schuster, 1946); Stefan T. Possony, *Lenin: the Compulsive Revolutionary* (Chicago: Henry Regnery Company, 1964); Christopher Hill, *Lenin and the Russian Revolution* (London: The English Universities Press Ltd., 1961); Bertram D. Wolfe, *Three Who Made a Revolution* (Boston: Beacon Press, 1955). For an analysis of the development of Communist theories of conflict and revolution from the time of Marx and Engels to Stalin, see Stefan T. Possony, *A Century of Conflict* (Chicago: Henry Regnery Company, 1953).

tial to the success of the revolution against the capitalist order. To Lenin, the Communist party, the "vanguard of the proletariat," was the most class-conscious, devoted, and self-sacrificing part of the proletariat.[16] Lenin held that the party must be centralized or hierarchical. It must be based on "democratic centralism"—that is, the party must provide for discussion and debate of issues before a decision was taken, while adopting iron-clad discipline in executing policy after a decision had been made.

Lenin saw imperialism as a special, advanced stage of capitalism. In capitalist systems, competition is eventually replaced by capitalist monopolies.[17] Imperialism is the monopoly stage of capitalism. The need to export capital arises from diminishing investment opportunities in capitalist countries themselves. The export of capital to achieve a higher rate of investment return hastens the development of capitalism elsewhere in the world. The countries which are the principal exporters of capital are able to obtain economic advantages based on the exploitation of peoples abroad. Moreover, the greater the development of capitalism, the greater the need for raw materials and markets, and hence the greater the scramble for colonies. The establishment of political control over overseas territories is designed to provide a dependable source of raw materials and cheap labor and to guarantee markets for the industrial combines of advanced capitalist countries.

Lenin held that imperialist policies would enable capitalist powers to stave off the inevitable revolution, since conditions of the domestic proletariat would be ameliorated by the exploitation of the working class in colonial territories. A portion of the proletariat in advanced capitalist countries even finds it possible to rise to the ranks of the bourgeoisie.

Writing in the spring of 1916, nearly two years after the outbreak of World War I, Lenin viewed the history of the previous generation as a struggle between the advanced capitalist powers for the control of colonies and markets. Capitalist countries have formed alliances for the exploitation of the underdeveloped areas. Especially in the Far East and Africa, the imperialist powers have claimed territories and spheres of influence. But such alliances are only "breathing spells" between wars, since the capitalist powers find it necessary to fight for control of limited overseas markets and raw materials. Because of the ultimate dependence of capitalist economic systems upon such markets and natural resources, international conflict is endemic in a world of capitalist states. The elimination of capitalist states, Lenin concluded, was the essential precondition to the abolition of international conflict.

For Lenin, capitalism developed at its own pace in each country, earlier in Holland, England and France, later in Germany and the United States, later still in Japan and Russia. But as it developed, monopolistic capital engaged in a feverishly competitive search for new markets, sources of raw materials

16. See V. I. Lenin, *Collected Works* (Moscow: Foreign Languages Publishing House, 1961), V, 425–529.

17. Lenin, *Imperialism: The Highest Stage of Capitalism,* pp. 16–30.

and cheap labor. Lenin was of the opinion that by this time the cartels had virtually completed the process of parceling out the territories of the world for exploitation. Because the planet has already been divided up, further expansion by some capitalists can occur only at the expense of other capitalists, and thus capitalistic imperialism provokes international wars.[18] Much later, in his famous "last thesis," issued on the eve of the 1952 meeting of the Communist Party of the Soviet Union, Stalin argued that the "frightful clashes" which Lenin had predicted between the capitalist and socialist camps were no longer inevitable, because such a war would jeopardize the very existence of capitalism. But Stalin went on to declare that contradictions within the capitalist system made the recurrence of war among capitalist states inevitable.[19] This was a rather unusual prophecy to utter at a time when, just a few years after the onset of the Cold War, the "capitalist world" appeared to be more unified than before World War II, as a result of the formation of the North Atlantic alliance.

Lenin, Stalin and War

Orthodox Leninist-Stalinist reasoning led inescapably to the conclusion that modern war is a function of capitalist imperialism; that if war should occur between the two systems it would be as a result of capitalist aggression and it would lead to the destruction of capitalism and the universal triumph of socialism; and that in an all-socialist world, once the dangers of "capitalist encirclement" had been eliminated, war would disappear. Stalin declared: "In order to destroy the inevitability of wars, it is necessary to destroy imperialism." [20] Stalin, of course, was not necessarily implying that the socialist camp must someday try to destroy the imperialist camp by carrying out an aggressive military attack across national boundaries. Stalin was, if anything, a cautious, conservative strategist; he certainly was not calling for a socialist holy war against a technologically superior Western state system. Both he and his successor, Khrushchev, propounded the thesis that "capitalist encirclement" must eventually give way to "socialist encirclement." Only in the sense that capitalism would undergo a revolutionary transformation into socialism should a communist contemplate the destruction of imperialism. Khrushchev is rather widely thought to have had a better appreciation than did Stalin of the implications of nuclear weapons technology for the "inevitability of war" problem, inasmuch as he formally recognized that general nuclear war could very well destroy not only capitalist society but communist society as well.

18. Lenin, *Collected Works*, XIX, 87 and 104.

19. Bernard Taurer, "Stalin's Last The-sis," *Foreign Affairs*, XXXI (April, 1953), 374.

20. Taurer, *op. cit.*, p. 378.

Thus while pursuing limited-risk arms control agreements with the capitalist West in order to render more manageable the strategic-military environment as reflected in international armaments competition, while at the same time continuing to develop Soviet military capabilities, both strategic and tactical, Khrushchev and his successors (Kosygin and Brezhnev) have lent support to "wars of national liberation" in the Third World. These are forms of warfare which are considered both "just" in terms of socialist ideology and "safe" from the standpoint of strategic analysis in an era of mutual nuclear deterrence.[21]

Nevertheless, whatever subtle modifications may have been made in recent decades by Communist leaders who have had to grapple with the realities of the international strategic environment, there has been no significant change in the Leninist theory of imperialism. Yet purely on grounds of politicoeconomic categorizations and correlations, this theory runs into several difficulties. While most of the advanced capitalistic countries did indeed engage in imperialistic adventures, not all of them did—witness Sweden and Switzerland—while Portugal, which lacked many of the essential characteristics of capitalist culture, remained one of the most important of the colonizing powers in the late nineteenth century, unchallenged in her territories by the more advanced capitalist states. Furthermore, the advanced capitalist countries invested more capital in other advanced countries than in undeveloped colonial territories, and they carried on much more trade with the former than with the latter. Foreign investment in the more advanced industrial countries is not always popular (unless it helps to cement a popular political-military alliance), but it cannot properly be regarded as unilaterally exploitative. If anything, the relationship is one of mutual exploitation, or what the classical economists call "comparative advantage." In the history of England and France, the two principal capitalist imperialist powers of modern Europe, it is not possible to draw convincing correlations between surges of imperialistic sentiment and activity on the one hand and the outward flow of investment funds on the other.[22] And even in those cases where the investment capital did go into colonial regions, and where the relationship between private capital and the colonial country was more onesidedly exploitative largely because of a great disparity in respect to development levels and economic

21. See Herbert S. Dinerstein, *War and the Soviet Union* (New York: Frederick A. Praeger, 1959), pp. 68–69 and 80–81; Frederick C. Barghoorn, *Soviet Foreign Propaganda* (Princeton: Princeton University Press, 1964), pp. 92–93; Frederic S. Burin, "The Communist Doctrine of the Inevitability of War," *American Political Science Review*, LVII (June, 1963), 352-354; Walter C. Clemens, Jr., "Ideology in Soviet Disarmament Policy," *Journal of Conflict Resolution*, VIII (March, 1964), 17–20.

22. William L. Langer, "A Critique of Imperialism," *Foreign Affairs*, XIV (October, 1935), 103–104. Langer notes that France sent most of her capital not to her colonies but to Russia, Rumania, Spain, Portugal, Egypt and the Ottoman Empire. "In 1902 only two and a half billion francs out of a total foreign investment of some 30 or 35 billion francs was placed in the colonies." *Ibid.*, p. 104.

power, the relationship between the capitalistic governments and the colonial peoples was far from a purely exploitative one. The colonial services of the Western imperialist governments even before World War I had brought to their overseas territories literacy and education, administrative-level systems, hospitals, medicine, hygiene and sanitary methods, and at least the rudiments of technology, technical competence and scientific knowledge, along with the softening effects of European civilization and the Christian religion, all of which constituted advantages beyond what would have accrued to the native populations had they remained closed to Western contacts.[23] An objective appraisal of imperialism would note its positive achievements as well as its sordid aspects,[24] but twentieth-century Marxists have been preoccupied with the latter. Notable among Western writers who were strongly influenced by the Marxist-Leninist interpretation of imperialism and who consequently took a rather narrow view of the phenomenon were the English socialist Harold J. Laski (1893–1950) and the American historian Parker T. Moon (1892–1936).[25]

Critics of the Economic Theories of Imperialism

Modern critics of the economic theories of imperialism have taken issue with Hobson, Lenin and their followers on grounds of both semantics and theoretical analysis. These critics have generally accused the Marxists of being so

23. See Luigi Sturzo, *Nationalism and Internationalism* (New York: Roy Publishers, 1946), p. 225. Sturzo, the founder of the modern Christian Democratic Party in Italy, became an exile after the rise of Mussolini to power.

24. The political impact of the West upon the colonial lands was in some respects greater than the economic. The very concepts of "independence," "self-determination," "freedom" and "sovereign equality" which the peoples of Asia and Africa employed with great effect after World War II to express their political aspirations were borrowed from the Western political vocabulary by native leaders who had received their university education in the West. See Hans Kohn, "Reflections on Colonialism," in Robert Strausz-Hupé and Harry W. Hazard, eds., *The Idea of Colonialism* (New York: Frederick A. Praeger, 1958), pp. 6–14.

25. Harold Laski went through a phase of revolutionary Marxism during the

1930s, in which he argued that the capitalist class will invariably resort to war to combat either domestic or foreign threats to its economic interests. He did not hold that the capitalists really want war, but he said that they puruse objectives which they refuse to abandon even if they cannot be attained except by war. See *The State in Theory and Practice* (New York: Viking Press, 1935), pp. 202–204. Nearly a decade earlier, Parker T. Moon had presented imperialism as a peculiarly Western phenomenon: "Imperialism . . . means domination of non-European native races by totally dissimilar European nations." *Imperialism and World Politics*, (New York: Macmillan Company, 1926), p. 33. Thus Moon reflected a widespread tendency in this century to identify imperialism with the foreign policies of the Western capitalist maritime powers involving the subjection of distant and alien peoples.

obsessed by their ideological aversion to finance capitalism as to confuse particular historic manifestation of the imperialistic impulse with a much more comprehensive sociological phenomenon which has assumed many different shapes throughout history. Moritz Julius Bonn (1873–1965), a German economist, defined imperialism as "a policy which aims at creating, organizing and maintaining an empire; that is, a state of vast size composed of various more or less distinct national units and subject to a single centralized will." [26] The American historian Charles A. Beard (1874–1948) wrote: "Imperialism is employment of the engines of government and diplomacy to acquire territories, protectorates, and/or spheres of influence occupied usually by other races or peoples, and to promote industrial, trade and investment opportunities." [27] Hans J. Morgenthau lamented the application of the term "imperialism" to any foreign policy which the user of the term found objectionable, and he urged the post-World War II generation of university students to accept an objective, ethically neutral definition of imperialism as "a policy that aims at the overthrow of the status quo, at a reversal of the power relations between two or more nations." [28] He denied that every increase in the international power of a nation is necessarily imperialistic. Moreover, he warned against the disposition to regard every foreign policy which aims conservatively at the maintenance of an already existing empire as imperialistic, when the term should properly be reserved for the dynamic process of changing the international status quo by acquiring an empire. [29]

The economic interpretation of imperialism, contends Morgenthau, errs in the attempt to build a universal law of history upon the limited experience of a few isolated cases. The theory not only ignores the problem of precapitalist imperialism (including the ancient empires of Egypt, Assyria, Persia and Rome; Arab imperialism of the seventh and eighth centuries; the European Christian imperialism of the Crusades; and the personal empires of such men as Alexander the Great, Napoleon and Hitler), but it also fails to provide a convincing explanation even of capitalist-age imperialism. Most of the major wars in the age of mature capitalism were not fought primarily for economic motives. The Boer War and the Chaco War between Bolivia and Paraguay (1932–1935) were, but not the Austro-Prussian War, the Franco-German War, the Crimean War, the Spanish-American War, the Russo-Japanese War and the Turco-Italian War, and certainly not the two world wars. Moreover, Europe's acquisition of colonial territories in the age of mature capitalism was small compared with that which occurred from the sixteenth to the

26. M. J. Bonn, "Imperialism," in the *Encyclopedia of the Social Sciences* (New York: Macmillan Company, 1937), VII, 605.

27. Charles A. Beard, *American Foreign Policy in the Making 1932–1940* (New Haven: Yale University Press, 1946), p. 113.

28. Hans J. Morgenthau, *Politics among Nations: The Struggle for Power and Peace,* 4th ed. (New York: Alfred A. Knopf, 1966), p. 42. This definition was carried in the 1948, 1954, 1960 and 1967 editions.

29. *Ibid.*

eighteenth century. Finally, since war involves the irrational and the unpredictable, while capitalism thrives best on rational foresight and planning, capitalists are partisans of peace rather than war.[30]

Raymond Aron notes that the Leninist theory of imperialism enjoys great prestige even among non-Marxists because of its intellectually satisfying ability to account for a variety of circumstances.[31] (Morgenthau would add that the intellectual climate of Western capitalist culture itself favors the reduction of politics to a matter of economics.) Like Morgenthau, Aron holds that, apart from the Boer War, none of the conflicts seriously engaging the interests of the European Powers between 1870 and 1914 was traceable to a desire for capitalist profits. In fact, "the actual relationship is most often the reverse of that accepted by the current theory of imperialism: the economic interests are only a pretext or a rationalization, whereas the profounder cause lies in the nations' will to power." [32] Aron illustrates his point by referring to the Russo-Japanese War, the establishment of the French protectorate in Tunisia, pressure from the Wilhelmstrasse for German banks to invest in the Berlin-Baghdad Railway and other pre-World War I examples. The late American economist Jacob Viner (1892–1970) substantially agreed with Aron:

> In almost all of these cases, the capitalist, instead of pushing his government into an imperialistic enterprise in pursuit of his own financial gain, was pushed, or dragged, or cajoled, or lured into it by his government, in order that, in its relations with the outside world and with its own people, this government might be able to point to an apparently real and legitimate economic stake in the territory involved which required military protection.[33]

Aron is particularly insistent that neither the First nor the Second World War could be explained adequately in economic terms. The fact that one of the results of World War I was a redistribution of Germany's colonial empire in no way proves that Frenchmen, Englishmen and Germans really fought the war to enable the capitalists of their respective countries to exact a larger share of an already divided up planet.[34] More important factors than economic competition in the two cataclysmic wars of this century were balance of power policies, unbridled political nationalism and the administrative-technological rivalry of military organizations.[35] Aron assigns a central place to Anglo-

30. *Ibid.*, pp. 46–49.

31. See Raymond Aron, *The Century of Total War* (Boston: Beacon Press, 1955), Chapter III, "The Leninist Myth of Imperialism," especially p. 57.

32. *Ibid.*, p. 59.

33. Jacob Viner, "International Relations Between State-Controlled Economies," in *Readings in the Theory of International Trade*, American Economic Association; Blakiston Series of Republished Articles

on Economics (Philadelphia: Blakiston Company, 1949), IV, 437–458.

34. Aron, *op. cit.*, p. 62.

35. *Ibid.*, pp. 62–73. The student who is interested in further research into the origins of World War I should consult the works of such specialists in the subject as Sidney Bradshaw Fay, G. P. Gooch, Harry Elmer Barnes, Camille Bloch, A. J. P. Taylor, Bernadotte E. Schmitt, Nicholas Mansergh and Ray-

German rivalry before World War I, but denies that this had much to do with capitalism. If capitalist imperialism had been the main motive for England's going to war in 1914, then she should have arrayed herself against her major capitalist competitor since the turn of the century—the United States.[36] The fact that this was unthinkable should serve to cast some doubt upon the explanatory power of a theory which subordinates international politics to international economics.

One of the most trenchant critiques of the Leninist theory came from the pen of the Austrian economist Joseph A. Schumpeter (1883–1950), who insisted that imperialism cannot be reduced to the pursuit of concrete economic interest, when history is replete with examples of societies "that seek expansion for the sake of expanding, war for the sake of fighting, victory for the sake of winning, dominion for the sake of ruling." [37] Wars are not fought in order to realize immediate utilitarian advantages, even if these are the professed purpose. Imperialism rather is "the objectless disposition on the part of a state to unlimited forcible expansion." [38] Like nationalism, it is irrational and unconscious, a calling into play of instincts from the dim past. Imperialism, in short, is an atavism in the social culture. If one wants to trace it to economic roots, he should realize that it stems from past rather than present relations of production. Undoubtedly it is the ruling classes in any state who take the decisions for war, but it is not the business bourgeoisie who comprise the principal foreign-policy decision-makers in the modern world; it is the vestigial aristocratic classes of an earlier regime who still fill the important governmental, diplomatic and military posts. Capitalism does not exhibit a particularly warlike disposition when compared to previous aristocratic, military and religious caste systems. In fact, competitive enterprise in the capitalist system absorbs tremendous amounts of human energy in purely economic pursuits, leaving little excess to be worked off in war and even less tendency

mond Sontag. Most of these specialists, as well as most leading general historians of modern Europe (e.g., J. Salwyn Schapiro, F. Lee Benns, Carlton J. H. Hayes, Ferdinand Schevill, Charles D. Hazen and William Stearns Davis) trace the coming of the war to the interaction of the European alliance systems; nationalism; irredentism; the political somewhat more than the economic aspects of imperialistic rivalry; militarism and armaments; and the condition of "international anarchy," i.e., the absence of organization adequate to enforce international law and ensure peaceful settlement of disputes. Subordinate but not insignificant factors were: the role of the press in the formation of popular attitudes, fears, suspicions and antipathies toward foreign nations and the impact of individual personalities and decisions. For an highly informative appraisal of five self-styled American "revisionist" historians and social scientists—Harry Elmer Barnes, Charles A. Beard, C. Hartley Grattan, Walter Millis, and Charles Callan Tansill—who took it upon themselves to persuade their countrymen that they should have not entered World War I, see Warren I. Cohen, *The American Revisionists: The Lessons of Intervention in World War I* (Chicago: University of Chicago Press, 1967).

36. Aron, *op. cit.,* p. 65.

37. Joseph A. Schumpeter, *Imperialism and Social Classes,* Heinz Norden, trans., Paul M. Sweezy, ed. (Oxford: Basil Blackwell, Ltd., 1951), p. 5.

38. *Ibid.,* p. 6.

to welcome war as a diversion from unpleasant activities or from boredom. Capitalist society, far from furnishing an environment conducive to imperialism, creates the sociological basis for a substantial opposition to war and armaments. Before the age of capitalism, pacifist principles had been taken seriously only by a few obscure religious sects. Pacifism emerges as a significant political movement only in capitalist society where organized parties begin to produce peace leaders, peace slogans and peace programs, along with a popular aversion to imperialism and popular support for arbitration of disputes, disarmament and international organization. In this respect Schumpeter is in basic agreement with Norman Angell and even, strangely enough, with Karl Marx and Friedrich Engels, who had noted in *The Communist Manifesto* that national differences and antagonisms between peoples were daily vanishing, owing to the development of the bourgeoisie, to freedom of commerce, to the world market, to the uniformity in the mode of production.[39] According to Schumpeter's line of reasoning, if the ruling classes of capitalist countries now and then opt for policies of imperialism and war, they do so because they are motivated not by the calculus of capitalist interest but rather by atavistic instincts inherited from a precapitalist age—instincts not yet driven out by the logic of capitalism.

Finally, Schumpeter cautions against the tendency of Marxist-Leninist analysis to appeal in a superficial way to the evidence of cases which are rarely if ever examined in detail. Such a tendency opens up the danger of "tautological solutions" which he describes in this passage:

> *France conquered Algeria, Tunisia and Morocco, and Italy conquered Abyssinia, by military force without there being any significant capitalist interest to press for it . . . . If that should not look very Marxist, it will be replied that action was taken under pressure of potential or anticipated capitalist interests or that in the last analysis some capitalist interest or objective necessity "must" have been at the bottom of it. And we can then hunt for corroboratory evidence that will never be entirely lacking, since capitalist interests, like any others, will in fact be affected by, and take advantage of, any situation whatsoever. . . . Evidently it is preconceived conviction and nothing else that keeps us going in a task as desperate as this. . . . And we really need not take the trouble; we might just as well say that "it must be so" and leave it at that.[40]*

To sum up, the Hobson-Leninist theory of imperialism is an analytic tool which has attracted the allegiance of many intellectuals probably more for its anticapitalist ideological content than for any validity it might possess as a result of careful empirical research. Nearly all analysts agree that the theory has a partial validity. It furnishes an adequate interpretation of a few instances

39. Marx and Engels, *The Communist Manifesto*, p. 28.
40. Joseph A. Schumpeter, *Capitalism, Socialism and Democracy,* 3rd ed. (New York: Harper and Brothers, 1950), fn. pp. 52–53.

of modern imperialism and would have a wider applicability if it did not, merely to "save the appearances" for Marxism, focus excessively upon economic factors to the exclusion of political, psychological and cultural determinants of human social action. The theory fails to come to grips with the question of whether modern imperialism is to be explained primarily by economic factors unique to the capitalist system or by a greater variety of factors more relevant to the universal phenomenon of social group expansionism in all historic periods. Nor does it face up to the question of whether violent conflict can really be adequately understood as a result of a capitalist imperialism which emanates from societies of strong pacifist inclinations. Granted that some capitalists undoubtedly profit from the waging of wars, this does not prove that they cause or originate wars, or that capitalists at a given time are more bellicose than pacifists, or that the small group who might have an interest in precipitating war actually possesses the power to galvanize the primitive impulses of enough people within the society to determine the choice for war. It could happen occasionally, but the serious student of international relations is not likely to accept such a simplistic solution for all modern wars. Nor is he likely to believe that an all-socialist world would be entirely nonimperialistic and peaceful.

Leninist Theory and Postwar International Relations

The history of international relations since World War II has not dealt too kindly to the Leninist theory of imperialism. That theory is hard-pressed to explain Soviet Communist imperialism in Eastern Europe. Stalin's last thesis concerning the inevitability of war within the capitalist camp has not been verified to the complete satisfaction of most observers. On the one hand, to be sure, the West has had its internal disagreements (eg., Suez, the Graeco-Turkish dispute over Cyprus and French policy toward NATO under de Gaulle) but none of these has been the internecine struggle which Stalin seemed to predict. On the other hand, the communist state system itself has known some serious conflicts. Soviet troops suppressed a workers' revolt in East Germany in 1953, crushed the Hungarian uprising in 1956, and with the Warsaw Pact allies invaded Czechoslovakia in 1968. North Korea attacked South Korea in 1950 and was later joined in the aggression by Communist China. The latter country launched a major military attack against Tibet in 1950 and against India in 1962, and by 1969 was engaged in hostilities with the Soviet Union along the Amur-Issurri Rivers. At the time of the Hungarian uprising, Khrushchev declared that the Soviet Union was putting down a counterrevolution. In 1961, he pledged the Soviet Union to support "wars of national liberation" in the developing world. In 1968, after the Soviet military move against Czechoslovakia, party leader Leonid Brezhnev announced the doctrine that the Soviet Union had the right to intervene for the defense of communism in any country of the socialist camp, with or without an invitation. While Marxists offer a theoretical explanation of the Soviet interventions in Eastern Europe and in such national liberation wars as Vietnam in terms of the struggle between the forces of socialism and the forces of capitalism, it is much more difficult to do this for the Sino-Indian War and impossible to do it for the Sino-Soviet conflict.

Since the 1950s, the Leninist theory of imperialism has been seriously strained by the process of decolonization carried out by the European powers —notably Britain, France, the Netherlands and Belgium. Although conflict has attended the independence of such states as Algeria, India, Pakistan, Cyprus, the Congo, and Kenya, more than two-score erstwhile colonial territories in Asia and Africa achieved status as independent states with relatively little conflict. According to the tenets of economic determinism, the capitalists should have fought much more tenaciously than they did to preserve their imperialist holdings. Furthermore, since the masses' standard of living in the Western capitalist states had been alleged to be artificially high because it was based substantially on the exploitation of colonial native populations, there should have been a perceptible decline in the West's standard of living as a result of disimperialism, but this did not occur. To the contrary, the formation of the European Economic Community or "Common Market" reflected a conviction on the part of Western capitalists that, regardless of how important trade with, and investment in, the overseas colonies may once have been, economic transactions among the advanced industrial countries of the West were now considerably more important for the continued development of the free "mixed enterprise" system of democratic social welfare states. Britain as the world's leading imperialist power undoubtedly felt most keenly of all the economic consequences of disimperialism, but as early as 1961, when the Macmillan Government announced that it would seek entry into the Common Market, the political leadership of Britain demonstrated its recognition of the fact that the European Continent had superseded the lands of the old British Empire (i. e., the modern Commonwealth of Nations) as vital to the British economy.

In the face of international political and economic developments within the last two decades, Communists and other Marxists have been compelled to modify their theories of imperialism and conflict in several compensatory ways. Despite the steady movement of Asia and Africa toward political decolonization, Nikita Khrushchev frequently warned that the Western nations would "halt the disintegration of the colonial system of imperialism and strangle the national liberation movements of the peoples for freedom and independence." [41] The West, said Khrushchev, was desperately seeking new forms for

41. Nikita S. Khrushchev, *For Victory in Peaceful Competition with Capitalism* (New York: E. P. Dutton and Company, 1960), p. 33. See also pp. 628–29.

keeping the peoples of economically underdeveloped countries in a state of permanent dependence. If any politically independent government in the Third World entered into a military assistance pact with a Western nation for defense against external attack or internal guerrilla subversion, this was simply a case, in Khrushchev's eyes, of fastening another control upon nominally independent states and propping up their "corrupt regimes" under the pretext of saving them from communism.[42] Khrushchev singled out the European Economic Community as an instrument of "neocolonialism" against which the new states had to be particularly on their guard. There was no doubt that official communist theory, while conceding that some economic development was now taking place in the Third World, still regarded the newly independent countries as part of the world subject to exploitation by the capitalist monopolies. Whereas the native populations had been previously oppressed by foreign capitalists and their colonial governments, they were now oppressed by foreign capitalists and their local allies—the national bourgeoisie, which found itself in the contradictory position of being itself an exploiting class, and thus dependent on international finance capital in the struggle against socialism, and of seeking to gain its own independence against foreign capitalistic imperialism.[43]

According to the strictly orthodox Marxist-Leninist theory, the affluence of Western society was due in substantial measure to the exploitation by European and American capitalism of the peoples of Asia, Africa and Latin America. Hence the West's standard of living should have declined after the loss of the colonial empires, but in actual fact it continued to rise. To offset this paradox, Marxists laid increasing emphasis on the argument that the Western economies were being artificially stimulated by the "arms race" and the fomenting of war hysteria for the enrichment of a handful of monopolists.[44] A corollary to this, of course, is the contention that the reluctance and the slowness with which Western governments enter into negotiations for arms limitation agreements are to be attributed to the fact that the so-called military-industrial complex (a sociological entity of somewhat dubious "viscosity") has such a large stake in ensuring continued military-technological competition.

The notion that colonial exploitation has been replaced by the "arms race" does not stand up too well under serious scrutiny. The United States, which had a very meager overseas empire compared to the European nations, would undoubtedly have become the principal military defender of Western civilization after World War II regardless of developments in the colonial world. The West European nations which renounced rather enormous colonial holdings have consistently allocated a much lower percentage of their gross national product to defense than has the United States, and the case could be made that the West European standard of living has risen more rapidly than that

42. *Ibid.*, pp. 750–751.
43. G. Mirsky, "Whither the Newly Independent Countries?" *International Affairs* (Moscow), XII (December, 1962), 2, 23–27.
44. Khrushchev, *op. cit.*, pp. 33–35.

of the United States during the last two decades. Furthermore, even though it is reasonable to expect that the cancellation of military contracts following upon a disarmament agreement would have an adverse multiplier effect upon prices, employment, public spending, and confidence in the health of a capitalist nation's economy, two important points must be made in this connection: 1) In terms of pure economics, the problem of disarmament is a soluble one.[45] 2) The primary obstacles to disarmament, far from being economic, are technical, strategic and political. The arms problem in the age of the nuclear missile can hardly be adequately explained by the old "devil theory" of war. It is not an aberration imposed upon the contemporary international system by the profiteering of certain industrialists (the "munitions-makers") or the innate aggressiveness of certain militarists. It is rather an intrinsic part of the system, deeply rooted in the essential characteristics of modern science and technology, of the decision-making and diplomatic processes of governments, of the global ideological-sociopolitical competition, and of a world structure in which nation-states seem driven by a law of their own nature to seek their security by engaging in some form of power balancing.[46] This at least is as plausible an explanation of the arms race as that furnished by the Marxists.

Contemporary Theories of Revolutionary Warfare

No study of communist theories would be complete without an examination of writings which have formed the theoretical basis of revolutionary warfare as practiced by such contemporary figures as Mao Tse-tung, Ho Chi Minh, and Ernesto "Che" Guevara. Several themes run through their official statements, as well as through the writings of General Vo Nguyen Giap, the archi-

45. See *Economic and Social Consequences of Disarmament*, Report of the Secretary-General, United Nations, Department of Economic and Social Affairs, New York, 1962; *Economic Impacts of Disarmament*, United States Arms Control and Disarmament Agency Publication 2 (Washington: Government Printing Office, 1962). Emile Benoit, "Economic Adjustments to Arms Control," *Journal of Arms Control*, I (April, 1963), 105–111; and Robert A. Levine, "General Disarmament as a Policy Goal: Economic Aspects," in *The Prospects for Arms Control*, James E. Dougherty, ed., with John F. Lehman, Jr. (New York: Macfadden-Bartell Corporation, 1965), pp. 163–170.

46. See the following works by James E. Dougherty: "Nuclear Weapons Control," *Current History*, XLVII (July, 1964), 31–38; "The Status of the Arms Negotiations," *Orbis*, IX (Spring, 1965), 49–97; "Soviet Disarmament Policy," Chapter 7 in Eleanor L. Dulles and Robert D. Crane, eds., *Détente: Cold War Strategies in Transition* (New York: Frederick A. Praeger, 1965), pp. 138–178; *Arms Control and Disarmament: The Critical Issues* (Washington: Center for Strategic Studies, Georgetown University, Special Report Series, 1966); and the introduction to James E. Dougherty and John F. Lehman, Jr., eds., *Arms Control for the Late Sixties* (Princeton: D. Van Nostrand, 1967), pp. xxi–xl.

tect of North Vietnamese military strategy in South Vietnam; Régis Debray, who has written on revolutionary warfare in Latin America; and Frantz Fanon, who sought to generalize from the experience of the Algerian War to a worldwide black revolution.[47]

Revolution is a long-term process by which a group of revolutionaries, initially inferior in numbers and capabilities, seizes power from a governing class by the use of guerrilla warfare. As set forth by Mao Tse-tung, the principles of operation are: (1) to attack isolated enemy forces first and to gain control of portions of the countryside from which further operations can be launched; (2) to seize small and medium cities and, only at a later stage, to take larger cities; (3) to make the eradication of the enemy's effective

47. There is an extensive primary and secondary literature on revolutionary warfare. Among the sources are: "On Protracted War," "Problems of Strategy in Guerrilla War against Japan," "The Role of the Chinese Communist Party in the National War," and "Problems of War and Strategy," in *Selected Works of Mao Tse-tung*, (Peking: Foreign Languages Press, 1965), II, 79–237; General Samuel B. Griffith, *Mao Tse-tung on Guerrilla Warfare* (New York: Frederick A. Praeger, 1961); Scott A. Boorman, *The Protracted Game* (New York: Oxford University Press, 1969); Mostafa Rejai, *Mao Tse-tung on Revolution and War* (New York: Doubleday and Company, 1969); Bruno Shaw, ed., *Selected Works of Mao Tse-tung* (New York: Harper [Colophon Books], 1970); Stuart Schram, *Political Leaders of the Twentieth Century: Mao Tse-tung* (Baltimore: Penguin Books, 1967); Robert Jay Lifton, *Revolutionary Immortality: Mao Tse-tung and the Chinese Cultural Revolution* (New York: Alfred A. Knopf [Vintage Books], 1968); H. C. Peterson, ed., *Che Guevara on Guerrilla Warfare* (New York: Frederick A. Praeger, 1961); Daniel James, ed., *The Complete Bolivian Diaries of Che Guevara and Other Captured Documents* (New York: Stein and Day, 1968); Rolando E. Bonachea and Nelson P. Valdes, eds., *Che: Selected Works of Ernesto Guevara* (Cambridge: M.I.T. Press, 1969); Jay Mallin, ed., *"Che" Guevara on Revolution: A Documentary Overview* (Coral Gables: University of Miami Press, 1969); George Lavan, ed., *Che Guevara Speaks: Selected Speeches and Writings* (New York: Grove Press, 1968); Régis Debray, *Revolution in the Revolution: Armed Struggle and Political Struggle in Latin America* (New York: Grove Press, 1967); Leo Huberman and Paul M. Sweezy, eds., *Régis Debray and the Latin American Revolution* (New York: Monthly Review Press, 1968); Robin Blackburn, ed., *Strategy for Revolution: Essays on Latin America* (New York: Monthly Review Press, 1970); Luis Mercier Vega, *Guerrillas in Latin America: The Technique of the Counter-State* (New York: Frederick A. Praeger, 1969); General Vo Nguyen Giap, *People's War; People's Army* (New York: Frederick A. Praeger, 1962); Bernard B. Fall, ed., *Ho Chi Minh on Revolution: Selected Writings, 1920–1966* (New York: Frederick A. Praeger, 1967); George K. Tanham, *Communist Revolutionary Warfare: The Vietminh in Indochina* (New York: Frederick A. Praeger, 1961); Sir Robert Thompson, *No Exit from Vietnam* (New York: David McKay, 1969); Charles W. Thayer, *Guerrilla* (New York: Harper and Row, 1962); Harry Eckstein, ed., *Internal War: Problems and Approaches* (New York: Free Press of Glencoe, 1964); Peter Paret and John W. Shy, *Guerrillas in the 1960's* (New York: Frederick A. Praeger, 1962); William J. Pomeroy, *Guerrilla and Counter-Guerrilla Warfare: Liberation and Suppression in the Present Period* (New York: International Publishers Company, 1964); Frantz Fanon, *The Wretched of the Earth* (New York: Grove Press, 1966); Henry Bienen, *Violence and Social Change* (Chicago: University of Chicago Press, 1968); Carl Leiden and Karl M. Schmitt, eds., *The Politics of Violence: Revolution in the Modern World* (Englewood Cliffs, N. J.: Prentice-Hall, 1968).

strength, rather than seizing or holding a city, the principal objective, since cities will fall to the insurgent forces once the enemy's military capabilities have been destroyed; (4) to concentrate superior force in battle and, whenever possible, to encircle and destroy the enemy forces; (5) to fight no battle which the guerrilla forces are not sure of winning; (6) to replenish the strength of guerrilla forces by arms captured from the enemy and to make effective use of the intervals between campaigns to rest, train and consolidate troops.[48] The revolutionary army makes use of invulnerable sanctuaries located either in remote parts of the country in which they are operating (e.g., Yenan Province in China in the 1930s and the Sierra Maestra in Cuba in the 1950s) or maintains elaborate facilities for this purpose in adjacent countries (Cambodia, Laos, and North Vietnam in the Vietnamese war).

Mao Tse-tung and General Giap characterize revolutionary war as a three-stage process which includes: Stage one, in which the guerrilla forces are inferior to those of the opponent and must use tactics designed to wear down the opponent; stage two, in which a strengthened revolutionary force begins to mount large-scale attacks against the opponent and assumes control of major sections of the countryside and small cities and towns; and stage three, in which the revolutionary force embarks on a strategic counteroffensive designed to overwhelm its opponent. As the revolutionary force moves from the first to the third stages, it fights first with small units and later with larger ones, moves from scattered encounters to concentrated battles, and changes from a form of fighting in which the principles of regular warfare gradually develop but still bear the character of guerrilla warfare.

The revolutionary army is politically indoctrinated so that it has an intimate understanding of the goals for which it fights. In this first stage, it establishes support among the population, for it must rely upon the local inhabitants both for daily sustenance and intelligence information about the opponent. According to Mao Tse-tung, support in the countryside is as important to the guerrilla force as water is to fish. The support of the local population is gained either by the exploitation of its grievances against the central government or by the use of terror and violence to remove key government supporters from the local governing structure or to instill fear of reprisals in the local population.

Whereas Mao Tse-tung and General Giap emphasized guerrilla warfare as the principal form of struggle only in the first of three stages of successful revolution, Che Guevara adapted the three-stage model to what he considered to be the circumstances of Latin America. While Mao and Giap postulated the evolution of guerrilla forces into a regular army, Guevara believed that the guerrilla force could itself ultimately seize power after decisive encounters in which the enemy army would be annihilated.

Revolutionary warfare, according to its principal theorists and practitioners,

---

48. See *Mao Tse-tung on Guerrilla Warfare,* trans. with an intro. by Samuel B. Griffith (New York: Frederick A. Praeger, 1961), pp. 41–114.

is a strategy designed to seize control of the countryside in order to mount a final, crushing offensive against the urban centers. Clearly, this was the strategy followed in the communist seizure of power in China and Cuba. The theorists of revolutionary warfare have extended their analysis to whole continents and even to the entire international system. Che Guevara held his theory of revolution, based on the Cuban experience, to be relevant to all of Latin America, and died in the hills of Bolivia in 1968 attempting to establish the validity of his theory. According to Régis Debray, the principal problem of revolutionary activity in Latin America is the destruction of the armed forces of Latin American oligarchies and the preparation of the masses for the building of a new socialist system. Debray calls for the establishment of a series of guerrilla *focos,* or bases, in the countryside. Unlike Mao Tse-tung and General Giap, Debray subordinates the party to the guerrilla force and argues that "the people's army will be the nucleus of the party, not vice versa." [49] Latin American guerrilla movements should be controlled by the guerrillas themselves, rather than by urban-based political parties. The guerrilla force is the nucleus of a revolutionary party and a revolutionary army. Debray considers the old communist parties of Latin America as "enfeebled political vanguards," to be replaced by a band of dedicated guerrilla revolutionaries. This new group will end "a divorce of several decades duration between Marxist theory and revolutionary practice." [50]

Revolutionary change would come about principally through the efforts of the guerrilla force itself rather than as a result of a mass popular movement. In contrast to Mao Tse-tung and General Giap, who stress the dependence of the guerrilla force upon the civilian population, Debray considers the civilian population as a danger. In Latin America, the guerrilla force must be clandestine, mobile, and independent of the civilian population.

If Debray focused on revolution of continental proportions in Latin America, Lin Piao, China's minister of defense, produced in 1965 a major statement describing the world as consisting of the rural, underdeveloped areas of Asia, the Middle East, Africa and Latin America, as contrasted with the developed, urban areas of Europe and North America.[51] Lin Piao characterized international relations as a struggle in which revolutionary governments, under China's leadership, would seize power in the underdeveloped areas before mounting a final offensive against the developed, urban areas and ultimately

49. Régis Debray, *Revolution in the Revolution: Armed Struggle and Political Struggle in Latin America* (New York: Grove Press, 1967), p. 116.

50. *Ibid.,* p. 107.

51. For major portions of the text of this statement, see *New York Times,* September 4, 1965. "Everything is divisible. And so is this colossus of U.S. imperialism. It can be split up and defeated. The peoples of Asia, Africa, Latin America and other regions can destroy it piece by piece, some striking at its head and others at its feet. That is why the greatest fear of U.S. imperialism is that people's wars will be launched in different parts of the world, and particularly in Asia, Africa and Latin America, and why it regards people's wars as a mortal danger."

destroying the United States itself as a principal bastion of "capitalist imperialism."

Like Lenin, Lin Piao saw the loss of the less developed, former colonial areas as crucial to the ultimate destruction of the industrialized, capitalist countries. From Lenin, the theoretician-practitioners of revolutionary warfare borrowed the concept of the highly trained, motivated and politicized activist, the "vanguard of the proletariat" as crucial to the seizure of power whether in the Soviet Union or China or Cuba. Lenin furnished a strategic doctrine designed to hasten the revolutionary change foreseen by Marx. If Lenin adapted the Marxian theory of class struggle from the industrialized setting of Western Europe to the less industrialized environment of pre-1917 Russia, revolutionary theoretician-practitioners such as Mao Tse-tung, General Giap, Che Guevara, and Régis Debray have sought to adapt communist theory to environments even more removed from those about which Marx wrote. Conceivably, the need to evolve strategies designed to achieve, through protracted political-military means, what Marx foresaw as inevitable points up the limited appeal of Marx's teachings in the absence of force.

In the final analysis, the doctrines espoused by Lenin, Stalin, Mao Tse-tung, Che Guevara, General Giap, Régis Debray, Frantz Fanon and Lin Piao are more than mere intellectual theories. They are doctrines of social conflict in which the use of force and violence in some form (but not necessarily any specific form such as armed uprising or nuclear war) plays an essential role, even though it may often be intermixed with nonviolent techniques. Since war for Lenin was not only a continuation but also a summation of politics, he held that socialists could not be pacifists without ceasing to be his kind of socialists.[52] Professor Stefan T. Possony, formerly of Georgetown University and later of the Hoover Institution on War, Revolution and Peace at Stanford University, wrote the following analysis in the early 1950s:

> The communists believe that class war is the essence of history and that old social orders die and new social orders emerge only through violence. Specifically, they do not believe that fundamental social transformations can take place in a gradual or evolutionary fashion. The historical process must carry through convulsion and crisis, revolution and war. The communist millenium will be prepared by a profound and long-lasting crisis of the capitalist system, but it can be ushered in only after the preceding social order has been destroyed by force.[53]

The authors are inclined to agree with Dr. Possony that practically all "good communists" did believe that in times past. Do they today? Are the leaders of the Soviet Union still "good communists" and do they adhere to such convictions? The future peace of the world and the well-being of mankind may depend heavily upon the answers which history will provide to these questions.

52. Possony, *op. cit.*, p. 89.   53. *Ibid.*, p. xxi.

Economic Theories of Imperialism and War   195

CHAPTER 7
Microcosmic Theories of Conflict

Human Motivations and Conflict

Many theories discussed in Chapters 5 and 6 pertained to man's conscious motivations, ethical evaluations and attitudes concerning conflict. Most of those earlier theories, whether derived from religious belief, philosophical reflection or political experience, are what we call "prescientific." But it would be wrong to imply that men in earlier times were content with superficial or mythical explanations. When Thucydides said that men go to war for reasons of honor, fear and interest; when the Christian fathers taught that war results from a deep-rooted disorder in human nature which they called "original sin"; when Hume wrote that nations go to war in order to preserve a balance of power, or to prevent one monarch from establishing international hegemony; when some nineteenth-century writers defended or extolled war as a catalyst against social stagnation; when Lenin and his followers traced the outbreak of wars to the profit-seeking of the imperialists—all of these were trying to go beyond purely conscious motivations and to probe the underlying reasons for human conflict. Some of them found their reasons in the "dark forces" which lurk within the individual psyche or soul; some found them in the characteristics of the larger social system, or certain aspects of it. Some even implied that men were ill-advised to look for the causes of war, when they should be looking for the causes of peace. This was the thrust of William James' argument that man could expect recurrences of war until he had discovered some moral-psychological equivalent of it.[1]

It was also the thrust of the argument of those historians who, in searching for the origins of World War I, cited as a cause the condition of "international anarchy" i.e., the absence of those instruments of world law and organization which would be efficacious for peacekeeping.[2] This is both a curious and a

1. See footnote 47 in Chapter 5.
2. Quincy Wright, *Causes of War and Conditions of Peace* (New York: Longmans, 1935). See also footnote 35 in Chapter 6.

provocative thought, that the nonexistence of one thing might be the "cause" of something else. It is closely linked to the thought that "the expectation of war" is a principal "cause of war," in other words, that war is such an intrinsic and unavoidable feature of the present nation-state system that it can be expected to recur until the existing system has been replaced by a set of conditions which does not yet exist.[3]

THE HISTORICAL RELATIVITY OF THEORY

Consider one of the earlier "prescientific" theories. A medieval Christian prince, deciding whether to declare war on a neighboring prince, would discuss the issue with his feudal advisors (some of whom might have had a clerical training). He would couch his own case in terms of "justice," or "the rights of the Church," or the need to correct some "wrong" perpetrated by the other party. These were the dominant mental categories of the age. We cannot know to what extent princes who employed this terminology really believed that such a formulation expressed their true motivations, but this was the public theoretical framework within which they acted. Today we might regard that kind of expression as romantic or naïve if it was believed, or merely a cynical rationalization if it was not believed. But no other theory was available in that culture, and contemporary judgment as to its superficiality merely indicates that in the modern world we have developed much more highly differentiated and sophisticated theories as to why men go to war. Today many social scientists are skeptical of nearly all the earlier theories about the "causes of war." Just consider the fate of the once highly respectable balance-of-power theory (examined in Chapter 1). Perhaps a century from now scientists will smile at the explanations of human conflict with which intellectuals entertained themselves in the 1970s.

MODERN STUDIES OF MOTIVATIONS AND WAR

In the twentieth century, social scientists have turned increasingly toward motives, reasons and causal factors which may be operative both in individual

3. See "War and the Expectation of War," Chapter 7 in Vernon Van Dyke, *International Politics* (New York: Appleton-Century-Crofts, 2nd ed., 1966); Gordon W. Allport, "The Role of Expectancy," in Hadley Cantril, ed., *Tensions That Cause War* (Urbana: University of Illinois Press, 1951); and Werner Levi, "On the Causes of War and the Conditions of Peace," *Journal of Conflict Resolution*, IV (December, 1960), 411–420.

Levi notes that war should be traced not to a specific factor but to a constellation of factors. Most attempts to understand the causes of war, he says, involve a "search for all possible elements present in the situation to explain the origins of war," but they reflect a failure "to try to discover whether there are missing elements whose presence would lead to the avoidance of the use of violence." *Ibid.*, p. 418.

human beings and in social collectivities even though men are not immediately aware of them and do not become consciously aware of them except as a result of scientific observation and methodical analysis. Frequently the efforts to understand the roots of conflict behavior have been addressed to the worthy object of eliminating war, at least in its most destructive forms. But many social scientists, including some identified with the peace movement, recognize that total elimination of conflict from the human situation is not only impossible but undesirable.[4] Some hope that nonviolent forms of competition and conflict will gradually replace violent conflict everywhere. For others pacifism as a political principle is highly selective: some Western intellectuals and students oppose nuclear war and every resort to military or police force by Western governments but readily support violent revolution on the campus or in the Third World.

WHY DO MEN BEHAVE AGGRESSIVELY? WHY DO STATES WAGE WARS?

The two questions, which serve to introduce this section, are related, but they are not exactly the same. The former pertains to the inner springs of action within individual human beings, the latter to the decision-making processes of national governments. Violent revolution constitutes yet another phenomenon, different from individual aggressiveness, which is rooted in the biological-psychological characteristics of man, and from the waging of international war, which is a highly politicized and institutionalized form of learned social behavior. Revolution itself, insofar as it requires organization, leadership, ideology and doctrine, propaganda, planning, strategy, tactics, communications, recruits and supplies, and very often a diplomacy for the acquisition of foreign support, assumes a highly politicized character with the passage of time. Thus an understanding of it requires more of a *macrocosmic* (i.e., political-sociological) than a *microcosmic* (individual psychological) analysis. Psychological and social psychological factors alone might go much further in helping to explain instances of anomic [5] violence, such as a food or language riot in India, the flareup of a group of students around the goalpost at the end of a hard-fought football game, or a racial disorder at a public beach. But even in these cases social psychologists would be wary of "the fallacy of the single factor," and political scientists would argue that some instances of apparently "anomic" violence might involve an element of political organiza-

4. "Human existence without conflict is unthinkable. Conflict gives life much of its meaning, so that its elimination, even if attainable, would not be desirable." Jerome D. Frank, "Human Nature and Non-Violent Resistance," in Quincy Wright *et al., Preventing World War III: Some Proposals* (New York: Simon and Schuster, 1962), p. 193. Kenneth Boulding suggests that in a given situation there may too much or too little conflict, or an optimal amount which lends to life a certain dramatic interest. *Conflict and Defense* (New York: Harper and Brothers, 1962), pp. 305–307.

5. The word "anomic" here refers to a condition of normless violence flaring up rather unexpectedly.

Contending Theories of International Relations

tion and can be adequately comprehended only when placed in their total political context.

The phenomenon of international war is the most complex and difficult to explain. It is impossible to describe the causes of war purely in terms of individual psychology, as if it were a case of psychic tensions within individuals mounting to the breaking point and then spilling over into large-scale conflict. Feelings of hostility might indeed be widespread within a nation *vis-à-vis* another nation and yet war might be averted by astute statesmanship. Conversely, a government can lead a people into a war for which there is no enthusiastic support. Professor Werner Levi of the University of Minnesota made several trenchant points on this subject:

> *When for instance will certain natural traits or psychological drives find outlets in war, and when in something more peaceful? . . . . What these explanations fail to do is to indicate how these human factors are translated into violent conflict involving all citizens, regardless of their individual nature, and performed through a highly complex machinery constructed over a period of years for just such purpose.*
>
> *There is always the missing link in these fascinating speculations about the psychological causes of war between the fundamental nature of man and the outbreak of war. . . . Usually, the psychological factors and human traits can be classified as conditions of war more correctly than as causes.*
>
> *. . . [There is] another distinction which might be equally difficult to make in practice, but which nevertheless raises questions unanswered by the theories on psychological causes of war. There are aggressive wars and defensive wars. . . . In fact, the failure of most psychological explanations of war to distinguish between different kinds of wars is another one of their weaknesses.*[6]

Throughout history, wars have been fought because of conscious human decisions, usually by political executives (monarchs, presidents, prime ministers, dictators)and their advisors, occasionally by larger bodies such as city-state assemblies, or warrior councils of the tribe, or parliamentary legislatures. This element of deliberate decision deserves to be stressed because it is often overlooked in the chain of causality. Men have long been convinced that there is an element of free choice in at least some decisions for war or peace, and that under certain circumstances the scales might be tipped either way, depending upon the way the individuals, comprising the die-casting body, perceive and evaluate the reasons for and against war. It is this conviction of freedom which lends genuine drama, sometimes even a tragic character, to the crucial debate before the decision is made. Thucydides captured this drama in the speech of the Athenian delegate at the Congress of the Peloponnesian Confederacy, who warned the Spartans not to heed the Corinthians' appeal for war:

6. Werner Levi, *op. cit.,* p. 415. Here the reader should also review the caution expressed by Herbert C. Kelman in the observation cited in Chapter 5, p. 142.

Take time then in forming your resolution, as the matter is of great importance; and do not be persuaded by the opinions and complaints of others to bring trouble on yourselves, but consider the vast influence of accident in war, before you are engaged in it. As it continues, it generally becomes an affair of chances, chances from which neither of us is exempt, and whose event we must risk in the dark. It is a common mistake in going to war to begin at the wrong end, to act first, and wait for disaster to discuss the matter. But we are not yet by any means so misguided, nor, so far as we can see, are you. . . .[7]

Thucydides astutely combined the role of the perceiving individual in the decisional process with the general, almost irresistible tendency of historical events. He did not overlook the part psychological factors played: the real cause of the Peloponnesian War was the "growth of the power of Athens, and the fear which this inspired in Lacedaemon." [8] But this fear does not remain a mere blind force. It leads to a rational calculation of the gains and losses which might be involved in war and a weighing of these risks against the imagined consequences of avoiding war.[9] The historian's reference in the above passage to the "vast influence of accident in war" applied to the unpredictability of events once the decision is made for war. It is wrong to infer that Thucydides subscribed to an "accidental theory" of the outbreak of war.

Since the emergence of the "delicate balance of nuclear terror" in the late 1950s, there has been an understandable increase of apprehensiveness over the possibility of "accidental war." [10] But few Western theorists would go so far as to agree with Bruce Russett that the causes of modern war might be analyzed through the application of an accounting scheme designed orginally to study the causes of automobile accidents.[11] It is especially difficult for those, including the Marxists, who believe that history is essentially a rational process, to accept the notion that the most cataclysmic event in history might occur purely by chance. Even if one willingly concedes the possibility that the world might end not with a whimper but with an accidental bang, nevertheless instead of dwelling on the futility of living in an accident-prone world he may prefer to work for a reduction of the dangers of unintended war, both by

7. Thucydides, *History of the Peloponnesian War*, trans. Richard Crawley, in Everyman's Library (New York: E. P. Dutton and Company, 1910), pp. 51–52.

8. *Ibid.*, p. 16.

9. See Peter H. Judd, "Thucydides and the Study of War," Andrew W. Cordier, ed., *Columbia Essays in International Affairs*, (New York: Columbia University Press, 1967), II, 161–191; and George Kateb, "Thucydides' History: A Manual of Statecraft," *Political Science Quarterly*, LXXIX (December, 1964), 481–503.

10. See Herman Kahn, "The Arms Race and Some of Its Hazards," Donald G. Brennan, ed., *Arms Control, Disarmament and National Security* (New York: George Braziller, 1961), pp. 89–121; J. David Singer, *Deterrence, Arms Control and Disarmament* (Columbus: Ohio State University Press, 1962), Chapter 4; and Henry A. Kissinger, *The Necessity for Choice* (Garden City, N.Y.: Doubleday and Company [Anchor Books], 1962), pp. 236–238.

11. Bruce M. Russett, "Cause, Surprise and No Escape," *Journal of Politics*, XXIV (February, 1962), 3–22.

minimizing the chance that accidents will happen and by minimizing the chances that such accidents, if they do occur, will lead to war. A decision must be made between accident and war. Even though man will never be able to assess accurately the objective risks of ultimate "accidental" disaster, it must be pointed out that history and the social sciences furnish abundant evidence that the initiation of war is a matter of conscious, deliberate choice, and scant evidence of decision-less outbreaks of war.[12] It is conceivable, of course, that a skirmish might start spontaneously between two hostile societies in proximity to each other, without an authoritative political decision having been made. But the skirmish does not become a sustained war until a political decision has been made by one side or both.

Social collectivities have at times gone to war for a variety of reasons, which have been to a great extent relative to historical-cultural circumstances. The Europeans, who plunged into war over religious issues less than four hundred years ago, would regard such a *casus belli* as unthinkable today. Today, the motives for which governments might conceivably ask their peoples to make war vary greatly among the more than 120 different nations of the world. Despite all that has been said about *lebensraum* in this century in the West, it would be very difficult to prove that any modern industrialized nation-states (such as Germany) have gone to war to relieve population and food pressures. But it is less difficult to imagine that such a motive might consciously enter into the decision-making of such an underindustrialized and thickly-populated power as China. Any analysis of the origins of war must consider the relativity and variety of relevant factors.

A persistent cause of war has been the readiness of societies to resort to organized force in order to reduce or remove a perceived threat to their security or to their religious, political, ideological, economic or sociocultural value systems. Undoubtedly there have been times when the threat perceived was real and proximate, or even imminent, just as there have been times when the threat was so remote as to be virtually imaginary. At recurring periods in history, one or more societies have acted more belligerently and aggressively than others, whether with or without what would appear to an "objective" observer to be good cause, or at least an understandable cause. (The term "aggressive" in this context carries no ethical connotations.) In any event, when this happens other societies become apprehensive. They seek their security and the preservation of their cultural integrity by engaging in some form of power balancing. Furthermore, the perception of an external enemy whose way of life contrasts sharply with that of the perceiving society serves to enhance the latter's sense of identity and social solidarity, even while giving rise to an anxiety which may tempt some on one side to contemplate the elimination of the adversary as a means to threat-reduction and anxiety-reduction. Political writers and other social theorists have long assumed that in certain

12. Theodore Abel, "The Elements of Decision in the Pattern of War," *Ameri-* *can Sociological Review,* VI (December, 1941), 853–859.

circumstances political leaders may deliberately provoke foreign conflict in order to buttress their own position and achieve greater internal cohesion by diverting domestic resentments abroad.[13]

"War," said Quincy Wright, "has politico-technological, juro-ideological, socio-religious, and psycho-economic causes."[14] Wright warns against adopting any simplistic approach to the problem. "A war, in reality, results from a total situation involving ultimately almost everything that has happened to the human race up to the time the war begins."[15] If we really wish to understand the phenomenon of war, we cannot ignore the political factors to which it is related: nationalism and internationalism; the nature of the international system of sovereign states; the sentiments of pacifism and militarism in various strata of society, and the total impact of public opinion on foreign decision-making processes; the tendency of governments to rely on force as an effective instrument of national policy; the stability of the international political-strategic environment at any given time; the quality of nations' leadership and diplomacy at critical junctures; and the presence or absence of political-legal-organizational mechanisms for settling disputes. Two writers closely associated with the quest for the conditions of international peace have acknowledged the utility of the institution of war. James T. Shotwell, a Columbia University professor who was an early advocate of what finally emerged as the Kellogg-Briand Pact of 1928, said, "War . . . has been the instrument by which most of the great facts of political national history have been established and maintained . . . It has been used to achieve liberty, to secure democracy. . . ."[16] Clyde Eagleton, professor of international law at New York University, wrote:

> War is a means for achieving an end, a weapon which can be used for good or for bad purposes. Some of these purposes for which war has been used have been accepted by humanity as worthwhile ends; indeed, war performs functions which are essential in any human society. It has been used to settle disputes, to uphold rights, to remedy wrongs; and these are surely functions which must be served . . . . One may say, without exaggeration, that no more stupid, brutal, wasteful or unfair method could ever have been imagined for such purposes, but this does not alter the situation.[17]

We must always return to the political level in order to place our analysis of contemporary conflict theories in a proper perspective. Provided that the

13. This observation, which is at least as old as Machiavelli, has been reiterated by modern social psychologists, e.g., Stephen Withey and Daniel Katz, "The Social Psychology of Human Conflict," Elton B. McNeil, ed., *The Nature of Human Conflict* (Englewood Cliffs, N.J.: Prentice-Hall, 1965), p. 81.

14. Quincy Wright, *A Study of War* (Chicago: University of Chicago, 1942), II, 739.

15. *Ibid.*, I, p. 17.

16. James T. Shotwell, *War as an Instrument of National Policy* (New York: Harcourt, Brace Company, 1929), p. 15.

17. Clyde Eagleton, *International Government*, rev. ed. (New York: Ronald Press, 1948), p. 393. See Quincy Wright on "The Political Utility of War," in *A Study of War*, II, 853–860.

student does not lose sight of the social superstructure in which war may be chosen or avoided in the contextual specifics of diplomacy, statesmanship and politics, an examination of present-day social science and behavioral efforts to contribute toward a scientific explanation of social conflict can be highly useful. They suggest many hypotheses which are awaiting verification and numerous insights which open up avenues for further theoretical integration. With these caveats and possibilities in mind, we turn now to data from disciplines other than political science, to see what light they might cast upon the nature of conflict for the student of politics.[18]

Biological and Psychological Theories

Neither the microcosm nor the macrocosm alone, neither individual nor collectivity alone, neither the biological-psychological nor the sociological-anthropological approach alone can furnish an adequate conceptual framework for understanding human conflict. Conflict arises out of external objective conditions and social structures, and also out of the psychological states of individuals acting singly or in small groups. At all levels of analysis, larger organized aggregates of human beings affect smaller aggregates and individuals, and vice versa. Individuals and groups are in constant and virtually inseparable interaction. At any given time, certain individuals and groups will wield greater political influence than others in the decision-making process which leads to the avoidance, postponement, initiation, exacerbation, control or termination of conflict. Whether the larger is more important than the smaller is a question which we may never be able to answer. Perhaps our only solution to the dilemma is to take social situations and individual inner processes as an organic whole. Class structures and communications patterns, as well as political, economic and cultural conditions, affect individual and group

18. Political scientists are usually readier than economists to probe the mysterious motivating forces of human action. Quincy Wright has offered the following interesting contrast between the two disciplines: "Economics . . . assumes that men are rational, at least in some of their activities; that in making choices, they will calculate the probable results and the relation of means to ends. . . . Politics, on the other hand, recognizes that men frequently act on the basis of irrational emotional drives and erroneous beliefs; consequently political scientists study attitudes and opinions as they are and the choices which they suggest. They often find that political behavior can best be explained by psychological analyses of masses and of individual leaders, and that insight may be obtained from infantile and neurotic behavior. They study biological and cultural drives and practices of ambivalence, repression, scapegoating, displacement, projection and rational adaptation of clearly defined means to clearly defined ends. . . . [Economists] tend to relegate the causation of war and of international relations to the realms of politics, sociology and psychology." *The Study of International Relations* (New York: Appleton-Century-Crofts, 1955), pp. 237–238. For a collection of readings from the contemporary literature on conflict at the international level, see Dean G. Pruitt and Richard C. Snyder, eds., *Theory and Research on the Causes of War* (Englewood Cliffs, N.J.: Prentice-Hall, 1969).

attitudes, images and moods. Conversely, the predominant psychological characteristics of "types" within a culture or even of a few personalities might be crucially important in determining whether a given society under given circumstances moves toward schism, revolution or war, or toward integration, nonviolent political development or peaceful settlement.

The key microcosmic concept for the explanation of conflict is aggression, i.e., a behavioral impulse directed toward the injury of some human or non-human object. Aggression studies have preoccupied many biologists,[19] psychologists and social psychologists. In recent years the biologist and psychologist have often crossed paths in the areas of "instinctive" behavior, innate behavior and aggressive or fighting behavior.

INSTINCT THEORIES

Generally, psychologists have long agreed that aggression is to be understood in some sort of stimulus-response framework. A basic issue that arose in their field four or five decades ago was whether aggressive tendencies are innate, instinctive and ever-present in man, or whether they appear only as a result of an externally produced frustration in man. The instinct theories were gradually replaced by the frustration-aggression hypothesis, still probably the dominant preferred explanation among psychologists and social psychologists. But a brief review of the older theory is relevant in view of the more recent writings of animal behaviorists.

Among the leading figures identified with the instinct theories of aggression during the early decades of the century were William James (1842–1910) and William McDougall (1871–1938). McDougall, the leading British psychologist of his day, considered instinct as a psychophysical process inherited by all members of a species; it was not learned, but could be modified by learning. McDougall, however, took issue with the psychoanalysts who considered the aggressive impulse as ever-present in man and constantly seeking release. McDougall insisted that the "instinct of pugnacity," as he called it, one of the eleven which he identified, became operative only when instigated by a frustrating condition.[20] He did not look upon human aggressiveness as a built-in impulse constantly seeking release. Thus he placed himself midway between the pure "instinctivists" and the "frustration-aggression" school to be treated presently, seeking his understanding of aggression in neither the organism nor the environment alone, but in their interaction.

The most famous and most controversial of the "instinct" theories was

19. Biologists might demur at being treated under the "micro" heading, insofar as they are interested not only in the individual organism but also in the whole species and its ecology. This would be a legitimate complaint. But although the biologist, like the psychologist, seeks to generalize to the whole species, he must obtain most of his data from the obser-

vation of individual members of the species, or small groups, in various habitats.

20. William McDougall, *An Introduction to Social Psychology* (Boston: Luce, 1926), especially pp. 30–45. See also his *Outline of Psychology* (New York: Charles Scribner's Sons, 1923), pp. 140–141.

Contending Theories of International Relations

that of the "death instinct," put forth by Sigmund Freud. Originally, Freud was inclined to the view that aggression results from frustration, especially the frustration of the sexual impulses.[21] But after World War I, Freud postulated the existence in man of a fundamental *Eros,* or life instinct, and a fundamental *Thanatos* or death instinct. For Freud, all instincts were directed toward the reduction or elimination of tension, stimulation and excitation. The motivation of pleasure-seeking activity is to attain an unstimulated condition—a sort of Oriental Nirvana or absence of all desire. Death involves the removal of all excitation. Hence all living things aspire to "the quiescence of the inorganic world." [22] But men go on living despite the death instinct because the life instinct channels the annihilative drive away from the self toward others. Aggressive behavior thus provides an outlet for destructive energies that might otherwise lead to suicide. According to this hypothesis, the recurrence of war and conflict becomes a necessary periodic release by which groups preserve themselves through diverting their self-destructive tendencies to outsiders. This, in brief, is the psychoanalytic foundation for Freud's view, which he exchanged in correspondence with Albert Einstein: that is, man contains within himself "an active instinct for hatred and aggression." [23] Hence Sigmund Freud and Émile Durkheim would appear to be not too far from agreement on the proposition that society harbors a certain amount of destructive energy which, if not diverted externally, manifests itself internally against either the individual or the group.

Most contemporary psychologists reject Freud's hypothesis of the death wish as the basis for aggression theory. Professor Leonard Berkowitz calls it "scientifically unwarranted." [24] He cites two principal grounds on which it is deemed deficient—one from positivist logic and one from modern experimental science. He maintains that Freudian theory is unacceptable because of its teleological character. In other words, the theory attributes the cause of present behavior to a future condition, i.e., the reduction or removal of excitation. "Claiming that some mysterious force—calling it an instinct, compulsion or drive does not help—seeking to attain a future state in some un-

21. Sigmund Freud, *A General Introduction to Psychoanalysis,* trans. G. S. Hall (New York: Boni and Liveright, 1920), pp. 170–174.

22. Sigmund Freud, *Beyond the Pleasure Principle* (London: International Psychoanalytical Press, 1922); (New York: Bantam Books, 1959), p. 198.

23. "Why War?" A letter from Sigmund Freud to Albert Einstein, written in 1932. Text in Robert A. Goldwin *et al., Readings in World Politics* (New York: Oxford University Press, 1959). After describing the "death instinct," Freud wrote: "The upshot of these observations . . . is that there is no likelihood of our being able to suppress humanity's aggressive tendencies. . . . The Bolshevists, too, aspire to do away with human aggressiveness by ensuring the satisfaction of material needs and enforcing equality between man and man. To me this hope seems vain." But then, paradoxically, he added that "complete suppression of man's aggressive tendencies is not in issue; what we may try is to divert it into a channel other than that of warfare." *Ibid.,* p. 29. This last statement seems to parallel William James' quest for a "moral equivalent of war." See also Freud's *Civilization and Its Discontents* (New York: Cape and Smith, 1930).

24. Leonard Berkowitz, *Aggression: A Social-Psychological Analysis* (New York: McGraw-Hill Book Company, 1962), p. 8.

known fashion produces certain behaviors is only the application of 'word magic.' " [25] As for the experimental evidence, Berkowitz argues that recent research performed with animals (principally cats, rats and mice) negates the validity of the notion that all behavior is aimed at tension-reduction, inasmuch as "organisms frequently go out of their way to obtain additional stimulation from their external environment." [26] This is an interesting observation insofar as it casts a different light on the question of why human beings willingly risk the dangers that often accompany conflict and violence. But it is cited here primarily as an argument *contra* Freud's death wish. One might wonder whether the evidence concerning the desire of living organisms, at least at times, for an increase of tension and stimulation completely invalidates the Freudian hypothesis, or merely introduces greater complexity into it, by suggesting dialectically that the increased excitation is an unconscious step toward the cessation of all stimuli. This latter interpretation, however, would still be open to the logical positivist objection summarized above. It should be remembered that Freud never adduced any compelling body of evidence in support of his hypothesis. Hence there is no scientific need to disprove it. Yet Freud's position in the field of psychoanalysis is so dominant, and his influence on modern Western thought so pervasive, that psychologists sometimes seem anxious to discredit this particular aspect of his theory because of the rather pessimistic connotations which it has for society.[27]

25. *Ibid.*, p. 9.

26. *Ibid.*, p. 10. D. O. Hebb has shown that there is an important relationship between excitation and the human being's mental development. Noting that a mere repetition of responses may weaken rather than strengthen them, he says that prolonged routinized learning has a negative, monotonous effect which often leads to a disturbance or reduction of motivation or loss of interest. Hebb argues that human behavior is dominated not by what is thoroughly familiar and arouses a "well-organized phase sequence," but rather by the "thought process that is not fully organized." He insists upon "the continued need of some degree of novelty, to maintain a wakefulness of choice." He adds that "some degree of novelty, combined with what is predominantly familiar, is stimulating and exciting over a wide range of activities." He also refers to the human "preoccupation with what is new but not too new, with the mildly frustrating or the mildly fear-provoking." As examples he cites the case of children seeking controllably frightening situations, the addiction of adults to dangerous sports or to "ghost stories," and the fascination of problem-solving challenges, even when they involve frustration. He concludes that conflict need not be regarded as "unpleasant and grossly disruptive of human behavior; on the contrary, some degree of conflict is stimulating and necessary to the maintenance of normal responsiveness to the environment." *The Organization of Behavior: A Neuropsychological Theory* (New York: John Wiley and Sons, 1949), pp. 224–234. It is interesting to note that, according to Hebb, human beings seek what may be "frustrating." Later in the same work, he suggests—somewhat contradictorily to what has just been shown—that behavior associated with unpleasant emotions (e.g., anger and fear) has "one constant function . . . to put an end to the original stimulation" through aggression, flight, avoidance or failure to respond. *Ibid.*, p. 254.

27. Contemporary psychoanalytic writers have adhered to the aggressive instinct theory. A few, such as Karl Menninger, retain the notion of death instinct. Others, such as Hartmann, Kris and Lowenstein, continue to postulate an aggressive instinct but do not trace it to the death wish. Still others, including Fenichel, have shifted back toward the frustration explanation of aggression. See Berkowitz, *op. cit.*, pp. 11–12.

Before making the transition from instinct to frustration theories, we must look at some of the results of animal research behavior. Human behavior and animal behavior are dissimilar; in some respects, though, they may be analogous. From a knowledge of animal behavior we cannot directly infer anything about human behavior. "Work on one species," according to Elton B. McNeil, "can serve as a model only for the formation of *hypotheses* about other species." [28] Thus while an examination of animal studies can furnish no proof as to the way human beings act, it can suggest fruitful areas for future research. The advantage of animal investigation is that it admits of a freedom of experimentation that would be impossible in the case of humans, and it permits the scientist to observe several generations of a species within a short time. The principal caveat to remember, of course, is that humans are vastly more complex than even the most highly developed animals, and that the computing organism of the human nervous system lends itself to individual learning and adaptation, while this is much more limited in the lower organisms. Simplicity makes it easier to isolate a factor for study, but harder to apply its implications to man.

In animals the causes of aggressive behavior are relatively few. They fight over food, females and territory; they fight to protect the young. It has been found that there is a relationship between aggressiveness and the production of the male hormone (even though in a few species the female is more aggressive than the male); that within a species, some breeds may be more aggressive than others; that the so-called "instinctive targets of aggression" (such as the mouse for the cat) appear to be more a matter of learning than of hereditary instinct; that fighting within a species may produce intricate patterns of submission and dominance; that an animal will fight rather than be deprived of status; that repeated success in fighting can make an animal more aggressive; and that various forms of electrical, chemical and surgical interventions into the brain can produce predictable alterations in animal aggressiveness.[29] It has also been noted that the same principles of learning on which the stimulation of conflict behavior is based may be applied in reserve, as it were, to control and reduce the aggressive urge.[30]

Berkowitz, in an effort to cast doubt upon the notion of instinctive aggressiveness, writes that:

28. See his chapter, "The Nature of Aggression," in Elton B. McNeil, ed., *op. cit.*, p. 15.

29. Students of animal behavior-physiology are producing some interesting insights into the problem of aggression, but they would be the first to admit difficulties in interpreting their data and to caution against the hasty application of their findings to the more mysterious realm of human affairs. A useful summary of findings on animal aggression can be found in *Ibid.*, pp. 15–27.

30. John Paul Scott, *Animal Behavior* (Garden City, N.Y.: Doubleday and Company, [Anchor Books], 1963), pp. 121–122. One should note that if human aggressiveness is to be reduced or inhibited, it will have to be by way of learning, since the avenues of electrical, hormonal, chemical and surgical interventions into the human body are of necessity, and fortunately, quite limited.

Microcosmic Theories of Conflict   207

> *Man presumably possesses an aggressive instinct because of his bio-*
> *logical heritage and his membership in the animal kingdom. . . . It*
> *certainly is unreasonable phylogenetically to maintain that human be-*
> *ings would have these biological tendencies if the other animals did*
> *not. This being the case, the advocate of the instinctive aggression*
> *doctrine is hard-pressed to defend himself against the essentially nega-*
> *tive evidence provided by biologists and psychologists.*[31]

John Paul Scott, an experimental biologist who has based his study of individual aggression and its causes on animal research, denies that there is any physiological evidence pointing to a spontaneous "instinct for fighting" within the body. There is no need for the organisms to fight, apart from happenings in the external environment. "There is, however, an internal physiological mechanism which has only to be stimulated to produce fighting." [32] As Scott sees it, aggression is the result of a learning process in which the motivation for fighting is increased by success; the longer success continues, the stronger the motivation becomes. He favors a multi-factor theory of aggression, based on a complex network of physiological causes which eventually are traced to external stimulation. If the stimulation is sufficiently high, it may activate unconscious motor centers for fighting which, in the absence of the stimulus, are usually repressed as a result of training. Scott, therefore, roots the aggressive impulse in physiological processes, but demands a stimulus from the environment and rejects the concept of self-activation.

Generally speaking, biologists have been less reluctant than psychologists to speak of "instinct"—not so much as an explanation of an inherited pattern of behavior (through genetic transmission) as a short-hand description of those behavior differences which are determined by the interaction of heredity and environment.[33] A growing number of biologists now definitely prefer the term "innate behavior" over the older "instinct."

Within the last decade, one of the most rapidly advancing branches of biological science has been ethology—the study of animal behavior in all its aspects, with particular emphasis on the four basic animal drives of reproduction, hunger, fear and aggression. It is quite possible that the findings of ethologists will eventually induce psychologists to wonder whether they dismissed the concept of instinct too quickly and too finally, instead of refining it and relating it to data from other disciplines.

Lorenz: Intra-Specific Aggression

In recent years new light has been cast upon the nature of aggression by Konrad Lorenz of the Max Planck Institute of Behavioral Physiology. Lorenz

31. Berkowitz, *op. cit.*, p. 15.

32. John P. Scott, *Aggression* (Chicago: University of Chicago Press, 1958), p. 62.

33. Scott, *Animal Behavior*, pp. 153–155.

believes that the "fixed motor patterns" of animal behavior follow Mendel's law of inherited characteristics, yet he recognizes that there is a subtle relationship between the two factors of evolutionary adaptation—innate behavior and learning in the environment. From studies of aggression in certain species of fish, dogs, birds, rats, deer and farmyard animals, Lorenz concludes that aggression is something very different from the destructive principle expressed in the Freudian hypothesis of *thanatos*. According to Lorenz, "aggression, the effects of which are frequently equated with those of the death wish, is an instinct like any other and in natural conditions it helps just as much as any other to ensure the survival of the individual and the species." [34]

Lorenz found that aggression, as he defines it, occurs primarily among members of the same species, not between members of different species. When an animal of one species kills an animal of another species for food, this is not aggression; in killing the prey, the food-gatherer exhibits none of the characteristics of genuinely aggressive behavior. The typical aggressive instinct, according to Lorenz, is not *inter*-specific, but *intra*-specific, and can best be illustrated by the tenacity with which a fish, an animal or a bird will defend its territory against members of its own species. Aggression is seen as serving a species-preserving function in the Darwinian sense:

> *The danger of too dense a population of an animal species settling in one part of the available biotope and exhausting all its sources of nutrition and so starving can be obviated by a mutual repulsion acting on the animals of the same species, effecting their regular spacing out, in much the same manner as electrical charges are regularly distributed all over the surface of a spherical conductor. This, in plain terms, is the most important survival value of intra-specific aggression.*[35]

Lorenz notes that among animals who hold sway over a particular territorial space, the readiness to offer combat to an intruder is greatest at the center of the individual's territory—the part of the habitat with which it is most familiar. Lorenz contends that "even the slightest decrease in aggression toward the neighboring fellow member of the species must be paid for with loss of territory and . . . of sources of food for the expected progeny." [36] Here we have a concept which Robert Ardrey has popularized as "the territorial imperative." Ardrey interprets the available evidence to mean that men, no less than lions, wolves, tigers, eagles, robins, mockingbirds, ring-tailed lemurs, herring gulls, callicebus monkeys and many other species, are territorial creatures. He is convinced that man's territorial drive—his fierce attachment both

34. Konrad Lorenz, *On Aggression,* trans. Marjorie Kerr Wilson (New York: Bantam Books, 1967), p. x.

35. *Ibid.,* p. 28. "In other words, the threshold value of fight-eliciting stimuli is at its lowest where the animal feels safest, that is, where its readiness to fight is least diminished by its readiness to escape. As the distance from this 'headquarters' increases, the readiness to fight decreases proportionately as the surroundings become stranger and more intimidating to the animal." *Ibid.,* p. 32.

36. *Ibid.,* p. 167.

to private property and to the national patrimony—is an innate behavior pattern of an ancient biological order, "placed in our nature by the selective necessities of our evolutionary history." [37] Yet paradoxically, the sexual and family bond must overcome the tendency toward repulsion that is at the very heart of an individual's territory, where intra-specific aggression ought to be strongest. Lorenz describes the intimate relationship between bond behavior and aggressiveness as follows:

> *(A)s far as is known, in all the multiplicity of animals inhabiting the earth not a single species exhibiting bond behavior is anything but highly aggressive. Some birds and animals form bonds only in the mating season and are unbonded after the young are reared. While bonded, these species are invariably aggressive, and at other times they are usually unaggressive. A good many aggressive, bond-forming species, especially among those that form the most nearly permanent bonds, have innate behavior patterns that reinforce the bond . . . . On the other hand, a good many very aggressive species that live socially show no real bond behavior. Thus it is permissible to speculate that aggressiveness precedes bond behavior in the evolutionary sequence. . . . In normal circumstances the bonded pair are partners in the safe rearing of the next generation. And the bond both cements the partnership and acts to shield one partner from the aggressiveness of the other. . . .[38]*

Besides helping to keep the species spread over the widest area, the aggressive urge as manifested in the rival fight, usually between males, contributes to the selection of the fittest for reproduction. But the aim of aggression, says Lorenz, is to ward off the intruder, or to take possession of the female, or to protect the brood. Its object is never to exterminate fellow members of the species. Among several species one can verify a phenomenon which Lorenz terms the "ritualization of aggression," by which he means a fixed motor pattern involving a ceremonialized series of inciting or menacing gestures by one individual to ward off an interloping member of the same species. This form of aggressive expression seems to be nature's design to achieve the positive species-preserving purpose of the aggressive instinct without resort to actual violence.[39]

37. Robert Ardrey, *The Territorial Imperative* (New York: Atheneum Publishers, 1966), p. 103; see also pp. 4–7, 110–117; as well as his book *African Genesis* (New York: Dell Publishing Company, 1967), p. 174. See also Robert Ardrey, *The Social Contract: A Personal Inquiry into the Evolutionary Sources of Order and Disorder* (New York: Atheneum Publishers, 1970).

38. Konrad Lorenz, as quoted by Joseph Alsop in "Profiles: A Condition of Enormous Improbability," *The New Yorker,* XLV (March 8, 1969), p. 84.

39. Lorenz, *On Aggression,* pp. 54–65, 69–81 and 99–110. He gives the familiar example of the ceremonial inciting by the female duck who will charge menacingly toward an "enemy couple" until, frightened by her own boldness, suddenly scurries back to her own protective drake to refurbish her courage before the next hostile foray. Thus without actually joining battle she delivers her warning message.

In sum, Lorenz makes aggression out to be a benign instinct among animals. He points out that several animal species have developed some remarkable aggression-inhibiting mechanisms or appeasement gestures. This is especially true among animals that are hunters of large prey and that are gregarious. The wolf, for example, is armed with such an array of powerful weapons that he had to develop strong aggression inhibitors (such as baring his neck to the fangs of a victorious foe, thus giving the latter pause); otherwise the species might have destroyed itself.[40] Lorenz and other scientists hope that man will manage to ritualize and control his aggressive impulses as well as some of the lower orders of animals have done. But weak creatures (e.g., doves, hares, chimpanzees and men) which normally lack the power to kill a foe of their own size and which can rely upon flight or other forms of evasion have not been under much pressure to develop inhibitions against killing their own kind. Lorenz gives this description of man's plight:

> In human evolution, no inhibitory mechanisms preventing sudden manslaughter were necessary, because quick killing was impossible anyhow; the potential victim had plenty of opportunity to elicit the pity of the aggressor by submissive gestures and appeasing attitudes. No selection pressure arose in the prehistory of mankind to breed inhibitory mechanisms preventing the killing of conspecifics until, all of a sudden, the invention of artificial weapons upset the equilibrium of killing potential and social inhibitions.[41]

Lorenz's studies might well prompt the psychologists to revive their interest in the discarded instinct theories, but his concept of the aggressive impulse should not be confused with that of the Freudians or others who subscribe to the notion of a self-stimulating urge to destroy. For Lorenz, the purpose of the instinct is to warn the outsider to keep his distance; it apparently comes into play only when the proper stimulus is applied, although it has been construed by some as a spontaneously operating urge.[42] The older instinct school, however, might be inclined to argue that Lorenz' hypothesis, if valid, really

40. *Ibid.*, p. 127. See also pp. 72–74, 122–132 and 232–23. For a further elaboration of Lorenz's views concerning the implications of biological findings for a knowledge of human social behavior, see "A Talk With Konrad Lorenz," *New York Times Magazine,* July 5, 1970, pp. 4–5, 27–30.

41. *Ibid.*, p. 233. See also Jerome D. Frank, *Sanity and Survival: Psychological Aspects of War and Peace* (New York: Random House [Vintage Books], 1968), pp. 42–45 in his Chapter 3, "Why Men Kill—Biological Roots." R. L. Holloway, Jr. suggests that the averting of eyes, cringing and tears may serve an inhibiting or appeasing function in man, even though they are quite weak. "Human Aggression: The Need for a Species-Specific Framework," *Natural History,* LXXVI (December 1, 1967), 41.

42. J. P. Scott, in reviewing the Lorenz book, criticized it for suggesting that destructive aggressive behavior arises from a spontaneous outburst of internal energy. "Actually," Scott reiterates, "there is no evidence that there is any physiological mechanism in any mammal which produces stimulation to fight in the absence of external stimulation. Rather there is much evidence indicating that mechanisms exist which are easily excited by external stimulation and which function to prolong and magnify the effects of this stimulation." "Fighting," in *Science,* CLIV (November 4, 1966), 636–637.

lends support to the theory of a modified aggressive instinct in every species—less destructive and more positive than Freud's, but nevertheless constantly operative for all practical purposes, since it can be activated by any member of the species outside of the individual's immediate biological unit.

Frustration-Aggression Hypothesis

Within recent decades, most psychological authorities have been inclined to trace the source of aggression to some form of frustration. The psychological concept of frustration and its effects deserves particularly close examination because of a widespread assumption that the high conflict potential of the developing areas is a function of frustration caused by economic deprivation.[43] Not infrequently, theorists of social revolution, in describing the attitudes which prevail in a prerevolutionary situation, relate such phenomena as "alienation" and "anomie" to a condition of "general frustration." [44] Rarely do those who explain the unrest in the developing regions by reference to "rising expectations" and economic frustrations present any careful analysis of the psychological processes involved, but they seem to take for granted some kind of undifferentiated frustration-aggression theory.

THE DOLLARD-DOOB HYPOTHESIS

The frustration-aggression theory is a relatively old one. McDougall, Freud and others had suggested it at one time or another. But this theory received its classic expression in the work of John Dollard and his colleagues at Yale shortly before the outbreak of World War II. The Yale group took "as its point of departure the assumption that *aggression is always a consequence of*

43. See e.g., George Pettee, "Revolution—Typology and Process," in Carl J. Friedrich, ed., *Revolution* (New York: Atherton Press, 1966), p. 19. Pettee likens the prerevolutionary situation to one of frustration or cramp. Robert C. Williamson writes: "Internecine warfare has been the end result of social, political and economic frustration as well as of personal anomie." "Toward a Theory of Political Violence: The Case of Rural Colombia," *Western Political Quarterly,* XVIII (March, 1965), 36.

44. Robert L. Heilbroner, describing the problems of economic development in the emerging nations, writes: "Above all, the necessity to hold down the level of consumption—to force savings—in order to free resources for the capital-building process will make for a rising level of frustration, even under the sternest discipline. This frustration will almost surely have to be channeled into directions other than that of economic expectations. . . . In a word, economic development has within it the potential, not alone of a revolutionary situation, but of heightened international friction." *The Great Ascent* (New York: Harper and Row, 1963), pp. 158–159. For a fuller discussion of the revolutionary potential of economic deprivation and development in the light of the frustration-aggression hypothesis, see Chapter 8 on revolution.

frustration." More specifically they took it for granted that "the occurrence of aggressive behavior always presupposes the existence of frustration and, contrariwise, that the existence of frustration always leads to some form of aggression." [45] Frustration they defined as "an interference with the occurrence of an instigated-goal response at its proper time in the behavior sequence." [46] Whenever a barrier is interposed between a person and his desired goal, an extra amount of energy is mobilized. Such energy mobilization, said Stagner, "if continued and unsuccessful, tends to flow over into generalized destructive behavior." [47] Maslow, however, pointed out a difference between mere deprivation that is unimportant to the organism and a threat to the personality or life-goal of the individual; only the latter, he said, causes aggression.[48]

According to the Dollard study, the strength of the instigation to aggression can be expected to vary with (a) the strength of instigation to the frustrated response, (b) the degree of interference with the frustrated response; and (c) the number of frustrated response-sequences.[49] Aggression occurs only if goal-directed activity is thwarted, not in cases of unperceived deprivation. Moreover, the Yale group pointed out, not every frustrating situation produces overt aggression. Acts of aggression can be inhibited, especially when their commission would lead to punishment or other undesirable consequences. The anticipation of punishment reduces overt aggression, and the greater the amount of punishment anticipated for an aggressive act, the less likely is that act to occur.[50]

The individual experiences an impulse to attack whatever barrier stands in the way of goal-directed behavior. The immediate barrier-target, however, may be physically, psychologically or socially immune to attack: the person who interposes himself may be stronger, vested with an aura of authority, sacred in character, capable of retaliating with a socially approved punishment, or in some other way rendered for all practical purposes invulnerable. The Dollard group focused primarily on the threat of punishment. The expectation of punishment interferes with the act of aggression and thus gives rise

45. John Dollard, Leonard W. Doob, Neal E. Miller, *et al., Frustration and Aggression* (New Haven: Yale University Press, 1939), p. 1. For another basic work in the field, see Norman R. F. Maier, *Frustration: The Study of Behavior Without a Goal* (New York: McGraw-Hill Book Company, 1949).

46. Dollard *et al., op. cit.,* p. 7.

47. Ross Stagner, "The Psychology of Human Conflict," Elton B. McNeil, ed., *The Nature of Human Conflict,* p. 53.

48. Abraham H. Maslow, "Deprivation, Threat and Frustration," *Psychological Review,* XLVIII (No. 6, 1941), reprinted in J. K. Zawodny, *Man and In-*

ternational Relations (San Francisco: Chandler, 1966), 2 vols., I: *Conflict,* pp. 17–19. Maslow writes: "It is only when a goal object represents love, prestige, respect or achievement that being deprived of it will have the bad effects ordinarily attributed to frustration in general." *Ibid.,* pp. 17–18.

49. Stagner, *op. cit.,* p. 28. Minor frustrations and the residual instigations from them can become cumulative and lead to a stronger aggressive response than would ordinarily be expected from the frustrating situation which immediately triggers the response. *Ibid.,* p. 31.

50. *Ibid.,* pp. 32–38.

to further frustration, which will intensify the pressure either for direct aggression against the interfering agent or for other indirect forms of aggression.[51] There may occur a displacement of aggression, in which case the individual directs his hostility toward someone or something not responsible for the original frustration. Alternatively, the individual who is both frustrated and inhibited may alter not the *object* but the *form* of aggression (for example, by imagining or wishing injury to someone instead of actually harming the interfering agent). Another form which indirect aggression may take is self-aggression, in which the individual castigates himself, injures himself or, in the most extreme cases, commits suicide.[52] Dollard and his colleagues point to the "greater tendency for inhibited direct aggression to be turned against the self when it is inhibited by the self than when it is inhibited by an external agent," but they add that self-aggression is not the preferred type of expression.[53] Finally, it is assumed that any act of aggression leads to catharsis— i.e., a release of tension and a reduction in the instigation to aggression. These, in brief, are the essential psychological principles which comprise the Dollard-Doob theory.

MODIFICATIONS OF THE DOLLARD-DOOB HYPOTHESIS

The Dollard-Doob hypothesis has undergone certain modifications and refinements at the hands of other psychologists and social psychologists since the early 1940s. The crucial question is not whether frustration always leads to some form of aggression; it is conceded that it may be worked off in other ways and that a more accurate statement of the Dollard thesis is "that frustration produces instigation to different types of responses, one of which may be aggression." [54] Rather the crucial question is whether all aggression is traceable to frustration. Several authorities, including Durbin and Bowlby, Karl Menninger and J. P. Seward, have criticized the frustration-aggression hypothesis on the grounds that there are other causes of aggression besides frustration; [55] and the studies of animal behavior made by Scott and Frederickson, as well as Lorenz, also point to such other causes as dominance strivings, the sight of a strange animal of the same species, human resentment at the intrusion of strangers, disputes over the possession of objects, pain, inter-

---

51. Norman R. F. Maier, from his study of the role of punishment in the learning process, was led to postulate a relationship between frustration and fixation. See "Frustration Theory: Restatement and Extension," *Psychological Review,* LXIII (No. 6, 1956), 370–388, in J. K. Zawodny, ed., *op. cit.,* pp. 20–29.

52. Dollard *et al., op. cit.,* pp. 39–47.

53. *Ibid.,* p. 48.

54. Elton B. McNeil, "Psychology and Aggression," *Journal of Conflict Resolution,* III (September, 1959), 204. McNeil here is following N. E. Miller, "The Frustration-Aggression Hypothesis," *Psychological Review,* XLVIII (July, 1941), 338.

55. Leonard Berkowitz, *op. cit.,* p. 29.

ference with comfort, and so forth. But the psychologists who subscribe to the Dollard hypothesis usually end up broadening the notion of frustration to encompass all these other aggression-arousing factors, or by attempting to reduce all these latter factors to forms of frustration.[56]

Even at the level of individual psychology, before we pass on to the realm of social psychology, several difficulties arise in connection with the frustration-aggression hypothesis. These difficulties do not necessarily vitiate the theory, but they certainly complicate it. First, psychologists are not agreed as to whether the frustration-aggression nexus is a simple and virtually automatic stimulus-response pattern or whether such emotional states as anger and fear must be or can be interposed. Similarly, there is some disagreement as to whether additional cues, releasers, or other triggering stimuli must be present for aggression actually to occur. Second, what constitutes a frustration is not a completely objective matter; it often depends upon cognition and interpretation by the individual.[57] Third, some writers distinguish between primary and secondary frustrations and between active and passive frustrations. It is held that the various types of frustrations lead to different kinds of aggressive reactions.[58] Fourth, no clear differentiation is made between frustrations stemming from interference with routinized or frequently repeated goal-oriented behaviors and frustrations arising from interference with novel or "one shot" goal-directed actions. Fifth, although it may be relatively easy to see the operation of the frustration-aggression syndrome in children, it is considerably more ambiguous in adults. Sixth, when aggressive behavior does occur, "it may be deflected from its original goal, disguised, displaced, delayed, or otherwise altered." [59] This, to say the least, makes for uncertainty as to the connection between a specific frustration and a specific act of aggression, particularly since we are not sure whether frustration "wears off" in time, even if it is not "worked off" in some way besides aggression. One sometimes gains the impression that the psychologists, like the Ptolemaic astronomers of old, are trying to "save the appearance" through the introduction of "epicycles" and that, no matter what kind of behavior is observed, it is interpreted in such a way as to allow the theory to remain intact. Such an impression is strengthened when one learns that not only does frustration fail to produce observable aggression in all cases, but sometimes it leads to the very opposite, i.e., to

56. *Ibid.*, p. 30. McNeil observes that "the contention that aggressive behavior always presupposes the existence of frustration" has "met with little resistance or criticism." "Psychology and Aggression," p. 204.

57. For an elaboration of these first two points, see Leonard Berkowitz, *op. cit.*, pp. 32–48.

58. Sanford Rosenzweig, "An Outline of Frustration Theory," J. McV. Hunt, ed., *Personality and the Behavior Disorders*

(New York: Ronald Press Company, 1944), pp. 381–382. Elton B. McNeil, following Rosenzweig, says: "The privation of being born into poverty poses a series of frustrations for the individual; but his reaction to them differs considerably from his responses to being deprived of wealth, once he has possessed it." "Psychology and Aggression," *op. cit.*, p. 203.

59. Elton B. McNeil, "Psychology and Aggression," p. 204.

Microcosmic Theories of Conflict   215

regression.[60] One must be cautious, therefore, in trying to explain social behavior through the application of a hypothesis drawn from individual psychological behavior which leaves something to be desired inasmuch as the phenomenon in question (in this case, frustration) sometimes—and for reasons which are not clear—produces an effect diametrically opposed to the one which the hypothesis requires. The frustration-aggression theory is supported by a convincing body of experimental evidence. There can be little doubt of its utility when it is applied to certain limited and simpler aspects of individual and perhaps group behavior. But it is perhaps more than the theory can bear to use it for the purpose of extrapolating from relatively simple stimulus-response experiments to an explanation of the more subtle and complex modes of human action, especially those which are politically organized.

From Individual to Societal Aggression

How do we pass from aggression in the individual to aggression in society? In view of Herbert C. Kelman's warning cited near the beginning of Chapter 5 (see p. 142), such a transition should not be taken for granted. Yet the Dollard group transferred the lessons of individual frustration-aggression to the much broader level of collective social behavior without expressing any doubt as to the validity of the transfer and without offering any substantiating evidence or arguments that the transfer can in fact be made. Dollard himself had applied the frustration-aggression principle to an analysis of Negro reactions to the frustrations imposed by the white group in a Southern community and thus "was able to reveal the psychological effects of the social structure upon the organization of personality and behavior." [61] The Dollard study carried the suggestion that even the Marxist theory of the class struggle depends implicitly upon the frustration-aggression principle.[62]

60. Otto Klineberg, *Tensions Affecting International Understanding* (New York: Social Science Research Council, 1950), especially in Chapter 5, "Influence Making for Aggression," p. 196. Bernard Berelson and Gary A. Steiner also have noted that prolonged or intense frustration sometimes produces flight from the goal rather than a further struggle toward the goal. They suggest that when survival is not at stake, and occasionally even when it is, people may give up and abandon the situation, physically or psychologically. *Human Behavior: An Inventory of Scientific Findings* (New York: Harcourt, Brace and World, 1964), p. 270. This phenomenon would seem to correspond to what the biologists describe as the "fight or flight" reactions of animals in states of anxiety. See Harley C. Shands, "Some Social and Biological Aspects of Anxiety," *Journal of Nervous and Mental Disease*, CXXV (No. 3, 1957), reprinted in J. K. Zawodny, *op. cit.*, especially pp. 9 and 15.

61. Dollard *et al.*, *op. cit.*, p. 2.

62. The Yale group notes that "when Marxists have described the dynamic human interrelationships involved in the class struggle and in the preservation and destruction of the state, they have introduced unwittingly a psychological system involving the assumption that aggression

There are a number of difficulties involved in shifting the analysis of frustration from the plane of the individual to that of the society. Such a shift gives rise to a major "level of observation" problem. While it may be quite easy to see the frustration-aggression hypothesis validated in experiments with individuals (e.g., withdrawing bottles from babies, or interfering with the completion of relatively simple goal-oriented behavior patterns), it is more difficult to verify the hypothesis at the level of large-group behavior. First of all, the time factor is quite different. The most clear-cut experimental evidence from the study of individuals would seem to indicate fairly rapid time sequences from the onset of frustration to the manifestation of aggressive responses—minutes or hours in most cases, and perhaps days or weeks in some, although it is hard to achieve certitude in these latter cases in view of the fact that the length of time it takes a frustration to "wear off" (if it does) is not known. We have already seen that a series of minor frustrations can lead to "pent up" aggressiveness. Presumably each minor frustration results from a distinct stimulus in the S-R pattern. It seems reasonable to conclude, however, that the longer the time interval between the interference with the goal-directed action and the commission of an aggressive act, the less certain is the connection between the frustration and the aggression, because several other steps may have intervened in the meantime—inhibitions, displacements, substitute responses and other outlets or adjustments.

At some point, a long series of minor frustrations may shade off toward a continually frustrating condition or set of conditions, every conscious adversion to which constitutes an additional stimulus. But no matter how the time factor for individual behavior is explained, it would seem that social psychological phenomena usually develop at a slower time rate. Frustrating situations are perceived more slowly; the perceptions are less uniform and the interpretations more diverse; the stretched out time provides greater opportunity for individuals to adjust; the variety of response is broader for large groups than for individuals; responses to frustrating situations are likely to vary according to the cultural values of different groups within the social structure; and, perhaps most importantly, a whole complex of external sociological (rather than internal psychological) factors contributes toward the determination of the response to frustration. Hence it may be possible to verify the frustration-aggression hypothesis in the behavior of smaller, unstructured groups (e.g., such anomic outbursts as the rioting of an unorganized mob), but it would seem much more difficult, and perhaps impossible, to apply the theory in any precise way to the behavior of larger, more highly institutionalized social entities.[63] Finally, it should be pointed out that most exponents of

is a response to frustration." *Ibid.*, p. 23. The frustrating agents, of course, are the bourgeoisie, and the aggressive response by the frustrated proletariat is the organization of a class which finally carries out a revolution.

63. Sociologists distinguish between the behavior of small groups and that of large groups. Herbert Blumer has called attention also to the differences between "collective behavior" (even by fairly large groups) in "undefined or unstruc-

the frustration-aggression explanation are careful to exclude "learned aggression" from the scope of their theory. This is important to remember in any consideration of organized conflict (such as war, revolution and guerrilla insurgency) in which training for aggressive conduct plays a significant role.

Socialization, Displacement and Projection

The frustration-aggression school has attempted to move from the individual to the social level more by logical inference than by experimentation. The principal conceptual mechanisms by which the transfer is made are "the socialization of aggression," "displacement" and "projection"—all closely related notions. It is important to understand how these mechanisms are supposed to operate, for they are crucial in the effort to apply the frustration-aggression explanation of conflict to social communities.

Psychologists hold that the process of acquiring social habits invariably gives rise to frustrations of one sort or another, inasmuch as every forced modification of spontaneous behavior from childhood to adulthood, it can be argued, interferes with goal-responses. This holds true for feeding habits, the suppression of crying, limitation of movement, cleanliness and toilet training, table and speech manners, sex behavior, sex typing, age grading, social behavior, the disciplines of schooling, restrictions on adolescents, and the various adjustments required in adulthood, such as marital, professional or occupational, and so forth.[64] Most of these examples, of course, are drawn from

tured situations" and organized social behavior which follows culturally prescribed norms. "Collective Behavior," in J. B. Gitter, ed., *Review of Sociology: Analysis of a Decade* (New York: John Wiley and Sons, 1957), p. 130. In the elementary forms of collective behavior, the individuals in the group stimulate each other and contribute toward the circular development of a sense of unrest and excitement. Frustration might play a role here, although sociologists generally do not refer to it; even if they did, they would probably subordinate it to the stimulation-reinforcement which occurs. Blumer shows that elementary collective behavior can gradually develop into a more complex social movement as it "acquires organization and form, a body of customs and traditions, established leadership, an enduring division of labor, social rules and social values—in short, a culture, a social organization, and a new scheme of life." *Ibid.*, p. 199. Neil J. Smelser, while modifying some of

Blumer's ideas, agrees with the distinction described above: "Collective behavior . . . is not institutionalized behavior. According to the degree to which it becomes institutionalized, it loses its distinctive character." *Theory of Collective Behavior* (New York: Free Press of Glencoe, 1963), p. 8. It is interesting to note that Smelser, in his chapter on "The Hostile Outburst," makes no mention of the frustration-aggression hypothesis in his efforts to explain aggression in society. *Ibid.*, pp. 222–269. He does, however, make a brief footnote reference to it elsewhere. See p. 107.

64. John Dollard *et al., op. cit.,* pp. 55–76. E. F. M. Durbin and John Bowlby contended that the conflict within the child arising out of the fear of punishment is an important source of aggressiveness in the adult, because aggression can be controlled but not destroyed. "The boy, instead of striking his father whom he fears, strikes a smaller boy whom he

Contending Theories of International Relations

middle-class American family life. Frustration-aggression patterns are culture-bound; both the factors which make for frustration in human beings and the directions in which aggressive impulses are turned—or the "targets of aggression"—will depend largely upon the values of the specific cultural systems. Every society imposes some sort of social controls upon the spontaneous behavior of individuals. Thus according to the hypothesis, every social system produces in its members frustrations which eventually lead to fear, hatred and violent aggression. Every culture must develop for itself its own solution to the problem of socially managing the aggressive impulses of its members.[65] The "socialization of aggression" takes place in all human societies, attenuating hostile action among members of the "in group" by directing aggressive impulses against "out-groups." [66]

A child who is frustrated by the decision of a parent may seek release by substituting a different object of aggression—such as a toy, a piece of furniture, a sibling, another child in the neighborhood, a teacher, a pet, or a neighbor's property. It is deemed preferable that the substituted object be similar, if possible, to the original cause of the frustration. But very often similar targets (such as other adult authority figures) will also be invulnerable because aggression against them will likewise lead to punishment. As one finds safer targets, they frequently bear less resemblance to the original objects. The repression of hostile impulses from the level of consciousness can help in the displacement process, by allowing the individual to forget the identity of the original source of the frustration.[67] Repression can lead to projection,

---

does not fear. . . . And in the same way revolutionaries who hate ordered government, nationalists who hate foreign policies, individuals who hate bankers, Jews, or their political opponents, may be exhibiting characteristics that have been formed by the suppression of simple aggression in their childhood education." (New York: Columbia University Press, 1939), excerpted in J. K. Zawodny, *op. cit.,* p. 97. For another study of the effect of child-rearing practices upon the cultural and personality patterns of adult populations, see John W. M. Whiting and Irwin L. Child, *Child Training and Personality* (New Haven: Yale University Press, 1953).

65. "Which mode or modes of control are selected depends to a great extent on the culture in which the individual participates. Among the Sioux, for example, an infant's tantrums were a matter of pride to his parents, and he was hurt and frustrated as a child to encourage his rage. Rages were later controlled by venting them against extra-tribal enemies

in forays which promised social rewards. Among the Alorese, on the other hand, aggression is suppressed at an early age and later finds expression in intra-tribal stealing." Martin Gold, "Suicide, Homicide and the Socialization of Aggression," in Bartlett H. Stoodley, ed., *Society and Self: A Reader in Social Psychology* (New York: Free Press of Glencoe, 1962), pp. 281–282.

66. Robert R. Sears, Eleanor Maccoby and Harry Levin, "The Socialization of Aggression," in Eleanor E. Maccoby, Theodore M. Newcomb and Eugene L. Hartley, eds., *Readings in Social Psychology* (New York: Henry Holt and Company, 1958), pp. 350–352. Robert A. Le Vine writes: "The linkage between socialization of the child and customary social behavior is most conspicuous in the case of the aggressive motive." "Socialization, Social Structure, and Inter-Societal Images," in Herbert C. Kelman, ed., *op. cit.,* p. 46.

67. Elton B. McNeil, "Psychology and Aggression," *op. cit.,* p. 212.

which involves an attribution to, and an exaggeration in, others of unfavorable qualities and malicious motives that one is reluctant to recognize in himself. Man seeks to reduce his guilt feelings by projecting his intolerable thoughts and feelings to others. Once he has fastened upon his target, perceptual distortion sets in; everything in the target's behavior confirms and justifies his suspicions.[68]

It is quite common for psychologists and social psychologists to cite the frustration-aggression-displacement syndrome as the explanation of hostile attitudes toward "scapegoat" groups within a society and toward foreign nations.[69] But it is not clear how the leap is made from individual psychiatric theory to the analysis of attitudes and behavior at the level of large sociological entities. One might readily agree that a system of rewards and punishments within a family structure will serve to deter overt aggression, which the growing child will then displace.[70] It can also be conceded that there may be significant differences between the personality effects of democratic and authoritarian child-rearing patterns, and that such factors as the relations between fathers and sons, unsatisfied sexual desires and the success-anxiety which a specific social culture breeds might contribute to the formation of an "authoritarian personality"[71] who harbors hostile suspicions toward selected groups within his own society and toward selected foreign nations. The psychologists call attention to the fact that the growing child assimilates the attitudes and prejudices of adults, especially parents, and thus the notion of "the enemy," whether internal or external, is perpetuated through transmission from one generation to another. When a critical yet undefined proportion of people within a society become sufficiently frustrated or anxious or authoritarian, the society allegedly opts for conflict in an unconscious quest for self-release.

The mechanism by which individual psychic attitudes and complexes of a quasi-pathological character are translated into the concrete political decisions of leaders building up toward the actual outbreak of organized conflict has not yet been adequately defined and described, much less experimentally tested, in a manner intelligible to political scientists. Undoubtedly the frustrations of human beings form an important part of the total matrix out of which social conflict arises. The presence of widespread frustration would seem to lend a conflict potential to any social situation. It might even be said to constitute such a highly "useful" prerequisite as to be almost a necessary condition, at least for certain forms of conflict. To admit this is not to deny that the hypothesis contains serious difficulties. We still do not know, for

---

68. *Ibid.*, p. 213; Ross Stagner, *op. cit.*, pp. 55–56.

69. *Ibid.*, p. 54; and Ralph K. White, "Images in the Context of International Conflict," in Herbert C. Kelman, ed., *op. cit.*, especially pp. 267–268.

70. Frieda L. Bornston and J. C. Coleman, "The Relationship between Certain Parents' Attitudes toward Child Rearing and the Direction of Aggression of Their Young Adult Offspring," *Journal of Clinical Psychology*, XII (1956), 41–44.

71. See T. W. Adorno, *et al.*, *The Authoritarian Personality* (New York: Harper and Brothers, 1950).

example, what exactly is the relationship between childhood frustration experiences (with their accompanying effects upon personality) and adult socio-political attitudes. Nor is there any way to determine whether childhood experiences or contemporary adult frustrations are more important as influences upon behavior. But the frustration-aggression-displacement syndrome alone would not appear to supply both the necessary and the sufficient conditions. Frustration might supply the potential for conflict, but a trigger mechanism is required, and the potential must somehow be organized and given specific direction. One of the most glaring deficiencies in the frustration-aggression-displacement theory is its failure to explain adequately why particular groups are selected as targets of displaced aggression, especially when alternate targets are available.[72] At various times it has been suggested that targets are selected because they are "safe," because they are highly "visible," because they are "different and strange," because they have been traditionally mistrusted and disliked, or because they are most feared. Yet the target which is singled out for the displacement of aggression is also supposed to have some degree of association with the original frustrater.

Learning Theory and International Conflict

Hadley Cantril's psycho-political research, "transactional psychology," emphasizes that people do not react directly in a simple mechanistic way to a situation but rather that their reaction is grounded upon assumptions formed by past experiences: "The way we look at things and the attitudes and opinions we form are grounded on assumptions we have learned from our experience in life . . . Once assumptions are formed and prove more or less effective, they serve both to focus attention and screen out what is apparently irrelevant and, as reinforcing agents, to intensify other aspects of the environment which seem to have a direct bearing on our purposes."[73]

This theory has important implications for the effective formulation of policy. It emphasizes "the importance of understanding the state of mind of people with whom the Government must deal, at home or abroad, in order to devise the right expression of policy at the right time or to decide the right moment to act." Understanding people's assumptions or states of mind involves knowing "their feelings, the whole complex of their hopes and aspirations, their frustrations and fears . . . traditions and customs."[74]

72. Leonard Berkowitz, *op. cit.*, pp. 139, 149 and 193–264; cf. also his "The Concept of Aggressive Drive," in Leonard Berkowitz, ed., *Advances in Experimental Social Psychology* (New York: Academic Press, 1965), II, 312.

73. Hadley Cantril, *The Human Dimension: Experiences in Policy Research* (New Brunswick, N.J.: Rutgers University Press, 1967), p. 16.

74. *Ibid.*, p. 156.

In 1947 Hadley Cantril organized a research program for UNESCO which enlisted the services of social scientists in the study of "Tensions Affecting International Understanding." In response to a resolution of the UNESCO General Assembly, which called for "an inquiry into the influences which predispose towards international understanding on the one hand and aggressive nationalism on the other," a small group of experts from different disciplines and different nations conferred and agreed to a common statement, published in *Tensions that Cause Wars.* A second resolution called for "inquiries into the conceptions which people of one nation entertain of their own and of other nations." Surveys were taken of the attitudes of people in Australia, Britain, France, Germany, Italy, the Netherlands, Norway, Mexico, and the United States toward people in other nations. The analysis, which appeared in *How Nations See Each Other,* suggested that "the stereotypes people have of people in other nations are largely results and not causes of the current relationship of their countries: people in one nation are hostile to people in other nations not because they have unfavorable stereotypes; rather they have these unfavorable stereotypes because they think these other people are interfering with their own or their nation's goals." [75]

Although considerable emphasis has been placed upon the quantitative study of international relations in the past decade, Harold Lasswell was among the first to suggest that international political phenomena could be so studied. With more adequate knowledge about trends, it would be possible to make predictions which could be altered by "preventive politics." Thus, Lasswell was concerned "with the organization of social knowledge to illuminate the margin of manipulable choice in the pattern of future events." [76] According to Lasswell, the utility of his theory lay in its potential for discovering the psychological and social roots of those human insecurities that cause wars and finding substitutes for violence as the means to gain security. In other words, Lasswell sought to develop a "policy science" for the study of international relations.

Lasswell also contended that a single theoretical framework could be devised to accommodate and unify the study of all political processes, whether domestic, comparative, or international. He called for the development of a framework sufficiently broad to accommodate future changes in the world political process.[77]

75. *Ibid.,* pp. 127–128. See also Hadley Cantril, ed., *Tensions that Cause Wars* (Urbana: University of Illinois Press, 1950), p. 7; Hadley Cantrill and William Buchanan, *How Nations See Each Other* (Urbana: University of Illinois Press, 1953).

76. William T. R. Fox, "Harold D. Lasswell and the Study of World Politics," in Arnold A. Rogow, ed., *Politics, Person-* *ality, and Social Science in the Twentieth Century* (Chicago: University of Chicago Press, 1969), pp. 376–7.

77. Lasswell's writings on the politics of biotechnology, astropolitics, and thinking machine-actors are found in "The Political Science of Science," *American Political Science Review,* L (December, 1956), 961–79; *The Future of Political Science* (New York: Atherton Press,

Contending Theories of International Relations

In every society the pattern of distribution of values—safety, income and deference—resembles a pyramid. In fact, Lasswell defined politics as the "study of the changing value hierarchy, the pyramids of safety, income, and deference," or the study of "who gets what, when and how." [78] World politics is the study of the "shape and composition of the value patterns of mankind as a whole." For this reason, Lasswell called for comparative studies of world elites and their values. The elite of the society receives most of its values and attempts to retain its position of ascendancy "by manipulating symbols, controlling supplies, and applying violence." [79] However, mass insecurities and discontent, especially heightened by shifts in the division of labor, in the distribution of the instrumentalities of violence, or in changes in symbols of identification, give rise to class struggles for a redistribution of values.

"Wars and revolutions are avenues of discharge for collective insecurities and stand in competition with every alternative means of dissipating mass tension." [80] An elite with vested interests might prefer a foreign war, rather than domestic social changes, for relieving its insecurities. As long as the present world political structure existed, violence would persist. Lasswell argues that since elites can be sustained not only by violence but also by manipulating symbols, what is needed for a stable world order is a world myth or a "universal body of symbols and practices sustaining an elite which propagates itself by peaceful methods. . . ." [81]

Social psychologists point out that the expression of aggression within a society may be either covert or overt. Physical aggression may be eschewed in favor of verbal aggression—i.e., murder, suicide and other forms of violence may be rather rare, while the culture sanctions malicious gossip, slander and the use of sorcery as means of retaliating against those one dislikes. Elton B. McNeil writes:

> *Starting with the premise that an average quantity of aggression is the inheritance of each individual, it becomes clear that a dependable relationship exists between the freedom for its overt expression and the degree to which covert forms of it will make their appearance. The quantity of aggression given in the beginning seems fixed and unalterable, and if it finds no overt channel for expression, it becomes covert . . . .*[82]

This suggests that some cultures may develop acceptable ways of allowing people to work off aggressive impulses—e.g., through intensely competitive

1962, No. 72); "Men in Space," *Annals of the New York Academy of Sciences* No. 72 (1958), pp. 180–194.

78. *World Politics and Personal Insecurity* (New York: McGraw-Hill Book Company, 1935), pp. 207 and 3.

79. *Ibid.,* p. 3.

80. *Ibid.,* p. 25.

81. *Ibid.,* p. 237.

82. Elton B. McNeil, "The Nature of Aggression," McNeil, ed., *op. cit.,* p. 35.

sports which provide a catharsis for both players and spectators. A society which does not develop such outlets and which seeks to protect itself against internecine strife may be more disposed to direct its accumulated hostility against external societies. At the very least it can be said that social scientists have long taken for granted an inverse relationship between internal and external social conflicts. (We shall return to this point below in the chapter on the macrocosmic theories.)

Image Theory

In their analysis of international conflict, psychologists frequently relate the phenomena of "displacement" and "projection" to the concept of "national images." These images reflect a process of selective perception (and, hence, some perceptual distortion) caused by the traditional historic view of other nations as transmitted through the educational system, folklore, the news media and other channels of socialization. There is nothing mysterious about an "image." The term, according to Kelman, merely refers to "the organized representation of an object in an individual's cognitive system . . . the individual's conception of what the object is like." [83] Intergroup tensions and the decisions that lead to intergroup or international conflict are often traced to individual states of mind, which are politically manipulable and where distorted perceptions may be more significant than accurate ones.

Kenneth Boulding (who is an economist rather than a psychologist by profession) has pointed out that the behavior of complex political organizations is determined by decisions which involve "the selection of a preferred position in a contemplated field of choice," and which is in turn the function of the decision-maker's *image*. The image is a product of messages received in the past—not a simple accumulation of messages but "a highly-structured piece of information-capital." Every nation is a complex of the images of the persons who think about it; hence the image is not one but many. Furthermore, there are in the nation the images of a relatively small group of powerful people who make the important decisions and the images of the ordinary people (the masses) who are affected by the decisions but only indirectly take part in making them—more so in democratic, less in dictatorial or totalitarian systems. Boulding then makes this important observation:

> *In the formation of the national images, however, it must be emphasized that impressions of nationality are formed mostly in childhood and usually in the family group. It would be quite fallacious to think of the images as being cleverly imposed on the mass by the powerful. If anything, the reverse is the case, the image is essentially*

83. Herbert C. Kelman in Kelman, ed., *op. cit.*, p. 24.

a mass image, or what might be called a "folk image," transmitted through the family and the intimate face-to-face group, both in the case of the powerful and in the case of ordinary persons. Especially in the case of the old, long-established nations, the powerful share the mass image rather than impose it . . . This is much less true in new nations which are striving to achieve nationality, where the family culture frequently does not include strong elements of national allegiance but rather stresses allegiance to religious ideals or to the family as such.[84]

"MIRROR IMAGES"

Within recent years, considerable attention has been devoted to the subject of "mirror images." This interest has been perhaps a natural outgrowth of the efforts of social psychologists to understand within the framework of their own discipline the Cold War between the United States and the Soviet Union. The notion of "mirror images" is based on the assumption that the peoples of two countries involved in a prolonged hostile confrontation develop fixed, distorted attitudes which are really quite similar. Each people sees itself as virtuous, restrained and peace-loving, and views the adversary nation as deceptive, imperialistic and warlike. One writer describes it in this way:

> *Each side believes the other to be bent on aggression and conquest, to be capable of great brutality and evil-doing, to be something less than human and therefore hardly deserving respect or consideration, to be insincere and untrustworthy, etc. To hold this conception of the enemy becomes the moral duty of every citizen, and those who question it are denounced. Each side prepares actively for the anticipated combat, striving to amass the greater military power for the destruction of the enemy . . . . The approaching war is seen as due entirely to the hostile intentions of the enemy.*[85]

According to the social psychologists, the perception of the enemy, even though it may be erroneous, can help to shape reality and bring on the self-fulfilling prophecy: when suspicions run high, a "defensive" move by one side may look "provocative" to the other, evoking from the latter a further "defensive" reaction which serves only to confirm the suspicions of the former.[86]

The concept of the "mirror image" seems to have been elaborated by American social psychologists almost exclusively for the purpose of explaining

84. Kenneth E. Boulding, "National Images and International Systems," *Journal of Conflict Resolution*, III (June, 1959), 120–131. This and the previous quotations are on pp. 121–122. See also his book, *The Image* (Ann Arbor: University of Michigan Press, 1956).

85. Arthur Gladstone, "The Conception of the Enemy," *Journal of Conflict Resolution*, III (June, 1959), 132.

86. Stagner, *op. cit.*, p. 46.

certain aspects of Soviet-American relations and perhaps of contrasting Khrushchev's behavior with that of Stalin in such a way as to make the former look "peaceful" and the latter "aggressive." Urie Bronfenbrenner, for example, in a well-known exposition of the idea, argues that both American and Russian citizens believe essentially the same things about each other's societies: *They* are the aggressors; *their* government exploits and deludes the people; the mass of *their* people are not really sympathetic to the regime; *they* cannot be trusted; and *their* policy verges on madness.[87] Even within the restricted context of Soviet-American relations, the concept of the "mirror image" has given rise to some serious difficulties. One of the difficulties associated with the notion of the mirror image is that it readily gives rise to pseudocorollaries in the minds of untrained observers—corollaries which are not necessarily implicit in the concept itself but which emerge by a process of insinuation: 1) The social and political values of the two sides are scarcely distinguishable from each other. 2) Neither party can properly be cast in the role of aggressor or defender. 3) Both sides are equally right, equally wrong, and equally responsible for pursuing policies that produce international tensions. 4) The strategic behavior of the two sides springs from thought processes that are essentially similar. 5) The reduction of image-distortion can be accomplished with equal ease on both sides. In fairness to the advocates of the "mirror image" theory, it should be pointed out that they often make some effort to dissociate themselves from the illogical inferences which can be drawn therefrom. Ralph K. White, for example, warns: "The proposition that 'there is probably some truth on both sides' should be distinguished from the quite different proposition that 'there is probably an equal amount of truth on both sides'. . . . (It is) entirely possible to attribute too much validity to the other's viewpoint, leaning over backward to avoid ethnocentrism. . ." [88] Urie Bronfenbrenner has called attention to an important asymmetry: "It proved far easier to get an American to change his picture of the Soviet Union than the reverse. Although showing some capacity for change, Soviet citizens were more likely than American to cling to their stereotypes and to defend them by denial and displacement. . . . I am persuaded that a comparative study of modes of adaptation in American and Soviet society would reveal a stronger predilection in the latter for black-and-white thinking, moral self-righteousness, mistrust, displacing of blame to others, perceptual distortion, and denial of reality." [89]

87. "The Mirror Image in Soviet-American Relations: A Social Psychologist's Report," *Journal of Social Issues,* XVII (No. 3), 46–48. See also William Eckhardt and Ralph K. White, "A Test of the Mirror Image Hypothesis: Kennedy and Khrushchev, *Journal of Conflict Resolution;* XI (September, 1967), 325–332; Charles E. Osgood, "Analysis of the Cold War Mentality," *Journal of Social Issues,* XVII (No. 3, 1961), 12–19.

88. *Op. cit.,* p. 240.

89. "Allowing for Soviet Perceptions," in Roger Fisher, ed., *International Conflict and Behavioral Science,* The Craigville Papers (New York: Basic Books, 1964), p. 172.

Other Psychological Theories of Conflict

In addition to the still dominant frustration-aggression hypothesis, there are several other psychological theories of conflict with which the student of international relations should be familiar. These theories often serve to complement and in some cases to modify the theories treated in the foregoing sections.

STEREOTYPES AND PREJUDICE

The student should be acquainted with the studies of Allport, Klineberg and others on such phenomena as bias, prejudice and stereotypes, and the part played by educational and mass communications systems in the shaping of intergroup attitudes.[90] He should be conversant with the phenomenon which Frenkel-Brunswik calls the "intolerance of ambiguity," or the tendency of human beings to reduce frustrating or anxiety-producing uncertainties and contradictions in the world as perceived by reducing social reality to nice, neat dichotomous categories—black and white, good and bad, friend and foe.[91] The student should also be aware of Karen Horney's concept of a neurotic search for glory by the individual who confuses with his real self an idealized self-image which demands personal triumph and visible success, often to vindicate humiliations experienced in childhood.[92] Also of significance for an understanding of certain aspects of national and international politics is Erich Fromm's thesis concerning the desire of modern man to escape the burdens of freedom. Feeling alone and powerless in the face of gigantic entities and social forces he cannot control, man, according to Fromm, is tempted masochistically to dissolve himself in the omnipotent state, to identify entirely with the state, and to seek his satisfaction vicariously in the fortunes of the larger collectivity. Himself ready to submit to power within his nation, he wants his nation to assert itself at the expense of the weak beyond its borders.[93] These psychoanalytic interpretations of political behavior cannot be examined here in detail, but merely citing them in this summary fashion should make it obvious to the reader that if either national leadership groups

90. Gordon W. Allport, *The Nature of Prejudice* (Cambridge: Addison-Wesley, 1954); and Otto Klineberg, *The Human Dimension in International Relations* (New York: Holt, Rinehart and Winston, 1964).

91. Else Frenkel-Brunswik, "Intolerance of Ambiguity as an Emotional and Perceptual Personality Variable," *Journal of Personality*, XVIII (September, 1949),

108–143; and "Social Tensions and the Inhibition of Thought," *Social Problems*, II (October, 1954), 75–81.

92. Karen Horney, *Neurosis and Human Growth* (New York: W. W. Norton and Company, 1950), pp. 21–27.

93. Erich Fromm, *Escape from Freedom* (New York: Rinehart and Company, 1941), pp. 21–22, 141–142, 164–168.

or large segments of their publics should lapse into pronounced forms of the neuroticism which these theories describe, it could have a profound impact upon the international behavior of states.

FESTINGER AND COGNITIVE DISSONANCE

One of the newer psychological theories which merits particular mention is the theory of cognitive dissonance and consistency advanced by Leon Festinger.[94] Stated in its simplest form, the theory refers to the normal tendency of the individual to reduce inconsistencies which may arise in his knowledge concerning his values, his environment and his behavior. Inconsistency might be reduced by modifying any one of the three. The problem of one's attitude toward smoking provides an apt illustration. The nonsmoker experiences no great difficulty when he learns that, according to contemporary scientific research, the smoking of cigarettes is considered a serious hazard to health and to life. The inveterate smoker, however, suffers cognitive dissonance when this is called to his attention. He has always considered personal health to be an important human good. If he is married and has children, he may feel a moral obligation to act prudently for the prolongation of his life. His wife might plead with him to stop smoking, and he is pained by the thought of displeasing her. He can attempt to reduce the inconsistencies in his knowledge by pursuing various courses.

First of all, he could stop smoking, but this may be difficult. He enjoys the pleasure of smoking and he might be convinced that it relaxes him and enhances his ability to concentrate creatively at his work. As for the issue of personal health, he might try to persuade himself that one should not be unduly concerned about longevity of life and sacrifice all sorts of present pleasures for the sake of a future benefit which might just as easily be snatched away as the result of a car accident, a disease unrelated to smoking or a nuclear war. If he perceives the deprivations of a fatherless family largely in economic terms, he may soothe his conscience by buying more life insurance. Should it be his wife's critical attitude which is producing the dissonance within him, he may marshal his arguments to change her opinion, perhaps by deprecating the validity of the hypothesis that correlates cigarettes with health hazards. To reinforce his own convictions, he might increasingly seek the company of smokers as well as information calculated to show the advantages of smoking. In rare cases, the individual may even obtain a research grant to prove a less perturbing hypothesis concerning cigarettes or to find a way to reduce the harmfulness of smoking. In each of the foregoing examples, the individual strives to reduce his inner dissonance by changing his behavior, his values or

94. Leon Festinger, *A Theory of Cognitive Dissonance* (Stanford: Stanford University Press, 1957); and *Conflict, Decision and Dissonance* (Stanford: Stanford University Press, 1964).

Contending Theories of International Relations

his environment. Usually, of course, restructuring of one's knowledge is an easier task than changing behavior or altering external reality.

Does this normal tendency away from cognitive dissonance and toward cognitive consistency have significant implications for the study of conflict at the level of international relations? Although the phenomenon seems readily verifiable through the introspection of personal experience, it is not yet demonstrable that it plays a significant part in interstate conflict, and perhaps it will never become so demonstrable in an empirical sense. We might speculate on how it could become operable. If this psychological mechanism does have significance at the level of international politics, it may be within the minds of key decision-makers. Suppose, for example, that the leaders of a particular nation were convinced on ideological grounds that their country could not achieve permanent security until the adversary who represented the antithesis of their national value system had been destroyed or disarmed as a result of a victorious war. But with the growth of nuclear weapon stockpiles, the same leadership group realizes that direct hostilities between the two powers might very well prove mutually suicidal. Most of the leaders, therefore, in an effort to reduce cognitive dissonance, begin to restructure their knowledge patterns concerning the world situation. Some abandon their earlier insistence upon the destruction of the enemy nation and derive satisfaction from the notion that henceforth their national security will be guaranteed by "the balance of terror." Others deprecate the antithetical character of the two national value systems and express the hope of eventual "convergence." Still others seek different avenues to dissonance reduction: some hope to disarm the foe by psychopolitical rather than military means; some try to persuade themselves that strategic superiority can be achieved, after which a bold first nuclear strike will bring a quick and tolerably cheap victory; some may perceive in the emergence of a third power a common threat which the two traditional enemies might now collaborate to contain. No sensible observer would attempt to predict how these various resolutions of the dissonance problem would distribute themselves among the leadership elites.

The theory of cognitive dissonance, which is perhaps related to the "intolerance of ambiguity" discussed earlier, might cast light on the phenomenon of internal revolution within a society. It is often suggested that when human beings perceive an intolerably wide gap between their social ideals and the operational reality of the existing political system, they become alienated from the latter and seek to reduce their inner dissonance by gravitating toward revolutionary organization for the purpose of restructuring the external environment according to their ideal vision. In revolutionary situations, of course, many individuals will hover precariously on the borderline between continuing to grant the system minimal or passive support and withdrawing from the system to oppose it actively by violence. This is partly a matter of weighing prospective rewards and punishments, and thus falls under the heading of what psychologists call "approach-avoidance" conflicts within the indi-

Microcosmic Theories of Conflict

vidual, where the antagonistic tendencies are both sufficiently strong to produce ambivalent or neurotic behavior.[95]

We might suggest the following hypothesis concerning the relationship between cognitive dissonance theory on the one hand and the theories of the causes of international war and internal revolutionary conflict on the other: modern technological developments, particularly in respect to nuclear missile weaponry and to the mass media of communications as a factor in social conflict, produce in the minds of both individuals and social aggregates a form of cognitive dissonance which seems likely to attenuate pressures for direct international military hostilities (at least between nuclear powers and their immediate allies) while increasing the probability of intrasocietal conflict and violence, both in nuclear and non-nuclear weapon countries. There are several different elements in confluence here: the impact of advanced weapons technology and of communications patterns upon the crucial inverse relationship, long hypothesized by social scientists but never conclusively demonstrated, between intrasocietal and extrasocietal violence.

Intrasocietal Violence and International Conflict

In this text we do not contend that the condition of mutual nuclear deterrence between the United States and the Soviet Union renders absolutely impossible direct general war between the two superpowers. We readily recognize that, even though the great majority of political-military leaders on both sides probably now reject the idea of deliberate nuclear attack as fraught with such frightful risks of unacceptable retaliatory damage as to be totally inappropriate as a rational instrument of policy, nevertheless several things could happen which might weaken the assumption that large-scale nuclear war will not occur. Although most experts would now agree that there exists a crude strategic parity between the Soviet Union and the United States, sufficient to induce the two superpowers that they should seek mutually advantageous arms control agreements, there always remains the possibility that one side or other may achieve a technological advance in weaponry which will convince an influential faction within the decision-making machinery that a strategic first-strike could be feasible. Beyond this contingency of deterrence-

95. Judson S. Brown, "Principles of Intrapersonal Conflict," *Journal of Conflict Resolution,* I (June, 1957), 137–138. For a different perspective of how psychological factors in the personal background of a political leader may affect his decision to "go revolutionary," see

E. Victor Wolfenstein, *Violence or Non-Violence: A Psychoanalytic Exploration of the Choice of Means in Social Change* (Monograph Series, Center for International Studies, Princeton University, 1965).

failure lie other possibilities: a catalytic war provoked by a third party; a war started as a result of the unauthorized use of nuclear weapons, psychic error, misinterpretation of intelligence, technical accident, or the uncontrollable escalation of a local conflict (between the superpowers, their allies or their clients).[96] Nevertheless, a theory of international relations cannot long dwell upon such speculative possibilities, except to recommend that responsible governments take unilateral, bilateral and multilateral steps toward arms control which are calculated to minimize the likelihood of such disastrous happenings. (Theories of nuclear deterrence and arms control will be discussed in Chapter 9.) The authors, instead of spending too much time describing what *might* happen in the nuclear age, are more disposed to examine the kind of conflict which *is* happening and which has become prominent in the nuclear age—namely, revolutionary warfare within nations. Although it is essentially "internal," such revolutionary conflict has significant implications for the international system.

Throughout the continents of Asia, Africa and Latin America, the so-called revolution of rising expectations has created a social-psychological climate conducive to indigenous discontent, alienation and conflict. Even within the industrially advanced countries, recent years have witnessed the development of a revolutionary mentality or temper among sectors of youth and of disadvantaged minorities. The technical communications media have produced a more widespread awareness of discrepancies, gaps and contradictions, both internationally and intranationally. In nearly every historic age, the existence of revolutionary conditions within states has led to external interventions by strong foreign powers.[97] Weaker revolutionary forces seek to augment their power by inviting outside aid. Furthermore, in view of the prevailing nuclear stalemate, great powers which are committed to a reversal of the international status quo are naturally attracted to the idea of supporting "national liberation warfare" (as the Soviets call it) or "people's war" (as the Chinese call it), since these are relatively safe methods of carrying on their revolutionary movement, compared to the more dangerous methods of direct confrontation with the West. Other factors have favored the rise of intrasocietal violence on the international scene within the last two decades

---

96. For representative works in the field of arms control literature, see Donald G. Brennan, ed., *Arms Control, Disarmament and National Security* (New York: George Braziller, 1961); Hedley Bull, *The Control of the Arms Race* (New York: Frederick A. Praeger, 1961); Thomas C. Schelling and Morton H. Halperin, *Strategy and Arms Control* (New York: The Twentieth Century Fund, 1961); and James E. Dougherty and John F. Lehman, Jr., eds., *Arms Control for the Late Sixties* (Princeton: D. Van Nostrand Company, 1967).

97. "That every internal war creates a demand for foreign intervention," writes George Modelski, is "implicit in the logic of the situation." "The International Relations of Internal War," James N. Rosenau, ed., *International Aspects of Civil Strife* (Princeton: Princeton University Press, 1964), p. 20.

—the after-effects of decolonization upon weak and inexperienced states structural deficiencies in the international economic system, the increasing availability of arms, and the diffusion of knowledge concerning revolutionary techniques, to refer to only a few. The mention of large-scale, organized violence, however, leads us to the macrocosmic theories of conflict, which are discussed in the following chapter.

Behaviorists and the Political Causes of War

We would conclude this chapter by reiterating that the causes of international war cannot be understood exclusively in terms of biological or psychological factors. One must always return to the level of political analysis to find out why a particular government regards certain foreign governments as allies and others as adversaries. It is out of a matrix of political communications—involving politicians and diplomats, the public, the press, the military, socioeconomic elites, special interest groups in the foreign policy-making process—that governments define their goals, interests, policies and strategies, weighing the likely consequences of acting or not acting in specific situations, as well as the prospects of success or failure in invoking force. When a government takes a decision for war, it may be for a great variety of conscious reasons, singly or in combination—to preserve its "prestige;" to establish hegemony within a larger area; to support an ally and thus safeguard an alliance against erosion; to maintain an "equilibrium" in a particular region; to fill a "power vacuum;" to protect an economic interest abroad; to dissuade future aggression; to gain control of territory deemed vital to national security; to consolidate the domestic position of a ruling elite or political party; or to enhance internal cohesion and head off domestic strife by deflecting conflict passions abroad. Many other political motives for war could be cited. But these examples will suffice to focus our attention upon an important conclusion: The findings of the behavioral scientists can serve as valuable illuminators to our understanding of the causes of war, provided that we place them in perspective as partial explanatory factors within the larger international political context in which those who wield the power of decision opt either to go to war or to refrain from it.[98]

98. For a thoughtful and critical analysis of the contributions which behavioral scientists had made prior to 1959 toward the control of interstate violence, see Kenneth N. Waltz, *Man, the State and War* (New York: Columbia University Press, 1959) pp. 42–79. Waltz anticipated the conclusion reached here, namely, that the behaviorists must take into greater account the political framework of war-peace issues.

CHAPTER 8

Macrocosmic Theories of Conflict: Revolution

Social scientists—especially sociologists, anthropologists, and political scientists—who adopt a macro approach to human phenomena tend to regard conflict as a normal concomitant of group existence. Those sociologists who follow Talcott Parsons in emphasizing social adjustment, "common-value orientation" and system maintenance are an exception. More interested in social order than social change, in social statics than dynamics, the Parsonians consider conflict as a disease with disruptive and dysfunctional consequences. However, most European sociologists from Karl Marx to Georg Simmel and Ralf Dahrendorf and most American sociologists in the pre-Parsonian era (e.g., Robert E. Park, John W. Burgess, William Graham Sumner, Charles H. Cooley, E. A. Ross and Albion W. Small) and some in recent decades (e.g., Jessie Bernard and Lewis A. Coser) have viewed conflict as serving positive social purposes.[1]

1. See Georg Simmel, *Conflict,* trans. Kurt H. Wolff in *Conflict and the Web of Group-Affiliations* (New York: Free Press of Glencoe, 1964); Lewis A. Coser, *The Functions of Social Conflict* (New York: Free Press of Glencoe, 1964), pp. 15–38; Jessie Bernard, "Parties and Issues in Conflict," *Journal of Conflict Resolution,* I (March, 1957); and Ralf Dahrendorf, "Toward a Theory of Social Conflict," *ibid.,* II (June, 1958), trans. Anatol Rapoport. Dahrendorf, a German sociologist, argues that when certain social-structural arrangements are given, conflict is bound to arise. He traces the responsibility for the shift of emphasis within the field of sociology from social conflict to social stability to Talcott Parsons and his structural-functional approach to the study of society. (For a discussion of the work of Parsons and structural-functionalism, see Chapter 4.) This approach contains the following implicit postulates: 1) Every society is a relatively persisting configuration of elements. 2) Every society is a well-integrated configuration of elements. 3) Every element in a society contributes to its functioning. 4) Every society rests on the consensus of its members. Dahrendorf thinks that this social equilibrium conception of society is not compatible with the serious study of conflict. The foregoing postulates not only fail to explain change and conflict, they exclude these phenomena altogether. When confronted with instances of con-

For these latter social theorists, conflict not only integrates, but it helps to establish group identity, clarifies group boundaries and contributes to group cohesion. Nearly every sociologist and social anthropologist postulates some degree of "in-group" hostility for the "out-group." When there are many out-groups, the political scientist can cast light upon why a particular one may be singled out at a particular time as the target of hostility. Historians of nationalism often describe the importance of the external *bête noire* in the formative period of a nation's consciousness. But beyond this well-known phenomenon, some social theorists contend that even within groups discord and opposition help to hold the groups together by providing inner relief and making the unbearable bearable.[2] Thus many thinkers in modern times accept conflict as something which is "structured into existence by the very fact of group identifications,"[3] and even "the central explanatory category for the analysis of social change and of 'progress.' "[4]

One of the most enduring hypotheses in social conflict theory is that which postulates an inverse relationship between internal and external conflict: internal violence within a group is expected to decrease as external aggression increases and vice versa. In the last century, Durkheim recognized this proposition.[5] More recently, Clyde Kluckhohn, an eminent American anthropologist, restated the hypothesis that if intragroup aggressive impulses become strong enough to threaten a nation with internal disruption, the nation may attempt to preserve its cohesion by displacing the aggressiveness through external war. Ordinarily, he says, "aggression release within a society is inversely proportional to outlets outside."[6] Robert F. Murphy, who studied the Mundurucú tribe of Brazil, notes that warfare once served that group as a

---

flict, the "structural-functional" school treats them as abnormal, deviant, pathological. In contrast to the "structural-functional" theory, Dahrendorf offers four different postulates: 1) Every society is subjected at every moment to change; change is ubiquitous. 2) Every society experiences at every moment social conflict; conflict is ubiquitous. 3) Every element in a society contributes to its change. 4) Every society rests on constraint of some of its members by others. Dahrendorf's postulates are not presented to replace the Parsonian view, but rather to complement it. The two organic models together, he suggests, would exhaust social reality, and a synthesis of the two would supply us with a complete theory of society in both its enduring and its changing aspects. Dahrendorf, *op. cit.*, especially pp. 173–175. See also Irving Louis Horowitz, "Consensus, Conflict and Cooperation: A Sociological Inventory,"

Special Forces, XLI (December, 1962), 177–188. Horowitz insists that conflict as well as consensus must be treated within the framework of social structure, not as a deviation from it.

2. Simmel, *op. cit.*, pp. 16–20.

3. R. L. Holloway, Jr., *op. cit.*, p. 42. Holloway is a physical anthropologist who specializes in the evolution of the brain and human behavior.

4. Coser, *op. cit.*, p. 8.

5. Émile Durkheim, *Suicide,* trans. J. A. Spaulding and G. Simpson (Glencoe, Ill.: Free Press, 1951).

6. Clyde Kluckhohn, *Mirror for Man* (Greenwich, Conn.: Fawcett Books, 1960), p. 212. The author observes that during wartime citizens readily suffer privations which in peacetime would bring on widespread social disturbances. *Ibid.,* p. 213.

'safety valve institution." Intrasocietal aggressiveness, especially among the males, was siphoned off by directing considerable hostility toward the outside world, all of which was regarded as inimical, and thus served the integration of the society. The contemporary Mundurucú, who do not make war, have undergone community fission.[7] Simmel noted the reciprocity between social-political centralization and the aggressive impulse to war. War promotes inner cohesiveness, yet internal political centralization increases the probability that external release of tensions will be sought through war.[8]

The empirical evidence for the reciprocal relationship between internal and external conflict, however, is not as conclusive as the theory suggests. Rudolph J. Rummel, for example, after running correlations, factor analysis and multiple regression on internal conflict data and external conflict data for seventy-seven nations over a period of three years (1955–1957), concluded that foreign conflict behavior is generally unrelated to domestic conflict behavior.[9] In a subsequent replication of the Rummel study, Raymond Tanter similarly found little positive relationship between foreign and domestic conflict behavior.[10] Later still, in a study of the United States domestic scene during the Vietnam war, Tanter suggested a positive correlation between a foreign war which continues without apparent success and the incidence of domestic turmoil.[11]

Both Rummel and Tanter in their studies took "domestic conflict behavior" to include such phenomena as assassinations, strikes, guerrilla warfare, government crises, purges, riots, revolutions, antigovernment demonstrations and lethal domestic violence. Under the heading of "foreign conflict behavior" they examine antiforeign demonstrations, diplomatic protests, severance of diplomatic relations, the expulsion or recall of diplomats, threats, military hostilities short of warfare, wars, troop movements, mobilizations and total war casualties.

7. Robert F. Murphy, "Intergroup Hostility and Social Cohesion," reprinted from *American Anthropologist*, LIX (No. 6, 1957), 1018–1035, in Zawodny, ed., *op. cit.*, pp. 602–603. R. F. Maher has reached a similar conclusion from his study of tribes in New Guinea. See Robert A. Le Vine, "Socialization, Social Structure and Intersocietal Images," Kelman, ed., *op. cit.*, p. 47.

8. Simmel, *Conflict, op. cit.*, pp. 88–89.

9. Rudolph J. Rummel, "Dimensions of Conflict Behavior Within and Between Nations," *General Systems Yearbook*, VIII (1963), 24. See also by the same author "Testing Some Possible Predictors of Conflict Behavior Within and Between Nations," *Peace Research Society, Papers I, Chicago Conference, 1963*.

10. Raymond Tanter, "Dimensions of Conflict Behavior Within and Between Nations, 1958–60," *Journal of Conflict Resolution*, X (March, 1966), 65–73.

11. Raymond Tanter, "International War and Domestic Turmoil: Some Contemporary Evidence," in *Violence in America: Historical and Comparative Perspectives,* A Report to the National Commission on the Causes and Prevention of Violence, June 1969, prepared under the direction of Hugh Davis Graham and Ted Robert Gurr (New York: New American Library, 1969). See also Ted Robert Gurr, *Why Men Rebel* (Princeton: Princeton University Press, 1970).

Macrocosmic Theories of Conflict: Revolution   235

Many pitfalls lurk in such an effort. First, the danger is that one may gather too much disparate data without having previously developed a theory to guide the investigation and to give meaning to the comparison. Second conflict statistics are extremely difficult to obtain for many countries, and every entry left blank skews the results. Third, one may find himself, in the absence of an adequate weighting scheme, comparing grapes and watermelons, or comparing the number of revolutions, strikes and demonstrations with the number killed in foreign wars. Further, serious analytical problems are likely to arise when we try to compare conflict behavior of countries which are far removed from each other on the scale of political-economic-social development, such as the United States, the Soviet Union, Britain, France, Germany and Japan at one end and Afghanistan, Ethiopia, Liberia, Nepal, Outer Mongolia and Yemen at the other, without the introduction of any compensators. Fifth, added deficiencies may arise from a failure to distinguish adequately between violent and symbolic conflict, anomic and organized or structured violence, between nonpolitical and politicized conflict, between extragovernmental and governmental activity, between outside-stimulated internal conflict and inside-stimulated external conflict. Although empirical studies in this area so far leave much to be desired, it would seem that the theory of an inverse linkage between intrasocietal and extrasocietal conflict will continue warranting careful analytical refinement and research by students of international relations.

Socioeconomic Gaps and Conflict

By examining the phenomenon of "revolution" one can determine the various ways in which contemporary social scientists approach the study of conflict behavior. A strong case can be made that the advent of nuclear weapons technology has greatly reduced the likelihood of direct military hostilities between the major powers, especially the nuclear powers; that the development of alliance systems has also helped to immunize the formal allies of the principal nuclear powers against the threat of overt military attack. Thus the international strategic-political situation militates in favor of a shift in the nature and often in the locus of politically significant conflict. At the same time, the conditions which social scientists usually cite as the source of human conflict potential—i.e., socioeconomic discrepancies, the aggressive impulses resulting from frustration, cognitive dissonance caused by measuring the actual against the ideal, withdrawal and alienation from existing social structures, and so on—are apparently becoming more rather than less common on a world scale. Almost everywhere, thanks to communications technology, the gap between expected (or desired) need fulfillment and actual need fulfillment is widening among large numbers of people. It may be that such a gap constitutes the most important single *necessary* (but not *sufficient*) condition for the occurrence of internal social conflict.

Especially in the Third World (Asia, Africa and Latin America), the process of social, economic and political development is seldom able to provide expanding satisfactions at a pace commensurate with the expanding aspirations of peoples. But even the most industrially advanced countries, including the United States, have their problems. It seems that the development process always produces nonsymmetrical effects in respect to the benefits which are bestowed upon peoples. The mass media of technical communications facilitate the drawing of invidious comparisons not only between the "have" and the "have-not" nations, but also within national societies between privileged and disadvantaged groups. In most highly developed—and most rapidly developing—countries, segments of the privileged groups revolt against the conditions of "affluence," become alienated from the institutions which produced the affluence, and cast their lot with the disadvantaged to bring down The Establishment. Both in less developed and in highly developed societies, the breakdown of traditional mechanisms and agencies of social integration plays a crucial role in the growth of revolutionary conflict potential.

Revolution is an old concept in social theory. In ancient Greece, Aristotle attributed revolutionary feelings to a discrepancy between men's desires and their perceived situation with respect to equality and inequality. In short, he saw revolution springing from a political disagreement over the basis on which society ought to be organized.[12] Thucydides, Polybius, Aquinas, Machiavelli, Bodin, Hobbes, Locke and other classical theorists were interested in the problems of cyclical change of governmental forms, foreign intervention into revolutions, the "natural causes" and moral-political justifications of revolutions, the dynamic process of revolution, the role of conspiracy in violent political change, and the monopolization of legitimate force by the state as a guarantor of internal stability against civil turmoil.

Before the French Revolution, rebellion in Europe against the ruler usually implied no more than a personnel change in government, hardly an attack upon the established political order. Hannah Arendt has pointed out that modern revolutions are of a strikingly different genre, for they aim at a spirit of freedom and of liberation from an old order of things. Marked by a "pathos of novelty," revolution involves "the notion that the course of history suddenly begins anew, that an entirely new story, a story never known or told before, is about to unfold." [13]

Without suggesting that ideology is the cause or motive of revolution, we can say that modern revolution is normally characterized by a set of emotion-

12. Aristotle, *Politics,* trans. Benjamin Jowett (New York: Random House [Modern Library], 1943), Book V, Chapter 2, p. 212. See also Chalmers Johnson, *Revolutionary Change* (Boston: Little, Brown and Company, 1966), p. 4.

13. Hannah Arendt, *On Revolution* (New York: Viking Press, 1965), p. 21.

laden utopian ideas—an expectation that the society is marching toward a profound transformation of values and structures, as well as of personal behavior. The revolutionary pictures a vastly improved pattern of human relationships in a future realization, then imparts his vision to the masses, hopefully to motivate them to revolutionary action. He describes a more perfect social situation—more freedom; more equality; more consciousness of community; more peace, justice and human dignity; more of the transcendentals which appeal to man. Unlike the utopians of old, who posited their idyllic states in unreachable geographic places ("nowhere"), the modern revolutionary locates his utopia in the future: its eventual achievement is not only possible but inevitable.[14] The revolutionary credo strengthens the motives for enduring the hardships of the struggle. The vision of a life free from every form of oppression justifies the suffering, terror and chaos which revolution brings. It does not matter that the present generation of men must endure pain for the sake of the cause, for without the revolution injustice will continue indefinitely, piling misery upon misery forever, but as a result of the revolution man will be lifted up to a higher and nobler plane of existence. Present deprived man suffers heroically so that future fulfilled man may be happy. Such has always been the ideological rationalization of revolutionaries.

James H. Meisel has presented a profound philosophical account of the role played by discontented intellectuals in historic revolutions. He suggests that the human mind is engaged in an endless quest for the triumph of reason in society, and this quest meets with both success and failure. Nearly every sudden intellectual leap forward seems to end up producing its own form of tyranny, liberating not the intellectuals but the barbarians, or the Organization Men and totalitarian bureaucrats. Throughout history, the intellectuals provide the breeding ground of revolution. Revolution begins when Mind proclaims some kind of New Dispensation of Freedom. But eventually mind or soul becomes an enemy of mind. Every revolution dies in overorganization, or terror, or oppression, or the restoration of the old order, or sheer boredom, or the final alienation from technical culture.[15]

According to pre-World War II theories, revolutions occur when the gap between distributed political power and distributed social power within a society becomes intolerable. Certain social classes which are experiencing some of the benefits of progress desire to develop more rapidly than the system will permit, and hence they feel cramped. Discontent spreads over the sharing of economic outputs, social prestige or political power. Traditional values are openly questioned, and a new social myth challenges the old one.

14. Frank E. Manuel, "Toward a Psychological History of Utopias," *Daedalus*, XCIV (Spring, 1965), especially pp. 303–309; Karl Mannheim, *Ideology and Utopia: An Introduction to the Sociology of Knowledge*, trans. Louis Wirth and Edward A. Shils (New York: Harcourt, Brace and World [Harvest Books], 1964).

15. James H. Meisel, *Counterrevolution: How Revolutions Die* (New York: Atherton Press, 1966), pp. 3–16, 209–220.

The intellectuals become alienated from the system. Gradually they move from mere criticism to a withdrawal of political loyalty. The governing elites begin to lose confidence in themselves, in their beliefs and in their ability to command and to solve society's problems. The old elites become too rigid to absorb the emerging elites into their ranks, and this accelerates the polarization. Propagandists assume the intelligentsia's sophisticated criticisms of established institutions, translating them into slogans for mass consumption. The intellectuals join forces with the new and disaffected elites, and demand for radical reforms increases. Moderate political elements prove too weak to strike viable compromises between those who agitate for rapid change and those who oppose all change. The breaking point is reached when the instruments of social control, especially the army and the police, collapse or shift their allegiance to the discontented elements, or when the incumbent government proves inept in using those instruments of social control. Such was the classic explanation of revolution advanced by Crane Brinton in 1938, of which it could be said three decades later that not much theoretical progress had been made beyond it.[16]

During the last decade, social scientists have realized that the older theories of political revolution no longer apply toward understanding conflict in the Third World, where most of the guerrilla insurgencies that have occurred since World War II have arisen out of a very different social environment from the historic revolutions of the West. Nevertheless, it would seem that the earlier and the later revolutions ought to have sufficient elements in common to permit at least a certain continuity in the development of conflict theory, with appropriate adjustments to take account of different social circumstances and new social science knowledge. Earlier in this book we noted that contemporary social scientists and policymakers generally look upon the high conflict potential of Asia, Africa and Latin America as a function of widespread frustration traceable to economic deprivation. (See footnotes 43 and 44 in Chapter 7.)

Professor Ted Robert Gurr of Princeton University argued that "the necessary precondition for violent civil conflict is deprivation, defined as actors' perception of discrepancy between their value expectations and their environment's apparent value capabilities."[17] The disparity between aspirations and fulfillment can be conceived of either as mere economic deprivation or as a combination of various types of deprivation, including economic, psychological, social and political. Perhaps the least sophisticated theory is that

16. See Crane Brinton, *Anatomy of Revolution* (New York: W. W. Norton and Company, 1938). The praise came from James C. Davies, "The Circumstances and Causes of Revolution: a Review," *Journal of Conflict Resolution*, XI (June, 1967), 248. For other pre-World War II theories of revolution, see Lyford P. Edwards, *The Natural History of Revolution* (Chicago: University of Chicago Press, 1927); and George Pettee, *The Process of Revolution* (New York: Harper and Brothers, 1938).

17. Ted Robert Gurr, "Psychological Factors in Civil Violence," *World Politics*, XX (January, 1968), 252–253.

Macrocosmic Theories of Conflict: Revolution

which makes poverty itself the prime frustrating agent. Efforts have often been made to correlate high conflict potential with absolutely low economic variables and with economic stagnation. Robert McNamara, when he was secretary of defense, once pointed out that from 1958 to 1966, 87 percent of the world's very poor nations, 69 percent of the poor nations, and 48 percent of the middle-income nations (based upon World Bank categories) had suffered serious violence. From these statistical data he concluded: "There can then, be no question but that there is an irrefutable relationship between violence and economic backwardness." [18] According to this hypothesis, one can predict the highest incidence of violence in the most poverty-striken countries measured in terms of per capita income.

Such a hypothesis contains several problems. Serious violence does indeed occur in many of the countries in the "very poor" category, but it occurs no more frequently in poorer countries than more affluent ones. The categories of "very poor," "poor" and "middle-income" are too imprecise to permit the drawing of firm conclusions. Taken as aggregates, these three groupings of countries may differ from each other in several significant ways besides level of income, and thus other factors besides the degree of poverty undoubtedly contribute to the incidence of conflict. Admittedly, generalization in the social sciences always involves a certain amount of oversimplification of complex phenomena, but there is probably too much oversimplification here. Violence proneness within a society declines only as a result of social development in many dimensions, of which the economic is only one, and not necessarily the centrally causative one. Furthermore, although conditions of poverty are frequently linked to criminal behavior and anomic conflict, it has often been pointed out that the most impoverished societies are usually not considered fertile breeding grounds for revolution.

> *As Zawadzki and Lazarsfeld have indicated, preoccupation with physical survival, even in industrial areas, is a force strongly militating against the establishment of the community-sense and consensus on joint political action which are necessary to induce a revolutionary state of mind. Far from making people into revolutionaries, enduring poverty makes for concern with one's solitary self or solitary family at best and resignation or mute despair at worst.[19]*

At any given time, one may be able to name several very poor countries in which a revolutionary upheaval is less likely than in a relatively advanced

18. Address to the American Society of Newspaper Editors, Montreal, May 18, 1966, Department of Defense News Release No. 422–66.

19. James C. Davies, "Toward a Theory of Revolution," *American Sociological Review,* XXVII (February, 1962), 7.

The study to which Davies refers is B. Zawadzki and P. F. Lazarsfeld, "The Psychological Consequences of Unemployment," *Journal of Social Psychology,* VI (May, 1935), 224–251. See also Ancel Keys *et al., The Biology of Human Starvation* (Minneapolis: University of Minnesota Press, 1950).

economic system. Economic factors undoubtedly play an important part in many revolutions, but they must be analyzed in relation to other important political, strategic, cultural and social psychological factors which are not reducible to pure economics. If one subscribes to an absolute economic explanation of revolution, he will very likely adopt a rather narrow economic approach to the development of policies for coping with revolutionary situations.

Socioeconomic Modernization and Conflict

A more interesting theory, somewhat better borne out by existing data, postulates conflict as a function not of poverty but of social development and change. James N. Rosenau contends that "the more rapid the rate of social change becomes, the greater the likelihood of intrasocietal violence." [20] Arnold Feldman has pointed out that "change contributes to revoltionary potential rather than eradicating dissatisfactions." [21] Many analysts now agree that social frustration and revolutionary potential are not as pronounced in the most backward areas as they are in areas economically and socially "on the move," although it should be pointed out that there are few regions left in the world which are not undergoing "modernization" to some degree. Modernization may be imposed artificially from without, for example, by foreign investors, or it may grow organically from within as a result of a shift of attitude from a fatalistic acceptance of things as they are to an active desire for change. "When the Middle Eastern peasant," writes Manfred Halpern, "realizes for the first time that the structure of life can be concretely improved, and that he is being denied the opportunity to improve his own lot, then the seeds of revolution will have been planted." [22] In short, as Crane Brinton perceived in 1938, revolutionists are more likely to be children of hope than of despair.[23] This should not be taken to mean, however, that the social psychological states of the revolutionary leaders, of active revolutionary followers, and of the masses to whom the revolutionary appeals are addressed are necessarily all the same. In the interaction of these elements, there may be a dialectical relationship between the social psychology of despair and the revolutionary politics of hope.

20. James N. Rosenau, ed., *International Aspects of Civil Strife* (Princeton: Princeton University Press, 1964), editor's introduction, p. 5.

21. Arnold Feldman, "Violence and Volatility: The Likelihood of Revolution," Harry Eckstein, ed., *Internal War: Problems and Approaches* (New York: Free Press of Glencoe, 1964), p. 119.

22. Manfred Halpern, *The Politics of Social Change in the Middle East and North Africa* (Princeton: Princeton University Press, 1963), p. 93.

23. *Anatomy of Revolution,* p. 115. On this point, see also Vernon Van Dyke, *International Politics,* 2nd ed., (New York: Appleton-Century-Crofts, 1966), p. 327.

"Rising Expectations" and Frustration

When people of "rising expectations" experience gradual progress at a sufficient rate to be able to perceive an improvement differential in their situation from year to year, they are not a likely target for the appeals of the revolutionary propagandist. But certain groups within the population may become frustrated as a result of nonsymmetrical change. Different sectors of the society, as they perceive the distribution of the benefits of development, are likely to be moving forward at different rates; some may perceive no motion or a loss of relative position. This phenomenon occurs constantly in all developing societies, including the most advanced. The spread of technical communications facilitates the process whereby some groups become keenly aware of discrepancies and draw comparisons between their own position and that of others (within the community, the nation and the world). Few groups in any country (even the most advanced) experience real improvements commensurate with their mounting aspirations. The question then becomes one of frustration-tolerance. James C. Davies has called attention to the fact that the gap between what people want and what they get may be tolerable or intolerable.[24] Unfortunately we cannot determine in advance the point at which the gap becomes so intolerable that revolution occurs, because this depends upon many other cultural, political and psychological variables in addition to factors which are economically measurable. The perception of the gap may depend largely upon the way in which the revolutionary organization can utilize the communications nets to dramatize the discrepancies. Davies also suggests that the danger of revolutionary conflict becomes most acute when a society which is on the long-term path toward development suddenly experiences a downturn in the economic process. Although Davies' study pertained to economic trends within whole national societies, his "J-curve" theory might well be even more useful if applied to more than economics and to less than nations—i.e., if it were applied to the way in which subnational groups perceive themselves as suffering a reversal of their total position within the social system as a result of developmental change.

Political Instability and Frustration

Ivo K. and Rosalind L. Feierabend have identified political instability with aggressive behavior, which they attribute to unrelieved social frustration. In situations of systemic frustration, they contend, political stability may still be predicted if certain conditions are met, namely, that the society is a non-participant one; or that constructive solutions to frustrations are available; or that the government is sufficiently coercive to prevent overt acts of hostility against itself; or that the aggressive impulse can be displaced against minority groups or other nations; or that individual acts of aggression are sufficiently

24. Davies, "Toward a Theory of Revolution," *op. cit.,* p. 6.

abundant to furnish an outlet. But in the absence of these conditions, aggressive behavior can be expected to result from systemic frustration. In the more extreme cases, political instability will take the form of riots, strikes, mass arrests, assassination of political figures, executions, terrorism and sabotage, guerrilla warfare, civil war, coup d'état and other forms of revolt.[25] Referring to the "essentially frustrating nature of the modernization process," the Feierabends offer the following generalization:

> *Furthermore, it may be postulated that the peak discrepancy between systemic goals and their satisfaction, and hence the maximum frustration, should come somewhere in the middle of the transitional phase between traditional society and the achievement of modernity. It is at this middle stage that awareness of modernity and exposure to modern patterns should be complete, that is, at a theoretical ceiling, whereas achievement levels would still be lagging far behind. Prior to this theoretical middle stage, exposure can no longer increase, since it already amounts to complete awareness, but achievement will continue to progress, thus carrying the nation eventually into the stage of modernity. Thus, in contrast to transitional societies, it may be postulated that traditional and modern societies will be less frustrated and therefore will tend to be more stable than transitional societies.[26]*

One can take issue with certain aspects of the previous formulation. It contains, for example, the uncritical assumption that there can be such a thing as "complete exposure" to or awareness of modernization, and it overlooks the fact that since increasingly rapid and profound social change is a permanent feature of the modernization process, there will always be, in every society, relatively traditional, transitional and modernized sectors. Nevertheless, the Feierabends have begun useful work of asking how the various subprocesses of modernization may be related to the occurrence of frustration and conflict. The phenomenon which they attempt to describe is a function of many complex factors which have been variously analyzed in the literature of developing societies.[27]

25. Ivo K. and Rosalind L. Feierabend, "Aggressive Behaviors Within Polities, 1948–1962: A Cross-National Study," *Journal of Conflict Resolution,* X (September, 1966), 250–256.

26. *Ibid.,* p. 257.

27. Only the most obvious works, beyond those previously mentioned, can be cited here: Eugene Staley, *The Future of Underdeveloped Countries* (New York: Harper and Brothers, 1954); Daniel Lerner, *The Passing of Traditional Society* (Glencoe, Ill.: Free Press, 1958); Gabriel A. Almond and James S. Coleman, eds., *The Politics of Developing Areas* (Princeton: Princeton University Press, 1960);

Bert F. Hoselitz, *Sociological Aspects of Economic Growth* (Glencoe, Ill.: Free Press, 1960); Lucian W. Pye, *Politics, Personality and Nation-Building* (New Haven: Yale University Press, 1962); Myron Weiner, *The Politics of Scarcity* (Chicago: University of Chicago Press, 1962); Leonard Binder, *The Ideological Revolution in the Middle East* (New York: John Wiley and Sons, 1964); Morris Janowitz, *The Military in the Political Development of New Nations* (Chicago: University of Chicago Press, 1964); David E. Apter, *The Politics of Modernization* (Chicago: University of Chicago Press, 1965); Lucian W. Pye, *Aspects of Political Development* (Boston: Little, Brown and Company, 1966).

It is impossible in international relations theory to examine in detail the various aspects of development which contribute to an environment conducive to conflict, but the student should keep these in mind. As population is drawn from rural to urban areas, traditional religious values and cultural patterns begin to break down among the intellectuals, professional classes, technically skilled groups and sectors of the urban masses. Technology is imported; transport and communication nets grow; literacy rates rise; social mobility is enhanced. Family and other social ties which formerly bound men together disintegrate. New socioeconomic classes of a functional nature begin to emerge, but they are weaker than the structures they replace when it comes to giving the individual a sense of belonging to community. This is what the German sociologist Ferdinand Tonnies referred to in the late nineteenth century as the movement from *Gemeinschaft* (community) to *Gesellschaft* (association). The contrast was overdrawn, but it is not without some validity.[28] The partially uprooted individual moves more rapidly and receives more varied impressions of the world from the communications media. He is forced to make profound adjustments but probably can find no satisfactory set of norms to guide him. Both fascinated and frightened by the changes he sees, he becomes psychologically troubled. Edward Shils has shown that the intellectual in underdeveloped countries has an ambivalent attitude toward things foreign and Western: he appreciates foreign culture but has a sense of inferiority with respect to his own.[29] Moreover, as intellectuals abandon traditional religious and cultural values, acting differently from the way they were taught in their youth, they may develop feelings of guilt from which they may try to escape by projecting hostility against the external agents of social change—the Western imperialist system. Assertive nationalism becomes a means of restoring self-respect.

Incumbent governments in the developing countries, lacking experience in economic planning, find it difficult to impress the unsophisticated masses with the need to accept present deprivations in order to promote long-range economic expansion. Development demands patience in many dimensions: the acquisition of technical skills; improvements in the educational system; the modification of social incentives; the emergence of managerial capabilities; the willingness of traditional elites to admit the new functional elites to a fair share of the system's benefits; responsible fiscal policies, administrative re-

28. Ferdinand Tonnies, *Community and Society—Gemeinschaft und Gesellschaft*, trans. and ed., Charles P. Loomis (East Lansing: Michigan State University Press, 1957).

29. Edward A. Shils, "The Intellectuals in the Political Development of the New States," *World Politics*, XII (April, 1960), 329–368. See also Robert Waelder, "Protest and Revolution Against Western Societies," in Morton A. Kaplan, ed., *The Revolution in World Politics* (New York: John Wiley and Sons, 1962).

forms, and so forth. All of these imperatives are frustrating to the impatient. Even gradual progress is frustrating to those whose appetites have been whetted to insist upon rapid and far-sweeping changes—instant progress. Meanwhile, population growth places added pressures upon developing systems, causing food shortages and nutritional deficiencies, as well as the pathological consequences which can accompany human overcrowding.[30]

Sociologists and anthropologists consider the likelihood of internal social conflict to be on the increase when the integrating mechanisms of a society break down. As immemorial religious-cultural traditions give way to secularization, emergent nationalism as expressed by a charismatic leader might prove powerful enough to preserve domestic solidarity, especially if there is an external *bête noire* against which aggressive feelings can be directed. (Israel serves this purpose for several of the neighboring states.) So long as national integration remains high, enemy groups do not become salient to each other within the society. But in the absence of an integrating principle, the changes wrought by development would seem to increase the potential for group conflict within nations. As new groups emerge, they forge their own consciousness of group interests and values; they establish their self-identity by directing hostility outward. At this point the configuration of the communications process takes on considerable importance. Since hostility may be aimed outward in many different directions and randomly distributes itself among so many targets as to become dissipated without the occurrence of serious politicized violence in a conflict with a single enemy, it is the function of political organization to channel the aggressive hostility inherent in discontented groups into one coherent direction. An incumbent government will attempt to divert it against a foreign adversary. (In some regions of the world, such as Latin America, it is difficult to do this, because of the cultural similarity of most members of the regional state system.) A revolutionary organization will attempt to channel it against the incumbent government. In either case, considerable strategic manipulation of social communications is presupposed. Neither external wars nor internal revolutions are typically spontaneous or accidental happenings; both require a high degree of organization and planning.

Macrocosmic social theorists are aware that, although every man is in some sense subject to the same laws of individual biological and psychological

30. Population experts attribute the frustration which breeds social unrest, political instability and violence in the underdeveloped areas to the fact that millions of individuals receive neither the caloric quantity nor protein quality of food required for a healthy life. See Frank Lorimer, "Issues of Population Policy," Philip M. Hauser, ed., *The Population Dilemma,* for the American Assembly (Englewood Cliffs, N.J.: Prentice-Hall, 1963), p. 144. See also *The World Food Problem,* Report of the President's Science Advisory Committee, The White House, May 1967, Vol. I, pp. 3 and 11. Recent evidence supplied by biologists suggests that serious and prolonged malnutrition may produce genetic damage. *New York Times,* March 2, 1967. For some effects of high population density, see George M. Carstairs, "Overcrowding and Human Aggression," in Graham and Gurr, eds., *Violence in America,* pp. 730–742.

Macrocosmic Theories of Conflict: Revolution

behavior, the development of an explanatory and predictive capability regard-ing social conflict requires a sensitive appreciation of the great variety of specific social contexts in which conflicts may arise or be avoided. Anthro-pologists remind us that some primitive peoples are highly belligerent and constantly disposed to war for almost any reason or no reason at all, while other primitives scarcely have a word for "war" in their language. We cannot say that human groups and societies are essentially either bellicist or pacifist. Most societies seem to oscillate between the two tendencies. At any given time, some are peaceful and some are not. The ratios of peaceful to warlike can change from one era to another, and a society or group which is quite belligerent in one period may become satisfied and docile in another. Thus we would do well to avoid the sweeping judgment of a Hobbes that the state of nature is one of war, from which man has been rescued by the institution of the state, and the equally sweeping judgment of a Rousseau that natural man is a peaceful, noble savage who has been corrupted by civilization. Both con-flict and cooperation are normal phases of the social process. Neither can be held to be more fundamental than the other, even though they manifest them-selves in varying proportions at any given time.

Moreover, a society which in one phase of its history may be highly inte-grated and disposed toward intense external conflict might at another time undergo domestic disintegration and experience serious internal disorders. But it must be admitted that when the social scientist attempts to determine whether a particular community is integrating or disintegrating he encounters difficult ambiguities. One observer, relying on such indicators as the growth of communications, the expansion of the national school system and the increasing provision of welfare services, might conclude that a given society is becoming more integrated. Another observer, focusing upon such indicators as crime rates, the decline of traditional institutional influences and the occur-rence of riots and demonstrations, might be led to the conclusion that the same society is disintegrating. Even the same data can be interpreted in opposite ways, depending upon the social philosophy of the analyst. In all social transi-tions, one can discern aspects of integration and disintegration unfolding side by side. If social scientists are divided in their opinions about these things, we are perhaps no worse off than the physicists who cannot agree whether the universe is building up or breaking down.

Societal Breakdown: The Crucial Questions

When a scientist asks too general a question, he often obtains an answer of very limited utility. Instead of trying to generalize about such large issues as integration or disintegration of a whole society, it may be more useful to select a small number of major social configurations and to examine them within a specific community. The political scientist, for example, would want to know such things as: 1) the degree to which various strata or groups within the population are being recruited into or are withdrawing from participation in the political system; 2) the ability of the political system to respond flexibly to the various demands made upon it and to produce outputs likely to inhibit the growth of pressures for revolutionary change; and 3) the extent and effectiveness of social and political control, as well as the acceptability of the methods whereby such control is maintained.

Specifically, the political scientist would be interested in securing data concerning the following characteristics: 1) the extent to which people in various social groups feel themselves more loyal to than critical of the system; 2) the extent to which they participate in elections, pay taxes, perform military service and give other expressions of support for the military system; 3) whether the intellectuals who are being educated within the system are also being satisfactorily absorbed by it, or whether they are being excluded and alienated from it; 4) whether the system contains built-in "safety-valves" for the orderly release of social energies (e.g., economic competition, channels for criticism and the expression of new ideas, outlets for religious and humanitarian motivations, sports rivalry, etc.); 5) what kind of relatively stable and cohesive social groups exist (church, army, trade unions, farmers' organizations, professional associations, political parties, etc.) and the direction they are taking within the system; 6) the pattern in which symbolic honors, political power and economic benefits are distributed among various groups within the system; and 7) the proportionate allocation by various groups of fear-hostility attitudes inside and outside the nation.

This latter factor, of course, is of particular interest to the student of international relations, because it bears upon the question of whether the conflict potential in a particular country is for international war or internal revolution. At this point we come back to the venerable hypothesis of political analysts, never conclusively proved, that a government can head off impending domestic strife by fomenting a popular foreign war. Whether this can be accomplished may depend upon the presence of readily perceptible and historically significant group differences—ethnic-linguistic, religious or tribal. If such differences are more pronounced across national borders than within the nation, the government will be in a better position to solidify the nation by going to war. But if such differences are more pronounced intranationally, they may very well constitute an important factor in the potential for domestic conflict. In the latter case, going to war with a neighbor is likely to exacerbate the internal conflict if group affiliations extend across the boundaries of two warring nations. Whether or not there is international war, serious ethnic differences within a country caught up in a revolutionary situation are likely to be exploited both by the incumbent government and by the revolutionary organization.[31]

31. In a study of forty-six Third World insurgencies from 1946 to 1966, it was found that ethnic-linguistic, religious or tribal differences played at least a mod-

The economic, psychological, sociological and political conditions mentioned above provide the matrix out of which revolutionary conflict arises,
but they cannot be set forth definitively as the causes of conflict. They are,
as it were, the necessary but not the sufficient conditions. Within a society
there may be fairly high levels of frustration, alienation, cognitive dissonance,
sense of threat and other attitudes of mind conducive to conflict. There may
be nonsymmetrical rates of change. There may be in proximity highly visible
groups which have a history of animosity toward each other. Communications between some groups may break down and reach a virtual vanishing
point. Yet politically structured conflict will not occur until deliberate decisions to invoke political violence have been taken, and these decisions will
normally not be taken until after there has developed a conflict organization
capable of managing violence and of supplying political direction to existing
resentments and aggressive impulses. The link between the social psychological state and the development of the conflict organization seems to be in the
first instance the personalities of a small number of revolutionary leaders,
combined with their life experiences in the environment which shaped them.

THE MAKING OF A REVOLUTIONARY

As Lawrence Stone has noted, we still do not know what makes a man go
revolutionary.[32] What identifiable elements in his personality (such as need for
achievement, sense of moral indignation and social mission, propensity for
risk-taking, desire for power, etc.) and in his personal background (childhood, relations with parents, socialization, education, religion, travel, reading,
previous military training, and contacts with other conflict organizers) impel
him to decide that he should attempt to overthrow the system by force instead
of working from within to reform it? It would be surprising if the leaders of a
revolution were motivated by the same psychic forces as are the masses—
i.e., that they are attracted to insurgency because they have suffered the depri-

---

erately significant part in thirty-one, or
two-thirds, of the total number. Ethnic
differences included Asians against Europeans or Americans; black Africans
against white Europeans; Greeks against
Turks and British; Nagas against Indians;
Kurds against Iraqis and Iranians; Ka-
bylian Tribesmen against Algerians; Rif
Berbers against the Central Moroccan
government; Quechua-speaking Indians
against Bolivians and Peruvians; Zanu-
Zimbabwes against Rhodesians; Simba
Tribesmen against the Congo Government, etc. Religious differences figured
in insurgencies in Indochina and Vietnam, Burma, India, Thailand, Algeria,
Angola, Lebanon, Mozambique, Chad,
Congo and Yemen. In some cases, the
existence of the differences was a necessary condition of the conflict. In others,
the differences contributed to the intensity or duration of the conflict, or
helped to shape strategic planning. James
E. Dougherty, "The External Appearance
of Insurgency," unpublished paper prepared for the Foreign Policy Research
Institute, University of Pennsylvania,
January, 1968.

32. Lawrence Stone, "Theories of Revolution," *World Politics*, XVIII (January,
1966), 168.

vations of economic poverty. Revolutions are usually led by "elites," and it is an essential attribute of elites that they are moved by more subtle personality factors than those predicable of the masses. Elites and masses differ significantly in their reactions to frustration, and in the sources of their frustration.[33] Revolutionary leaders seldom come from the poorest classes. More typically, they derive from middle-class families that have not known economic hardship. Their deprivations are more likely to be psychological rather than economic. What they want frequently are intangible rewards—prestige, a share in political power, fame as part of a charismatic movement struggling for justice, even the stimulation of excitement and danger. In the case of some revolutionary terrorists, the presence of psychopathological elements cannot be discounted.[34]

Once a student of revolutionary conflict gets beyond the difficult problem of trying to develop not only an explanatory theory of the general causes of revolution but also a predictive theory of revolutionary occurrences of a sizeable scale—a task in which social science shades into strategic intelligence—there are many other questions about the revolutionary process worthy of study.

Political Objectives. What are the avowed political purposes for which the conflict is waged? Modern revolutions have been fought to expel a colonial power and achieve national independence; to change the political system without radically altering the social systems; to terminate an intolerable minority status by achieving either local autonomy or territorial secession from the system; to determine the succession after the expected departure of a colonial regime; to bring pressure to bear from one political system upon another. An insurgency ostensibly begun for one objective may undergo either a *de facto* or an avowed change of purpose during the course of the conflict. Avowed objectives while the revolution is in course are usually a matter of propaganda

33. Even individuals differ in their reactions. Frustration tolerance varies, and different people are frustrated by different things. Gardner Lindzey, "Frustration Tolerance, Frustration Susceptibility and Overt Disturbance," reprinted in Zawodny, *op. cit.,* I, pp. 30–34. It is known, too, that a relationship exists between class background and modes of expressing aggressiveness: poorer, less-educated classes are more prone to commit physical aggression; better-educated middle classes to psychological aggression. Martin Gold, "Suicide, Homicide and the Socialization of Aggression," in Bartlett H. Stoodley, ed., *op. cit.,* pp. 278–293.

34. In André Malraux's great novel about the Chinese Revolution, published in 1933, we are given a picture of the revolutionary terrorist Ch'en who conceives of himself as a sacrificial priest before he kills his victims, who despises those who do not kill, who contemplates assassination with ecstasy, and who makes terror the whole meaning of life. *Man's Fate,* trans. Haakon M. Chevalier (New York: Random House [Vintage Books], 1967), pp. 10, 64, 163, 233. "There was a world of murder, and it held him with a kind of warmth." *Ibid.,* p. 10. For an analysis of Malraux's novel, consult Irving Howe, *Politics and the Novel* (New York: Fawcett Books, 1967), pp. 209–221. For an expansive discussion of *Man's Fate* as well as of Malraux's ideological posture as novelist, revolutionary, and minister, see David Wilkinson, "Malraux, Revolutionist and Minister," Walter Laqueur and George L. Mosse, eds., *The Left-Wing Intellectuals Between the Wars, 1919–1939* (New York: Harper and Row [Torchbooks], 1967).

designed to gain political support. Some objectives of the revolutionary program are usually left unspoken. But a comparison of avowed objectives with actual outcomes can be an interesting exercise.

Duration of Revolutionary Conflict. We are all familiar with the relatively sudden *coup d'état,* carried out by a small group of high-status individuals to effect a personnel change in the top echelon of government. The *coup* itself is a conflict phenomenon worthy of investigation,[35] but it is not a genuine revolution. The total revolutionary process is of fairly long duration—usually a matter of years. Mao Tse-tung insisted upon deliberate protraction and the avoidance of eschatological adventurism as essential elements in the strategy of revolutionary warfare.[36] The history of Third World insurgencies since World War II indicates that guerrilla conflicts which were terminated in substantially less than three years were usually not successful; duration of from three to nine years is marked by about a half-and-half chance of success; conflicts which are prolonged beyond ten years show a perceptible decline in the prospects for revolutionary success, but an increase in the probability of compromise settlement.

The Terrain of Revolutionary Insurgency. The impression has long been common that revolutionary insurgency is a predominantly rural phenomenon, but this notion can be misleading. Social scientists are not at all agreed as to where revolutionary discontent is more likely to manifest itself—in the cities or in the countryside. In recent years there has been a growing tendency to question the stereotyped generalization of the "peasant revolution." Rural peasants are more tradition-bound and apathetic toward the political process than are urban dwellers. The dissatisfied peasant is more likely to migrate to the city than to revolt. Moreover, peasant insurrections, when they occur, are often led by revolutionaries from an urban background. In any event, as the sharp dichotomy between rural and urban cultures dissolves under the impact of modern communications, our earlier ideas of the "peasant revolution" will begin to lose their relevance.[37]

Revolutionary insurgency as a social-psychological process with important previolent stages seems likely to begin in urban centers where social mobility is high, where traditional norms are weakest and anomie is greatest, where ideas circulate more rapidly, and where certain psychological states such as frustration and dissonance may be more pronounced. But as an externalized strategic process, we often find that the violent stages of guerrilla insurgency

35. See William G. Andrews and Uri Ra'anan, eds., *The Politics of the Coup d'État* (New York: Van Nostrand Reinhold Company, 1969).

36. On Protracted War, in *Selected Works of Mao Tse-tung* (London: Lawrence and Wishart, Ltd., 1954), II, 188 and 201–202.

37. See A. F. K. Organski, *The Stages of Political Development* (New York: Alfred A. Knopf, 1965), especially pp 132–133; Karl W. Deutsch, "Social Mobilization and Political Development," *American Political Science Review,* LV (September, 1961); Gil Carl Alroy, *The Involvement of Peasants in Internal War.* (Princeton: Center of International Studies, Princeton University), 1966.

Contending Theories of International Relations

begin in rural areas geographically remote from the political capital of the country.

Several considerations help to determine the location of revolutionary conflict. Insurgents are disposed to establish bases in regions with a record of previous revolutionary activity or sentiment.[38] They want access to major political targets, as well as economic self-sufficiency. They are anxious to secure a base in zones of weak political control, not easily accessible to and penetrable by government forces. Hence they are attracted to provinces not served efficiently by road, rail and air transport and to terrain which, while lending cover to small guerrilla bands, proves hostile to the movement of larger and more cumbersome conventional military forces—mountains, jungles, forests, river deltas, swamplands and deserts. Not only physical geography but political geography as well enters the picture. Whenever possible, insurgents usually find it advantageous to establish headquarters, training camps and supply routes close to or across the borders of friendly or neutral countries. The guerrillas may then seek legal sanctuary or political haven when subjected to hot pursuit, thus compelling incumbent government forces to incur international censure if they carry their punitive action to the area of retreat. Moreover, borderlands are frequently zones of ethnic heterogeneity and diversity of political loyalties—factors which revolutionists may find helpful. Quite naturally, logistical considerations always loom large. Sources and routes of foreign supply are extremely important factors in the political geography of guerrilla revolution.

Revolutionary Behavior: Major Issues for Investigation

Various other internal and external aspects of revolutionary conflict are worthy of study, some of which may forever prove elusive because of the extreme difficulties of data-gathering. The student would like to know about the factors that influence the morale of revolutionary forces and about the weapons and communications technology available to each side, and how these compare as outcome determinants with the quality of intelligence, strategic doctrine and political decision-making of the parties involved in the conflict. How effectively do incumbent regimes and revolutionary organizations utilize communications media, such as newspapers, radio, motion pictures, television, social institutions and informal channels? The analyst will wonder about the pattern in which the economic benefits and penalties of revolutionary conflict are distributed; about the fund-raising and supply-gathering activities of the revolutionists; about the way in which various segments of the population are

38. Robert W. McColl, "A Political Geography of Revolution: China, Vietnam and Thailand," *Journal of Conflict Resolution,* I (June, 1967), 153–167.

selected as targets of economic pressure, political propaganda or violent attack. He will inquire into the effect of changing rates of recruitment, defection and casualties, as indicators of power, motivation and morale, and whether time favors one side over the other. He will attempt to gauge the impact of the revolution upon the political life and the economic development of the country.[39] He will examine the way in which the established system responds to the revolutionary challenge, whether with self-strengthening policies of social improvement and control. He will investigate the ways in which the revolutionary process terminates and either fades into oblivion or consolidates itself with the creation of new revolutionary and postrevolutionary institutions.

Externally, the analyst will be interested in the internationalization of conflict. In the contemporary world, virtually every conflict which occurs within the ken of newsgathering agencies becomes an item in the environment of international relations. A revolution may produce a spillover effect in a neighboring country. There may be spontaneous or organized demonstrations in distant foreign countries to support one side or to protest against the other. The world communications net plays a crucial role in the internationalization of conflict. Revolutionaries must strive to acquire by slow degrees some semblance of an international personality as an object of potential foreign support in the forms of money, arms, diplomatic backing, organized political sympathy and other kinds of assistance. Conflicts are drawn into the vortex of world politics when they become items in the decision-making processes of foreign governments, international organizations (such as the United Nations), regional alliances (such as NATO, SEATO or OAS), associations of political parties (such as Communists and Socialists), churches, ethnic organizations, economic interest groups and private organizations of interested individuals. The possible forms of outside intervention and aid are myriad, and defy inventory.

External and Internal Factors: A Summary

What is perhaps more important for our purposes is the question of the relative weight to be assigned in a given revolutionary conflict to external and internal factors as determinants of the outcome.[40] Without implying that any one form of external aid (such as military assistance), however massive, can

39. Peter A. R. Calvert warns against the assumption that there is an intrinsic connection between revolution and significant social change. "Revolution: The Politics of Violence," *Political Studies,* V (February, 1967), 3.

40. See Karl W. Deutsch, "External Involvement in Internal War," Harry Eckstein, ed., *Internal War,* pp. 100–110.

play an overriding role in ensuring either the success or failure of a revolutionary insurgency, then what begins as or appears to be an indigenous conflict may become the focal point of international intervention, overt or clandestine, to such an extent that the conflict can no longer be regarded as an internal one. "If outside manpower, motives, money, and other resources appear to constitute the main capabilities committed to the struggle on both sides," writes Karl W. Deutsch, "then we are inclined to speak of a 'war by proxy'—an international conflict between two foreign powers, fought out on the soil of a third country; disguised as conflict over an internal issue of that country; and using some or all of that country's manpower, resources and territory as means for achieving preponderantly foreign goals and foreign strategies." [41] In this case, local parties to the conflict lose the power of initiative and control to a complex international process of strategic planning, diplomatic bargaining and negotiation, and political-military decision-making—a process in which the local parties within the conflict-ridden nation may play only a subordinate client role. Once the international political prestige of two great powers becomes engaged, their rivalry may very well overshadow in importance the social psychological attitudes of the inhabitants of the country on whose soil the conflict is being waged, at least in respect to the magnitude and duration of the revolutionary conflict, until a strategic stalemate (in the total political rather than merely in the military sense) is attained.

41. *Ibid.*, p. 102.

CHAPTER 9
Macrocosmic Theories of Conflict: Nuclear Deterrence and Arms Control

The Nature of Deterrence

No single concept has dominated international strategic theory during the last two decades so much as that of deterrence. The word "deterrence" rarely appeared in international relations textbooks written before World War II, and when used it did not have the meaning it has in the nuclear age. Bernard Brodie has pointed out that the threat of war, whether explicit or implicit, has always been an instrument of policy whereby one government dissuaded another from pursuing certain courses of action. But "since the development of nuclear weapons, the term has acquired not only special emphasis but also a distinctive connotation."[1] In recent literature, the term has usually implied the holding of nuclear weapons capabilities for the purpose of confronting a nuclear aggressor with the threat of an unacceptable level of nuclear retaliation even after he had struck a counterforce blow. Among several but by no means all analysts, the term has also been employed to include the deterrence of conventional military attack through posing a risk that nuclear weapons will be introduced into the conflict. This is a more controversial concept, and will be discussed presently. Practically all would agree that the concept of deterrence has no relevance in respect to conflict below the conventional military level, such as guerrilla insurgency.[2]

1. Bernard Brodie, "The Anatomy of Deterrence," *World Politics,* XI (January, 1959), 174. See also Stephen Maxwell, "Rationality in Deterrence," Adelphi Papers No. 50 (London: Institute for Strategic Studies, 1968), p. 1.

2. See Frederick H. Gareau, "Nuclear Deterrence: A Discussion of the Doctrine," *Orbis,* V (Summer, 1961), 183; Sir John Slessor, "A New Look at Strategy for the West," *Orbis* II (Fall, 1958), 321; and Glenn H. Snyder, "The Balance of Power and the Power of Terror" in Paul Seabury, ed., *The Balance of Power* (San Francisco: Chandler Publishing Company, 1965), pp. 184–201.

It is not our purpose here to discuss the technical requirements for maintaining a successful deterrent, or successful mutual deterrence. The authors recognize that the calculus of deterrence is intimately connected to advanced weapons technology and that this technology constantly changes. In 1945 there was a quantum leap in firepower from the conventional 2,000 pound air-delivered bomb to the 20-kiloton atomic bomb of the Hiroshima-Nagasaki type. Less than ten years later, not long after the Soviet Union had acquired atomic capabilities, the world's two principal military powers had taken another quantum leap in firepower from the kiloton to the megaton weapon, and those who were convinced that kiloton weapons were sufficient to guarantee mutual deterrence became more confident then ever that the two superpowers, recognizing nuclear embroilment as a mutual-suicide encounter, would adhere to a policy of war-avoidance. By the late 1950s, the area of radical technological change had shifted from firepower to delivery speed, when intercontinental strategic missiles, capable of traveling thirty times faster than strategic bombers, began to become available.

At this point voices were raised in warning against the assumptions of strategic stability and the automaticity of deterrence. In 1959 Albert Wohlstetter warned that impending technological developments would render strategic weapons more vulnerable to surprise attack and that the maintenance of deterrence, while nevertheless feasible, could be achieved only through difficult defense choices pertaining to the dispersal, mobility and protection of missile systems.[3] By the mid-1960s, there was a widespread assumption among strategic analysts that both the Soviet Union and the United States had achieved a condition of stable mutual deterrence as a result of deploying such numbers of ICBMs as to make it impossible for either power to consider itself capable of launching a surprise first-strike against the other's missile forces without incurring a heavy level of damage in retaliation. Although it was often conceded that no precise quantitative tag could be placed upon the notion of "unacceptable level of retaliatory damage" since one nation cannot

3. Albert Wohlstetter, "The Delicate Balance of Terror," *Foreign Affairs,* XXXVIII (January, 1959), 211–234. For the view that the goal of arms control policy should be to find ways not of eliminating retaliatory forces but of maintaining a balance between them, and thereby reduce the incentive to a preemptive first strike, see Henry A. Kissinger, "Arms Control, Inspection and Surprise Attack," *Foreign Affairs,* XXXVIII (July, 1960), 557–575. Others warned that if nations were to reduce arms to levels too low the incentive for attack might be raised. See Hedley Bull, *The Control of the Arms Race* (New York: Frederick A. Praeger, 1961), pp. 32 and 168–169; Thomas C. Schelling and Morton H. Halperin, *Strategy and Arms Control* (New York: The Twentieth Century Fund, 1961), pp. 3 and 56–57; and Glenn H. Snyder, *Deterrence and Defense* (Princeton: Princeton University Press, 1961), pp. 97–103. See also Thomas C. Schelling, "Surprise Attack and Disarmament," *Bulletin of the Atomic Scientists,* XV (December, 1959) 413–418.

define this for itself, much less for an adversary, most strategic analysts were convinced that the motivations on either side to contemplate initiating a deliberate first strike were infinitesimally low. To policymakers, at least, nuclear war had become "unthinkable," even if not to theoretical analysts whose job it was to "think about the unthinkable" for the purpose of keeping it that way.[4]

OFFENSIVE-DEFENSIVE SYSTEMS

By the late 1960s new military-technological advances in the fields of ballistic missile defense and multiple warheads once again prompted writers to worry about the possibility that the international strategic situation, viewed in objective mathematical terms, was becoming less stable. It was feared that land-based missile complexes were becoming more vulnerable, and that the advent of antiballistic missiles (ABM) and multiple independently-targeted reentry vehicles (MIRV) might bring about a situation in which one side would be tempted to initiate a nuclear strike on the expectation of a lop-sided exchange.[5] Other writers held that political leaders, in contrast to strategic theoreticians, would continue to regard the balance of terror "overwhelmingly persuasive" for the foreseeable future, and would view an increasingly costly form of armaments competition increasingly unattractive since it would not appreciably affect either security or the ability to deter.[6]

4. Raymond Aron suggested that the most effective, though least visible, result of the thermonuclear stalemate was to make the policymakers of the two superpowers much more cautious in their relations with each other. *The Great Debate: Theories of Nuclear Strategy,* trans. Ernst Pawel (Garden City, N.Y.: Doubleday and Company, 1965), p. 26. See also Raymond Aron, *On War,* trans. Terence Kilmartin (Garden City, N.Y.: Doubleday and Company, 1959), pp. 35–43. Herbert S. Dinerstein noted that political goals were superseding military goals in international alliance diplomacy. "The determination of the major powers to avoid war . . . has caused a qualitative change in international relations. The expectation that war can be avoided makes the primary purpose of alliances deterrence of war rather than preparation for its conduct." "The Transformation of Alliance Systems," *American Political Science Review,* LIX (September, 1965), 593. Vincent P. Rock went so far as to suggest that the condition of mutual deterrence combined with the awareness of still-lingering dangers of breakdown into mutual catastrophe would lead to the transformation of deterrence into interdependence. *A Strategy of Interdependence* (New York: Charles Scribner's Sons, 1964), pp. 330–331. For a less optimistic assessment, see Herman Kahn, *Thinking About the Unthinkable* (New York: Horizon Press, 1962).

5. See, e.g., Carl Kaysen, "Keeping the Strategic Balance," *Foreign Affairs,* XLVI (July, 1968), 665–675; Harold Brown, "Security Through Limitations" and Donald G. Brennan, "The Case for Missile Defense," *Foreign Affairs,* XLVII (April, 1969), 422–432 and 443–448, respectively; and "Missiles and Anti-Missiles: Six Views," *Bulletin of the Atomic Scientists,* XXV (June, 1969), 20–28.

6. William R. Kintner, ed., *Safeguard: Why the ABM Makes Sense* (New York: Hawthorn Books, 1969); Abram Chayes and Jerome B. Wiesner, eds., *ABM: An Evaluation of the Decision to Deploy an Antiballistic Missile System* (New York: Harper and Row, 1969). McGeorge Bundy, "To Cap the Volcano," *Foreign Affairs,* XLVIII (October, 1969), 1–20.

As indicated previously, our concern here is not primarily with the missile "numbers game" or with precise details of size and multiplicity of warheads, degrees of hardening, dispersal and mobility, command and control systems, reliability and guidance-system accuracy of missiles, length of warning times, effectiveness of surveillance, performance characteristics of various offensive and defensive types of weapons, and other quantifiable factors. These are important in the strategic calculus of deterrence capabilities, and they will undoubtedly continue to change with advancing technology. But for purposes of our present discussion, certain theoretical questions should be posed. The following schema advances some of the principal theoretical problems associated with nuclear deterrence.

DETERRENCE AND THE BALANCE OF POWER

The concept of mutual deterrence is, in a sense, the classical notion of "balance of power" in modern guise. Many writers, including Bernard Brodie, Hedley Bull, William R. Kintner, Henry A. Kissinger, Robert Bowie, Robert Osgood, Donald G. Brennan, Thomas C. Schelling and Herman Kahn have treated "mutual deterrence," "stable deterrence," "balanced deterrence," and "stable arms balance" in terms curiously reminiscent of earlier treatises on the balance of power, and they reflect a keen awareness of the same difficulties which plagued the older theory. It has often been said that the balance of power does not furnish a good theoretical basis for foreign-policy decision-making because it is uncertain (since there are no reliable criteria for measuring comparative power) and because it is unreal (since nations, feeling uncertain, are not content to aim at achieving a balance but seek instead a margin of superiority, or a unilaterally "favorable balance of power").[7] Thus contemporary statesmen and their advisors have difficulty in determining whether "stable mutual deterrence" *describes* that which is or *prescribes* that which should be pursued; whether it is an objective situation best achieved automatically by the continued efforts of both sides to attain superiority in military technology, or whether it is a policy requiring a cooperative conscious quest for a balanced parity by rival governments. It has never been entirely clear whether the balance of power represents an inexorable application of the laws of nature or a norm which men can freely choose or reject; a mechanistic explanation of what is actually happening, or an ethical exhortation to what should be happening, something to be wrought by the workings of an "invisible hand" or something to be sought through voluntary, intelligent coordination.[8] (For a discussion of classical theories of balance of power, see Chapter 1.)

7. Hans J. Morgenthau, *Politics Among Nations,* 4th ed. (New York: Alfred A. Knopf, 1967), pp. 197–205.

8. See Ernst B. Haas, "The Balance of Power: Prescription, Concept or Propaganda?" *World Politics,* V (October, 1953), 442–477.

In the final analysis, a stable military equilibrium is probably the product of the interaction of technological trends and policy choices, in combination with a variety of other conscious and unconscious elements.

THE RELATION BETWEEN KNOWLEDGE AND DETERRENCE

A deterrent capability to be effective cannot be kept secret. A certain amount of knowledge about it must be communicated to the adversary. If one side deploys additional weapons or modernizes its weapons arsenal in total secrecy, then it has not really upgraded the effectiveness of its deterrent force. At any given time, of course, governmental policymakers may feel comfortable with their estimates of the existing military situation. All governments carry on intelligence-gathering activities, and expect others to do likewise. But different departments and agencies of a government will disagree among themselves concerning intelligence estimates. Individuals will fear inadequate data, contradictions in the data, deliberate deception or distortion of data, and interpretations of the data which he deems unduly optimistic or pessimistic. Although deterrence requires that some knowledge be communicated to the other side, the transmission of too much intelligence might weaken the deterrent if it were to facilitate the planning of an attack. Uncertainties increase as military technology becomes more complex. But the question arises as to whether an increase in uncertainty in the calculus of possible nuclear exchange effects, resulting from the deployment of new weapons systems, is more likely to strengthen or to weaken the condition of mutual deterrence. This remains a subject for debate among the experts.

Robert E. Osgood has aptly described the part played by uncertainty in the delicate and fragile calculus of deterrence—a calculus which involves a process of "mutual mind reading" in an effort to second-guess an opponent in respect to intentions, values assigned to an objective, estimated costs and effectiveness of certain actions and the probability of specific interactive responses. He notes that up to a point the element of uncertainty in nuclear deterrence, taken together with the frightful implications of miscalculation, may contribute to caution and restraint, and thus to international stability. But he warns against an excessive reliance upon uncertainty:

> *It leads to a kind of strategic monism that relies too heavily upon the undeviating self-restraint and low risk-taking propensities of statesmen. It ignores the provocative effect of the fearful uncertainties themselves. It overlooks the tendency of any apparently stable military balance, even one based on great uncertainties and risks, to breed unwarranted confidence in the regularity and predictability of that balance, which in turn diminishes the restraints upon military action.*[9]

9. Robert E. Osgood, "Stabilizing the Military Environment," in Dale J. Hekhuis, Charles G. McClintock and Arthur L. Burns, eds., *International Stability*

It seems logical at first glance to assume a close relationship between balanced deterrence and equality of strategic weapons between two rival powers. Some writers have urged a renunciation of the quest for military "superiority" not only as meaningless or futile, but especially as a threat to stable deterrence.[10] President Nixon, seeking to steer a middle (and perhaps less clearly defined semantically) course between "parity" and "superiority," advocated a policy of "nuclear sufficiency." Actually, the size of the U.S. strategic bomber, missile and submarine forces was officially established at the beginning of the decade of the 1960s and remained relatively constant throughout. In the late sixties there was a widespread assumption that a crude parity prevailed between the strategic forces of the two superpowers, and that this situation was more conducive to meaningful strategic arms limitation talks (the SALT) than a situation of substantial strategic inequality would have been.[11]

Strategic parity is in the first instance a mathematical concept, yet it is difficult to define with mathematical precision. Several years ago, advocates of "finite deterrence" frequently suggested that the two superpowers should agree either to limit or to cut back the size of their strategic missile arsenals to levels much lower than they were economically capable of sustaining but which would be sufficient, so the argument ran, to preserve the condition of mutual deterrence. The most commonly proposed measure of subsaturation parity was the number of ICBMs. There were several deficiencies in such a measure, however. First, Soviet missiles were capable of carrying warheads of substantially higher megatonnage than U.S. missiles. Second, the term ICBM did not mean exactly the same as the term "strategic weapon" for these reasons: a) There was a time when the number of deployed U.S. strategic weapons fluctuated dependently upon the location of Polaris submarines in the oceanic areas of the world. b) The Soviets had several hundred midrange missiles in western Russia and, although these were neither ICBMs nor "strategic weapons" (in the sense that they could reach the United States), nevertheless they were targeted upon Western Europe and they were "strategic" in relation to an area which the United States was politically committed to defend. c) Even

(New York: John Wiley and Sons, 1964), p. 87. For other views on uncertainty, see A. R. Hibbs, "ABM and the Algebra of Uncertainty," *Bulletin of the Atomic Scientists*, XXIV (March, 1968), 31–33; D. G. Brennan, "Uncertainty is Not the Issue," *ibid.*, 33–34; Freeman Dyson, "A Case for Missile Defense," *ibid.*, XXV (April, 1969), 31–33.

10. See, e.g., Rock, *A Strategy for Independence*, pp. 118–126.

11. James E. Dougherty, "A Nuclear Arms Agreement: What Shape Might It Take?" *War/Peace Report*, IX (December, 1969), 8–11, 16–18; Herbert Scoville, Jr., *Toward a Strategic Arms Limitation Agreement* (New York: Carnegie Endowment for International Peace, 1970); Alexander De Volpi, "Expectations from SALT," *Bulletin of the Atomic Scientists*, XXVI (April, 1970), 6–8, 30–34; *Yearbook of World Armaments and Disarmaments*, prepared by the Stockholm International Peace Research Institute (New York: Humanities Press, 1970).

if only land-based ICBMs had been involved, and even if warhead sizes and other technical weapons factors had been more or less equivalent, U.S. strategists of deterrence would undoubtedly have argued that parity of missile numbers at low or finite levels would have been in fact inequitable from the standpoint of the United States because the latter had not only a land mass half the size of the Soviet Union but also a pattern of population distribution and urbanization with much higher concentrations in certain regions. d) Planes which the United States called "tactical aircraft" for the defense of NATO Europe were regarded by the Soviets as "strategic" because they were capable of striking at targets in Russia. In short, there were in the geostrategic situations of the two superpowers fundamental asymmetries which made it impossible to reduce their military security requirements to formulas of mathematical parity. If parity was to be assumed, it had to be based upon the notion of fluctuating and compensating imbalances in various weapons sectors.

But let us assume for a moment that mathematical parity of disparate weapons systems can be computed, achieved and believed. Even then there would be no guarantee that balanced mutual deterrence would obtain. In a situation of mathematical equality between the two superpowers, one side might still be able to enjoy a psychological or a political-strategic advantage over the other. An example of a psychological advantage would be a greater willingness to employ the threat of force in close support of diplomacy, especially in time of crisis. One side, in virtue of its ethical tradition, its political ideology and its military doctrine, as well as its psychologcal attitude, might be more defensive while the other is more aggressive, more willing to take risks, more willing to probe the reliability of the other's commitments to defend intermediate areas, and more confident of its ability to control the crisis and to gauge the other's likely reactions. William R. Kintner has argued that if the status-quo power enjoys strategic superiority, this is likely to make for a safer world than would be the case if the anti-status-quo state possessed strategic preponderance. He also contends that parity, in respect of weapons quantities, will not provide assurance that the deterrent will remain in balance at all levels of the political, psychological and strategic spectrum.[12]

The Extension of Deterrence: Western Europe

Strategists are generally agreed that deterrence is strongest in respect to the direct confrontation of the two superpowers. Without implying that any degree of nuclear deterrence is absolutely guaranteed to be permanently effective,

12. William R. Kintner, *Peace and the Strategy Conflict* (New York: Frederick A. Praeger, 1967), especially Chapter 1.

Contending Theories of International Relations

we can say that deterrence is most likely to prevent both the United States and the Soviet Union from carrying out direct, deliberate, strategic attacks against each other's territory and forces. But aside from this contingency, a good portion of the strategic literature of the last two decades has been concerned with the more difficult problem of extending the deterrent for the purpose of protecting allies against attack. Specifically, the main concern of American and Western European writers has pertained to the feasibility of relying upon U.S. nuclear power to inhibit Soviet aggression against those parts of Europe incorporated into the North Atlantic Treaty Organization (NATO).[13]

Nuclear Deterrence and Flexible Response

The members of NATO felt compelled to rely upon United States nuclear power almost from the beginning of the alliance because of what was presumed to be a serious Soviet-Western conventional force imbalance. The magnitude of the imbalance has sometimes been called into question, notably after the Hungarian uprising highlighted the political unreliability of Eastern European national military forces. But generally speaking, the Western Europeans have been sufficiently satisfied with the effectiveness of the United States' nuclear guarantee that they have been unwilling to bring their conventional force contributions up to the levels urged by the United States. In fact, the principal reason why many Europeans were disturbed by the Kennedy Administration's desire to deemphasize "massive nuclear retaliation" and to move toward a strategy of "flexible response" was that they feared that the Soviet Union might interpret this as a prelude to the withdrawal of the United States' nuclear guarantee. Western Europeans were apprehensive lest the Soviets begin to think that the Americans were so determined to avoid nuclear war in Europe that they would denuclearize the region. In the view of many European strategists, this would have been a serious mistake because it would have so altered the environment that a Soviet conventional attack, hitherto "unthinkable" might become "thinkable." American policymakers exhorted the European allies to depend less upon immutable deterrence and to begin contemplating the realities of defense planning. But most Europeans vastly preferred deterrence to defense.

There is something to be said for the positions of both the United States and the allied governments of Western Europe during the early 1960s. The

13. Within recent years, a few revisionist historians have questioned whether the Soviets ever did intend to attack Western Europe, but the fact remains that the overwhelming majority of Western statesmen and strategic analysts have been convinced for more than twenty years that United States power and treaty commitments have been of decisive significance in the maintenance of an equilibrium in Europe.

advent of nuclear-tipped missiles had greatly transformed the international military situation, and it took time to adjust to the new realities. American and Soviet policymakers were well aware of certain Western military vulnerabilities in Europe, particularly in Berlin. (After the downgrading of the Soviet bloc's conventional capabilities in the wake of the Hungarian uprising, there was still a lingering tendency in the West to confuse the problem of defending Western Europe with the much more serious problem of defending West Berlin.) American strategists were asking how many million American lives an American President would be willing to risk by ordering an armored column armed with tactical nuclear weapons to open up a closed corridor to Berlin, knowing that this might lead to the launching of Soviet ICBMs against American cities. The air was filled in those days with talk about a "conventional pause," "dual-capability forces," "graduated deterrence" and "tactical" or "limited" nuclear war. In trying to separate nuclear from conventional forces and responses by time, geography and command and control systems, the United States was pursuing what many American policymakers at the time deemed the prudent and responsible way of reducing the chances of nuclear war and increasing the options between the extreme alternatives of holocaust and surrender.

The West Europeans were quite understandably of two minds on the subject. At times their principal fear was that if a genuine crisis came the United States would be unwilling to defend them with nuclear weapons; at other times their fear was that it would be willing to do so. Their ambivalent attitude was not as contradictory as it seemed. Put more precisely, what they probably wanted was this: In advance of and in the midst of a crisis, they wanted the Soviet leaders to be convinced that any conventional aggression from the east would meet with an early nuclear response. But if an attack actually came, the Europeans would probably not favor a nuclear response at all unless they were convinced that a minimal nuclear reply (or what the British called a "nuclear shot across the bow") would quickly bring all parties sufficiently to their senses to terminate the war with little or no nuclear destruction. In other words, the Europeans preferred maximum reliance upon deterrence so that there would be no war at all. They were reluctant to contemplate the possibility of tactical or limited nuclear war in the event of attack. Some American policymakers undoubtedly regarded the European attitude as illogical, unrealistic or ostrich-like in its avoidance of thinking through the potential consequences of relying upon a nuclear strategy. But in the minds of many Europeans, the Americans were being too logical and too mathematical, and not sufficiently psychologically and politically intelligent in European terms. The strategy of deterrence had worked, the Europeans argued. By taking a remote hypothesis of how deterrence might break down, and making that the basis of a new strategic doctrine which was to be substituted for the older one, the United States in the Europeans' view would increase the probability that some kind of military conflict would occur, and once a conflict involving Soviet and American forces had been joined there would be strong pressures for escalation to the nuclear level. Thus the American desire to reduce the likelihood of nuclear conflict had produced a new strategic doctrine which, in the eyes of many European strategists, might well have just the opposite effect.

THE ROLE OF TACTICAL NUCLEAR WEAPONS

The strategic theorists were never able to prove that nuclear war could be limited (say, by posing the specter of strategic superiority in the background, along with the attendant threat of a tactical nuclear response in Europe highly credible). Nor could the strategic theorists ever prove that nuclear war could *not* be limited, i.e., that it was bound to escalate uncontrollably to general or strategic nuclear war. Most European analysts, while hoping that the deterrent could be retained at the highest level, were not very enthusiastic about the neoscholastic arguments concerning the possibility of keeping nuclear war limited to tactical weapons. Nearly all those who thought that it could be limited at all were more or less in agreement that it could not be limited for very long—probably not beyond a few days, by which time the superpowers would either negotiate or escalate. But Europeans were fond of pointing out that, so far as they were concerned, any use of nuclear weapons beyond the purpose of demonstrating a Western resolve to invoke nuclear power if needed would bring on a degree of devastation in densely populated Western Europe which would be of "strategic" proportions, even if the Soviets and the Americans could speak euphemistically of "tactical nuclear war."

In the final analysis, despite the speculation over the possibility of tactical nuclear war and flexible response in Europe, United States defense planners did not really reduce their dependence upon a nuclear strategy for NATO as much as the public rhetoric seemed to indicate. Even in the early 1960s, American policymakers recognized that the maintenance of the Europeans' confidence in NATO and in the dependability of the U.S. nuclear guarantee would serve the arms control purpose of discouraging the proliferation of additional national nuclear deterrent forces in Europe, especially in Germany. Toward the latter 1960s, when the Non-Proliferation Treaty was a major objective of U.S. diplomacy, U.S. Defense Secretaries frequently called attention to the number of nuclear warheads which the United States had deployed in the NATO area. Moreover, although the withdrawal of France from the integrated military command of NATO made it possible for the alliance to shift officially from a doctrine of "massive retaliation" to one of "flexible response," it was widely realized that the defense planning consequences of France's departure, combined with the implications of Soviet military redeployments during the invasion of Czechoslovakia, had increased the probability that any attack upon Western Europe would provoke an early nuclear response.[14]

DETERRENCE AND RATIONALITY

The theory of nuclear deterrence, ever since it became prominent in thinking about international politics, has always presupposed a high degree of rationality on the part of national decision-making structures—especially in the United States, the Soviet Union and Britain, less so in the case of France (under de Gaulle) and Communist China. (Paradoxically, France and China as inferior nuclear powers had good reasons throughout the 1960s to be extremely cautious, and their governments were probably more rational than they were generally credited with being by policymakers in Moscow and

14. The literature dealing with the theoretical issues discussed in this section is vast and can only be sampled. See the following books: Alastair Buchan, *NATO in the 1960's* (New York: Frederick A. Praeger, 1960); Alastair Buchan, ed., *Europe's Futures, Europe's Choices: Models of Western Europe in the 1970s* (New York: Columbia University Press, 1969); Alastair Buchan and Philip Windsor, *Arms and Stability in Europe* (New York: Frederick A. Praeger, 1963); Alvin J. Cottrell and James E. Dougherty, *The Politics of the Atlantic Alliance* (New York: Frederick A. Praeger, 1964), Chap. 3; Henry A. Kissinger, *The Necessity for Choice* (New York: Harper and Brothers, 1961), Chaps. II–IV, and *The Troubled Partnership: A Reappraisal of the Atlantic Alliance* (New York: McGraw-Hill Book Company, 1965); Herman Kahn, *On Thermonuclear War* (Princeton: Princeton University Press, 1960); Klaus Knorr, ed., *NATO and American Security* (Princeton: Princeton University Press, 1959); General André Beaufre, *NATO and Europe*, trans. Joseph Green (New York: Random House [Vintage Books], 1966); Thomas W. Wolfe, *Soviet Power and Europe, 1945–1970* (Baltimore: Johns Hopkins Press, 1970); F. W. Mulley, *The Politics of Western Defense* (London: Thames and Hudson, Ltd., 1962); Robert L. Pfaltzgraff, Jr., *The Atlantic Community: A Complex Imbalance* (New York: Van Nostrand Reinhold Company, 1969); James L. Richardson, *Germany and the Atlantic Alliance* (Cambridge: Harvard University Press, 1966), Chaps. 7–10; Helmut Schmidt, *Defense of Retaliation* (New York: Frederick A. Praeger, 1962), Chaps. 3, 6, 11; Robert E. Osgood, *NATO: The Entangling Alliance* (Chicago: University of Chicago Press, 1962), Chaps. 5–9; Timothy W. Stanley, *NATO in Transition* (New York: Frederick A. Praeger, 1965), Chaps. 3–5; Robert Strausz-Hupé, James E. Dougherty and William R. Kintner, *Building the Atlantic World* (New York: Harper and Row, 1963), Chaps. 3, 5; See also the following representative and important articles: Michael Brower, "Nuclear Strategy of the Kennedy Administration," *Bulletin of the Atomic Scientists*, XVIII (October, 1962), 34–41; the Symposium by Raymond Aron, Klaus Knorr and Alastair Buchan, "The Future of Western Deterrent Power," *Bulletin of the Atomic Scientists*, XVI (September, 1960), 266–282; Bernard Brodie, "What Price Conventional Capabilities in Europe?" *The Reporter*, XXVIII (May 23, 1963), 25–33; Kai-Uwe von Hassel, "Détente Through Firmness," *Foreign Affairs*, XLII (January, 1964), 184–194; Herman Kahn, "The Arms Race and Some of Its Hazards," *Daedalus*, LXXXIX (Autumn, 1960), 744–780; Thomas C. Schelling, "Nuclear Strategy in Europe," *World Politics*, XIV (April, 1962), 421–432; and Albert Wohlstetter, "Nuclear Sharing: NATO and the N plus 1 Country," *Foreign Affairs*, XXXIX (April, 1961), 355–387.

within the Anglo-American alliance who resented and feared the independent courses of action charted by the French and the Chinese.)

The rationality implicit in the theory of mutual nuclear deterrence seems to be essentially of the Hobbesian variety.[15] According to the theory, what the two superpowers are saying to each other in effect is this:

> *'I want peace (in the sense that I do not wish to become embroiled in a nuclear war with you). I have the same kind of selfish rationality which you have, and I know that you are just as interested in surviving as I am. Therefore we are both driven by a fundamental law of nature to seek at least this kind of peace, even if not other kinds. We seek peace, not because we trust each other, or share each other's values, but rather because we fear each other.*
>
> *'We both know that the outcome of a nuclear exchange is incalculable in advance, because if such an exchange occurs, we shall probably prove incapable of limiting the damage, whether we consider ourselves under those circumstances to be rational or irrational. For on one side or the other or both there will be "rationalists" who will say that to stop now is to accept defeat. They will be joined by the irrationalists who are primarily driven by the desire for excitement, revenge or suicide, or something else. Thus we both face the danger of escalation to mutual extinction, simply because we shall exercise all the advantages of war once we are in it.'*

To be perfect disciples of Thomas Hobbes in this instance, the two superpowers need not convenant between them to create a political sovereign to take them out of the state of nature. The atom itself is the common power which holds them both in awe.[16]

15. Rationality is a transcendental notion which cannot be precisely defined. It pertains to the fundamental norms of human thought. In practical areas of human activity (such as politics) where human choices must be made, we usually think of "rationality" as involving some proportionate relationship between ends and means, or between goals and policies. To say that this or that course of action is "rational" or "irrational" presupposes a prior judgment or assumption concerning objectives or goals, and in the final analysis these are based upon values which lie beyond "rational" evaluation. See Hoffmann, *The State of War*, pp. 12–13; and William A. Scott, "Rationality and Non-Rationality of International Attitudes," *Journal of Conflict Resolution*, II (March, 1958), 8–16. Scott regards as rational attitudes resulting from a logical means-end relationship between external events and a person's goals or values, as both are perceived by the individual. Nonrational attitudes, as seen by psychologists, result primarily from influences outside the individual's cognitive system—i.e., either from unconscious processes within the person or from influences of the external environment, such as direct social reinforcement. *Ibid.*, p. 9.

16. See Thomas Hobbes, *Leviathan*, Everyman's Library (New York: E. P. Dutton and Company, 1950), Part I, Chap. 14, pp. 106–118. Many analysts of deterrence have attempted to describe the kinds of rational policy estimations which are made in terms of utility and probability of success on the one hand and disutility and probability of failure on the other, in relation to calculated choices for aggression. They have concluded that the nations committed to a philosophy and doctrine of deterrence are not motivated to initiate attacks, but they are more strongly motivated to respond with nuclear retaliation to nuclear

The concept of "rationality" may be defined in different ways. Some people may think of "rational" policy choices in moral or ethical terms. Some may contrast the term to behavior of an "insane" or "reckless" nature. Some may contend that any nonviolent resolution of a conflict situation constitutes a "rational" course, while the option for a violent solution is "irrational." Still others may look upon rationality as an ends-means relationship involving a fairly heavy dose of economic (or gains versus cost) analysis. According to this notion, we must try to estimate the value assigned by policymakers to a particular objective before we can estimate the chances that they will, in active pursuit of that objective, adopt a course of action likely to lead to the necessity of *initiating* nuclear war and exposing themselves to nuclear retaliation. Throughout the analysis, we must remember that deterrence theory is not a causal-explanatory theory. It enables us to predict the occurrence or non-occurrence of nuclear war only within a framework of rational strategic decision-making.[17]

But the question is whether the effort to deter, if carried too far, might generate irrational fears which will in times of crisis decision-making weaken the assumptions of rationality on which deterrence is based. We have reason to suspect that the threat of punishment, instead of controlling or inhibiting individual behavior in desired directions, may sometimes have the effect of producing a more intransigeant opposition. Thomas W. Milburn has written:

> *However much pain (or punishment) might appear to be the logical opposite of satisfaction (or reward), its behavioral consequences are simply not opposite. Rewards may change the direction of an organism's effort and motives; punishments (or threat of them), while they may tend to suppress behavior, serve little to change underlying motives. Punishments are less than ideal means for influencing behavioral change, especially when used alone, because they increase anxiety and hostility in those upon whom they are used.*[18]

---

attacks and probably even to large-scale nonnuclear attacks. All of these factors enter into the calculation of what is known as the "credibility" of the deterrent, which is a matter of both mathematics (numbers and quantifiable characteristics of weapons) and psychology (the estimated intentions of the adversary). Generally speaking, the analysts also recognize the paradoxical necessity of preserving "credibility" through the maintenance of an operational readiness and constant technological-administrative perfection of a strategic weapons force which, if effective as a deterrent, will remain in permanent condition of non-use.

See Brodie, *op. cit.;* Singer, *Deterrence, Arms Control and Disarmament,* Chaps. 2 and 3; Morton A. Kaplan, "The Calculus of Nuclear Deterrence," *World Politics,* XI (October, 1958), especially p. 34, where Kaplan argues that a decision to abstain from or limit nuclear war might be irrational in those causes where such a decision leads to defeat.

17. Maxwell, *op. cit.,* p. 3.

18. Thomas W. Milburn, "What Constitutes Effective Deterrence?" *Journal of Conflict Resolution,* III (June, 1959), 139–140.

Milburn has also argued that deterrence is not really a military concept; it belongs to the realm of psychology, since it involves an effort to influence the behavior of others through dissuasion. He suggests that an understanding of deterrence requires an understanding of at least four concepts: influence process, hostageship, trust and the personal responsibility of leaders. Like many other writers, he calls for shifts of emphasis in U.S. policy: narrowing the range of Soviet actions which the United States would rely upon nuclear power to deter; reducing the reliance upon the acquisition of "overkill" capacity in favor of "finite" or "minimum" deterrence; and mixing the threat of punishment for undesirable with the prospect of reward for more desirable forms of behavior.[19]

Charles E. Osgood has similarly cast doubt upon the notion of rational decision-making in the nuclear age. He notes that as emotional stress increases beyond an optimum level, nonrational mechanisms become more prevalent in human thinking. "Faced with an overwhelming threat over which he feels he has no control, the human individual typically denies the reality of the danger rather than keeping it in mind and trying to cope with it." [20] M. G. Raskin has gone so far as to revive the discredited Freudian "death instinct" as the explanation of international competition in nuclear armaments.[21] Jerome Frank has contended that the basic dilemma of deterrence policy—namely, how to make an essentially incredible threat look credible to an opponent—leads to a sort of ritualization of irrational gestures by the two superpowers in times of crisis since each is determined to demonstrate its ultimate resoluteness.[22]

This brings us full circle to the seemingly contradictory concept used by many strategic writers—"the rationality of the irrational." [23] Fortunately for the world, the two superpowers during the last two decades have not proved quite as reckless in hurling threats of nuclear attack as one might be led to expect from a reading of the more pessimistic psychological literature. To be

19. Thomas J. Milburn, "The Concept of Deterrence: Some Logical and Psychological Considerations," *Journal of Social Issues*, XVII (No. 3, 1961), 3–11.

20. Charles E. Osgood, "Questioning Some Unquestioned Assumptions about National Defense," *Journal of Arms Control*, I (January, 1963), 3. For experimental evidence of the phenomenon which psychologists call "defensive avoidance," see I. L. Janis and R. F. Terivilliger, "An Experimental Study of Psychological Resistance to Fear Arousing Communications," *Journal of Abnormal and Social Psychology*, LXV (1962), 402–410.

21. M. G. Raskin, "Political Anxiety and Nuclear Reality," *American Journal of Psychiatry*, CXX (March, 1964), 831–836.

22. Jerome D. Frank, *Sanity and Survival, op. cit.*, pp. 140–141.

23. Kahn, *On Thermonuclear War*, pp. 291–295; Thomas C. Schelling, *Arms and Influence* (New Haven: Yale University Press, 1966), pp. 37–38; Maxwell, *op. cit.*, pp. 2–10. Paul Ramsey, distinguishing between "the unthinkable" and "the un-do-able," rejects on moral grounds a "committal" strategy which is based upon the rationality of the irrational and which is designed precisely to adopt in advance a posture which will make it impossible to choose a limited ethical course of action when the crisis comes. *The Limits of Nuclear War*, pp. 12–17.

Nuclear Deterrence and Arms Control

sure, in the thermonuclear age the "self-fulfilling prophecy" may need to be fulfilled only once to cause a serious disruption of history. But the United States and the Soviet Union have carefully worked out the rules governing their strategic interaction with a view toward minimizing the risks of direct confrontation and embroilment. The utterance of a nuclear threat by one side has usually been couched in sufficiently restricted or ambiguous terms as to convey to the other side an appreciation of the importance which is attached to a specific foreign policy commitment or security position without frightening the other side into a precipitate response. The usual decoded form of the threat is as follows: "If you take that military initiative which I think you may be contemplating, you will be doing something offensive to me in such a sensitive area that I may feel compelled, even against my better judgment, to take forms of counteraction which might put us into direct hostile contact with each other, and thus pose the risk of nuclear war. Please consider this a fair warning, and act accordingly with prudence." Perhaps Lorenz better than the latter-day Freudians can understand this ritualized and rationalized form of aggressive communication designed to avert rather than spark violent conflict.

Deterrence and Arms Control

It may well be that the political leaders of the five nuclear powers have been overly optimistic about their ability to remain in rational control of their foreign policy choices and defense responses, and thereby to avoid nuclear holocaust. Certainly the theoretical analysts of conflict in the nuclear age have spent more time worrying, or at least thinking, about a broad range of frightful contingencies that might occur than have the practical politicians. In time of noncrisis, the theoreticians have postulated many ways in which deterrence could break down and unintended nuclear war could begin, irrespective of the basic assumption of rationality on the part of Soviet and American leadership so far as a deliberately planned nuclear attack is concerned. One might hypothesize that in times of acute crisis and dangerous confrontations between nuclear powers, responsible political decision-makers have to "sweat the situation out" while the more abstract "think tank" analysts can calmly comfort each other with sophisticated reasons why they expect a nuclear war to be avoided. Such a hypothetical contrast suggests that there may be a significant difference between perceptions of the situation under various circumstances as between social and policy scientists on the one hand and governmental policymakers on the other.

Since the dawn of the atomic era, many voices have been raised to insist that unless the nations can achieve complete nuclear disarmament, they will eventually find themselves driven into nuclear war as something inevitable.

Contending Theories of International Relations

Nevertheless, although there is no compelling reason to think that any one of the five existing nuclear weapon states wants nuclear war within the foreseeable future, but good reason to think that they all prefer to avoid it because of its unpredictably costly consequences, none of the nuclear powers acts consistently as if it looks upon total nuclear disarmament as the optimum means of guaranteeing its security. It may be that there are varying numbers and proportions of governmental officials in all five states who really look upon general and complete disarmament as a desirable goal. But probably even some of these, and certainly many others, are convinced that the very same advanced weapons technology which makes disarmament appear to many as a more imperative objective than ever before also makes disarmament more difficult than ever to attain. At least at the present time, the political, technical and strategic obstacles to general disarmament seem insuperable.

Among the nuclear weapon states, there are serious asymmetries of power which render "pentagonal" negotiations unlikely. Given the discrepancies of geostrategic requirements among the five, it is difficult to determine in what weapons sectors the process of arms limitation should begin, in what ratios the reductions should be made, and how far down the scale reductions might be carried before the condition of mutual deterrence might give way to renascent incentives for surprise attack in order to achieve decisive advantages. Both of the superpowers are constrained in their negotiating policies by considerations of coalition diplomacy, inasmuch as their allies often become nervous at the prospect of alterations in the political-military situation, despite their constant professions of interest in change. (This has been particularly true in the West. On the Soviet side, the problem has been different: when the Soviet Union conducts arms negotiations with the United States, it comes under ideological attack from China for conniving with the capitalist foe.) Moreover, there are still rather serious disagreements between the Western and the Communist states over such issues as inspection for disarmament, as well as the development of an effective international peacekeeping organization in lieu of national military establishments for safeguarding external security. Other obstacles could be cited, but the ones cited have been quite sufficient to hamper progress toward genuine disarmament. To date the nuclear powers have not been willing to move away from an international political-military environment in which the conditions of the "equilibrium game" have been relatively familiar toward a radically transformed and less predictable system of "disarmed" states. This fact may be traced to the cautious conservatism of governmental institutions, the nature of the nation-state system itself, the difficulties of controlling modern military technology by the written devices of traditional diplomacy, and the intractability of the political, ideological, cultural and other value conflicts dividing nations.

The fact that presently each nuclear power attaches a higher priority to policy objectives other than general disarmament has not led governments to despair. Political leaders in the five nuclear weapon countries, even if they cannot arrive at formal agreements among themselves, seem to be aware that the conditions of the nuclear age impose upon them requirements to be cautious in their dealings with each other.[24] They take for granted the continued existence, for the indefinite future, of national military establishments. But they appear to be interested in rendering the international environment in which they operate safe against the danger of unintended war.

Several American writers warned against the danger that the nuclear superpowers might stumble into war unpremeditatedly, virtually by accident. Herman Kahn, for example, warned of the widespread fear "that a button may be pressed accidentally, an electrical circuit short, a relay stick, a telephone call or other message be misunderstood, an aurora borealis or meteor or flock of geese be mistaken for an attack, a switch fail, some ICBMs launched through mechanical or human error, some stockpile weapons accidentally exploded. . . ." [25] Bruce M. Russett tried to analyze the causes of World War I through the application of an accounting scheme designed originally to study the causes of automobile accidents, and there was a clear implication that in the nuclear age a mishap due to technical malfunctioning or human exhaustion and misinterpretation of signals could lead to cataclysmic consequences.[26] A Soviet writer sharply criticized Russett's theory of accidental war as being intrinsically related to the imperialists' purpose of proving that, since war is a fatal inevitability, there is no point in resisting the warmongers.[27]

24. For the history of disarmament efforts in the twentieth century and an analysis of the political, economic, technical and military-strategic problems associated with these efforts, see: Philip Noel-Baker, *The Arms Race: A Programme for World Disarmament* (New York: Oceana Publications, 1960); Bernhard G. Bechhoefer, *Postwar Negotiations for Arms Control* (Washington: The Brookings Institution, 1961); Seymour Melman, ed., *Inspection for Disarmament* (New York: Columbia University Press, 1958) and *Disarmament: Its Politics and Economics* (Boston: American Academy of Arts and Sciences, 1962); Michael Wright, *Disarm and Verify* (New York: Frederick A. Praeger, 1964); Arnold Wolfers *et al.,* *The United States in a Disarmed World* (Baltimore: Johns Hopkins Press, 1966); Richard A. Falk and Richard J. Barnet, *Security in Disarmament* (Princeton: Princeton University Press, 1965); Evan Luard, *First Steps to Disarmament* (New York: Basic Books, 1965); James E. Dougherty, *Arms Control and Disarmament: The Critical Issues* (Washington: Center for Strategic Studies, 1966), and

"Soviet Disarmament Policy: Illusion and Reality," in Eleanor L. Dulles and Robert D. Crane, eds., *Détente: Cold War Strategies in Transition* (New York: Frederick A. Praeger, 1965); J. I. Coffey, "The Soviet View of a Disarmed World," *Journal of Conflict Resolution,* VIII (March, 1964), 1–6.

25. Herman Kahn, "The Arms Race and Some of Its Hazards," in Donald G. Brennan, ed., *Arms Control, Disarmament and National Security* (New York: George Braziller, 1961), p. 91.

26. Bruce M. Russett, "Cause, Surprise and No Escape," *Journal of Politics,* XXIV (February, 1962).

27. "In our day the danger of world war —this time with the employment of thermonuclear weapons—has become greater still, due to the reactionary forces' pathological hatred of socialism and everything progressive. And the war danger is not accidental, as Russett would have us believe. It is part of imperialism, of its profit lust and drive for world supremacy." V. Berezhkov, "The 'Automobile Accident' Theory of War," *New Times,* Moscow, April 18, 1962.

Whether or not the Soviet leaders were more fearful of deliberately planned war than of an accidental occurrence leading to war, it appears that United States policymakers did begin to become concerned about the risks of unexpected events which might reduce the options available to decision-makers in times of crisis. Both administrative and physical safeguards were developed to minimize the chance of any unauthorized detonation of nuclear weapons. There were "fail safe" measures for the dispatch of strategic bombing missions, permitting recall as long as possible, and "two key" systems to control nuclear weapons on the territory of allies abroad. There was a "two man" rule to verify proper handling at every level of operations involving nuclear weapons. Personnel responsible for handling nuclear weapons were subject to careful psychological screening to reduce the risks of personal psychic failure. Permissive action links were refined to make detonation impossible without the reception of proper electronic signals. More broadly, an effort was made to ensure more time for decision-making by eliminating weapons systems of "hair trigger nervousness" (due to lack of protection or forward position) which might someday create a pressure for preemptive attack because of their vulnerability to surprise attack. The United States moved toward the creation of an "invulnerable second strike capability" and more flexible, survivable command and control systems.[28] It was also thought that the improvement of emergency communication capabilities between the superpowers would help to reduce the danger of war by miscalculation of the adversary's intentions or by precipitate response to ambiguous perceptions of adversary actions. (The Washington-Moscow "hot line," agreed upon in 1963, represented an effort in this direction.)

THE ARMS RACE AND ARMS CONTROL

Several advocates of arms control have recognized a certain degree of validity in the phenomenon known as Richardson processes when applied to international armaments competition. Lewis F. Richardson used differential equations to determine the reaction coefficient in friendliness-hostility relations, with particular reference to arms races.[29] If A exhibits distrust of and hostility toward B by increasing his rate of self-armament, how does B respond? Does he react slowly, calmly and moderately, making his own necessary adjustments

28. John T. McNaughton, "Arms Restraint in Military Decisions," J. David Singer, ed., *Weapons Management in World Politics*, Proceedings of the International Arms Control Symposium, *Journal of Conflict Resolution*, VII (September, 1963), 228–234.

29. Lewis F. Richardson, *Arms and Insecurity* (Pittsburgh: Boxwood, 1960),

and *Statistics of Deadly Quarrels* (Chicago: Quadrangle Books, 1960); "Movement Toward War: From Motives and Perceptions to Actions," Introduction to Part Three, Dean G. Pruitt and Richard C. Snyder, eds., *Theory and Research on the Causes of War* (Englewood Cliffs, N.J.: Prentice-Hall, 1969), pp. 49–59.

at a reduced rate, or does he become alarmed, increasing his armaments at a more rapid pace, thus setting in motion the "self-fulfilling prophecy" by further arousing and apparently justifying A's fears and hostility? In the latter case, the reaction coefficient is greater than unity, and the result is likely to be an intensive arms race culminating in war, according to Richardson.

One of the objectives of arms control, therefore, is to moderate the pace of international armaments competition. This may be accomplished in several different ways, whether by formal diplomatic agreements or by unilateral but tacitly reciprocated moves. Thus the concept of arms control might embrace any of the following policies:

> *a) A program of weapons research, development and deployment, as well as a strategic doctrine, which stresses the nonprovocative and defensive aspects of national security postures. (Examples of this include abstention from civil defense; abstention from building ever larger warheads despite their technological feasibility; a nuclear test ban; agreement not to emplace weapons of mass destruction in outer space or on the ocean bed.)*
>
> *b) Holding quantitative rates of weapons production below the levels which rival powers are economically and technically capable of sustaining in an all-out "arms race." (Examples of this include holding steady or reducing military budgets while gross national product is growing; a formal verified freeze on the production of specified items, such as fissionable materials for weapons purposes or strategic delivery vehicles.)*
>
> *c) Tension-reducing agreements or arrangements, such as a "no-first-use of nuclear weapons" pledge, a "nonaggression pact," and proposals for disengagement or "thinning out" of forces in intermediate regions, the creation of demilitarized or nuclear-free zones (e.g., the Antarctica Treaty and the Latin America Nuclear Free Zone Agreement), and prohibitions on the sale and delivery of conventional arms to countries in "tinderbox areas" (e.g., the Middle East).*[30]

30. For further discussion of the types of arms control proposals mentioned in these three paragraphs, see: Donald G. Brennan, *op. cit.;* Hedley Bull, *The Control of the Arms Race* (New York: Frederick A. Praeger, 1961); J. David Singer, ed., *op. cit.;* David H. Frisch, ed., *Arms Reduction: Program and Issues* (New York: The Twentieth Century Fund, 1961); Donald G. Brennan, "Arms and Arms Control in Outer Space," in Lincoln P. Bloomfield, ed., *Outer Space,* for the American Assembly (Englewood Cliffs, N.J.: Prentice-Hall, 1962); Buchan and Windsor, *op. cit.;* Karol Lapter, "Nuclear Freeze in Central Europe," *Disarmament and Arms Control,* II (Summer, 1964); Morton H. Halperin, "A Proposal for a Ban on the First Use of Nuclear Weapons," *Journal of Arms Control,* I (April, 1963); James Dougherty, "Zonal Arms Limitation in Europe," *Orbis,* VII (Fall, 1963), 478–517; and "The Status of the Arms Negotiations," *Orbis,* IX (Spring, 1965), 49–97; James E. Dougherty and John F. Lehman, Jr., eds., *The Prospects for Arms Control* (New York: Mcfadden-Bartell Company, 1965) and *Arms Control for the Late Sixties* (Princeton: D. Van Nostrand Company, 1967).

During the 1960s, arms control analysts exhibited serious concern over the dangers of further proliferation of nuclear weapons to countries not already possessing them. Specifically, the fear was that a small nuclear power might someday act as a "catalyst" of an unwanted war between larger nuclear powers. Especially in the United States and Britain, and probably to a considerable extent in the Soviet Union, many persons seemed to take it for granted that the possibility of nuclear war would increase in geometric proportion to the number of independent nuclear powers in the world. This might be expressed mathematically by the formula $R = N^2$ where R stands for the risk of war and N for the number of nuclear weapon states. The difficulty with such a formula, of course, is that it fails to take into account the different political qualities of governments acquiring control over nuclear arsenals and the character of their foreign policies. Some states would undoubtedly be more responsible and less reckless than others. A few writers criticized the concept that the danger would increase with the growth of membership in the "nuclear club," contending instead that acquisition of nuclear weapons might just as well compel a militant power to become more cautious and that a world of many nuclear powers might be stabler than a world of a few.[31] Nevertheless, most arms control analysts were inclined to think that a world of twelve or fifteen nuclear states would be less stable than a world of four or five because the former would contain a greater statistical probability of technical accident, unauthorized use, strategic miscalculation or uncontrolled escalation from a limited to a general war.[32]

Three of the nuclear powers (the United States, the Soviet Union and Great Britain) negotiated a nonproliferation treaty while France and China remained aloof, but it is possible that even the latter two countries were in tacit agreement with the other three that it was not in the interest of any of them to

31. See, e.g., Pierre Gallois, *The Balance of Terror: Strategy for the Nuclear Age,* trans. Richard Howard (Boston: Houghton Mifflin Company, 1961). Fred Charles Iklé argued that while it was understandable for the leading nuclear powers to discourage proliferation, they could not prevent it, and that it would be easier to control the dangers from small nuclear powers when they begin to manifest themselves rather than to try to prevent proliferation. Iklé specifically rejected the "statistical" and "catalytic war" theories. "Nth Countries and Disarmament," *Bulletin of the Atomic Scientists,* XVI (December, 1960), 391–394.

32. William C. Davidon and others, *The*

Nth Country Problem and Arms Control (Washington: National Planning Association, 1960); Robert W. Tucker, *Stability and the Nth Country Problem* (Washington: Institute for Defense Analyses, 1961); Arnold Kramish, *The Peaceful Atom in Foreign Policy* (New York: Harper and Row, 1963); Leonard Beaton and John Maddox, *The Spread of Nuclear Weapons* (London: Chatto and Windus, Ltd., 1962); R. N. Rosecrance, ed., *The Dispersion of Nuclear Weapons* (New York: Columbia University Press, 1964); Alastair Buchan, ed., *A World of Nuclear Powers?* (Englewood Cliffs, N.J.: Prentice-Hall, 1966); Leonard Beaton, *Must the Bomb Spread?* (Harmondsworth: Penguin Books, 1966).

dilute the currency of nuclear prestige. During the negotiation of the treaty, the European allies of the United States were apprehensive about the possible weakening of the Western alliance, placing obstacles in the way of future European unity, and arousing German security fears. After the treaty was negotiated, several nonnuclear states of the world signed the treaty reluctantly, or postponed signature (or ratification) until they had more time to judge developments in the international system which had a bearing upon their national interests. West Germany did not wish to bargain away too much prior to the settlement of the question concerning Germany's future status in Europe, although the German Federal Republic did sign the treaty in 1969. Such countries as Israel, the United Arab Republic, Switzerland, India, Pakistan, Japan and Australia were far from enthusiastic when it came to closing out future options that might be vital to national defense.

Several nonnuclear states raised serious questions: Why should they renounce the nuclear option before the present nuclear powers make substantial progress toward decreasing the symbolic importance of nuclear weapons in world politics? Is the nonproliferation treaty an instrument for buttressing the privileged position of the five countries which were assigned the veto power in the United Nations Charter? Will the treaty render permanent the dependence of the nuclear "have-nots" upon the nuclear "haves" for developing the peaceful applications of atomic energy? Will the present nuclear powers, or those which drafted the treaty, provide credible defense guarantees to signatory nonnuclear states which might in the future find themselves subjected to "nuclear blackmail" or to threats of massive conventional attack from aggressive powers? These difficult questions penetrated to the very heart of the future international system.[33]

THEORY IN THE ERA OF THE SALT

As the decade of the 1970s began, the United States and the Soviet Union entered a new phase of negotiations—the strategic arms limitation talks (known as the SALT). This development led to novel challenges for international theorists interested in a variety of subjects: the impact of technology on foreign and defense policies; linkages between domestic and international politics; theories of negotiations and bargaining; international interactive processes—e.g., the relationship between superpower talks in one important functional dimension (arms control) and their political-strategic confrontation in specific geographic regions such as Berlin, Southeast Asia and the Middle East; and the relations of the superpowers to other powers—great, middle

33. James E. Dougherty, "The Non-Proliferation Treaty," *Russian Review,* XXV (January, 1966), 10–23 and "The Treaty and the Non-nuclear States," *Orbis,* XI (Summer, 1967), 360–377; Eliza-beth Young, "The Control of Proliferation: The 1968 Treaty in Hindsight and Forecast," Adelphi Paper No. 56 (London: Institute for Strategic Studies, April, 1969).

Contending Theories of International Relations

and small. Some of the specific types of questions to which the new super-power negotiations give rise are the following:

1) What effect will the SALT have on the choices to be made in the future by states which possess both the capability and the motivation to move toward the acquisition of nuclear weapons? During the negotiations for the Non-Proliferation Treaty, several non-nuclear-weapon states called for an end to "vertical proliferation" (among the nuclear-weapon states) as well as "horizontal proliferation" (to other countries beyond the present five). But to what extent do the leaders of the non-nuclear weapon states really expect or want the two superpowers to embark on the path of nuclear arms reduction before China has entered as a serious participant into the arms negotiations? Furthermore, granted that the total collapse or failure of the SALT would probably have an adverse effect upon the continued viability of the Non-Proliferation Treaty, is there any assurance that progress in the SALT —which if it occurs at all is likely to be rather slow and gradual—will prove decisive so far as the willingness of other states to abstain from the choice of nuclear weapons acquisition is concerned? [34]

2) In terms of the overall structure of the problems of arms control and disarmament, are the strategic arms limitation talks between the two super-powers the most theoretically logical and politically appropriate follow-up to the Non-Proliferation Treaty?

3) The governments of the United States and the Soviet Union do not appear at the present time to labor under fears of a deliberate surprise attack by the other side. What, then, are their motives for undertaking the SALT? Is it because they are both beset by internal and external uncertainties only indirectly related to nuclear armaments (e.g., domestic unrest in the United States and the Soviet Union's dispute with Communist China)? Is it because, despite the present presumptions of "strategic stalemate," they fear the technological uncertainties of the future and the danger of an interaction process in which one side may overreact in respect to development and deployment of weapons, creating a temporary imbalance which may tempt one party to behave imprudently in time of crisis? Are they moved by the economic consideration that it would be futile to go on investing in costly new weapons systems if such expansion is likely to produce only a mutually cancelling effect upon the strategic equation? Are the superpowers afraid that their failure to negotiate would increase the likelihood of nuclear proliferation to other countries? Do they merely wish to placate "world public opinion?" Do they perceive the SALT as a preliminary step toward a radically different international system from the one that now exists? Can we ever determine satisfactorily what the motivations of the two governments are? Do motiva-

34. See the three articles by George H. Quester: "Israel and the Non-Proliferation Treaty," Bulletin of the Atomic Scientists, XXV (June, 1969), 7–9, 44– 45; "India Contemplates the Bomb," ibid., XXVI (January, 1970), 13–16, 48; and "Paris, Pretoria, Peking—Proliferation?" ibid., XXVI (October, 1970), 12–16.

tions make a substantial difference with regard to outcomes? In which directions are the motivations likely to change?

4) Under what circumstances would other nuclear powers such as France and China be willing to enter as serious partners into the arms negotiations? What effect would their admission have upon other countries? What is to be the eventual role of non-nuclear-weapon states, including relatively small powers, in planning the kind of international order in which disarmament would make more sense than it has up to now?

5) What effects will the SALT have upon the relationships of the United States with its European NATO allies, and of the Soviet Union with its Warsaw Pact partners in East Europe. In an era of increasing talk about "European security" (east and west), will the SALT lead to a dissolution of the alliance systems which have up to now served as the guarantors of peace and stability in Europe? If so, what will replace them?

6) What is the connection between concessions designed to create a climate conducive to the conduct of international arms negotiations and the bargaining process itself? Within recent years, some American political leaders have argued that the United States should refrain from deploying antimissile defense systems and multiple warhead systems lest these deployments ruin the chances for agreement with the Soviets. Others have argued that the United States should confront the Soviet Union with the choice of reaching a negotiated agreement or facing a continuation of a costly arms competition. The first school says: Threats will wreck the SALT. The second says: The Soviets have no incentive to negotiate the inevitable. The SALT might cast some light on the validity of these two approaches to negotiations, but developments will probably be sufficiently ambiguous to enable partisans of both positions to claim vindication for their theory.

7) Finally, what will be the scope, form and substance of agreements which the superpowers are likely to achieve? Hedley Bull, professor of international relations at the Australian National University, has suggested that the United States and the Soviet Union find themselves in an enduring but nonetheless limited political détente. They perceive a common interest in the avoidance of nuclear war, and thus of any mutual armed conflict. They remain wary of directly intervening with military force in each other's principal spheres of influence. They are interested in containing those conflicts in Asia, the Middle East and Africa in which they might become unwillingly embroiled. They have certain common objectives in respect to Germany—to see that she does not acquire control of nuclear weapons, nor alter her present boundaries by force.[35] But, says Bull, there is no evidence emanating from the superpowers "that would justify speculations that they might agree to establish, or to work towards, some kind of joint hegemony of the globe."[36]

35. Hedley Bull, "The Scope for Super-Power Agreements," *Arms Control and National Security* (An International Journal), I (1969), 1–23. See esp. pp. 1–5.

36. *Ibid.,* p. 6.

Given the complexity of contemporary military technology and the pace of political change now going on in the international system, Bull doubts that any single agreement can be negotiated which will in itself fully contain strategic arms competition, but he holds out some hope for a simple proposal such as a freeze on the total number of launch vehicles deployed by each side, despite the fact that such an agreement would leave wide loopholes for qualitative changes in weapons technology.[37]

Nuclear Weapons: Implications for International Behavior

Despite all that has been written and debated about nuclear deterrence, no one can yet say without appearing arrogant that our theoretical knowledge in this crucial dimension is satisfactory. It will take a great deal more ratiocination before we can confidently claim to understand, even with a minimal adequacy, the impact of nuclear technology on foreign policy decision-making. We really do not yet know all the political, psychological and sociological subtleties which may enter into that process whereby theory is translated into practice, and whereby the practitioners of power—"statesmen," "rulers" and "politicians" (whose scope of action is limited by myriad constraints)—try to respond to the full spectrum of dangers described and analyzed for them exhaustively by theoreticians who deal primarily in abstract ideas rather than the pragmatic placation of human interest-and-goal seeking.

From the dawn of the atomic era in 1945 until today, man's attitudes toward nuclear war have undergone remarkable change. Each increment in the size of nuclear stockpiles makes nuclear war a bit less thinkable among decision-makers invested with functioning reason. Great powers now resolve or suffer without resort to war provocations that once would certainly have led to international war. Yet it would be premature to say that the fear of nuclear holocaust has reduced international tension, rivalry and hostility. Serious conflict continues in forms that have thus far remained below the threshold of nuclear exchanges—insurgency and counterinsurgency, border disputes, infiltration and subversion, invasion of nations for suppressive purposes, air and maritime incidents, threats, cold war, and the support of client states or proxy states at war. Meanwhile, despite the frequent criticisms which are leveled at governments for accumulating "nuclear overkill" capabilities, political decision-makers seem unwilling to be content with the assumption that weapons technology has reached a plateau. Rather it is true that fears of new

37. *Ibid.*, pp. 21–23. In addition to the works cited above in Footnote 11, see also Jeremy J. Stone, "When and How to Use SALT," *Foreign Affairs*, XLVIII (January, 1970), 262–273; and Matthew P. Gallagher, "The Uneasy Balance: Soviet Attitudes Toward the Missile Talks," *Interplay*, III (December, 1969/January, 1970), 21–25.

scientific breakthroughs, fears of surprise attack, and uncertainties concerning the performance of weapons systems as well as the consequences of an actual exchange leave decision-makers in doubt that they have now achieved "enoughness." Hence if any form of conflict which is now assumed to be controllable should under certain critical circumstances suddenly become uncontrollable, the risks of cataclysm for the human race will be great. Some theoreticians hold that nuclear war is for all practical purposes a statistical certainty, and that this justifies even unilateral disarmament if reciprocal disarmament cannot be achieved. Others contend that every day that passes without nuclear war, instead of bringing the world closer to extinction, strengthens the rational presumption that war will not occur and furnishes an increment of time for the international system to move toward higher forms of organization than have hitherto existed. But whether the world is moving toward political-psychological integration or physical-biological disintegration is essentially unpredictable from the standpoint of a purely scientific methodology.

DETERRENCE THEORY: TRADITIONAL WISDOM V. SCIENTIFIC METHOD

There is a growing dichotomy between those who theorize about such things as power, deterrence and war in terms of either traditional political wisdom or of modern scientific method and those on the other hand who would break away from these modes of "rational" analysis in favor of an approach to the problems of mankind which emphasizes the suprarational or intuitive values of ethics, humanitarianism and religion. At the birth of the modern era in the early seventeenth century, *avant-garde* intellectuals bent their efforts to separate science from what they regarded as the dead hand of religious faith and philosophical certitude, both vestiges of an outmoded medieval civilization which had been founded upon the Judaeo-Christian spiritual heritage and categories of thinking received from ancient Greece. Men became convinced that the scientific method for discovering new knowledge and penetrating the innermost secrets of the universe proved to be such a brilliant success precisely because it was "value-free." Thus it may be that in a sense the Faust legend was historically verified. In time, the conscious, observing subjective microcosm classified itself with the unconscious, observed, objective macrocosm; the former proceeded to deduce from the latter general deterministic laws which it assumed to be applicable to itself and to social aggregations. Today perhaps we are witnessing a growing unwillingness to measure man along with the atoms and the stars.

CHAPTER 10

Theories of International Integration, Regionalism and Alliance Cohesion

Consensus, Force and Political Community

Central to the study of politics is the identification and analysis of forces which contribute to the integration of political communities. Like the study of conflict, another major focal point in the study of politics, political integration cuts across the traditional fields into which political science is organized, and is as relevant to the student of politics at the local and metropolitan level as to the student of comparative and international politics.[1]

Two problems are fundamental to the study of integration and politics: (1) obtaining from subjects or citizens deference and devotion to the political unit within which they live; (2) achieving procedural and substantive consensus within political systems. It is possible to outline essentially two theories of political integration. First, political systems gain and retain their cohesiveness because of widely shared values among their members and general agreement about the framework of the system. Thus systems have procedural consensus. Moreover, systems survive because of the substantive consensus, that is, general agreement about the solutions to problems which the political system is called upon to solve. The greater the procedural and substantive consensus, the greater the integration of the political system.

As an alternative theory, it has been argued that political systems become or remain cohesive because of the presence, or threat, of force. Writers such as Hobbes, and in contemporary sociology, Dahrendorf, have argued for a recognition of the importance of coercive power in the integration of political communities.[2] In the study of international relations, proponents of world

1. For an analysis which cuts across traditional fields, see Philip E. Jacob and James V. Toscano, eds., *The Integration of Political Communities* (Philadelphia: J. B. Lippincott Company, 1964).

2. Thomas Hobbes, *Leviathan* (Oxford:

Basil H. Blackwell, 1967), p. 109, 174. Ralf Dahrendorf, *Class and Class Conflict in Industrial Society* (Stanford: Stanford University Press, 1959), p. 157; by the same author, *Essays in the Theory of Society* (Stanford: Stanford University

government have often seen in the monopolization of power at the international level the key to the reduction of violence, and so-called political realists such as Niebuhr and Morgenthau have argued that world government is not possible without the development of greater consensus at the global level.[3]

Functionalism and the Integrative Process

Contemporary students of political integration owe a considerable intellectual debt to the concept of functionalism. In the study of political science functionalism has assumed several meanings. Eclectic functionalists, widespread in political science, ask what function a political party, an international organization, or an office holder performs. Depending on the analyst functionalism may only provide a list of activities in which "X" is engaged, or it may answer questions regarding "X" 's contributions to the performance of certain purposes or activities.[4]

Although structural-functional analysis, as suggested in Chapter 4, now occupies a vital place in the study of political science it differs fundamentally from functionalism as used by David Mitrany (1888–   ), a British political scientist whose writings have greatly influenced contemporary integration theorists. Mitrany, who wrote mostly during the interwar years, suggested that the growing complexity of governmental systems had increased greatly the essentially technical, nonpolitical tasks facing governments. Such tasks not only created a demand for highly trained specialists at the national level, but contributed to technical problems at the international level. If such problems could be assigned to specialists and somehow separated from the political sector, it would be possible to achieve international integration. The growth in technical problems which could not be solved exclusively at the national level, would contribute to the proliferation of international collaboration in technical fields. In Mitrany's theory there is a doctrine of "ramification," whereby the development of collaboration in one technical field contributes to collaboration in other technical fields. Functional collaboration in one sector results from a felt need, and generates a felt need for functional collabora-

Press, 1968), pp. 147–150. See Chapter 5 for an examination of other writers, traditional and contemporary, who have posited the existence of relationships between conflict and the integration of political and social units.

3. Reinhold Niebuhr, "The Illusion of World Government," *Bulletin of the Atomic Scientists,* V (October, 1949), 289–292. Hans J. Morgenthau, *Politics among Nations* (New York: Alfred A.

Knopf, 1967), pp. 500–516. For an examination of literature on world government, see Inis L. Claude, Jr., *Power and International Relations* (New York: Random House, 1962), pp. 205–285.

4. William Flanigan and Edwin Fogelman, "Functional Analysis," James C. Charlesworth, ed., *Contemporary Political Analysis* (New York: Free Press, 1967), p. 73.

tion in another sector. Mitrany assumed that functional activity could reorient international activity and contribute to world peace. Eventually such collaboration would encroach upon, even absorb, the political sector. In particular, "economic unification would build up the foundation for political agreement, even if it did not make it superfluous." [5] In short, his basic strategy was to shift the focus of attention from divisive political issues to noncontroversial technical problems.[6]

As a result of World War I, Mitrany saw the nation-state to be lacking in its ability either to preserve peace or to improve the social and economic well-being of its inhabitants. Conflict and war spring from the division of the world into separate and competing national units. As an alternative to conflict, Mitrany suggested the gradual creation of a transnational web of economic and social organizations and the remolding of attitudes and allegiances to make the masses of people more amenable to international integration.

INTEGRATION AS A PROCESS AND CONDITION

Thus Mitrany was concerned with the process by which political communities become integrated. Although more recent students of integration have drawn upon Mitrany's work, they have developed their own definitions of integration. Ernst Haas, professor of political science at the University of California, Berkeley, defines integration as a *process* "whereby political actors in several distinct national settings are persuaded to shift their loyalties, expectations and political activities toward a new centre, whose institutions possess or demand jurisdiction over the pre-existing national states." [7] In a later work, Haas conceives of integration as "referring *exclusively* to a process that links a given concrete international system with a dimly discernible future concrete system. If the present international scene is conceived of as a series of interacting and mingling national environments, and in terms of their participation in international organizations, then integration would describe the process of increasing the interaction and the mingling so as to obscure the boundaries between the system of international organizations and the environment provided by their nation-state members." [8]

Referring to integration as a *condition,* Amitai Etzioni, professor of sociology at Columbia University, asserts that a political community which possesses effective control over the use of the means of violence is integrated. Such a community has a center of decision-making that allocates resources and rewards throughout the community and forms the dominant focus of political

5. David Mitrany, *A Working Peace System* (Chicago: Quadrangle Books, 1966), p. 97.

6. David Mitrany, "The Functional Approach to World Organization," *International Affairs,* XXIV (July, 1948), 359.

7. Ernst B. Haas, *The Uniting of Europe* (Stanford: Stanford University Press, 1958), p. 16.

8. Ernst B. Haas, *Beyond the Nation-State* (Stanford: Stanford University Press, 1964), p. 29, italics in original.

identification for the large majority of politically aware citizens.[9] In Etzioni's scheme, political unification is the process whereby political integration as a condition is achieved. Unification increases or strengthens the bonds among the units which form a system.[10] Making use of Haas's definition, Leon N. Lindberg of the University of Wisconsin, in his work on the European Community, defines integration as "(1) the process whereby nations forgo the desire and ability to conduct foreign and key domestic policies independently of each other, seeking instead to make *joint decisions* or to *delegate* the decision-making process to new central organs; and (2) the process whereby political actors in several distinct settings are persuaded to shift their expectations and political activities to a new center." [11] Karl W. Deutsch refers to political integration as a condition in which a group of people have "attained within a territory a sense of community and of institutions and practices strong enough and widespread enough to assure, for a long time, dependable expectations of peaceful change among its population." [12] Deutsch suggests that "integration is a matter of fact, not of time." [13]

While Deutsch emphasizes integration as a condition in which people seek peaceful settlement of their disputes, rather than resorting to war, Haas focuses on a shift in loyalties to a new political unit. Etzioni suggests that an integrated political community effectively controls force, has a decision-making center that allocates rewards and resources and forms the dominant focus of popular political identification.

In another analysis, Philip E. Jacob, University of Hawaii, suggests that political integration "generally implies a relationship of *community* among people within the same political entity. That is, they are held together by mutual ties of one kind or another which give the group a feeling of identity and self-awareness." [14]

Spill-over, which will be examined in the work of Haas later in this chapter, involves the learning theory principle that frequency of association or reinforcement contributes to the strengthening of habits. Moreover, spill-over includes from learning theory the process of generalization: namely that

9. Amitai Etzioni, *Political Unification* (New York: Holt, Rinehart and Winston, 1965), p. 4. "A political community is a community that possesses three kinds of integration: (a) it has an effective control over the use of the means of violence (though it may 'delegate' some of this monopoly to member-units); (b) it has a center of decision-making that is able to affect significantly the allocation of resources and rewards throughout the community; and (c) it is the dominant focus of political identification for the large majority of politically aware citizens." *Ibid.*, p. 329.

10. *Ibid.*, p. 332.

11. Leon N. Lindberg, *The Political Dynamics of European Economic Integration* (Stanford: Stanford University Press, 1963), p. 6.

12. Karl W. Deutsch, *et al.*, *Political Community and the North Atlantic Area* (Princeton: Princeton University Press, 1957), p. 5.

13. *Ibid.*, p. 6.

14. Philip E. Jacob and Henry Teune, "The Integrative Process: Guidelines for Analysis of the Bases of Political Community," Jacob and Toscano, eds., *op. cit.*, p. 4.

agreements in one sector are likely to be generalized to other agreements in similar sectors.

CONDITIONS FOR INTEGRATION

After criticizing contemporary theories for allegedly confusing conditions promoting integration and consequences resulting from integration, Johan Galtung, director of the International Peace Research Institute at Oslo and editor of the *Journal of Peace Research,* defines integration as "the process whereby two or more actors form a new actor. When the process is completed, the actors are said to be integrated. Conversely, disintegration is the process whereby one actor splits into two or more actors. When the process is completed, the actor is said to be disintegrated." [15] Galtung sketches several models designed to establish conditions for integration.

First, integration may be viewed as value-integration. In this category, Galtung sets forth two models. An egalitarian model provides for the integration of values in the sense that actors have "coinciding interests." A second model, the hierarchical model, includes the integration of values which are arranged so that dilemmas and conflicts can be resolved by choosing the value highest in the hierarchy.

In a second category of conditions, Galtung conceptualizes integration as actor-integration. Here he sets forth a similarity model, in which integration consists of increasing similarity between actors in rank, demographic composition, and economic and political structure. Similarity is viewed as homology, that is, each member of an actor may find an "opposite number" in the other actor. In this category, there is a second model, the interdependence model. Integration is a process by which cultural, political and economic interdependence between actors is increased. Actors become linked to such an extent that what harms one actor injures the other.

A third category provides for integration as exchanges between parts and whole. Here Galtung sets forth two models. In the loyalty model, integration develops and endures so long as the unit is supported by its component parts. Support forms an input such as acts of allegiance or the allocation of resources from the parts to the whole. Finally, Galtung describes an allocation model. The existence of the integrated unit depends upon its ability to offer outputs to its parts. Such outputs include the provision by a nation of a sense of identity to individuals, ensuring protection from enemies, or furnishing economic gains such as markets and high living standards.

In itself, none of these conditions is necessary and sufficient for integration. Integration is a process in which great importance is attached both to the con-

15. Johan Galtung, "A Structural Theory of Integration." *Journal of Peace Research,* Vol. 5, No. 4 (1968), 377.

stituent actors and their environment. According to Galtung, "only when the new actor is so firmly integrated that the images formed by self and others coincide, is the integration process completed." [16]

Galtung distinguishes three types of integration: territorial, organizational, and associational. Territorial integration gives way to organizational integration as a result of demands for higher output. Organizations are the essential prerequisite for production. Organizational integration yields to associational integration because of demands for equality and justice, as well as a need for association with people similar to oneself. In turn, associational integration leads to territorial integration because of a felt need for a measure of heterogeneity and variety. Territorial and associational integration make possible the reconciliation of needs for diversity and homogeneity. Nations as well as the international system can be analyzed in order to determine how these processes of integration are combined.

Although all three types of integration can be present at the same time, Galtung suggests that in the contemporary world, organizations and associations tend to increase more rapidly than territories. If organizations create webs of interdependence and associations produce new points of identification that transcend the territorial nation state, the problem facing mankind is the development of an alternative to existing forms of territorial integration.

Writers on integration have several features in common. All are concerned with the process by which loyalty is shifted from one center to another. They share an interest in communications within units to be integrated. According to Deutsch and Etzioni, peoples learn to consider themselves members of a community as a result of human communications patterns. In general, integration theorists hold that persons adopt integrative behavior because of expectations of joint rewards or penalties. Initially, such expectations are developed among elite groups both in the governmental and private sectors. Successful integration depends upon a people's ability to "internalize" the integrative process, that is, for member elites, rather than external elites, to assume direction of an integrative process. Deutsch, Etzioni and Haas use systems theory in developing integration models. In the work of each of these theorists there is emphasis upon the effect of integration in one sector upon the ability of participating units to achieve integration in other sectors.

Transactions and Communications: Implications for Security Communities

To a greater extent than other writers on integration, Karl Deutsch uses both communications and systems theory, drawing upon the mathematician Norbert Wiener's writings on cybernetics and on sociologist Talcott Parsons's work on general systems. Deutsch quotes with approval the following passage from Wiener.

16. *Ibid.*, p. 378.

Contending Theories of International Relations

The existence of social science is based on the ability to treat a social group as an organization and not as an agglomeration. Communication is the cement that makes organizations. Communication alone enables a group to think together, to see together and to act together. All sociology requires the understanding of communication.[17]

Communications among people can produce either friendship or hostility depending upon the extent to which the memories of communications are associated with more or less favorable emotions. Nevertheless, in Deutsch's scheme political systems endure as a result of their ability to abstract and code incoming information into appropriate symbols, to store coded symbols, to disassociate certain important information from the rest, to recall stored information when needed, and to recombine stored information into new patterns which were not present when the information entered as an input into the system. The building of political units depends upon the flow of communications within the unit, as well as between the unit and the outside world.

Deutsch is concerned with the relationship between communications and the integration of political communities.[18] Countries are "clusters of population, united by grids of communication flows and transport systems, and separated by thinly settled or nearly empty territories." [19] Peoples are groups of persons united by an ability to communicate on many kinds of topics; they have complementary habits of communication. Generally, boundaries are areas where the density of population and communications decline sharply. Peoples become integrated as they become interdependent. "Wherever there is immediate interdependence, not for just one or two specialized goods or services but for a very wide range of different goods and services, you may suspect that you are dealing with a country." [20] Interdependence among nations is far lower than interdependence within nations. In fact, in some respects, as in the case of foreign trade, most countries are less interdependent today than they were in the nineteenth century. Trade, as a percentage of GNP, has declined.[21]

Deutsch's major substantive contribution to integration theory is found in

17. Quoted in Karl W. Deutsch, *The Nerves of Government* (New York: The Free Press, 1964), p. 77. See Norbert Wiener, *Cybernetics* (Cambridge: MIT Press, 1965).

18. In his work on nationalism, Deutsch wrote: "The community which permits a common history to be experienced as common, is a community of complementary habits and facilities of communication. It requires, so to speak, equipment for a job. This job consists in the storage, recall, transmission, recombination, and reapplication of relatively wide ranges of information, and the "equipment" consists in such learned memories, symbols, habits, operating preferences, and facilities as will in fact be sufficiently complementary to permit the performance of these functions. *A larger group of persons linked by such complementary habits and facilities of communication* we may call a people." Karl W. Deutsch, *Nationalism and Social Communication* (Cambridge: MIT Press, 1953), p. 96. Italics in original.

19. Karl W. Deutsch, "The Impact of Communications upon International Relations Theory," Abdul Said, ed., *Theory of International Relations: The Crisis of Relevance* (Englewood Cliffs, N.J.: Prentice-Hall, 1968), p. 75.

20. *Ibid.*, p. 76.

21. *Ibid.*, pp. 84–90.

his work on the conditions for political community in the North Atlantic area. Drawing upon historical data, Deutsch and his collaborators examined ten cases of integration and disintegration at the national level.[22] Since Deutsch's cases, in contrast to Etzioni's, are examples of the building of political communities at the national level, the implicit assumption of his work is that generalizations derived from these comparative studies are relevant to an understanding of integration at the international level, that there are similarities or isomorphism, between the process of community building both at the national level and beyond the nation-state. Research and analysis undertaken in this work yielded several important conclusions about the conditions for the formulation of amalgamated security communities and pluralistic security communities. Deutsch and his associates set forth two kinds of security communities: "amalgamated," in which previously independent political units have formed a single unit with a common government; and "pluralistic," in which separate governments retain legal independence. The United States is used as an example of an amalgamated security community, while the United States-Canada, or France-Germany since World War II, may be called pluralistic security communities.[23]

For the formation of an amalgamated security community, several conditions were found to be necessary: (1) mutual compatibility of major values; (2) a distinctive way of life; (3) expectations of joint rewards timed so as to come before the imposition of burdens from amalgamation; (4) a marked increase in political and administrative capabilities of at least some participating units; (5) superior economic growth on the part of at least some participating units and the development of so-called "core areas" around which are grouped comparatively weaker areas; (6) unbroken links of social communication, both geographically between territories and between different social strata; (7) a broadening of the political elite; (8) mobility of persons, at least among the politically relevant strata; (9) a multiplicity of communications and transactions.[24]

PLURALISTIC SECURITY COMMUNITIES

For the formation of "pluralistic security communities" three conditions were found to be essential: (1) compatibility of values among decision-makers;

22. They included the formation of the United States, its breakup in the Civil War, and the reunion which followed, the union of Scotland and England, the disintegration of the Anglo-Irish union, German unification, Italian unification, the Hapsburg Empire, the union of Norway and Sweden, and the Swiss Confederation. Two other cases, the union of Wales and England, and the formation of England itself in the Middle Ages, were studied "less intensively."

23. Here the reader may wish to refer to Chapter 1, where the point is made concerning John H. Herz's theory to the effect that in the nuclear age the ability of the territorial state to provide its citizens with a sense of security has been put in doubt.

24. Deutsch, *et al.*, *Political Community and the North Atlantic Area*, p. 58.

Contending Theories of International Relations

(2) mutual predictability of behavior among decision-makers of units to be integrated; [25] (3) mutual responsiveness. Governments must be able to respond quickly, without resort to violence, to the actions and communications of other governments. In a pluralistic security community, the member units forgo war as a means toward the settlement of disputes.

In their study of political community and the North Atlantic area, Deutsch and his collaborators examined cases such as the Austro-Hungarian Empire, the Anglo-Irish Union, and the union between Norway and Sweden, in which political communities disintegrated. From such investigations, several tentative conclusions emerged about conditions conducive to disintegration: (1) extended military commitments; (2) an increase in political participation on the part of a previously passive group; (3) the growth of ethnic or linguistic differentiation; (4) prolonged economic decline or stagnation; (5) relative closure of political elites; (6) excessive delay in social, economic, or political reforms; (7) failure of a formerly privileged group to adjust to its loss of dominance.

In Deutsch's conception the integrative process is not unilinear in nature. The essential background conditions do not come into existence at the same time, nor are they established in any special sequence. "Rather it appears to us from our cases that they may be assembled in almost any sequence, so long as all of them come into being and take effect." [26]

On the basis of findings concerning the building and disintegration of national units, Deutsch and his associates suggest that the North Atlantic area, "although it is far from integrated, seems already to have moved a long way toward becoming so." [27] Several countries have achieved "pluralistic integration:" the United States and Canada; the United Kingdom and Ireland. An essential condition for integration in the North Atlantic area is the development among countries of a greater volume of transactions and communications, especially those associated with rewards and expectations of reward. Deutsch and his collaborators suggested the need to develop new functional organizations within the North Atlantic area and to "make NATO more than a military alliance" by developing the "economic and social potentialities of this unique organization." [28]

Etzioni and the Stages of Political Unification

While Deutsch and his collaborators have completed historical cases of the integration and disintegration of nation-states, Amitai Etzioni has examined four contemporary efforts to form political units at a level beyond the nation-

---

25. This idea is similar to Parsons' social system in which persons develop expectations about each other's behavior. See Chapter 4, pp. 106–110.

26. *Ibid.*, p. 70.
27. *Ibid.*, p. 199.
28. *Ibid.*, p. 203.

state. He suggests that any study of political unification may pose four major questions:

Under what conditions is it initiated? What forces direct its development? What path does it take? And what is the state of the system affected by the process once it is terminated? [29]

Etzioni's objective in asking such questions is to trace the evolution of a unification process from its inception to maturity. One of his principal efforts has been to develop a model of integration. His unification model involves four stages: (1) the preunification state; (2) the unification process, i.e., integrating power; (3) the unification process, i.e., integrated sectors; (4) the termination state. He juxtaposes the propositions contained in his model with such entities as the West Indies Federation (1958–1962), the Nordic associational web (1953–1964), the United Arab Republic (1958–1961), and the European Economic Community (1958–1964).

For integration to occur, it is necessary to have "interdependence among the participating units." [30] In the preunification state, there is a gradual expansion in the scope of the system "in terms of the sectors that are controlled on a system rather than a unit level." [31] Etzioni is far from explicit about the shared properties to be found in the preunification system. Properties such as cultural homogeneity, economic interdependence, or territorial contiguity may influence the unification process. Members of preunification unions do not necessarily belong to the same international organizations or share membership in the same bloc. At the first stage external elites play a major role in the unification process. Such elites are often the primary proponents of unification.

The second stage is characterized by the presence of integrating power which may be coercive, utilitarian or identitive. Such power is wielded by elites within the system. In fact, at this stage elites within the system, rather than outside elites, become the principal advocates of integration. Etzioni refers to the process by which control of a system is taken over by member-elites from external elite units as internalization. Coercive power includes weapons, police, or the military. Utilitarian power consists of economic factors and technical and administrative capabilities. Identitive power comprises values, symbols, or rituals which may be utilized in the unification process.

In the third stage of the unification process, the flow of goods, persons, and communications among the units of the system shows a marked increase. Moreover, unification in one sector "spills over" into other sectors. In a process of "secondary priming," unification in one sector leads to unification in another sector. Thus Etzioni's model, especially at this stage, includes com-

29. Etzioni, *Political Unification*, p. 14.   31. *Ibid*.
30. *Ibid*., p. 34.

munications and functionalist theories found respectively in the work of Deutsch and Haas.

Finally, there is the termination state. According to Etzioni, a union "takes off" and "spills over" until it reaches the termination state. At that time the processes which have been described in earlier stages of the model have run their course and come to an end. Mature unions, i.e., those which have reached their termination state, differ greatly "in the levels of unification at which they stabilize, that is, stop increasing their integration and expanding their scope." [32]

After utilizing his paradigm in the study of the four cases chosen for examination, Etzioni presents several findings about the unification process. His proposition about the importance of external elites was confirmed. External elites enhanced the prospects for unification if their objectives coincided with those of the elite units within the union. In the case of the West Indies Federation and the EEC, external elites, Britain and the United States, respectively, had an effect upon the unification process. The West Indies Federation failed primarily because Britain did not use her influence to develop a federal structure which would have reflected more accurately the power of Jamaica and Trinidad as compared with the weaker members. In contrast, in Western Europe "American influence was compatible with the evolving European power structure. . . . The rapid reconstruction of Western Germany, its large contribution to NATO, its important albeit secondary role in the ECSC and the EEC, and its support of positions favored by America, suggest that the United States was 'betting on the right horse' . . . . Thus American assistance to Germany was an instance of an external elite endorsing a rising internal one, rather than trying to erect or to block such an elite." [33] Moreover, both the West Indies Federation and the EEC cases confirmed the proposition that, as the level of integration and the scope for union increase, the elite units of the union must internalize both the functions performed and the authority held by the external elite. In the West Indies, failure of the Federation was attributed in part to the inability, and the unwillingness, of elite units to assume functions performed by Britain, the external elite. In contrast, in Western Europe internal elites, rather than the United States, became the principal activists on behalf of unification. Under three conditions, however, internalization places stresses upon the union: (1) if the functions internalized are taken over by member units rather than by the union itself (e.g., France rather than the European Community); (2) if some members' gains are not matched by the gains of other members, opposition to member-unit internalization is likely to mount; and (3) if internalization among sectors, such as the military and the economic, is uneven.

Etzioni advances the proposition that unions with fewer elite units are more likely to succeed than unions with many elite units, since the greater the num-

32. *Ibid.*, p. 60.　　　　　33. *Ibid.*, p. 287.

ber of elite units, the more formidable are likely to be the problems which must be resolved.[34] In a related proposition, Etzioni contends that egalitarian unions, like unions with few elite units, are more likely to succeed than non-egalitarian unions. The UAR disintegrated despite the fact that it had fewer elite units than the EEC. However, the UAR did not have an effective elite unit, since Egypt possessed neither the assets nor the will to preserve the union. Both the initiative to form the union and to dissolve it came from Syria, rather than Egypt. Compared to the UAR, the EEC was

> *comparatively egalitarian in utilitarian matters and elitist in political issues. The new element the EEC introduces is that of the system-elite. We need to augment our propositions by stating that the most effective unions are expected to be ruled by system-elites rather than by member-elites. A system-elite combines the decisiveness found in member-elites with the ability to generate commitment found in egalitarian unions; the decisiveness is gained from the existence of one superior center of decision-making, while commitments are generated because the system elite represents all the members of the union as well as the union as a collectivity.[35]*

The Nordic Union, which survived, was an egalitarian union. In the case of the West Indies Federation, which failed, the external elite, Britain, was unable to develop an internal elite unit in support of the Federation. In the EEC, Etzioni found the development of a system elite. He hypothesized that "the most effective unions are expected to be ruled by system-elites rather than by member-elites." [36]

In comparing the four cases chosen for examination, Etzioni concludes that the EEC is most advanced in the level and scope of its integration, while the failure of other unification efforts is attributed largely to their deficiencies in utilitarian and identitive assets and capabilities.[37] He hypothesizes: "The more utilitarian power the elites initiating and guiding unification command or the more the union-system builds up, the more successful unification will be." This hypothesis was tentatively confirmed. In the EEC the utilitarian power of the union increased, and this in turn advanced the identitive power of the system-unit, and prepared the way for further commitment. In the West Indies, in contrast, the union did not command utilitarian power, and the distribution of power was such that it led to opposition to the union on the part of the two largest members, Trinidad and Jamaica. Therefore, he suggests: "It is

34. Etzioni hypothesizes: "In particular, unions having one elite will be more successful than those having two, those with two more than those with three." *Ibid.*, p. 69.

35. *Ibid.*, pp. 296–297.

36. *Ibid.*, p. 296.

37. In Etzioni's scheme, utilitarian assets include technical and administrative capabilities, manpower, and economic possessions. The term identitive assets refers to "the characteristics of a unit or units that might be used to build up an identitive power. These identitive potentials are usually values or symbols, built up by educational or religious institutions, national rituals, and other mechanisms." *Ibid.*, pp. 38–39.

Contending Theories of International Relations

hardly surprising that the more utilitarian and identitive power supporting a particular unification effort, the farther it advances, and vice versa." [38] But Etzioni does not ignore coercive power as a factor in the unification process. The lack of coercive power, he concludes, hastened the disintegration of the West Indies Federation and the use of such force might have extended the life of the UAR.

Like Deutsch, Etzioni emphasizes communications in the development of unions. In the case of the West Indies Federation and the UAR, communications were distorted, and there was inadequate responsiveness among the units to be unified. In contrast, the EEC had channels for more rapid and effective communication, responsiveness, and representation. He concludes that adequate representation is a prerequisite for adequate responsiveness and that extensive vertical communication and representation, together with responsiveness at intermediate levels, enhance the prospects for unification.

Etzioni is concerned with the dynamics of unification. He suggests that efforts to unify underdeveloped countries are less likely to succeed than efforts to unify industrially advanced peoples. Underdeveloped countries are characterized by widespread illiteracy among peoples whose outlook is parochial. Such peoples lack the organizational and political skills needed to cope with problems of regional unification. Both of the cases where unifica- period of crisis, an effort was made to accelerate the movement toward unifi- tion failed, the West Indies and the UAR, consisted of underdeveloped units. Put differently, Etzioni, like Deutsch and Haas, gives a prominent place in his scheme to politically aware elites as moving forces in a unification process.

In another proposition, Etzioni suggests that the deceleration of unification efforts will be more effective when resistance to the union is great, and accel- eration more effective when the union has reached the stage of maturity, the termination stage in his paradigm. (Deceleration is the curtailing of changes introduced in order to allow additional time for adjustment and to reduce pressures for deunification. Acceleration consists of speeding up changes so as to make the benefits of the union more tangible and to increase support for it.) In the case of the West Indies and the UAR, he concludes, the propo- sition was confirmed. The disintegrative process was hastened when, in a cation. In the case of the mature Nordic Union, deceleration of an already slow process had the effect of halting unification, although Etzioni believes that an acceleration policy would probably not have had a different effect. In the case of the EEC acceleration was initiated at the moment of success, with beneficial effects upon the union.

In yet another proposition, Etzioni views the rewarding of as many units and subunits as possible as important to ultimate success. Widespread rewards contribute to widespread support by creating vested interests in the Union and making it possible to withstand the inevitable strains of adjustment. In the West Indies and UAR cases, the adjustment was attempted before widespread

38. *Ibid.,* p. 306.

rewards were evident to participating units. In the case of the Nordic Union, there was no reallocation and no new integration, while the EEC "quite systematically delayed reallocation until the integrating power was built up."

In a later examination of unifying forces at the international level, Etzioni viewed the world as a "small set of subglobal systems."

> *These post-modern sub-global systems differ from earlier, especially colonial, empires in several ways: (a) Their power mix is relatively more balanced; they rely less on direct coercive control (though this is still used frequently as compared to its use in the intranational systems of the superpowers themselves): (b) Utilitarian exchanges seem relatively less exploitive (though there is some "colonial" residue), in that relatively more genuine technical and economic aid is given, more indigenous development—including some industrialization—is allowed, more of the benefits of production remain in the countries, and a considerable increase in autonomous local administration is tolerated. (c) Relatively higher stress is put on normative control, in the forms of various extended elite-controlled educational and propaganda facilities, a rhetoric of equality, and a facade of multilateralism and formal equality of representation in the General Assembly of the United Nations and various regional bodies. (d) There is also an increase in the upward communication from the non-elite countries to the elite, more "downward" knowledge of the non-elite countries on the part of the elite, and even some increase in responsiveness.*[39]

Etzioni views unification on a global scale as a dialectical process including essentially three stages. In the first, so-called subcommunities containing heterogeneous and conflicting units are formed. Only after the unification of subcommunities has been completed are the member units prepared to build a political community. In the second stage, the subcommunities furnish the "middle tier" for a "multitier consensus formation structure."[40] In the third stage, a community comes into existence linking and, to a large degree, superseding the subcommunities. Thus, because Etzioni sees regional units as crucial to unification at the global level, he has focused his empirically based work on the model building and the comparative analysis of contemporary unification efforts, successful and unsuccessful, in widely separated regions of the world.

Functionalism and Sector Integration

In contrast to the more comparative focus of Deutsch and Etzioni, the work of Haas deals with specific cases, which Haas analyzes with the use of an

39. Amitai Etzioni, *The Active Society: A Theory of Societal and Political Processes* (New York: Free Press, 1968), pp. 585–586.

40. *Ibid.*, p. 599.

elaborate theoretical framework. In his work on the European Coal and Steel Community, Haas postulates that the decision to proceed with integration, or to oppose it, depends upon the expectations of gain or loss held by major groups within the unit to be integrated. "Rather than relying upon a scheme of integration which posits 'altruistic' motives as the conditioners of conduct, it seems more reasonable to focus on the interests and values defended by them as far too complex to be described in such simple terms as 'the desire for Franco-German peace' or the 'will to a United Europe.' " [41] Haas assumes that integration proceeds as a result of the work of relevant elites in the governmental and private sector, who support integration for essentially pragmatic rather than altruistic reasons. Elites having expectations of gain from activity within a supranational organizational framework are likely to seek out similarly minded elites across national frontiers.

Haas attempts to refine functionalist theory about integration. Criticizing Mitrany for having taken insufficient account of the "power" element, Haas postulates that power is not separable from welfare. Since few men make the pursuit of power an objection, power may be described as "merely a convenient term for describing violence-laden means used for the realization of welfare aims." [42] But Haas advances the proposition that "functionally specific international programs, if organizationally separated from diffuse orientations, maximize both welfare and integration." Such programs give rise to organizations whose "powers and competences gradually grow in line with the expansion of the conscious task, or in proportion to the development of unintended consequences arising from earlier task conceptions."

Moreover, as a result of a learning process, power-oriented governmental activities can evolve toward welfare-oriented action. As actors realize that their interests are best served by a commitment to a larger organization, learning contributes to integration. Conceptions of self-interest and welfare are redefined. Haas advances the corollary: "Integrative lessons learned in one functional context will be applied in others, thus eventually supplanting international politics." [43]

Crucial to integration is the "gradual politicization of the actors' purposes which were initially considered "technical" or "noncontroversial." [44] The actors become politicized, Haas asserts, because, in response to initial "technical" purposes, they "agree to consider the spectrum of means considered appropriate to attain them."

41. Ernst B. Haas, op. cit., p. 13. For an analysis of expectations of British official and nonofficial elite groups from European Integration, see Robert L. Pfaltzgraff, Jr., Britain Faces Europe, 1957–1967 (Philadelphia: University of Pennsylvania Press, 1969).

42. Haas, Beyond the Nation-State, p. 47.

43. Ibid., p. 48.

44. Ernst B. Haas and Philippe Schmitter, "Economics and Differential Patterns of Political Integration: Projections about Unity in Latin America," International Organization, XVIII (Autumn, 1964), 707. Reprinted in International Political Communities (New York: Doubleday and Company, 1966), p. 262.

To the functionalist proposition that a welfare-orientation is achieved most readily by leaving the work of international integration to experts or voluntary groups, Haas offers two qualifications: (1) that voluntary groups from a regional setting, such as Western Europe, are more likely to achieve integration than an organization with representatives from all over the world; and (2) that experts responsible to no one at the national level may find that their recommendations are ignored. Therefore, he suggests that expert managers of functionally specific national bureaucracies joined together to meet a specific need are likely to be the most effective carriers of integration. Haas rephrases the functionalist proposition to read: "International integration is advanced most rapidly by a dedication to welfare, through measures elaborated by experts aware of the political implications of their task and representative of homogeneous and symmetrical social aggregates, public or private." [45]

Again with qualification, Haas accepts the functionalist proposition that political loyalties are the result of satisfaction with the performance of important functions by a governmental agency. Since it is possible for peoples to be loyal to several agencies simultaneously, there may be a gradual transfer of loyalty to international organizations performing important tasks. Haas accepts this proposition with the caveat that it is not likely to hold if the integrative process is influenced by nations with ascriptive status patterns, or traditional or charismatic leadership.[46]

"SPILLOVER" AND THE INTEGRATIVE PROCESS

Central to Haas's work is the concept of "spillover," [47] or what Mitrany called the doctrine of ramification. In his examination of the European Coal and Steel Community, Haas found that among European elites directly concerned with coal and steel, there were relatively few persons who initially were strong supporters of the ECSC. Only after the ECSC had been in operation for several years did the bulk of leaders in trade unions and political parties—both Socialist and Christian Democrat—become proponents of the Community. Moreover such groups, as a result of gains which they experienced from the ECSC, placed themselves in the vanguard of other efforts for European integration, including the Common Market. Thus there was a marked tendency for persons who had experienced gains from supranational institutions in one sector to favor integration in other sectors. Moreover, Haas suggests that decisions made in organizations at the international level may be integrative. "Earlier

---

45. Haas, *The Uniting of Europe,* p. 49.

46. *Ibid.,* p. 50.

47. Haas refers to "spillover" as "the expansive logic of sector integration," and suggests: if actors, on the basis of

their interest-inspired perceptions, *desire* to adapt integrative lessons learned in one context to a new situation, the lesson will be generalized." *Beyond the Nation-State* (Stanford: Stanford University Press, 1964), p. 48.

decisions spill-over into new functional contexts, involve more and more people, call for more and more interbureaucratic contact and consultations, meeting the new problems which grow out of the earlier compromises." [48] Thus there was an "expansive logic" which contributed to "spill-over" from one sector to another. The process is one whereby the nations "upgrade" their common interests.

In his work on the International Labor Organization, Haas develops a model which brings together the functional analysis of general systems theory and refines the "spill-over" concept found both in his earlier work and in Mitrany's writings in the form of the doctrine of ramification. Haas is concerned with the extent to which an international organization can transcend national boundaries and thus transform the international system. Governmental policies, the product of the interaction of national actors and their environment, constitute inputs into the international system. The organizations and accepted body of law form the structure of the international system. The structures receive inputs and convert them from tasks into actions. Collective decisions are the outputs of the international system. Such outputs may change the international environment in such a way as either to produce integrative or disintegrative tendencies within the international system. If the weak structures of the international system are inadequate to the tasks given them, their outputs enter an international environment in which national actors are predisposed either to strengthen or weaken institutions for collaborative action at the international level. In either eventuality, the purposes (defined as consciously willed action patterns) of the actors are likely to produce new functions (defined as the results of actions, which may bring unintended consequences). Purposes and functions may transform the international system by (1) producing a form of learning that enhances the original purposes of the actors and thus leads to integration; and (2) results in a learning experience that contributes to a reevaluation of purposes and thus disintegration.[49]

In collaboration with Philippe Schmitter, Haas has set forth three sets of variables "which seem to intervene more or less consistently between the act of economic union and the possible end product we label political union." [50] The first set, the "background variables," include the size of member-units, the extent of social pluralism within the units, elite complementarity, and

48. Ernst B. Haas, "International Integration: The European and the Universal Process," *International Organization,* XV (Autumn, 1961), 372.

49. Haas, *Beyond the Nation-State* p. 81. According to Haas: "The major and perhaps the sole justification for using systems theory in the discussion of international politics is its ability to link the will of governments with the shape of the world to come. It is policy that produces the 'system,' though the system then goes on to constrain future policy or dictate its limits." Ernst B. Haas, *The Web of Interdependence: The United States and International Organizations* (Englewood Cliffs, N.J.: Prentice-Hall, 1970), p. 106; and by the same author, *Tangle of Hopes: American Commitments and World Order* (Englewood Cliffs, N.J.: Prentice-Hall, 1969), pp. 10–12.

50. Haas and Schmitter, *op. cit.,* p. 266.

transaction rates among units. The second set consists of "variables" at the moment of economic union, such as the powers delegated to the union and the level of shared government purposes. The third set is termed process variables. Included are decision-making style, rates of transactions after integration, and the ability of governments to adapt in response to crisis. According to Haas and Schmitter, the higher the scores for each variable, the more likely it is that economic union will "spill-over" into political integration.[51] Moreover, economic issues in a democratic, pluralist, industrial setting are most likely to spill-over into political integration. Thus Haas has focused much of his investigation upon the international region which most fully meets these criteria, namely, Western Europe, although he has sought to find "functional equivalents" in Latin America for phenomena isolated in a European context.

In this work Haas found again that the growth of "legitimate and authoritative international tasks" was related to a "high degree of functional specificity: the task must relate to directly experienced needs and demands of important national elites." Some functionally specific issues, such as human rights, Haas found, are more likely to lead to spill-over than others, such as trade union issues. "An over concentration on trade union issues would seriously delay the growth of a genuine functional law of human rights because once trade union demands have been established and ratified, there is little left to spill over from mundane contract negotiation to civil liberties. Integration in the field of human rights requires an enlargement of the functionally specific realm to comprehend more and varied aspects of freedom. . . ."[52] In yet another way Haas acknowledged that there is no automaticity about "spill-over." Instead, "spill-over" will occur only if "actors, on the basis of their interest-inspired perception, *desire* to adapt integrative lessons learned in one context to a new situation."[53] The integration experience of Western Europe in the 1960s led Haas to modify further the "spill-over" concept.

POLITICAL LEADERSHIP: IMPLICATIONS FOR SECTOR INTEGRATION

Examining the European integration movement in the 1960s Haas concludes that there was some "spill-over." The progress of the Common Market in achieving such objectives as a common external tariff, uniform rules of competition, a freer market for foreign labor, and a Community agricultural policy have "come close to voiding the power of the national state in all realms other than defense, education and foreign policy."[54] Although major decisions are made by the EEC Council of Ministers, which represents the member governments, the agreements reached have usually resulted in "in-

51. *Ibid.,* p. 274.
52. Haas, *Beyond the Nation-State* p. 409.
53. *Ibid.,* p. 48.

54. Ernst B. Haas, "The 'Uniting of Europe' and the Uniting of Latin America," *Journal of Common Market Studies,* V (June, 1967), 324.

Contending Theories of International Relations

creased powers for the Commission to make possible the implementation of what was decided."

Despite these developments, Haas concluded that the "phenomenon of de Gaulle" was missing from his earlier integration framework. Events of the 1960s showed that "pragmatic interest politics concerned with economic welfare has its own built-in limits." This earlier work, it will be recalled, emphasized the development of expectations of gain among elites in the units to be integrated. The integrative experience of Western Europe after 1957 led Haas to conclude that interest based upon pragmatic considerations—e.g., expectations of economic gain—is "ephemeral," since it is not "reinforced with deep ideological or philosophical commitment." A political process which is "built and projected from pragmatic interests, therefore, is bound to be a frail process, susceptible to reversal." If it proves possible to satisfy pragmatically based expectations with modest advances in integration, support for dramatic integrative steps will be lacking. Herein, Haas admits, lies one of the important limitations of pragmatically based expectations of gain.

In addition, Haas contends that a shared political commitment between major elites and governmental leaders is needed if integration is to move forward smoothly.

> This is precisely the condition that, in a pluralistic setting, cannot be expected to occur very often. Otherwise, integration can go forward gradually and haltingly if both leaders and major elites share an incremental commitment to modest aims and pragmatic steps. The difficulty arises when the consensus between statesmen and major non-governmental elites is more elusive and temporary incremental commitment to economic aims among the leaders will not lead to smooth integration if the major elites are committed to dramatic political steps. More commonly, a political commitment to integration by the statesman will rest on very shaky ground if the interests of the major elites are economic. They rest on an even weaker basis if the statesman's commitment is to national grandeur and the elites' to economic gradualism, as in the case of contemporary France.[55]

Haas contends that "the functional logic which leads from national frustration to economic unity, and eventually to political unification, presupposes that national consciousness is weak and that the national situation is perceived as gloomy. To be sure, the situation may improve. If integration has gone very far by then, no harm is done to the union; but in Europe it had not gone far enough before the national situation improved once more, before self-confidence rose, thus making the political healing power of unions once

---

55. *Ibid.*, p. 329. But the opposite may be argued, namely that pragmatically-based integration in the so-called technical areas is the most enduring, not the most ephemeral, form of integration. The most technical functions, such as telecommunications and postal service, were the first to achieve integration without "spill-over" into other fields. See James A. Caporoso, *Functionalism, Spill-Over, and International Integration.* Doctoral Dissertation in Political Science, University of Pennsylvania, 1968.

more questionable." [56] In such a situation the strong political leader becomes crucial, for he can either press forward the integration process or offer rewards at the national level which satisfy pragmatically inspired proponents of integration and thus weaken the integration movement.

In sum, although Haas has developed an integration framework which embodies features of systems theory and functionalism, he has sought to point up some of the major limitations as well as the potential utility of functionalism in explaining integration at the international level. Therefore, in addition to his own work in the study of international organizations and integration, Haas has provided a critique and elaboration of functionalism.

Delineating International Regions: A Quantitative Analysis

In an effort to develop empirical evidence about factors which aid or hinder the process of integration, Bruce M. Russett poses the following questions:

(1) How many groups ("regions") are necessary for an adequate summary description of the similarities and differences among types of national political and social systems? (2) What countries are to be found in each group? (3) How do these groups compare with the groupings, including the area groupings we call regions, now in use by social scientists? (4) What are the discriminating variables for distinguishing groups in general, and in distinguishing between specific groups? (5) What is the relevance of our groupings to theories of comparative and international politics? [57]

In a quest for tentative answers to such questions, Russett focuses attention on regions of social and cultural homogeneity, on regions of states which share similar political attitudes or external behavior as identified by the voting patterns of governments in the United Nations, on regions of political interdependence where countries are joined together by a network of supranational or intergovernmental political institutions, on regions of economic interdependence as identified by intraregional trade as a proportion of a nation's national income, and on regions of geographical proximity. Such analysis may make possible the identification of those areas of the world where the potential for further integration is great as well as areas with little prospect for further integration.

Russett uses factor analysis to delineate regional groupings. He fac-

56. Haas, "The 'Uniting of Europe' and the Uniting of Latin America," *op. cit.,* 331. A study by Karl Deutsch and others led similarly to the conclusion that de Gaulle, although he did not reverse the integrative process in the European Community, did bring it to a halt. *France, Germany and the Western Alliance* (New York: Charles Scribner's Sons, 1967), p. 223.

57. Bruce M. Russett, *International Regions and the International System: A Study in Political Ecology* (Chicago: Rand McNally and Company, 1967), pp. 7–8.

tor analyzes fifty-four social and cultural variables on eighty-two countries. Included are such variables as GNP per capita, primary and secondary school pupils as a percentage of population, percentage of adult literacy, foreign mail per capita, infant mortality rate, different religious groups as a percentage of population, and rates of population increase. Using factor analysis, Russett reduced the fifty-four separate variables to four dimensions or factors. In other words, he produced four clusters from the fifty-four separate variables. The factors, or dimensions or clusters he termed as follows: (1) economic development; (2) communism; (3) Catholic culture; (4) intensive agriculture. For example, the first factor, economic development, was so labelled because Russett found that many variables loaded heavily on it, that is, were highly correlated with it. These included per capita GNP, newspapers, and radios per capita, life expectancy, pupils in primary and secondary schools, hospital beds and physicians per capita. After following a similar procedure to derive the other four factors, Russett grouped countries in accordance with the extent to which they resembled each other over a variety of variables. He grouped countries which loaded most heavily on each factor and gave them regional names. Thus a grouping called "Afro-Asia" loaded heavily on Factor One, economic development. Countries in this region resembled each other in levels of economic development. A grouping called "Western Community" loaded highly on a factor which included such variables as governmental expenditure and revenue, total voting turnout, rate in increase of GNP per capita. The "Western Community" consisted of Atlantic nations, as well as New Zealand, Argentina, Japan, Israel, and Trinidad and Tobago. A grouping called "Latin America" but which includes the Philippines, as well as another grouping termed "semideveloped Latins," loaded heavily on the factor called "Catholic Culture." In this factor were such variables as Christians as a percentage of population, votes for socialist parties, speakers of the dominant language, and land inequality. A grouping designated "Eastern Europe" loaded heavily on a factor called "intensive agriculture." This factor included such variables as overall population density and population density as related to farming land. For each of the regions delineated, it is possible to provide the mean and standard deviation for each set of factor scores. The smaller the standard deviation, the greater the homogeneity of the regional grouping for that factor. Thus the Afro-Asian group has the following profile: very underdeveloped, moderately noncommunist, non-Catholic in culture, and population densities and agricultural patterns which vary widely. The "Western Community" grouping contains states that vary greatly in the intensive agriculture and Catholic culture factors but have generally low scores on the communism factor, and a high level of economic development. In the "Eastern European" grouping communism is the "most sharply discriminating dimension," with moderate levels of economic development and a low level of Catholic culture.[58] Some of Russett's

58. *Ibid.*, pp. 30–34.

conclusions concerning regional groupings might appear obvious to the reader, but there may be some utility in the compilation of statistical evidence to demonstrate the validity of the "conventional wisdom" of scholars in respect to the characteristics of regions.

In other analyses, Russett discovered that in United Nations voting, most of the groups voting together are not defined solely by geographical location, e.g., the Brazzaville group included, in fact, non-African underdeveloped states which tend to be pro-Western on cold war issues. However, factor analysis revealed a strong correlation between membership in an international organization and the geographical location of a state. Proximity may contribute to common interest in the solution of problems which cannot be solved at the national level. He found that both membership in international organizations and voting patterns were stable.

Russett considers trading patterns as but one indicator of political integration. Indeed, countries which are interdependent economically, as in the case of a metropolitan power and its colony, may be highly differentiated on the sociocultural dimension. He contends that only "under conditions of relatively equal impact in the two countries concerned" can one consider trade to induce mutual responsiveness. Most important is the degree of *interdependence* not simply dependence. The measure of trade must be tied not to an index of relative acceptance but rather to the ratio of trade between the two countries to national income or GNP.

A factor analysis of trade among states reveals that although geography exercises a powerful influence on trade, the role of proximity can be exaggerated. Nearly half the countries examined are joined to one or more clusters not identified primarily with their geographic neighbors. Both political orientation and culture have major effects on commercial choice. Nor is trade simply the product of a division of labor between industrial and primary-producing nations. Many of the world's trade groupings are composed overwhelmingly of either developed or underdeveloped nations.

In discussing integration, Russett does not limit his definition of integration to the presence or absence of violence. He suggests that states be considered more integrated the higher the ratio of capabilities to loads or burdens in their relationship. Responsiveness is the behavioral consequence of that ratio, and in turn the responsiveness of states to one another can be defined as the probability that the requests or demands of one will be met favorably. He concludes that a reexamination of theories of international conflict and of international integration must begin with the understanding that war has not necessarily been eliminated within the groupings delineated by the variables examined in this study. Russett suggests that his clusters alone do not tell us where integration has been or will be achieved. They tell us only that for countries within a grouping the prospects for integration are greater than between a typical country within the group and one outside of it. Physical space or geography may be less crucial than social space or sociocultural considerations to the integration of political communities.

Alliance Cohesion

Both at the international level and domestic level, groups are formed to enable their members to achieve a shared objective. Since such groups are disbanded when the objective for which they were created has been achieved, they are far less enduring than the political communities whose formation and structure are of concern to writers whose work has been discussed earlier in this chapter. Because of the historic importance of alliances in the international system, and the widespread use of coalitions by political groups intent upon attaining elective office, such collaborative efforts have been the object of scholarly investigation especially by the political realists examined in Chapter 3, but also by writers concerned more specifically with the dynamics and operation of alliances.

Two scholars in particular, George F. Liska, professor of political science at Johns Hopkins University, and William Riker, professor of political science at the University of Rochester, have developed theories of alliance behavior. In their theoretical frameworks, Liska and Riker are similar in several respects. First, they agree that alliances or coalitions disband once they have achieved their objective, because they are formed essentially "against, and only derivatively for, someone or something." [59] Although a "sense of community" may reinforce alliances or coalitions, it seldom brings them into existence. In forming alliances to achieve some desired objective, decision-makers weigh the costs and rewards of alignment. A decision to join an alliance is based upon perception of rewards in excess of costs. Each country considers the marginal utility from alliance membership, as contrasted with unilateral action. Ultimately, the cohesiveness of an alliance "rests on the relationship between internal and external pressures, bearing on the ratio of gains to liabilities for individual allies." [60] Once costs exceed rewards, the decision to realign is taken. According to Liska, nations join alliances for security, stability and

59. George F. Liska, *Nations in Alliance: The Limits of Interdependence* (Baltimore: Johns Hopkins Press, 1962), p. 12. William H. Riker, *The Theory of Political Coalitions* (New Haven: Yale University Press, 1962), pp. 32–76. See also Bruce M. Russett, "Components of an Operational Theory of International Alliance Formation," *Journal of Conflict Resolution,* XII (September, 1968), 285–

301. For a selection of essays from the literature on alliances, see Julian R. Friedman, Christopher Bladen, and Steven Rosen, eds., *Alliance in International Politics* (Boston: Allyn and Bacon, 1970); Francis A. Beer, ed., *Alliances: Latent War Communities in the Contemporary World* (New York: Holt, Rinehart and Winston, 1970).

60. Liska, *op. cit.,* p. 175.

status. In Liska's theory a primary prerequisite for alliance cohesion is the development of an "alliance ideology." The function of alliance ideology is to provide a rationalization for alliance. In performing this function, ideology "feeds on selective memory of the past and outlines a program for the future." [61] Periodic consultation, especially between a leading member and its allies, both on procedural and substantive issues, contributes to the development and preservation of alliance ideology and thus alliance cohesion.

After victory, the size of the alliance or coalition must be reduced if additional gains are to accrue to the remaining participants. Second, alliances or coalitions are crucial to the attainment of a balance of power. In Riker's framework, the formation of one coalition contributes to the formation of an opposing coalition. When one coalition is on the verge of victory, neutral actors often join the weaker of the coalitions to prevent the stronger from attaining hegemony. If neutral members do not align themselves with the weaker side, some members of the leading coalition must shift to the weaker of the two coalitions if the system is to regain equilibrium. Equilibrium is the likely result of the existence of two "quasipermanent blocking coalitions," or the presence of such coalitions that "play the role of balancer if a temporary winning coalition sets the stakes too high." [62] In establishing his rules for equilibrium Riker draws upon rules set by Kaplan in his balance of power system.[63] Moreover, in relating alliances or coalitions to balance of power, Liska and Riker incorporate into their theories ideas found in realist international relations theory.

THE OPTIMUM SIZE OF ALLIANCES

Liska and Riker suggest that alliance builders, if they act "economically," do not form alliances haphazardly with all available allies. Instead, Liska considers the "marginal utility of the last unit of commitment to a particular ally and the last unit of cost in implementing commitments." [64] Riker stresses

61. *Ibid.*, p. 61.

62. *Op. cit.*, p. 188. For another application of Riker's framework, see Martin Southwold, "Riker's Theory and the Analysis of Coalitions in Precolonial Africa," Sven Groennings, E. W. Kelley, and Michael Leiserson, eds., *The Study of Coalition Behavior: Theoretical Perspectives and Cases from Four Continents* (New York: Holt, Rinehart and Winston, 1970), pp. 336–350. For an effort to relate Riker's framework to balance of power literature, see Dina A. Zinnes, "Coalition Theories and the Balance of Power," in the same volume, pp. 351–368.

63. For an examination of Kaplan's rules for the balance of power system see Chapter 4.

64. Liska, *Nations in Alliance,* p. 27. In recent years writers on alliances have borrowed terminology and models from economics. For a selection of economics writings on national choice, market structure, collective bargaining, the pursuit of benefits, and criteria for inclusion, see Bruce M. Russett, ed., *Economic Theories of International Politics* (Chicago: Markham Publishing Company, 1968).

the "size principle," according to which participants create coalitions adequate to union and no larger than necessary to achieve their commonly shared objective. If actors have perfect information, they will create a coalition of exactly the minimum size needed to win. Without complete information, members of a winning coalition create a larger coalition than necessary to achieve their objectives. The less complete the information, the larger the coalition. This fact, which Riker observes both at national and international levels, contributes to the short life-span of alliances or coalitions.

Liska and Riker address themselves to the question of rewards from joining an alliance or coalition. According to Liska, the gains and liabilities associated with alignment can be grouped into pairs. For example, the pair peculiar to security is protection and provocation—"the first to be derived from a particular alliance and the second producing counter-action and counter alliance." Burdens and gains, as well as potential for status enhancement and possible losses in capacity for independent action, must be balanced. Liska contends that "in order to assess a particular alignment all these factors must be compared with hypothetical gains and liabilities of other alignments, with non-alignment, or at least with a different implementation of an unavoidable alliance." [65] In Riker's theory, actors join alliances or coalitions for several reasons: the threat of reprisal if they refuse to align themselves; to receive payments of one kind or another; to obtain promises about policy or about subsequent decisions; or to gain emotional satisfaction.

ALLIANCE COHESION AND DISINTEGRATION

In the building of theory about alliance behavior, Liska employs historical data, while Riker uses game theory and a mathematical model of coalitions which he then applies to historical data at both the international and American national levels. Both theories give an important place to instability as characteristic of alliance systems. According to Liska, a common factor leading to the disintegration of alliance systems is the conclusion of a separate peace by an ally in war. To induce a member of an opposing alliance to make a separate peace is a major strategic concern of political actors. For both dealignment and realignment, "the basic techniques are coercion, enticement, or combination of the two, unless force alone suffices to compel a separate peace which is tantamount to unconditional surrender. To force defection by means short of the enemy's destruction, pressure has to be applied at the militarily or psychologically weakest part of the adversary alliance." [66]

In Riker's theory, there are two necessary conditions for disequilibrium in alliances or coalitions: (1) a change in the weight of participants, or (2) a willingness on the part of the winner to set high stakes. There is, in Riker's scheme, a "disequilibrium principle" which derives from his "size principle."

65. *Ibid.*, p. 30.   66. *Ibid.*, p. 43.

In bodies where the size principle is operative, participants tend to remove from the coalition those actors deemed unessential for attaining the goals of the coalition. This factor contributes to the instability of coalitions.

Despite the existence of many important differences, one or the other theories of alliance behavior have certain features in common with theories of integration. Riker emphasizes the importance of communications among actors in the formation of coalitions of optimal size. The absence of adequate communications among members contributes to the formation of coalitions larger than needed to achieve their initial objective. In the theory of integration advanced by Deutsch and Etzioni importance is attached to communications within the unit to be integrated. In Deutsch's theory, moreover, the existence of core areas is crucial to the formation of "amalgamated security communities." Liska suggests that the cohesiveness of alliances is related to the existence of a "core power." As in Haas' earlier formulations, pragmatic interests play a major role in leading nations to align themselves. The fact that such interests do not endure contributes to the disintegration of alliances, as well as the ephemeral nature of support for integration which Haas noted in his more recent work.

The roles and claims of alliance members change with alterations in their respective national capabilities. An increase in the strength of the core power is likely to contribute to alliance cohesion and efficacy. Like the French strategist Pierre Gallois,[67] Liska contends that nuclear weapons have increased the vulnerability of core powers to attack and thus contributed to the decline in alliance cohesion.

In addition, Liska has addressed himself to the concept of equilibrium in an international context.[68] Drawing upon "the idea of the economic firm in equilibrium," Liska examines equilibrium in international organization as illustrative of the more general application of this concept to international politics. Liska specified several conditions for "structural equilibrium" in international organizations:

> *A composite organization is in structural equilibrium if there is an overall correspondence between the margins of restraints it imposes on members and their willingness to tolerate them; if the ratios between the influence exercised by individual members and their actual power are not too unequal; and if the respective powers of the different organs correspond to the composition of their membership. . . . More important than structure is the commitment of states participating in an international organization—in our case mainly that for*

67. Pierre Gallois, *The Balance of Terror* (Boston: Houghton Mifflin Company, 1961), Chapter 1.

68. George Liska, *International Equilibrium: A Theoretical Essay on the Politics and Organization of Security* (Cambridge: Harvard University Press, 1957). Liska uses the concept of equilibrium in two ways: as a "theoretical norm or point of reference," and as "denoting an actual tendency toward changing states of temporary equilibrium in political institutions," p. 13.

mutual assistance against threats to security. What matters is that the actual readiness and obligation results in pressure on the commitment toward its reduction, decentralization, or evasion, which tends to be cumulative. And, lastly, an international organization is in equilibrium with respect to its functional scope when the functions and jurisdiction which it actually exercises correspond to the extent of the needs relevant to its purpose. Depending on the adequacy of the area covered by the organization, its geographic scope can be analyzed in analogous terms.[69]

Basic to structural equilibrium is the inclusion in the organization of powerful states which can affect its purpose.

In Liska's theory, equilibrium in the international system has similar features. Like domestic politics, international politics consists essentially of efforts to "control the oscillations of a dynamic balance." According to Liska, "a workable organization on national, regional, or global scale requires that institutional, military-political, and socioeconomic factors and pressures for and against stability be deliberately equilibrated." Therefore, international organization is part of a "dynamic interplay of institutional, military-political, and socioeconomic factors and pressures, constituting a *multiple equilibrium.*"

Integration Theory: Problems of Conceptualization and Definition

Although the theorists examined in this chapter have suggested a series of indicators for assessing the level of integration, theory is not sufficiently advanced that there exists either a commonly accepted definition of integration or general agreement on the relevant indicators of integration. Given the fact, as Joseph S. Nye, Jr., of Harvard University, has pointed out, that dynamic or causal models have preceded static or measurement models, it is not surprising to find different authors defining integration differently and each developing his own set of indicators.[70] Some writers, as we have seen, emphasize transaction flows such as trade, travel, mail, telephone, radio and other forms of technical communication, as indicators of integration. In examining transactions flow, or communications, Haas suggests that the question remains whether a rise in transactions precedes, reinforces, results from, or causes integration. According to Haas, the question of *when* these conditions are expected is vital when we try to devise a rigorous theoretical framework to explain the causes of integration. Especially in the case of indicators based on

69. *Ibid.,* pp. 13–14.

70. Joseph S. Nye, Jr., "Comparative Regional Integration: Concept and Measurement," *International Organization* XXII (Autumn, 1968), 857. For a collection of contemporary writings on integration at the international level, see, by the same author, *International Regionalism: Readings* (Boston: Little, Brown and Company, 1968).

social communication we must know whether the transactions measure among the elites to be integrated preceded the integrative process or whether they are a result of events which characterize the region after integration has occurred for several years. In the latter case, we have merely defined an existing community in terms of communications theory, but we have not explored the necessary steps for arriving there.[71]

INDICATORS OF INTEGRATION

In the mid-1960s Deutsch, using transaction flows as one of his indicators to assess the level of European integration, concluded that "European integration has slowed since the mid-1950s and it has stopped or reached a plateau since 1957–58." In part, he based this conclusion on the fact that since then there had been no increases in transactions flow "beyond what one would expect from mere random probability and increase in prosperity in the countries concerned." [72] In support of his conclusion Deutsch marshalls other evidence, including elite interviews and content analysis of selected key newspapers in France and Germany. Thus, in addition to transactions flow, statistical analysis of opinions expressed by elites and attention accorded in the press form indicators of integration.

Other scholars employing in some cases different indicators, and in other instances similar ones, have reached conclusions about the status of European integration which are diametrically opposed to Deutsch's. For example, if integration is defined as Leon Lindberg conceives it, namely, as "the process whereby nations forgo the desire and ability to conduct foreign and key domestic policies independently of each other, seeking instead to make joint decisions or to delegate the decision-making process to a new central organ," it is possible to reach conclusions different from Deutsch's. Using such a definition in an examination of the EEC during the five-year period after its formation in 1958, Lindberg notes substantial progress toward European integration.[73]

Another study, using different attitudinal data, concluded that, European

71. Ernst B. Haas, "The Challenge of Regionalism," *International Organization,* XII (Autumn, 1958), 445.

72. Karl W. Deutsch, *France, Germany and the Western Alliance* (New York: Charles Scribner's Sons, 1967), pp. 218–220. Deutsch bases his findings on the Relative Acceptance Index, which purports to separate "the actual results of preferential behavior and structural integration from the mere effects of the size and prosperity of the country."

73. According to Lindberg "Significant national powers have been thrust into a new institutional setting in which powerful pressures are exerted for Community solutions: that is, solutions which approximate the up-grading-of-common interests type. Our case studies have revealed that important and divergent national interests have been consistently accommodated in order to achieve a decision." Moreover, since the founding of the EEC, there has been a shift in political activities and expectations—another part of Lindberg's definition of integration: "This has been most striking at the level of high policy-makers and civil servants, for the EEC policy

ntegration, far from having halted after 1958, may have moved, in some
espects, into full gear only since then.[74] Professor Ronald Inglehart of the
everal schools considered to be representative of important social and economic groups in Britain, France, the Netherlands and Germany. In a self-
administered questionnaire in 1964–65, incorporating questions from previous
adult surveys, he concluded that a majority—transcending all differences of
University of Michigan, bases his findings upon a sample of youths from
social class, sex, and religion—were overwhelmingly favorable to European
unification; that although there was substantial reluctance among adults,
especially in France, the younger generation strongly encouraged it.[75] His
assumption attributes the differing attitudes among age groups to the fact that
the adults in the sample received their basic political orientation during
nationalist periods and that these attitudes are not easily changed. The youth
in the sample received their political orientation when nationalism was less in
favor. Given the stability of such attitudes, it is possible to project from these
data and anticipate that the current generation of youth in these countries
will manifest a relatively "European" outlook when they become adults because
this accords with conditions existing at that point in time when their basic
political orientations were instilled.

Using other indicators, Professor Carl J. Friedrich of Harvard University
concludes that Western Europe has become more integrated since 1957, the
year of the signing of the Rome Treaty for the creation of the Common
Market.[76] Criticizing Deutsch's contention, and his indicators, that integration
has slowed, Friedrich examines the development of sentiment and contacts
at the European level in business, agriculture, the trade union movement,
and the academic community. In each of these areas he finds a marked increase
in contacts across frontiers and support among such groups for European
integration. Moreover, Friedrich criticizes Deutsch and his associates both
for their choice of indicators and their use of statistical data in supporting their
conclusions.[77]

Other writers have suggested still other indicators of integration. Professor
Claude Ake of Columbia University, for example, has proposed the develop-

making process, by its very nature, engages an over-expanding circle of national officials." Leon N. Lindberg, *The Political Dynamics of European Economic Integration* (Stanford: Stanford University Press, 1963), pp. 6, 286–288. See also Leon N. Lindberg and Stuart A. Scheingold, *Europe's Would-Be Polity: Patterns of Change in the European Community* (Englewood Cliffs, N.J.: Prentice-Hall, 1970), pp. 24–100.

74. Ronald Inglehart, "An End to European Integration," *American Political Science Review,* LXI (March, 1967), 91. For a study of continuity and change in foreign policy attitudes, see Neal E. Cut-

ler, "Generational Succession as a Source of Foreign Policy Attitudes: A Cohort Analysis of American Opinion, 1946–1966," *Journal of Peace Research,* VII (1970), 33–47; by the same author, but not related specifically to foreign policy, "Generation, Maturation, and Party Affiliation: A Cohort Analysis," *Public Opinion Quarterly,* XXXIII (Winter, 1969–70), 583–588.

75. Inglehart, *op. cit.,* p. 92.

76. Carl J. Friedrich, *Europe: An Emergent Nation?* (New York: Harper and Row, 1969), especially pp. 196–215.

77. *Ibid.,* pp. 35–46.

ment of quantitative indicators, including: (1) the legitimacy score or the extent to which citizens give loyalty to the state and see it as the embodiment of their interest; (2) the extraconstitutional behavioral score or the frequency distribution of the preference of political actors between constitutional and extraconstitutional behavior; (3) the political violence score or the extent to which actors resort to violence to attain objectives; (4) the secessionist demand score; (5) the alignment pattern score or the extent to which major groups competing for power draw their support from more than one geographical area and ethnic, religious, social and economic groups; (6) bureaucratic ethos score or the extent to which the members of a political system are prepared to give their loyalty to their political unit and its office-holders in spite of personal feelings about them; and (7) the authority score, or the degree to which the people accept their political unit as legitimate and are prepared to accept its rule without coercion.[78]

Professor Philip E. Jacob suggests ten "integrative factors" which might contribute to the development of more reliable indicators. These factors include: (1) proximity, based on the hypothesis that the closer people live geographically, the greater the prospects for integration; (2) homogeneity, with the hypothesis that communities whose members are similar to each other are more likely than those whose members are different to become integrated; (3) transactions, with the hypothesis that cohesiveness can be measured by the volume of transactions among individuals and groups; (4) mutual knowledge or cognitive proximity, with the hypothesis that essential to integration is mutual knowledge or understanding; (5) functional interest, with the hypothesis that essential to integration is the extent to which the dominant functional interests are broadly shared in each of the communities and thus stand to be advanced by the integration of the communities; (6) communal "character" or social "motive," with the hypothesis that communities characterized by a high "affiliation" motive are most likely to develop integrative behavior; (7) structural frame, with the hypothesis that political structures that permit broad participation in decision-making are more cohesive than those which permit little such participation; (8) sovereignty-dependency status, with the proposition that the more sovereign the political unit, the less disposed will it be to integration; (9) governmental effectiveness, or the hypothesis that the more effective the government of a political community in meeting popular demands and expectations, the more integrated it will be; and (10) previous integrative experience, with the proposition, similar to Haas' "spill-over," that previous integrative experience is conducive to further steps toward integration.[79]

Finally, the definition of community found in the works of Deutsch and Haas has been the object of criticism. According to Haas and Deutsch, there is either an absence of, or minimal resort to, violence in the resolution of con-

---

78. Claude Ake, *A Theory of Political Integration* (Homewood, Ill.: Dorsey Press, 1967), pp. 8–11.

79. Jacob and Toscano, eds., *op. cit.,* pp. 16–44.

Contending Theories of International Relations

flict in an integrated community. Herbert Spiro suggests that such a focus leads to a preoccupation with questions of "obedience" which seems obsolescent.[80] His notion of community "requires as a minimum only awareness of the pursuit of common goals, and of members' inability to solve alone the problems arising out of these goals." Thus, there may be "a community between the parties to a civil or international war, as indeed between the contestants in the current Cold War, e.g., with regard to the goal of the survival of mankind." [81]

INTERNATIONAL SYSTEMIC FACTORS AND INTEGRATION

Integration theorists have been criticized for having given insufficient emphasis to factors in the international environment which affect the integration process. Hoffmann, for example, argues that the apparent failure of spill-over in Western Europe may be attributed at least in part to two variables, namely, the diversity of the national units and the bipolar international system of the postwar period. The success of the Common Market in achieving economic growth has strengthened the capacity of national units for national action. Changes in the international environment have affected West European national outlooks toward integration. While the Benelux countries were prepared to rely almost exclusively upon the United States for defense, France sought to accelerate tendencies in the international system toward multipolarity. France's ambivalence toward European integration reflected the attitude that "integration is good if it leads to an entity that will emancipate Europe from any bipolar system, bad if it does not and merely chains France to German national desiderata." [82] In European integration Germany found a device for regaining a place of respectability among the Western nations as well as an outlet for national energies. Britain's outlook toward European integration was strongly influenced by British global perspectives of foreign policy. In short, Hoffmann contends, relations among West European nations have been "subordinated to their divergences about the outside world;" the "regional subsystem becomes a stake in the rivalry of its members about the system as a whole." [83] Beyond Hoffmann's analysis, it is possible to adduce additional

80. Herbert J. Spiro, "Comprehensive Politics: A Comprehensive Approach," *American Political Science Review,* LVI (September, 1962), 589.

81. *Ibid.*

82. Stanley Hoffmann, *Gulliver's Troubles, or the Setting of American Foreign Policy* (New York: McGraw-Hill Book Company, 1968), p. 401. At various times European and American analysts have speculated on the feasibility of a European nuclear deterrent, which presumably would reduce the bipolarity of the international system. See, for example, Henry A. Kissinger, *The Necessity for Choice* (Garden City, N.Y.: Doubleday and Company, 1962), pp. 129–131; Robert Strausz-Hupé, James E. Dougherty, and William R. Kintner, *Building the Atlantic World* (New York: Harper and Row, 1962), Chapter 5. For an analysis of European elite attitudes toward a European nuclear force, see Deutsch, *Arms Control and the Atlantic Alliance*, pp. 34, 99, 136.

83. Stanley Hoffmann, "The Fate of the Nation-State," *Daedalus,* VC (Summer, 1966), 865.

examples of variables from the international environment which appear to exert a major influence upon the integrative movement in a region such as Western Europe.

In fact, the lower the regional autonomy of a regional subsystem such as the European Community, the greater the importance of "exogenous factors," maintains a critic of Haas. The integrative experience in Western Europe, and especially those of Latin America and East Africa, "reflect a dynamic inter-action between an internal regional dialectic, analyzed by present theory, and changing international environmental pressures relatively unexplored in current neofunctionalist literature." [84]

Research on integration has been criticized not only on the basis of the variables and indicators chosen for examination, but also for the lack of an appropriate theoretical framework. In particular, such criticism has been directed toward research, such as that undertaken by Russett, which relies heavily upon factor analysis in the development of inductive theory.[85] In the absence of a deductive theoretical framework, Young argues, empirical investigation is not likely to provide an adequate basis for predictive theory, to take account of intervening variables, or offer adequate explanation of relationships among variables. Such a discussion reflects the disagreement among scholars about the nature of theory noted in Chapter 1.

LIMITATIONS OF FUNCTIONALISM

Functionalism itself has been the object of several kinds of criticism: (1) that it is difficult, if not impossible, to separate the economic and social tasks from the political; (2) that governments have shown themselves unwilling to hand over to international authority tasks which encroach upon the political; (3) that certain economic and social tasks do not "ramify" or "spill-over" into the political sector; (4) that the road to political integration lies through political "acts of will" rather than functional integration in economic and social sectors. Research conducted thus far has not produced agreement among students of integration about "spill-over," or about the catalysts which initiate and sustain the integrative process. There is no widely accepted deductive model about integration in which definitions and conditions for integration as well as processual steps and transformation rules are set forth. To a con-

84. Roger D. Hansen, "Regional Integration: Reflections on a Decade of Theoretical Efforts." *World Politics,* XXI (January, 1969), 270. For another review and critique of the Haas-Schmitter work, see J. S. Nye, Jr., "Patterns and Catalysts in Regional Integration," *International Organization,* XIX (Autumn, 1965), 870–884.

85. Oran R. Young, "Professor Russett: Industrious Tailor to a Naked Emperor," *World Politics,* XXI (April, 1969), 486–511. For Russett's reply, see "The Young Science of International Politics," *World Politics,* XXII (October, 1969), 87–94.

siderable extent, the disagreement about functionalism may be reduced to a debate between the proponents and opponents, respectively, of the coercion and consensus theories of community discussed earlier in this chapter.

The Development of Integration Theory

What is needed is a model which incorporates propositions from neofunctionalist literature as well as writings which give greater importance to the role of coercion and the impact of the international environment upon integration. Current integration models may be faulted for their relative neglect of the role of conflict as an integrating force. Students of postwar Europe agree, in general, that the experience of World War II was important, if not crucial, as a catalyst in the postwar European integration movement. Yet the phenomenon of conflict—perhaps like the "phenomenon of de Gaulle" in Haas' critique of *his* earlier works—is missing from models of integration, even when they are applied to the postwar European experience. Except perhaps as a result of normative biases of students of integration, it is difficult to understand the reason for this oversight, since both traditional and contemporary writers in the field of conflict have examined in considerable depth the integrative role of conflict. Moreover, the integrative impetus of postwar Europe was based largely upon disillusionment with the nation-state as a result of World War II. Thus, even in the European context, conflict may have played an integrative role which is given less prominent consideration than it deserves in the integration literature on Europe.

There is need, as Nye has suggested, for integration as a concept to be broken down into economic, political, and social components; these components, in turn, might be divided into subtypes, each of which could be measured. "Rather than allowing us to talk about integration in general and confusing terms, this disaggregation will tend to force us to make more qualified, and more readily falsified, generalizations with the *ceteris paribus* clauses filled in, so to speak, and thus pave the way for more meaningful comparative analysis than that provided by the general schemes used so far." [86] In sum, major conceptual problems, as well as disagreement about definitions, variables, and indicators, remain, despite the contributions of scholars, especially during the past generation, to theoretical knowledge about integration at the international level.

86. Joseph S. Nye, Jr., "Comparative Regional Integration: Concept and Measurement," *op. cit.*, 858.

CHAPTER 11
Decision-Making Theories

Decision-Making Analysis: Its Nature and Origins

Since World War II interest has increased in *decisions* as a central element in the political process and as a focal point for study by social scientists. Decisions are, in David Easton's terminology, the "outputs" of the political system, by which values are authoritatively allocated within a society. The concept of decision-making had long been at least vaguely implicit in some of the older descriptive approaches to diplomatic history and the activities of governmental institutions. But the process of decision-making was first made the subject of systematic investigation in other disciplinary fields outside of political science. Psychologists were interested in the motives underlying an individual's decisions and why some individuals had greater difficulty than others in making decisions. Economists focused their attention on the decisions of consumers, producers, investors and others whose choices affected the economy. Students of business administration sought to increase the efficiency of the executive's decision-making organization. The concept was later taken over by political scientists interested in analyzing the decisional behavior of voters, legislators, executive officials, politicians, leaders of interest groups and other actors in the political arena.[1] The study of foreign policy decision-making, with which we are primarily concerned in this chapter, concentrates on one special sector of the more general political phenomenon.

Decision-making is simply the act of choosing among available alternatives, about which a certain amount of uncertainty exists. This is not to imply that in the decision-making model the policy official or unit empowered to make an authoritative choice is presented a neat set of alternatives from which to select after carefully weighing the consequences of each possible action ac-

1. See Paul Wasserman and Fred S. Silander, *Decision-Making: An Annotated Bibliography* (Ithaca, N.Y.: Graduate School of Business and Public Administration, Cornell University, 1958).

cording to a fixed utility scale. In foreign policy perhaps even more than in national politics—because the terrain of the former is usually less familiar—policy alternatives are seldom "given." They must often be gropingly formulated in the context of a total situation in which disagreements will arise over which estimate of the situation is most valid, which alternatives exist, what consequences are likely to flow from various choices, and the values which should serve as criteria for ranking the various alternatives from most preferred to least preferred. Later, we shall see that there are controversies among the theorists over the nature of the decision-making process. We can say now that the essence of the process is choice among possibilities—not an abstract or ideal choice but a practical one appropriate to the circumstances. Rarely are policymakers confronted with the absolute and inescapable necessity of a single response, with no other alternatives conceivable. As we shall examine it in this chapter, the total decision-making process involves a "before" and "after," and the theory must take adequate account of these elements.

EARLY APPROACHES TO DECISION-MAKING ANALYSIS

Thus the decision-making approach to an understanding of international politics is not novel. Twenty-four centuries ago the Greek historian Thucydides, writing *The Peloponnesian War,* was very much interested in the factors which led the leaders of various city-states to decide the issues of war and peace, alliance and empire, as precisely as they did under the circumstances confronting them. He examined not only the conscious strategic reasons for statesmen's choices and their picture of the systemic environment—both of which are reflected in the speeches which he attributes to them—but also the deeper psychological forces of fear, honor and interest which in varying combinations motivated them as individuals and set the prevailing tone of their particular societies. Thus Thucydides was indeed an early decision-making theorist.

Many other political writers—classical and modern—have given princes and policymakers substantive advice on the kinds of decisions they should make. Machiavelli provided many aphoristic recommendations for the ruler who would be successful in the pursuit, consolidation and extension of power: It is safer to be feared than loved, but make yourself feared without incurring hatred . . . Imitate the fox and the lion . . . Do not keep your pledged word when it is against your interest . . . Do not place your trust in mercenaries . . . It is wrong to remain neutral when your neighbors are at war . . . and so on.[2] In our own day, several writers on international politics have offered useful counsel to foreign policy-makers. Walter Lippmann, for example, has warned

2. Niccolò Machiavelli, *The Prince* and the *Discourses,* introduction by Max Lerner (New York: Random House [Modern Library], 1950); Herbert Butterfield, *The Statecraft of Machiavelli* (New York: Macmillan Company, 1956).

against allowing a nation's commitments to get out of balance with its power.[3] Hans Morgenthau has reminded the postwar generation of the cardinal rules of diplomatic flexibility and compromise, including these: Do not permit a weak ally to make decisions for you, and do not place yourself in a position from which you cannot move forward without incurring the risk of war.[4] While Machiavelli is often too vague or too rigid to be helpful, the conventional wisdom of such writers as Lippmann and Morgenthau has often proved valuable as a stimulant to rational reflection on the part of decision-makers and students who might one day fill a foreign policymaking role. But the older substantive theories of foreign policy, irrespective of how valuable they continue to be as intellectual guidelines, did not attempt to probe systematically into the phenomenon of decision-making as what we might call a dynamic psychopolitical process, carried on within an identifiable institutional framework. It is to the newer theoretical approaches that we must now turn.

THE ASSUMPTIONS OF MODERN APPROACHES TO DECISION-MAKING ANALYSIS

Modern decision-making theorists are not inclined to claim too much for the theory. They neither assert that it is brand new, nor that it represents an exclusively valid set of insights into the nature of international politics, nor that it embodies any startlingly explanatory theories that have been adequately tested and verified, nor that it facilitates prediction. Decision-making theories, if they are genuine theories, are such only in the sense that the concept of "theory" is broad enough to encompass conceptual frameworks. A conceptual framework is not at all like a verified hypothesis or set of verified hypotheses. It arises out of an effort to order a mass of data, but it does not depend primarily upon statistically significant correlations, nor can it be stated as an "if-then" proposition—i.e., "if such and such conditions are verifiably present, then this or that will occur (either absolutely or with a specified probability)."

When we say that decision-making theory is basically a conceptual framework, we mean that it furnishes a comprehensive and useful checklist of the factors which one ought to take into account in any attempt to analyze policymaking, either as a generalized process or as a process in a specific case. The theory serves to identify a large number of relevant variables, and it suggests interesting possible interrelationships among these variables, but it does not establish precise correlational linkages among the variables, nor does it necessarily contain hypotheses that would lead to a predictive capability concerning the kind of substantive policy which a decision-maker might choose in a given

3. Walter Lippmann, *U.S. Foreign Policy: Shield of the Republic* (Boston: Little, Brown and Company, 1943), pp. 9–10.

4. Hans J. Morgenthau, *Politics Among Nations,* 4th ed. (New York: Alfred A. Knopf, 1967), p. 545.

situation.[5] But to say this is not to vitiate the theory. The decision-making approach provides valuable insights into politics and is a helpful guide to certain types of research (one of the most important functions of theory). The study of individual decisions provides much of the basic knowledge on which the scientific analysis of politics is founded. No one should undertake a case study of a specific political decision without having acquired a familiarity with decision-making theory.

DM theory (as we shall occasionally refer to it) may be considered more appropriately as a form of micro analysis rather than macro analysis.[6] Its central focus is upon something much smaller than the whole political system, viz., upon a relatively limited and well-defined decisional unit. This marks a significant shift from traditional political analysis, in which writers on international politics have been prone to reify or personify nation-states as the basic actors within the international system. The irrepressible tendency to speak of "the Great Powers" and to say that France did this, or Egypt decided to pursue such and such a course, or that Britain and the United States consulted with each other and reached a particular agreement reflects the extent to which the language of modern politics has been cast in the mold of nationalism and influenced by the thought-molds of Hegel, for whom the nation-state was the march of God through world history. DM theory directs attention not to states as metaphysical abstractions or to governments or even to such broadly labeled institutions as "the Executive," but instead seeks to highlight the behavior of the human decision-makers who shape governmental policy:

> *It is one of our basic methodological choices to define the state as its official decision-makers—those whose authoritative acts are, to all intents and purposes, the acts of the state.* State action is the action taken by those acting in the name of the state.[7]

By narrowing the subject of investigation from the larger, abstract collectivity to a much smaller group of persons who are ultimately responsible for making policy decisions, DM theorists hope to make the locus of political analysis more concrete and more precise, and thus more amenable to the application

5. See James N. Rosenau, "The Premises and Promises of Decision-Making Analysis," James C. Charlesworth, ed., *Contemporary Political Analysis* (New York: Free Press, 1967), pp. 208–209. To call something a "check list" of relevant variables is not to demean it. Secretary of State Rusk, ruminating upon the check list used by airline pilots, once confessed that if the "No Smoking-Fasten Seat Belts" sign failed to flash on before take-off, he always nervously wondered what else had been forgotten—such as fuel or landing wheels. "The Anatomy of Foreign Policy Decisions," Address to the American Political Science Asso-

ciation, Washington, D.C., September 7, 1965, *Department of State Bulletin,* September, 1965, p. 503.

6. See the remarks of Richard C. Snyder quoted in Ithiel de Sola Pool, ed., *Contemporary Political Science: Toward Empirical Theory* (New York: McGraw-Hill Book Company, 1967), p. ix.

7. "Decision-making as an approach to the Study of International Politics," in Richard C. Snyder, H. W. Bruck, and Burton Sapin, eds., *Foreign Policy Decision-Making* (New York: Free Press of Glencoe, 1963), p. 65. See also pp. 85–86.

of scientific method. It is logical to assume that a carefully circumscribed group of individuals ought to lend itself, more readily than a whole nation-state, to the kind of data-gathering required for scientific ratiocination. But whether this is actually the case remains to be seen, especially in view of the fact that the theory itself demands a study of the decisional unit within a vaster systemic context. The decision-maker makes his decisions within a total perceived environment which includes the salient features of his national political system and of the international system as a whole. Thus DM theory is linked to systems theory, and the micro is joined to the macro, through the perceptions of the decision-maker, who presumably is aware of his existence at various concentric systemic levels.

We can see, then, that the psychological concept of perception plays a crucial role in DM theory, but whether the theory requires reliance upon perception as its exclusive foundation is a matter of controversy. The Snyder team, for example, when dealing with the "definition of the situation" in which the decision is to be made shuns the *objective* situation as it might be defined by the judgment of the observer, and insists upon restricting the inquiry to the world as it is viewed by the decision-makers.[8] But an English analyst, Joseph Frankel, argues that DM theory must take the objective environment into account, for even though factors which are not present in the minds of the policymaker cannot influence his decisions, nevertheless these may be important for the outcome of his decisions insofar as they set limits to what he can really do.[9] Frankel accepts the distinction, drawn by Harold and Margaret Sprout, between the "psychological environment" and the "operational environment."[10] The two environments may be quite dissimilar: the policymaker's perception of the range of action possible in a certain situation may be either wider or narrower than the conditions of objective political reality will tolerate. There remains, of course, the epistemological problem of determining what the objective situation is at any given time. Naturally, most decision-makers take it for granted that what they perceive is the objective situation. Later, in retrospect, policymakers and scholars might reach substantial agreement—in the light of accumulated data and the process of sifting and weighing various interpretations—that the decision-makers in specific cases were guilty of having vitiated their analysis by overlooking certain crucial factors. Thus the definition of a previous objective situation can be approached more or less adequately as historical knowledge grows. It will always be more difficult to achieve a consensus as to what the present objective situation is.

Next we must raise the question as to whether the theories with which we are dealing in this chapter presuppose the rationality of the DM process, and whether they confine themselves to the rational components of that process. For many decades, the Western intellectual's faith in the essential rationality

8. *Ibid.*, p. 65.
9. Joseph Frankel, *The Making of Foreign Policy: An Analysis of Decision-Making* (New York: Oxford University Press, 1963), p. 4.
10. *Ibid.*

of human behavior (inherited from the Enlightenment) has steadily disintegrated. Freud virtually completed the erosion process with his discoveries concerning the powerful role which the unconscious plays in human life. Yet all students of political science and international relations, while usually rejecting the old naive rationalism, are nevertheless disposed to assume that there are some rational elements in all political processes, insofar as men verbalize their political goals and operations in the form of rationally intelligible ideas. Moreover, if our knowledge of the individual prompts us to postulate irrationality, the demands of social organization require us to grope in the direction of rationality, and to employ the criteria of "rationality" in order to identify and understand "the irrational." The assumption of rational behavior, handled properly, is more productive for theory building than a denial of it would be. In their effort to explain political processes, social scientists have no choice but to assume that in human affairs the rational generally predominates over the irrational, even though the two orders are often closely meshed. The social scientist is compelled to believe that even man's irrational behavior must be at least partly penetrable by rational insights. Otherwise he may as well shift to another profession, for the ultimate irrationality is neither explicable nor predictable.

The theory developed by the Snyder group does not assume the actual rationality of decision-makers. In this schema, rationality is an element to be discovered rather than taken for granted. But there is in the theory an assumption of purposeful behavior and explicit motivation; behavior is seen not as a merely random activity.[11] There is also a tendency to recognize that the DM process combines rational elements, value considerations in which the rational may be synthesized with the nonrational, the irrational or the suprarational, and such irrational or nonrational factors as the psychic complexes of the policymakers. J. David Singer, among others, has pointed out that under conditions of stress and anxiety decision-makers may not act at all according to standards of utility that could be called rational,[12] and Martin Patchen has suggested the need for greater attention to the presence of nonrational and partly conscious factors in the personalities of those who make national decisions.[13] DM theory recognizes the interplay of both rational and irrational factors in the DM process, but necessarily focuses primarily upon the rational factors, since they are always more easily accessible to the observer.

DECISION-MAKING AND RATIONALITY

Joseph Frankel performs a useful service when he points out that some foreign policy decisions may be highly irrational while others approach much closer

11. Snyder *et al., op. cit.,* p. 8.

12. J. David Singer, "Inter-Nation Influence: A Formal Model," *American Political Science Review,* LVII (June, 1963), 428–430.

13. Martin Patchen, "Decision Theory in the Study of National Action," *Journal of Conflict Resolution,* IX (June, 1965), 165–169.

to rationality. Especially during periods of crisis, he notes, such issues as the Irish Question, or Alsace-Lorraine, or Israel, or the anti-imperial movement in Indonesia and Kenya, do not lend themselves entirely to rational analysis. But in most cases, and over the long haul, governments with limited resources are constrained by the imperatives of economy and diplomatic prudence to strike a rational balance between the principle of minimum cost and maximum comprehensiveness in which no important political values are ignored. While cautioning against the excesses of the rationalist method, Frankel concludes that foreign policy bureaucracies generally strive toward the application of reason for the sake of avoiding error. His final comment on the question:

> *Every specific decision usually leads to action which requires explanation to the general public in the traditional terms of rationality. This often leads to rationalization, a spurious explanation on rational grounds of decisions taken for other reasons; but at the same time it constitutes a powerful argument for the decision-makers to take into account these rational considerations before their final decision. Rationalization is generally considered a debasement of reason but actually it is also a powerful rational influence.*[14]

LIMITATIONS OF DECISION-MAKING THEORY

Decision-making theory is vulnerable to a number of objections, but the leading DM theorists have anticipated most of them. They readily admit that, because of national security and secrecy policies, inadequate records, faulty memories, and the perennial tendency of human beings to color the facts after the event, the scholar who sets out to study foreign policy decisions often encounters serious data problems. But this difficulty places a limiting effect upon all academic approaches to the study of international political relations, not only upon DM theory. Second, the political behavior of states appears to be affected by many variables which only with the greatest difficulty can be sorted out and assigned their proper weights in an orderly analytic scheme. Third, although the world presents us with a great diversity of cultures, we still do not know too much about the influence of cultural factors in national policy formation. Knowing most about our own "national character" and its impact upon the making of foreign policy, we sometimes run the risk of assuming the same rational-irrational mix in the DM process of other nations and cultures. Fourth, when we seek to understand how foreign policy decisions are made, we encounter two significant unknowns: a) the problem of chance or accidental occurrence in the creation of international patterns of

14. Joseph Frankel, *op. cit.,* p. 174. For his discussion of the other points briefly summarized in the paragraph above, see his Chapter XII, "Rationality and its Limitations," *ibid.,* pp. 166–175. The distinction between rational and irrational behavior will be treated more precisely in Chapter 12, where we examine Game Theory.

Contending Theories of International Relations

conflict; and b) the problem of simultaneity, by which is meant that "no state engages in separate, isolated actions, with one following the other in chronological sequence." [15] Decisions do not occur in a vacuum, even though we sometimes study single decisions as if they did. Many decisions are being made or carried out at the same time both within one country and in foreign countries, and all of these feed into the pattern of action and interaction.

It is not accurate, therefore, to imagine decision-makers making clear-cut choices at given points in time and then sitting back to await the results. All decisions occur in a fluid context. The effects of previous decisions impinge upon present decisions. Policymakers are constantly being affected by the internal setting of their own political system and by the external setting— i.e., the international environment. Governments experience the impact of their own and others' foreign policy decisions, fed back through the communications net. Snyder and his colleagues concede that this requires an analytic scheme of the broadest sort—intercultural, intersocietal and intergovernmental.[16] They do not furnish such a framework, but focus more precisely upon governmental decision-making as the pivotal link. They acknowledge that time is a troublesome factor in the theory. Action is not a series of discrete phenomena; rather it is a continuum. Estimates of the situation and definitions of the problem change from Time A to Time B. Even the goals may change as on-going progress is assessed, or as the decision-makers note discrepancies between expected consequences and actual consequences, or as new information prompts them to revise their estimate of the situation. Thus DM involves both prediction and testing, often with frequent modifications of the original hypothesis as the unfolding action is evaluated.[17]

The Decision Situation (or Occasion) [18]

We have said previously that DM theory focuses attention primarily, even if not exclusively, upon the "situation" or the "problem" as perceived in the minds of the decision-makers. Braybrooke and Lindblom suggest that decision-making, although it cannot be perfectly identified with, nevertheless may be

15. Snyder *et al., op. cit.,* p. 59. For a discussion of other points summarized in the above paragraph, see *ibid.,* pp. 56–59.

16. *Ibid.,* p. 70.

17. *Ibid.,* p. 76.

18. Students of decision-making have suggested several different ways of analyzing the phenomenon. Harold Lasswell, e.g., presents seven functional stages: information; recommendation; prescription; invocation; application; appraisal and

termination. *The Decision Process: Seven Categories of Functional Analysis* (College Park: University of Maryland Press, 1956). See also James A. Robinson and R. Roger Majak, "The Theory of Decision-Making," James C. Charlesworth, ed., *op. cit.,* pp. 178–181, including bibliographical references; John P. Lovell, *Foreign Policy in Perspective: Strategy, Adaptation, Decision-Making* (New York: Holt, Rinehart and Winston, 1970), especially pp. 205–261.

generally equated with, rational problem-solving.[19] The question now arises as to how the decision-makers define the situation in relation to the problem confronting them. How do they see objects, conditions, other actors and their intentions? How do they define the goals of their own government? What values strike them as most important, not in the abstract but insofar as they appear to be at stake in this particular situation?

Snyder observes that some situations are more highly structured than others. Some are readily grasped in their meaning while others may be more fluctuating and ambiguous. The urgency of situations, or the pressure to take action, will also vary widely. Whether a problem is considered primarily political, economic, military, or something else will normally have a great deal to do with how it is to be handled and by whom.[20] Abdul Said (professor of international relations, School of International Service, American University) and the late Charles Lerche noted that decision-makers must consider carefully three clusters of factors: (1) the pattern of forces in the given situation, including those which a single state might control and those which it cannot; (2) the policies which are being pursued by other states active in the situation; and (3) the capabilities of the DM's state for carrying out various policies in the light of the total situational context.[21] It is difficult enough, out of the welter of opinions from professional diplomats, scholars, journalists and others, to arrive at a relatively accurate assessment of the various trends and forces active in a foreign situation (and here foreign policy decision-making is more complex than domestic). Analyzing another state's intentions can be an even more treacherous business. The decision-makers in one state, anticipating a policy initiative by their counterparts in another, may regard their own move to deter or preclude as a purely defensive response. But if the DMs in the second state had not really intended to take the expected action, they will probably look upon the first state's action as an initiative, not a response. At this point, the discrepancy between the perceived situation as it is defined by the policymakers and the actual situation as it exists "out there" may be quite considerable. But the publication and execution of the decision, even if founded upon erroneous conceptions of reality, may change reality. In this sense perhaps every decision is a "self-fulfilling prophecy," for it induces other perceptions and reactions that conform with its own dialectic.

How do foreign policy decision-makers define or interpret problematic situations? On what basis do they formulate their national policies? Snyder complains that much-used terms such as "policy" and "objective" are taken for granted and escape clarification. An objective somehow is a projection into the unknown. To formulate an objective, according to Snyder, is "to

19. David Braybrooke and Charles E. Lindblom, *A Strategy of Decision* (New York: Free Press of Glencoe, 1963), p. 40.

20. Snyder, *et al., op. cit.,* p. 81.

21. Charles O. Lerche, Jr., and Abdul Said, *Concepts of International Politics* (Englewood Cliffs, N.J.: Prentice-Hall, 1963), p. 32.

rehearse the future in imagination." [22] He might have added, and certainly understood, that the rehearsal occurs frequently amidst the tension which actors experience when both their lines and the plot itself are being tampered with by several parties, most of whom have conflicting ideas as to how the actors should play their roles and how the drama should end. Within the foreign policy bureaucracies of governments there will always be a dichotomy between those who believe that the most men can hope to achieve is improvement of a given situation by a marginal increment and those who strive to effect a more fundamental transformation. This is sometimes (but not only) a matter of the time frame in which postulated objectives are conceived and also of the optimistic or pessimistic outlook which colors men's estimates of the degree and rate of change that can be expected in human affairs.

THE "NATIONAL INTEREST" AND DECISION-MAKING

One of the most frequently invoked criteria by which policymakers attempt to interpret international situations and formulate policies suitable to them is "national interest." [23] This concept, which has figured prominently in the discussion between "realists" and "idealists," especially during the 1950s, is generally admitted to be an elusive one, having both a fixed and a variable content. The fixed and irreducible content of the idea of the national interest would normally include the preservation of the nation as an independent political community, capable of maintaining the integrity of its territory and population and of safeguarding the autonomous development of its institutions. The variable content is a function of myriad factors—the traditional national mythos, or set of ideals, on which most people agree, the personality of political leaders, the differing political philosophies of rival political parties, the international conditions prevailing at a given time, contemporary trends in public opinion, the impact of changing technology, and so forth. All of these factors might influence the decision-maker's attitudes toward what "the national interest" demands in respect to military security, defense alliances, international peacekeeping organization and foreign aid.

During the last decade or so, the idea of "the national interest" has been subjected to a great deal of criticism. It has been attacked on the grounds that

22. Snyder *et. al., op. cit.,* p. 23.

23. For the more traditionalist exposition of this notion, see Charles A. Beard, *The Idea of National Interest* (New York: Macmillan Company, 1934); Hans J. Morgenthau, *In Defense of the National Interest* (New York: Alfred A. Knopf, 1951); Norman D. Palmer, ed., *The National Interest—Alone or With Others?, The Annals of the American Academy of Political and Social Science,* Vol. CCLXXXII (July, 1952), 1–118; Robert E. Osgood, *Ideals and Self Interest in America's Foreign Relations* (Chicago: University of Chicago Press, 1953); Charles O. Lerche, Jr., *Foreign Policy of the American People,* 2nd ed., (Englewood Cliffs, N.J.: Prentice-Hall, 1961), Chapters 1 and 6, and W. W. Rostow, *The United States in the World Arena* (New York: Harper and Brothers, 1960), Appendix A., pp. 543–550.

if it ever had any validity it was in the days of the classical balance of power, when there was (despite nationalism) a certain degree of intellectual and value consensus within the diplomatic mechanisms of the state system of Europe, but that it has become irrelevant in a global era of cultural discrepancies and ideological hostilities. (For a discussion of "national interest" in realist writings, see Chapter 3.) It has been questioned not only by behaviorists who deny its objective character and narrow it entirely to the subjective prejudices of individuals, but even by more traditional theoreticians who point out that it is always difficult to distinguish "the national interest" from subnational interests or from the interests of the decision-makers themselves, and who are perhaps inclined to think that the concept represents a rather parochial type of calculus in an age when nations (or at least their elites) are searching for larger unities, whether regional or universal.[24]

The Decisional Setting

Many other aspects of the decision situation deserve consideration. What they amount to is the total "internal setting" and "external setting" in which the decision must be made. Are decision-makers part of a system in which they are expected to respond to "cues from above" (e.g., a strong leader or a single ideological party) or "cues from below" (including shifts of public opinion, the demands of organized pressure groups, and the interventions of influential politicians on behalf of their constituents)?[25] Is an election pending? Are important foreign allies trying to make an input to the decision? From what sources do decision-makers derive their impressions of the situation, as well as ideas about how it should be handled? To what extent do decision-makers rely upon the wire services and the press and to what extent do they rely upon diplomatic, intelligence and other in-house channels of information and evaluation concerning the situation?[26] Finally, there is the question of the temporal-psychological context in which the need for making the decision arises. Whether the requirement for reaching a decision comes as a complete surprise or as the result of prior planning; whether the time available for deliberation and choice is adequate to the demands of the situation;

24. Some of the foregoing criticisms were honestly anticipated by the traditional analysts cited in Footnote 23. See also Stanley Hoffmann, ed., *Contemporary Theory in International Relations* (Englewood Cliffs, N.J.: Prentice-Hall, 1960), pp. 33–34, 73–79, 86–89, and 282–283; and Morton A. Kaplan, "The National Interest and Other Interests," Chapter 8 in his *System and Process in International Politics* (New York: John Wiley and Sons, 1957), pp. 151–161.

25. Snyder, *op. cit.,* p. 86.

26. See, e.g., Bernard C. Cohen, *The Press and Foreign Policy* (Princeton: Princeton University Press, 1963); and Roger Hilsman, Jr., *Strategic Intelligence and National Decisions* (Glencoe, Ill.: The Free Press, 1956).

Contending Theories of International Relations

and how important the values at issue are thought by the decision-makers to be—these factors have much to do with the quality and intensity of the choosing process, and they may be used to distinguish critical from noncritical decisions. Crisis-like decisions have been defined as those which "arise without prior planning, allow short time for response, and have high value consequences." [27] More will be said about crisis decisions later.

The Organization of Decision-Making

Decision-making occurs in an organizational or institutional context which imposes limitations upon the process, and which is shaped by the basic constitutional structure of the system or what we might regard as the formal aspect of the internal setting.[28] DM theory emphasizes the importance of the "decisional unit." Before anyone can analyze a foreign policy decision, he must be able to identify the group of individuals who made it and to locate that group in its proper institutional setting.

The decision-making process, then, is a function of organizational structure; the action or behavior of the system is intimately related to its form. Democratic and totalitarian states make foreign policy in very diverse ways. Even among the Western constitutional states, considerable differences exist in the organization of governments for the conduct of foreign affairs. Historically, executives of governments have virtually monopolized foreign policy decision-making because of their natural advantages in respect to the control of the instruments of diplomacy, war and peace—i.e., unity, secrecy, strategic intelligence, and the ability to act quickly in emergencies without the necessity of public debate. But in modern democratic states, although many decisions must still be made within the area of executive discretion and beyond the effective reach of the public, the executive branch has experienced some limitation of its freedom by legislatures, political parties, interest groups, public opinion and the mass media of communications. At the formal level of analysis, one needs to know to what extent the executive is subject to legislative limitations in this field. Legislatures usually wield their influence through such devices as the power to ratify treaties, to approve appointments, to authorize appropriations and question expenditures, to define the organizational structure and powers of departments and agencies, and to act as a mediator between the people and the executive by conducting public hearings and passing

27. James A. Robinson and Richard C. Snyder, "Decision-Making in International Politics," Herbert C. Kelman, ed., *International Behavior: A Social-Psychological Analysis* (New York: Holt, Rinehart and Winston, 1965), p. 442. See also Footnote 66.

28. See *ibid.*, pp. 448–456; Snyder, *et al., op. cit.,* pp. 87–105; Frankel, *op. cit.,* pp. 10–17.

resolutions which support or criticize executive policies and decisions. Several scholars have noted that, among the leading powers, the United States—as a result of the constitutional concept of "checks and balances"—exhibits in the highest degree a division of responsibility between executive and legislature which may produce at one time uncertainty and contradiction, at other times a remarkable consensus.[29]

Within the executive branch itself, the study of the DM process requires an accurate knowledge of the relationship between the head of state and his foreign secretary; between both of them and other special foreign policy advisers in the executive establishment; between both of them and ambassadors in the field; between the foreign secretary and the defense minister, the chief of intelligence, the nation's representatives to international organizations (such as the United Nations), and the chairmen of key foreign policy committees in the legislature. What formal and informal lines of authority, jurisdiction and communication have been established among the leading *dramatis personae*? Does the president or the prime minister prefer to centralize the control of foreign policy in his own hands (as Roosevelt, Churchill and Kennedy did) or does he rely heavily upon his foreign secretary (as Eisenhower did upon John Foster Dulles)? Does he make extensive use of "informal" personal representatives to communicate with foreign heads of government (as Woodrow Wilson did in the case of Colonel House and Franklin Roosevelt did with Harry Hopkins)? Does the president or the prime minister depend upon the collective advice of a National Security Council or a cabinet? Does the secretary of state accept the situational assessments of the ambassadors in the field, or would he rather fly to a trouble spot himself? The foregoing questions by no means exhaust those which could be asked, but they show that organizational structure must be scrutinized in both its formal and informal aspects, and that the *modus operandi* of both cannot be fully understood except in the light of "leadership styles," at any level of governmental decision-making.[30] Personality styles at the top will gradually filter down and shape the role expectations of individuals at all echelons of the bureaucracy.

29. See, e.g., Hans J. Morgenthau, "Conduct of American Foreign Policy," in Hans J. Morgenthau and Kenneth W. Thompson, eds., *Principles and Problems of International Politics* (New York: Alfred A. Knopf, 1950); Charles O. Lerche, *op. cit.,* pp. 76–85; Roger Hilsman, Jr., "Congressional-Executive Relations and the Foreign Policy Consensus," *The American Political Science Review,* LII September, 1958), 725–744; James A. Robinson, *Congress and Foreign Policy-Making* (Homewood, Ill.: Dorsey Press, 1962); Joseph Frankel, *op. cit.,* pp. 25–28.

30. See Edward S. Corwin, *The President: Office and Powers,* 4th ed. (New York: New York University Press, 1957); Louis W. Koenig, *The Invisible Presidency* (New York: Holt, Rinehart and Winston, 1960); Richard E. Neustadt, *Presidential Power* (New York: John Wiley and Sons, 1960); Theodore C. Sorensen, *Decision-Making in the White House* (New York: Columbia University Press, 1963); Alexander de Conde, *The American Secretary of Sta'e: An Interpretation* (New York: Frederick A. Praeger, 1962); Don K. Price ed., *The Secretary of State,* for the American Assembly (Englewood Cliffs, N.J.: Prentice-Hall, 1960); Norman A. Graebner,

It is often difficult to determine at precisely what level a policy decision originated. The flow of foreign policy ideas into the government from outside, the generation of ideas within the bureaucracy, and the dissemination and evolution of ideas within the offices of government are subjects about which relatively little is known. The awarding of contracts by governmental departments and agencies for the performance of specialized foreign policy and defense studies, as well as the solicitation of expert opinion from nongovernmental consultants, and how these practices vary from one part of the organization to another, represent areas of possible future social science research.[31]

A number of additional technical problems might be mentioned. In nations which understand fiscal responsibility, governmental offices or "decisional units" usually operate under strict budgetary restraints. Advocates of various types of foreign policy programs find themselves in constant competition for scarce resources. Furthermore, both within and between governmental units, conflicts are bound to arise among individuals, factions, and modes of substantive expertise for influence, prestige and ultimate dominance.[32] Who rivals whom may, therefore, be an important item of information in decision assessment. So may be the distinctive thought patterns which are "institutionalized" in the form of memoranda, directives, statements of objectives, intelligence estimates and strategic plans which members of the agency may take more or less seriously.[33] How seriously the individual decision-maker may regard the fixed policy guidelines which he receives from the past in comparison with the dynamic facts of an unfolding situation may be a function not only of his own personality but also of the personnel recruitment policies of the organization to which he belongs. Finally, there is the matter of the adequacy of a

---

ed., *An Uncertain Tradition: American Secretaries of State in the Twentieth Century* (New York: McGraw-Hill Book Company, 1961); Henry W. Wriston, "The Special Envoy," *Foreign Affairs,* XXXVIII (January, 1960), 219–237; Dean Rusk, "The President," *Foreign Affairs,* XXXVIII (April, 1960), 353–369; Henry M. Jackson, ed., *The National Security Council* (New York: Frederick A. Praeger, 1965).

31. A start in this direction has been made in some areas, notably in respect to the kind of scientific advice which the government seeks and receives in an age of complex technological developments bearing upon national security and foreign policy. See Robert C. Gilpin, *American Scientists and Nuclear Weapons Policy* (Princeton: Princeton University Press, 1962); Robert C. Gilpin and Christopher Wright, eds., *Scientists and National Policy-Making* (New York: Columbia University Press, 1964); and Harold Karan Jacobson and Eric Stein, *Diplomats, Scientists and Politicians* (Ann Arbor: University of Michigan Press, 1966); and Eugene B. Skolnikoff, *Science, Technology and American Foreign Policy* (Cambridge: MIT Press, 1967).

32. See Robinson and Snyder, *op. cit.,* p. 450. The authors stress the need for the resolution of conflicts between governmental units through argument and persuasion, clearance or approval requirements, bargaining and decision by higher authority.

33. All decision-makers in established (as distinct from entirely new) systems can draw upon a fund of previous practices, or what David Easton calls a "social memory bank, encapsulated in the traditional modes of operation of the system." *A Systems Analysis of Political Life* (New York: John Wiley and Sons, 1965), p. 456.

Decision-Making Theories

decisional unit's staff for the kind of tasks which are imposed upon it. If an organization is strained by burdens of rapid decision-making which significantly transcend its capabilities for efficient evaluation, this factor will certainly have an adverse effect upon the quality of its total performance. This is not to imply, of course, that there is any necessary connection between the quantity of bureaucratic personnel and the quality of decisions.

In a sense, every organization may be considered as a system in action, and a subsystem of a more comprehensive system. Gabriel A. Almond, borrowing from the social theory of Max Weber and Talcott Parsons, has defined every political system as a system of action, with "the role" as the unit of the political system which determines what a person within a specific structure and process is expected to do, why he does what he does, and how this is related to what others do.[34] Richard C. Snyder has something similar in mind when he speaks of "competence" as the totality of "the activities of the decision-maker relevant and necessary to the achievement of the organizational objective"—activities carried on according to a set of explicitly prescribed and conventionally accepted rules.[35] Whether we are talking about foreign policy-making in the Soviet, British, French, American, Japanese or Indian political system, we must remember that "the role" is shaped by both the system and by the individual's interpretation of it, and that the influence of personality in comparison with social ideology will vary markedly from one system to another. Actually, social scientists now know more about the organizational context of foreign policy decision-making in the United States than in any other country.[36]

Motivations and Characteristics of Decision-Makers

Richard C. Snyder has emphasized the importance of motivational analysis as a major determinant of the decision-making process.[37] Men constantly attribute motives to the behavior of states, and these are really not separable from the motives of individual decision-makers who speak on behalf of states and

34. Gabriel A. Almond, "Comparative Political Systems," *Journal of Politics,* XVIII (August, 1956), 391–409.

35. Snyder, *op. cit.,* p. 106.

36. See Robinson and Snyder, *op cit.,* p. 452. It would be unfair, however, to imply that no significant progress has been made in laying the foundations for a comparative study of foreign policy decision-making. See Philip W. Buck and Martin W. Travis, Jr., *Control of Foreign Relations in Modern Nations* (New York: W. W. Norton and Company, 1957); Joseph E. Black and Kenneth W. Thomp-

son, eds., *Foreign Policies in a World of Change* (New York: Harper and Row, 1963); Roy C. Macridis, ed., *Foreign Policy in World Politics,* 3rd ed. (Englewood Cliffs, N.J.: Prentice-Hall, 1967). The new theoretical approach to comparative foreign policy analysis is exemplified by James N. Rosenau, "Foreign Policy as Adaptive Behavior," *Comparative Politics,* II (April, 1970), 365–387. There is also a growing body of literature on foreign government decision-making in specific situations. See below, Footnote 59 and 60.

37. Snyder, *op. cit.,* pp. 137–171.

rationalize their policy actions. We can bypass the perennial argument as to whether historical social forces shape the leader or whether the leader can move history in a new direction through his choices. But we can certainly say that most decision-makers in any political system are likely to be swept along by the collective impulses of their society and their times, whereas only a minority will prove to be strongwilled and creative personalities who refuse to be dictated to by their environment and who strive to escape from the inescapable and recast their destiny. In Snyder's view, motivation is only one component of action. It is not to be equated with causation, which is a broader concept. He assumes a multiplicity of motives of differing strengths, as well as the likelihood of conflict among motives, within organizational units and within the individual decision-maker. He realizes that motives, although they are related to something in the external order, lie hidden in an internal psychic structure. Hence they cannot be observed directly, but only inferred indirectly from the symbolic, verbal acts by which diplomats and statesmen are forever explaining the basis of their decisional behavior both to their own constituencies and to their foreign counterparts.

Snyder has drawn a useful distinction between two types of motivation—"in order to" motives and "because of" motives.[38] The former are conscious and verbalizable: the decision-makers are taking this particular decision in order to accomplish such and such an objective of the state which they serve. For example, the administration of President Johnson sought a nonproliferation treaty "in order to" promote international stability by restricting the number of states that might independently opt for the initiation of nuclear hostilities. "Because of" motives, on the other hand, are unconscious or semiconscious motives, those which arise out of the previous life experience of the decision-makers, and which predispose or impel them toward certain kinds of policy orientations for private psychological reasons. In the example cited previously, if one would fully understand the motivations of those who worked for the conclusion of the Nonproliferation Treaty, he would have to probe the biographies of those policymakers who most assiduously pressed for the negotiation of the treaty and search out those elements in the childhood, social background, education, life experience and previous organizational conditioning of the treaty's most ardent proponents.

Originally, Snyder thought that DM theorists ought to be concerned primarily with the postulated future consequences of an act, and to shy away from a psychoanalytic inquiry into the decision-maker's personal past.[39] James N. Rosenau paraphrases Snyder's position as follows:

Snyder contends that usually the behavior of officials can be satisfactorily explained through an exploration of motives derived from their

---

38. *Ibid.,* p. 144.

39. "This relieves us of the necessity to connect what the Secretary of State had for breakfast with his conduct at meetings of the National Security Council." Snyder, *op. cit.,* p. 161.

decision-making organization, from their interpretations of the society's goals, and from their reactions to demands of situations in the internal and external settings—and that therefore it is usually not necessary to investigate their "because of" motives.[40]

But later, although he remained justifiably suspicious of indiscriminate borrowings from the field of psychological research by persons trained as political scientists, Snyder showed heightened interest in such personality characteristics of decision-makers as "propensity to assume high risks, tolerance of ambiguity and uncertainty, intelligence, creativity, self-esteem, dominance, submissiveness, need for power, need for achievement and need for affiliation." [41] Most decision-making theorists, like most political historians, would agree that knowledge about the biographical pattern of policymakers, their social backgrounds, education, religion, critical life experiences, professional training, foreign travel, residence or service, previous political activities, and so on—might help to cast light upon the deepest motives and values of those who make specific decisions. However, little is known about the relationship between the total inner psychic experience of an individual and his overt policy choices in an organizational context. Probably few DM theorists would be willing to go so far as Martin Patchen, who, in commenting upon the delicate task of measuring personal motivations in the U-2 crisis of 1960, offered the following provocative suggestion:

One approach is to analyze projectively verbal materials—such as informal interviews, speeches, articles, letters, etc. A second, and perhaps more promising, method is to analyze conditions of reward and punishment in a person's past history which are known to contribute to various motives. For example, we might be able to assess the strength of Khrushchev's motivation to avoid war on the basis of our knowledge of his past experience with war. Did he suffer personally in the past wars? Did he lose a son? Did he witness horrible scenes? His motivation for personal success and achievement might be assessed from knowledge of the learning conditions of his own childhood, if such information is available; or if it is not, one could rely on knowledge of the child-raising practices of the Ukrainian peasant society from which he came.[42]

Although the foregoing passage is highly imaginative and contains ideas which should by no means be lightly dismissed, nevertheless it would seem prudent to conclude that political scientists should be extremely careful when

40. Rosenau, *op. cit.*, p. 201. But Rosenau goes on to say that in Snyder's analytic scheme "in order to" motives may not always produce satisfactory explanations and that there may be times when the more idiosyncratic "because of" motives will have to be explored. Nevertheless, he adds, time and energy can normally be saved by studying "in order to" motives first and regarding as a residual category the more deep-rooted psychological factors which need be taken into account only under unusual circumstances. *Ibid.*

41. Robinson and Snyder, *op. cit.*, p. 444.

42. Martin Patchen, *op. cit.*, p. 173.

it comes to extrapolating from personal psychological experiences in the past to "official role" participation in present group decision-making in a governmental-institutional setting. It is one thing to acknowledge that an individual's background may be significant, especially in cases where there are unusual behavioral aberrations from what would "normally" be expected on the basis of the analysis of known social processes. But it is quite another thing to draw a definite causal line between the previous psychic event (perhaps years earlier) and the present deviant action. It may be possible to forge such a connecting link, but this should be done only when thorough research and consultation indicates a strong consensus among competent psychological authorities.

The Decision-Making Process

David Easton has defined the proper object of political science research as "the authoritative allocation of values for a society." [43] This, in essence, is what political decision-making is all about. But DM theorists are not in general agreement as to whether the process of political decision-making is fundamentally the same as the process of nonpublic or private decision-making. As political scientists, the authors of this book are strongly inclined to agree with those who postulate important differences between decisions in a family, in a university, in a business corporation, and in a government department.[44] Even though private and public decision-making are both characterized by various mixes of individual and collective processes, nevertheless the frames of reference and the "rules of the game" exhibit rather unique properties at various echelons.

It was said earlier that a decision involves a choice among alternatives. Now the question is how this expression of intent is arrived at. Is it basically a psychological-intellectual process which goes on in the minds of policymakers, or is it a social bargaining process in which various competing, conflicting and accommodating forces and pressures in the external environment clash to produce a synthesis?

43. David Easton, *The Political System* (New York: Alfred A. Knopf, 1953), p. 129.

44. Paul Diesing attributes a distinctive rationality to economic, social, technical, legal and political decisions. *Reason in Society: Five Types of Decisions and Their Social Conditions* (Urbana: University of Illinois Press, 1962). Others, too, including R. C. Wood and William L. C. Wheaton, have cautioned against extrapolating from private to public decision behavior. Cf. Robinson and Majak in Charlesworth, ed., *op. cit.,* pp. 177–178. Anthony Downs, on the other hand, is thought to equate private with public decision-making. *Ibid.,* p. 178. But even he differentiates sharply between individual and organizational decision-making. See *Inside Bureaucracy,* A RAND Corporation Research Study (Boston: Little, Brown and Company, 1967), pp. 178–179.

Since economists and students of business administration made significant early inputs to DM theory, the theory as originally developed reflected many of the assumptions of the Enlightenment and Benthamite Utilitarianism, with their emphasis upon reason and education in the making of human social choices. It assumed a rational man who is clearly aware of all the alternatives available to him and who is capable both of calculating their respective outcomes and then of freely choosing according to his order of value preferences. Such assumptions, as we shall see presently, have been seriously questioned in recent times.

In the specific field of foreign policymaking, the concept of rational decision-making long held sway, and a great many authorities still refuse to abandon it, because most of the alternative theories lead inexorably to rather pessimistic conclusions about the future of man and international society. Compared to the era in which the balance of power theory prevailed in the minds of statesmen and diplomats as the most rational basis for the conduct of foreign policy, our contemporary age is witness to keen competition among different rational modes of decision-making. Both capitalists and Marxists believe in arriving at decisions in a rational way, but their rational philosophies diverge. Even within Western society, experienced diplomats can argue spiritedly over what constitutes a rational decision, just as in academic circles today traditional political analysts and behavioral scientists are sometimes disagreed as to what reason demands in a particular situation. Most decision-making theorists are perforce inclined toward some form of rationalism, although they too sometimes disagree over the basic premises of rational behavior.

Lerche and Said may be somewhat excessively rationalistic in describing the foreign policymaking process as follows (even while admitting that in practice the procedure is never quite so clearcut):

> *If foreign policy thus consists of the application of a set of internalized criteria of judgment to a dynamic external situation, we may conceptualize the process as consisting of the following steps: (1) the establishment of the original criteria; (2) the determination of the relevant variables in the situation; (3) the measurement of the variables by the criteria; (4) the selection of an objective; (5) the elaboration of a strategy to reach the objective; (6) the decision to act; (7) the action itself; (8) the evaluation of the results of the action in terms of the original criteria.*[45]

But the formulation of Lerche and Said is useful for several reasons. It points to the importance of a clear definition of the situation by policymakers, who must frame for themselves as accurately as they can the central questions to be answered. This is the sort of advice with which professional practitioners of the diplomatic art are quick to concur, for they know that the search for information depends upon asking the right questions.[46] The Lerche-Said

45. Lerche and Said, *op. cit.*, p. 31.   46. See Rusk, *op. cit.*, pp. 503–504.

schema suggests that the decisional process should be made an intellectual affair throughout, as far removed from emotionalism as possible. It ought to be a calm ordering of national values and necessities, of rationally perceived interests and prudently framed objectives, of long-term goals and short-term exigencies. Such a schema is easy to criticize if we take it to be a description of the DM process as this actually and usually unfolds in most foreign offices round the world. But if we regard the schema as a theoretical statement of what foreign policymaking at its rational finest ought to be, and of the heights to which the "pros" do manage to rise on more or less rare occasions, then it is not at all a bad model. We must admit, however, that many decisions fall far short of the ideals which are embodied in abstract models.

According to the classic model of decision-making, policymakers make a calculation in two basic dimensions—utility and probability—and, assuming that they are "rational," they will attempt to maximize expected utility. In other words, after all the available alternatives have been surveyed and the product of weighted values and assessed probabilities has been obtained, the decision-maker can choose his optimal course.[47] Snyder points out that "decision-makers may be assumed to act in terms of clearcut preferences," but that these preferences, instead of being entirely individual, derive from the rules of the organizational system, shared organizational experience over a period of time, and the information available to the decisional unit, as well as from the biographies of individuals.[48] Snyder, however, refrained from subscribing fully to the classic explanatory formula of "maximization of expected utility," which had already been subject to question before he wrote his principal essay on the subject.[49]

Braybrooke and Lindblom reject as unsatisfactory for most important decisions (i. e., those which affect significant changes in the external social world) the "synoptic conception" of decision-making, by which the policymaker is presumed to spread out before him all his available alternatives and to measure, against his scale of preferred values, all the probable consequences of the social changes implicit in the various courses of action under consideration. This synoptic schema, in their view, simply does not conform to reality. It presupposes omniscience and a kind of comprehensive analysis which is prohibitively costly and which time pressures normally do not permit. Every

47. See, e.g., Marshall Dimock, *A Philosophy of Administration*, (New York: Harper and Brothers, 1958), p. 140; J. David Singer, "Inter-Nation Influence: A Formal Model," *American Political Science Review*, LVII (June, 1963), 424; Bruce M. Russett, "The Calculus of Deterrence," *Journal of Conflict Resolution*, VII (June, 1963), 97–109.

48. Snyder, *op. cit.*, p. 176. Snyder emphasizes that the explanation of DM motivation implies a concept of multiple membership of the individual in a culture and society, in such social groupings as the profession and class, in the total political institutional structure and in the decisional unit. *Ibid.*, p. 172.

49. Snyder had earlier accepted the notion of "maximization of expected utility." See his "Game Theory and the Analysis of Political Behavior," in *Research Frontiers and Government* (Washington: The Brookings Institution, 1955), pp. 73–74.

solution, they assert, must be limited by several factors, including man's problem-solving capacities, by the amount of information available, by the cost of analysis (in personnel, resources, and time), and by the practical inseparability of fact and value.[50]

No one has challenged the classic model of rational decision-making more fundamentally, while yet remaining within a rational framework, than the eminent theorist of public administration, Herbert Simon, who postulates a world of "bounded rationality." For the classic concept of *maximizing* or *optimizing* behavior, he substitutes the notion of *"satisficing"* behavior. This presupposes that the policymakers do not really design for themselves a matrix which shows all available alternatives, the value "pro" and "cons" of each, and the probability assessments of expected consequences. Instead, Simon suggests, decision-making units examine alternatives sequentially until they come upon one which meets their minimum standards of acceptability.[51] In other words, men keep rejecting unsatisfactory solutions until they find one which they can agree is sufficiently satisfactory to enable them to act. This explanation is not likely to prove adequate in the eyes of Platonic idealists and others who seek "the best," but even Platonists are willing to admit that the average bureaucratic official is seldom trained in the ways of perfection. Braybrooke and Lindblom, who are partial both to Simon's "satisficing" model and to Karl Popper's idea of "piecemeal engineering," suggest that the pragmatic experimentalism which is so important a component of the philosophies of Western democracies dictates to democratic decision-makers a strategy of "disjointed incrementalism." Put in its simplest form, this means that democratic policymakers prefer to slice their decision-making problems into small segments which enable them to make "incremental" or "marginal" rather than far-reaching or profound choices.[52]

Another factor which deserves mention in this context is the phenomenon known as "decisional conflict," a term which has been defined by Irving L. Janis as referring to "opposing tendencies within an individual, which interfere with the formulation, acceptance or execution of a decision." [53] Such conflicts might arise either out of the psychological personality of the individual policymaker, or out of the intensity of cross-pressures on the part of competing groups, or out of both. In other words, external pressures for contrary or contradictory policy courses might produce within the individual policymaker

50. Braybrooke and Lindblom, *op. cit.,* Chapter 4.

51. See Herbert A. Simon, *Administrative Behavior* (New York: Macmillan Company, 1959); "A Behavioral Model of Rational Choice," *Quarterly Journal of Economics,* LXIX (February, 1955), 99–118; and "A Behavioral Model of Rational Choice," in Simon, ed., *Models of Man: Social and Rational* (New York: John Wiley and Sons, 1957), pp. 241–

260. See also William D. Coplin, *Introduction to International Politics: A Theoretical Overview* (Chicago: Markham Publishing Company, 1971), pp. 32–37.

52. Braybrooke and Lindblom, *op. cit.,* pp. 71–79 and Chapter 5.

53. Irving L. Janis, "Decisional Conflicts: A Theoretical Analysis," *Journal of Conflict Resolution,* III (March, 1959), 7.

symptoms of uncertainty, vacillation and tension, or even issue-avoidance. Moreover, intrapersonal conflicts might be a cause of intergroup or international conflicts. In acute cases, individual negotiators might reach international agreements which are repudiated by their home governments and suffer such postdecisional conflicts as to induce them to withdraw altogether from subsequent negotiating roles.[54]

The foregoing consideration serves to remind us that decision-making is not only an intellectual process involving the insight, perception and creative intuition of policymakers, but it is also a matter of social and quasi-mechanical processes.[55] Among political scientists, Arthur F. Bentley and David B. Truman have done much to stress the importance of interest groups in the decisional process, while William F. Riker, in his study of coalitions, suggests that decision-making may depend at least partially upon quasi-mechanical processes in which the actors are unconscious of their decision-making roles.[56] A striking example of group conflict in U.S. policy in the Middle East can be seen in the divergent interests of pro-Israeli elements and the oil industry. Quasi-mechanical processes may be illustrated in the case of individuals who, for motives of personal economic advantage, engage in international economic transactions such as importing, foreign investment, travel or capital flight to overseas banks, which virtually compel governmental policymakers to adopt regulatory decisions (e. g., in a balance-of-payments crisis). Robinson and Majak conclude that decisions can normally best be understood in the light of the three types of processes (intellectual, social, and quasi-mechanical), even though all three may not be equally relevant in a given instance.[57]

Finally, in an effort to understand the process, it is necessary to remember that decision-makers are not finished once they have made their choices. There is incumbent upon them an obligation to keep monitoring and assessing the consequences of their earlier decisions, so that they can evaluate the success or failure of those decisions, reexamine their assumptions and their information base, as well as the theoretical model by which they judge the total environment and the specific situation which required a policy, and modify their subsequent decisions accordingly.

Social scientists will probably never be able to agree whether the decision-making process originates in the minds of men or whether it is adventitious, i. e., arises out of the external social situation, whether man on balance affects reality more than he reflects it. Decision-making is an aspect of human culture,

54. *Ibid.*, pp. 7–13, where the author contrasts the reactions of two negotiators, President Wilson and Count Bernstorff, to the setback which the Zimmermann telegram represented to their peace efforts.

55. Robinson and Majak, *op. cit.*, pp. 180–183.

56. *Ibid.*, p. 182. The references are to

Arthur F. Bentley, *The Process of Government* (Chicago: University of Chicago Press, 1908); David B. Truman, *The Governmental Process* (Chicago: University of Chicago Press, 1951); and William H. Riker, *The Theory of Political Coalitions* (New Haven: Yale University Press, 1962).

57. *Ibid.*, pp. 182–184.

which is in turn a product of the organic interaction of man and his environment. What may prove to be more interesting and more researchable questions for the future are whether decision-makers have convictions that they are playing a causal role and can work substantial effects in the external order; what personality factors affect these convictions; whether the conviction of a causal relationship is stronger in crisis or in noncrisis situations; whether the conviction of causality is stronger before than after the decision; and whether attitudes about human ability to control and predict the outcomes of policy situations differ significantly between such groups as "experts" and laymen, "politicians" and "career bureaucrats," pragmatists and those who are more ideologically oriented, and younger and older decision-makers. Merely posing these questions serves to indicate that there is still a broad area of fruitful research in respect to the decision-making process.

Decision-Making in Crisis: Case Studies

Since the mid-1950s, a considerable amount of literature has appeared on foreign policy decisions, primarily American and British. Most of it has been in the form of case studies of specific decisions which were telescoped in time and circumscribed as to the number of decision-makers—the outbreak of World War I, Britain's decision to intervene in Suez in 1956, the United States decision to withdraw Aswan Dam assistance from Egypt in 1956, the United States decision in 1950 to resist aggression in Korea, President Truman's decision to fire General MacArthur in 1951, President Eisenhower's policy in the Quemoy crisis, and President Kennedy's decisions in the Bay of Pigs and Cuban Missile crises.[58] There have, of course, been some broader

58. See Erskine B. Childers, *The Road to Suez* (London: MacGibbon and Kee, Ltd., 1962); Hugh Thomas, *Suez* (New York: Harper and Row, 1966); James E. Dougherty, "The Aswan Decision in Perspective," *Political Science Quarterly,* LXXIV (March, 1959), 21–45; Alexander L. George, "American Policy-Making and the North Korean Aggression," *World Politics,* VII (January, 1955), 21–45; Glenn D. Paige, *The Korean Decision, June 24–30, 1950* (New York: Free Press, 1968); Harry S. Truman, *Memoirs* (Garden City, N.Y.: Doubleday and Company, 1956), II, Chapters 22–24; Richard E. Neustadt, *Presidential Power* (New York: John Wiley and Sons, 1960), Chapter 6; Charles A. McClelland, "Decisional Opportunity and Political Controversy: The Quemoy Case," *Journal of Conflict Resolution,* VI (September, 1962), 201–213; Elie Abel, *The Missile Crisis* (Philadelphia: J. B. Lippincott Company, 1966); Theodore C. Sorensen, *Kennedy* (New York: Harper and Row, 1965), Chapters XI and XXIV; Arthur M. Schlesinger, Jr., *A Thousand Days: John F. Kennedy in the White House* (Boston: Houghton Mifflin Company, 1965), Chapters VII, XXX, XXXI; Graham T. Allison, "Conceptual Models and the Cuban Missile Crisis," *American Political Science Review,* LXIII (September, 1969), 689–718; Dean G. Acheson, *Present at the Creation: My Years in the State Department* (New York: W. W. Norton and Company, 1969). These are mere representative samples. For a fuller bibliography of the literature in decision-making, see James A. Robinson and Richard C. Snyder in Kelman, *op. cit.,* pp. 458–463.

studies of decisions which were characterized by longer time frames and larger, more complex groups of actors: e.g., the French scuttling of the European Defense Community in 1954; the making of the U. S.-Japanese Peace Treaty of 1951; the British decision to seek entry into the European Economic Community; and U. S. policy in the negotiation and ratification of the Partial Nuclear Test Ban Treaty.[59] It must be admitted that the latter, more comprehensive type of study is considerably more difficult than the former to cast in a mold of precise decision-making analysis. It can probably also be expected that most students of the decision-making process in the future will continue, because of the problem of limited resources, to apply the theoretical model to readily identifiable and isolatable decisions, and this means that they will be attracted to more or less dramatic, critical decisions, rather than a harder-to-research kind of routine, cumulative process which takes place in a sprawling bureaucratic labyrinth over a longer time period.

THE U.S. DECISION TO INTERVENE IN KOREA

Among the case studies mentioned earlier, one which was consciously designed for the purpose of applying a theoretical DM model was Glenn D. Paige's account of seven days of U. S. national decision-making in response to the Korean crisis. Professor Paige reflects an awareness of the problem of applying to a single case the Snyder-Bruck-Sapin model, and of trying to verify any hypotheses merely on the basis of the Korean decision. He acknowledges that the single case produces lessons than can lead only to "a relatively low level of abstraction." [60] But he argues that the single-case method can have pedagogical as well as theoretical uses and can lay part of the empirical foundation for the subsequent comparative study of decision-making. Throughout the work, Paige is concerned with establishing an objective methodology. He approaches his task as would an historian who seeks a better understanding of crisis decision-making by reconstructing an actual instance of it. Using the materials on which any student of decision-making must primarily rely—newspaper accounts, official governmental publications, the diaries, memoirs and records of policymakers who were involved in the decision, interviews with key figures, and the comment of other experts—Snyder

59. See Daniel Lerner and Raymond Aron, *France Defeats EDC* (New York: Frederick A. Praeger, 1957); Bernard C. Cohen, *The Political Process and Foreign Policy: The Making of the Japanese Peace Settlement* (Princeton: Princeton University Press, 1957); Robert L. Pfaltzgraff, Jr., *Britain Faces Europe, 1957–1967* (Philadelphia: University of Pennsylvania Press, 1969); Harold Karan Jacobson and Eric Stein, *Diplomats, Scientists and Politicians: The United States and The Nuclear Test Ban Negotiations* (Ann Arbor: University of Michigan Press, 1966); and James H. McBride, *The Test Ban Treaty* (Chicago: Henry Regnery Company, 1967).

60. Paige, *op. cit.,* p. 10.

seeks to improve his objectivity by "decontaminating" the narrative, i.e., separating his own analytical interpretations and normative judgments from the reconstruction of the historical events.[61]

Paige is essentially faithful to the Snyder-Bruck-Sapin model, with its emphasis upon such concepts as "spheres of competence," "motivation," "communication and information," "feedback," and the "path of action." He begins by placing the Korean decision in the context of its internal and external setting and devotes to each a chapter covering the political-historical background from 1945 to 1950. Within the domestic setting are included biographical sketches of three principals: the President (Harry S. Truman), the Secretary of State (Dean Acheson) and the Secretary of Defense (Louis A. Johnson). The author touches briefly on their learning experiences, their views on such subjects as history and "power," and their conceptions of office, insofar as these might have a bearing upon their decisional behavior. He then discusses the state of relations existing between the Executive policymakers and the Congress, the impending Congressional election of 1950, and some salient features of public opinion at the time.[62] The treatment of the external environment stresses the bipolarity of the world, the postwar development of the "containment policy," national security estimates and requirements, and the policy posture of the United States toward Asia, especially Korea.[63]

Paige then presents nearly two hundred pages of meticulously reconstructed narrative—sometimes on an hour-by-hour basis—of the decision-making events which transpired in Washington between Saturday, June 24, and Friday, June 30, 1950. It would not be possible to summarize those events here without doing an injustice to the work, which should be read in its entirety. More relevant to our present purposes are the empirical propositions derived from the case study, which are set forth not so much as valid generalizations but rather as hypotheses which might be tested in other studies of crisis DM.[64] The Korean decision, Paige concludes, can be viewed either as a unified phenomenon or as a developmental sequence of choices (of which most decision-makers were aware) which contributed "to a stage-like progression toward an analytically defined outcome"—a sequence in which policymakers were apparently affected by "positive reinforcement" in the form of supporting

61. *Ibid.*, p. 14. Paige's empirical analysis, normative analysis and suggested implications for future crisis management are reserved to three chapters at the end.

62. *Ibid.*, pp. 21–49.

63. *Ibid.*, pp. 51–76.

64. Paige cites Charles F. Hermann's definition of a *crisis* as "A situation that (1) threatened high priority goals of the decisional unit, (2) restricted the amount of time in which a response could be made, and (3) was unexpected or unanticipated by the members of the decision-making unit." *Ibid.*, p. 276. Paige himself notes that a crisis is "thrust upon the decision-makers from outside their organization and from outside the territory and population over which they exercise official control." *Ibid.*, p. 275. Alastair Buchan has suggested that a crisis is a situation in which one country attempts to force a decision upon another in a specific matter. *Crisis Management: The New Diplomacy* (Boulogne-sur-Seine, France: The Atlantic Institute, 1966), pp. 20–22.

UN action, favorable editorial opinion and Congressional and international expressions of approval, as well as evidence of a temperate Soviet response.[65] Only a few of Paige's numerous propositions can be cited here:

> *Crisis decisions tend to be reached by* ad hoc *decisional units.*
> *The greater the crisis, the greater the felt need for face-to-face proximity among decision-makers.*
> *The greater the crisis, the more the leader's solicitation of subordinate advice.*
> *The more prolonged the crisis, the greater the sense of adequacy of the information about it.*
> *Costly responses to crisis tend to be followed by decline in the salience of the values associated with them.*
> *The greater the crisis, the greater the efforts of decision-makers to diminish popular anxieties.*
> *The greater the crisis, the more frequent and the more direct the interactions with friendly leaders in the external setting.*[66]

There are many other hypotheses which postulate relationships among the nature of the decision-making group, the perceived threat to values, the role of leadership, the quest for information, the framework of past responses, the shared willingness to make a positive response, the effort to secure international support, and so forth. Some of the propositions are novel and interesting; some might strike the reader as slightly tedious confirmations of what might otherwise be deduced logically—but it should be remembered that genuine confirmation of "obvious" truths, based on solid data, can be useful in the development of scientific theory.

PERCEPTION AND DECISION-MAKING: THE OUTBREAK OF WORLD WAR I

The use of content analysis with a stimulus-response model represents a quite different methodological approach to the study of decision-making. In studies of the outbreak of World War I and the Cuban Missile Crisis, Ole R. Holsti, Robert C. North, and Richard A. Brody have attempted to measure the perceptions of statesmen from the statements contained in messages exchanged during crisis situations.

The model used in these studies relates perceptions to behavior $(S\text{-}r\text{:}s\text{-}R)$. The symbol S is the stimulus or input behavior: it is a physical event or a verbal act. The symbol R represents the response action. Both S and R are nonevaluative and nonaffective. r is the decision-maker's perception of the stimulus (S), and s is his expression of intentions or attitude. Both r and s include factors such as personality, role, organization and system, which affect perceptual variables.

65. Paige, *op. cit.*, pp. 276–279.

66. *Ibid.*, pp. 281, 288, 290, 293, 301, 303, and 312.

The 1914 crisis was selected as the initial case because of the large amount of available documentation and because it was a classic example of the outbreak of war through escalation. The perception units for analysis were abstracted from the historical documents in the following terms: "the perceiving party or actor; the perceived party or actors; the action or attitude; and the target party or actor." [67] Over 5,000 such perception units were extracted from the 1914 documents. The documents used were those authored by selected British, French, Russian, German, and Austro-Hungarian decision-makers.

Initial studies were done based solely upon perceptual data. Using only the frequency of themes for analysis of the relationships between perceptions of threat and perceptions of capability in international crisis, support was found for the hypothesis: "If perceptions of anxiety, fear, threat, or injury are great enough, even the perceptions of one's own inferior capability will fail to deter a nation from going to war." [68] When it became evident that not only the frequency of perceptions is important, but also their intensity, the documents were coded again to measure the intensity of the perceptions of "hostility, friendship, frustration, satisfaction, and desire to change the status quo." [69] The results were then aggregated into twelve time periods. Results showed that "decision-makers of each nation most strongly felt themselves to be victims of injury precisely at that time when its leaders were making policy decisions of the most crucial nature." [70]

Next, the authors of the study undertook correlational analyses between the perception data and various types of "hard" and action data, since they recognized that the value of content analysis depends upon the relationship between the statements and the actual decisions made by statesmen. Thus, the authors attempted to find correlations between the results of the content analysis and such actions as mobilization, troop movements, and the breaking of diplomatic relations. Other actions, such as the financial indicators—gold movements and the price of securities, which are sensitive to international tension levels—were examined. "Given fluctuations of financial indicators, correlated with increases and decreases in international tension, these indicators can be used to check the validity of content analysis data. If the latter covary both with the political/military actions of nations participating in the crisis and with fluctuations of financial indicators that respond to the tensions born of these actions, confidence in the content analysis techniques is substantially enhanced." [71]

The next step was to combine the perception and action data to test the

67. Ole R. Holsti, Robert C. North, and Richard A. Brody, "Perception and Action in the 1914 Crisis" in J. David Singer, ed., *Quantitative International Politics* (New York: Free Press, 1968), p. 136.

68. *Ibid.*, p. 136.

69. *Ibid.*, p. 137.

70. *Ibid.*

71. *Ibid.*, p. 138.

basic interaction model $(S\text{-}r\text{:}s\text{-}R)$. Correlating the 1914 perception data with the spiral of military mobilizations, the authors concluded that a rise in hostility preceded acts of mobilization. Stated differently, decision-makers responded "to verbal threats and diplomatic moves, rather than troop movements." [72]

The action data, S and R, included all military events of the 1914 crisis. The action data were coded both in terms of frequency and intensity. It was assumed that a given amount of violence or action (S) will yield an appropriate level of expressed response (r), expressed intent (s), and a response (R) at about the same level of violence as the original stimulus (S). However, when the 1914 crisis data were divided into the two coalitions, a consistent lack of congruence was found in the actions of the two alliances. The difference corresponded to the different levels of involvement of the respective coalitions. This finding raises doubt about the classical theories built on a simple $S\text{-}R$ model. The hypothesis that "the correlation between input action (S) and policy response (R) will be better in a situation of low involvement than in one of high involvement" [73] was tested with the 1914 crisis data. The Triple Entente was less involved, having only 40 perceptions of hostility compared to 171 for the Dual Alliance. As the hypothesis suggested, it was found that the degree of congruence between S and R was high for the less engaged Triple Entente, and lower for the highly engaged Dual Alliance. This suggests that perceptions $(s$ and $r)$ may be less crucial in low involvement situations but are important in high involvement situations.

A second hypothesis, concerned not only with congruence or lack of congruence but also with the direction of the differences, was tested: "In a situation of low involvement, policy response (R) will tend to be at a lower level of violence than the input action (S), whereas in a high involvement situation, the policy response (R) will tend to be at a higher level of violence than the input action (S)." [74] It was found that the highly involved Dual Alliance was indeed consistently over-reacting to the threats, whereas the less involved Triple Entente under-reacted.

Since the action variables, S and R, alone failed to account for the escalation of war, the intervening perceptual variables, r and s, were analyzed. No significant difference was found between the two coalitions in the $s\text{-}R$ step. In both low and high involvement cases, the response action (R) was at a higher level of violence than was suggested by their leaders' statements of intent (s). Moreover, in the $r\text{-}s$ link, there was again little difference between

72. *Ibid.*, p. 46. The phenomenon described here is similar to the hostility-friendliness continuum and the unstable reaction coefficients studied by Lewis F. Richardson in his research on the arms races of 1908–1914 and 1929–1939. See *Arms and Insecurity* (Pittsburgh: Box-wood, 1960), and *Statistics of Deadly Quarrels* (Chicago: Quadrangle Books, 1960).

73. Holsti *et al.*, in Singer, *op. cit.*, p. 52.

74. *Ibid.*, p. 152.

the Triple Entente and Dual Alliance: in both groupings of nations the level of hostility was perceived to be consistently greater in the other's policy (r) than in their own statements of intent (s).

However, a significant difference appeared in the S-r step which could account for the escalation. In the low-involvement situation, r tended to be at a lower level than S, while in the high-involvement situation, r tended to be higher than S. Decision-makers in the highly involved Dual Alliance consistently overperceived the level of violence of the Triple Entente. The leaders of the less deeply involved Triple Entente underperceived the actions of the Dual Alliance. Moreover, in the latter stages of the crisis, after both alliances had become highly involved, there was less difference between the two coalitions in the way actions (S) were perceived (r) than before. The authors concluded, therefore, that intervening perceptions may perform an accelerating or decelerating function. In this case, the S-r link served a "magnifying" function. "This difference in perceiving the environment (the S-r link) is consistent with the pronounced tendency of the Dual Alliance to respond at a higher level of violence than the Triple Entente." [75]

PERCEPTION AND DECISION-MAKING: THE CUBAN MISSILE CRISIS

Using the same interaction model, Holsti, Brody, and North investigated the Cuban Missile Crisis of 1962. An example of escalation conflict like the 1914 case, the Cuban Missile Crisis provides an opportunity, therefore, both for comparison and contrast with the earlier study. An effort was made to find "patterns of behavior that distinguish the situation which escalated into general war (as in the 1914 crisis) from those in which the process of escalation is reversed" [76] (as in the Cuban Missile Crisis).

The source materials for the analysis of perceptions (s and r) consisted of fifteen American, ten Soviet, and ten Chinese documents. The documents were content analyzed. Action data (S and R) were coded from a 0 to 10 level of violence or potential violence. Objective financial indices, which had revealed a striking correlation to the perceptions and expressions of hostility in the 1914 crisis and which were available on a day-to-day basis, were also incorporated into the analysis of the Cuban Missile Crisis.

It was found that the actions of the United States and the Soviet Union correlated closely; each increase or decrease in the level of violence of one party was followed by a similar pattern of action by the other. "The pattern of perceptions was relatively consistent with the course of events surrounding the Cuban crisis. In each case October 25–26 was the point at which mutual

75. *Ibid.*, p. 157.

76. Ole R. Holsti, Richard A. Brody, and Robert C. North, "Measuring Affect and Action in the International Reaction Models: Empirical Materials from the 1962 Cuban Crisis," *Journal of Peace Research,* I (1964), 174.

perceptions appeared to change." [77] Thus, at this point the trend reversed from escalation to deescalation.

In the case of the Cuban Missile Crisis, unlike the 1914 crisis, there was found to be "close correspondence between the actions of the other party (S) and perceptions of the adversary's actions (r)." Here both sides perceived accurately the nature of the adversary's actions and acted at an appropriate level. Efforts made by either party "to delay or reverse the escalation were generally perceived as such and responded to in a like manner." [78] Such behavior differed from that of the 1914 crisis in which, at the beginning, the Dual Alliance consistently reacted at a higher level than the Triple Entente and also consistently overperceived the level of violence taken by the Triple Entente. Subsequently, this difference in the S-r link between the two coalitions lessened as both were drawn into escalation and war.

From the analysis of the 1914 crisis, the 1962 Cuban Missile Crisis, and from other similar studies, such as Sino-Soviet relations and Communist bloc integration, "in general there are indications that, the more intense the interaction between parties, the more important it is to incorporate perceptual data into the analysis." [79] Moreover, it was found that in the S-r:s-R model, the link between perception and action, S-r could perform an accelerating or decelerating function, that is, the "relationship between one coalition's actions, the other coalition's perceptions of those actions, and the resulting policies was apparently the crucial one." [80]

Psychological Components of Decision-Making

It can be said that all crisis decisions entail a particular kind of psychological component. They give rise to situations of threat and counterthreat which produce tension within the participants, whether in the form of excitement, fear, anxiety, frustration, dissonance, or some other psychic state. A knowledge of how conditions of stress affect the solidarity and problem-solving ability of small groups may cast light on the way leaders behave at crucial decision-making junctures.

Stress is a function of many different variables. In the internal setting, these might include: the pressure of time in which critical decisions have to be made; the necessity of having to attend to several different policy problems simultaneously; the simplicity or complexity of the organization for decision-making; the demands of conflicting interest groups; the existence of public opinion unfavorable to courses of action which the policy-makers feel compelled to consider; serious disagreements over the assessment of the situation, the values at stake, and the anticipated consequences of various courses of action; the fear of war and its consequences on the part of the decision-

77. *Ibid.*, p. 177.
78. *Ibid.*
79. *Ibid.*, p. 158.
80. *Ibid.*

makers; and the clash of personalities within the decisional unit. In the external setting, the variables might include: the total strategic power position of the contesting parties; the strategic doctrines and cultural-psychological attitudes of the adversary; the assessment of the adversary's objectives, intentions and "staying power;" the efficiency of the international communications system and the intelligence system on which the decision-makers depend for the flow of information; and the attitudes of allies and neutrals, or "world public opinion." Some of these factors will cause greater stress than others, and will be more significant for one individual, or one decisional unit, or one side, than the other. In any given international conflict situation, the stress experienced by decision-making groups at any critical juncture will vary qualitatively among the parties according to their perceptions of the total situation and their own reactions to it.

Psychologists have designed experiments to test the effects of stress upon group integration and the problem-solving efficiency of groups. It has been found, as one might expect, that individuals in groups react differently to stress from the way isolated individuals react. With the latter, increased stress usually leads to aggression, withdrawal or escape behavior, regression or various neurotic symptoms. But in the case of groups, the opposite result is often obtained. John T. Lanzetta has furnished the following description of his experiments:

> *It was found that as stress increased there was a decrease in behaviors associated with friction in the group; a decrease in the number of disagreements, arguments, aggressions, deflations and other negative social-emotional behaviors, as well as a decrease in self-oriented behaviors. Concomitant with this decrease was an increase in behaviors which would tend to result in decreased friction and better integration of the group; an increase in collaborating, mediating, cooperating behaviors.*[81]

Lanzetta suggests that the reason for this phenomenon is to be found in the tendency of group members, faced with conditions that produce stress and anxiety, to seek psychological security in the group through cooperative behavior. But the hypothesis of group integration under stress seems to be valid only up to a point. It may be that group members provide mutual reinforcement for each other only while they expect to be able to find a solution to their common problem. Robert L. Hamblin designed an experiment which led him to suggest that group integration during a crisis will begin to decrease if no likely solution appears to be available. Cooperation is likely while it is

---

81. John T. Lanzetta, "Group Behavior Under Stress," *Human Relations,* VIII (1955), reprinted in J. David Singer, ed., *Human Behavior and International Poli-* *tics: Contributions from the Social-Psychological Sciences* (Chicago: Rand McNally and Company, 1965), pp. 216–217.

potentially profitable, but when the members of the group meet one failure after another no matter what they do, they experience a frustration which leads to the displacement of antagonism against one another. In some cases, individuals attempt to resolve the crisis problem for themselves by withdrawing and leaving the other members to work out their own solution if they can —a process tantamount to group disintegration.[82]

Hamblin's findings may prove relevant for an understanding of the behavior of leadership groups in international conflict when they perceive that the tide is beginning to turn against them, regardless of which strategy or tactics they pursue. But here a caveat is in order. The behavior of national or other political leadership groups is a more complex phenomenon than the behavior of a small *ad hoc* group playing an experimental game. The stress conditions encountered during the course of a struggle that lasts for weeks or months or even years are much more intricate psychologically than those experienced in a two-hour game. The internal and external settings are infinitely richer in variety, as are the values, perceptions, cross-pressures, information, and political-cultural guidelines which impinge upon the decision-makers. In a larger-scale and more prolonged crisis, the time factor may permit various subtle adjustment mechanisms to come into play which can never operate in a brief experiment.

One cannot deny, however, that there is some relationship between stress and problem-solving efficiency. Dean G. Pruitt, synthesizing the findings of several writers in the field, concludes that the relationship is probably curvilinear, some stress being necessary to motivate activity but too much stress causing a reduction in efficiency.[83] Crisis inevitably brings in its wake a foreshortened perspective, a difficulty in thinking ahead and calculating consequences, and a tendency to select for consideration only a narrow range of alternatives—those which occur most readily to the decision-makers.[84] Naturally, if more time were available a wider spectrum of choices could be evaluated, but the preciousness of time is built into the definition of crisis. Contingency planning can help, but the crisis which comes is invariably somewhat different, at least in its details, from the crisis which was abstractly anticipated.

There is no reason, on the basis of available psychological data, to be unduly optimistic or unduly pessimistic about the ability of decision-making groups to conduct cooperative, rational problem-solving operations under conditions of crisis. This observation may be of small comfort in a nuclear age of international relations, when recurring crisis has become a normal and

82. Robert L. Hamblin, "Group Integration During a Crisis," *Human Relations,* XI (1958), in Singer, ed., *op. cit.,* pp. 226–228.

83. Dean G. Pruitt, "Definition of the Situation as a Determinant of International Action," Kelman, ed., *op. cit.,* p. 395.

84. See *ibid.,* p. 396, where Pruitt refers to the work of M. J. Driver and Charles E. Osgood.

expected feature of the world's political-strategic landscape.[85] The two leading members of the international system have begun to accumulate a certain amount of steadying experience in the restrained management of those crises in which they confront each other directly. The pessimist cites every new crisis as evidence that mankind's luck is running out and that the leaders of the powers cannot be expected to weather another storm like the last one without making fatally absurd moves. The optimist, on the other hand, regards each passing crisis as a gained experience, and thus a contribution, however meager, toward the developing of a maturing and stabilizing process. At the very least, we can say that the foreign policy decisions of national governmental institutions occur in a context which normally minimizes the influence of personal and emotional factors and makes it likely that the collective political decision will embody a more practical wisdom than do most every-day personal decisions of individuals.

85. The social science literature on crisis is growing. In addition to the works already cited in this section, see Charles A. McClelland, "The Acute International Crisis," *World Politics,* XIV (October, 1961), 182–204; Charles A. McClelland, "Access to Berlin: The Quantity and Variety of Events, 1948–1963," Singer, ed., *op. cit.,* pp. 159–186; Charles A. McClelland, "Action Structures and Communication in Two International Crises: Quemoy and Berlin," James N. Rosenau, ed., *International Politics and Foreign Policy,* rev. ed. (New York: Free Press, 1969), pp. 473–483; Charles F. Hermann, "International Crisis as a Situational Variable," Rosenau, ed., *ibid.,* pp. 409–422; Robert C. North, "Decision-Making in Crises: An Introduction;" Richard R. Fagen, "Calculation and Emotion in Foreign Policy: The Cuban Case;" Dinna A. Zinnes, "Hostility in International Decision-Making;" all in the *Journal of Conflict Resolution,* VI (September, 1962), 197–199, 214–221, 236–243.

CHAPTER 12
Game Theory, Bargaining, and Gaming

Game Theory and the Study of Political Phenomena

Some people are either shocked or offended or both at the suggestion that such serious phenomena as politics and human conflict should be treated as "games." The analogy seems almost sacreligious insofar as it implies a conceptual reduction of important human affairs to a sport or recreation. Yet throughout history generals and strategists have engaged in a practice known as "war gaming," which involves an effort to second-guess the opponent in advance, and many a party politician and government official has referred to his profession at times as part of "the great game of politics." Johan Huizinga (1872–1945), a distinguished Dutch philosopher-historian, argued that human culture cannot be fully comprehended unless we realize that man is a "player," *homo ludens*, and that human beings play games from childhood through old age in all dimensions of life from making love to making war.[1] Today it is assumed that many human behaviors often acquire a game-like quality. This is true for labor-management bargaining, price competition among large industrial firms, the rivalry of two suitors for a woman's hand, the strategy of guerrilla insurgency, or the conduct of international arms control negotiations, as well as buying a house or deterring tantrums in a child.[2]

GAME THEORY AS DECISION-MAKING

Game theory is a specialized form of decision-making theory and a controversial one at that. Some condemn it out of hand as useless simply because

1. See Johan Huizinga, *Homo Ludens: A Study of the Play Element in Culture* (Boston: Beacon Press, 1955).

2. These and other game-like situations are cited for heuristic purposes by Thomas C. Schelling, whose theories are summarized in a subsequent section of this chapter.

they do not understand it. Others who are infatuated with it but who do not fully understand the problems of applying it to the social order do a disservice to game theory by pretending that it can provide precise answers to the policymaker's dilemma when it cannot. The analysis of games will not furnish a normative code of how to behave ethically in any concrete situation. Nor does it give us a complete empirical theory of how people actually do behave in real-life situations. Hence, we do not expect from game theory a reliable predictive capability in international politics. The authors of this book disagree with those who contend that a political problem is incomprehensible unless expressed in mathematical terms. We are even farther from those enthusiasts who seem to regard game theory and experimental gaming as indispensable keys to social salvation. Nevertheless, we believe that after its deficiencies have been discounted and its limitations recognized, game theory remains a useful analytical tool in the field of international relations. Managed skillfully, it can help to provide new insights into certain decision-making situations which contain elements of conflict or collaboration and which call for the adoption of a "strategic" approach to the solution of the problem.

Not all foreign policy decisions require a strategic approach. In many situations the policymaker finds himself pitted not against an opposing strategic intelligence but rather against characteristics of human nature, society, and the physical environment which do not really constitute "conflict parties" in the strict sense of the term. This would hold particularly true, for example, in respect to many decisions concerning foreign aid and international economic development, in which the "adversaries" to be overcome are seen as human sickness, hunger, illiteracy, unfavorable weather conditions, soil poverty, chronic foreign exchange deficits, and similar factors. Although we often speak metaphorically of "strategies" against disease, hunger, ignorance and poverty—and the use of the term is not entirely inappropriate when applied to man's struggle against these impersonal forces—still, it must be borne in mind that "conflict" in the parlance of the social sciences presupposes a kind of contest among human parties who are consciously seeking objectives which are, at least for the time being, incompatible.[3] When we are dealing with international strategic situations, game theory helps us to clarify our thought about available choices, suggests novel possibilities which might not otherwise have occurred to us, and induces us to penetrate beyond a mere verbal description of a problem to a deeper, more generalized level of comprehension at which more powerful analytic methodologies might usefully be brought into play. As Anatol Rapoport writes:

3. The foreign aid example might be misleading. Often the opponents of foreign aid decision-making are individuals or groups striving to thwart development programs—land reform, tax reform, edu- cation, restrictions on capital flight abroad, etc. These are genuine strategic adversaries, and they require a well-conceived strategic approach.

Contending Theories of International Relations

Game theory, when it is pursued beyond its elementary paradox-free formulations, teaches us what we must be able to do in order to bring the intellect to bear on a science of human conflict. To analyze a conflict scientifically, we must be able to agree on relative values (to assign utilities). We must learn to be perceptive (evaluate the other's assignment of utilities). Furthermore, in order to engage in a conflict thus formalized, we must be able to communicate (give a credible indication to the other of how we assign utilities to outcomes).[4]

Here an earlier caveat bears reiteration: Game theory is an interesting and potentially productive way of looking at certain classes of decision-making problems; it is not a *ouija* board for a magical science which is capable of supplying instant solutions for specific complex situations.

INTELLECTUAL ORIGINS AND DEFINITIONS

Martin Shubik's definition of game theory as a method of studying decision-making in conflict situations is a good point of departure.[5] This theory, says Thomas C. Schelling, "is concerned with situations—games of 'strategy,' in contrast to games of skill or games of chance—in which the best course of action for each participant depends on what he expects the other participants to do." [6] Both Shubik and Schelling, along with other game theorists, have built upon the foundation laid in the pioneering work of John von Neumann and Oskar Morgenstern.[7] The latter pair, one a mathematician and the other an economist, analyzed the various strategies that might be pursued by players in relatively simple games and found that mathematical methods enabled one to identify all possible sequences of moves and to select an optimum strategy for playing.[8] They suggested that some of the lessons to be learned from game theory may be applicable to more complex social situations.

Game theory is based upon an abstract form of reasoning, arising from a

4. Anatol Rapoport, "The Use and Misuse of Game Theory," *Scientific American,* CCVII (December, 1962), 118. See also Martin Shubik, "Game Theory and the Study of Social Behavior: An Introductory Exposition," Martin Shubik, ed., *Game Theory and Related Approaches to Social Behavior* (New York: John Wiley and Sons, 1964), pp. 4–5.

5. *Ibid.,* p. 8.

6. Thomas C. Schelling, *The Strategy of Conflict* (New York: Oxford University Press [Galaxy Books], 1963), pp. 9–10. According to Richard C. Snyder, the purpose of game theory is to formulate mathematically complete principles that will specify rational choices when it is

impossible to control all the factors governing outcomes because of the decisions of others. "Game Theory and the Analysis of Political Behavior," *op. cit.,* pp. 73–75.

7. John von Neumann and Oskar Morgenstern, *Theory of Games and Economic Behavior* (Princeton: Princeton University Press, 1944, 1953).

8. It should be stressed that this holds for simpler games. It has not yet proved possible, even with computers, to work out the "perfect" strategy for such a game as chess which potentially involves trillions of alternate choices, depending upon the interaction of the two players' choices. See Shubik, *op. cit.,* p. 12.

Game Theory, Bargaining, and Gaming

combination of mathematics and logic. Nearly all game theorists would agree that the theory with which they deal is addressed to what is "rationally correct" behavior in conflict situations in which the participants are trying to "win," rather than to the way individuals actually do behave in conflict situations. Individuals can and often do conduct themselves irrationally and emotionally in conflict situations, but for the sake of their theoretical analysis, games theorists assume rational behavior, simply because they find this assumption more profitable for theory-building than the obverse of it. If we were to assume that all human behavior is fundamentally absurd, neurotic or psychotic, then there could be no theory, either of games or of any other social phenomena. Games theorists, then, subscribe to some such notion as the following: If people in a certain situation wish to "win"—i.e., to accomplish an objective which the other party seeks to deny them—we can sort out the intellectual processes by which they calculate what kind of action is most likely to be advantageous to them, assuming that they believe their opponents also to be rational calculators like themselves, equally interested in "second-guessing" and trying to outwit the opponent.[9]

In some contemporary circles, the notion of "winning" is regarded as irrational. But games theorists have to assume that "winning" is the goal of game-

9. As Anatol Rapoport has asserted quite cogently, a theory is a collection of theorems, and a theorem "is a proposition which is a strict logical consequence of certain definitions and other propositions." "Various Meanings of 'Theory',", *American Political Science Review,* LII (December, 1958), 973. He notes that Freudian "depth psychology" is "singularly poor in predictive capacity, either deterministic or statistical" (*ibid.,* p. 982) but he does not suggest that the reason for this perhaps resides in the basic irrationality of the subject matter. If one really assumes the irrationality of behavior, he must at the same time accept its unpredictability, at least for the time being, until the behavior becomes rationally penetrable. In the social universe, the observer can ascribe no greater rationality to his own theoretical explanation of a phenomenon than he is willing to attribute to the "decision-makers" who collectively comprise the action-situation or process he is trying to describe and explain. Rapoport does concede, however, that the special merits of game theory derive from its assumption of "perfectly rational players" (*ibid.,* p. 984). This may, of course, also constitute a major weakness if, in contrast to Freudian psychoanalytic theory which emphasizes irrationality, game theory runs to the opposite extreme and places excessive stress upon the mathematically rational factors which enter into human decisional behavior. The notion of "second-guessing" may be more psychological than logical-mathematical. Which strategic philosophy does the good strategist adopt? Does he play the board, or does he play the opponent? Does he formulate his strategy on the basis of a mathematical computation of available moves, or does he formulate it much as a psychological warfare expert would try to size up his adversary? Anatol Rapoport, a mathematician-psychologist-game theorist at the University of Michigan, concedes that pure game theory is essentially mathematical and hence contains no uncertainties. "Although the drama of games of strategy is strongly linked with the psychological aspects of the conflict, game theory is not concerned with these aspects. Game theory, so to speak, plays the board. It is concerned only with the logical aspects of strategy. It prescribes the same line of play against a master as it does against a beginner." "The Use and Misuse of Game Theory," *Scientific American,* CCVII (December, 1962), 110.

Contending Theories of International Relations

sters. Presumably if a player is deliberately trying to lose, he is either psychi-
cally peculiar or else he is playing a different game. Take, for example, the
case of a father who frequently plays a parlor game with three of his children.
If two of the children have been steadily winning, while the third has been
getting out of sorts over losing, the father may try to lose deliberately so that
the third child can move into the winner's circle. When he does this, the father
is not playing according to the assumptions underlying the rules of the game
as printed on the inside of the box cover. But at this point the father is playing
his own game—a different and in a sense a larger game.

A few rudimentary concepts should be considered. Every game is characterized by the following elements: 1) two or more players who are trying in
some sense either (a zero-sum game) to get the best of each other or (a non-
zero-sum game) to achieve a solution which is best for both; 2) a payoff or
a set of payoffs which may mean various things to the players because of
discrepancies in their value systems; 3) a set of ground rules or guidelines
which must be observed if the game is to be played according to the definition
of the game; 4) information conditions which determine the quality and quantity of knowledge which each player has of the environment and of the choices
made by the other player(s); 5) the total environment in which the game is
played, whether fully perceived by the players or not; and 6) the interaction
of competing moves, in which every choice by one may prompt the other(s)
to modify subsequent choices. Eventually, each of these elements will have to
be elaborated upon in their applicability to "the game" of international strategic relations. For the moment, it is sufficient to point out that a game might
be compared to a "system" insofar as it has "roles," "inputs" and "outputs,"
"parameters," a "communications flow," an "external environment," and a
set of interacting variables—in this case, rival strategies.

ZERO-SUM GAMES

The most commonly drawn preliminary distinction in game theory is that
between a zero-sum game and a non-zero-sum game, with variations of each.
In a zero-sum game between A and B, what A wins, B loses. Chess, checkers,
mill, two-person poker, stratego, two-man blackjack—all of these are two-
person zero-sum games. Each game ends with one player having a score of
plus one and the other minus one, and the value of "one" for the game
depends upon the "stakes" or the size of the "pot." Examples of real-life
situations which contain aspects of zero-sum games would include an electoral
race between two candidates for a Congressional seat, most military tactical
situations in which the objective which one side seizes is lost to the other at
least temporarily, such as an "air duel" or a battle over a hill, and the rivalry
of two men for the hand of the same woman, assuming that she is a woman
of honor. It should be noted that a three-man race for an elective office is not

really a zero-sum game unless we break it down into two different contests between the winner and each loser. Some analysts would also point out that there is a difference between a ZSG in which what one player loses he previously possesses (as in poker) and a ZSG in which the loss is a prize which was being sought (as in an election campaign). But game theory does not consider these differences significant. We might also observe that in a tactical military situation the ground gained by one side equals the ground lost by the other, but there might have been a considerable discrepancy in the cost to each side, measured in casualties. The same notion holds true for the election campaign and for courting a fair lady: there is a single payoff, but the contending parties may spend widely varying sums in the effort to win. Payoff should not be confused with cost, although it is often necessary to compare the one with the other to determine "whether the game is worth the candle."

Two-Person Zero-Sum Games

In most of the literature on the subject, games are schematically represented in a "normalized" form in which no details of the game are given but in which the strategies for each player and the accompanying payoffs are depicted in a matrix. Moreover, the payoff values are often assigned in a purely arbitrary manner, merely to facilitate the illustration of a point. (The student, therefore, need not worry too much about how the payoff values were arrived at—at least not yet.) Moreover, the strategies may consist of fairly complex plans and yet be designated simply as Strategy 1 or Strategy 2 or Strategy N for each player. Thus, in mathematical theory, both strategies and payoffs are treated abstractly. In the most helpful form of notation, each matrix contains the payoff which each player receives when he chooses one of the two strategies that converge at that point. The student may, however, come across a matrix which shows only the payoffs to one player. The following three simplified 2 × 2 matrices, borrowed or adapted from Shubik, will be sufficient to illustrate our discussion of two-person zero-sum games:

Matrix I		Strategy for Player 2	
		A	B
Strategy for	A	+4,−4	−3,+3
Player 1	B	−3,+3	+4,−4

Matrix II		Strategy for Player 2	
		A	B
Strategy for	A	−5,+5	−7,+7
Player 1	B	+8,−8	+1,−1

Matrix III			Strategy for Player 2	
			A	B
Strategy for	A		−20, −20	+5, −5
Player 1	B		−5, +5	−2, −2

Matrix I refers to a game in which there is no "saddlepoint." First it will be noticed that in each matrix the sum of the payoffs is zero.[10] But there is no point at which the strategies of the competing players logically converge. If both players opt for the A strategy, No. 1 wins 4 and the other loses 4. If No. 1 plays his B strategy and No. 2 chooses the A strategy, the former loses and the latter gains 3. If the student analyzes this payoff matrix for a minute, he will see that the best strategy for each player in a long series of runs is a random strategy, determined by the toss of a coin, for this will eventually produce a balancing out of the wins and losses of 4's and 3's. In other words, the game schematized in Matrix I reduces to a game of chance with which game theory is not directly concerned.

Matrix II refers to a ZSG in which there is a saddlepoint. This is the point at which the minimum values in the rows (across) and the maximum values in the columns (up and down) converge at equality, or where the maximum values in the rows and the minimum values in the columns converge. The point of convergence is known as the minimax value. It is an axiom of game theory that in a two-person zero-sum game, a rational strategy is based on the minimax principle: Each player should seek to maximize the minimum gain of which he can be assured, or to minimize the maximum loss which he need sustain. Let us suppose, again following Shubik, that Player 1 is a police force in a country torn by guerrilla insurgency, and Player 2 is the guerrilla force. The police in this particular game can choose either to go into the jungle in pursuit of the insurgents (Strategy A) or to avoid the jungle and to protect key areas (Strategy B). The choice of open battle or attritional skirmishes is up to the guerrilla force. The police do better out of the jungle than in it, where they stand to lose in both battles, and skirmishes (−5 and −7, respectively). The guerrillas' preferred strategy, whether in or out of the jungle, is to skirmish, for in this way they can maximize their gains (+8) or hold their losses to a minimum (−1). In the simplified game described, two rational players would tend to converge at the saddlepoint of +1, −1—i.e., the police would probably choose key areas outside the jungle, while the guerrillas would skirmish and eschew open battle, thus holding their losses

10. Details of a simple game may help the student to envisage the game. Let us call it Defenders and Attackers. The latter can strike at either of two towns. The Defenders can fully protect only one. If the Defenders select the right town and meet the Attackers, the latter will be destroyed. If Defenders select one town and Attackers select the other, the town is destroyed. Martin Shubik, "The Uses of Game Theory," Charlesworth, ed., *op. cit.*, p. 247.

Game Theory, Bargaining, and Gaming

to -1 instead of -8.[11] This, of course, only describes the tactical encounters between guerrillas and police. For an insight into the strategic outcome of a guerrilla insurgency, something much more complex than a simple 2×2 matrix would be required. (In real life, the guerrillas might lose most tactical exchanges and yet win strategically, because of psychopolitical factors.)

The minimax strategy is a cautious strategy. There are five points to be remembered in connection with the minimax strategy: 1) It applies only to zero-sum games. 2) It is proof against information leakage. 3) It is useful and normative only against an opponent who is presumed to be playing a rational game. If the adversary is stupid, prone to make blunders or usually motivated by emotional factors (which might, for example, incline him to play his "hunches") then the minimax strategy is not necessarily the optimum one to pursue. 4) The utility of the minimax strategy is validated in a series of plays, not in a one-shot game. 5) It is a rather dull, no-fun strategy, but it may be unavoidable. Shubik offers the following caveat:

> *Apart from appreciating the two-person zero-sum game as the definition of a strictly competitive situation, the general political scientist will not gain too much insight from an intense study of this topic . . . There is also a considerable amount of misinterpretation concerning the role in general game theory of the famous result concerning two-person zero-sum games known as the* minimax *or* saddlepoint theorem. *Zero-sum games are of extremely limited interest in the behavioral sciences in general.*[12]

The type of game referred to in Matrix III above leads us partially out of two-person zero-sum games toward the non-zero-sum or nonconstant-sum game. The essential characteristic of a non-zero-sum (NZSG) is that it is not exclusively competitive in the sense that what one gains another must lose. The sum of gains and losses need not add up to zero. There is room in this type of game for elements of both conflict and cooperation; on some plays, both parties might win, and at the end of the game both parties might be ahead by varying amounts. In a non-zero-sum game there are often several different payoffs, some of which may be very good or very bad, some marginally good or bad. The payoffs depend upon whether the players cooperate with each other, cut each other's throats, or mix their strategies of conflict and cooperation in varying combinations.

What is interesting about Matrix III (on p. 351) is the fact that it refers to a game which might be a ZSG under some circumstances and a NZSG under others, depending upon the outcome. Actually, this matrix depicts the possible payoffs in a game of "chicken," in which two youths drive toward each other in their fathers' automobiles at eighty miles an hour, each with his left set of wheels on the highway dividing line. If neither one swerves to the right they

---

11. Martin Shubik, "Game Theory and the Study of Social Behavior," *op. cit.*, pp. 15–17.

12. Martin Shubik, "The Uses of Game Theory," Charlesworth, ed., *op. cit.*, p. 248.

will both be killed in the crash—an outcome which is arbitrarily assigned a numerical value of -20 for each. It could just as easily have been -200 or another figure, but in any event this becomes a "minus-sum game in which both players lose as heavily as possible." If one stays on the course and the other veers, one gains esteem and the other loses in the eyes of the peer group. The latter is "chicken." This condition is indicated in the two matrices containing a $+5$ and -5. Thus if either driver swerves and the other holds to the course, the game turns out to be zero-sum. If both veer to the right, each suffers dishonor in the eyes of the peer group, but since the reputation for being "chicken" is shared between them, so that no invidious comparisons can be drawn, each suffers only a -2.[13] We should hasten to point out that the payoff matrix as shown is partly a function of the distorted value system of the youthful peer group, as perceived by the two drivers. Actually, the peer group chiefly craves the excitement of the game, and regrets the tragic outcome later. Certainly the parents and fiancées of the two youths would assign a larger negative valuation to their deaths and a high positive valuation to an outcome in which both have enough sense to veer off course before it is too late.[14] It ought to be made clear that the game of "chicken," played with human life at stake, is a game that is entered into only by irrational players, one or both of whom may become rational enough during the course of the game to save their lives.

NON-ZERO-SUM GAMES

Two-person non-zero-sum games can be played either "cooperatively" or "noncooperatively." In a "cooperative" game, the players are permitted to communicate with each other directly and to exchange information in advance concerning their intended choices. In a "noncooperative" game, overt communication is not permitted but the choice of each becomes obvious to

13. See *Ibid.*, pp. 242–243.

14. The mathematicization of utilities or value preferences is always a tenuous business. Even in respect to zero-sum games, Thomas C. Schelling notes that the value systems of two individuals are incommensurate. "If two feudal noblemen play a game of cards, one to lose his thumb if he loses and the other to lose his eyesight, the game is 'zero-sum' (as long as neither cares about the other's loss) though nobody's loss is the other's gain and there may be no way of comparing what they risk losing. It is precisely *because* their value systems are incommensurable that, if their interests are strictly opposed, we can arbitrarily represent them by scales of value that make the scores of payoffs add up in every cell to zero." "What is Game Theory," Charlesworth, *op. cit.*, p. 216. An approach which contrasts with that of Schelling is presented by Morton A. Kaplan in his discussion of the work of Duncan Luce and Howard Raiffa. In a discussion of some variant games, Kaplan agrees with Luce and Raiffa that in certain games the outcome will be determined by the *psychologies* of the players. "A Note on Game Theory and Bargaining," Morton A. Kaplan, ed., *New Approaches to International Relations* (New York: St. Martin's Press, 1968), pp. 507–509.

the other after the play. There is, however, a slight ambiguity in this terminology. Even if a game is "noncooperative" insofar as the rules prohibit overt or direct communication, it is possible for the players to cooperate tacitly through inferred communication, by which one player interprets the other's intentions from the kinds of choices he makes in a long series of plays.

The "Prisoner's Dilemma" Game. Perhaps the best known example of a two-person NZSG is "Prisoner's Dilemma." Two individuals are taken into police custody and accused of a crime. Since they are interrogated separately, neither knows what the other will tell the district attorney. Each is aware that if both remain silent or deny all allegations, the worst they can expect is a sentence of sixty days in the county jail for vagrancy. If one turns state's evidence and the other remains silent, the former will receive a one-year commuted sentence and the other will be sent to the state penitentiary for ten years. If both confess, both will receive from five to eight years in prison. Their optimum strategy, of course, is a tacit agreement to remain silent, but in the absence of communication, neither can trust the other. Each makes the following assessment of the situation: If I remain silent, I will get either sixty days or ten years, depending upon whether my partner confesses. If I confess, I will receive a commuted sentence or five to eight years, depending upon whether he confesses. In either case I can assure myself of a lighter sentence by confessing. Since he is undoubtedly making the same sort of calculation, the chances are that he will confess, and hence I would be foolish to remain silent and count upon the slim chance that he would do likewise. Thus each, by choosing what seems to be the safer course, contributes to an outcome highly disadvantageous to both.[15]

Game theorists have devised several variations of "Prisoner's Dilemma," one of which will be described and analyzed below. But at this juncture the student should be reminded of two points which, though often made in pass-

15. Many descriptions of "Prisoner's Dilemma" can be found. See A. W. Tucker and P. Wolfe, eds., *Contributions to the Theory of Games,* III, *Annals of Mathematic Studies,* No. 39 (Princeton: Princeton University Press, 1957); R. Duncan Luce and Howard Raiffa, *Games and Decisions,* (New York: John Wiley and Sons, 1957); pp. 94 ff; Anatol Rapoport and A. M. Ghammah, *Prisoner's Dilemma* (Ann Arbor: University of Michigan Press, 1965); and Martin Shubik, "The Uses of Game Theory," in Charlesworth, ed., *op. cit.,* pp. 264–268. The problem of "trust" and "suspicion" between players in mixed motive games has been dealt with by Morton Deutsch, "Trust and Suspicion," *Journal of Conflict Resolution,* IV (December, 1958), and by Anatol Rapoport, "Formal Games as Probing Tools for Investigating Behavior Motivated by Trust and Suspicion," *Journal of Conflict Resolution,* VII (September, 1963), pp. 570–579. Two psychologists at Kent State University conducted gaming experiments on a variation of "Prisoner's Dilemma" in which they separated "temptation" (i.e. the desire to obtain the largest payoff by being the only defector) from "mistrust" (i.e., the fear that the other would like to be the lone defector), and found that "temptation" is a more likely source of noncooperative behavior than is "mistrust." V. Edwin Bizenstine and Hazel Blundell, "Control of Choices Exerted by Structural Factors in Two-Person, Non-Zero-Sum Games," *Journal of Conflict Resolution,* X (December, 1966), especially p. 482.

ing in the literature on game theory and games, are seldom stressed as much as they deserve to be. First, there is an important difference between game theory, which is based on mathematical-logical analysis and which purports to show what kind of strategy a rational player *should* play (when he presumes his opponent rational), and experimental gaming, which is designed to furnish empirical evidence of how individuals *actually do behave* in game situations. Second, there is an important difference between "one-shot" games and games which are played over a series of runs by the same players who, as a result of experience, acquire insight into the strategic thought processes of each other.

In one variation of "Prisoner's Dilemma," pairs of college students played fifty trials of a game in which the payoffs depended upon whether they pursued competitive or cooperative strategies. The subjects were seated on opposite sides of a partition. Each had in front of him a panel with a red button and a black button. The experimenter gave the following instructions:

> *Each of you will have a chance to make some money in this situation . . . You see in front of you a red button and a black button. On each trial you will press either the black button or the red button. If you press the black button, two things can happen. If you press the black button and the other person also presses the black button, you get three cents and he gets three cents. If you press the black button and he presses the red button, you get nothing and he gets five cents. Suppose you push the red button. Again, two things can happen. If you push the red button and the other person presses the black button, you get five cents and he gets nothing. If you push the red and the other person also pushes red, you get one cent and the other person gets one cent.*[16]

The subjects were not allowed to communicate directly with each other, but since the payoffs were made after each trial, each player knew which button the other had chosen.

The reader will note immediately that in such a game the best way to maximize monetary gains is for the two players to cooperate tacitly and to choose black on every trial. This, however, is not what happened in the experiments at Ohio State University. Only a few pairs sought to maximize monetary returns in this manner. The great majority played competitively; they were out to win more than their opponents even if this meant losing some money. In other words, the dominant strategy was to choose red most of the time, apparently on the assumption that this was the best way to do the opponent in, regardless of whether he was a beneficent or maleficent adversary. It is possible, of course, that people might play more cooperatively as the economic payoffs are increased (say, from cents to dollars), but this becomes a costly

16. Alvin Scodel, J. Sayer Minas, Philburn Ratoosh and Milton Lipetz, "Some Descriptive Aspects of Two-Person Non-Zero-Sum Games," *Journal of Conflict Resolution*, III (June, 1959), 115. See also p. 118.

method of playing experimental games which few supporters of scholarly research are eager to underwrite.[17] It is also possible that many people play games for a satisfaction which is not readily reducible to economics. "Winning" is often much more fun than cooperation to optimize financial gains. Whether in this type of situation the competitive desire to win is any less "rational" than the cooperative desire to maximize economic income is a question for the philosophers of game theory to debate.

Anatol Rapoport has constructed a variation of "Prisoner's Dilemma" to illustrate a problem of international politics between nuclear powers A and B which are considering two alternatives—total disarmament (TD) versus an arms race (AR). In his simplified model, the military capabilities of other countries can be ignored. When both are involved in the arms race, each is satisfied that mutual deterrence based on a "balance of power" provides a security assurance against attack, but this is very costly. If both countries are disarmed, each is likewise satisfied that it is secure from attack, and this condition is highly advantageous from an economic standpoint. But *unilateral* disarmament is highly disadvantageous to the disarmed nation and highly advantageous to the nation which remained armed, or rearmed while the other remained disarmed.

17. In "Prisoner's Dilemma" experiments at Pennsylvania State University, larger payoffs varying from $2 to $5 were used in games which were run through ninety-eight trials for each pair of subjects. Because of high costs, however, it was not possible to make a payoff after each trial. Only a single payoff was made for a single trial selected by a random procedure after the completion of all the trials. The result was "a tendency toward cooperative choice." Robert Radlow, "An Experimental Study of 'Cooperation' in the Prisoner's Dilemma Game," *Journal of Conflict Resolution,* IX (June, 1965), 223. There would seem to be grounds for holding that the concept of a single-shot payoff may have altered the game structure and the motivation of the players so as to furnish an artificial inducement for more frequent cooperation. If so, Radlow's results, while interesting in themselves, would be somewhat inconclusive as a refutation of the Ohio State findings concerning the dominance of competitiveness over cooperation for maximization of gain. In another series of experiments at Ohio State University involving the choice of red (competitive) with black (cooperative), no significant differences were noted between mixed-sex and same-sex pairs, and it was concluded that sex role does not influence cooperative and competitive behavior in this type of game. Daniel R. Lutzker, "Sex Role, Cooperation and Competition in a Two-Person, Non-zero-sum-Game," *Journal of Conflict Resolution,* V (December 1961), 366–368. See also Philip S. Gallo, Jr., and Charles G. McClintock, "Cooperative and Competitive Behavior in Mixed-Motive Games," *Journal of Conflict Resolution,"* IX (March, 1965), 68–78; and Harold H. Kelley, "Experimental Studies of Threats in Interpersonal Negotiations," *ibid.,* 79–105. Malvern Lumsden conducted experiments in Norway to raise the stakes in a different way. He tried to make the game of "prisoners' dilemma" more realistic by casting it in terms of resistance to German occupation in World War II. He sought to do the same for a game of "chicken" by expressing it in terms of a nuclear confrontation over Cuba. He thus introduced an element of "higher stakes" by a simulated appeal to the imagination of the players and found that this led to a substantial increase in cooperative behavior. "Perception and Information in Strategic Thinking," *Journal of Peace Research,* III (1966), 255–277.

The "game" described in the preceding paragraph is represented in the following matrix:

		Strategy for County B	
		TD	AR
Strategy for Country A	TD	5, −5	−10, 10
	AR	10, −10	−5 , 5

Strategy AR proves dominating for both players because it is certain to be better than the other no matter what the opponent chooses, if we ignore the cost factor. If B remains armed, A must remain armed; if B disarms, A then becomes stronger than B. But if both remain armed, they are worse off in this game than if they had both disarmed. (This may not be the case in a real-life situation, but for purposes of the game it is.) The way this game is structured, each player chooses his own strategy. There is no "agreement" to disarm under terms and controls to satisfy both sides. Strategy AR is dictated by national self-interest. Strategy TD is based upon the perception of collective interest. Both parties might prefer to benefit through cooperation (just as in the case of the two prisoners) but neither one knows what the other will do. Neither can choose collective interest over self-interest because it is forced to assume that the other will follow the most prudent course.[18]

N-PERSON GAMES

This brings us to N-Person non-zero-sum games, involving three or more players. As might be expected, much less is known about these than about two-person games, because the number of permutations or interacting strategies increases at an exponential rate with the number of players. Hence it is not surprising that no single theory has yet been developed for N-Person games. Probably the must fruitful avenue of inquiry to date has been in the area of coalition formation. (For an examination of literature on alliances and coalitions, see Chapter 10.) When several players are in a game, it becomes quite natural for two or more to form a coalition against the others, in which case the others are induced to do likewise in order to ensure their survival and maximize their gains. Sometimes the rules of the game may encourage the alignment of coalitions before starting to play; sometimes coalitions are formed, either tacitly or overtly, after the game is in progress. If two coalitions emerge, forcing all players to choose one or the other, the game in effect is reduced to a two-person zero-sum game.[19] It is conceivable, how-

18. Anatol Rapoport, *Strategy and Conscience* (New York: Harper and Row, 1964), pp. 48–52.

19. Anatol Rapoport and C. Orwant, "Experimental Games: A Review," *Behavioral Science*, VII (January, 1962), 1–37.

ever, that at a particular stage of the game there might be three coalitions, one of which would eventually find itself under pressure to coalesce with one of the other two. The crucial question, it would appear, is to work out to the satisfaction of all the allies "a rational division of the spoils." [20] If coalitions are formed before the start of the game, all the partners should be considered equal and entitled to an equal share of the payoff. What is much more interesting, of course, is a situation in which the payoff is divided according to the contribution which each partner makes to the victory of the coalition, and where the contribution is in some sense a function of "power" and "weakness." Sometimes there may be "founding members" of the coalitions with others permitted to join later after bargaining for terms which reflect both the power of the coalition leaders and the more desperate straits of the applicants for entry. In addition to the division of the payoff and to the circumstances under which coalitions are formed, other questions worthy of the attention of games theorists pertain to the motives which might drive a member of one coalition to defect to another and whether it is possible for a coalition to enforce against its own members any sanction that is stronger and more efficacious than the bond of mutual interest.[21]

International Relations as a "Game"

It is now time to ask what all this has to do with international relations or, more narrowly, with international politics. First, it should be made clear that international relations—or the operation of the international system—cannot be fully comprehended merely within the analytical framework of a "game." But the patterns and processes of international relations undeniably manifest certain gamelike characteristics. The application of analytical techniques derived from game theory, therefore, can aid in improving our understanding of the subject, provided that this approach is employed with the balanced

20. Abraham Kaplan, "Mathematics and Social Analysis," *Commentary*, VII (September, 1952), 284. The mathematical and psycho-strategic intricacies of the three-person game can be appreciated by reading William H. Riker, "Bargaining in a Three-Person Game," *American Political Science Review*, LXI (September, 1967), 642–656.

21. For theoretical insights into the formation and dissolution of coalitions, see Chapter 10 and the following works: George F. Liska, *Nations in Alliance:* *The Limits of Interdependence* (Baltimore: Johns Hopkins Press, 1962); William R. Riker, *The Theory of Political Coalitions* (New Haven: Yale University Press, 1962); Julian R. Friedman, Christopher Bladen and Steven Rosen, *Alliance in International Studies* (Boston: Allyn and Bacon, 1970); Sven Groennings, E. W. Kelley and Michael Leiserson, eds., *The Study of Coalition Behavior: Theoretical Perspectives and Cases from Four Continents* (New York: Holt, Rinehart and Winston, 1970).

intellectual perspective of those who regard it as one among several useful tools. Within the last decade or so, some have ascribed too many wonderful problem-solving powers to game theory; others have condemned it, especially when applied to such strategic issues as nuclear deterrence, the prevention of local aggression and the conduct of limited war.[22] The authors of this book prefer to pursue a *via media* between these extreme views.

Virtually all game theorists agree that international relations can best be conceptualized as an N-person non-zero-sum game, in which a gain by one party is not necessarily at the expense of other parties. An example of this, drawn from international economics, can be seen in the fact that the more advanced industrialized countries of the West, as well as Japan and the Soviet system states, do not suffer a loss in their absolute or relative economic position as the national economies of Asia, Latin America and Africa develop. Indeed, economic expansion in less developed countries often leads to an intensification of trade, aid and investment relations with the wealthier countries of the Western system. But it is to be noted that this example, which is quite clearcut, comes from the realm of economics. Several writers who have pioneered in the effort to apply game theory to the social sciences (e.g., Oskar Morgenstern, Thomas C. Schelling, Martin Shubik and J. C. Harsanyi) have had economic training or have done extensive research into problems of economic competition. Competition between economic firms can be either a zero-sum or a non-zero-sum game. Economic analysts see the latter as the preferable, more rational alternative because both firms stand to gain, at least in the shorter run, if the mutual wounds of excessive competition can be avoided. Perhaps it is not too much to say that within the American economy the desirable has gradually become, or is becoming, the actual: The rivalry among the largest corporations in a field is looked upon as a non-zero-sum game.

22. James Newman, for example, has written: "The theory of games can fairly be said to have laid the foundation for a systematic and penetrating mathematical treatment of a vast range of problems in social science. . . . The theory of games is today regarded as the most promising mathematical tool yet devised for the analysis of man's social relations." *The World of Mathematics* (New York: Simon and Schuster, 1956), II, 1265. See also Colonel Francis X. Kane, U.S.A.F., "Security Is too Important to Be Left to Computers," *Fortune*, LXX (April, 1964), 146–147. "In order to construct models and manipulate them mathematically, we need masses of data on repeated events. This necessitates the discarding of data on individual events that do not fit into the mass. Such "unique" events lie principally in the field of decisions that have occurred only once in history—e.g., the Japanese decision to attack Pearl Harbor, the United States decision to defend South Korea, the Soviet decision to put missiles into Communist Cuba. These individual acts cannot be handled by scientific methodology." In England, R. H. S. Crossman, P. M. S. Blackett, Sir Solly Zuckerman and Bertrand Russell, and in the United States, Stuart Hughes, David Reisman, Michael Macoby, Arthur Waskow and Eugene Rabinowitch have been numbered among the critics of "game theory" strategists. See Albert Wohlstetter, "Sin and Games in America," Shubik, ed., *op. cit.*, 209–225.

But whether international politics can be as readily reduced as international economics to a non-zero-sum game will probably be for a long time a subject of debate between political scientists and economists. To be sure, there are some political scientists who do not sharply distinguish between politics and economics—or, for that matter, between politics and psychology. But the authors of this work are convinced that "the political" is not perfectly interchangeable with "the economic" or the "psychological." As we pointed out in a previous chapter, there are important differences between political decisions and decisions made by business firms or by individuals.[23] Hence we caution against efforts to make a hasty and uncritical transfer of the NZSG concept to international politics by those who do not offer any convincing scientific demonstration beyond a simple illustration of highly restricted applicability. In our view, international politics (as a distinctive segment of the more comprehensive phenomenon of "international relations") can best be understood within the game theoretical framework as involving a complex and fluctuating mixture of tendencies toward zero-sumness and non-zero-sumness.

There can be no doubt that it is highly desirable in the nuclear age to stress the elements of mutual interest and tacit cooperation in the avoidance of general war, in the hope that these will outweigh the elements of divergent interests and conflict. But the understandable desire to attenuate the dangerous excesses of international ideological conflict has perhaps led some analysts to overlook the fundamental difference between the *ought* and the *is*. The conduct of international politics would probably be more restrained if the political leaders of all the major powers were convinced that international politics is a non-zero-sum game in the nuclear age. But for scholars to assert that it always has been so, and always will be necessarily so, is to propound conclusions which serious study of history does not substantiate.

It might be more accurate to say that international politics is usually a non-zero-sum game for most "players," because most governments normally tend to observe rational limits in their decision-making processes. But in every age there may be a few political-strategic adversaries who view their confrontation with each other as having certain characteristics analogous to those encountered in a two-person zero-sum game. History is replete with instances of this phenomenon, from Rome's Catonic strategy toward Carthage to the insistence of contemporary extreme Arab nationalists that Israel must eventually be "driven into the sea." Undoubtedly, much of the zero-sum quality that marks certain bilateral interstate relations in this century is a function of ideological attitudes combined with the dialectics of communications systems and mass politics. In some cases, leaders may feel compelled to pay lip service to the ideological objective of "the annihilation of the

23. See Chap. 11, pp. 329–334.

enemy" even if they have no serious intention of embarking upon an Armageddon during their tenure of rule. But if individuals and groups in one country speak frequently as if the bilateral relationship is a zero-sum game, their counterparts in the second country will sooner or later do likewise. It will always be important to distinguish the way in which a bilateral conflict is viewed by the governmental policymakers, by various politically conscious social groups, and by individuals. If an ideologically oriented group which perceives the conflict as a zero-sum game should seize control of the government, the conflict may indeed become a zero-sum game.

Instead of viewing international politics as a single n-person game, it might be appropriate to think of it as an almost infinite variety of subgames striving to become a universal game. The subgames themselves may be two-person games (e.g., Soviet-American, Franco-German, Arab-Israeli or UAR-Israeli relations, and so on) or n-person games of a coalition character (e.g., NATO and the Warsaw Pact) or of a universalist character (the League of Nations and the United Nations). Thus, international politics appears as a continuous series of simultaneous subgames in which the number, identity, and perhaps even the nature of the players, as well as the payoffs which they seek, undergo changes from time to time. These changes, which some try to facilitate and others to prevent, have much to do with whether the subgames are zero-sum or non-zero-sum.

INTERNATIONAL RELATIONS: LIMITATIONS OF GAME THEORY

Those who would apply the game theoretical framework to the analysis of international politics require a greater precision of language than they have sometimes employed in the past. It is not enough to say merely that we are dealing with a non-zero-sum-game. We must carefully define the structure of the game we are discussing: the players, the rules and objectives of the game, the pay-offs and the values which the players attach to them, the whole context in which the game is played, and the interaction of the various strategies pursued. A specific game might appear to be a zero-sum game in the eyes of a country's leaders but not in the eyes of the whole people. Take, for example, World War II as it was waged between Germany and the Allied Powers. The strategic objective of "unconditional surrender" enunciated by Roosevelt and Churchill certainly made the war look like a zero-sum-game to Hitler's Nazi regime because the latter could not possibly accept such terms and still survive politically, even though the German people could survive "unconditional surrender" and endure as a nation, albeit a divided one.

It might be argued that many of the anticolonial revolutions which have occurred since World War II were, in a sense, zero-sum encounters, assuming that the metropolitan countries were aiming at the preservation of their political control within the overseas territories while the insurgents were seeking to eliminate foreign control and to establish their own independent status. In short, when two parties are striving toward mutually exclusive objectives and one succeeds and the other fails, this is a zero-sum game. If the contest ends in a complex compromise which leaves neither party entirely satisfied but where both parties are willing to settle for less than their original objectives rather than bear the cost of prolonging the struggle, then this is a non-zero-sum game. Thus the zero-sumness or non-zero-sumness of a subgame in international politics must be defined in terms of the various alternative payoffs and outcomes as these are perceived by the players.

The difference between a ZSG and a NZSG does not, contrary to popular opinion, depend on whether the game is conceptualized in such a way that one side must survive while the other perishes. Extreme Communist ideologues might see their conflict with "capitalism" in this way, and so might extreme Arab nationalists describe the solution of the problem of "Israeli-occupied Palestine." But zero-sumness pertains to the exclusive winning or losing of a payoff, not necessarily to the survival of the players except in a weird game of tic-tac-toe in which the loser forfeits his life, or in a game of Russian Roulette which goes on until one player dies. Fortunately, most zero-sum games are not so absurd, either in the parlor or in the international arena. Take, for example, the conflict between India and Pakistan over Kashmir. Control over this region is the payoff in a zero-sum game; so long as India retains control, Pakistan is deprived of it. But the Pakistanis may continue to hope that someday the situation may be reversed, just as a person who has lost a chess game to his opponent may aspire to win the next round. This raises the interesting question as to when both parties in a specific international conflict recognize that the zero-sum game is over and is not to be replayed. This might require an uncommonly high degree of political rationality. The frequent historic replay of zero-sum games between two states over the control of a disputed territory might eventually arouse political passions to such a point that the stakes are escalated far beyond the original objective of the game to include the physical integrity of the players.

GAME THEORY AND SOVIET-AMERICAN RELATIONS

During the last decade, much of the discussion concerning game theory and international politics has centered on the Cold War between the Soviet Union and the United States. Nearly all game theorists have regarded this bilateral conflict relationship as a non-zero-sum game. On the other hand, it must be admitted that the more ideologically oriented on each side (i.e., the militant communists and the militant anticommunists) have been inclined to view the contest as a zero-sum game in which neither side can finally enjoy full security while the other continues to exist in its distinctive form. The zero-sum mentality on either side is suspicious in outlook. It is not readily disposed to speak

Contending Theories of International Relations

of such concepts as the conflict-cooperation mix, coexistence, convergence, the "limited adversary" relationship, and détente. But it is quick to believe that any improvement in the position of the one must be entered upon the ledger as a liability by its rival.

Whether an advance by one side—military, political, psychological or economic—will be seen as a loss, a gain or a matter of indifference by the other depends upon the assumptions and the mode of analysis. Let us take as a hypothetical example the question of the GNP growth rates of the two superpowers. This was an issue of public concern and widespread debate in the United States during the 1959–61 period, when many observers thought that the American economy was growing at a rate of about 3 percent per year while the Soviet economy, less than half the size of ours, was thought to be expanding at about 6 percent. Those figures were themselves controversial, but they can be accepted for the sake of this illustration.

The debate about growth rates was carried on in several directions.[24] Some contended that our national output was so much larger in absolute volume that it would take the Soviets at least a few decades to match us, even on the doubtful assumption that they could maintain a superior growth rate over many years. (As a matter of fact, the United States' rate soon surpassed that of a lagging Soviet economy.) But there were many people in this country, and not only conservatives, who by 1960 were fearful lest our national interest be imperiled by a sustained higher Soviet growth rate. This was held to be an unfavorable situation regardless of whether one was thinking of the Cold War in terms of peaceful economic competition between the two systems for the allegiance of the world's people or in terms of a race for superiority in advanced weapons technology.

Those who saw the Cold War as a zero-sum game argued along the following lines. Even though the output of the American economy was more than twice as large by volume, there was cause for concern in a comparison of "softness" and "toughness" in the two economies. Whereas the United States emphasized consumer satisfactions as the ultimate determinant of national planning and investment, the more centralized Soviet system placed stress upon heavy industry and military production, where a high degree of efficiency had already been achieved. If the Soviet Union should grow more rapidly than the United States for several years, the former would be able to devote increasing resources to strategic weapons programs until it achieved military technological superiority over the United States. Furthermore, it was pointed out, a high Soviet growth rate would strengthen the loyalty of the

24. For the principal contending arguments about the prospects of the United States and the Soviet Union for achieving and maintaining high growth rates, see *Comparisons of the United States and Soviet Economies.* Joint Economic Committee, 36th Congress, First Session (Washington: Government Printing Office, 1959). For selections from the testimony of Professor G. Warren Nutter and Walt W. Rostow, see Harold and Margaret Sprout, *Foundations of International Politics* (Princeton: D. Van Nostrand Company, 1962), pp. 442–449.

Russian population to a totalitarian political system and provide an expanding capability to compete with the United States in aid and trade, to put on "spectaculars" in space, and to deploy an impressive navy on the world's oceans, thereby enhancing the Soviets' international political influence.

Those, on the other hand, who interpreted the United States-Soviet rivalry as a non-zero-sum game took positions which can be summarized as follows. The growth of the Soviet economy need not be feared under all circumstances as adverse to American interests. The Soviet Union, as it becomes a more advanced industrial nation, is also likely to become a more satisfied and less aggressive power. It will have more to lose and less to gain from war—certainly from nuclear war. It will probably think of itself increasingly as a status-quo power, particularly *vis-à-vis* the less developed and more militantly revolutionary Chinese Communists. Material development may help to bring about an internal mellowing in the Soviet Union and Eastern Europe, thus paving the way for the relaxation of totalitarian controls, the transformation of the communist monolith into a socialist "commonwealth of nations," and the gradual rise of liberalizing pressures which the leadership of the communist countries could not entirely resist or suppress. Judgments about utilities and payoffs depend upon one's philosophical values, his convictions about the nature of international politics, his political opinions about the Cold War, and his interpretations of the international objectives of the two superpowers. Such judgments are functions of deeprooted, perhaps intuitive political preconceptions as much as they are of detached scientific inquiry into the objective reality of the social universe.

Bargaining Theory

Thomas C. Schelling of Harvard University, although widely regarded as a leading game theorist, is not primarily concerned with the mathematics of games. Like Morgenstern, he began as an economist and soon began to focus his attention upon bargaining.[25] In Schelling's work we find a combination of the social-psychological and the logical-strategic approaches to the subject of human conflict—conflict viewed not exclusively as the opposition of hostile forces but rather as a more complex and delicate phenomenon in which antagonism and cooperation subtly interact in the adversary relationship. His theory seeks to make use of game theory, organization and communication theory, and theory of evidence, choice and collective decision. This strategic theory, according to Schelling:

25. Thomas C. Schelling, *National Income Behavior: An Introduction to Algebraic Analysis* (New York: McGraw-Hill Book Company, 1951); and "An Essay on Bargaining," *American Economic Review*, XLVI (June, 1956), 281–306.

takes conflict for granted, but also assumes common interest between the adversaries; it assumes a "rational" value-maximizing mode of behavior; and it focuses on the fact that each participant's "best" choice of action depends on what he expects the other to do, and that "strategic behavior" is concerned with influencing another's choice by working on his expectation of how one's own behavior is related to his.[26]

Schelling, then, is mainly interested in such problems as the conduct of negotiations, the maintenance of credible deterrence, the making of threats and promises, bluffing, double-crossing, the waging of limited conflict, and the formulation of formal or tacit arms control policies. His writing reflects a conviction that in most international strategic situations the notion of the zero-sum game is simply irrelevant. In his view, the two superpowers cannot rationally suppose themselves engaged in a zero-sum rivalry which could be played out to the bitter end of a full-scale nuclear exchange. The resultant score of such a game would in all probability be not zero but minus two. (If one asks "minus two what?" the answer is, at the very least, "minus two superpowers.") Schelling, therefore, does not devote much attention to the rational analysis of this ultimate irrationality. Indeed, his "theory of inter-dependent decisions," as he prefers to call it, is addressed less to the *application* than to the *threat* of violence as a means of influencing another party's behavior. Going to war might be the height of folly under certain circumstances, but posing a controlled threat or risk of war might prove to be a strategically shrewd move.[27]

While Schelling is very much interested in what constitutes rational behavior between parties to a conflict, he shies away from the notion that rationality can be neatly measured along a quantitative utility scale. This may be possible in respect to human action in the economic order where a precise monetary standard is available. But he deems the concept of utility as applied to international political and strategic decision-making much more ambiguous and fluid, and hence less relevant. Thus, instead of looking for the "minimax solution" to conflict situations, Schelling is more interested in what we might not inaptly call "motivational dialectics." He goes so far as to suggest that even though rationality is a desirable commodity, it is not always and under all circumstances desirable to *appear* rational.

[It] is not a universal advantage in situations of conflict to be inalienably and manifestly rational in decision and motivation . . . . It

26. Thomas C. Schelling, *The Strategy of Conflict* (New York: Oxford University Press, 1963), p. 15.

27. *Ibid.*, p. 15. Schelling notes that "inmates of mental hospitals often seem to cultivate, deliberately or instinctively, value systems that make them less susceptible to disciplinary threats and more capable of exercising coercion themselves." A self-destructive attitude expressed as a threat ("I'll cut a vein in my arm if you don't let me . . .") can put an "irrational" person in an advantageous position *vis-à-vis* a "rational" one. *Ibid.*, p. 17.

is not true, as illustrated in the example of extortion, that in the face of a threat it is invariably an advantage to be rational, particularly if the fact of being rational or irrational cannot be concealed. It is not invariably an advantage, in the face of a threat, to have a communication system in good order, to have complete information, or to be in full command of one's own actions or of one's own assets . . . The very notion that it may be a strategic advantage to relinquish certain options deliberately, or even to give up all control over one's future actions and make his responses automatic, seems to be a hard one to swallow.[28]

Schelling focuses particularly upon what is sometimes called the "limited adversary" relationship, or what he himself refers to as "the theory of precarious partnership or . . . incomplete antagonism."[29] This implies a situation in which parties to a conflict, despite their strategic opposition to each other, perceive some minimum mutual interest, even if this amounts to no more than the avoidance of reciprocal annihilation. Even when, for one reason or another, parties cannot carry on direct or overt communication with each other, they can nevertheless tacitly coordinate their moves by fixing upon certain salient points of common interest and converging expectation. He illustrates the possibility of tacit communication by citing several examples from non-hostile relationships in which two parties share an interest in finally arriving at the same meeting place.

If a husband and wife become separated in a department store each might try to figure out where the other is most likely to go with a view to rendezvous. In another situation, two parachutists drop into the same vicinity at some distance from each other. In order to be rescued, they must get together quickly, but they cannot communicate directly concerning their exact location. Each one knows, however, that the other carries a copy of the same map of the area, showing a central salient feature (such as a bridge) which furnishes a focal point for coordinated behavior. In a third example, a number of people in New Haven, Connecticut were told that they were to meet someone in New York City on a specified date, but they received no instructions as to the exact place or time. Since they could not communicate with the other party, they had to make an intelligent guess. A majority of those queried chose the information booth in Grand Central Station at high noon on the date given.[30]

It might be objected in reference to this last illustration that people taking the train from New Haven to New York always pass through Grand Central. But this need not vitiate the validity of Schelling's theory. Perhaps it only serves to demonstrate that choices based upon mutual expectation of convergent decisions reflect not merely abstract logic but also concrete historical experience—an input which might help to render prediction more reliable. There is no guarantee, of course, that this method of tacit bargaining will

28. *Ibid.*, pp. 18–19.
29. *Ibid.*, p. 15.

30. For these and analogous examples, see *ibid.*, pp. 53–58.

Contending Theories of International Relations

work in any particular two-party situation. Schelling modestly claims no more than that the shrewd selection of those points of convergence which seem likely, in the mind of one party, to be relatively unique and unambiguous in the mind of the other is superior to a system of purely random guesses as to a focal point of agreement.

Bargaining parties are not motivated solely by a desire to agree. Divergent interests skew the quest for convergence. But if agreement is finally reached, it means that forces for agreement proved stronger than forces for severance of negotiations. Moreover, although tacit coordination does not at first glance seem applicable to explicit bargaining in which formal communication is normal, nevertheless it is probably present even under explicit bargaining conditions. As examples, Schelling cites the tendency to "split the difference" in price haggling, and the recurring willingness to follow a conspicuous precedent embodied in an earlier compromise. Although the power to communicate alters a bargaining situation, it does not repeal the relevance of convergent expectations and the role of objective coordinating signals. Granted that in bargaining contests one side often manifests either greater power or a stronger determination to press for a unilaterally favorable settlement, still Schelling notes that the outcome can often be predicted "on some basis of some 'obvious' focus for agreement, some strong suggestion contained in the situation itself, without much regard to the merits of the case . . . ."[31]

Schelling contends that the limitation of conflict is not only theoretically possible but also historically actual. Recent cases in point include the mutual abstention from the use of gas weaponry in World War II and the various restrictions imposed upon the conduct of the Korean War with respect to geographical boundaries, the political identification of parties involved, the kinds of weapons employed and the types of military operations permitted. Tacit agreements, he argues, require terms of reference which can be distinguished qualitatively, not just quantitatively. In short, the step levels of conflict limitation must be unambiguous so that they can be clearly perceived under the pressures of time and emotional confusion which crisis generates in any decision-making system.[32]

Schelling also suggests that it may be possible to make arrangements prior to the outbreak of conflict which increase the likelihood that limits could be observed once hostilities are under way. This involves keeping channels of communication open, clarifying in advance the authority and authenticity of messages calculated to reduce the pressures for uncontrollable escalation, and identifying parties who might plausibly act as intermediaries. But he concedes that there are certain exigencies in the strategy of threats, bluffs and deterrents which may render one or both superpowers in the nuclear age

31. *Ibid.*, p. 68. See also pp. 71–74, where he speaks of the "mutually identifiable resting place," the search for which characterizes both tacit and explicit bargaining. "If one is to make a finite concession that is not to be interpreted as capitulation, he needs an obvious place to stop." *Ibid.*, p. 71.

32. *Ibid.*, pp. 74–77.

reluctant to enter into such contingency plans as might reduce the fear of unrestrained war. In other words, the strategic condition of mutual nuclear deterrence might be gradually undermined by a growing assumption that one or both adversaries would seek desperately to keep it limited once it had been initiated and to terminate it as soon as possible. But the fact that advance preparations by one side are not reciprocated by the other at the time does not necessarily mean that they are useless. Unilateral prior signalling might later prove advantageous if the message is remembered by the adversary after the onset of the crisis.[33]

Perhaps Schelling's principal contribution to this sector of international relations theory is his stress upon the necessity of avoiding extreme formulations. At one extreme of the spectrum he sees the zero-sum game as the limiting case of pure conflict, not as a point of departure for realistic strategic analysis. At the opposite extreme he places the "pure collaboration" game in which there is no divergent interest because the players always win or lose together. Schelling is primarily interested in the situations which lie in between—i.e., in those bargaining or "mixed-motive" games that contain elements of both conflict and mutual dependence, of divergence and convergence of interest, of secrecy and revelation—all in what he calls the "spiral of reciprocal expectations," [34] which is usually a matter more of psychological than of mathematical calculus.

The major objective in bargaining, Schelling constantly reiterates, is for each party to make his commitments, threats and promises credible to the other party, so that the latter cannot conclude that the former is bluffing. If your adversary thinks that you are leaving yourself an avenue of retreat, he will take neither your commitment nor your threat seriously. Hence there may be a strategic advantage in making an overt commitment from which there can be no retreat and by communicating this clearly to the adversary. This can be achieved by staking your reputation on the adherence to the commitment or the execution of the threat, or by making it clear that if the other party commits an act which you wish to deter, you will have no flexibility in respect to punishing him simply because you have already set up an automatic response which is irreversible. This makes the threat of punishment not merely probable but certain, and the adversary must take this into account before he decides to make his move.[35] It is the rich variety of subtle signaling prob-

33. *Ibid.*, pp. 77–80. For other discussions by Schelling of the problems of limiting conflict, see his "Reciprocal Measures for Arms Stabilization," Donald G. Brennan, ed., *Arms Control, Disarmament and National Security* (New York: George Braziller, 1961); see also Thomas C. Schelling and Morton H. Halperin, *Strategy and Arms Control* (New York: The Twentieth Century Fund, 1961), especially Chapters 2 and 8.

34. Schelling, *The Strategy of Conflict*, p. 87.
35. *Ibid.*, pp. 22–46 and 119–139. "Hardly anything epitomizes strategic behavior in the mixed motive game so much as the advantage of being able to adopt a mode of behavior that the other party will take for granted." *Ibid.*, p. 160.

lems associated with this type of political game that makes *The Strategy of Conflict* one of the most interesting and readable works in international relations theory.

Simulation in International Relations

Simulation is different from game theory and gaming, although related to them. Whereas game theory seeks the optimum mathematically rational strategy for playing a game (purely as a game, with no reference to the "real world"), simulation theory deals with a "let's pretend" situation. A simulation experiment is a game which has been designed not merely for the sake of "playing the game" but rather for the purpose of demonstrating a valid truth about actual social processes through the unfolding of an artificially constructed yet dynamic model. Thus, simulation techniques are essentially laboratory techniques or nonlaboratory contrivances which permit the study of replicated human behavior. Through the use of these techniques the researcher attempts to learn something significant about a complex phenomenon "out there," which he cannot control, by creating "in here" a more simplified version of that phenomenon which he can control and which is in some way analogous or isomorphic. Social scientists have long complained that it is virtually impossible to obtain from the real world certain kinds of data needed to verify their hypotheses. The experimental method of simulation represents an effort to compensate for these data deficiencies.[36]

WAR GAMING AND THE VARIETIES OF SIMULATION

Simulation techniques have found many uses in this century. War games and other exercises in strategic analysis have a long history which perhaps reflects the disposition of men in widely separated cultures to regard war itself as containing a "play element." [37] Every strategic planner has some sort of model or simulation in mind when he attempts to forecast the outcome of a contest. The notion of a "scenario" to describe the situation at the start of the game (even though the term "scenario" is a modern importation) was always implicit in military gaming. Formalized political-military gaming with government personnel as participants made its appearance in the period between the two world wars, and became quite common after 1945 in the work of the

36. Richard C. Snyder, "Some Perspectives on the Use of Experimental Techniques in the Study of International Relations," in Harold Guetzkow and others, *Simulation in International Rela-* *tions: Developments for Research and Teaching* (Englewood Cliffs, N.J.: Prentice-Hall, 1963), pp. 2–5.

37. Huizinga, *op. cit.,* Chapter V, "Play and War," pp. 89–104.

RAND Corporation and other institutes.[38] Simulation devices—including moot courts, mock nominating conventions—were familiar fixtures of the American educational scene before World War II.[39] Since the late 1950s, simulation has become a widely accepted teaching tool in international relations at both collegiate and high school levels.

Simulation may assume a variety of forms, depending upon the political knowledge-level and experience of the participants; the total resources available, including personnel, physical facilities and administrative support; and the purpose intended to be served by the exercise. Simulation experiments in the field of international relations are commonly designed with a view toward one or perhaps a combination of the following objectives: 1) teaching and training students; 2) advancing the policy sciences and clarifying policy alternatives through the interaction of professional practitioners; 3) promoting theoretical research and analysis through the testing of social science hypotheses. It is important to keep distinct these three functions of "political gaming," at least conceptually.

THE USES AND LIMITATIONS OF SIMULATION

Many proponents of simulation techniques are convinced that their greatest utility is in teaching. In one rather well-known version, Inter-Nation Simulation which was developed as an educational device by Harold Guetzkow (professor of political science, psychology, and sociology, Northwestern University), participants role play the key domestic and foreign policy decision-makers of five or six fictitious states. (Fictitious rather than real states are used so that subjects can make their decisions in response to the interactive process of the game, uncomplicated by presuppositions and theories as to how the leaders of actual countries ought to act in various situations.) Players learn about their roles and their country situations by reading background papers. They learn the game both by orienting themselves to its rules and even more by playing it. This, like the great majority of all political games, is characterized by the compression of real time—e.g., a few hours of play might be made to represent a month or a year of historical time. National goals may either be given at the outset or defined by the participants as play proceeds. Periodically, each nation is assigned basic resources which can be allocated by the leaders' choices to internal or external purposes. Aside from national goals, action is guided by the presumed desire of the decision-makers to remain in office. They can be replaced if either domestic consumer satisfaction or national security falls below a minimum standard which fluctuates somewhat

38. Herbert Goldhamer and Hans Speier, "Some Observations on Political Gaming," World Politics, XII (October, 1959), reprinted in James N. Rosenau, ed., International Politics and Foreign Policy: A Reader in Research and Theory (New York: Free Press, 1961), pp. 498–499.

39. Lincoln P. Bloomfield and Norman J. Padelford, "Three Experiments in Political Gaming," American Political Science Review, LIII (December, 1959), 1105.

arbitrarily according to rules that permit differentiation of democratic from totalitarian regimes. Interaction among nations includes holding conferences, entering into treaties, extending aid, issuing threats, declaring war, developing international organizations, and so forth. The game permits both bilateral and multilateral communications—the former through "restricted messages" and the latter through a "world newspaper." [40] Simulation experiments may involve the periodic feeding of game results to a computer for the purpose of speeding up the evaluation of decision-consequences according to a preprogrammed formula, but computerization is not a necessary part of simulation.

Simulation as a Teaching Device. Advocates of simulation for teaching purposes argue that participation in a game enables a student to become actively involved in an interactive process which emulates selected basic features of international reality. Those educators who evaluate gaming most highly are likely to be those who believe that "doing something" is a superior learning experience to "hearing something." They point out that games stimulate interest and motivation essentially because they are "fun;" they provide an opportunity for the student to test his theoretical knowledge gained from reading, lectures, and other sources; they introduce the student to the concrete pressures which impinge upon the policymaker, the dilemmas which face him, and the constrictions which limited resources place upon him; they enable the student to experience decision-making in a group context; the game furnishes a glimpse into a model world which the student can grasp more easily than he can the real international system. [41]

Simulation as a heuristic device, however, is not without its critics. It has been pointed out that a substantial proportion of students can be expected to be uninterested or skeptical; that gaming may arouse interest in the fun of the game without producing a serious attitude toward the study of international relations; that students seldom know enough about either the real political world or the roles they are supposed to play to act "even remotely as real-world politicians do in making their institutions and their political machinery work." [42] In view of these pros and cons, the promises and the problems, each

40. Harold Guetzkow, "A Use of Simulation in the Study of Inter-Nation Relations," in Guetzkow *et al., op. cit.,* pp. 24–38. This is a reprint of his article which appeared in *Behavioral Science,* V (July, 1959). For a description of student games which involved a specific international crisis, see Bloomfield and Padelford, *op. cit.,* pp. 1107 ff.

41. Chadwick F. Alger, "Use of the Inter-Nation Simulation in Undergraduate Teaching," in Guetzkow *et al., op. cit.,* pp. 152–154.

42. Bernard C. Cohen, "Political Gaming in the Classroom," *Journal of Poli-* *tics,* XXIV (May, 1962), 374. Cohen is quite skeptical in regard to what it is that the students find interesting about the game, as well as their level of political knowledge, their serious desire to emulate real decision-makers, and their willingness even to observe the basic rules of the game, compared with their determination to make sport of their personal acquaintances who are supposed to represent "foreign countries." For evidence that simulation is not superior to the case study as a teaching device, see James A. Robinson, *et al.,* "Teaching with Inter-Nation Simulation and Case Studies," *American Political Science Review,* LX (March, 1966), 53–65.

teacher has to decide for himself whether the students will approach the game with sufficient maturity and seriousness of purpose to warrant the investment of teaching time which simulation requires.

Gaming and the Policy Sciences. In games designed to serve the policy sciences, an effort is usually made to achieve as much "realism" as possible. Professional policymakers generally derive greater profit by representing officials not of fictitious countries but of actual states engaged in the subtleties and complexities of the international interactive process which professionals understand best. Players might be instructed to play either "predicted strategies" (based upon the way specific governments would be expected to behave from historical experience) or "optimal strategies" (based upon what the individual deems best under the circumstances, regardless of existing domestic and other constraints) or a combination of the two approaches. Frequently the element of "Nature" or "Fate" is introduced into the game by allowing the control group to provide for such unexpected events as technological breakthroughs, the death of key leaders, and the outbreak of civil turbulence. Occasionally the "scenario" will be used to project the opening of the game sufficiently far into the future to prevent the simulation from being overtaken by daily news developments. Participants have found that by participating in a gaming experiment of a critical international problem they have acquired fresh insights into the complexities of situations, into the unexpected turns which events might take, and into the psychological-moral-intellectual pressures and uncertainties which accompany the making of foreign policy decisions.[43] It is impossible, however, from the outcome of a "crisis game" to predict the actual outcome of a real-world political encounter.

Gaming and Theory-Building. The third principal use of political gaming is in the area of research and theory-building. Here the primary objective is not to provide a worthwhile personal experience via the gaming process either to students or to policymakers, but rather to test social science hypotheses. The utility of simulation as a tool for confirming or disconfirming theoretical propositions about the international system is a matter of considerable controversy within the field of international relations theorists and among the "simulators" themselves. One might admit that from a careful observation of the behavior of a group of experienced policymakers in a realistically simulated crisis (e.g., a future Berlin crisis), he might be able to make some interesting inferences concerning the political values, strategic preconceptions, psychological attitudes and preferred methods of conflict management which would be likely to characterize those particular policymakers if a real crisis were soon to arise

---

43. Goldhamer and Speier, in Rosenau, ed., *op. cit.,* pp. 499–502. Richard E. Barringer and Barton Whaley report that "the political-military game is a most intense and vivid experience, seemingly for even the most sophisticated individuals," that the insights gained depend largely upon the knowledge and experience of the participant and that the game suggests *unanticipated* policy alternatives. "The M.I.T. Political-Military Gaming Experience," *Orbis,* IX (Summer, 1965), 444–448.

in a closely similar form. But this, after all, would be a highly particularized and concretized kind of prediction, more appropriate to diplomatic intelligence than to social science. The social scientist is much more interested in universally applicable generalizations than in those subtle nuances of unique historical situations which comprise the special intellectual competence of the country or area expert. The policymaker wishes to know as much as possible about "this" particular crisis or policy situation, so that he can favorably influence its outcome. The social scientist, on the other hand, is not primarily oriented to "this" situation. His principal concern is with universal generalizations and probabilities. Of what use can simulation be to him in this more comprehensive quest?

The crucial question is: What is the relation between a game and reality? What can we learn about the real political world from empirically observing the results of political gaming? A game, after all, is only an analogical model, which may or may not be partially parallel to the real world in respect to both elements and interactive processes depending upon the intelligence that has gone into the construction of the model, combined with the maturity and seriousness with which the model is played out. Eugene J. Meehan of Brandeis University lays down the following useful guidelines:

> *If a model is used as an aid to explanation, then the interaction of elements in the system is prime; if the model is used for prediction, the outcome of dynamic processes in model and empirical world must be similar . . . Models are always partial and approximate, as are analogies. It follows that there will be properties of observed reality not duplicated in the model, at least potentially, and it is always possible that models have properties that are not duplicated in the empirical world. Furthermore, models and analogies may be useful in creating some expectations with regard to reality (supposing them to have congruence with reality) but may be quite useless and even misleading in other respects.*[44]

THE GAME WORLD AND THE REAL WORLD

The first question to be asked is whether the game is "isomorphic" or congruent with reality? Richard E. Dawson (Washington University) has implicitly recognized the need for traditional political knowledge in simulation experiments when he noted that before a researcher can validly model a real political system, he has to know a great deal about the workings of that system.[45] It is not enough that a game be "realistic" in flavor. In its substan-

44. Eugene J. Meehan, *Contemporary Political Thought: A Critical Study* (Homewood, Ill.: Dorsey Press, 1967), pp. 31–32.

45. Richard E. Dawson, "Simulation in the Social Sciences," in Harold Guetzkow, ed., *Simulation in Social Sciences* (Englewood Cliffs, N.J.: Prentice-Hall, 1962), pp. 13 ff.

tive details, a game might bear a superficial resemblance to a real-world political situation and yet be quite unlike reality in the playing—i.e., in its basic dynamic processual features.

Snyder asks whether participants can ever escape the realization that what they are involved in is only a game and not "the real thing." He then cites evidence to the effect that people can become totally absorbed in the simulation exercise.[46] But the fact remains that total absorption in a game does not necessarily bridge the gap between simulation and reality. We are faced here with such problems as the compression of time and the concomitant pressure of hurried decisions from a sketchy information base; the selection of a small number of nations out of the whole complex international system; the cultural provincialism of nearly all gaming experiments to date—virtually all decision-makers have been Americans; the fact that national decisions are made by a small number of decision-makers, completely abstracted from an institutionalized context; and the realization that the reward-punishment matrix and indeed the whole socio-psychological environment of decision-making in a game are quite different from those in real life.

For guidance in constructing models and evaluating the results of simulated international interaction, students of simulation have turned to the writings of scholars in other fields, both traditional and contemporary, who have theorized about international relations. In the literature of international relations, as we have seen in other chapters, several scholars have engaged in "macro-level" analysis, that is, the study of several kinds of relationships among several kinds of actors over time. Similarly, models of international simulation have provided for the observation of the behavior of actor participants in differing environments and in a multiplicity of relationships over time. Although simulation models have necessarily been more parsimonious than the literature of international relations in general, both in variables under investigation and in the description of international relationships, students of simulation have attempted to use the work of other international relations scholars (1) to compare simulation models with models, often implicitly stated, in international relations literature; (2) to compare the *results* of simulation runs with empirically derived descriptions of international behavior, for example, in crisis simulations.[47]

46. Richard C. Snyder, "Some Perspectives on the Use of Experimental Techniques in the Study of International Relations," *op. cit.*, pp. 12–14.

47. See, for example, William D. Coplin, "Inter-Nation Simulation and Contemporary Theories of International Relations," *American Political Science Review*, IX (September, 1966), 562–578; Richard W. Chadwick, "An Empirical Test of Five Assumptions in an Inter-Nation Simulation about National Political Systems," *General Systems*, XII (1967), 177–192; Walter C. Clemens, Jr., "A Propositional Analysis of the International Relations Theory in Temper—A Computer Simulation of Cold War Conflict." In William D. Coplin, ed., *Simulation in the Study of Politics* (Chicago: Markham Publishing Company, 1968), pp. 59–101.

Among many scholars there is agreement that simulation can benefit from the literature of international relations theory. Richard A. Brody of Stanford University, for example, has suggested that "the complementary role of verbal and mathematical theory in the construction of operating models cannot be overemphasized. Verbal theory guides the selection of crucial components. Mathematical theory aids in specifying the relationship between components." [48] Moreover, the structure (i.e., the form, rules, and function) of simulations often reflects the assumptions of a variety of other theories.

There are differences, not only between simulations and theories from international relations literature, but also among the simulation models themselves. Each simulation model has a distinctive emphasis and has borrowed its assumptions from different sources. William Coplin of Wayne State University warns that since simulation is itself a theory, or theories, "consequently, the comparison is more a reliability check on simulation and verbal theorists than a validity check on either. "Any lack of congruence between the assumptions of simulations and those of verbal theories," Coplin maintains, "does not indicate that either theory lacks validity since neither has a monopoly on valid hypotheses." [49]

Whereas those who design simulations can employ and benefit from the theories found in international relations literature, simulation also has model-building values of its own, beyond what it borrows from other theories. "Although iconic, verbal, and mathematical devices are very useful in developing a simulation, their limitations are precisely the reason why one moves to an operating representation . . ." [50] Some of the advantages of simulation techniques in theory-building over other models are its dynamic operating quality and its ability to control elements enabling replication and variation. Furthermore, simulation can go beyond individual verbal theories because of its eclectic quality and its ability "to build syntheses beyond the capability of the individual." [51] As Guetzkow speculates: "in the long run, the use of simulation as a theory-building device may provide an effective vehicle within a very complex area of behavior, allowing us to elaborate on a holistic, all-encompassing model with ever increasing differentiation of its components." [52]

Yet another contribution of simulation theory to international relations

48. Richard A. Brody, "Varieties of Simulations in International Relations Research," *Simulation in International Relations* (Englewood Cliffs, N.J.: Prentice-Hall, 1963), p. 219.

49. William D. Coplin, "Inter-Nation Simulation and Contemporary Theories of International Relations," *op. cit.*, 562.

50. Richard A. Brody, *op. cit.*, p. 196.

51. Harold Guetzkow, "Simulation and Realities," Morton A. Kaplan, ed., *New Approaches to International Relations* (New York: St. Martin's Press, 1968), p. 205.

52. *Ibid.*, p. 257.

theory is its demand for greater explicitness. Guetzkow has argued that "although it (simulation) is but one of alternative ways of building models about the operation of social systems, its operating character demands a greater clarity in formulation than is often necessitated in literary and mathematical formulation."[53] Similarly, Schelling has stated that during the construction of the game what had appeared beforehand to be plausible concepts "had to be abandoned when an effort to incorporate them in the game revealed that they were meaningless, or innocuous, or that they rested on inessential distinctions."[54]

Although simulation models appear to have several advantages over verbal and mathematical theories of international relations, they have their deficiencies. Brody warns that "a typical disadvantage of the approach (simulation) is its potential for misrepresentation due to the lack of empirical grounding of the model . . . By providing pressure for more or less definitive conceptualization, simulation may force premature modeling in areas in which empirical research has been sparse."[55]

Sidney Verba has argued that simulation may serve as an important link between verbal or mathematical theories and the real world. Ordinarily one deduces hypotheses directly from a verbal or mathematical theory. A simulation designed to work as if a particular verbal or mathematical theory were correct, could generate the implications of that theory while having complete control over the processes. "A simulation study that matches a real-world situation thus involves the testing of the hypothesis twice, in the simulation and in the real world, with the real-world test having the advantage of reality and the simulation test the advantage of lack of ambiguity."[56]

Similarly, Guetzkow writes: "When the simulation constructions are realized in action, they are an operation vehicle through which many implicit consequences of theory may be exposed, although not tested, in the sense of providing a situation which permits verification of facets of the theory they constitute."[57] Simulation theory "provides no short-cut or magical route to the 'proof' of the validity of the verbal and mathematical components it contains."[58] Similarly, the validity of simulations cannot be established simply by a comparison with other theories of international relations; in order to establish simulation theory, "it is imperative to make checks against empirical observations, not merely against another set of theories."[59]

53. Harold Guetzkow, "A Use of Simulation in the Study of Inter-Nation Relations," in *Simulation in International Relations, op. cit.*, p. 33.

54. Thomas C. Schelling, "An Experimental Game for the Study of Bargaining" *World Politics*, XIV (1961), 57.

55. Richard A. Brody, *op. cit.*, p. 219.

56. Sidney Verba, "Simulation, Reality, and Theory in International Relations," *World Politics*, XVI (1964), 517, 519.

57. Harold Guetzkow, "A Use of Simulation in the Study of Inter-Nation Relations." *op. cit.*, p. 90.

58. Harold Guetzkow, "Simulation and Realities," *op. cit.*, p. 205.

59. *Ibid.*, p. 256.

In Guetzkow's assessment of the correspondence between INS simulations and empirical materials, no firm conclusions are drawn because of the fragmentary nature of the evidence available. As Guetzkow notes, it is yet too early to attempt to assess the validity of aspects of extant simulations because of the "inadequate state of both verbal theory and empirical work within international relations as a discipline." [60] Guetzkow admits the possibility of errors in such studies, including the possible unreliability of the reference data, the many incomparabilities, and the intuitive method of assessing correspondence between simulations and "reality." Nevertheless, he urges that extant simulations should be checked, to the extent possible, and that further work in simulation should be more carefully guided in the future by concurrent validity checks.

Guetzkow himself attempts to assess the correspondence between Inter-Nation Simulation and reference materials in areas such as human surrogates or actors, surrogate groups, and relations among nations. The assessments of correspondence were rated on a five-point scale: "Much," "Some," "Little," "None," and "Incongruent." Reference materials included (1) studies of processes made in the field and laboratory, and (2) data gathered from operations within the international system. Three-fourths of the reference materials are of the latter type. Moreover, both the internal processes and the outputs of simulations were examined with references concerned with processes and outcomes, thus increasing the credibility of the simulation. The reference materials ranged from anecdotal, illustrative materials to rigorous, systematic materials.

The impact of the personal characteristics of the actors, culture/nationalism, and training/professionalism/background upon decision-making observed in the INS runs was compared to the findings in the general materials from field and laboratory and in the materials from international relations. It was found that the surrogates or actors in simulations bore similarity to the decision-makers of the international scene, but even more closely resembled ordinary people observed in field situations and within the laboratory. The similarities held for crisis and noncrisis situations. "Correspondences are found for the outputs, as in terms of the inter-entity production of violence and alliance; correspondences are found, also for the intervening processes, as for perception and nationalism. However, only a few of the multitude of components comprising the varying personalities, diverse background and multinationalities have been assessed." [61]

Instead of trying to verify macrocosmic propositions through simulation, it may be more useful to rely upon games to learn something about microcosmic decision-making processes. Some analysts are interested in examining the pictures of politics in the heads of the participants. They see the game as a controlled experiment in individual decision-making, a process worthy of study

60. *Ibid.,* p. 256.　　　　　　　　　61. *Ibid.,* p. 223.

in itself regardless of our present inability to extrapolate from the results of games to the behaviors of national bureaucratic decision-making structures.[62]

Gaming and Simulation: The Development of International Relations

To summarize, it can be said that simulation experiments are regarded as potentially useful heuristic devices by many teachers of international relations, provided that suitable facilities are available and the students are properly motivated to learn from them. But games are time-consuming and they require very careful planning and administration. The teacher should not take it for granted that simulation is in all circumstances worthwhile merely because it gets the students "actively involved." Policy-oriented games played by experienced decision-makers can also prove valuable tools for the improved understanding of specific foreign policy problems, insofar as they may cast light upon factors and suggest alternatives which might otherwise be overlooked. But here, too, it must be recognized that the best games take several days or even a few weeks to run, and the time which government officials can devote to such exercises is strictly limited. As for the use of simulation in research and theory-building, some writers are more optimistic than others about the possibility of using political games to validate hypotheses about the real political world. But nearly all the authorities in this area cautiously refrain from asserting that simulation techniques can produce any predictive capability. Most would probably agree that much more needs to be known before simulation can be accepted as a reliable tool for the verification of theory.

62. David C. Schwartz, "Problems in Political Gaming," *Orbis,* IX (Fall, 1965), 677–693. Schwartz argues that differences of behavior and choice both in games and in the real political world are partially due to personality factors, about which something could be learned if personality tests were administered to the participants prior to the game and post-move questionnaires were employed to probe the relationship of perception to action. *Ibid.,* pp. 686 and 690. The principle of relating game decisions to personality factors was given an interest-ing reverse application in a study designed to investigate the use of an actual historical situation to validate simulation. An effort was made (with somewhat inconclusive results) to select participants for the roles of such figures as Edward Grey, Raymond Poincaré, the Kaiser and the Tsar by matching personality characteristics as much as possible. See Charles F. Hermann and Margaret G. Hermann, "An Attempt to Simulate the Outbreak of World War I," *American Political Science Review,* LXI (June, 1967), especially pp. 404–405.

CHAPTER 13
International Studies in the 1970s

International Relations: Stages of Development

E. H. Carr has suggested that "when the human mind begins to exercise itself in some fresh field an initial stage occurs in which the element of wish or purpose is overwhelmingly strong, and the inclination to analyze facts and means weak or nonexistent." [1] Whatever the validity of this statement in the development of other disciplines it describes the growth of international relations, especially in its formative years between the two world wars.[2] Although the study of international relations has always had a normative element and the study of the causes of conflict and its resolution has been of continuing concern to students of international relations, the focus both of teaching and research has shifted, especially since World War II. The study of international relations has passed through three stages which may be characterized as utopian, realist, and behavioral, or stated differently, normative, empirical-normative, and behavioral-quantitative.[3] On the threshold of the 1970s the study of international relations appears to be entering a fourth, or postbehavioral phase.[4] In this fourth stage an effort will be made to synthesize concepts and findings

1. E. H. Carr, *The Twenty-Years' Crisis, 1919–1939* (New York: Harper and Row [Torchbooks], 1964), p. 4.

2. See Kenneth W. Thompson, *Political Realism and the Crisis of World Politics* (Princeton: Princeton University Press, 1960); William T. R. Fox, *The American Study of International Relations* (Columbia: University of South Carolina Press, 1968), pp. 1–35.

3. This is not to suggest that the concerns of students of international relations during each of these stages have been mutually exclusive. Examples of

each can be found at every stage of the development of international relations.

4. For an examination of current trends in political science, see David Easton, "The New Revolution in Political Science," *American Political Science Review,* LXIII (December, 1969), 1051–1061. Because the study of international relations has been closely linked to political science, the methodological, conceptual and substantive trends of political science can be expected, as they have in the recent past, to influence the development of international relations.

from existing literature and to develop theories and methodologies "relevant" to major international issues facing mankind over the next decade, while at the same time pressing the quest for theories with greater explanatory and predictive capabilities. The period which lies ahead is likely to be characterized by a continued search for concepts and methodologies from other disciplines, and by attempts to engage in comparative studies at many levels and units of analysis, but also by a greater effort to bridge the gap between normative and behavioral-quantitative theories, and between theory and policy.

THE BEHAVIORAL CRITIQUE

If by the end of the 1940s political realism had largely replaced a utopian, or normative, orientation in the study of international relations and thus the field had moved from its first to its second stage of development, a rising generation of scholars was no more satisfied with prevailing modes of analysis than its predecessors. Over the past two decades, much of the proliferating literature of international relations has reflected dissatisfaction with the state of the field.[5] In this literature, and in academic discussion, and thus in the behavioral-quantitative stage of the development of international relations, the following critical themes prevailed: (1) Earlier approaches had only limited ability to enable the researcher to identify and analyze important problems, since the research tools available to the practitioner of traditional research were crude. Even when traditionally oriented scholars had identified the most important problems, they had not stated them in such a way as to enhance the prospects for their investigation. (2) Traditional theory has been based upon international systems which differed fundamentally from the contemporary international system. Because it inadequately describes the contemporary system, it provides inadequate conceptualization or hypotheses for the building of theory. (3) The explanatory and predictive capacity of theories is limited. Therefore, much of what passes for international relations theory is largely irrelevant to the scholar and especially the policymaker, when evaluating the present or predicting the future. Scholars, and to an even greater extent policymakers, therefore, revert to pragmatic solutions for specific problems. (4) Existing literature is replete with untested and implicit assumptions about human behavior and international conduct. (5) Many of the most widely used terms of international relations, such as balance of power and collective security, are used in virtually incompatible ways by scholars, and even by the same scholar. Such usage contributes not only to theoretical fuzziness but to the difficulty of communication within the discipline.[6] (6) Because research efforts have not been based upon powerful and broadly based theoretical frame-

5. See Andrew M. Scott, *The Functioning of the International System* (New York: Macmillan Company, 1967), pp. 2–6.

6. See Inis L. Claude, Jr., *Power and In-*

ternational Relations (New York: Random House, 1962), pp. 11–39; Ernst B. Haas, "Balance of Power: Prescription or Propaganda," *World Politics*, V (1953), 442–447.

works, they have not contributed adequately to a cumulative literature of international relations. Because scholars have not addressed themselves to similar hypotheses and have indeed assumed instead the uniqueness of events, they have not contributed to the building of a body of generalizations about international phenomena. (7) The availability of quantitative methodologies and conceptual frameworks borrowed or adapted from other disciplines provides the tools for major breakthroughs in the building of theory. The advent of the computer and advanced technologies of information storage, retrieval, and analysis enhance the prospects for testing theory. Given the research techniques now available, today's scholars have an opportunity to make a major contribution to international relations theory. Since the conduct of research in international relations has been strongly influenced by younger scholars impatient with the conventional wisdom, a "credibility gap" and a "generation gap" have emerged in the study of international relations.

Although the assumptions of individual traditional writers were sometimes not explicitly stated, the "conventional wisdom" of international relations has contained a series of assumptions which scholars over the past generation have questioned and sought to subject to more systematic examination: (1) It was assumed that nations were sovereign in their domestic affairs and that foreign powers could not exert major internal influence upon them. If such a model corresponded to the international system before the twentieth century, it does not fit the contemporary international system. In fact, there is a burgeoning literature whose authors seek to examine the "linkage" between national and international systems, and to examine what are called "penetrated" political systems whose domestic policies are influenced by developments beyond their frontiers.[7] (2) Decision-making units, it was assumed, were not subject to major internal strains and conflicts as to objectives, policies, and the nature of the national interest. Especially since World War II, however, literature on foreign policy has accorded a position of considerable prominence to the domestic factors which impinge upon foreign relations.[8] (3) The traditional assumption was that only the nation-states could be the actors of international politics. The rise of international organization at the global and regional level, the increasing importance of the multinational corporation, the expansion of transnational contacts has given a new set of dimensions to international relations which has been reflected in the literature. (4) Political behavior in an international context, it was once assumed, differs

7. See, e.g., James N. Rosenau, ed., *Linkage Politics: Essays on the Convergence of National and International Systems* (New York: Free Press, 1969); "Compatibility, Consensus, and an Emerging Political Science of Adaptation," *American Political Science Review*, LXI (December, 1967), 983–988; and Wolfram F. Hanrieder, "Compatibility and Consensus: A Proposal for the Conceptual Linkage of External and Internal Dimensions of Foreign Policy" in the same issue of the *American Political Science Review*, LXI (December, 1967), 971–982.

8. See, e.g., Gabriel Almond, *The American People and Foreign Policy* (New York: Harcourt, Brace and World, 1950). For a more recent example of such literature, see James N. Rosenau, ed., *Domestic Sources of Foreign Policy* (New York: Free Press, 1967).

fundamentally from political behavior within the national unit. Therefore, there was justification for the separation academically of studies of international political behavior from the analysis of political behavior within the national unit. The distinction between domestic and international behavior stemmed principally from a model in which decision-making was centralized. Governments within the national units held a monopoly of the coercive capabilities of the units, in contrast to the decentralization of decision-making and the coercive capabilities within the international system. Increasingly, scholars have stressed the similarities rather than differences between the political process at the national and international levels. Scholarly interest in the political systems of less developed areas, where tribal loyalties often compete with modernizing forces, and effective political power remains decentralized, has contributed to a reassessment of older notions about the uniqueness of international political processes.

In short, much of the criticism of international relations theory has been based upon both a questioning of the relevance of older assumptions as well as technique and methodology. Such dissatisfaction has led to a proliferation of literature designed to remedy perceived deficiencies in the study of international relations.

THE NATURE OF QUANTITATIVE-BEHAVIORAL RESEARCH

The basic trends which have characterized international relations in its behavioral-quantitative stage may be summarized as follows: (1) the adaptation of theories, propositions, conceptual frameworks, methodologies, and ideas from other disciplines, including in particular sociology, social psychology, management-administrative science, psychology, anthropology, economics, and mathematics; (2) an attempt to relate phenomena from other disciplines to allegedly similar phenomena at the international level, which takes the essentially two mutually reinforcing forms of the examination of international phenomena by (a) the use of conceptual frameworks, theories, and propositions by which similar phenomena in other disciplines have been examined; and (b) the comparative analysis of phenomena such as conflict, integration, bargaining, negotiation, and deterrence in an international context and other fields; (3) a focus upon problems of units of analysis, including attempts to distinguish conceptually and methodologically among such units as the individual decision-maker, the decisional unit, the state, international subsystems, and the international system itself; (4) a concern about problems of level of analysis, including an effort to draw clearcut distinctions between macrotheory or grand theory, and the so-called middle ranges of theorizing, and a tendency for scholars to focus explicitly upon one or the other levels of theorizing; (5) a greater effort to become comparative *within* the study of International Relations, which has essentially two dimensions: (a) great comparative

Contending Theories of International Relations

analysis of phenomena in a contemporary context, and (b) attempts systematically to compare various aspects of international relations in a historic context and to draw comparisons between contemporary and historic international phenomena; (6) a focus upon problems of data collection, an attempt to exploit more skillfully existing data, to develop new resources, and to build archives or data banks equipped with facilities for the storage and retrieval of materials for scholarly use; (7) an increase in the range of methodologies, but a lack of consensus as to those most appropriate for the study of international phenomena; and (8) a more conscious effort to link research to theory building, including the development of criteria of relevance for research, the statement of problems and their investigation in such a fashion as to make it possible for other scholars to replicate, or duplicate, such research and attempt to develop knowledge that is cumulative.

The problems of scope, methodology, the nature of theory, and the relevance of other disciplines to the study of international relations are by no means resolved. Critics of certain of the trends outlined above have doubted the extent to which events or other political phenomena can be treated as similar and the ability of the researcher to make hypotheses operational. Skepticism remains as to whether the most important problems of international relations can be made operational so that indicators of a quantitative nature [9] can be developed. The authors of this volume maintain that dogmatism, either "traditional" or "behavioral," does little to enhance the development of international relations. Such dogmatism, as well as the focus upon questions of method and scope, indicates the uncertainty of students of international relations about the appropriate techniques and focal points for analysis. The issue is not *whether* one methodology or another, one form of theorizing or another, one analytical focal point or another, is relevant. Far from being mutually exclusive, alternative methodologies and research interests have the potential of becoming mutually reinforcing and contributing to the advance of knowledge.[10] The question is less one of their appropriateness, than of the extent to which one methodology or approach to theory fulfills the specific research task set for it by the individual scholar.[11]

9. For an examination of this debate, see Klaus Knorr and James N. Rosenau, "Tradition and Science in the Study of International Politics"; Hedley Bull, "International Theory: The Case for a Classical Approach"; Morton A. Kaplan, "The New Great Debate: Traditionalism vs. Science in International Relations"; J. David Singer, "The Incompleat Theorist: Insight without Evidence"; Marion J. Levy, Jr., " 'Does It Matter if He's Naked?' Bawled the Child?" in Klaus Knorr and James N. Rosenau, eds., *Contending Approaches to International Politics* (Princeton: Princeton University Press, 1969), pp. 3–110.

10. See Johan Galtung, "The Social Sciences: An Essay on Polarization and Integration," in Knorr and Rosenau eds., *op. cit.*, pp. 243–285.

11. There is, of course, a need for criteria both for the establishment of research agendas and for the conduct of research itself. Given the differing conceptions of the nature of theory and the disparate research and methodological interests of students of international relations, prospects for reaching agreement upon such criteria are not great.

Several major focal points of research over the past generation are indicative of the interests of scholars in the behavioral-quantitative stage of international relations. General systems theory, theories of conflict, decision-making, and game theory are illustrative of borrowings from other disciplines. General systems theory, for example, has had a major impact upon theorizing efforts at a macro-level as well as the middle-range theories of decision-making, conflict and integration. Writings in conflict and integration illustrate the growth of both a comparative and quantitative focus, and the rise in interest in the comparison of such phenomena in an international context with supposedly similar phenomena in other contexts. Writings in these fields, as well as those using systems theory, indicate the growth of interest in broadening both the data base and the focus of concern, not only to comparative materials, but to points of time in the recent and distant past. Studies employing general systems theory and decision-making theory, in particular, reflect the concern with developing more explicitly defined units of analysis.

Both in political science and international relations, theorizing efforts of the past generation have produced macrotheories, or grand theories, within which major categories of variables can be analyzed. In political science, both Almond's and Easton's formulations provide schema which include major categories of variables. In international relations, realist theory and general systems theory represent approximations to macro-theory.[12] Realism is a grand theorizing effort because its proponents have generally sought to isolate one, or a few, variables capable of explaining and predicting a broad range of international behavior. In addition to its focus on power as a crucially important variable, realism provided frameworks for the analysis both of international politics and foreign policy. At the level of the international system, realist writers used a framework based upon balance of power quite similar to the balance of power model subsequently developed more formally by Morton A. Kaplan. At the national level of analysis, realists concerned themselves with the elements of national power and for comparative purposes developed a classificatory scheme for analyzing the respective capabilities of nations. The proponents of realism were aware of what J. David Singer has termed the "level of analysis problem" in international relations;[13] they concerned themselves with analysis both at the level of interaction between and among states, and with the behavior of individual states and their foreign policies.

Those more recent students who have used general systems theory have

12. The word "theory" itself has been used in several ways in the field of international relations, and there is disagreement among scholars about the nature of theory. See Chapter 1 for a discussion of the various uses of the term "theory."

13. See J. David Singer, "The Level-of-Analysis Problem in International Relations," Klaus Knorr and Sidney Verba, eds., *The Internationl System: Theoretical Essays* (Princeton: Princeton University Press, 1961), pp. 77–92. See also the treatment by the authors of this text in Chapter 1, pp. 17–20.

Contending Theories of International Relations

sought not only to develop more clearly delineated levels of analysis, but to advance a framework broadly enough based to encompass most, if not all, of international behavior. If realism brought to bear materials and insights from history as well as other disciplines, including geography, strategic studies, economics, and political science, general systems theory provides a framework for the utilization of data, concepts and propositions from many disciplines. But among their distinguishing characteristics realism and general systems theory differ in that the former seeks great explanatory and predictive capacity using power as a variable, and general systems theory provides a framework for the analysis of relationships among many, or a few, variables, and seeks to develop explanatory and predictive constructs.

Other theorizing efforts represent "islands" of theory which may (or may not) be linked one day into a grand theory of international relations. How such linking will take place, whether by the enlargement of existing "islands" or new "islands" of theory, or by a major breakthrough toward a macro-theory within which middle-range theories can be linked, is an object of debate among social scientists. It is an issue which remains unresolved as the study of international relations enters its fourth stage.

The Postbehavioral Study of International Relations

Given the focus of interest over the past decade, it is possible to suggest several trends in international relations which will be operative in the "postbehavioral" stage. Such trends are likely to reflect several major problems confronting international relations. They include (1) not only the continuing effort to delineate the nature and scope of international relations but also an attempt to establish international relations more firmly as an "autonomous" field of study; (2) the kinds of theorizing appropriate to the building of theories with greater explanatory and predictive capacity; (3) the methodological tools appropriate for research and especially the relationship between quantitative and qualitative research; (4) the division of labor between "basic" and "applied" research and the question of the "relevance" of international relations research to the crucial international problems of the next decade; and (5) efforts to develop more precise linkages between various levels of analysis (or "actors") along the continuum from the microcosmic (the individual person) to the macrocosmic (the international system).

METHODOLOGICAL CONCERNS

The development and exploitation of new methodologies for research, as well as new research and substantive interests, have given new stature to international relations as a field of study, although other, older disciplines have focused upon problems of international relations such as conflict and "peace research" in such fields as psychology, sociology, social psychology, and economics. Students in such disciplines as sociology or psychology who study conflict will continue to center their efforts at least in part upon conflict in an international context. Ideally, international relations provides the framework for an emerging discipline for the integration of concepts, propositions, and methodologies from many disciplines, as well as the development of whatever concepts, propositions and methodologies may be relevant specifically to the study of problems at the international level.[14] Ultimately, international relations may become a discipline which incorporates, builds upon, and synthesizes insights discovered by most, if not all, of the social sciences.[15] It is possible to envisage such a development in international relations in the stage which it is now entering.

EMERGING SUBSTANTIVE INTERESTS

Given the continuation, and even the strengthening, of international relations as a field of study, several substantive interests are likely to be dominant. Because of the *raison d'être* of international relations from its early years, the problems of war and peace can be expected to continue to attract principal attention. In particular, students of international relations are likely to retain an interest in the problem of conflict, which has been of central concern since its beginning as an organized field of study. In the years ahead, the study of conflict will differ from earlier approches by the techniques, methodologies, conceptual frameworks, and data bases employed in theory-building. For example, the research of neuro-physiologists on the midbrain and forebrain relating to how inputs, such as injury, removal and electrical stimulation, produce passivity and rage in animals may lead to advances in knowledge about conflict. Moreover, the use of economic models to develop exchange or barter ratios for pairs of noneconomic goods, together with the utilization of insights from psychology about personality theory and the effects of organizational variables upon social and political behavior, may contribute to a greater understanding of several important problems of international relations, namely, conflict, community building, and decision-making.[16]

14. For a useful effort to delineate the boundaries of international relations, see E. Raymond Platig, *International Relations Research: Problems of Evaluation and Advancement* (Santa Barbara: Clio Press, for the Carnegie Endowment for International Peace, 1967), esp. pp. 26–44.

15. One contemporary student of International Relations, Johan Galtung, has suggested: "One may say that the relationship between international relations and political science is the same as the relationship between sociology and psychology: it is the transition from the meticulous study of one unit at the time to the study of the interaction structure between the units that characterize the relation between these pairs of sciences." Johan Galtung, "Small Group Theory and the Theory of International Relations," Morton A. Kaplan, ed., *New Approaches to International Relations* (New York: St. Martin's Press, 1968), p. 271.

16. See Walter Isard, in association with Tony E. Smith, Peter Isard, Tze Hsiung Tung, and Michael Dacey, *General Theory: Social, Political, Economic, and Regional* (Cambridge, Mass.: MIT Press, 1969).

Contending Theories of International Relations

Conflict. It is to be hoped that the 1970s will witness a refinement of research and theory-building techniques in respect to the phenomenon of human conflict. We very much need reliable knowledge concerning the interrelationship between international and intrasocietal aggressive behavior. As the conditions of the nuclear age increasingly inhibit tendencies toward overt military hostilities among the Great Powers, is it inevitable that the latter—or at least the more democratic and less socially controlled nations—will experience a rise of intranational revolutionary discontent? What are the implications of various modes of socio-economic development for the incidence of tensions, conflict and violence, as well as for stability or instability, within the international system? In view of suggestions advanced by social scientists in recent years relative to racial and campus disturbances in the United States, with specific reference to the part played by the mass media in the transmission of information and the shaping of attitudes, what role do these media now play and will they be likely to play in the future in international cooperation and conflict, détente and crisis? What can our still fitful forays into the science of ecology teach us about the likely consequences of the challenges and problems posed to man by his environment—population growth, the politics of food and hunger, and the chemical-industrial tainting of the human ambient? Questions such as these will be high on the priority lists of international relations specialists in the 1970s.

Integration. The study of integration, of long-standing concern to students of international relations, especially since the work of David Mitrany in the period between the two world wars, is likely to attract the attention of many scholars. Over the past generation, the creation of international organizations at the global and regional levels not only contributed to the rise in interest in the study of integration, but also provided an important source of data for scholarly investigation. The growing importance of the multinational corporation adds yet another dimension to the study of integration, and is already becoming the object of scholarly investigation by students of integration at the international level.

Existing theories of political integration owe a considerable intellectual debt to earlier studies of nationalism as well as cybernetics and systems theory. The study of the normative conditions for political community, characteristic of the study of international relations in its first stage, has given way to specific case studies and comparative analyses of integration, both at the global and regional levels. Like conflict, the study of integration cuts across the traditional boundaries of political science, and links the work of scholars in other disciplines. To the extent that scholars focus upon such phenomena as conflict and integration, the controversy about "relevance" which gained prominence in political science at the end of the decade of the 1960s is likely to be minimized in the field of international relations, although students of international relations can be expected in this fourth stage to concern themselves, perhaps even more than in the recent past, with the policy implications of their work.

In the integration literature, there is need for greater definitional and conceptual clarity. This is a task to which students of international relations can be expected to turn their attention in the next decade. Existing integration models will be decomposed and, where possible and feasible, made operational so that they may be tested. The achievement of greater agreement among writers about the nature of integration, its necessary components, and the stages and transformation rules by which it is achieved, would contribute to major breakthroughs in knowledge about the building and disintegration of political communities.

Transnational Forces. Students of integration at the international level, from Mitrany to Deutsch, have had as a major concern transnational forces. Although our knowledge about the precise effect of such forces upon national foreign policies is not great, few students would deny their importance to the policymaker, and hence the need for their inclusion in international studies. In the next decade, the number and importance of transnational actors, especially in the form of the multinational corporation, can be expected to grow. The fact that the majority of nation-states have annual GNPs which are less than the total assets of the leading multinational corporations is but one indicator of the emerging importance of this sector of international business. The multinational corporation as a catalyst for international integration or the reinforcement of residual nationalism, its implications for international monetary policy and for alignment patterns of nation-states is an appropriate and likely focal point for scholarly investigation in the 1970s.[17]

Subnational Forces. If the thrust of scholarly literature and thought in the policy community has been the building of political units beyond the nation-state, there is evidence that scholars and policymakers have neglected a phenomenon of the past decade—the emergence of centrifugal forces within the existing national units. Neither the so-called developed nations nor the developing states have been immune from the rise of linguistic-ethnic nationalism. Even units such as Great Britain, France, and the United States, where the literature of political science, in its conventional wisdom, long ago dismissed forces making for separateness in favor of assumptions about the homogeneity of population and the "melting pot," have faced disintegrative elements. Other countries, including, for example, Canada, Belgium, Nigeria, India, Pakistan, Vietnam, and Cyprus, have been beset with deep cleavages resulting in sepa-

17. See, for example, Sidney E. Rolfe, *The International Corporation,* XXIInd Congress of the International Chamber of Commerce, Istanbul, May 31-June 7, 1969; Jack N. Behrman, *Some Patterns in the Rise of the Multinational Enterprise* (Chapel Hill: University of North Carolina Press, 1969); Werner J. Feld, *Transnational Business Collaboration among Common Market Countries: Its Implication for Political Integration* (New York: Praeger Publishers, 1970); C. F. Kindleberger, ed., *The International Corporation* (Cambridge: The MIT Press, 1970); Endel J. Kolde, *International Business Enterprise* (Englewood Cliffs, N.J.: Prentice-Hall, 1968); Sidney Rolfe and Walter Damm, eds., *The Multinational Corporation in the World Economy* (New York: Praeger Publishers, 1970); Virgil Salera, *Multinational Business* (Boston: Houghton-Mifflin Company, 1969).

Contending Theories of International Relations

ratist movements. If the decade following World War II was characterized by a movement toward regional organization reflected in the literature of international relations, we have now entered a period of dissatisfaction by peoples around the world with the political units in which they live. Although the causes of this ferment are complex, those who express dissatisfaction with the status quo seek (1) to gain a greater voice in the decision-making process of existing units; (2) to achieve greater decentralization of power; or (3) to replace existing units with wholly new structures. It is conceivable that we have entered a period of opposition to the bigness of units which reflect the impersonal forces of bureaucracy and technology. As the world approaches the year 2000, we face several conflicting forces, some of which, such as technology, give impetus to larger political units; others of which contribute to the perpetuation of existing political units; and still others enhance the prospects for the fragmentation of present units. The study of such forces, together with the devising of political forms which reconcile the need for bigness with the desire of peoples for freedom from centralized controls, is a task which will confront both scholars of international relations and policymakers over the decade ahead.

The effort to examine linkages between foreign policy and domestic policy, as well as to understand the domestic and international determinants of foreign policy, reflects the growth of interest in comparative international studies. In the stage which international relations research is now entering, greater emphasis is likely to be placed, in particular, on the comparative study of foreign policy, although such interest is by no means new to international relations. The quest for theoretical frameworks for decision-making and notably the conceptualization and research nearly a generation ago of Richard C. Snyder [18] and his associates as well as more recent efforts such as those of Wolfram F. Hanrieder and James N. Rosenau,[19] are indicative of such interest. In the 1970s, the study of foreign policy can be expected to be subjected to conceptual and research tendencies similar to those which have characterized research elsewhere in the field.

Closely related to the comparative study of foreign policy is the need for a theory of strategic policy. Although the study of military strategy and the development of strategic theories have concerned the scholarly community since World War II, and although the role of power in international behavior has been the focal point of much of international relations theorizing, little effort has been expended to create frameworks for the comparative study of

18. See Richard C. Snyder, H. W. Bruck and Burton Sapin eds., *Foreign Policy Decision Making* (New York: Free Press of Glencoe, 1963).

19. See Hanrieder, *op. cit.,* James N. Rosenau, "External Influences on the Internal Behavior of States," R. Barry Farrell ed., *Approaches to Comparative*

and International Politics (Evanston, Ill.: Northwestern University Press, 1966), pp. 27–92; James N. Rosenau, *Comparative Foreign Policy—Fad, Fantasy, or Field.* Paper prepared for presentation at the Conference-Seminar of the Committee on Comparative Politics, University of Michigan, 1967.

strategic policy or to employ such frameworks for systematic examination including several national units.[20] Such a study could be conducted either as part of a larger model of international interaction, or as an important component of a decision-making framework. More reliable knowledge about the relationship between military force and other national capabilities, the development of strategic doctrine, and the propensity of nations to use specific types of power unilaterally or in collaboration with other nations would represent a significant contribution to international relations theory. If the study of foreign policy continues to become more comparative, it is not difficult to anticipate similar trends in the study of national security policy.

Comparative and Cross-National Research. Over the past decade the tendency toward a more comparative focus in international relations research has been manifested in a growth of interest in cross-national analyses at the subnational level.[21] Such problems include ecological change and its implications for the social and political order, urban studies and violence, and the political values of elites. The growth of issue areas of common concern to postindustrial, industrial, or industrializing societies is likely to accelerate the tendency toward comparative studies of problems which until recently have not been considered central to the field of international relations, or what as a result of such interests is now called "international studies."

As in the past, students of international relations will be faced with both too much and too little data for the validation of theories. On the one hand, vast amounts of data have always been available to the student of politics; on the other hand, the development of quantitative research techniques, together with elaborate theoretical frameworks, increases the need for large new amounts of data. Many of the most important kinds of data relevant, for example, to the study of comparative foreign policy (including health records of decision-makers) [22] are not easily gathered, and, in fact, may never be available to the scholar. This, in turn, will increase the need for indirect or "unobtrusive" measures of political behavior.[23]

TECHNIQUES FOR THE STORAGE AND RETRIEVAL OF DATA

Undoubtedly the development of new techniques for information storage and analysis will help to ease the problems of data availability. The growth of

20. For one notable exception, see Edward A. Kolodziej, "Contemporary International Relations and Military Power: A Comparative Approach," mimeo. (University of Virginia, 1968).

21. See, for example, Robert T. Holt and John E. Turner, *The Methodology of Comparative Research* (New York: Free Press, 1970).

22. However, there are two volumes of potential use in a study of decision-making which takes account of the medical histories of key participants. They include Hugh L'Etang, *The Pathology of Leadership* (London: William Heinemann Medical Books, Ltd., 1969); Lord Moran, *Churchill: Taken from the Diaries of Lord Moran, The Struggle for Survival, 1940–1965* (Boston: Houghton Mifflin Company, 1966).

23. See Eugene J. Webb, Donald T. Campbell, Richard D. Schwartz, and Lee Sechrest, *Unobtrusive Measures: Non-reactive Research in the Social Sciences* (Chicago: Rand McNally and Company, 1966).

data banks, linked by computer consoles, is making new data archives available to researchers in many parts of the world. Technically advanced storage and retrieval systems now make it possible to desensitize data from governmental sources for the use of the scholarly community. The creation of a national archive consisting of data from government sources, would contribute greatly to the conduct of research in international relations and the other social sciences. Such a project, funded by the United States government, is deserving of official consideration at the highest level. It has been estimated that, in the State Department alone, "original" items and distributed copies of "communications" were of the order of sixty-four million in one year.[24] Such archives, to the extent that they lessened the need for the collection of new data for research projects, would lower the cost of conducting research and bring a wider range of research problems within the capabilities of the individual scholar. A factor which undoubtedly contributed to quantitative research was the unprecedented availability of large-scale funds without which such research would have been all but impossible. If the decade of the 1970s is a period of reduced foundation and government emphasis upon international affairs research funding, the need for data archives becomes even more vital if the cost of such research is to be reduced to fit slimmer research budgets and grants.

The computer has already enhanced man's ability to engage in the quantitative and qualitative analysis of political materials, and to test theories containing causal and noncausal relationships. Although aggregate analysis has been used in examining relations among nations, there is scope for applying such techniques and methodologies to phenomena such as violence by employing data about units within nations. In the 1970s such research is likely to be conducted. At this stage, however, there is no widespread consensus within the academic community about the extent to which aggregate analysis will contribute significantly to the development of international relations theory.

A Qualitative-Quantitative Synthesis? Implications for Teaching

It is not difficult to anticipate greater efforts to develop more refined indicators and to introduce a greater qualitative element to quantitative studies. The quest for a greater balance between quantitative and qualitative theory-building efforts can be expected to have important implications for the teaching of international relations. One example will suffice. In the postwar period, the so-called area program took hold in political science and international

24. Willard Fazan, "Federal Information Communities: the Systems Approach." Paper prepared for the annual meeting of the American Political Science Association (September, 1966). Quoted in Davis B. Bobrow and Judah L. Schwartz "Computers and International Relations," Bobrow and Schwartz, eds., *Computers and the Policy-Making Community: Applications to International Relations* (Englewood Cliffs, N.J.: Prentice-Hall, 1968), p. 9.

relations programs in American universities. Such programs developed at a time of increasing United States interest both in the official and private sectors in international affairs. Because of their emphasis on governmental systems as well as on the intellectual and political history, literature, language and economic problems of specified regions, such programs attracted not only students preparing themselves for academic careers, but persons in training for governmental and business careers abroad. In recent years, the orientation of international relations toward a more comparative and empirical focus diminished interest in area programs, as the emphasis of academic training in international relations shifted toward the development of techniques and methods for the examination of political phenomena, such as conflict and integration, on a comparative basis which cuts across older delineations both geographically and academically.[25] Nevertheless, a regional focus is useful to the extent that data about problems under examination can be found only in one region. For example, the study of historical political development, integration at the international level, and the behavior of nations in alliance, of necessity must be based largely upon the experience of the North Atlantic area.

Over the next decade, skepticism about the utility of area studies may be replaced by a growing awareness of their potential qualitative contribution to the quantitative study of political phenomena. For example, the area specialist is likely to have expertise needed both to propose hypotheses and interpret the findings of persons engaged in bivariate or multivariate analysis. The area specialist may be able to give meaning to both the correlations presented by quantitatively oriented students of politics, and a qualitative dimension to the quantitative flows of information and transactions which are contained in certain of the literature on integration, conflict, and alignment.[26] Area specialists can add dimensions to our knowledge of international processes and make us properly wary of sweeping generalizations.

The Quest for Relevance

In the third stage of the development of international relations, the focus of research upon empirical-analytical theory has contributed to a reduction in interest among scholars and policymakers in each other's immediate problems, although much of the funding of social science research in the behavioral sciences has come from the United States government. To the policymaker charged with the formulation of immediate responses to pressing problems, the methodologically laden writings of international relations scholars some-

25. In addition, area programs have been affected by reduced government funding.

26. For a recent critique of such literature and an attempt to engage in qualitative analysis of transnational interaction and integration in Europe, see Carl J. Friedrich, *Europe: An Emergent Nation?* (Boston: Little, Brown and Company, 1969), pp. 24–25. See also Oran R. Young, *Systems of Political Science* (Englewood Cliffs, N.J.: Prentice-Hall, 1967), pp. 60–62.

times appear to provide few, if any, solutions, even though much of the research of the field has been focused upon issues of war and peace which have relevance to the policymaker. For their part, many scholars are concerned with basic research and long-range problems rather than with solutions to the pressing, every-day problems of governments. Because of research both techniques and problem orientation, much of international relations research may appear not only unintelligible but also irrelevant to the immediate concerns of the policymaker. Although it is difficult to assess with precision the impact of international relations research upon policymakers, nevertheless, there is considerable evidence to suggest that the policy community has made some use of academic writings. In particular the development in international relations of a subfield in strategic affairs, especially deterrence and defense, has furnished a body of literature upon which policymakers have drawn for insights.

The longer range outcome of basic research, including theory building and testing, if the proponents of such research have their way, will be to produce a body of knowledge which will explain and perhaps even predict political phenomena. For example, it may eventually be possible to specify the conditions essential to political integration within a national or international context, or it may be possible to state with a greater degree of precision within carefully specified parameters, the conditions which give rise to particular forms of international conflict. If the study of international relations theory reaches this stage of development, we will have achieved an understanding of those international phenomena deemed most important to scholars. In addition, moreover, we will have developed a body of theories of considerable importance in the building of a new science of international relations. Although the quest for such an understanding of international phenomena is likely to be pressed in the 1970s, the research conducted thus far holds promise of only limited success in reaching such a goal in the forseeable future.

If it were possible to develop and test theories, for example, about such phenomena as political integration or international conflict, it might be possible to advance a series of "if-then" propositions relevant to the needs of scholars and policymakers. For example, a greater understanding of the essential conditions for integration or conflict would make possible an understanding of alternative outcomes of various policy choices, since certain kinds of policy choices could be expected to produce certain kinds of outcomes. In short, with the development of a body of empirical-analytic theory, the problems of concern to scholars would have relevance to the interests of policymakers. A new linkage between international relations theory and policy formulation would have been forged.

POLICYMAKING AND INTERNATIONAL RELATIONS THEORY

The literature of international relations, traditional and contemporary, qualitative and quantitative, contains assumptions and conclusions which may have relevance to the policymaker. Policy decisions are frequently dictated by the underlying assumptions of the policymaker. For this reason there is need to engage in a systematic examination of the assumptions which guide policymakers in the formulation of major policies. Therefore, the statements of policymakers and the memoirs of statesmen should be analyzed to develop a check list of assumptions which guide their thinking on policy. An effort should be made to match such assumptions, as well as policies, with assumptions and policies contained in theoretically oriented literature of international relations. A major systematic effort is needed to make international relations literature, especially the writings of the past generation, more relevant to the policymaker. An inventory and matching of major assumptions, theories and findings about international phenomena from policy statements and the literature of international relations would enhance the relevance of academic research to the needs of the policymaker. Such an inventory would contribute to a greater understanding of the current status of international relations theory and provide an indication of those areas where concentrated new efforts are needed. Such a matching exercise would provide much needed insights into the theories, explicit or implicit, which guide policymakers, and would contribute to a greater understanding of those theories of international relations which have had the largest impact upon thought in the policy community.

THEORIZING ABOUT THE FUTURE

Of the highest importance to a study of international relations which purports to be "revelant" is the development of conceptual and methodological tools to anticipate change, for change must be anticipated if it is to be moderated for beneficial purposes. The speed of change as a result of technology has become a major concern of political leaders everywhere. Changes in the nature of the nation-state and the transformation of the international system make urgent the development of more systematic knowledge about the future. In the development of weapons systems and in the designing of policies, whether in foreign affairs or the urban field, an understanding of future technological developments is of crucial importance.[27] Such knowledge is needed if governments are to develop means to influence change.

Although for centuries men have attempted to set forth their conceptions of the future, the need for more systematic forecasts has grown as the lead-time for policy planning, the complexity of issues facing policymakers, and the urgency of problems have increased. The result has been the emergence of the "futurologist," who seeks to "invent the future" by technological fore-

27. As a *New York Times* writer has suggested: "Because of the lead-time in building new strategic systems, the decisions we make today substantially determine our military posture—and thus our security—five years from now. This places a premium on foresight and planning." *New York Times*, February 19, 1970.

casting.[28] If technological forecasting can clarify the choices available to nations by reducing uncertainty about the future, it will contribute to innovative efficiency by making it possible to calculate more accurately the lead-time and the resources needed for alternative policy choices. It may lead also to a more precise understanding of the outcomes of alternative policy choices. The urgency of problems facing political systems—advanced and less developed—together with the quest for a more "relevant" field of inquiry could combine over the next decade to give increasing impetus to the development within international relations of a subfield called "futurology."

This is not to suggest that it is even dimly foreseeable that theories of international relations will achieve a level of predictability which will make possible a high degree of specificity of alternative policy choices. To expect a high level of predictability in international relations theory, given the many variables which must be considered until and unless more parsimonious and reliable theories are developed, would be to anticipate from international relations theories a level of performance which exceeds even theories in the physical sciences. As Morton Kaplan has suggested:

> *Modern theoretical physical science has reared its present lofty edifice by setting itself problems that it has the tools or techniques to solve. When necessary, it has limited ruthlessly the scope of its inquiry. It has not attempted to predict the path a flipped chair will take, the*

28. There are three general types of technological forecasts: the exploratory, opportunity and normative. The *exploratory* forecast suggests future technology likely if the current level of support continues. The *opportunity* forecast depicts probable effects of increased effort in one technological "problem area" or another. The *normative* forecast combines desired goals and technological possibilities, using the goals as a guide for the allocation of resources.

Numerous techniques have been used to obtain such forecasts. The most frequently used is still the trend extrapolation, and its variations: trend correlation in several fields and growth analogy. A new technique for obtaining "intuitive" rather than statistical forecasts is the Delphi method, an elaborate polling device for obtaining an expert consensus without a conference or panel discussion. Systems analysis, such as Program Evaluation and Research Technique (PERT), originally developed by the United States Navy, has been especially helpful for opportunity forecasting as well as R&D administration. Finally, mathematical modelling and the "feedback" concept are intended to aid normative forecasting in correlating the goals of government and industry with technological capabilities.

The most comprehensive general treatment of technological forecasting is Eric Jantsch, *Technological Forecasting in Perspective* (Paris: OECD Publication, 1967). An explanation of forecasting techniques may be found in Robert V. Ayres, *Technological Forecasting and Long-Range Planning* (New York: McGraw-Hill Book Company, 1969). See also James R. Bright, *Technological Forecasting for Industry and Government: Methods & Applications* (Englewood Cliffs, N.J.: Prentice-Hall, 1968). For the more literary and speculative side of the movement, see Bertrand de Jouvenel, *The Art of Conjecture,* N. Lary, trans. (New York: Basic Books, 1967), Herman Kahn and A. J. Wiener, *The Year 2000: A Framework for Speculation* (New York: Macmillan Company, 1967), Dennis Gabor, *Inventing the Future* (New York: Alfred A. Knopf, 1964) and Daniel Bell, ed., *Toward the Year 2000: Work in Progress* (Boston: Houghton Mifflin Company and the American Academy of Arts and Sciences, 1968).

paths of the individual particles of an exploded grenade, or the paths of the individual molecules of gas in a chamber. In the last case, there are laws dealing with the behavior of gases under given conditions of temperature and pressure, but these deal with the aggregate behavior of gases and not the behaviors of individual particles. The physicist does not make predictions with respect to matter in general but only with respect to the aspects of matter that physics deals with; and these, by definition, are the physical aspects of matter.[29]

The Role of Normative Theory

In the fourth stage of its development, however, international relations may experience efforts to establish linkages between normative theory on the one hand, and empirical-analytic theory on the other. The question of a value-free study of politics is of longstanding interest to students of politics. Although normative assumptions may underlie empirical research, the quest for a value-free science of politics has diminished interest over the past generation in normative theory. If political scientists choose to emphasize empirical-analytic theory, to the relative neglect of normative theory, they will have removed themselves from a problem area which historically has been of great concern to them. They will have chosen to ignore the task of defining the meaning of "the good life," the designing of political structures and the establishment of normative standards for mankind in a future which is fraught with growing problems and even peril. The pressing problems created by the impact of technology upon political institutions, changes in the political environment brought about by changing techniques, nationalism and ideology, and the implications of increasing popular pressures and demands upon existing political structures, are likely to lead students of international relations to a greater interest in normative theory. Empirical-analytic theories will not necessarily provide answers to the question of the kinds of institutions and norms appropriate to the world of the future, although from the findings of such studies the student of policy and the policymaker may gain insights vital to the solving of pressing problems.

In almost dialectical reaction against the so-called behavioral revolution, those political scientists who have called for a greater "politicization" of their profession have had as a concern the question of values, goals, or preferences. The "new revolution" of post behavioralism which, according to David Easton, is sweeping political science contains the following arguments: (1) it is more important to be relevant to contemporary needs than to be methodologically sophisticated; (2) behavioral science conceals an ideology based upon empirical conservatism; (3) behavioral research, by its focus upon abstraction,

29. Morton A. Kaplan, "Problems of Theory Building and Theory Confirmation in International Politics," Klaus Knorr and Sidney Verba, eds., *The* *International System: Theoretical Essays* (Princeton: Princeton University Press, 1961), p. 7.

loses touch with reality; (4) the political scientist has the obligation to make his knowledge available for the general benefit of society.[30]

Because of the close (according to some, all too close) identification of international relations with political science, it will be difficult, if not impossible, for international relations to be unaffected by the "postbehavioral" revolution of political science. Over the past generation international relations has experienced many of the same shifts in theoretical and methodological focus as political science, although scholars for the most part have retained a major interest in "relevant" problems. Research on the causes of war and the resolution of conflict; theories of deterrence; arms control and negotiations about armaments; and the integration of political communities, cannot be said to fail the test of relevance.

In the field of international relations there have always been groups of scholars whose principal interest was the development and analysis of public policy. In its utopian and realist phases, international relations study was strongly focused upon policy. Over the past generation, the efforts of scholars to give the field a more theoretical orientation and to emphasize the methodological basis of inquiry have represented more a supplement to, rather than a replacement of, a concern for policy problems.[31] Indeed, considerable emphasis has been placed on the development of more rigorous techniques for the analysis of public policy, especially in the form of systems analysis.[32] The goal of such work has been to devise criteria to aid in choosing and evaluating alternative policies or strategies, or mixes of policies or strategies, for the attainment of specified objectives. The effort has been to find "optimal" or preferable solutions among a series of alternatives based upon relative costs and benefits by the use of such techniques as mathematical models, human gaming, and the canvasing of expert opinion. Such cost-benefit studies

30. David Easton, "The New Revolution in Political Science," *American Political Science Review*, LXIII (December, 1969), 1052. Similarly, Easton was among the first to discern the behavioral revolution in political science. See David Easton: *The Political System: An Inquiry into the State of Political Science* (New York: Alfred A. Knopf, 1954), especially pp. 37–125; by the same author, *A Framework for Political Analysis* (Englewood Cliffs, N.J.: Prentice-Hall, 1965), pp. 6–9.

31. For a collection of essays by scholars concerned with the relationship between social science and public policy in the post-World War II period, see Daniel Lerner and Harold D. Lasswell, eds., *The Policy Sciences* (Stanford, Calif.: Stanford University Press, 1951). For a more recent discussion, see Norman D.

Palmer, ed., *A Design for International Relations Research: Scope, Theory, Methods, and Relevance*. Monograph 10, The American Academy of Political and Social Science (October, 1970), especially pp. 154–274.

32. Charles J. Hitch and Ronald N. McKean, *The Economics of Defense in the Nuclear Age* (Cambridge: Harvard University Press, 1963); Ronald McKean, *Efficiency in Government through Systems Analysis* (New York: John Wiley and Sons, 1958); Raymond A. Bauer and Kenneth J. Gergen, eds., *The Study of Policy Formation* (New York: Free Press, 1968); Harold Lasswell, "Policy Sciences," in *International Encyclopedia of the Social Sciences* (New York: Macmillan Company and the Free Press, 1968), XII, 181–189.

International Studies in the 1970s

represented a reaction against policy recommendations based upon unstated assumptions, untested hypotheses, and uncertainty as to the implications of alternative choices and outcomes. The deficiencies of systems analysis in dealing with such irrational forces as charisma and ideology, or the propensity of actors to adopt high-risk or low-risk strategies, and its inadequacies in explicating the value assumptions of analysis, all serve to point up the need for additional work in the decade ahead toward the development of a policy science field either within international relations or as a separate discipline or "interdiscipline." [33]

Given the likely increase in pressing political problems, it will be necessary to strike a balance between empirical-analytic theory and normative theory, and between basic and applied research in the fourth stage of development, which international relations is now entering. Indeed, despite the tendency over the past generation to deemphasize normative theory, it has been a major thesis of this chapter that normative and empirical theory and basic and applied research are by no means incompatible. Normative theory can suggest alternative goals and preferences for political institutions and can also provide propositions for testing, and empirical-analytic theory can furnish guidance as to the kinds of political behavior which are essential for the attainment of desired goals. At present a strong tide seems to be running in favor of normative (or ethical) analysis, especially regarding the problem of war. This can have a humanizing effect provided it does not become so emotional that it loses contact with the philosophical and scientific bases of traditional Western political wisdom.

By focusing upon the building of theories of conflict, integration, and decision-making, scholars have chosen problem areas of central concern not only to the study of political science, but also to the development of a policy science. The outcome of such research is of transcending importance to both scholars and policymakers.

Conceivably, just as the study of international relations has moved from the extreme preoccupation with the normative theory of the 1920s to preoccupation with empirical-analytic theory of the 1960s, the coming generation of scholars will hopefully try to achieve a better and less pendular balance and seek to assure the relevance of international theory to the manifold problems facing international society, while at the same time pursuing the needed quest for broadly-based theories that explain and predict political behavior at the international level. Thus international relations, or international studies, will have achieved in its next stage of development, a greater synthesis among those concerns that have been of principal importance in the stages through which the field has passed since its beginnings in the early years of this century.

---

33. See Yehezkel Dror, *Analytical Approaches and Applied Social Sciences* (Santa Monica, Calif.: The RAND Corporation, November, 1969), monograph.

Index of Names

Leoni, Bruno, 9n
Lerche, Charles O., Jr., 320, 320n, 321n, 324, 330, 330n
Lerner, Daniel, 24n, 147, 147n, 243n, 335n, 397n
Levi, Werner, 18n, 143, 197, 199, 199n
Levin, Henry, 219n
Le Vine, Robert A., 191, 219n
Levy, Marion J., 113, 113n, 383n
Lewin, Kurt, 42n
Lifton, Robert Jay, 192n
Lijhart, Arend, 30n
Lin Piao, 194, 195
Lincoln, George A., 12n
Lindberg, Leon N., 119n, 282, 282n, 306, 306n, 307n
Lindblom, Charles E., 320n, 331, 332, 332n
Lindzey, Gardner, 249n
Lipetz, Milton, 355n
Lippmann, Walter, 164n, 313, 314, 314n
Liska, George, 13, 301, 301n, 302, 302n, 303, 303n, 304, 304n, 305, 305n, 358n
Locke, John, 237
Loomis, Charles P., 244n
Lorenz, Konrad, 208-212, 209n-211n, 214, 268
Lorimer, Frank, 245n
Lowenstein, K., 206n
Luard, Evan, 270n
Luce, R. Duncan, 353n, 354n
Lumsden, Malvern, 356n
Lutzker, Daniel R., 356n
Luxembourg, Rosa, 176, 178

MacArthur, Douglas, 334n
Maccoby, Eleanor E., 219n
Machiavelli, Niccolò, 2, 2n, 67, 67n, 68, 68n, 149n, 160, 160n, 161, 162, 202n, 237, 312, 313n
Mack, Raymond W., 144n, 146n
Mackinder, Sir Halford, 5, 47, 50, 52-54, 53n, 54n, 56, 62, 63, 73, 92
Macoby, Michael, 359n
Macridis, Roy C., 326n
Maddox, John, 273n
Mahan, Alfred Thayer, 5, 47, 51-52, 51n, 63, 163, 164n
Maher, R. F., 235n
Maier, R. F., 213n, 214n
Majak, A. Roger, 319n, 329n, 333, 333n
Malatesta, Errico, 166
Malinowski, Bronislaw, 112
Mallin, Jay, 192n
Malraux, André, 249n
Mannheim, Karl, 238n
Manning, C. A. W., 8n
Manu, 148n
Manuel, Frank E., 238n

Mansergh, Nicholas, 185n
Mao Tse-tung, 148n, 191, 192, 192n, 193, 193n, 194, 195, 250, 250n
Marcellinus, 151n
Marchant, P. D., 8n
Marcion, 150n
Marlborough, Duke of, 155
Marshall, Charles Burton, 70, 70n, 81n, 84n
Martin, Kingsley, 156n
Marx, Karl, 141n, 172-176, 174n, 175n, 178, 179, 179n, 187, 187n, 195, 233
Masaryk, Thomas, 166n
Maslow, Abraham H., 213, 213n
Masters, Roger D., 10n
Maxwell, Stephen, 254n, 266n, 267n
McBride, James H., 335n
McClelland, Charles A., 13, 13n, 40n, 45n, 114, 115, 115n, 116, 116n, 117, 118, 119-120, 120n, 121, 212n, 235
McClintock, Charles G., 258n, 356n
McColl, Robert W., 251n
McDougall, William, 204, 204n, 212
McKean, Ronald N., 397n
McKenna, Joseph C., 169n
McLaughlin, Charles H., 12n
McNamara, Robert, 240
McNaughton, John T., 271n
McNeil, Elton B., 115n, 141n, 142n, 202n, 207, 207n, 213n, 214n, 215n, 219n, 223, 223n
Meehan, Eugene J., 373, 373n
Meinecke, Fredrich, 2n, 68n
Meisel, James H., 238, 238n
Melman, Seymour, 270n
Mencius, 67, 148
Mendel, Gregor, 209
Menninger, Karl, 206n, 214
Merritt, Richard L., 37n, 61, 61n
Merton, Robert K., 112, 113, 113n, 136, 136n
Metternich, Klemens von, 22, 33
Milburn, Thomas W., 266, 266n, 267, 267n
Mill, John Stuart, 172
Miller, Neal E., 213n
Millis, Walter, 186n
Mills, Leonard A., 12n
Minas, J. Sayer, 355n
Mirsky, G., 190n
Mitchell, General William, 51
Mitrany, David, 280, 281, 281n, 293, 294, 388
Modelski, George, 19, 19n, 21n, 27, 115, 115n, 116, 117, 118, 123-125, 124n, 135, 149n, 231n
Mohammed, 48, 149
Monnerot, Jules, 172n
Montesquieu, Baron de, 46, 47n, 156

Reisman, David, 369n
Rejaik, Mostafa, 192n
Reynolds, P. A., 112n
Richardson, James L., 264n
Richardson, Lewis F., 271, 271n, 339n
Riggs, Fred W., 123n
Riker, William H., 19, 19n, 301, 301n, 302, 302n, 303, 304, 333, 333n, 358n
Ritchie-Calder, Lord, 64n
Robbins, Lionel, 5, 5n
Robinson, James A., 319n, 323n, 324n, 325n, 326n, 328n, 329n, 333, 333n, 334n, 371n
Rocco, Alfredo, 165
Rock, Vincent P., 256n, 259n
Rogow, Arnold A., 222n
Rokkan, Stein, 37n
Rolfe, Sidney E., 388n
Rollins, Abbie A., 73n
Rommen, Heinrich A., 153n
Roosevelt, President Franklin D., 22, 324, 361
Roosevelt, President Theodore, 22, 51
Rosecrance, Richard N., 13, 115, 115n, 116, 117, 118, 121-123, 121n-123n, 130, 133, 133n, 373n
Rosen, Steven, 301n, 358n
Rosenau, James N., 13n, 19n, 24n, 37n, 61n, 94n, 109n, 114n, 136n, 231n, 241, 241n, 315n, 326n, 327, 328n, 344n, 370n, 372n, 380n, 381n, 383n, 389, 389n
Rosenweig, Sanford, 215n
Ross, E. A., 233
Rostow, Walt W., 74n, 321n, 363n
Roucek, Joseph S., 6n
Rousseau, Jean-Jacques, 2, 155, 156n
Rummel, Rudolph J., 37n, 41, 41n, 42, 146n, 235, 235n
Rusk, Dean, 325n, 330n
Russell, Bertrand, 160n, 163n, 359n
Russell, Frank M., 2n, 5, 5n, 148n, 152n
Russett, Bruce M., 37n, 39n, 200, 200n, 270, 270n, 298, 298n, 299n, 300, 301n, 310, 310n, 331n
Ryan, John A., 152n

Said, Abdul, 285n, 320, 320n, 330, 330n
Sapin, Burton, 315n, 316, 316n, 317, 317n, 319n, 320n, 321n, 322n, 323n, 335, 336, 389n
Saul, 149
Schapiro, Salwyn, 186n
Scheingold, Stuart A., 307n
Schelling, Thomas C., 231n, 255n, 257, 264n, 267n, 345n, 347, 347n, 353n, 359, 364, 364n, 365, 365n, 366, 366n, 367, 367n, 368, 376, 376n, 378n

Schevill, Ferdinand, 186n
Schleicher, Charles P., 12n, 32n, 34, 34n
Schlesinger, Arthur M., 334n
Schmidt, Helmut, 264n
Schmitt, Bernadotte E., 4n, 185n
Schmitter, Philippe, 293n, 295, 295n, 296, 296n, 310n
Schram, Stuart, 192n
Schuman, Frederich L., 6n, 12n, 14n, 66, 67n, 74-75, 74n-75n
Schumpeter, Joseph A., 186, 186n, 187, 187n
Schwartz, David C., 378n
Schwartz, Judah L., 391n
Schwartz, Richard D., 390n
Schwarzenberger, Georg, 6n, 11, 11n
Scodel, Alvin J., 355n
Scott, Andrew M., 49n
Scott, James Brown, 154n
Scott, John Paul, 207, 208, 208n, 211n, 214
Scott, William A., 265n
Scoville, Herbert, Jr., 259n
Seabury, Paul, 32n, 254n
Sears, Robert R., 219n
Sechrest, Lee, 390n
Seidenberg, Bernard, 141n
Semple, Ellen Churchill, 51
Seward, J. P., 214
Shands, Harley, 216n
Shang, Lord, 148n
Shaw, Bruno, 192n
Shils, Edward A., 106n, 107n, 108n, 238n, 244, 244n
Shotwell, James T., 5, 5n, 202, 202n
Shubik, Martin, 347, 347n, 351n, 352n, 359
Shy, John W., 192n
Sibley, Mulford Q., 169, 169n
Siffin, William J., 123n
Silander, Fred S., 312n
Simmel, George, 144n, 233, 233n, 234n, 235, 235n
Simon, Herbert, 332, 332n
Simonds, Frank H., 5, 5n, 6n
Singer, J. David, 18n, 19, 20, 28, 28n, 37n, 103n, 104n, 118n, 121n, 130, 131, 131n, 132, 132n, 133, 141, 200n, 271n, 272n, 317n, 331n, 338n, 339n, 341, 342n, 343n, 344n, 383n, 384n
Skolnikoff, Eugene B., 325n
Slessor, Sir John, 254n
Small, Albion W., 233
Small, Melvin, 132, 132n
Smelser, Neil J., 218n
Smith, Adam, 7, 7n, 172
Smith, Tony E., 387n
Snyder, Glenn H., 36n, 254n, 255n
Snyder, Richard C., 13, 13n, 27, 144n,

Index of Names

Whaley, Barton, 372n
Wheaton, William L. C., 329n
Wheeler-Bennett, J. W., 5, 5n
Weidner, Edward W., 14n
White, Lynn, Jr., 64n
White, Ralph K., 220n, 226, 226n
Whiting, Allen S., 12n
Whiting, John W. M., 219n
Whittlesey, Derwent, 57n
Wiener, A. J., 395n
Wiener, Norbert, 117, 284, 285n
Wiesner, Jerome B., 256n
Wight, Martin, 2, 2n, 3, 3n, 11, 11n
Wikenfield, Jonathan, 42, 42n
Wilcox, Francis O., 119n
Wilkinson, David, 249n
Williamson, Robert C., 212n
Wilson, Marjorie Kerr, 209n
Wilson, President Woodrow, 3, 22, 85, 324, 333n
Winberg, Chai, 148n
Windsor, Philip, 264n, 272n
Winslow, E. M., 177, 177n
Withey, Stephen, 142, 142n, 202n
Wittfogel, Karl A., 51
Wohlstetter, Albert, 255n, 264n, 359n
Wolfe, Bertram D., 179n

Wolfe, P., 354n
Wolfe, Thomas W., 264n
Wolfenstein, E. Victor, 230n
Wolfers, Arnold, 7n, 17, 18, 18n, 67, 67n, 85-87, 85n-87n, 270n
Wolff, Robert P., 21
Wolin, Sheldon, 21n
Wood, R. C., 329n
Wright, Christopher, 325n
Wright, Michael, 270n
Wright, Quincy, 9n, 12n, 13, 14n, 17, 17n, 29, 29n, 30, 30n, 40n, 42, 42n, 43, 43n, 152n, 196n, 198n, 202, 202n, 203n
Wriston, Henry W., 325n

Young, Elizabeth, 274n
Young, Oran, 94n, 116n, 134, 134n, 136n, 137, 137n, 310, 310n, 392n

Zawadzi, B., 240, 240n
Zawodny, J. K., 141, 142n, 213n, 214n, 216n, 219n, 235n, 249n
Zeiller, Jacques, 151n
Zimmern, Alfred, 8n
Zinnes, Dina A., 302n, 344n
Zuckerman, Sir Solly, 359n

Index of Subjects

ABM (Anti-Ballistic Missile system), 256
Agraria (and Industria), 19, 116
Aggression
    a learned response, 208; and economic deprivation, 212; and preservation of species, 210-211; cause of conflict, 204; critique of instinct theories, 207-208; instinct theories, 204-206; intraspecific, 208-212; social outlets, 223-224; the "territorial imperative," 209
Aggression-frustration, 212-214
    and displacement, 220; and projection, 219-220; and repression, 219; critiques of the concept, 214-216; culture bound, 218-219; from individual to group, 216-218, 220-221
Alliances, 7, 10, 13, 32
    and integration patterns, 338; cohesion, 301-302; cohesion and power, 304; diplomacy, 14; ideology, 302; instability, 303-305; optimum size, 302-303; and World War I, 339; *See also* Coalitions
American foreign policy, 54
    and Germany, 276; and Korea, 335-337; and the Middle East, 33; and South Vietnam, 79; based on national experiences, 81; containment policy, 84-85; distinct periods, 80-82; geographic factors, 81-82; legalistic-moralistic orientation, 81; neglect of less developed areas, 84; prescription for, 73, 267; spirit of romanticism, 82
American constitution, 80
American-Japanese Peace Treaty, 335
American Journal of International Law, 84
American security
    and Russo-German relations, 84
Anarchism, 165-167

Antarctica Treaty, 272
Anthropogeographie, 55
Appeasement, 71
Area programs
    in international relations, 392; *See also* International Relations
Arms Control, 32, 35-36, 231, 254-278
Arms race
    substitute for imperialism, 190-191; *See also* Disarmament, Non-Proliferation Treaty, SALT
Atlantic Alliance, *See* NATO
Augustinian theology, 77
Austro-Hungarian empire, 22

Balanced deterrence, 257-259
    and peace, 260; and strategic parity, 260; *See also* Deterrence
Balance of payments, 24
Balance of power, 5, 7, 15, 20, 22, 28, 30-36, 185, 332, 356, 384
    American policy in South East Asia, 79; and coalition formation, 61; and alliances, 302; and the Realist School, 66; an English theory, 33-34; as foreign policy prescription, 257; classical conception, 137; consensus for effectiveness, 79; confusion of meanings, 100-101; contemporary models, 35-36; criticism of, 34-35, 100-101; defined, 30-32, 79, 86; effect of geography, 75; functions of, 32-33; guide for statesmen, 34; "holder of the balance," 33, 34
Balance of power system, *See* Balance of power
Bargaining theory, 364-369, 382
Basic interest, *See* National interest
Behavioral School, 20, 39; *See also* Behavioralism

409

Behavioralism
critique of Utopianism and Realism, 380-382; orientation of, 382-383
Bellicism, 159-164
main doctrines, 164-165; *See also* War
Berlin crisis
American deterrence, 262; simulation of, 372
Bipolarity, 14, 86, 336
maintenance of equilibrium, 109; *See also* International system
Bipolar system
contrasted to multipolar system, 96-97; operation of, 79; *See also* International system
Bipolarization
type of balance of power, 79
Britain, 52
and disimperialism, 189; "holder of the balance," 33
British empire, 52
British foreign policy
and Finland, 76-77

Capitalism
and imperialism, 176-177; stage in Marxian dialectic, 174-176
"Capitalist encirclement"
threat to socialism, 181
Challenge and response, 49-50
Coalitions, 19, 269, 333
Britain, 62; size principle, 303-304; *See also* Balance of power
Coalition theory, *See* Coalitions
Cognitive dissonance, 228-230
Cold war, 10
and game theory, 362-364; mirror images, 225
Collective security
Korea, 87
Colonialism, 13
Commitment
credibility of, 368
Communication
international, 43; tacit, 366-367
Communism, 72
democratic centralism, 179-180; *See also* Marxism
Communist Manifesto, 179, 187
Communist Party, 179-180
Communist strategy, 93-94
Community
defined, 308-309
Concert of Europe
Pax Britannica, 157
Concurrent validity, 377
Conflict theories, 138-278
anarchist explanation, 167; and class

struggle, 173; and consensus, 88; and cooperation, 364; and game theory, 246-247; and national interest, 78; balance of power, 75; conceptualizations, 203-204; containment of, 367; cross-national comparisons, 226; contrasted with cooperation, 72; dialectics of antagonism, 97; decision-making, 332; defined, 98; functional, 233-236; guerrilla, 28; ideological, 14, 35, 360; in international relations, 386-387; intrapersonal, 33; learned, 221; motivations of, 91, 196-197; psychic, 69; related to social development, 241; revolution of rising expectations, 231
Containment, 357
in Korea, 87; response to Soviet policy, 84-85
Content analysis
World War I analyzed, 237-240
Conventional pause, 262
Cooperation, 12
Counterinsurgency, 28
Coup
distinguished from revolution, 250
Credibility
defined, 97
Crisis
decision-making, 323, 334-335; gaming, 372; rational decision-making, 317-318
Cuban missile crisis, 337
an interaction model, 340-341
Czechoslovakia
invasion of, 264; Soviet involvement in 1968, 188-189
Cybernetics, 117
and integration, 387

Data-retrieval systems
in international relations, 391; *See also* International Relations
Death instinct, 205
and the arms race, 267
Decision-making, 14, 17, 27, 384, 398
a microlevel analysis, 315; and "folk knowledge," 105; and Korea, 335-337; conceptual framework, 314-315; cognitive dissonance, 229; crisis situations, 334-335; critique of, 328-329; defined, 312-313; early approaches, 313-314; environment of, 322-323; in systems theory, 316; maximization contrasted to optimization, 332; modern approaches, 314-317; organizational structure, 323-326; political scope, 329; processes of, 326-329; psychological components, 341-344; role of motivations, 326-329; situational variables, 319-320; synoptic contrasted to incremental, 331-332;

Index of Subjects

perceptions, 316; World War I: a case study, 337-340

Decision-making theory, *See* Decision-making

Declaration of Independence, 80

Decolonization, 14

Demands, 111; *See also* Input-output analysis

Democratic centralism, 179-180

Deterrence, 14, 254-278, 365, 368
and arms control, 268-270; and nuclear war, 367-368; and nuclear weapons, 254; and parity, 259; arms superiority, 259; balance of power, 257; balance of terror, 256; defined, 97; finite, 259; likelihood of war, 230-231; limitation of wars, 170; nuclear sufficiency, 259; rationality of decision-makers, 264-268; related to technology, 255-256

Dimensionality of Nations Project (DON), 41-43

Diplomacy, 3, 5
and the superpowers, 90; management of power, 80; "peace through accommodation," 79-80; recent role, 79-80; resolution of conflict, 90

Disarmament, 5, 13, 14, 25, 40
negotiations, 268-269

Disputes, 32

Distribution of wealth, 48

"Dominant minority"
defined, 49

Dual Alliance, 339, 340, 341

Dual-capability forces, 262

Ecological perspectives, 47

Economic development, 10

ECSC (European Coal and Steel Community), 289
and integration, 293; spill-over effect, 290

EEC (European Economic Community), 22, 310
case study in integration, 288-292; degree of integration, 306; economic growth, 309; imperialism of, 189-190; role of elites, 288-289; spill-over effect, 290

Elan vital, 49

Elites
and system stability, 117; and war, 223; decision-making, 117; foreign policy, 14; integration, 289, 293; revolutionary, 248-249

Enlightenment, 47

Environment, 47
challenge and response, 49-50

Equilibrium, *See* Systems and General systems theory

Eurasia, 53-54, 62, 73

Ethiopia
Italian invasion, 71

European Defense Community, 335

European state system, 33

Factor analysis, 41-43, 298-300

Feedback, *See* Systems and Systems theory

Fellowship of Reconciliation, 71

Feudal system, 93

Field theory, 42

Flexible response, 261

Franco-Prussian War, 97

Freedom
psychological burden, 227

French foreign policy, 52
challenge to existing order, 88

French Revolution, 96

Frustration
defined, 213; goals and satisfactions, 243

Foreign Affairs, 6

Foreign aid, 347

Foreign policy
and aspirations, 83; changing opponent behavior, 92; conceptualization, 86; decision-making, 313; defined, 23-24; determinants, 390; domestic linkages, 381, 389; elite assumptions, 394; impact of technology, 277; psychological context, 344; state's goals, 92; strategic approach, 346; struggle for power, 83

Foreign policy goals
a classification, 85

Foreign Policy Reports, 6

Functional equivalents, 113

Functionalism
approach to integration, 293-294; contrasted to structural-functional analysis, 280-281; critique, 310-311

Functional requisites, 113

Functions
compared to dysfunctions, 113

Game theory, 384
and decision-making, 345-347; and social phenomena, 346; application to international relations, 358-361; application to the Cold War, 362-364; components of, 349; defined, 347; example of "chicken," 352-353; minimax and maximin strategies, 351-352; normal form, 350; rationality, 348-349; prisoner's dilemma, 354-355; related to systems, 349

Gaming, 397
aid in theory construction, 372-373; analogical model, 373; and decision-

Gaming (*Continued*)
  making, 377-378; and simulation, 369-370; contrasted to game theory, 355; isomorphic to reality, 373-374; realism in reconstruction, 372
Gemeinschaft, 244
General systems theory, 107-114
  integration of disciplines, 105-106; purpose of, 103-104; the Parsonian subsystems, 107
Geographic mobility, 52
Geographic "possibilist" school, 50-51
Geography
  and individual choice, 57-59; cognitive behavioralism, 58
Geophysics, 52
Geopolitical school, *See* Geopolitics
Geopolitics, 54
  and German national expansion, 56; and national power, 55-57; British and Japanese policies, 61; critiques of, 61-62; current research, 60-61; defined, 56; effect of technology, 62-63; effect on behavior, 77; flexible frontiers, 56-57; inevitability of conflict, 56; insular and noninsular, 61; *lebensraum,* 56; line of least resistance, 73; related concepts, 57; the "rimland" hypothesis, 54; theoretical development, 55
German geopolitical school, 46
German-Japanese alliance
  threat to American security, 73
Gesellschaft, 244
Graduated deterrence, 262; *See also* Deterrence
Great powers, 12, 29

Hague Conferences, 81
Heartland
  defined, 53; inner crescent, 62; outer crescent, 53; rimland, 62; river crescent, 53; *See also* Geopolitics
Hegelian dialectic, 10
Heisenberg's principle of indeterminacy, 38
Homeostasis, 118
Hostility
  and war, 271-272
Human behavior
  basis of international relations, 85; Nietzsche's "will to power," 161
Human nature
  characteristics of, 82-83; *See also* Political behavior
Hungarian uprising, 262

ICBM (Intercontinental Ballistic Missiles), 255, 270
  Soviet-American parity, 259-260

Ideology, 13, 43
  stability of the international system, 90
Image, 105
  a selection process, 224
Imperialism, 7, 13, 15, 22
  American, 72; and Eastern Europe, 188; and "human instincts," 179; and the economic order, 175; as objective, 78; costs and benefits, 177; critique, 183-190; defined, 184, 186; finance capitalism, 178; investments, 182; J. A. Hobson's theory, 176-178; Lenin's theory, 178-183; monopoly capitalism, 182; policies of, 78
Industria (and Agraria), 19, 116
Industrial Revolution, 173-174
Input-output analysis, 111; *See also* General systems theory, Systems, Systems theory
Instability
  regime, 43
Integration, 384, 398
  a learning process, 284; and alliances, 304; and EEC, 22; and geographic distance, 61; and interdependence, 300; and subnational forces, 388-390; basic approaches, 279-280; conceptualization, 305-306; critique, 386-387; cybernetic approach, 284-287; defined, 281-283, 300, 305-306; disaggregation of, 311; elite commitment, 297-298; elite units, 289-290; Etzioni's four stages, 288-292; European, 297-298, 306-309; functional, 13, 29; Galtung's three conditions, 283-284; historical and contemporary, 292; indicators of, 306-309; Malaysia, 61; political, 29; regional, 13, 14, 292, 298-300; structural-functional approach, 280; transnational forces, 388; United Arab Republic, 61; West Indies Federation, 61
Interest, *See* National interest
International behavior
  defined, 8
International community, 2
International Conciliation, 6
International economics, 14
International investment, 11
International Labor Organization, 295
International law, 2, 3, 10, 13
  and disputes, 83; teaching of, 5
International morality, 7
International order
  and legitimacy, 88; and balance of power, 88-89
International organization, 2, 4, 10, 13, 40, 47, 381
  structural equilibrium, 304-305
International political system, *See* International system

International politics
contrasted to national, 382; zero-sum or non zero-sum, 360-361; *See also* International relations
International relations, 375
action-reaction processes, 13, 23; as equilibrium process, 13; as power struggle, 10; as social communication process, 13; concern of, 95; contrasted to national politics, 9-10, 95; compared to foreign policy, 23-24; compared to policy sciences, 24; cross-national research, 390-391; early theoretical approaches, 1-3; field of study, 8, 9; influence of Realist School, 68-101; limitation of game theoretic approach, 11; neurophysiologist concepts, 386; reification, 58-59; related to history, 75-76; relation to international law and organization, 4; role of economics, 5; role of environment, 47-64; scope of, 15-17; some conventional assumptions, 381-382; struggle for power, 69; study of, 10, 13, 75-86; teaching of, 14-15, 65; use of history, 20
International relations theory
appropriate time-span, 20; coalitions approach, 19; conceptualization, 44; different approaches, 30; dimensionality of nations project, 41-43; decision-making approach, 18; definition of "general" theory, 29-30; field theory, 42; levels of analysis, 17-20, 43-44; "minds-of-men" approach, 18; purpose, 44; quantitative or qualitative data, 44; Realist School, 15; scope and nature, 15-30; scope, 40-41; textbooks of, 15-16; theory and practice, 21-24; traditional and behavioral schools, 28; units of analysis, 43-44
International Studies Quarterly, 14
International system, 13, 19, 21, 24, 33, 44, 375, 383
and legitimacy, 111-112; balance of power, 75; competition among nations, 74, 79; decentralization, 66-67, 74; defined, 94, 96, 115; definition of subsystems, 119; degree of centralization, 112; different approaches and theories, 114-119; distinguished from other systems, 114-119; elite effect on stability, 117-118; heterogeneous, 96; homogeneous, 96; nationalism and stability, 118; outputs, 295; related to the national, 111; stability and resources, 117; working of, 72
International theory
speculative tradition, 3
Internation simulation
assessment, 377

Interstate relations, 2, 44
Intervention, 32
International trade, 11
Isolationism, 11
Italian State System, 20

"Just war," 154-155
and nuclear age, 167-171; consensus, 170
John Hopkins Center for Foreign Policy, 85
Journal of Peace Research, 14

Kashmir dispute
and game theory, 362
Kellogg-Briand Treaty, 3, 81, 202
Korean conflict, 367

Latin America Nuclear Free Zone Agreement, 272
Law
relation to force, 163
League of Nations, 2, 3, 22, 112
as conceived by France and Britain, 86-87
Lebensraum, 47, 62, 201; *See also* Geopolitics
Legalistic-moralistic approach
to international relations, 76, 81
Legal system, 43
Legitimacy
defined, 88
Level of analysis, 382
in international relations, 384-385; *See also* International Relations
Leviathan
early use of systems analysis, 103
Limited war
effective implementation, 89; role of diplomacy, 89; guide for American foreign policy, 89
Linkage
of national and international politics, 91

Marxism, 172-176; *See also* Communism
adaptations to new circumstances, 195; and imperialism, 189-191; dialectical materialism, 174; "inevitability of war," 181-182
Mayas, 49
Methodology
and international relations, 383; factor analysis, 41; observer-observed relationship, 40; spatial analysis, 43; Traditional and Behavioral Schools, 14, 28; Utopian and Realist Schools, 14; "value-free," 40
Military capabilities, 43
Mirror-images, 225-226
MIRV (Multiple Independently-Targeted Reentry Vehicles), 256

Politics
defined, 9, 223; of development, 14
Policy science, 24
Pollution
and international relations, 63-64
Post-behavioralism
approach to international relations, 385-386; assumptions of, 396-397
Power, 2, 15, 43, 68, 77, 293
and conflict, 91-92; and moral principles, 75; and political order, 91; criticized as a concept, 87, 100; defined, 76; determinant of political behavior, 66-67; goal of states, 74; in coalitions, 358; Machiavelli, 67; related to commitment, 314; related to means of production, 174; related to military strength, 24; the Realist School, 91-92
Power politics, 12
Prestige
as foreign policy objective, 78; means of achieving in foreign policy, 78
Prisoner's dilemma
applied to disarmament, 356-357
Promise
credibility, 368; element of bargaining theory, 365
Propaganda, 13
Protracted conflict
defined, 93-94
Public opinion
the Realist School, 7

Rand Corporation, 14, 102
war gaming, 370
Rationality
and irrationality, 267-268, 365-366; defined, 266; in decision-making, 316-318; See also Deterrence
Realism
a tool of analysis, 384; attempt at grand theory, 384; contrasted to general systems theory, 385; in international relations, 379; See also Realist School
Realist School, 47, 68-99
a critique, 99-101; and morality, 70; and national interest, 70-71; autonomy of the political sphere, 77; balance of power, 66; concept of man, 66, 70; concept of power, 65; contemporary relevance, 100; contrasted to Utopian School, 5-8, 65-66; criticism of American foreign policy, 70; geopolitical influence, 54, 66; intellectual antecedents, 67-68; international morality, 66; nation-state as unit of analysis, 65; national versus universal morality, 77; normative orientation, 98; power and

national interest, 10-24; prospects of world government, 70; state sovereignty, 74; sin and anxiety, 69; state preservation, 72-73; use of history, 63; See also International relations
Realists, See Realist School
Reformation, 93
Renaissance, 20, 93
Reinsurance Treaty, 22
Review of Politics, 14
Revolution
aspirations and fulfillment, 239-240; collective insecurities, 223; cognitive dissonance, 229-230; choice of terrain, 250-251; duration, 250; historical and contemporary, 237-238; J-curve, 242; needs and desires, 236-237; internal and external factors, 251-253; political objectives, 249-250; role of intellectuals, 239; social and political power, 238-239
Revolutionary warfare
contemporary theories, 191-195; differences in, 193
Russian foreign policy
ideological orientation, 52, 84

SALT (Strategic Arms Limitation Talks), 259
implications of, 274-277
Saddlepoint
solution to a zero-sum game, 350-351
Scenario, 373
Scientific method, 37
and values, 278
Science, 36
Seapower, 51-52, 54
Security, 5
Security communities
amalgamated, 304; conditions for amalgamated type, 286; conditions for pluralistic type, 286-287
Simulation
and hypothesis testing, 372-373; as a teaching device, 370-372, 378; approach critiqued, 378; compared to verbal theories, 375; contrasted to game theory and gaming, 369; defined as a theory, 375; related to verbal and mathematical theories, 376; strengths and weaknesses in theory building, 375-376; uses and limitations, 370-371
Social influence, 48
Social revolution, 50
Socialist thought, 3
Sovereignty, 74
Spatial analysis, 43
Spheres of influence, 32

Spill-over, 282, 289, 309
  process of integration, 294-296; *See also* Integration
Stability
  and legitimacy, 88
Stable arms balance, 257; *See also* **Deterrence**
Stable deterrence, 257, 259; *See also* **Deterrence**
State
  defined, 55

Technology
  in geopolitics, 59-60; military, 15
Territorial compensation, 33
Theory, 41-43, 45
  deductive, 45; defined, 25-26; formulation of, 36-37; "grand," 28-29, 45, 382-385; inductive, 45; macro, 45, 384, 392; middle-range, 29, 45, 382, 384, 385; natural and social science, 37-41; predictability, 38-39; purpose, 95; specific, 45; verbal and mathematical, 375
Theory-building
  in natural and social sciences, 43-44
Third world, 13
  revolutionary insurgencies, 299
Thirty Years' War, 96
Threat, 382
  and bargaining theory, 365; credibility, 97, 368
Totalitarianism, 43
Traditional School, 20, 39
Treaty of Rome, 307
Treaty of Versailles, 4
Treaty of Westphalia
  balance of power, 155
Triple Entente, 339, 340, 341

U-2 crisis, 328
UNESCO
  studies on tensions and war, 222
Unification, *See* Integration
United Arab Republic
  case study in integration, 288-292
United Nations, 112, 336
  East-West problems, 83; Korea, 87; voting patterns, 300
United States, 52
  Department of Defense, 102; Department of State, 23
Unit veto system, 97
U.S. foreign policy
  geopolitical considerations, 54

Utopianism
  in international relations, 379
Utopians, *See* Utopian school
Utopian school, 10, 47
  contrasted to Realist, 5-8

Values
  and order, 109-110; Lasswell's categories, 223
Versailles Peace Treaty, 22
Violence
  and economic backwardness, 240

War
  accidental, 271; a deliberate choice, 197-201; and civilizations, 161; and national cohesion, 201-202; causes, 203; collective insecurities, 223; "devil theory," 157, 191; economic basis, 158-159; gaming, 345; national self-preservation, 162-163; psychological theories of, 196-232; related to imperialism, 181-183; total, 10
Warfare
  economic factors, 5
Warsaw Pact, 361
  implications for SALT, 276
Weapons technology, 14
Western Europe, 46
  defense of, 259
West Indies Federation
  case study in integrations, 288-292
What is to be Done?, 179
World government, 47
  prospects of, 70
World law, 25
World peace, 25
  defined, 97; types, 97
World politics
  defined, 223
World Politics, 14
World War I, 270, 335
  and imperialism, 173, 180; analysis of, 337-340
World War II, 10, 361, 367, 370
  and European integration, 311; and regional integration, 389

Zeitschrift für Geopolitik, 56
Zero-sum
  application, 352; contrasted to non zero-sum, 252, 349-50